Chronology
of
The People's Republic of
CHINA
1970-1979

by Peter P. Cheng

Scarecrow Press, Inc.
Metuchen, N.J., & London   1986

Library of Congress Cataloging in Publication Data

Cheng, Peter, 1930–
    Chronology of the People's Republic of China, 1970–
1979.

    Continues: A chronology of the People's Republic of
China from October 1, 1949.
    Bibliography: p.
    Includes indexes.
    1. China--History--1949-   --Chronology. I. Cheng,
Peter, 1930-   . Chronology of the People's Republic of
China from October 1, 1949. II. Title.
DS777.55.C445669   1986   951.05   84-20231
ISBN 0-8108-1751-9

TABLE OF CONTENTS

PREFACE

This Chronology provides a day-to-day chronicle of kaleidoscopic events which occurred in the People's Republic of
China during the 1970's. The accounts have been compiled
from reports appearing in publications in China, England,
France, the United States, India, and Japan. This volume
is a continuous work to the author's book, A Chronology of
the People's Republic of China from October 1, 1949, published by Rowman & Littlefield.

I am grateful to the University Research Council of the
University of Nebraska for a travel grant to the Library of
Congress in Washington, DC, and a semester-leave with Fac-
ulty Development Fund to complete research work at the office of the New China News Agency (Xinhua News Agency)
in Tokyo, Japan.

Finally, I'd like to thank my lovely wife, Nelly, and our
three daughters, Margaret, Elizabeth, and Patricia, for their
patience and affection which made the preparation of this
book possible.

P.P.C.
December 1983

[v]

ABBREVIATIONS

AEC	Atomic Energy Commission (USA)
ASEAN	Association of Southeast Asian Nations
CAAC	Civil Aviation Administration of China
CC	Central Committee
CCP/CPC	Chinese Communist Party
CPPCC	Chinese People's Political Consultative Conference
CPSU	Communist Party of the Soviet Union
CYLCC	Communist Youth League Central Committee
DPRK	Democratic People's Republic of Korea (North)
DRVN	Democratic Republic of Vietnam
ECAFE	Economic Commission for Asia and the Far East (UN)
EEC	European Economic Community
ESCAP	Economic and Social Council Action Program (UN)
FAO	Food and Agricultural Organization (UN)
GDR	German Democratic Republic (East)
GEMS	Global Environmental Monitoring System
GMD	Guomindang
GPCR	Great Proletarian Cultural Revolution
IOC	International Olympic Committee
JETRO	Japan External Trade Organization
MFN	Most Favored Nation
NCNA	New China News Agency
NLF	National Liberation Front
NPC	National People's Congress
OAU	Organization of African Union
OECD	Organization for Economic Cooperation and Development
PLA	People's Liberation Army
politburo	Political Bureau
PRC	People's Republic of China
RC	Revolutionary Committee

RMB	Renminbi
SC	State Council
SVNFL	South Vietnam, National Front for the Liberation of
SWAPO	South West African People's Organization
TASS	Telegraphic Agency of the Soviet Union
UNCTAD	United Nations Conference on Trade and Development
UNDP	United Nations Development Program
Unesco	United Nations Educational, Scientific and Cultural Organization
UNHCR	United Nations High Commissioners for Refugees
UNIDO	United Nations Industrial Development Organization
WHO	World Health Organization

Unless otherwise indicated all references to Korea mean North Korea, those to Vietnam mean North Vietnam, and those to Germany mean East Germany

ROMANIZATION

The system of romanization for Chinese characters used in this book is the Pinyin system. The system is used by the People's Republic of China and is increasingly used by scholars in the West. The system is simple to read except for two letters:

Q is pronounced like the ch in chicken, and x is pronounced like the s in simple.

Chapter I

1970

THE FINAL CAP ON CHINA'S CULTURAL REVOLUTION

The final cap was put on China's tumultuous Great Proletarian Cultural Revolution in 1970, and the world's most populous nation set about repairing the damage caused by that upheaval. On the domestic front, China cooled the political temperature of the past years and attempted to get its economy moving forward again. Internationally, China launched one of its most successful diplomatic campaigns ever.

Beginning with the New Year's Day editorial, official statements consistently emphasized China's willingness to establish or improve diplomatic relations with all countries, regardless of their social systems, on the basis of the "Five Principles of Peaceful Coexistence." Accordingly, China received a large number of foreign delegations during the year, including President Yahya Khan of Pakistan; French Minister Delegate to the prime minister for planning and territorial development, Andre Bettencourt; Rumanian Defense Minister Ion Jonits; Palestine Liberation Organization leader Yasir Arafat, who hailed the Chinese as being the first to provide military assistance to the Palestine guerrillas; and high-level officials from Tanzania, Zambia, Sudan, and Syria. At this time China also expressed renewed interest in joining the United Nations, signed aid agreements with North Vietnam, Albania, and North Korea, and extended loans to Tanzania, Zambia, Ceylon, and Rumania. China began to repair its relations with enemies both long-standing (Yugoslavia) and recent (Burma and India). Finally, by year's end, Chinese ambassadors had returned to nearly three-quarters of China's overseas embassies.

The nation whose relations with China improved most

1

noticeably was the Soviet Union. Following the American invasion of Cambodia in April, the two nations apparently decided to disassociate four groups of issues in their relationship: ideology, the border, diplomatic relations, and economics. By keeping the issues separate, China and the Soviet Union were able to ameliorate their diplomatic relations,
even though little progress was made in resolving ideological
and border issues. The Americans, not the Russians, became China's principal opponents. Although Mao's statement
of May 20 condemned "American imperialism," it made no mention of either revisionism or the Soviet Union. In July, it
was announced that the two nations would exchange ambassadors. The new Soviet Ambassador to China, V.S. Tolstikov, arrived in Beijing on October 10, and the Chinese
Ambassador, Liu Xinchuan, left for Moscow on November 22.
A Sino-Soviet Trade Agreement (the first since 1967) was
signed in Beijing on November 22, and the annual protocol
on border-river navigation was signed late in December at
Heiho. Border talks, which had been in progress, intermittently since November 1969, continued in Beijing without any
official statement about what was being discussed. In addition, the Soviet Union made a last-minute appeal for the admission of Beijing to the United Nations, reversing an apparent decision to abstain from the debate as it had done in
1969.

    Nevertheless, a strong undercurrent of mutual criticism
and bitterness persisted. The Soviet message on China's
National Day was one of very few addressed to the "Chairman
of the Chinese People's Republic," while the Chinese message
on the Soviet National Day referred to the Soviet people as
having been educated by the "great Lenin and Stalin." Both
messages, however, contained feelings about improving state
relations. The message said that "differences of principle
... should not hinder the two countries from maintaining and
developing normal State relations...." The Soviet message
had said that they were in favor of "the normalization of
State relations and ... the restoration of good neighbourly
relations and friendship...."

    The American invasion of Cambodia halted the ameliora-
tion of Sino-American relations which had been indicated by
the resumption of the ambassadorial talks in Warsaw on January 20. China's response to the Cambodian situation itself

was cautious. Premier Zhou Enlai did not announce his support for Sihanouk's government-in-exile until April 5, almost
two-and-a-half weeks after Sihanouk had arrived in Beijing,
and well after similar expressions of support had been issued
by North Vietnam, the NLF, and the Pathet Lao. While China
played host to the "summit conference of the three Indochinese peoples," the official Chinese statement hailing the conference stated only that China would "provide powerful backing for the three Indochinese peoples in their war," thereby
implying that Chinese aid would not include active combat
support. And while Mao gave Sihanouk the place of honor
during the May Day celebrations in Beijing, Mao's own statement on the Cambodian situation, published on May 20, was
extremely mild. Mao felt a major change had taken place in
Indo-Chino which contributed to the increasing international
isolation of the US; China's role in America's defeat would be
one of a gratified spectator rather than an active participant.
On May 18, China postponed the ambassadorial discussion
which had been scheduled for May 20 with the US. The
sessions still remained in recess by the end of the year.

The Japanese-American agreement on the reversion of
Okinawa, statements that both South Korea and Taiwan were
essential to Japanese national security, the launching of
Japan's first earth satellite in February, the automatic extension of the Japanese-American Mutual Security Treaty in
June, the Japanese government's defense white paper in October, the improvement of Japanese economic relations with
the Soviet Union, and the increasing Japanese investment in
Taiwan and Southeast Asia all increased Beijing's fear of a
resurgent, nationalistic Japan. Although Sino-Japanese trade
reported an overall increase of twenty-five percent during
1970, the Chinese began to undertake punitive measures
against Japanese firms who had close ties with Nationalist
China or the US. Japan's growing interest in the Korean
peninsula led to an improvement of relations between China
and North Korea. The meetings of Chinese and Korean military delegations during the year included contingency planning for joint military action against an American or Japanese
attack on North Korea.

The big payoff in China's campaign to improve international relations and image, came during the latter part of the
year. In October, Canada and Equatorial Guinea extended

diplomatic recognition to Beijing. Italy, Ethiopia, and Chile followed in November and December. At the United Nations, China, for the first time, won a majority on the question of whether it should replace Nationalist China. The results of the vote were: fifty-one for Beijing, forty-nine against, and twenty-five abstentions. Beijing remained out of the UN for another year, however. The Assembly earlier had voted sixty-five to fifty-two (with seven abstentions) in favor of a US-backed resolution declaring that the China issue was an "important question," requiring a two-thirds majority.

As part of its new diplomatic offensive, the Chinese also increased their foreign aid to other developing countries. The main focus was on Africa, and the largest of the Chinese commitments was to a 1,080 mile long railroad costing $408 million. This railroad would connect the rich copper mines of landlocked Zambia with the Tanzanian port of Dar es Salaam on the Indian Ocean. Work on the railroad officially began in October.

In 1970, a number of foreigners connected with China made the news. American-born writer, Anna Louise Strong died in Beijing at the age of eighty-four. Miss Strong had lived in China for a number of years and was often received by Mao, Zhou Enlai and other high-ranking Chinese officials. Catholic Bishop James Walsh, who had been imprisoned in China in the late 1950's and was serving a twenty-year sentence, was released. British engineer George Watt, apprehended during the Cultural Revolution for alleged spying activities while supervising construction of a chemical plant in Lanzhou, was also released. He had served nearly three years in prison.

The year also saw a considerable restoration of order to China's domestic situation. China's economic policy appeared to be a program of gradual, proportional economic development, stressing agriculture, light industry, geographical balance, and egalitarian distribution. Despite the lack of hard statistics, which China had not published since 1960, analysts concluded that the Chinese economy in 1970 probably regained the levels that existed just before the Cultural Revolution. According to reports from Beijing, the country enjoyed a good harvest for the eighth consecutive

year. The improved economic situation was reflected to some
extent in China's foreign trade, which topped $4,400 million.
After some six weeks of negotiations, China and Japan
signed a new trade agreement. Japan was China's largest
trading partner, and the two-way flow of goods was estimated at a total of $800 million in 1970, a marked increase
as compared to $625 million in 1969. As 1970 drew to an
end, there were increasing signs that Beijing was preparing
to launch its fourth five-year plan in 1971. The third plan
had been abandoned shortly after it was introduced because
of disruptions caused by political disturbances in the country.

Two important developments occurred on the scientific
and technological fronts in 1970. First, on April 24, Chinese
scientists succeeded in launching China's first earth satellite.
The 380-pound probe circled the globe every 114 minutes,
blaring out "The East Is Red," a short version of China's
popular song praising Mao Zedong. Second, on October 14,
Beijing's scientists conducted an atmospheric explosion over
testing grounds in Xinjiang Province in northwest China.
The test was detected and announced by the US Atomic
Energy Commission. The AEC estimated that the explosion
had a force of about three megatons. This test, the eleventh
since China entered the nuclear age in October 1964, was
not officially disclosed by Beijing. By the year's end, China
was believed not only to have developed a few medium-range
(600-1,000 miles), nuclear-tipped missiles, but to be con-
centrating its efforts in developing an intermediate-range
(1,500-2,500 miles) missile capable of striking targets in
Russia.

In education, schools at all levels began functioning
for the first time in four years. China's colleges and universities resumed classes in the autumn. Although politics
still played an important role in school curricula, more attention was being given to traditional subjects such as science, mathematics, and languages. The continued campaign
to send students to the countryside created a series of political and social problems. Peasants resent the influx of students to their villages and communes, and many young people tried to return to the cities illegally. The educational
policy appeared to create serious social tensions.

Finally, the Chinese Communist party celebrated its forty-ninth anniversary on July 1. On August 23, the party's Ninth Central Committee held its second plenary session. The communique issued at the close of the meeting on September 6 announced that preparations were under way for the long-delayed Fourth National People's Congress. In the meantime, the reestablishment of the machinery of government was apparent by 1970 in the party administration, the government bureaucracy and the economy. The first post-Cultural Revolution provincial party committees were established. There were signs that the ministerial structure of the government was being simplified. Against this trend of steady consolidation, however, the continued absence of a number of senior party leaders cast doubt on the stability of the central leadership.

January 1 The New Year editorial published jointly by the People's Daily, the Red Flag and the Liberation Army Daily, entitled "Usher in the great 1970s," attacked the Soviet leaders by name, saying: "The Soviet revisionist renegade clique--the centre of modern revisionism--is heading for total bankruptcy at an accelerated tempo. Khrushchev, the clown, who swaggered like a conquering hero not long ago, is now a heap of dirt beneath the contempt of mankind. His successors, Brezhnev and company, are faring even worse, and their conditions are deteriorating year after year; they are saddled with crises both at home and abroad."
  • A group of Chinese engineering and technical personnel arrived in Dar es Salaam, Tanzania by the Chinese oceangoing passenger ship Yaohua to help build Tanzania-Zambia railways. The team left Tanzania for home after completing the survey of the Tanzanian section of the Tanzanian-Zambian Railway on April 23.

January 2 V.V. Kuznetsov, head of the Soviet government delegation in the Sino-Soviet boundary negotiations, returned to Beijing from Moscow. It was noticed that, whereas he had been seen off on his departure (December 14, 1969) by the leader of the Chinese delegation, Qiao Guanhua, he was not welcomed by Qiao on his return. It was also noticed that, during Kuznetsov's absence from Beijing, there was an increase in the polemic on both sides. This started with a Tass (Telegraphic

Agency of the Soviet Union) commentary of December
30, which implied that China was becoming a military
dictatorship, and was continued by the People's Daily
New Year editorial which, for the first time, attacked
the Soviet leaders by name, saying, "...the so-called
'Brezhnev doctrine' is nothing but a variation of mori-
bund neo-colonialism."

January 3   China and Albania signed a protocol on scientific
and technical cooperation.

January 5   A strong earthquake with a shock of seven magnitude occurred in the area south of Kunming in Yunnan province.
   • China and Zambia signed and exchanged letters
stating that China would provide gratis broadcast trans-
mitters for Zambia.
   • An article published in the first 1970 issue of the
Red Flag rejected the contention that extremists belonging to radical mass organizations should automatically be
given party membership because of their participation
in the Cultural Revolution. The article called for an
end to political factionalism.

January 13   Beijing Hospital made a portable transistor ultra-
violet-ray therapy machine. It could be operated only
by trained technicians.

January 14   The People's Daily charged that "the Japanese
reactionaries are organizing a modern army with a view
to carrying out aggression and expansion in Asia."

January 19   Negotiations for the establishment of diplomatic
relations continued in Stockholm between China and
Canada. The Canadian Secretary of State for External
Affairs, Mr. Sharp, said that agreement might be
reached later in the year and also that China had accepted Canada's terms for discussion which included
bypassing the issue of Taiwan.

January 20   Sino-Albanian barter and payment protocol for
1970 and protocol on the use of Chinese credits in 1970
by Albania were signed in Tirana.
   • The 135th Sino-American Ambassadorial talk was
held in the Chinese Embassy in Warsaw. No details of
what took place at the meeting were issued.

January 21 The problem of people relaxing vigilance on the
assumption that the Cultural Revolution was over clearly
worried the leadership. A joint editorial in the two
Shanghai papers, Wenhui Bao and Jiefang Ribao, warned
that "when your ears are filled with the noise of machines, you will not be able to listen to the sound of
the handful of class enemies sharpening their swords."

January 30 At his press conference, President Richard Nixon
said that while the US sought to make some normalization of our relationships with Communist China, it was
necessary to expand the proposed antiballistic missile
system because of possible Chinese nuclear threat
against the US or its Pacific allies.
  • China and Zambia signed and exchanged in Lusaka
the summary minutes of talks on the construction of
Lusaka-Kaoma Highway and the letter on treatment and
working conditions for the Chinese technical personnel.

January 31 The Pentagon announced that it would supply
thirty-four F-100 Super-Sabre Fighter Bombers to Taiwan.
  • The 1970 Sino-Finnish Trade Agreement was signed
in Beijing.

February 1 China pledged support to the Arabs in their
struggle against Israel in a letter handed to Egyptian
Ambassador Salah el Abid by Premier Zhou Enlai in
Beijing. The message, addressed to President Nasser,
said, "The Chinese people will forever remain the most
reliable friend of the UAR, Palestine, and other Arab
countries."
  • The 1970 Sino-Guinean trade protocol was signed
in Guinea.

February 2 A major policy article appeared in the Red Flag,
entitled "The Road Forward for China's Socialist Agriculture." Dealing with the present, the emphasis was
on gradual development with no sudden changes in the
existing pattern of commune organization. Western analysts viewed the article as a sign that moderates had
overcome demands by radicals for changes in agricultural policy.
  • On Sino-Soviet border talks, according to the Moscow correspondent of Agence France Presse, the Chi-

nese delegation proposed that there should be mutual troop withdrawal from the frontier and agreement on the nonuse of nuclear weapons. The Russians had responded by proposing that troops stay where they were and that there should be an agreement on the nonuse of all weapons, conventional or nuclear.

February 3 NCNA released reports on new success in Chinese scientific research work on glaciers, frozen soil, and deserts.

• A Chinese economic and technical survey team arrived at Aden, as did a Chinese medical team, at the request of the government of the People's Republic of Southern Yemen.

February 5 According to the New York Times, two sets of proposals were said to have been presented at the January meeting of Sino-American Ambassadorial talks. The US had offered exchanges of travellers in order to broaden contacts prior to any political agreements. Financial and trade agreements also were reported to have been included in the US proposal. Beijing was said to have proposed political negotiations in an effort to achieve formal agreement on principles of peaceful coexistence.

February 8 China and Ceylon exchanged letters in Colombo on building a cotton-spinning and weaving mill at Minneriya of Ceylon with China's assistance.

February 9 Talks between Canada and China on the establishment of diplomatic relations were resumed in Stockholm. The discussions had been halted in December 1969 by China's insistence that Canada accept the so-called "one-China policy." On February 14, External Affairs Minister Mitchel Sharp reiterated the Canadian view: "The question of the limits of sovereignty of any particular government is not at issue in the exchange of diplomats."

February 10 A US military pilotless high-altitude reconnaissance plane was shot down by an air defense unit of the PLA Navy over Hainan Island, according to an NCNA report.

February 15 Mr. William McBain (age seventy-nine) crossed
the Hong Kong border from China. He was arrested on
October 25, 1969 in Shanghai for "violation of law." It
was generally assumed that his release was due to his
age and ill-health.

February 20 The 136th meeting of Sino-American Ambassadorial talks were held in Warsaw.
• A detailed analysis of the present and projected
military strength of the Soviet Union and China was
given by Secretary of Defense Melvin Laird in his report on the US defense program in the fiscal year 1970–
71, presented before a joint session of the Senate Arms
Services and Appropriation Committee. On China, the
report said, "Chinese strategic forces are comprised of
both offensive and defensive components. Expansion of
both components has been progressing and is expected
to continue in the foreseeable future. On the offensive
side, the threat is currently limited to air-delivered
nuclear weapons, but an operational medium-range bal-
listic missile could be deployed at any time. They probably also are seeking improvement of defensive forces
by deploying increased numbers of surface-to-air-missile
and fighter interceptors."

February 28 The Red Flag published an article describing
Mao's speech at the National Conference on Propaganda
Work of the Chinese Communist party in which he out-
lined a program for creating proletarian intellectuals.

March 1 Two officers from British merchant ships in Shanghai were detained in March: Captain Ray of the
Anchises on March 1 and second officer Duff of the
Glen Falloch on March 9. Both were released on March
26.

March 2 A protocol on the mutual delivery of goods for 1970
was signed in Pyongyang between China and North
Korea.

March 3 NCNA released a report of a conference on cotton
production convened by the State Council. The report
said that cotton production from 1966–69 had exceeded
all previous records. Compared with 1965, the average
annual output of the three years had increased by 12.2

percent, the per-mu yield by 12.5 percent, and state
purchasing by 8.4 percent.

March 7 Yoshimi Furui, representative of the Japan-China
Memorandum Trade Office, and four other delegation
members arrived in Beijing. The delegation was later
joined by Kenzo Matsumura and former Foreign Minister
Aiichiro Fujiyama (March 22). As in the previous year,
the talks appeared to go slowly in their initial stages,
with the Chinese delegation making great play with
Sato's remark about Taiwan during his visit to the
United States in November 1969. Premier Zhou Enlai
received the delegation on April 19, and the delegation
left Beijing for home on April 21.

March 9 A friendship delegation, headed by Guo Moruo, arrived in Pakistan for a visit at the invitation of the
Pakistan government. The delegation was received by
President Yayha Khan on March 11 and left Pakistan
for home on March 12.

March 10 A protocol for medical cooperation between China
and Guinea was signed in Conakry.

March 12 An article, written by the "writing group" of the
Anhui Provincial Revolutionary Committee and published
in the Red Flag, was given front-page treatment in the
People's Daily. The article, entitled "The Great Programme for Building Up Contingents of Proletarian Intellectuals," was in commemoration of Mao's speech at a
party conference in propaganda work in the early stages
of the Hundred Flowers Campaign. Emphasis was placed
on the long-term nature of remolding the intellectuals
and the necessity of using persuasion, not compulsion.

March 14 A protocol for agreement on scientific and technical cooperation between China and North Vietnam for
1970 was signed in Hanoi.

March 16 NCNA issued the following statement: "The rumors
which appeared in Phnom Penh are complete fabrications
created with ulterior motives. When Premier Zhou Enlai
received Nay Valentin, Ambassador of the Kingdom of
Cambodia to China, in the early hours of March 15, he
pointed this out and expressed uneasiness and regret at
the incident that had taken place in Phnom Penh."

March 17   A protocol on medical cooperation between Algeria and China was signed in Algiers.

March 18   The coup d'état in Cambodia on March 18 took place as Prince Norodom Sihanouk was preparing to fly to Beijing after a visit to the Soviet Union. He eventually arrived in Beijing on March 19 and was welcomed as head of state and met by a large number of Chinese dignitaries led by Premier Zhou Enlai. However, no official statement was given in support of Sihanouk prior to the speech made by Premier Zhou Enlai in Pyongyang on April 7.

March 19   A protocol for trade agreement between China and United Arab Republic (UAR) for 1970 was signed in Cairo.

March 23   China and Zambia signed in Lusaka the minutes of talks between the two broadcasting technical investigation teams.

March 26   The Chinese Foreign Ministry issued a statement expressing firm support for the statement issued on March 21 by the spokesman of the Central Committee of the Laotian Patriotic Front, condemning the "intensified expansion of the war of aggression against Lao by US imperialism and the reactionaries of Thailand."

March 28   China and Rumania signed the trade agreement for 1970 in Beijing.

March 29   Anna Louise Strong died of heart disease in Beijing at the age of eighty-four. Beijing held a ceremony to pay last respects to her on April 2.

April 2   A British subject, Mrs. Constance Martin age seventy-two, who was arrested on October 25, 1969, crossed the Hong Kong border, having been released by the Chinese authorities without any charges being formulated against her.
● Chinese Government Economic and Friendship Delegation with Fang Yi, minister of the Commission for Economic Relations with Foreign Countries, as its leader, left Beijing for Pakistan at the invitation of the Pakistan government. President Yahya Khan received the delega-

tion on April 5 and inaugurated a Chinese-aid project on April 6. Sino-Pakistan protocol on economic and technical cooperation was signed in Rawalpindi on April 9.

April 3   A nine-member Japanese delegation of seven trading firms arrived in Beijing for a friendly visit at the invitation of the China Council for the Promotion of International Trade. A joint statement was signed on April 14 to condemn the Japan-US communiqué of November 21, 1969 (on Okinawa) and the "revival of militarism." Premier Zhou Enlai received the delegation on April 15. The delegation left Beijing for home on April 19.

April 5   Premier Zhou Enlai paid a three-day official visit to the Democratic People's Republic of Korea at the invitation of President Kim Il Sung. A grand rally was held in Pyongyang in his honor on April 7. The lengthy joint communique issued at the end of his visit was devoted largely to a denunciation of US "imperialism" and also of Japanese "militarism." (April 7)
   • Jewhar Rice and Tobacco Experimental Station, built with Chinese assistance, was handed over to the Somali government.

April 9   China and Albania signed a shipping protocol in Beijing.

April 11   The Red Flag carried an article entitled "Advertising Bourgeois Art and Literature Means Restoration of Capitalism," criticizing Zhou Yang's "reactionary" theories which praised renaissance and critical realism.

April 15   V.G. Wilcox, general secretary, and Ron Taylor, acting national chairman, of the Communist party of New Zealand, arrived in Beijing for a friendly visit at the invitation of the CCP Central Committee. Premier Zhou Enlai gave a banquet in their honor on April 16. They left Beijing for home on April 25.

April 19   The question of Japan's relations with Taiwan reported to have influenced the Memorandum talks. Premier Zhou Enlai emphasized on April 15 that China would not trade with Japanese firms engaged in transactions with Taiwan. Prime Minister Sato said on April 17 that the Memorandum talks would be considered a "big pipe" connecting China and Japan, and that Janapese Import-Export Bank credits to finance trade between the two countries could be studied on a case-by-case basis. Prime Minister Sato's statement cast doubt on Japan's continued adherence to "Yoshida's letter," a private note by Yoshida to the Nationalist Chinese government in March 1964, promising not to permit use of such credits for trade with China. Furthermore, in the communiqué issued on April 19, the Japanese delegation concurred in condemnation of the Japan-US communiqué of November 21, 1969. However, Japan expressed the hope that China would respond to Japan's call for closer contact instead of repeating criticism of the Japanese government.

April 20 Chinese personnel arrived in Lusaka, Zambia, for the construction of the Lusaka-Kaoma Highway.

April 21 Editorial departments of the People's Daily, the Red Flag, and the Liberation Army Daily published an editorial entitled "Leninism or Social-Imperialism," in commemoration of the centenary of the birth of Lenin. The article accused the present Soviet leadership of being worse than Hitler.

April 22 NCNA released a report on the inauguration of the Afghan Lapis Lazuli Carving Works, built with Chinese assistance.

April 23 NCNA reported that a new 15,000-ton tanker known as "Taqing No. 29," designed and built entirely by Chinese-made rolled steel, was recently launched at the Hungqi (Red Flag) shipyard in Shanghai.

April 24 The successful launching of China's first man-made earth satellite was announced. The Beijing announcement stated that the satellite weighed 173 kilograms (380 lbs), that it was circling the earth every 114 minutes along a trajectory with an apogee of 2,384 kilometers (1,430 miles) and a perigee of 439 kilometers (263 miles), and that it was broadcasting the music of "The East Is Red" on a frequency of 20,000 megacycles.

April 25 Chinese Workers Delegation, headed by Wang Hongwen, member of the CCP Central Committee and vice chairman of the Shanghai Municipal Revolutionary Committee, left Beijing for Albania for a ten-day visit. The delegation left Tirana for home on May 6 after meeting with Albanian leaders, including Mehmet Shehu, on April 30.

• A summit conference of the Indochinese People was held in the frontier region of Laos, Vietnam, and China from April 24-26. Premier Zhou Enlai attended banquets at the conference on April 25 and 26 but his presence there was not announced in the Chinese press until May 2 (after the text of his speech had been broadcast by Hanoi Radio). In his speech of April 25, Premier Zhou Enlai pledged Chinese support, saying, "The three fraternal Indo-Chinese peoples may rest assured that in the common struggle against US imperialism, the Chinese people will always stand by their side."

April 27   NCNA announced that the 137th meeting of Sino-American Ambassadorial talks would be held in Warsaw on May 20, 1970.

April 28   The Chinese government issued a statement on the summit conference of the Indo-Chinese peoples. The statement declared support for the conference, and the struggle of the people of Cambodia, Laos, and Vietnam, but without mentioning China as a "reliable rear area" as Premier Zhou Enlai did in his speech.

April 30   American and South Vietnamese troops invaded Cambodia.

May 1   Chairman Mao and Vice Chairman Lin Biao received Prince Norodom Sihanouk and his wife.
• NCNA released reports on restaging of model revolutionary theatrical works to mark the twenty-eighth anniversary of the publication of Chairman Mao's "Talks at the Yanan Forum on Literature and Art." The Red Flag carried the text of the May 1970 version of the libretto of the opera The Red Lantern.

May 4   Prince Norodom Sihanouk established his Royal Government of National Union of Kampuchea in Beijing.
• The Chinese government issued a statement denoucing the US-troop movement into Cambodia as "not

only frantic provocations against the Indo-Chinese people, but also frantic provocations against the Chinese people, the Southeast Asian people and the revolutionary people of the world."

May 5 The Chinese government formally recognized the Royal Government of National Union of Cambodia under the leadership of the National United Front of Kampuchea. Premier Zhou Enlai congratulated Prince Sihanouk on the formation of the Royal Government.
  • China and Pakistan signed a trade protocol for 1970 in Beijing.

May 8 China and Tanzania signed minutes of talks on construction of the Tanzanian Mbarali State Farm with Chinese assistance.
  • A ceremony was held at Kombe near Brazzaville to lay the cornerstone of the Kombe State Farm to be built with Chinese assistance.

May 10 Le Duan, first secretary of the Central Committee of the Vietnam Workers' Party, arrived in Beijing. Before his departure on May 13, he met Chairman Mao, Vice Chairman Lin Biao, Premier Zhou Enlai, and Prince Sihanouk.

May 14 An Albanian delegation, led by Kadri Hazbiu, alternate member of Political Bureau of the Central Committee of the Albanian Party of Labour, arrived in Beijing for a forty-day visit to China. Premier Zhou Enlai held talks with the delegation on June 16. The delegation left Beijing for home on June 22.

May 18 China notified the US of the postponement of the 137th meeting of Sino-American Ambassadorial talks.

May 20 Guinea held an inauguration ceremony for Dabola Oil-Processing Works, built with Chinese assistance.
  • NCNA reported that a big water conservancy project on China's Huaibei Plain, north of the Huai River, was recently completed. The twenty-five kilometer canal put an end to the calamities brought by the Huai River.
  • Chairman Mao Zedong issued a statement on Cambodia, entitled "People of the World, Unite and Defeat

the US Aggressors and All Their Running Dogs." This was followed by massive rallies throughout China in support of the statement, in which 400 million people were said to have taken part. Mao's statement gave general, but no specific, support to Prince Sihanouk, emphasizing the need for the people of Indo-China to support each other and the power of revolution as the "main trend in the world today."

May 21 Chairman Mao Zedong and Vice Chairman Lin Biao attended the Beijing rally in support of the struggle of the people of the world against "US imperialism."
• Letters on the further development of border trade between China and Pakistan were signed in Rawalpindi.
• A trade protocol between China and Sudan for 1970 was signed in Khartoum.

May 22 The People's Daily, the Red Flag, and the Liberation Army Daily carried a joint editorial entitled "Remold World Outlook" in commemoration of the twenty-eighth anniversary of the publication of "Talks at the Yanan Forum of Literature and Art." The editorial stressed continuation of the drive to move officials and other intellectuals to the countryside.

May 25 The Red Flag carried the text of the May 1970 version of the libretto of the Beijing opera Shachiapang (Shajiabang).
• Premier Zhou Enlai wrote a letter to Chairman Yasir Arafat expressing high admiration for the Palestinian guerrillas' revolutionary spirit in resisting US-Israel aggression. The letter was handed to PLO Chief Housni Younes in Beijing by the Chinese vice foreign minister.
• Prince Norodom Sihanouk left Beijing for a fourteen-day visit to North Vietnam. He returned to a rousing welcome in Beijing on June 8.

May 26 A supplementary protocol of China's gratuitous aid to North Vietnam was signed in Beijing.

May 31 The Commander-in-Chief of the Pakistan Air Force, Air Marshal Audul Rahim Khan, visited China from May 31 to June 7 at the invitation of his Chinese counterpart, Wu Faxian. Premier Zhou Enlai held talks with him on June 3.

June 8 The Red Flag carried an article intended to define
a shift in Chinese economic policy towards strengthening agriculture and small industries. It said that the
so-called "walking-on-two-legs" policy was to be defined
as "the simultaneous development of industry and agriculture. In industry, this meant the simultaneous development of heavy and light industry, with priority
given to the development of heavy industry, the simultaneous development of industries run by central authorities and of local industries, the simultaneous development of large, medium and small industries, and
the simultaneous application of foreign and indigenous
methods for production under centralized leadership."
● The Delegation of the Japan-China Fishery Association, headed by Jisaku Eguchi, arrived in Beijing
for talks on matters related to the Sino-Japanese nongovernmental fishery agreement. A communiqué on the
talks was signed on June 20 and the delegation left
Beijing for home on June 27.

June 9 The Delegation of the Grand National Assembly and
the State Council of Rumania arrived in Beijing from
Pyongyang after concluding its visit to North Korea.
Premier Zhou Enlai held talks with the delegation on
June 9 and 10. Chairman Mao and Vice Chairman Lin
Biao received the delegation on June 11. The delega-
tion left Beijing for home on June 12. According to
Bucharest Radio, China agreed to give Rumania $21
million in aid to help repair flood damage.

June 10 Sino-Czechoslovakian agreement for goods exchange
and payments for 1970 was signed in Beijing.
● Soviet Premier Aleksey Kosygin, in a speech in
Moscow, said that no progress was being made in the
Sino-Soviet border talks.

June 13 Premier Zhou Enlai sent a telegram to Premier Kosygin expressing sympathy and condolences over earthquakes and floods in the Soviet Union.

June 14 The delegation from Somalia, led by Mohamed Ain-
anshe, vice president of the Supreme Revolutionary
Council, arrived in Beijing for a one-week visit. Premier Zhou Enlai met the delegation on June 17; Chairman Mao and Vice Chairman Lin Biao did so on June 19.

A protocol of economic and technical cooperation between the two nations was signed on June 19. The delegation left Beijing for home on June 20.

June 18   The Chinese Military Delegation, led by Su Yu, vice minister of National Defense, left Beijing for the People's Republic of Congo for a fourteen-day visit. President Marian Ngouabi received the delegation on June 24. The delegation returned home on July 1.

June 20   China notified the US of further postponement of the 137th Sino-American Ambassadorial talks.

June 21   The Sudanese Government Friendship Delegation led by Mansour Mangoub, minister of treasury, arrived in Beijing for a five-day visit. Chairman Mao met the delegation on June 26.

June 24   The Chinese Delegation with Huang Yongsheng as leader left Beijing for Pyongyang to attend the commemoration of the twentieth anniversary of the Korean War. On the same day, the North Korean delegation, with Foreign Minister Pak Sung Chul as leader, arrived in Beijing to join the Chinese people in commemorating the occasion. A mass rally of 100,000 people was held in Beijing on June 25. Chairman Mao and Vice Chairman Lin Biao received the Korean delegation on June 27. The Korean delegation left Beijing for home on June 29.

June 25   The Chinese Government Trade Delegation, headed by Zhou Huamin, vice minister of Foreign Trade, left Beijing for Berlin on a ten-day visit. A Sino-German goods exchange and payment agreement for 1970 was signed on June 30.
   • The tenth session of the shareholders' meeting of the Chinese-Polish Shipbrokers Company was held in Beijing from June 25 to July 4.

June 27   The Polish Government Trade Delegation headed by M. Dnochowski, vice minister of foreign trade, arrived in Beijing for a nine-day visit. A Sino-Polish goods exchange and payment for 1970 was signed on July 2.

June 29   A protocol of China's gratuitous aid to Rumania was signed in Beijing.

June 30   The 1970 trade protocol between China and Cuba
was signed in Havana. The senior Soviet delegate to
Sino-Soviet border talks, Kuznetsov, returned to Moscow for medical treatment.

July 1   The 753.3-kilometer railway from Jiaozuo (Henan) to
Zhicheng (Hubei) was completed. The 1085-kilometer
Chengdu-Kunming railway was formally opened to traf-
fic.
• The forty-ninth anniversary of the founding of the
CCP was marked by a joint editorial of the People's
Daily, the Red Flag, and the Liberation Army Daily,
which concentrated almost entirely on the question of
the type of person to be admitted to the party.

July 2   The Red Flag carried several articles on rebuilding
the party. The articles attacked tendencies from the
Right (abolition of ideological struggle and an unprin-
cipled peace) and the extreme Left (encouragement of
absolutism and denial of everything) and said that even
those who made serious mistakes could still play an important role.
• Prince Norodom Sihanouk arrived in Beijing on a
special train after concluding a state visit to North
Korea. Several hundred thousand people lined the
route in Beijing to welcome him.

July 3   China completed a big new canal, 110 kilometers
long, 200-700 meters wide, and seven meters deep.
The man-made canal, named the Hanbei, and seven flood
outlet gates were the first stage for the main project of
the water conservancy construction in Wuhan area,
north of the Hanjiang River. The water conservancy
construction was aimed at all-round harnessing of the
rivers and lakes in the area.

July 4   Upon the withdrawal of US troops from Cambodia (an-
nounced by President Nixon on June 30) the People's
Daily said that Nixon had suffered a "big defeat" in
Cambodia and the withdrawal was only "a smokescreen."

July 5   Premier Zhou Enlai gave a banquet to welcome Prince
Norodom Sihanouk to mark his return from North Korea
and said that "the vast expanse of China's territory
will forever remain the reliable rear area of the Khmer
and other Indo-Chinese People."

• The Tanzanian Government Delegation, led by Amir Habib Jamal, minister of Finance, and Zambian Government Delegation, led by E.H.K. Mudenda, minister of Development and Finance, arrived in Beijing for discussion on the Tanzania-Zambia railway. Premier Zhou Enlai met the delegations on July 9. Chairman Mao and Vice Chairman Lin Biao met them on July 11. Protocols and minutes of the talks were signed on July 12. After touring other parts of China, the delegations left Guangzhou for home on July 18. According to an official announcement in Dar es Salaam on July 12, China was to grant Tanzania an interest-free loan of 2,866 million Tanzanian shillings (about £169 million) repayable over thirty years from 1973.

July 7 The official French Delegation, led by Andre Betterncourt, arrived in Beijing for a fourteen-day visit. This was the first governmental delegation to visit China since the establishment of diplomatic relations in 1964 and it was given a high-level welcome, including interviews with Chairman Mao and Vice Chairman Lin Biao on July 13 and Premier Zhou Enlai on July 10. The delegation left Beijing for other parts of China on July 15 and left Guangzhou for home on July 22. On July 14, Premier Zhou Enlai talked with François Debre and Michel Parbot, correspondents of "Agence Française des Images." A text of the talk was published in the People's Daily on July 29. Premier Zhou Enlai said that such visits from countries with "different social systems" encouraged mutual understanding.

July 9 A new protocol on sending Chinese medical team to Congo (B) was signed in Brassaville.

July 10 Talks were held between China and the Soviet Union about the navigation of border rivers at Heihe in Heilongjiang. In September, the Soviet Union announced that agreement had been reached on settling trading accounts for border trade, but no such announcement was made from the Chinese side.
• Bishop James Edward Walsh, the former bishop of Shanghai who had been sentenced in 1958 to twenty years of imprisonment for "espionage and sabotage under the cloak of religion," was released. The official announcement said that he had "confessed his crimes

while serving his sentence." At the same time it was announced that another American, Hugh Redmond, who had been arrested in 1954 and sentenced to life imprisonment, had committed suicide on April 13.

July 13 The Chinese Government Delegation, headed by Jian Zhiguang, minister of Light Industry, arrived in Baghdad to attend the National Day celebrations of the Republic of Iraq at the invitation of the Iraqi government. The delegation returned to Beijing on July 22.

July 14 A protocol on the mutual supply of goods for 1970 between China and Mongolia was signed in Beijing.
 • The Congolian Delegation, led by Vice President Alfred Raoul of Congo (B) arrived in Shanghai for a seven-day visit to China. Premier Zhou Enlai held talks with him in Beijing on July 15, 16 and 18; Chairman Mao and Vice Chairman Lin Biao met with him on July 20. The delegation left Shanghai for home on July 22.

July 15 The People's Daily carried a commentary calling for popularizing Model Revolutionary Theatrical Works, a campaign to expand performance of the operas both by professionals and amateurs.

July 19 The Hungarian Government Trade Delegation, headed by Tordai Jeno, arrived in Beijing for a six-day visit. A Sino-Hungarian goods exchange and payment agreement was signed on July 23.

July 21 NCNA announced the resumption of regular classes at Qinghua University in Beijing. It was the first-known instance of a university's return to normal activity, since most schools stopped admitting new students four years before. The Red Flag carried an article to emphasize "running universities in close connection with factories, and recruiting students chiefly from workers, peasants, and PLA."
 • The New York Times reported that China and the Soviet Union recently had undertaken intensive military moves along their borders. The Soviet Union was said to have deployed at least thirty-five divisions and to have had the ability to reinforce this number with an additional twenty-five divisions, while the total number

of Chinese soldiers in border area was estimated at two million.

July 22 The Chinese Delegation, led by Zhang Weilian, left Beijing for Havana to attend the seventeenth anniversary of the National Insurrection Day of Cuba. The delegation returned to Beijing on August 19.

July 23 The Rumanian Military Delegation, led by Minister of Armed Forces Ion Ionita, visited China from July 23 to August 2 at the invitation of Huang Yongsheng, chief of Chinese PLA general staff. Chairman Mao and Vice Chairman Lin Biao met the delegation on July 29; Premier Zhou Enlai met it on August 1.

July 25 The North Korean Military Delegation, led by General Oh Jin Woo, the Korean chief of the general staff, visited China from July 25 to August 4. Premier Zhou Enlai met the delegation on July 26; Chairman Mao and Vice Chairman Lin Biao met it on August 1.

July 30 George Watt, engineer of the British Vickers-Zimmer, Ltd., who was arrested in September of 1967 and sentenced to three years of imprisonment, was released before the expiration of his term and deported from China.

July 31 A Sino-South Yemen protocol on economic and technical cooperation and letters of exchange on the dispatch of Chinese engineering and technical personnel were signed in Aden.

August 1 An official delegation from Southern Yemen, led by President Salem Robaya Ali, visited China from August 1-13. An agreement on economic aid was signed on August 7. Premier Zhou Enlai agreed to visit Southern Yemen at a time to be decided later. Chairman Mao met the delegation in Shanghai on August 11. The delegation left Shanghai for home on August 13.

August 6 The Sudanese Friendship Delegation, led by President Gaafar Mohamed Nimeri (P.S.C.), arrived in Beijing for a state visit from August 6-13 at the invitation of the Chinese government. Premier Zhou Enlai gave a banquet on August 7 and Chairman Mao met the delegation in Shanghai on August 12. Sino-Sudanese agreements on economic and technical cooperation were signed. The delegation left Shanghai for home on August 13.

August 7   A ten-member delegation of the local activists of the Japanese Socialist party, led by Hisao Kuroda, arrived in Beijing at the invitation of the China-Japan Friendship Association. Premier Zhou Enlai met the delegation on August 18.

August 10   The 10,000-ton class freighter Dong Feng (East Wind), which was designed and built completely by China, docked at the port of Vancouver, Canada after a transatlantic voyage. This was the first time a Chinese oceangoing freighter entered a Canadian port.

August 12   An eight-member delegation led by Kozo Sasaki, former Chairman of Japanese Socialist party, arrived in Beijing at the invitation of the China-Japan Friendship Association. Premier Zhou Enlai met the delegation on August 20. The delegation left Beijing for home on August 24.
• A six-member Chinese technical team arrived in Colombo, Ceylon to assist in the construction of the Bandarannaike Memorial Hall. The Ceylonese government held an inauguration ceremony for construction on November 25.

August 13   The Albanian Government Delegation, led by Abdyle Kellezi, an alternate member of the politburo of the Central Committee of the Albanian Party of Labour, visited China from August 13 to October 17. Premier Zhou Enlai met the delegation on August 18; Chairman Mao met it on September 28. Agreements on a long-term interest-free Chinese loan to Albania and on goods exchange and payments for 1971-75 were signed on October 16. The delegation left Beijing for home on October 17.

August 15   L.F. Ilyichev, deputy foreign minister of the Soviet Union, arrived in Beijing to take part in the negotiations on the Sino-Soviet boundary question.

August 17   A Sino-Cambodian agreement on providing gratu-

itous military aid from China to Cambodia was signed
in Beijing.

• Full diplomatic relations at the ambassadorial level
with Yugoslavia were restored for the first time since
1958 with the arrival of the Chinese Ambassador Zeng
Tao in Belgrade.

• Premier Zhou Enlai met Edgar Snow and his wife.

August 23 The second plenary session of the Ninth Central
Committee of CCP was held in Lushan (Jiangxi) from
August 23 to September 6. One hundred and fifty-five
full members (out of 170) and 100 alternate members
(out of 109) were present. A communiqué was published in the People's Daily on September 10, which
said that the task set by the Ninth Congress had been
carried out with great success, that Chairman Mao had
personally presided over the session, and that both he
and Lin Biao had spoken.

August 31 The 1970 Sino-Bulgarian agreement for goods exchange and payments was signed in Sofia.

September 1 The Ministry of Foreign Trade issued a statement on the fact that China had not conducted any
trade, direct or indirect, with South Africa or Rhodesia.

September 3 On the twenty-fifth anniversary of Japan's defeat, a large-character editorial was published jointly
by the People's Daily, and the Liberation Army Daily,
entitled "Down with Revived Japanese Militarism." The
editorial listed nine points to demonstrate the revival of
"militarism" in Japan and said that its existence was
now an "indisputable reality."

September 5 A Sino-Uganda protocol to the agreement on
economic and technical cooperation was signed in Entebbe, Uganda.

September 7 The Ceylonese Economic Delegation, headed by
Tikiri Banda Llangaratne, minister of Foreign and International Trade, visited China from September 7-12.
Premier Zhou Enlai met the delegation on September 12,
and a loan agreement between the two nations was signed
on the same day.

September 10   Premier Zhou Enlai met writer Madame Han
Suyin and her husband, Mr. Vincent Ruthnaswamy.

September 12   DRVN (Democratic Republic of Viet Nam) Government Economic Delegation, led by Vice President
Nguyen Con, visited China from September 12 to October 7. Premier Zhou Enlai met the delegation on September 15; Chairman Mao and Vice Chairman Lin Biao
met it on September 25. Agreement on Chinese economic and technical aid to DRVN and a protocol on Chinese aid to DRVN were signed on October 6.

September 15   Chairman Mao Zedong issued a letter to the
entire party, calling for a campaign to criticize Chen
Boda.

September 17   The Chinese Government Delegation, headed
by Xie Xinhe, vice minister of Light Industry, attended
the National Day celebrations of the Republic of Mali.
The delegation left Bamako for home on September 29.

September 18   Vice Admiral Mazaffar Hasan, Commander-in-
Chief of the Pakistan Navy, and six other Pakistan
guests visited China from September 18-26 at the invitation of Xiao Jingguang. Premier Zhou Enlai met the
delegation on September 20; Chairman Mao met it on
September 26.

September 22   The Red Flag gave additional information on
the criteria for enrollment in Chinese universities, saying: "New students should be selected among the
young activists who have distinguished themselves during the three major revolutionary movements: the
class struggle, the struggle for production, and the
struggle for scientific research." An NCNA report
said on September 24 that Qinghua University and Beijing University together had enrolled 4,000 students
since regular admission resumed in July.

September 23   The People's Daily published an editorial entitled "In Agriculture Learn from Dazhai." Although
praising the Dazhai model of "putting politics in command" and relying on one's own effort, the editorial
also pointed out that it was important to pay attention
to local conditions and that a slavish adherence to the
methods of others could lead one astray.

September 26 The Delegation of the Chinese Academy of
Sciences, headed by Yue Zhijian, left Beijing for a visit
to Albania from September 26 to October 24. The 1970–
71 plan for scientific cooperation between the two nations was signed on October 18.

• The Pakistan Government Friendship Delegation,
led by Lieutenant General Mohammad Atiqur Rahman,
governor of Punjum, arrived in Shanghai for a visit to
China from September 26 to October 3 at the invitation
of the Chinese government. Premier Zhou Enlai met the
delegation in Beijing on September 30.

• The Pakistan Agricultural Delegation, led by Abul
Keram Mohammad Ahsan, minister of Agriculture, arrived in Beijing for a visit from September 26 to October 5 at the invitation of the Chinese Ministry of Agriculture. Premier Zhou Enlai met the delegation on
September 30.

September 28 The Tanzanian Military Delegation, led by
Colonel Ali Manfudh, chief of operation and training of
the Tanzanian People's Defense Forces, arrived in Beijing for a visit from September 28 to October 29 at the
invitation of the Chinese Ministry of National Defense.
Premier Zhou Enlai met the delegation on September 30.

• The delegation of the Japan–China Cultural Exchange Association, led by Kenzoo Nakajima, arrived in
Beijing for a visit from September 28 to October 14.
Premier Zhou Enlai met the delegation on October 6,
and Mr. Nakajima spoke at the Beijing rally in commemoration of the tenth anniversary of the assassination
of Mr. Inejiro Asanuma on October 12.

• A Persian translation of the second volume of the
"Selected Works of Mao Zedong," an Arabic translation
of the third volume and a Hindi translation of the "Selected Military Writing of Mao Zedong" came off the
press.

September 29 Vice Chairman Dong Biwu and Premier Zhou
Enlai expressed sympathy on President Nasser's death
at the UAR Embassy in Beijing. Chinese government
institutions and harbors flew flags at half-mast in
mourning for President Nasser.

September 30 Premier Zhou Enlai gave a reception in the
banquet hall of the Great Hall of the People celebrating
the twenty-first anniversary of the founding of the

People's Republic of China. In a brief speech at the
reception, he made the first official reference to the
coming fourth five-year plan.

October 1   The twenty-first anniversary of the founding of
the People's Republic of China was celebrated with the
traditional parade at Tiananmen Square in the morning
and fireworks display in the evening. Chairman Mao
Zedong, Vice Chairman Lin Biao and other dignitaries
mounted the rostrum to review the parade. Vice
Chairman Lin Biao delivered the National Day speech
at the rally. Chairman Mao and Vice Chairman Lin Biao
also joined the Army and civilians in the evening festiv-
ities.

October 3   The Soviet message on China's National Day
stressed the point that they were in favor of "the normalization of state relations."

October 4   The thirteenth session of the Sino-Rumanian
Joint Commission on Scientific and Technical Cooperation
was held in Bucharest from October 4-21. A protocol
on the session was signed on October 21.

October 5   The Cambodian Senate and National Assembly
voted unanimously to abolish the monarchy and proclaimed "Khmer Republic" on October 9 (to go into effect
on November 1, 1970). On October 10, the Chinese
government issued a statement condemning the proclamation and calling on other governments to refuse to recognize "Khmer Republic" de facto or dejure. On the
same day, Prince Norodom Sihanouk, in Beijing, protested against the proclamation as "illegal and anti-
constitutional."

October 6   Former French Prime Minister Maurice Couve de
Murville and his wife arrived in Beijing for a visit from
October 6-25 at the invitation of the Chinese govern-
ment. Premier Zhou Enlai met them on October 8;
Chairman Mao met them on October 14.

October 10   Vasily Sergeevich Tolstikov, newly appointed
ambassador of the Soviet Union, arrived in Beijing, and
presented his credentials to Vice Chairman Dong Biwu
on October 13.

October 13   After many months of negotiations, Canada established diplomatic relations with the People's Republic
of China.   On the status of Taiwan, the joint communiqué said that "the Chinese government reaffirmed that
Taiwan is an inalienable part of the territory of the
People's Republic of China.   The Canadian government
takes note of this position of the Chinese government."

October 14   In what the US AEC regarded as an unusual
coincidence, the US, the USSR, and China exploded
nuclear devices within hours of each other.   The Chinese test, the first since September 1969 and the tenth
since China's first nuclear explosion in October, 1964,
was conducted at the Lop Nor test site in Xinjiang
province.   It was in the three-megaton range and estimated by the AEC to have been carried out in the
atmosphere.
   • The North Korean Government Delegation, led by
Chong Jun Taek, arrived in Beijing for a visit from
October 14-23.   Premier Zhou Enlai met the delegation
on October 17.   An agreement on Chinese economic and
technical aid to North Korea, and an agreement on mutual supply of main items of goods from 1971 to 1976
were signed on October 17.

October 15   The PRC and the Republic of Equatorial Guinea
decided to establish diplomatic relations at the ambassadorial rank.   No specific mention was made of Taiwan
in the communiqué.

October 17   The Chinese Government Delegation, led by Li
Shurong, vice minister of Agriculture, left Beijing for
Mogadishu to attend the National Day celebrations of
Somalia.   The delegation returned to Beijing on Novem-
ber 2.

October 19   The People's Daily commented on the "direction
of China's socialist commerce" and criticized the fallacy
"put profit in command" thoroughly.

October 20   The Guinean Government Economic Delegation,
headed by Tibou Toumkara, arrived in Beijing for a
visit from October 20 to November 11.   Premier Zhou
Enlai met the delegation on November 1.   A protocol of
an agreement on the economic and technical cooperation
between the two nations was signed on November 2.

October 22   The Cuban press agency, Prensa Latina, established an office in Beijing.

• The Chinese Government Delegation, led by Fang
Yi, minister of the Commission for Economic Relations
with Foreign Countries, left Beijing for Tanzania and
Zambia to attend the ground-breaking ceremony of the
Tanzanian-Zambian Railway. On October 26, President
Kaunda of Zambia officially inaugurated the construction
of the Tanzania-Zambia railway. The delegation returned
Beijing on November 21.

October 23   The Chinese People's Friendship Delegation, led
by Zeng Siyu, left Beijing for Pyongyang to attend
Korean activities marking the twentieth anniversary of
the entry of Chinese People's Volunteers into the Korean
War. The delegation returned to Beijing on October 27.

October 24   The Delegation of the Japanese Socialist party,
led by Tomomi Narita, arrived in Beijing for a visit from
October 24 to November 1. Premier Zhou Enlai met the
delegation on October 26. The final joint communiqué
attacked "the revival of Japanese militarism." It also
made an interesting reference to "the stand of China"
saying that it would never be the first to use nuclear
weapons.

October 28   Premier Zhou Enlai sent a telegram congratulating Salvador Allende Gossens on his being elected
president of the Republic of Chile. The Chinese Workers' Delegation, headed by Ni Jifu, left Beijing for
Chile on the following day to take part in celebrations
for his inauguration. The delegation returned to Beijing on November 14.

October 30   A People's Daily editorial, entitled "Study Chairman Mao's Philosophical Works Conscientiously," laid
down guidelines for studying Mao's philosophical works.

October 31   A Sino-Vietnamese agreement on mutual supply
of goods and payments for 1971 was signed in Beijing.

November 6   The PRC and Italy established diplomatic relations effective on November 6, 1970. In referring to
Taiwan, the joint communiqué was similar to that signed
by Canada, except that the Chinese government's views

were referred to as a statement, not as a position.

- The National People's Congress Standing Committee and the State Council sent a message to the Presidium of the Supreme Soviet and the Council of Ministers of the USSR, greeting the fifty-third anniversary of the October Socialist Revolution. Soviet Ambassador to China Vasily Sergeevich Tolstikov gave a reception in celebration of the occasion.

November 10   President Yahya Khan of Pakistan arrived in Beijing for a visit from November 10-14. Premier Zhou Enlai called him at the guest house on November 11, and Chairman Mao met him on November 13. A Sino-Pakistan agreement on economic and technical cooperation was signed on November 14. The joint communiqué following his visit repeated China's support for the Pakistan position on Kashmir.

November 11   Chairman Mao Zedong sent a message of condolences to Madame De Gaulle on the passing away of General Charles De Gaulle. The Chinese flag was flown at half-mast at Tiananmen Square, and over the building of the Chinese Ministry of Foreign Affairs in Beijing.

November 12   The Government Trade Delegation of the Soviet Union, headed by Ivan Grishin, vice minister of Foreign Trade, arrived in Beijing for a visit from November 12-29. A Sino-Soviet agreement (the first since 1967) on the exchange of goods and payments for 1971 was signed on November 22.

November 14   Exchange of letters concerning the supply of commodities by China to Afghanistan was signed in Kabul. According to the Kabul Radio, China agreed to provide $1 million to purchase consumer goods.

November 16   Burma's new ambassador, U Tein Maung, the first since 1967, arrived in Beijing, and presented his credentials to Vice Chairman Dong Biwu on November 21.

November 17   The Red Flag published an article, entitled "Rely on the Working Class to Institute Rational Rules and Regulations," to simplify former regulations and abandoned the fallacy of "one-man leadership" under an "expert" for a system in which the workers and the party played a greater role.

November 18   Premier Zhou Enlai met the new Soviet Ambassador to China Vasily Sergeevich Tolstikov.

November 20   For the first time there was a simple majority in the General Assembly of the United Nations for the resolution stating that the PRC should occupy the China seat and that Nationalist China should be expelled. The vote was 51-49-25. However, Beijing was not admitted, since a previous procedural motion declaring the issue to be an "important question" requiring a two-thirds majority also passed by 65-52-7.

• The Rumanian Government Delegation, led by Cheorghe Radulescu, arrived in Beijing after a visit to North Vietnam. Premier Zhou Enlai met the delegation on November 21. A Sino-Rumanian agreement on a long-term interest-free loan provided by China to Rumania was signed on November 25. The delegation left Beijing for home on November 26.

• Yang Shouzheng, representative of the government of the PRC and Chinese ambassador to Sudan, paid a visit to Ethiopia at the invitation of the Imperial Ethiopian government. Diplomatic relations at the ambassadorial level were established by a joint communiqué signed in Addis Ababa on November 24, but not published by the People's Daily until December 2. No specific reference was made to Taiwan in the communiqué.

November 22   The eleventh session of the Sino-Korean Scientific and Technical Cooperation Committee was held in Beijing from November 22 to December 10. A protocol of the session was signed on December 9.

November 24   The Third Hunan Provincial Congress of the CCP was held in Changsha between November 24 and December 4. Hua Guofeng was elected as the first secretary.

November 26   The PRC Government Delegation, headed by Lai Jifa, minister of Building Material Industry, left Beijing for Aden to attend the National Day celebrations of the People's Republic of Southern Yemen. The delegation returned to Beijing on December 7.

November 28   Chairman Mao Zedong, Vice Chairman Lin Biao,
and Premier Zhou Enlai greeted the twenty-sixth anniversary of the liberation of Albania.
• The PRC Government Delegation, headed by Sha
Feng, left Beijing for Mauritania to attend the celebrations of the tenth anniversary of the independence of
the Islamic Republic of Mauritania. The delegation returned to Beijing on December 15.
• The Delegation of the Chile-China Cultural Association, led by Antonic Tavulari, president of the association, arrived in Beijing for a visit from November 28
to December 16. Premier Zhou Enlai met the delegation
on December 14.

November 30   The first Canadian Chargé d'Affaires, John
Fraser, arrived in Beijing. It was agreed that ambassadors would be exchanged before April, 1971.

December 9   In Japan, pressure for normalizing relations with
Beijing was increasing. On December 9, 344 members
of the Diet from all parties adopted a resolution calling
for the establishment of diplomatic relations.

December 13   The CCP Central Committee and the government
of the PRC issued a statement supporting the appeal issued on December 10 by Hanoi. The People's Daily carried an editorial entitled "Resolutely Support the Vietnamese People in Carrying the War Against US Aggression and for National Salvation to Complete Victory."

December 14   A Sino-Sudanese protocol on dispatching a Chinese medical team was signed in Khartoum.
• In New York, the PRC and Cyprus signed a joint
communiqué (published on January 12, 1971) on their
decision to establish diplomatic relations.

December 15   Chile established diplomatic relations with the
PRC. A joint communiqué was signed in Paris on December 15 but was not published in the People's Daily
until January 6, 1971. The communiqué contained a
statement on Taiwan similar to that in the cases of Italian and Canadian recognition.
• The Mali Government Delegation, led by Foreign
Minister Charles Samba Sissoko, arrived in Shanghai for
a ten-day visit to China at the invitation of the Chinese

government. Premier Zhou Enlai met the delegation on December 20. Sino-Mali agreement on economic and technical cooperation was signed on December 21.

December 18   The Third Jiangxi CCP Provincial Congress was held from December 18-26.
* The Third Guangdong CCP Provincial Congress was held in Guangzhou from December 18-26.
* The Delegation of the Central Committee of the South Vietnam National Front for Liberation, led by Dang Thi, arrived in Beijing for a visit from December 18 to January 11, 1911. Hundreds of thousands of people in Beijing lined streets in rousing welcome to the delegation. Chairman Mao Zedong, Vice Chairman Lin Biao, and Premier Zhou Enlai greeted the tenth anniversary of the founding of South Vietnam National Front for Liberation on December 19. Premier Zhou Enlai gave a grand banquet to welcome the delegation on December 20.

December 19   The Third Jiangsu CCP Provincial Congress was held from December 19 to 26.

December 22   The Delegation of the Communist Party of Britain (Marxist-Leninist), led by Reg Birch, arrived in Beijing for a visit from December 22 to January 2. Premier Zhou Enlai held talks with the delegation on December 31.

December 23   Chairman Mao Zedong met Edgar Snow.

December 24   Letters of exchange on the construction of a power transmission and transformation project with the Chinese government's assistance was signed in Kathmandu, Nepal.

December 29   The People's Daily published an article condemning the decision of December 21 to carry out joint investigation and development of oil and mineral resources in the seabed near Taiwan by Japan, South Korea, and Nationalist China. The article further said that the islands in the area in question--Diaoyu, Huangwei, Qiwei, Nanxiao and Beixiao islands--were China's "sacred territory."

Chapter II

1971

A DRAMATIC YEAR FOR THE PEOPLE'S
REPUBLIC OF CHINA

The year 1971 was a dramatic one for the People's Republic of China. It saw new departures from Chinese foreign policy, symbolized by Henry Kissinger's two visits to Peking and the announcement that President Nixon would visit China in February 1972. It also saw the most sweeping surge of the central leadership of the Chinese Communist party since 1967. Of the twenty-one full members of the politburo, nine appeared to have been purged or demoted by the end of October. Of these, the most significant victim was Lin Biao who, until September 12, had been Chairman Mao's "close comrade-in-arms and worthy successor." As in 1966, the designated success to Mao had been cast aside.

The Chinese have a saying that a journey of 10,000 li begins with a single step. That first step was taken when Chairman Mao, in his interview with Edgar Snow in December 1970, indicated his desire to have President Nixon visit China. In return, President Nixon, in his State of the World report of February 25, expressed his desire to begin a "dialogue with Beijing" but cautioned that such a dialogue could not be conducted solely on China's terms. The invasion of Laos in March did not interfere with the amelioration of Sino-American relations. Unlike the 1970 incursion into Cambodia, the invasion of Laos produced neither a condemnatory statement by Mao, nor Chinese participation in an Indo-Chinese summit meeting. Premier Zhou Enlai did travel to Hanoi, though, to promise supplementary Chinese aid to North Vietnam. On April 10, an American ping-pong team, which had been participating in a tournament in Japan, arrived in China to open, as Zhou Enlai put it, a "new page

in the relations of the Chinese and American people." In
response, four days later, the United States relaxed its embargo on trade with China. About the same time, serious
planning began for Kissinger's visit to China in July. Kissinger made a secret trip to Beijing and held talks with
Zhou Enlai from July 9-11. When he returned, Nixon and
Zhou jointly announced on July 15 that the American chief
executive would be going to Beijing sometime before May 1972
to discuss "normalization of relations" and other subjects of
concern to both countries.

In seeking to form a coalition of "small" and "medium-
sized" powers, China supported the claims of Latin American
nations to a 200-mile territorial sea, and the attempts of the
oil-producing nations to raise the world market price of crude
oil. China also sought to improve its political relations and
increase its trade with virtually all nations. As a result,
China was admitted to the United Nations in October, and
signed a large number of trade agreements during 1971. A
dozen nations established diplomatic relations with China, including Nigeria, Austria, Turkey, Iran, Belgium, Peru, and
Lebanon.

China offered both positive and negative incentives for
improving Sino-Japanese relations. China had announced
that it would not trade with Japanese firms which had large
investments in Taiwan or South Korea, which supplied arms
or ammunition to American forces in Indo-China, or which
were connected with American enterprises. On the other
hand, if Japan acceded to the Chinese position, China had
promised expanded trade, a peace treaty, a nonaggression
pact with Japan, and even support for the Japanese claims
to the "northern islands" seized by the Soviet Union after
World War II. Finally, China seemed to be relying strongly
on a partial rapprochement with the United States to bolster
China's deterrence against the Soviet Union.

In the domestic field, the provincial party committees
formed between December 1970 and August 1971, were mainly
dominated by the military and had only a few representatives
of the masses appointed as party secretaries. Under the
principle of the "three-in-one combination," representatives
of the masses would serve on revolutionary committees alongside military and civilian cadres. However, in 1971, their
role on the committees was sharply circumscribed. Many of

these representatives were told to return to their production
units and improve their ability to relay the opinions of their
constituents. In a redefinition of the "three-in-one combination" which was to be applied to the reconstruction of the
party, the new party committees would be composed of "the
old, the middle-aged, and the young." Representatives of
the masses were thus effectively removed from active committee membership. Although military men occupied the majority of the provincial party secretaryships, their influence
on provincial, social and economic policies was marginal because they were still responsible for the State Council and
the party center, and were constrained by their fellow committee members.

The economic policies of 1971 strongly resembled those
of 1970 with their emphasis on stimulating production. There
were more specific programs announced for increasing output
in all sectors of economy. In heavy industry, the major emphasis was placed on a more efficient use of available resources. In agriculture, 1971 saw a renewed interest in
mechanization as a means of increasing productivity, in raising peasant income, and in releasing manpower for work in
rural factories. On economic redistribution, attempts to reduce inequalities among provinces focused on promoting provincial self-sufficiency and self-reliance, rather than on central reallocation of resources from province to province. A
drive for provincial self-sufficiency in grain production was
particularly evident during 1971, with several northern
provinces declaring themselves "basically self-sufficient in
grain."

In 1971, the criticism of idealism and metaphysics which
began in the last quarter of 1970, developed into an intensive
campaign against "phony Marxists." The campaign was directed at the May 16th Group, at radicals in the provincial
revolutionary committees, and, in particular, at Chen Boda,
a member of the Standing Committee of the politburo and
head of the Central Cultural Revolution Group. Chen and
the May 16th Group were blamed for the 1967 and early 1968
violence and anarchism of the Red Guards and revolutionary
rebels. Although Chen was purged, other major radicals
such as Jiang Qing, Zhang Chunqiao, Yao Wenyuan, and
Wang Hongwen remained extremely active.

On the night of September 12, a Chinese Air Force

plane crashed in Mongolia with nine people on board. The death of Lin Biao, which had been rumored for months, was confirmed in July 1972. The official version, as told by Mao and Zhou Enlai to visiting foreign dignitaries, was that Lin aspired to immediate power, and that even though the party's revised 1969 constitution named him Mao's heir, he plotted to overthrow Mao. When the conspiracy was discovered in mid-September of 1971, so the story went, Lin's son commandeered an airliner, which headed for Moscow via Mongolia. It ran out of fuel, though, and when it crashed deep inside Mongolia, all aboard, including Lin, his wife, Ye Zhun, and his son, died.

The "personality cult" of Mao Zedong was deemphasized in 1971. According to Edgar Snow, "The Chairman criticized the ritualism of the Mao's personality cult, explained why it had been a necessary nuisance during the Cultural Revolution, and forecasted its gradual modification." Visitors to China reported that portraits of Mao and placards bearing quotations from his writings, were gradually being removed from public places. This was not to say that Mao's thought was also being set aside. It only meant that Mao would be made one among equals rather than raised above his political associates and venerated, as he had been for years, as a demigod.

January 1   The New Year editorial, "Advance Victoriously Along Chairman Mao's Revolutionary Line," published jointly by the People's Daily, the Red Flag and the Liberation Army Daily referred to the successful conclusion of the third five-year plan (details of which had not been revealed) and the launching of the fourth five-year plan.

January 4   NCNA published a report on the completion of the first highway bridge across the Yellow River in the Ningxia Hui Autonomous Region.
   • The fourth CCP Shanghai Municipal Congress was held from January 4-10. Zhang Chunqiao was elected as the first secretary.

January 9   The Fourth Liaoning CCP Provincial Congress was held from January 9-13. Chen Xilian was elected as the first secretary.

January 12 The Chinese Government Delegation, led by Bai
Xiangguo, minister of Foreign Trade, left Beijing for a
visit to Ceylon. Sino-Ceylonese protocol on commodity
exchanges was signed on January 22. The delegation
returned to Beijing on January 26.

January 13 The Chinese Government Trade Delegation, led
by Sun Zhun, deputy director of the Bureau of the
Ministry of Foreign Trade, left Beijing for a visit to
Helsinki, Finland. The 1971 Sino-Finish trade agreement was signed on February 10.

January 15 The Third Anhui CCP Provincial Congress was
held from January 15-21. Li Desheng was elected as
the first secretary.

January 17 The Equatorial Guinean Government Delegation,
led by Jesus Alfonso Oyono Alogo, arrived in Beijing
for a seven-day visit at the invitation of the Chinese
government. Premier Zhou Enlai met the delegation on
January 19. Agreements on economic and technical cooperation, and on trade between the two nations were
signed on January 22.

January 20 The Fourth Zhejiang CCP Provincial Congress
was held from January 20-26. Nan Ping was elected as
the first secretary.

January 22 Minutes of the tenth meeting of the Sino-Korean
Committee for Cooperation in Border River Transport
were signed in Pyongyang. The meeting was held from
December 26, 1970 to January 22, 1971.

January 23 The People's Daily carried an editorial entitled
"Down with the Doctrine of Big-Nation Hegemony" in
opposition to the "hegemony" of "one or two superpowers" coupled with the assertion that China would
"never seek big-power status."

January 25 The PRC Ministry of Foreign Affairs issued a
statement condemning the US for "stepping up the expansion of the war of aggression in Indo-China and plotting new military adventures." This statement was made
to support statements of January 19 and 20 by Prince
Norodom Sihanouk, North Vietnam and Vietcong.

January 26 The UAR Goodwill Delegation, led by Mohamed Labib Shaukeir, speaker of the National Assembly, arrived in Beijing for a four-day visit. Premier Zhou Enlai met the delegation on January 27.
• The Chinese Government Trade Delegation, led by Zhou Huamin, left Beijing for a visit to Guinea. The Sino-Guinean trade protocol for 1971 was signed on February 9. The delegation left Guinea for home on February 11.

January 27 The PRC and the People's Republic of Congo signed minutes of talks concerning the construction of Fort-Rousset Hospital with Chinese aid.
• Premier showings took place of the color films of the "model" Beijing opera, The Red Lantern, and ballet, The Red Detachment of Women.

January 31 The People's Daily published an article, "Victory for Chairman Mao's Line on Party Building," to salute the formation of provincial party committees. It emphasized the need to be "modest and prudent" by carrying out "open door rectification campaigns."

February 3 An NCNA report indicated that since October 1968, 90,000 cadres had attended May 7 schools run by the Central Committee of the CCP or State Council. There were more than 100 such schools.

February 4 The PRC Ministry of Foreign Affairs issued a statement strongly attacking the US and their South Vietnamese "lackeys" for the invasion of southern Laos.

February 9 The Third Guangxi CCP Provincial Congress was held from February 9-16. Wei Guoqing was elected as the first secretary.
• Figures published by the Damascus office of the Chinese News Agency showed that Chinese exports to the Arab states in 1970 had been ten percent higher than in the 1967-69 period. The increased totaled about $200 million. Countries showing the largest increases in imports from China were Southern Yemen (up seventy-two percent), Sudan (up sixty-three percent), and Lebanon (up fifty-eight percent). The principal Chinese exports to the Arab states were tea, frozen foods, chemicals, and some industrial products. Kuwait re-

mained the chief Arab importer of Chinese products, followed by Syria and Libya.

February 10 The PRC and Nigeria signed a joint communiqué to establish diplomatic relations at the ambassadorial level.

• The Cuban Government Delegation, led by Herminio García Iazo, arrived in Beijing for a visit from February 10 to May 13. A new five-year trade agreement, payment agreement, and the 1971 trade protocol were signed on May 11. Premier Zhou Enlai met the delegation on May 12.

• The Chinese Government Trade Delegation, led by Bai Xiangguo, left Beijing for Rumania. Sino-Rumanian trade, payment agreements, and a long-term trade agreement on exchange of main goods were signed on February 19. The delegation left Rumania for home on February 23.

February 11 The Fifth Gansu CCP Provincial Congress was held from February 11-17. Xiang Henghan was elected first secretary.

• The DRVN Government Economic Delegation, led by Vice Premier Le Thanh Nghi, arrived in Beijing for a visit from February 11-23. An agreement on Chinese supplementary economic and military aid to Vietnam in 1971 was signed on February 15.

• The meetings of the boards of directors and supervisors of the China-Korea Yalu River-Electric Power Company were held from February 11 to March 17. Minutes of the meetings were signed on March 17.

February 12 The PRC issued a statement on the new situation in Indo-China. The statement warned that the attack on Laos was a "grave menace to China."

February 13 Aiichiro Fujiyama and other members of the delegation arrived in Beijing for talks on the Japan-China memorandum trade. Premier Zhou Enlai met the delegation on March 1. A communiqué on the talks was signed on March 1. The communiqué denounced "the revival of Japanese militarism." Later, unofficial reports said that the trade between China and Japan was likely to be about the same level or slightly higher than the previous year (about $70 million), with a decrease

of Japan's exports of about $6 million matched by a
similar increase in imports.

February 21   The first stage of the waste-water irrigation
project in Shanghai was completed.

February 25   In his annual State of the World Affairs message, President Nixon called China by its official name,
the People's Republic of China, and was conciliatory
toward normal relations with Beijing.   This was the
first official US statement to do so.

February 28   The Fifth Shaanxi CCP Provincial Congress
was held from February 28 to March 5.   Li Ruishan
was elected first secretary.
    • The first official statistics on the state of the Chi-
nese economy in thirteen years was given by Premier
Zhou Enlai in an interview with Edgar Snow.   The interview article was published in its entirety in the
Milan journal Epoca in February.
    • Agricultural production was worth $30 billion and
industrial production and transport was worth $90 bil-
lion.   Premier Zhou Enlai said that, although the Cultural Revolution had been more beneficial than harm-
ful, industrial production had dropped during 1967-68.

March 2   The British representative in Beijing, John Denson,
was received by Premier Zhou Enlai.   The meeting was
the first exchange at this level since the Cultural Revolution.   It was later revealed in London that, during
the meeting, Premier Zhou Enlai had agreed that China
would pay for the rebuilding of the British mission offices which had been destroyed by Red Guards in August, 1967.
    • The Third Henan CCP Provincial Congress was
held from March 2-8.   Liu Jianxun was elected first
secretary.

March 3   China's second successful launching of an earth
satellite took place.   The satellite, weighing 121 kg,
was heavier than the first and required a powerful
rocket to place it in orbit.
    • China and Nepal signed, in Katmandu, letters of
exchange regarding the repair work of Arankio Highway.

March 5   The Chinese Party and Government Delegation, led
          by Premier Zhou Enlai, left Beijing for a visit to Hanoi.
          A joint communiqué was issued on March 8 before the
          delegation's departure from Hanoi.   The visit was not
          made public in the Chinese press until after the return
          of the delegation to Beijing.

March 6   The First Qinghai CCP Provincial Congress was
          held from March 6-11.   Liu Xianzhuan was elected first
          secretary.

March 8   Gong Dafei, Chinese ambassador to Iraq, paid a
          visit to Kuwait from March 8-22.   An agreement to es-
          tablish diplomatic relations at ambassadorial level was
          signed on March 22.

March 9   The Sino-Sudan trade protocol for 1971 was signed
          in Khartoum.

March 10 The Fourth Beijing CCP Municipal Congress was
          held from March 10-15.   Xie Fuzhi was elected first
          secretary.

March 11 The People's Daily carried an editorial entitled
          "Long Live the Great Friendship and Military Unity be-
          tween the Chinese and Vietnamese Peoples."   The edi-
          torial contained this remark by Chairman Mao: "If any-
          one among us should say that we should not help the
          Vietnamese people in their struggle against US aggres-
          sion and for national salvation, that will be a betrayal
          of revolution."

March 13 Sun Jizhou, third secretary of the Nationalist
          Chinese Embassy in Senegal, who crossed over on March
          5 in Geneva, arrived in Beijing.

March 15 All travel restrictions on US citizens going to
          China were finally removed.   The State Department said
          that US citizens should no longer need special permis-
          sion to visit mainland China.

March 16 The Rumanian Government Delegation, led by
          Cheorghe Radulescu, arrived in Beijing for a visit from
          March 16-27.   Premier Zhou Enlai met the delegation on
          March 22.   China and Rumania signed a protocol con-

cerning supplying Rumania with whole plants and technical aid from China, a protocol concerning the conditions of delivering complete sets of equipment and material supplied by China for Rumania, and a protocol concerning the treatment and work conditions for the Chinese engineering and technical personnel to be sent to Rumania on March 22.

March 17   A large, Chinese table tennis delegation of sixty people left Beijing for Japan to take part in the Thirty-First World Table Tennis Championships. The delegation returned to Beijing on May 15 after touring Nagoya, Osaka, Kyoto, Tokyo.

• The People's Daily, the Red Flag, and the Liberation Army Daily published a joint article marking the centenary of the Paris Commune. The article, entitled "Long Live the Victory of the Dictatorship of the Proletariat," attacked the Soviet Union for being soviet in name only.

March 18   The Third Jilin CCP Provincial Congress was held from March 18-24. Wang Huaixiang was elected first secretary.

March 21   The Agence France-Presses, quoting Soviet sources, reported that Premier Zhou Enlai had introduced Ji Pengfei to the Soviet ambassador as the acting foreign minister.

• A People's Daily commentator article, entitled "Hail the Splendid Victory of Lao Patriotic Army and People," claimed that the Lao Patriotic Armed Forces had wiped out more than eight battalions and twenty companies of enemy troops and, incidently, that the South Vietnamese had never reached the town of Tehepone. The article said that the defeat in Laos marked the failure of Vietnamization.

• Premier Zhou Enlai received the leader of the Sino-Soviet border talk delegation, Ilyichev, and Soviet Ambassador Tolstikov.

• Premier Zhou Enlai gave a grand banquet welcoming the Goodwill Delegation of the Nepalese National Panchayat led by its Chairman Ram Hari Sharma.

March 22   Feng Yuqiu, Chinese ambassador to Mauritania, visited Yaounde from March 22-26. At the end of his visit, a communiqué was signed announcing that China and Cameroon had agreed to establish diplomatic relations.

March 23   The Third Hubei CCP Provincial Congress was held between March 23-28. Zeng Siyu was elected first secretary.

March 26   The CCP Central Committee and State Council gave a banquet celebrating the victories by the people of the three Indo-Chinese countries and welcoming the arrival of Le Duan, Kaysone Phomvihan, Nguyen Van Hieu (on their way to Moscow). Premier Zhou Enlai, Prince Norodom Sihanouk and all three guests spoke at the banquet.

March 29   The Mauritanian Government Delegation, led by Foreign Minister Hamdi Ould Mouknass, arrived in Beijing after visiting Shanghai for two days. Premier Zhou Enlai met the delegation on April 1. An agreement on economic and technical cooperation between the two nations was signed on April 1. The delegation left Beijing for home on April 10.

March 30   The Second Fujian CCP Provincial Congress was held from March 30 to April 3. Han Xianchu was elected first secretary.
   • The Chinese Government Trade Delegation, led by Zhou Huamin, left Beijing for a worldwide tour from March 30 to June 8. A Sino-Chilean trade agreement was signed on April 28; Budapest, Hungary was visited from May 19–27; the Sino-Polish agreement on goods exchange and payments for 1971 was signed on May 31; and the Sino-Mongolian protocol on goods exchanges for 1971 was signed on June 6.
   • The Chinese Government Trade Delegation, led by Xi Yesheng, left Beijing for Morocco. The Sino-Moroccan trade protocol for 1971 was signed on April 27.

March 31   The Bulgarian Government Trade Delegation, led by Dobri Alexiev, arrived in Beijing for a visit from March 31 to April 10. The Sino-Bulgarian agreement on exchange of goods and payments for 1971 was signed on April 10.

April 1   A Central Work Conference took place to extend
          criticism of Chen Boda--part of the movement against
          the ultra-leftist May 16 group.
             • The Third Shandong CCP Provincial Congress was
          held from April 1-5. Yang Dezhi was elected first
          secretary.

April 2   The thirteenth meeting of Sino-Vietnamese Boundary
          Railway Commission was held in Hanoi from April 2-11.

April 7   The Chinese Embassy in India strongly protested
          against the "Indian Government's connivance" with pro-
          tests in front of the Embassy on March 29.
             • The Third Shanxi CCP Provincial Congress was
          held from April 7-11. Xie Zhenhua was elected first
          secretary.

April 8   The Delegation of the Chinese Academy of Sciences,
          led by Yue Zhijian, left Beijing for a visit to North
          Korea from April 8-24. An executive plan for 1971-72
          scientific cooperation between the two nations was
          signed on April 23.

April 10 A US table tennis delegation, led by Graham
          Steenhoven, president of the US Table Tennis Associa-
          tion, arrived in Beijing for a visit from April 10-17.
          It was the first semi-official American group to visit
          China since 1949. The All-China Sports Federation
          gave a banquet on April 11 to welcome the delegation.
          Chinese and American players played friendly matches
          on April 13. Premier Zhou Enlai met the delegation
          along with the delegations from Canada, Colombia, Eng-
          land, and Nigeria on April 14. In his remark, Premier
          Zhou Enlai said that the delegation had opened "a new
          chapter in the relations of the American and Chinese
          people." The delegation left Beijing to tour Shanghai
          and Guangzhou on April 17 and left Guangzhou for
          home on April 27.

April 13 The People's Daily published an editorial entitled
          "Advance from Victory to Victory Along the Brilliant
          Road of Learning from Dazhai in Agriculture," to reaf-
          firm ownership by the production team as the basic
          form in the three-level ownership of the means of pro-
          duction in the people's commune.

April 14   President Nixon announced that the embargo on direct trade with China and travel regulations would be
relaxed as follows: (1) The US was prepared to expedite visas for visitors or groups of visitors from
China to the US; (2) US currency controls would be
relaxed to permit the use of dollars by China; (3) Restrictions would be ended on American companies providing fuel to ships or aircraft proceeding to or from
China except on Chinese-owned or Chinese-chartered
carriers bound to or from North Vietnam, North Korea
or Cuba; (4) US vessels or aircraft would carry Chinese cargoes between non-Chinese ports, and US-owned
foreign flag-carriers could call at Chinese ports.

   • After a lapse of 22 years, the reopening of direct
telephone communication between China and Britain was
announced.   Calls could be made by high-frequency
radio link between London and Shanghai, connecting
with other parts of China, between the hours of 9 am
and noon each day.

   • The Laotian Patriotic Front Delegation, led by Kaysone Phomvihan, vice chairman of the Central Committee
of the Laotian Front, arrived in Beijing for a visit from
April 14-26.   Premier Zhou Enlai met the delegation on
April 22.

   • Her Royal Highness Princess Ashraf Pahlavi, sister
of His Majesty Mohammed Reza Pahlavi, the Shahanshah
of Iran, arrived in Beijing for a visit at the invitation
of the Chinese government from April 14-19.   Premier
Zhou Enlai met her on April 14.

April 21   V.S. Ailcox, general secretary of the Communist
party of New Zealand, arrived in Beijing for a visit at
the invitation of the CCP Central Committee from April
21 to May 6.   Premier Zhou Enlai met him on May 4.

April 23   At a Washington press conference, Secretary of
State William Rogers said that he hoped that recent
ping-pong diplomacy signaled the beginning of new relations between the US and China.

   • The Chinese Workers' Delegation, led by Pan Shigao, left Beijing for Tirana to attend the May Day celebration.   The delegation returned to Beijing on May 19.

April 25   Prince Norodom Sihanouk gave a banquet in Beijing
to celebrate the anniversary of the summit conference

of the Indo-Chinese peoples. The People's Daily car-
ried an editorial, "The Fifty Million Indo-Chinese People
Are Invincible," to reaffirm Chinese people's determina-
tion to "go all out in their support for the war against
US aggression and for national salvation of the three
Indo-Chinese peoples."

April 27   The Malian Government Delegation, led by Captain
Charles Samba Sissoko, arrived in Shanghai for a visit
to China from April 27 to May 6 at the invitation of the
Chinese Government. Premier Zhou Enlai met the delegation on May 3 in Beijing.

April 28   A State Department spokesman said that the status
of Taiwan was "an unsettled question subject to future
international solution" and that the question should be
settled by an agreement between the "two Chinese governments."
    • Sino-Pakistan minutes of the talks on building a
sugar mill (for Pakistan) was signed in Karachi.

April 29   William N. Hinton and his wife arrived in Beijing
for a visit at the invitation of the Chinese People's Association for Friendship with Foreign Countries from
April 29 to November 15. Premier Zhou Enlai met them
on May 24 and November 13.

April 30   Princess Fatemeh Pahlavi, third younger sister of
Mohammed Reza Pahlavi, the Shahanshah of Iran, ar-
rived in Beijing for a visit at the invitation of the
Chinese government from April 30 to May 12. Premier
Zhou Enlai met the delegation on April 30.

May 1   Chairman Mao Zedong and Vice Chairman Lin Biao
mounted the Tiananmen rostrum to join the people in
celebrating May Day. The People's Daily carried an
editorial, entitled "Long Live the Great Unity of the
People of the World," indicating that China's foreign
policy be concentrated on "united front" tactics.

May 2   The Delegation of the Palestine Liberation Organization, led by Abu Ammar Salad, arrived in Beijing to
take part in the activities of the "Palestine International
Week" (May 3-8) and for a visit to China from May 2-11.
Premier Zhou Enlai met the delegation on May 9.

May 4 The People's Daily carried a commentator's article entitled "Fresh Evidence of the US Government's Hostility
Toward the Chinese People," to denounce the State Department statement of April 28 on Taiwan. The article
said that Taiwan was part of Chinese territory from
"time immemorial."

May 5 The fourteen-member Trade Mission of the Chamber
of Commerce of the Philippines visited Beijing from May
5-9. Premier Zhou Enlai met the delegation on May 7.

May 6 A protocol was signed in Paris by the PRC and the
Republic of San Marino on the establishment of official
relations at consular level.

May 7 The Second Xinjiang Unighur Autonomous Region CCP
Congress was held from May 7-14. Long Shujin was
elected first secretary.
    • The Third Guizhou CCP Provincial Congress was
held from May 7-11. Lan Yinong was elected first secretary.

May 8 NCNA released a full text of the press communiqué
in reference to the starting of talks by the PRC and
Turkey for the establishment of diplomatic relations.
    • The Malaysian Trade Delegation arrived in Guang-
zhou to visit China's 1971 Spring Export Commodities
Fair. The delegation arrived in Beijing on May 13 for
a four-day visit. Premier Zhou Enlai met the delegation
on May 15.

May 11 On the events in East Pakistan, the People's Daily
carried a commentator's article saying that the present
problems were "the internal affairs of Pakistan, in
which no country should or had the right to interfere."

May 13 The Third Inner-Mongolian Autonomous Region CCP
Congress was held from May 13-18. You Taizhong was
elected first secretary.
    • Professor Arthur W. Galston, plant physiologist,
and Professor Ethan R. Signer, microbiologist, of the
US arrived in Beijing for a seven-day visit at the invitation of the Chinese government. Premier Zhou Enlai
met the two professors on May 19.

May 14 Thai Foreign Minister Thanat Khoman disclosed that
Thailand was seeking to improve relations with the PRC
through the mediation of an unnamed third country.
Thanat said: "There are indications that these contacts are bringing better results."

May 15 The Government Trade Delegation of the German
Democratic Republic, led by Kurt Fenske, arrived in
Beijing for a ten-day visit. The Sino-GDR agreement
on exchange of goods and payments was signed on May
18.

May 16 The New York Times reported that the PRC manufactured for the first time a jet fighter of its own de-
sign.

May 17 The Second Hebei CCP Provincial Congress was held
from May 17-20. Liu Zihou was elected first secretary.
• The Chinese Military Friendship Delegation, led by
Zhang Daqi, left Beijing for a visit to Guinea and Mali.
Guinean President Sekou Toure received the delegation
on May 29, and Mali President Moussa Traore received
the delegation on June 8. The delegation returned to
Beijing on June 17.

May 18 The Italian Government Economic Delegation, led by
Mario Eagari, minister of Foreign Trade, arrived in Beijing for a seven-day visit. Premier Zhou Enlai met the
delegation on May 22. A joint press communiqué on the
visit was issued on May 25. The communiqué indicated
that a trade and payments agreement for three years
would be negotiated and that exhibition and visits would
be encouraged.

May 22 The Third Tianjin CCP Municipal Congress was held
from May 22-26. Xie Xuegong was elected first secretary.

May 25 The Vietnamese Government Civil Aviation Delegation, led by Ngo Thuyen, arrived in Beijing for a visit.
An agreement on civil air transport between the two nations was signed on May 30.

May 26 In Bucharest, China and Austria signed a joint communiqué on their decision to establish diplomatic relations at the ambassadorial level, effective May 28.

May 27 China and Ceylon signed, in Colombo, an agreement
on the provision of a convertible currency loan by the
former to the latter. China agreed to provide Ceylon
with an interest-free loan of 150 million rupees in convertible currency, repayable over 12 years after a
grace period of three years.

May 29 The Somali Government Delegation, led by Mohamed
Aden Scek, arrived in Beijing for a visit from May 29
to June 12. An agreement on economic and technical cooperation between the two nations was signed on June 7.

May 30 A Chinese economic and technical study group, led
by Lian Tianzhun, arrived in Santo Isable, capital of
Equatorial Guinea, for a visit. The delegation returned
to Beijing on September 8.

May 31 The Second Yunnan CCP Provincial Congress was
held from May 31 to June 3. Zhou Xing was elected
first secretary.

June 1 The Rumanian Party and Government Delegation, led
by President Nicolae Ceausescu, arrived in Beijing for
a visit at the invitation of Chinese government and
CCP Central Committee. The CCP Central Committee
and State Council gave a welcoming banquet on June 1.
Prince Norodom Sihanouk met President Ceausescu on
June 2; Chairman Mao and Vice Chairman Lin Biao met
him on June 3. Accompanied by Premier Zhou Enlai,
President Ceausescu left Beijing for a tour to Nanjing
and Shanghai on June 5. The delegation left Beijing
for North Korea on June 9. A joint communiqué was
issued before departure to stress the idea of national
independence.
 • The Red Flag published a special issue on the proletarian revolution in education. A major campaign appeared to be in progress at the philosophical-political
level to study Marxist philosophy and to criticize certain "erroneous" ideas, notably apriorism.

June 8 The Yugoslav Government Delegation, led by Foreign
Minister Mirko Tapavac, arrived in Shanghai on their
way to Beijing for a seven-day visit. Premier Zhou Enlai
met the delegation on June 12.

June 10 A list was announced, by the US government, of
goods which could be sold freely to China, including

wheat and a wide range of manufactured goods, but excluding goods of strategic importance.
• The Peruvian Trade Delegation, led by Carlos Alzamora Traverso, arrived in Beijing for a seven-day visit. Premier Zhou Enlai met the delegation on June 14. Minutes of talks between the two nations were signed on June 16.
• Dutch film director Joris Ivens and French film worker Marceline Loridan arrived in Beijing for a visit from June 10 to August 21. Premier Zhou Enlai met them on July 29 and August 11.

June 13   The People's Daily carried a commentator's article entitled "Warning to the US-Japanese Reactionaries," to denounce the joint military exercise of the 7th Fleet and the Naval Self-Defense Forces of Japan held in the sea of Korea.

June 17   The nine-member delegation of Komeito of Japan, led by Yoshokatsu Takeiri, arrived in Beijing for a visit at the invitation of the China-Japan Friendship Association from June 17 to July 2. Premier Zhou Enlai met the delegation on June 28. A joint communiqué was signed on July 2.
• The Iraqi economic and technical delegation, led by Sadoua Hammadi, arrived in Beijing for a seven-day visit. Premier Zhou Enlai met the delegation on June 21. An agreement on economic and technical cooperation between the two nations was signed on June 21.

June 20   The People's Daily carried a commentator's article, entitled "A Dirty Deal, a Despicable Fraud," to denounce US-Japanese agreement for the reversion of Okinawa (signed on June 17). It said that the idea that Okinawa would be nuclear-free after reversion was "a lie," since nothing was clearly written down about withdrawing nuclear weapons or not sending them there.

June 23   A contract on buying diesel locomotives from France was signed in Beijing.

June 24   The DRVN Military Delegation, led by Tran Sam, arrived in Beijing for a ten-day visit. Premier Zhou Enlai met the delegation on July 4. A protocol on supplementary gratuitous supply of military equipment and materials to DRVN in 1971 was signed on July 4.

June 25 Premier Zhou Enlai met Nguyen Van Hien, a member of Presidium of SVN Central Committee, and Ambassador Nguyen Van Quang.

June 29 The Canadian Government Mission, led by Jean-Lue Pepin, arrived in Beijing for a five-day visit. Premier Zhou Enlai met the delegation on July 2. A press communiqué of the visit was issued on July 2.

July 1 The entire party, the Army, and the people of all nationalities in China celebrated the fiftieth anniversary of the founding of the CCP. A joint editorial by the People's Daily, the Red Flag, and the Liberation Army Daily was longer than usual and constituted a brief revised historical sketch of the party's development. Liu Shaoqi was blamed for both "leftist" and "rightist" errors dating back to the 1930's. The reference to "a big careerist" was thought to be a direct criticism of Chen Boda.

July 3 The Delegation of the Australian Labour Party, led by Gough Whitlam, arrived in Beijing for a nine-day visit at the invitation of the Chinese People's Institute of Foreign Affairs. Premier Zhou Enlai met the delegation on July 5.

July 5 The fifteen-member friendship delegation of American members of the Committee of Concerned Asian Scholars arrived in Beijing for a visit from July 5-23. Premier Zhou Enlai met the group on July 21.

July 6 In Aden, the PRC and the People's Republic of Yemen signed minutes of talks on the establishment of the Yemen Cotton Textile Printing-Dyeing Combine Enterprise and minutes of talks on the reconstruction of the Khormakasar Salt Works.

July 9 Premier Zhou Enlai and Dr. Henry Kissinger, President Nixon's assistant for national security affairs, held secret talks in Beijing from July 9-11. Premier Zhou Enlai extended, on behalf of the Chinese government, an invitation to President Nixon to visit China at an appropriate date before May 1972.
   • Beijing held a grand ceremony to inaugurate the "China-Korea Friendship Week" marking the tenth an-

niversary of the signing of the Sino-Korean Treaty of Friendship, Cooperation and Mutual Assistance. Chairman Mao Zedong, Vice Chairman Lin Biao, and Premier Zhou Enlai greeted the occasion. The Chinese Party and Government Delegation, led by Vice Premier Li Xiannian, left Beijing for Pyongyang to attend the celebration of the occasion on July 10. Li Xiannian spoke at the Pyongyang rally on July 11. The delegation returned to Beijing on July 16.

July 14   The French Parliamentary Delegation, led by Alain Peyrefitte, arrived in Beijing for a visit from July 14-31. Premier Zhou Enlai met the delegation on July 18.

July 15   The announcement, which was made in person by President Nixon on television, read as follows: "Premier Zhou Enlai and Dr. Henry Kissinger, President Nixon's Assistant for National Security Affairs, held talks in Beijing from July 9-11, 1971. Knowing of President Nixon's expressed desire to visit the People's Republic of China, Premier Zhou Enlai has extended an invitation to President Nixon to visit China at an appropriate date before May 1972. President Nixon has accepted this invitation with pleasure. The meeting between the leaders of China and the United States is to seek the normalization of relations between the two countries and also to exchange views on questions of concern to the two sides." The same announcement was carried on page one of the People's Daily on July 16.

July 16   China and Nepal signed letters of exchange on road building, and cotton planting in Katmandu.

July 20   The People's Daily carried an editorial, entitled "The National Aspirations of the Vietnamese People Will Surely Be Realized," to commemorate the seventeenth anniversary of the Geneva Agreement.
    • The Algerian Government Delegation, led by Abdel Aziz Bouteflike, arrived in Beijing for an eleven-day visit. Premier Zhou Enlai met the delegation on July 23. The Sino-Algerian agreement on economic and technical cooperation was signed on July 27.
    • The Delegation of the Black Workers' Congress from the United States, led by James Fourman, arrived in Beijing for a twenty-five day visit at the invitation

of the Chinese People's Association for Friendship with
Foreign Countries. Zhang Chunqiao met the delegation
on July 23.

July 23   In Ottawa, Prime Minister Pierre Trudeau of Canada
received the Trade Mission of China National Cereals,
Oils and Foodstuffs Import and Export Corporation,
headed by Zhu Jinzhang.

July 24   The Government Delegation of Sierra Leone, led by
Finance Minister C.A. Kamara-Taylor, arrived in Shanghai for a seven-day visit at the invitation of the Chinese government. Premier Zhou Enlai met the delegation
in Beijing on July 29. A communiqué on establishment
of diplomatic relations between the two nations, and
agreements on economic and technical cooperation, trade,
and payments by the two nations were signed on July 30.
   • The Delegation of the People's Liberation Movement
of Angola, led by Agostinho Neto, arrived in Beijing
for a visit from July 24 to August 6. Premier Zhou
Enlai met the delegation on August 3.

July 25   The discovery of the earliest known manuscript of
the Analects of Confucius was announced by NCNA,
which at the same time gave details of a number of important archaeological discoveries made in different
parts of China between 1967 and 1970, during the Cultural Revolution.

July 27   According to a statistical report issued in Paris,
four-fifths of Chinese foreign trade was with capitalist
countries in 1970, compared to only one-fifth in 1960.
The information was provided by OECD (Organization for
Economic Cooperation and Development), and the French
National Center for Foreign Trade. According to the report, West Germany was China's largest trading partner
in Western Europe in 1970 with imports and exports at
$160 million; British and French exports to China had
totaled $100 million, slightly higher than imports. Bei-
jing's trade with Asian countries had increased sharply
since 1966. Singapore, the largest market for China,
imported $1.2 billion worth of China's products in the
five-year period and exported $216 million worth of
goods. Japan was China's largest supplier, with exports totalling $564 million, while Beijing sales to Japan
totalled $250 million.

• The UAR Government Trade Delegation, led by Mohamed Abdullah Merziban, arrived in Beijing for a visit from July 27 to August 8. Premier Zhou Enlai met the delegation on August 2. Instruments for extending trade and payment agreements were signed on August 2.

July 28   The US government announced a suspension of American intelligence-gathering missions over the PRC by manned SR-71 reconnaissance planes and unmanned drones.

• Writer Han Suyin and her husband, Vincent Ruthnaswamy arrived in Beijing for a visit from July 28 to October 8. Premier Zhou Enlai met them on October 6.

July 29   In Pyongyang, Prince Norodom Sihanouk issued his twenty-fourth message to the Khmer nation. In the message, he said that Premier Zhou Enlai had assured him that "China did not break her word" and would maintain the policy of support for the three peoples of Indo-China. Sihanouk's views were given explicit support from China by the publication of the full text of his message in the People's Daily.

• The PRC government issued a statement concerning the Soviet proposal on the convening of a conference of the five nuclear powers. The statement condemned such a monopolistic conference and repeated China's demand for a conference of all countries to discuss the complete prohibition and thorough destruction of all nuclear weapons.

July 31   The 1971 Sino-Vietnamese protocol for scientific and technological cooperation plan was signed in Beijing.

August 1   Army Day was celebrated by a banquet attended by the senior Chinese leaders the previous evening. A joint editorial of the People's Daily, the Red Flag, and Liberation Army Daily pointed to the success of Chinese foreign policy and emphasized the growing strength of medium-sized and small powers in opposing the "hegemony" of the super-powers.

• The twenty-two member Albanian Agricultural Delegation, led by Pirro Dodbiba, arrived in Beijing for a visit from August 1-31. Premier Zhou Enlai met the delegation on August 29.

August 2 The United States ended twenty years of opposition to the PRC's presence in the United Nations by
announcing it would support actions at the General Assembly this fall calling for seating the PRC. At the
same time, the US emphasized its continued resistance
to any move to expel Nationalist China, or otherwise
deprive it of representation in the United Nations.
On August 4 NCNA accused the US of playing a "clumsy
two-Chinas trick" that was "absolutely illegal and fu-
tile."

August 3 Jiang Qing, Zhang Chunqiao and Yao Wenyuan
accompanied Dutch film director Joris Ivens, French
film worker Marceline Loridan, writer Han Suyin, and
her husband, Vincent Ruthnaswamy to attend an experimental performance of Ode to Yimeng, a modern
revolutionary dance opera.

August 4 The PRC and Turkey issued, in Paris, a joint
communiqué on the establishment of diplomatic relations
between the two nations.
 • The Chinese Government Trade Delegation, led by
Zhou Huamin, left Beijing for Moscow. The Sino-Soviet
goods exchange and payment agreement was signed on
August 5. The delegation returned to Beijing on August 11.

August 5 Premier Zhou Enlai met James Reston, vice president of the New York Times, and Mrs. Reston in Beijing.

August 6 Kim Il Sung made the first public reference (in
Pyongyang) to President Nixon's proposed visit to Beijing. He said that Nixon was "going to turn up in Beijing with a white flag." He also said that China "would
continue to actively support and encourage the fighting
revolutionary people."
 • Ne Win, chairman of the Revolutionary Council and
prime minister of the government of the Union of Burma,
and Madame Ne Win arrived in Beijing for a visit to
China from August 6-11. Premier Zhou Enlai gave a
banquet to welcome them on August 6. Chairman Mao
Zedong met them on August 7. Describing his visit
later, Ne Win said that Premier Zhou Enlai had agreed
that overseas Chinese should be either citizens of China

or their country of domicile, not both, and that mixed and pure Chinese of the second generation should be offered Burmese citizenship.

August 7   The First Tibet Autonomous Region CCP Congress was held from August 7-12. Ren Rong was elected first secretary.

August 8   The Korean Government Economic Delegation, led by Chong Jun Taek, arrived in Beijing for an eight-day visit. Premier Zhou Enlai met the delegation on August 8. An agreement on economic cooperation between the two nations was signed on August 15.
   • The Chinese Delegation for Cooperation in Telecommunications, led by Zhong Fuxiang, left Beijing for a visit to Chile from August 8-20. The Sino-Chilian agreement for telecommunications services between the two nations was signed on August 19.

August 12   The Second Sichuan CCP Provincial Congress was held from August 12-16. Zhang Guohua was elected first secretary.

August 14   The PRC and the Democratic Republic of Yemen signed, in Aden, minutes of talks on construction of a road from Ain to Manfid, minutes of talks on construction of Zingibar Bridge, and minutes of talks on drilling wells.

August 15   The Third Ningxia Hui Autonomous Region CCP Congress was held from August 15-18. Kang Jianmin was elected first secretary.
   • The PRC Military Friendship Delegation, led by Li Desheng, arrived in Tirana, Albania for a visit August 15-22. Enver Hoxha and Mehmet Shehu met the delegation on August 20. The delegation arrived in Bucharest, Rumania on August 22 for a visit. Nicolae Ceausescu met the delegation on August 31. The delegation returned to Beijing on September 2.

August 16   The Third Heilongjiang CCP Provincial Congress was held from August 16-19. Wang Jiadao was elected first secretary.
   • In Islamabad, China and Iran signed a joint communiqué to establish diplomatic relations at the ambassadorial level.

August 17   China issued a statement after the US officially
requested to add a "two-Chinas" item to the UN agenda
(August 17). The Foreign Ministry statement, dated
August 20, said: "Should a situation of 'two Chinas',
'one China, one Taiwan' or 'the status of Taiwan remaining to be determined' or any other similar situation
occurs in the United Nations, the Government of the
PRC will absolutely have nothing to do with the United
Nations."
   •Premier Zhou Enlai met Dara Janekovic, correspondent of the Yugoslav newspaper Vjesnik.

August 18   The Korean Military Delegation, led by Army
General O Jin U, arrived in Beijing for a visit from
August 18 to September 7. An agreement on China
providing Korea with gratis military aid was signed on
September 7.

August 19   NCNA reported the completion of a new canal
opening a new outlet to the sea for two of the four
tributaries of the Haihe River system in Hebei province.

August 22   Chairman Mao Zedong, Vice Chairman Lin Biao
and Premier Zhou Enlai greeted the twenty-seventh anniversary of the liberation of Rumania.
   • The Trade Delegation of the China Council for the
Promotion of International Trade, led by Zhang Guang-
dou, arrived in Kuala Lumpur, Malaysia. A joint communiqué signed on the last day of the visit on August
28 said that China had agreed to purchase 40,000 tons
of rubber, 5,000 tons of palm oil and 50,000 c.u.m. of
logs, as well as other items.

August 23   NCNA announced the publication by the People's
Publishing House of the thirty-fifth and the thirty-
seventh volumes of the "Complete Works of Marx and
Engels," translated into Chinese by the Bureau for the
Translation of Marx-Engels-Lenin-Stalin's Work under
the CCP Central Committee.

August 24   The Chinese Government Trade Delegation, led
by Zhou Huamin, left Beijing for Guyana for a visit
from August 24 to September 7.
   • The Delegation of the Liberation Front of Mozambique, led by Samora Moises Machel, arrived in Beijing

for a visit from August 24 to September 7. Premier
Zhou Enlai met the delegation on September 5.

August 27   The People's Daily carried an editorial, entitled
"Our Party Is Advancing Vigorously," to mark the conclusion of the reconstruction of the party structure at
the provincial levels in China. The editorial said that
a few "proven renegades" had been thrown out of the
party and new blood had been brought in.

August 31   The People's Daily carried an editorial, entitled
"Smash the US Imperialists' Military Adventure of Aggression in Laos," to support statements by Prince
Souphanouvong which had denounced the Americans for
instigating Lao and Thai troops to make "nibbling attacks on the Lao Liberated zone."
   • The State Council and the Military Commission of
the CCP Central Committee issued a circular introducing
a new routine of physical exercise throughout the country on a trial basis.

September 3   The 141-member Beijing Opera Troup, led by
Tian Guangwen left Beijing for a performance tour in
North Korea from September 3-28.

September 4   The China Dance Drama Troups headed by
Zhou Jiuyan left Beijing for a performance tour in Al-
bania (September 14-October 5), Rumania (October 5-
November 1), and Yugoslavia (November 1-November 29).

September 5   NCNA released a report on the crossing over
to Beijing of Zhang Shuangzhao, confidential secretary
of the Taiwan Provincial Department of Finance after he
finished his post-retained study in the US.

September 9   NCNA released a report on the petroleum industry. It said that national output of crude oil had risen
by thirty percent every year from 1966-70.

September 10   The Republic of Togo decided to establish
diplomatic relations with the PRC.
   • The Delegation of the Japanese Communist Party
(left), led by Masayoshi Fukuda, arrived in Beijing for
a visit from September 10-22 at the invitation of the
CCP Central Committee. Premier Zhou Enlai met the
delegation on September 20.

September 11   A meeting between Premier Zhou Enlai and the delegation of new Diet members of the Liberal Democrat party, headed by Hideji Kawasaki, was suddenly postponed without explanation. It was rescheduled for September 16.

    • NCNA announced distribution of fifty colored photographs of Mao Zedong taken in different historical periods to mark the fiftieth anniversary of the founding of the CCP.

    • The Chinese Communist Trade Delegation, headed by Zhou Huamin, left Beijing to visit Finland (September 13-18), Sweden (September 19-26), Norway (September 27 to October 4), and Denmark (October 4-11).

September 12   Lin Biao's attempt to have Mao Zedong assassinated failed.

September 13   The Mongolian newspaper Unen, reported that a Chinese military aircraft with nine persons on board had crashed in Mongolian territory in the early hours of September 13.

September 15   The foreign press reported, in mid-September, that the traditional National Day parade in Beijing would not be held this year. Preparations for such a parade had been apparent in early September and the decision to cancel it only leaked out gradually (starting September 15) and appeared in the foreign press on September 20.

    • Marcel A. Naville, president of the International Committee of the Red Cross, and his wife arrived in Beijing for a visit from September 15-21. Vice Premier Li Xiannian met them on September 20.

September 16   AT&T announced that on the previous day the Chinese authorities had agreed to the company's request for the restoration of direct telephone communication between the US and the PRC, and that the Shanghai-Oakland radio-telephone circuit would be restored accordingly.

September 18   On the fortieth anniversary of the Shenyang Incident (September 18, 1931), the People's Daily published an editorial delivering a sharp attack on Japan for its revival of militarism.

• The twenty-two-member delegation of the Japanese
Dietmen's League for Promotion of the Restoration of
Japan-China Diplomatic Relations, led by Aiichiro Fuji-
yama, arrived in Beijing for a fifteen-day visit. Pre-
mier Zhou Enlai met the delegation on September 29.
A joint statement was signed on October 2.

September 19   The Delegation of the PLO, led by Abou Jihad,
arrived in Beijing for a fourteen-day visit. Premier
Zhou Enlai met the delegation on September 28.

September 21   Japan decided to cosponsor the American "two
Chinas" resolution at the United Nations. This produced a strong reaction from Beijing. A People's Daily
article of September 26 said that the so-called improvement of Japan-China relations was entirely "a smokescreen."

September 23   The fourteenth meeting of the Joint China-
Albania Committee for Cooperation in Technology and
Technical Sciences was held in Beijing from September
23 to October 19. A protocol of the meeting was signed
on October 19.

September 24   The PRC Ministry of Foreign Affairs issued a
statement expressing indignation at the bombing of
Quang Binh province in North Vietnam by a large number of US aircraft on September 21.
• The Chinese Government Economic Delegation, led
by Vice Premier Li Xiannian, left Beijing for Hanoi on
a five-day visit. The 1972 agreement on China's economic, military, and material assistance to North Vietnam was signed on September 27.

September 25   The Japanese Matsuyama Ballet Group, led by
Masao Shimizu, arrived in Beijing for a performance
tour in Beijing, Xian, Yanan, Wuhan, Shanghai, and
Guangzhou. The group left Guangzhou for home on December 2.

September 27   NCNA released a report dealing with iron and
steel production, saying that, during the first eight
months of 1971, production of steel, pig iron, and iron
ore was 19.6, 22, and 31.4 percent higher respectively
than in 1970.

• The Chinese Government Delegation, led by Bai Xiangguo, left Beijing for Paris on a fourteen-day tour. President Pompidou gave a welcome luncheon on October 2. This was the first Chinese group to visit Western Europe at the full ministerial level since 1949.

September 28 The 350-member Pyongyang National Opera troup of Korea, headed by Sin In Ha, arrived in Beijing for a performance tour in Beijing, Shenyang, Nanjing, Shanghai, Hangzhou, and Guangzhou. The troup left Guangzhou for home on December 9.

September 29 Leaders of the American Black-Panther Party, Huey Newton, Elain Brown, and Robert Ray, arrived in Beijing for an eleven-day visit.

September 30 The PRC Foreign Ministry gave a reception in Beijing celebrating the twenty-second anniversary of the founding of the PRC. Ji Pengfei acted as host at the reception.

October 1 People in Beijing celebrated the twenty-second anniversary of the founding of the PRC at gala parties in the parks. The Cultural Group under the State Council and the Chinese People's Association for Friendship with Foreign Countries gave a reception for the occasion. Premier Zhou Enlai, Jiang Qing, and Zhang Chunqiao were present.
    • Four new theatrical works were announced by NCNA. These were the revolutionary operas Fighting on the Plains, The Duzhuan Mountain, and Ode to the Dragon River, and the revolutionary dance-drama Ode to Yimen.

October 5 Premier Zhou Enlai and Guo Moruo met more than seventy Americans visiting or working in Beijing.
    • His Imperial Majesty Haile Selassie I, emperor of the Empire of Ethiopia, and his entourage arrived in Guangzhou for a state visit to China. The delegation arrived in Beijing on October 6. Vice Chairman Dong Biwu and Premier Zhou Enlai gave a grand welcome banquet on October 6. Prince Norodom Sihanouk met the emperor on October 7. Chairman Mao Zedong met the emperor on October 8. Economic, technical, and trade agreements between the two nations were signed on October 9. The delegation left Beiging for a visit to

Shanghai in the company of Premier Zhou Enlai on October 10.   The delegation left Guangzhou for home on
October 13.

October 6   The Doena Art Group of the Armed Forces of
Rumania, led by Major General Dinu Stelian, arrived in
Beijing for a performance tour in Beijing, Nanjing, and
Hangzhou.   The group left Beijing for home on October
30.

October 7   Letters on the Sino-Burmese economic and technical cooperation were exchanged in Rangoon.   China
agreed, at Burma's request, to extend the terms of its
loan agreement of January 1961, allowing for use of the
stipulated loans up to September 30, 1975, and for re-
payment by installments over the ten-year-period 1980-
90.
   • The Rumanian Government Delegation, led by Ioan
Avram, arrived in Beijing on their way to Hanoi.   The
delegation returned to Beijing on October 14.   Premier
Zhou Enlai met the delegation on October 15.   The Sino-
Rumanian protocol for China's supply of complete project and technical assistance to Rumania was signed on
October 16.   The delegation left Beijing for home on
October 16.

October 8   The People's Daily published an article entitled
"All Products Must Be of Good Quality," to argue
against the view that the greater the quantity, the
greater the achievement.
   • The PRC and Ceylon signed in Colombo an agreement providing an interest free loan from China to Ceylon in the form of 100,000 metric tons of rice.

October 11   Guo Moruo, special envoy of the PRC, and his
eight assistants, left Beijing by special plane to attend
the celebrations of the 2,500th anniversary of the founding of the Persian Empire.   The Shahanshah of Iran received the group on October 16.   They left Iran for
home on October 19.

October 13   The PRC and Burundi signed a joint communique
to restore diplomatic relations between the two nations.

October 14   The Chinese Government Delegation, led by Sha

Feng, left Beijing for Magadishu to attend the celebrations of the second anniversary of the Somali Revolution. The delegation left Somalia on October 28.

October 15   A Sino-Korean broadcast and television cooperation agreement was signed in Pyongyang.

October 17   The 1971 regular meeting of the Sino-Korean Border Railway Joint Committee was held in Shenyang from September 27 to October 17. A protocol was signed at the meeting on October 17.

October 19   The Chinese Government Trade Delegation, led by Bai Xiangguo, left Beijing for a visit to Algeria (October 20-28), and Italy (October 28-November 6). A long-term trade agreement between China and Algeria was signed on October 27, and a joint press communiqué on the visit was issued on October 28. A Sino-Italian trade and payment agreement was signed on October 29.

October 20   Henry Kissinger and his party of thirteen members arrived in Beijing to make final arrangements for the visit to China by President Nixon. Premier Zhou Enlai, Ye Jianying, and Ji Pengfei held talks with the delegation on October 20. The delegation left Beijing for home on October 26.

October 25   The PRC and Belgium signed a joing communiqué in Paris to establish diplomatic relations at the ambassadorial level.
   • The United Nations General Assembly adopted, by a vote of 76-35-7, a resolution to admit the PRC to the United Nations, including a permanent seat in the Security Council and at the same time to expel the Chinese Nationalist regime on Taiwan. Before adopting this resolution, the General Assembly rejected a US resolution asking the General Assembly that any proposal to deprive the Chinese Nationalist representation in the United Nations was "important matter" requiring a two-thirds majority for adoption. The vote on the resolution was 55-59-15.

October 27   China and Nepal signed letters of exchange regarding the surveys on mineral deposits in Nepal.

October 28   The People's Daily carried an editorial, entitled
"Historical Trend Is Irresistible," saying: "The vote
at the UN General Assembly reflects the general trend
and popular feelings in demand for friendship with the
Chinese people.   This is a historical trend that no force
on earth can hold back."
   • China and Rumania signed, in Beijing, an agreement on China providing Rumania with a long-term, interest-free loan.

October 29   Foreign Minister Gaston Thorn announced that
Luxembourg had decided to recognize the PRC, but had
not taken steps to set up diplomatic relations.
   • Unesco decided to admit Chinese representatives
in place of those from Taiwan.
   • Acting Foreign Minister Ji Pengfei sent a telegram
to U Thant, secretary general of the UN, informing
him that the PRC government would send a delegation
in the near future to attend the twenty-sixth session
of the General Assembly.

November 1   El Salvador Foreign Minister Walter Beneke and
Carlos de Sola, his assistant, arrived in Beijing for a
visit from November 1-5.   Ji Pengfei met them on November 4.
   • The People's Literary Publishing House published
Guo Moruo's Li Bai Yu Du Fu (Li Bai and Du Fu), the
first book on classical literature published in China
since 1965.

November 2   The Afro-Asian Table Tennis Friendship Invitational Tournament was held in Beijing from November 2-
14.
   • In a joint communiqué signed in Ottawa, the PRC
and Peru agreed to establish diplomatic relations at the
ambassadorial level.
   • The FAO (Food and Agriculture Organization) of the
UN adopted a resolution to admit Chinese representatives
in place of those from Taiwan.
   • Acting Foreign Minister Ji Pengfei informed U
Thant of the composition of the PRC delegation to the
Twenty-sixth Session of the General Assembly and the
appointment of Huang Hua as the permanent representative (ambassadorial rank) to the Security Council.

November 3   The PRC Ministry of Foreign Affairs gave a

banquet thanking Albania, Algeria and twenty-one other sponsor countries and other friendly countries for their support of the restoration to China of all her legitimate rights in the United Nations and the expulsion of the "Chiang Kai-shek clique."
  • The Government delegation from Finland arrived in Beijing for a seventeen-day visit. Premier Zhou Enlai met the delegation on November 18. The 1972 Sino-Finnish trade agreement was signed on November 18.

November 4 Ryokichi Minobe, governor of Metropolitan Tokyo of Japan, and his assistants, arrived in Beijing for a nine-day visit. Premier Zhou Enlai met them on November 10.

November 5 Soviet Ambassador Vasily Sergeevich Tolstikov gave a reception in Beijing to mark the fifty-fourth anniversary of the October Socialist Revolution.
  • The Pakistan Delegation, headed by Z.A. Bhutto, arrived in Beijing for a visit at the invitation of the Chinese government. Premier Zhou Enlai met the delegation on November 5. At a banquet given by Ji Pengfei on November 7, China reiterated her opposition to "any country interfering in the internal affairs of other countries."

November 6 The Standing Committee of the National People's Congress and the State Council sent a message congratulating the Soviet people on the fifty-fourth anniversary of the October Socialist Revolution. The message stated that China held a view that "the controversies of principles between China and the Soviet Union should not affect their state relations."

November 8 The Trade Mission from Guyana, led by David A. Singh, arrived in Beijing for a seven-day visit. A Sino-Guyana agreement on the development of trade relations, the mutual establishment of trade missions, and an agreement relating to import and export commodities of the two nations were signed on November 14.

November 9 The PRC Delegation to the Twenty-sixth Session of the General Assembly of the United Nations, headed by Qiao Guanhua, deputy minister of Foreign Affairs, left Beijing for New York. The delegation arrived in New York on November 11.

    • The PRC and Lebanon signed, in Paris, a joint communiqué to establish diplomatic relations at the ambassadorial level.

    • Premier Zhou Enlai and Prince Norodom Sihanouk spoke at the reception marking the eighteenth anniversary of the independence of Cambodia. Both stated that a new Geneva Conference or a political solution proposed by others would serve no purpose in solving the problem of Cambodia. It became known that Sihanouk planned to visit Hanoi at the same time President Nixon visited China.

    • Chinese Ambassador to Tanzania Zhang Xidong paid a visit to Kigali, capital of Rwanda, at the invitation of President Gregoire Kayibanda. The PRC and Rwanda signed a joint communiqué to establish diplomatic relations at the ambassadorial level on November 12.

November 10 Stanley Karnow of Washington Post wrote an article entitled "Lin Seemed Purged in Beijing Power Struggle" describing a "plot" against Chairman Mao in which Lin and his supporters had been involved. The "plot" had taken place in the first half of September and was in some way connected to the mysterious crash of the Chinese Trident jet in Mongolia on September 13, 1971.

November 13 The Government Trade Delegation from Burma, led by Colonel Maung Lwin, arrived in Beijing for a seven-day visit. A trade agreement and a commodity loan agreement between the two nations were signed on November 19.

November 15 Qiao Guanhua spoke at the plenary meeting of the Twenty-sixth Session of the UN General Assembly. He stated the basic principles of Chinese foreign policy in his speech, namely, "China belongs to the third world."

November 16 The Mexican government severed diplomatic relations with Nationalist China in Taiwan.

    • The International Labour Organization of the UN decided to admit Chinese representatives in place of those from Taiwan. Taiwan also lost its observer status in the General Agreement on Tariff and Trade Conference; however, it was left up to the PRC to apply to participate.

• The Chinese Government Economic Delegation, led by Fang Yi, left Beijing to visit Albania from November 16 to December 14. The protocol on the exchange of goods and payments for 1972, and the protocol on the use of Chinese loan by Albania for 1972 were signed on December 5.

• China voted for a resolution in the UN General Assembly calling on the US not to import chrome from Rhodesia.

November 17 Sino-Korean agreement on cooperation in overhauling of ships was signed in Pyongyang.

• The Ecuadorian government decided to sever diplomatic relations with Nationalist China in Taiwan.

November 18 China announced that a nuclear test was carried out in its western region. According to the US Atomic Energy Commission, it was a small test of about twenty kilotons, similar in size to the bomb dropped in Hiroshima.

November 20 The DRVN Workers' Party and the Government Delegation, led by Pham Van Dong, arrived in Beijing for a seven-day visit and received a grand rousing welcome. The CCP Central Committee and State Council gave a welcome banquet on November 20. Chairman Mao Zedong met the delegation on November 22; Prince Sihanouk met it on November 25. The Sino-Vietnamese communiqué on the visit was issued on November 26 in Shanghai.

November 23 The PRC was elected as a member of the UN Economic and Social Council.

• The Chinese Government Delegation, led by Li Shuiqing, left Beijing for Pakistan to attend the inaugural ceremony of a heavy plant and the ground-breaking ceremony of a foundry and forge factory from November 23-30.

• The Peruvian Delegation, led by General Jorge Fernandez Maloonado Solari, arrived in Beijing for a seven-day visit. An agreement on economic and technical cooperation between the two nations was signed on November 28.

November 24 Qiao Guanhua spoke at the plenary meeting
of the UN General Assembly in connection with the proposal of the Soviet Delegation to convene a world disarmament conference. He reiterated China's call, first
made on July 31, 1963, for a world conference to discuss the complete prohibition and destruction of all
nuclear weapons. Qiao called for full consultations on
the subject in order to make "a new start."
• Huang Hua spoke at a UN Security Council meeting
condemning Portuguese aggression against Senegal,
Guinea, Tanzania, and Zambia, and reaffirming China's
support for the just struggle of the people of Guinea
Bissau, Angola, and Mozambique against colonialism.
Later, the UN Security Council adopted a resolution
condemning Portugal's violation of the sovereignty and
territorial integrity of Senegal.
• In an interview with an Italian visitor which was
reported in Le Monde, Premier Zhou Enlai was said to
have complained that the Soviet Union had stationed
1.2 million troops along the frontier without any explanation.
• A regular meeting of the Sino-Mongolian Boundary
Through Railway Traffic was held in Huhehot.
• The Rumanian Government Trade Delegation, led
by Cornel Burtica, arrived in Beijing for a seven-day
visit. A protocol on the exchange of goods and payment for 1972 between the two nations was signed on
November 26.

November 28 Chairman Mao Zedong, Vice Chairman Dong
Biwu, and Premier Zhou Enlai greeted the twenty-
seventh anniversary of the liberation of Albania.

November 29 A joint Washington-Beijing announcement stated
that President Nixon's visit to China would begin on
February 21, 1972. According to Henry Kissinger in a
press conference on November 30, the president would
spend seven days in China, including at least four days
in Beijing, and visits to Shanghai and Hangzhou. "The
major thrust of the discussion," said Kissinger, "will
be on bilateral issues."

November 30 In his speech on the Palestine question at the
Special Political Committee of the UN General Assembly,
Fu Hao condemned the "aggression committed by the

Israeli Zionists against the Palestinian and other Arab
peoples."

• The Chinese PLA Delegation, led by Zhung Hui,
left Beijing for Tanzania to attend the celebration of the
tenth anniversary of independence of Tanganyika. The
delegation returned to Beijing on December 17.

December 1 A joint editorial by the People's Daily, the
Red Flag, and the Liberation Army Daily stressed that
the "class struggle" continued to be very acute and
that it should not be treated lightly.

• News was published on the excavation of archaeological sites and antiquities during and since the Cultural Revolution. These included an important discovery
of the artifacts of prehistoric culture, dating back to
five and six thousand years ago in Gansu province.

December 2 Minutes of talks on matters concerning the de-
sign and construction of a refractory in Pakistan with
the assistance of China was signed in Karachi.

• Chinese Ambassador to Mauritania Fang Youqiu
paid a visit to Senegal from December 2-7. A joint
communiqué was signed on December 5 to establish diplomatic relations between the two nations.

December 4 Chinese comment on the development of the war
situation was restrained until the full-scale Indian offensive was launched in the last week of November. In
the Security Council meetings between December 4 and
6, China exercised its first veto against a Soviet resolution favoring the Indian case. China voted in favor
of the two resolutions (vetoed by the Soviet Union) calling for a ceasefire.

December 5 No British-China agreement had been reached
in the negotiations to upgrade diplomatic relations at the
ambassadorial level. Britain was willing to "take note"
of the Chinese position on Taiwan, using the same formula employed by Canada and other nations which had
recognized China in the past year, but this was not acceptable to the Chinese. As Premier Zhou Enlai explained in an interview with Neville Maxwell, "Britain
is different from Canada. It is a signatory of the Cairo
Declaration and the Potsdam Declaration."

• In an interview with Neville Maxwell, Premier Zhou

Enlai said: "We should not expect too much to come out of President Nixon's visit."

• Huang Hua submitted a draft resolution concerning the tension on the Indo-Pakistan subcontinent and condemned the Indian government's armed aggression in Pakistan.

December 6   Huang Hua denounced the Soviet and Indian representatives for scheming to inject the representatives of Bangladesh into the Security Council meeting.

• The twelfth session of the China-Korea Committee for Scientific and Technical Cooperation was held in Pyongyang from December 6-29. A protocol of the meeting was signed on December 28.

December 8   A joint communiqué was signed in Copenhagen by the PRC and Iceland to establish diplomatic relations at the ambassadorial level.

• Premier Zhou Enlai informed the president of the United Arab Emirates (Zayid Bin Sultan Al Nuhayyan) of the Chinese government's decision to recognize his country.

• During a debate over an Afro-Asian proposal to revive the Jarring Mission in the Mideast, Qiao Guanhua stated that "we are not opposed to the Jewish people or the people of Israel, but we are firmly opposed to the Zionist policies of expansion and aggression." China abstained in the voting.

December 9   In the First Committee of the UN General Assembly, China voted against three resolutions calling for a total ban on all nuclear tests. On the following day, Chen Zhu said that China would abstain on the resolution concerned with the treaty for the prohibition of nuclear weapons in Latin America, but would vote in favor of a proposal to declare the Indian Ocean to be a "peace zone."

• The Japanese Delegation for Japan-China Memorandum Trade Talks, headed by Yoshimi Furui, arrived in Beijing for a thirteen-day visit. Premier Zhou Enlai met the delegation on December 20. A communiqué on the talks was signed on December 21.

December 10   After a visit to China, Santiago Carrillo, secretary general of the Communist party of Spain, said that

both parties had agreed to reestablish relations.   He
also reported that the CCP regarded his party as a
revolutionary one and that the CCP accepted the right
of every party to work out their own revolutionary
road.

December 13   China abstained from voting on a resolution in
the Security Council extending the operations of the UN
peacekeeping force in Cyprus.
    • An agreement on China's assistance to Syria for
the construction of a spinning mill was signed in Damascus.
    • China decided to commute the sentence of John
Thomas Downey to five years' imprisonment.   Richard
George Fecteau and Mary Ann Harbert were set free
and left China via Shunzhun.

December 14   The Chinese Government Delegation, led by
Yang Jie, left Shanghai for Tanzania and Zambia to
participate in the fifth round of talks on the Tanzania-
Zambia railway.   The three government delegations
signed the summary of tripartite talks on December 23.
The Chinese delegation concluded its visit on January
10, 1972.

December 15   According to the Financial Times, the first 500
kilometers of the Tanzania-Zambia railway had been basically completed (13,000 Chinese were reported to be
at work on the railway).   China would eventually provide 102 locomotives, 100 passenger wagons and over
2,000 freight wagons.
    • The Cuban Trade Delegation, led by Ismael Bello
Rios, arrived in Beijing for talks on the 1972 Sino-
Cuban trade.   The delegation left Beijing for home on
February 16, 1972.

December 16   China lodged a strong protest with the Indian
government against the crossing of the China-Sikkim
boundary and intrusion by Indian personnel into Chinese territory for reconnaissance.

December 18   Qiao Guanhua and some members of the PRC
delegation left New York for home.

December 19   Chairman Mao Zedong, Vice Chairman Dong

Biwu, and Premier Zhou Enlai greeted the eleventh anniversary of the founding of the South Vietnam National
Front for Liberation.

December 20   It was reported that Japanese entry permits
could now be supplied to Chinese citizens at the Japan-
China Memorandum Trade Office in Beijing.
• Premier Zhou Enlai met the Sudanese High Status
Official Delegation, led by Deputy President Khalid
Hassan Abbas.   An agreement on economic and technical
cooperation between the two nations was signed on De-
cember 20.

December 21   China took part in a decision by the Security
Council to recommend Mr. Kurt Waldheim as the new
secretary general.

December 22   Premier Zhou Enlai sent a message of congratulations to Z.A. Bhutto on his assumption of the presidency of the Islamic Republic of Pakistan.   He also met
the Pakistan Ambassador to China K.M. Kaiser.

December 23   Former French Prime Minister and Madame Pierre Mendes-France arrived in Beijing for a twenty-day
visit.   Premier Zhou Enlai met them on December 25.

December 24   The People's Daily carried an article entitled
"Foil US Imperialism's New Act of War," to denounce
the US resumption of bombing against North Vietnam.

December 26   The thirty-nine member Japanese Haguruma
(Gear) Theater, led by Natsuko Fujikawa, arrived in
Beijing for a performance tour in ten cities.   Premier
Zhou Enlai and other Chinese high officials saw the per-
formance in Beijing on January 19.   The group left
Guangzhou for home on April 3.

December 27   The Chinese government lodged protest with
the Indian government against the intrusions into
China's territory by armed Indian personnel and into
China's airspace by Indian aircraft.
• The Chinese Government Trade Delegation, led by
Li Qiang, arrived in Pyongyang for a nine-day visit.
The 1972 Sino-Korean protocol on goods exchange was
signed on December 30.

December 28   China and Ceylon signed an agreement on par-
cel post in Colombo.

  • Huang Hua sent a letter to the president of the
UN Security Council pointing out that the "aggressive
slaughter and persecution of the Pakistan people by
Indian troops" constituted a serious violation of the
Security Council Resolution 307 (1971).

December 29   On the American bombing of North Vietnam,
the Chinese Ministry of Foreign Affairs issued a statement saying that the Chinese were "closely watching"
the American moves and would "exert utmost" efforts to
assist the Vietnamese.

  • The PRC Embassy in India lodged protest with the
Indian Ministry of External Affairs against the "provocations carried out by Indian and Tibetan rebel bandits"
in front of the Chinese Embassy in India.

December 30   In a Security Council meeting, Huang Hua condemned the South regime "for colluding with the South
African and Portuguese colonialist authorities in jointly
suppressing the national liberation movement of the people of Southern Africa."

  • The PRC Ministry of Foreign Affairs issued a
statement to denounce the inclusion of the Diaoyu and
neighboring islands in the area of reversion as "a gross
encroachment upon China's territorial integrity and
sovereignty." It said that the islands, located between
Okinawa and Taiwan, had been part of China's territory
in the Ming Dynasty and were taken over together with
Taiwan when China ceded Taiwan to Japan in 1895.

Chapter III

1972

THE YEAR OF THE VISIT

President Richard M. Nixon's state visit to Beijing in February, the first such visit by an American president, proved to be an event of historic importance. The long-awaited trip was the fulfillment of a prediction made by Premier Zhou Enlai ten months earlier to American table tennis players and newsmen on their breakthrough visit to the mainland, that Sino-American relations would enter a new, warmer phase.

The President's visit had been arranged by Washington for maximum effect. A US press corps of eighty-seven newsmen, photographers, and radio and television reporters gave it full coverage. Hours after the restrained welcome at the airport the atmosphere gave way to one of warmth. The Nixon-Mao discussions were described as "serious and frank." In the week that followed, Nixon and Zhou held seven rounds of talks. In the time between these talks, the president toured the Ming Tombs, the Forbidden City and the Great Wall of China. At his farewell banquet in Beijing, Nixon said the Wall reminded him "that for almost a generation there has been a wall between the People's Republic of China and the United States of America." The process of removing that wall, he said, had begun.

In the joint communiqué signed in Shanghai on February 27, Nixon and Zhou took note of their differences, but said that these should not prevent the normalization of Sino-American relationships. The document stopped short of diplomatic recognition but formalized agreements usually concluded between allies. Among these agreements were the acceptance of the principles of peaceful coexistence, renunciation of the use of force, and refusal to seek domination of the Pacific area. The communiqué also touched on the Taiwan problem. Nixon acknowledged that the Nationalist-held island was part of China and recognized that its future was for the Chinese themselves to settle. He said that the US objective was to withdraw all US military men (about 9,000) from the island. With the continued deescalation of the Vietnam War in mind, he said that he would "progressively reduce" American forces "as the tension in the area diminished."

People-to-people exchanges, increased trade, and periodic consultations at a high level were also included in the agreement. The preeminent exchange took place in June, when presidential advisor Henry Kissinger returned to Beijing for five days of talks with Zhou. The exchanges markedly increased in the months following the summit meeting. By December, more than 500 Americans—journalists, physicians, scientists, scholars, and "friendly personages"—had made the journey to the mainland. Chinese visits to the United States were less frequent. By the end of the year, though, following a successful tour by the Chinese ping-pong team, others began to cross the Pacific. Among them were Chinese scientists, physicians and acrobats.

Although no one foresaw that US-China trade would be substantial at the outset, the first hesitant steps were promising. Americans appeared for the first time at the Guangzhou Trade Fair. And in September, US officials announced the first sale in twenty-two years of American wheat to China. While in September a total of fifteen million bushels were sold, this number increased to 18,700,000 bushels by November. During this same autumn period, unofficial indications that China anticipated a two-year boom in construction and air transportation were present in the flurry of Chinese buying in the United States and the United Kingdom. Purchases included ten Boeing 707's, valued at $125 million and Pratt and Whitney engines worth $25 million. Britain's Hawker-Siddeley group sold the Chinese twenty Trident jets, valued at approximately $159,800,000. The advent of Chinese participation in international air transport seemed imminent.

On November 22, Nixon cleared away another important barrier to Sino-American trade and travel when he lifted US-imposed restrictions which for more than two decades had

barred US planes and ships from visiting the mainland. It
was the start of a process of establishing regular air and
sea service between the United States and China. Major US
airlines quickly expressed interest.

Nixon's China visit, formalizing as it did a dramatic
about-face in US policy toward the People's Republic, had a
domino effect on American-Asian allies. For Japan, a long-
time follower of US efforts to bolster Taiwan and deny Beijing
a seat in the United Nations, the effect was close to being
traumatic. Prime Minister Sato Eisaku belatedly tried to
clamber aboard the China bandwagon, only to be rebuffed
by Beijing. By July his popularity among those Japanese
who favored a China rapprochement had decreased significantly. In subsequent party elections, Sato was succeeded
by a pro-China coalition led by Minister of International
Trade and Industry Kakuei Tanaka. Tanaka made the desired journey to Beijing late in September. After five days
of talks with Zhou and then with Mao, he signed a communiqué establishing diplomatic relations. Preparations were
soon launched for the conclusion of a peace treaty and for
trade, commerce and air agreements. Although diplomatic
ties with Taiwan, with which it had done an annual trade in
excess of $1 billion were broken, Japan sought to keep eco-
nomic and cultural ties with Taipei alive.

It was not long before more than twenty other countries recognized the People's Republic of China. Shortly
after Tanaka's successful visit, West German Foreign Minister Walter Scheel visited Beijing. Scheel formalized Bonn's
diplomatic recognition, and this left the United States alone
among the major world powers in recognizing the Republic
of China in Taiwan. In October, the Chinese took a step
toward improving their frayed relations with Great Britain.
The process of rapprochement had begun with the increase
of the two countries' respective diplomatic missions from the
chargé d'affaires level (existing since 1949) to the full ambassadorial one. A visit by Foreign Secretary Sir Alec
Douglas-Home produced public expressions of friendship and
hopes for more rewarding exchanges. Finally, the Sino-
American initiative and the change in Sino-Japanese relations
enabled Beijing to approve the beginning of peace and unity
negotiations between North and South Korea, and to join the
US and the Soviet Union in pressuring the North Vietnamese
to negotiate seriously on a cease-fire in Indo-China.

By late 1972, China had become an active member of
the United Nations. China's prime concern was the Soviet
threat. Thus, China opposed the European security conference and SALTs I and II, vetoed Bangladesh's application
for membership, refused to stop testing nuclear weapons,
and supported the Arab countries against Israel (although
she did speak out against terrorism and hijacking after the
Munich Incident in August). China's other concern involved
an attempt to break apart the perceived Soviet-American
"collusion" and, as a substitute for nuclear duopoly, offer
itself as the organizer, if not the leader, of the Third World
numerical majority. China therefore supported the claims of
Peru and other countries to a 200-mile coastal waters belt at
the United Nations Conference on Trade and Development in
Santiago in April, spoke at the UN-sponsored ecology conference in Stockholm on the rights of the Third World countries
to redress the imbalance among industrialized versus developing countries, and, in the corridors of the UN, sought
out delegations of developing countries. By the year's end,
China was generally regarded as a regular member of the UN
who had gone to the length of not only hosting the new
Secretary General Kurt Waldheim in Beijing, but establishing
a Geneva office in order to supply delegates to those specialized agencies of which it was already a member and to
make its interests known in others.

In the field of foreign aid, five new countries--Burundi,
Mauritius, Chile, Guyana, and Ruwanda--signed their first
aid agreement with China in 1972, and Malta became the first
non-Communist European country to receive Chinese aid.
China also offered to provide military equipment and training
to Sudan following the counter-coup in that country in 1971.
The year was also noteworthy for the flow of visitors to
China. Aside from the American and Japanese extravaganzas,
and the Waldheim visit, 1972 saw many visits from heads of
state (or in some cases, their wives) and foreign ministers
in Beijing, as well as a host of lesser trade, military, and
diplomatic missions. China also signed air transport agreements with Turkey, Albania, Rumania, and Ethiopia.

Domestically, China continued to consolidate its economic gains, with emphasis on agriculture and light industry.
Grain production for 1971 reached an all-time high of 246
million tons. With this as a foundation, heavy industry was
also able to move forward. Steel production totaled twenty-

one million tons, ranking China as seventh in world output. Foreign trade reflected China's determination to keep imports and exports close to the balancing point. The total trade amount of $4,611,000,000 was nine percent more than in 1970. Exports were fifteen percent greater at a total amount of $2,364 billion, and imports were only a scant three percent greater, at a total figure of $2,247 billion. Due to the 1972 drought which was the worst drought in China in the last ten years, total agricultural production, according to a late-year estimate given by Premier Zhou Enlai, would amount to four percent less than the 1971 harvest. Although this decline in agricultural production was probably responsible for the decrease in the total economic growth of the year, industry continued to expand at a rapid rate (about ten percent for industrial output).

Politically, the surviving leadership continued its efforts to tighten control over the Army, a source of disaffection not only in the 1966-69 Cultural Revolution but also in the aftermath. As 1972 drew to a close, China had no chief of state, no defense minister, and no chief of army general staff. The five-man standing committee of the party politburo, the most powerful organ in the country, had been whittled down to two--Chairman Mao and Premier Zhou Enlai. While one of the members, Kang Sheng, was ill, the other two, Defense Minister Lin Biao and Mao's old secretary, Chen Boda, had been purged.

The death of Lin Biao, Mao's designated successor, had been rumored for months. It was confirmed in July. The official version as told by Mao and Zhou to visiting foreign dignitaries, was that Lin aspired to immediate power, even though the party's revised 1969 constitution named him as Mao's heir. He plotted to overthrow his aging chief. When the conspiracy was discovered in mid-September of 1971, so the story went, Lin's son commandeered an airliner, which headed for Moscow via Mongolia. It ran out of fuel, though, and when it crashed deep inside Mongolia, all aboard, including Lin, his wife, Ye Zhun (a member of the politburo), and his son (a military officer) died. Equally mysterious was the disappearance of Chen Boda, the firebrand of the Cultural Revolution who counted Madame Mao as his ally. In October, party officials in Shanghai reported that he was associated with the Lin Biao plot in some unspecified way.

There was a campaign to restore old party cadres and technicians to their posts on grounds of administrative need and as their reeducation through the May 7 school experience drew to a close. It was now declared that "ultraleftism" involved opposing this restoration of "veteran comrade-in-arms," whose prior mistakes were now regarded as "contradictions among the people." At many local levels, it was reported that by 1972, more than ninety percent of the cadres criticized during the Cultural Revolution had returned to their previous posts.

The Lin Biao affair had, indeed, weakened the Army as a whole in its relations with the party. If the Army continued to remain without a head and if its influence had generally declined, the power of Zhou Enlai would increase dramatically. He no doubt felt exposed, especially politically, given the absence of a buffer between himself and Mao, and given the tightrope he had to walk between various ideological sins. Nevertheless, Zhou seemed to be able to carry out policies representative of the meliorating tendencies that have always been his hallmark. As for Mao Zedong, there were many indications of a net decline in his power. Moreover, the cult of Maoism--stressed repeatedly during the Cultural Revolution--had abated. By the spring of 1971, the process of returning Mao to his position as a symbol rather than a glorified proletarian saint, had begun. By late autumn of 1972, fewer Mao portraits, statues and quotations were present. The "Thought of Mao Zedong" was no longer singled out but was only mentioned along with the thoughts of other Communist saints.

There were more changes in educational policy. By the end of 1971, three new elements in the series of changes which had been underway since the end of the Cultural Revolution, were announced, and in 1972 they were put into effect. The first element involved the goal of providing universal five-year education in the countryside and seven-year education in cities. The second element involved a reduction in the emphasis of an admissions policy in higher education, which favored only those with impeccable ideological and class qualifications; emphasis was now placed on admitting the more academically well-prepared. The final element was the restoration of examinations in the classroom to avoid a severe decline in the quality of output in education.

January 1   The Burundi Government Delegation, led by
      Arthemon Simbanaiye, arrived in Beijing for a twelve-
      day visit.   Premier Zhou Enlai met the delegation on
      January 6.   An economic and technical cooperation
      agreement between the two nations was signed on
      January 8.
            • NCNA announced a new agreement (signed in Bei-
      jing on December 30, 1971) authorizing Air France to
      double the number of its Paris-Shanghai flights to two
      flights a week.   Air France was the only western air-
      line to provide regular service to China.
            • The People's Daily anounced some statistics on
      economic performance in 1971, the first official nation-
      wide statistics for ten years.   The total value of in-
      dustrial output in 1971 was about ten percent more
      than in 1970.   Steel production was 21 million tons,
      an increase of eighteen percent over the previous
      year.   Other increases were shown in pig iron (twen-
      ty-three percent), crude oil (27.2 percent), chemical
      fertilizer (20.2 percent), cement (16.5 percent), min-
      ing equipment (68.8 percent), metallurgical equipment
      (24.7 percent), and coal (over eight percent).   Total
      grain output had reached 246 million tons, "surpassing
      that of the rich harvest year of 1970."   No percentage
      increase was recorded for cotton.   Water conservancy
      and land reclamation on works were said to have
      added over 30 million mu more of land--this was the
      biggest figure in the last ten years.   In 1971, the
      state purchase prices for peanuts, sesame, grapeseed,
      and oils went up 16.7 percent on the average, while
      the selling prices for the processed products from
      these crops remained unchanged.   Price reductions
      were recorded in chemical fertilizer, insecticide, kero-
      sene and diesel oil, and farm machinery.   This process
      of "gradual reduction in the gap in parity prices be-
      tween industrial and agricultural products" had pro-
      duced a net benefit to the Chinese consumer of one
      thousand million yuan.

January 3   The nineteen-member advance party, headed by
      Brigadier General Alexander M. Haig, arrived in Bei-
      jing to make technical arrangements for President
      Nixon's visit to China.   The delegation left Shanghai
      for home on January 10.

January 6   Chen Yi, member of the Ninth Central Committee
         of the CCP, vice chairman of the CCP Central Commit-
         tee Military Commission, vice premier and foreign min-
         ister, died of cancer in Beijing at the age of seventy-
         one. Beijing held a ceremony to pay last respects to
         him on January 10. Chairman Mao Zedong attended
         the ceremony. Premier Zhou Enlai made a memorial
         speech.

January 7   A number of articles in the Peking Review (no.
         1) quoted Chairman Mao as saying that party cadres
         should be "open and above-board." They should not
         "intrigue and conspire."
             • China announced a nuclear test. The US Atomic
         Energy Commission estimated its yield as about 20,000
         kilotons--equivalent to 20,000 tons of TNT.
             • An Zhiyan endorsed, at the organizational meeting
         of the Fifty-second Session of the UN Economic and
         Social Council, the enlargement of the Council's mem-
         bership from twenty-seven to fifty-four.

January 11   NCNA announced that China's 1971 crude oil
         production was twenty-eight percent and natural gas
         twenty-five percent above the 1970 levels and topped
         the year's plan. It also reported that China's power
         industry set an all-time record in output and sur-
         passed the 1970 output by eighteen percent.

January 12   In a letter to Secretary General Kurt Waldheim,
         Huang Hua urged that the UN and all its related bodies
         should take immediate steps to cease all contacts, in-
         cluding programs of aid, to Taiwan. Later it was de-
         cided to suspend all aid under the UN development
         programs to Taiwan, withdrawing twenty-six experts
         from the island.

January 13   Minutes of talks between the PRC and the Peo-
         ple's Democratic Republic of Yemen on building a fac-
         tory of small agricultural implements and hardware with
         China's assistance was signed in Aden.

January 19   The People's Daily carried an article entitled
         "Refuting Malik," to defend Chinese policy on dis-
         armament. It said: We cannot agree to a world dis-
         armament conference the Soviet Union proposed to con-

vene, which has neither set a clear aim nor put forward practical steps for its attainment." The treaty
on the prohibition of bacterial weapons was also criticized for failing to prohibit chemical weapons, thus
allowing both superpowers to retain their stocks.

• The Official Delegation of the Foreign Affairs
Committee of the National Assembly of France, led by
Jean de Broglie, arrived in Beijing for a twelve-day
visit. Premier Zhou Enlai met the delegation on January 22.

January 21   In an interview with a delegation from Okinawa
on January 21, Premier Zhou Enlai said that China had
conducted thirteen nuclear tests thus far, one of which
was unsuccessful. He did not believe that the two
superpowers would ever abolish the nuclear systems on
which they had spent so much money, but they would
never use them without killing the working class on
whom they depended for expansion of their markets.

• The PRC Ministry of Foreign Affairs issued a
statement demanding that "the US government must
stop its 'Vietnamization' scheme, stop its war of aggression against Vietnam and the other Indo-Chinese
countries, immediately withdraw all the US aggressive
armed forces and its vassal troops and immediately
cease supporting the puppet regime in South Vietnam,
the Lon Nol-Sirik Matak clique in Cambodia and the
rightists in Laos."

January 22   The 1972 Sino-Vietnamese protocol on supplementary gratuitous supply of military equipment and economic materials by China to Vietnam was signed in
Beijing.

January 26   The Guinean Government Trade Delegation, led
by Aboubacar Couatey, arrived in Beijing for a ten-day
visit. The 1972 Sino-Guinean trade protocol was signed
on February 5.

January 27   NCNA reported discovery of a pair of three-
meter-long incisors as well as other teeth and bones of
an ancient elephant (elephus namadicus) in Zhengzhou,
Henan province.

• In a letter to UN Secretary General Kurt Waldheim,
Foreign Minister Ji Pengfei held that racial discrimina-

tion and apartheid were "the products of the policy of
colonialism and imperialism." The struggle of the peoples of Africa against these evils was "wholly just,
and they should be given energetic, moral, political,
and material support by all countries."

  • Huang Hua arrived in Addis Ababa, Ethiopia, to
attend the Special Meetings of the UN Security Council.
The meetings were held from January to February 5.
Huang stated Chinese policy toward Africa in a speech
on January 31. "The affairs of Africa," he said, "can
only be settled by the African countries and people
themselves," and he called for vigorous UN opposition
to the South African and Rhodesian regimes.

January 29 The Czechoslovak Government Trade Delegation,
led by M. Bursa, arrived in Beijing for a fourteen-day
visit. The 1972 Sino-Czechoslovak agreement on exchange of goods and payment was signed on February
10.

  • The French Air Force monthly magazine reported
that China's Air Force had eighty operational F-9
supersonic jet fighters. The magazine, Air Actualities,
said the aircraft, capable of flying at 1,400 miles per
hour, had been on the Chinese assembly line since
April, 1971. The Chinese Air Force had about 3,600
combat planes, including 2,900 fighters, 440 bombers,
300 helicopters and 400 transports, the magazine said.

January 30 The People's Daily carried an article entitled
"Comments on US President's Message," to describe
"US imperialism as riddled with insuperable contradic-
tions at home and abroad."

  • A Reuters report from Hong Kong said that twenty-seven Chinese Army officers had been arrested in
1971 during attempt to escape from the mainland to
Hong Kong. All twenty-seven were allegedly linked
with Lin Biao, who had not been mentioned officially
since October 8, 1971.

January 31 Chinese Ambassador to Italy Shen Ping and
Representative of Malta, G.J. Mallia, signed, in Rome,
a joint communiqué to establish diplomatic relations between the two nations at the ambassadorial level.

  • Pakistan President Z.A. Bhutto arrived in Beijing
for a state visit from January 31 to February 2. Pre-

mier Zhou Enlai met him on January 31; Chairman Mao
met him on February 1. A joint communiqué was
signed by Bhutto and Zhou to record a detailed exchange of views between them. It included China's
agreement to convert into outright grants the four
loans already being provided, and to defer the repay-
ment period of the 1970 loan for twenty years.

February 1   The Red Flag published the revised version of
the "model" Beijing opera Haigang (On the Docks).

February 11   The 1972 Sino-Cambodian (the Royal Government) agreement on China's provision of economic aid
and military supplies to Cambodia was signed in Beijing.

February 12   Prince Norodom Sihanouk left Beijing for Hanoi
to pay an unofficial visit. He remained in Hanoi during President Nixon's visit to China. The news of his
trip was not officially announced until his return to
Shanghai on March 5. He remained in Shanghai until
March 14, arriving in Beijing on the next day to a
full-scale welcome by Premier Zhou Enlai and other
Chinese leaders.

February 14   In New York, China and Mexico signed a joint
communiqué to establish diplomatic relations at the
ambassadorial level.
   • A further relaxation was announced in US restrictions on trade with China. China was now placed in
"Country Group V," which had the effect of putting
China on the same footing for the export of nonstrate-
gic goods as the Soviet Union and most Eastern European countries. The American Company RCA Globcom
had already been allowed under special license to sell,
for $2.9 million, a satellite earth station to China,
which was installed in Shanghai for immediate linkup
with Intesat facilities to provide direct television coverage of the Presidential visit.

February 15   Mrs. Lois Snow, wife of Edgar Snow, and their
children sent a message to Chairman Mao Zedong and
Premier Zhou Enlai to inform them of the death of Edgar Snow. Chairman Mao Zedong, Premier Zhou Enlai,
and Song Qingling sent separate messages of condolences to Mrs. Snow on February 16. A ceremony was

held in Beijing to pay last respects to Edgar Snow on February 19.

February 16   Chinese Ambassador Zhang Haifeng and Argentine Ambassador José Maris Ruda signed, in Bucharest, a joint communiqué to establish diplomatic relations at the ambassadorial level beginning February 16.
• The Delegation of the Chinese Academy of Science, led by Jin Lisheng, left Beijing for Havana to attend the celebrations of the tenth anniversary of the founding of the Cuban Science Academy. The delegation returned to Beijing on March 11.

February 17   President Nixon and Mrs. Nixon left Washington on their way to China, with scheduled stops in Hawaii and Guam. Three days before departing, President Nixon had talks with André Malraux, the French writer and specialist in Chinese affairs.

February 18   The 1972 Sino-Ceylonese trade protocol was signed in Colombo.
• According to a Hangzhou radio broadcast in Zhejiang province, the total number of primary school students in 1971 was thirty-eight percent more than in 1966, while the total number of middle school students was nearly 100 percent more. The radio broadcast also announced that more than eighty percent of the school-age children were enrolled in primary schools.

February 19   The PRC Ministry of Foreign Affairs issued a statement to condemn the American bombing of North Vietnam.

February 20   The PRC Ministry of Foreign Affairs accused Premier Sato Eisaku and other Japanese of plotting to establish a pro-Japanese puppet regime in Taiwan that would demand independence, not rule by Nationalist China, for the island.

February 21   President Nixon arrived in Beijing, accompanied by his wife and an official party of thirteen, including Secretary of State William Rogers and Henry Kissinger. President Nixon was greeted by Premier Zhou Enlai at the airport and met with Chairman Mao Zedong. President Nixon's meeting with Chairman Mao, which took place in his Zhong-nan-hai residence, lasted one hour and was described afterwards as "frank and serious." Observers were struck by the relatively optimistic tone of the speeches delivered at the banquet by Premier Zhou Enlai and President Nixon.

February 22 Nixon, Kissinger and Zhou met for four hours of political discussion, while Rogers and Ji Pengfei held a separate conference. In the evening, after a private dinner, the Nixons attended a special performance of the Red Detachment of Women, a revolutionary opera fashioned by Jiang Qing, Mao's wife. The People's Daily, after publishing only a formal announcement of Nixon's visit the previous day, devoted two of its six pages to the president's arrival, featuring photos of Nixon and Mao shaking hands. Chinese television, which had ignored the event in its evening news bulletin February 21, carried a ten-minute film of Nixon's activities.

• The Chinese Government Trade Delegation led by Zhou Huamin, left Beijing for Havana for a visit from February 22 to March 13. The 1972 Sino-Cuban trade protocol was signed on March 4.

February 23 President Nixon and Premier Zhou Enlai met for four hours of talks. The talks were followed by exhibitions of gymnastics and table tennis in the evening. Mrs. Nixon visited the Evergreen People's commune, and the Beijing glassware factory.

• Colonel V.I. Ivancy, military attaché of the Soviet Embassy in Beijing, gave a reception for the fifty-fourth anniversary of the founding of the Soviet Army and Navy.

February 24 President Nixon made an excursion to the Great Wall of China and to the Ming Tombs. He then had talks with Premier Zhou for another three hours.

• Beijing Radio announced that Dong Biwu, eighty-six years of age, had been named acting chief of state. He filled the vacancy created by the ouster of Liu Shaoqi.

• NCNA reported an "unusual increase" in the total of urban and rural bank savings, which was up by 13.8 percent in 1971 over the previous year.

• Beijing journalists gave a reception in Beijing to

welcome the American journalists accompanying President Nixon.

February 25 On their last day in Beijing, the Nixon group visited the Forbidden City. Later in the afternoon, President Nixon and Premier Zhou Enlai met for about an hour of private talks. That night, at the Great Hall of the People, President Nixon gave a banquet for Premier Zhou Enlai at which their mutual toasts suggested the substance of the communiqué released on February 27. American journalists accompanying President Nixon gave a cocktail party in Beijing for Beijing journalists.

February 26 President and Mrs. Nixon and the presidential party, accompanied by Premier Zhou Enlai and others, left Beijing for Hangzhou by special plane, and made an excursion to the West Lake in the afternoon. Mrs. Nixon visited the Linyin Monastery in the company of Madame Xu Hanbing. Chairman Nan Ping of Zhejiang Provincial Revolutionary Committee gave a banquet for the Nixon group in the evening.

February 27 In the company of Premier Zhou, the Nixons arrived in Shanghai from Hangzhou by special plane. Chairman Zhang Chunqiao of the Shanghai Municipal Revolutionary Committee gave a banquet to welcome the Nixons in the evening. Dr. Henry Kissinger, the president's assistant for national security affairs, held a news conference in Shanghai on the aspects of the Shanghai communiqué. According to an account given by him, he and Vice Foreign Minister Qiao Guanhua, who were the only officials on the both sides to attend all the Nixon-Zhou meetings, acted as "go-betweens" between their leaders.

February 28 President Nixon, Mrs. Nixon, and the presidential party left Shanghai for home by special plane. President Nixon and Premier Zhou released a joint communiqué indicating that their talks had resulted in agreement on the need for increased Sino-American contacts, and for eventual withdrawal of US troops from Taiwan as the tension in the area diminishes. On the status of Taiwan, the US acknowledged that "all Chinese on either side of the Taiwan Strait main-

tain there is but one China and that Taiwan is a part
of China" and "does not challenge that position."
  • The official Soviet News Agency, Tass, gave a
long account of the Shanghai communiqué, noting that
the communiqué had stressed "essential differences between China and the US."
  • Both India and Pakistan reacted to the Chinese
statement in the Shanghai communiqué pledging support
for the people of Kashmir "in their struggle for the
right of self-determination." Indian Prime Minister
Indira Gandhi said her country "will not tolerate any
interference in the Kashmir matter." The Pakistan
Foreign Ministry hailed the communiqué.
  • Marshal Green, assistant secretary of state in Far
Eastern Affairs, and John H. Holdridge, an Asian specialist for the National Security Council staff, arrived
in Tokyo from Shanghai to discuss President Nixon's
visit to China with Japanese officials.

February 29 The White House announced that Senate Lead-
    ers Mike Mansfield and Hugh Scott would visit China
    at the invitation of Premier Zhou Enlai. The Senators'
    visit was expected to take place during the summer.
      • Commenting indirectly on the Shanghai communiqué,
    Pyongyang Radio asked: "Why is the Nixon clique to-
    day shouting so hysterically about 'peace,' 'negotia-
    tion,' and 'exchange'? The reason has something to do
    with his 'sinister and sly objectives' of gaining a fav-
    ourable position for the forthcoming presidential elec-
    tion."
      • China and Ghana issued a communiqué on the re-
    sumption of diplomatic relations between the two na-
    tions. Chinese diplomats left Accra on November 5,
    1966.

March 1 The Red Flag published the revised version of the
    'model' Beijing opera Longjiang Song (Ode to Dragon
    River).

March 2 The People's Daily published an investigation re-
    port entitled "Do a Good Job of Enterprise Manage-
    ment in a Practical Way" from No. 2 cotton mill in
    Nandong (Jiangsu). The report called for more party
    leadership over "enterprise management."
      • China and Rumania signed a radio and television

cooperation agreement in Bucharest.

• Marshal Green, accompanied by John H. Holdridge, arrived in Taipei from South Korea for talks with leaders of Nationalist China. In Washington, James G.H. Shen, Nationalist Chinese ambassador to the US, said that Secretary William Rogers had assured him of the American commitment to the 1954 Taiwan Defense Treaty.

• According to a high administrative briefing in Washington, the statement in section (a), number 4 of the Shanghai communiqué implied some degree of Chinese acquiescence in avoiding the use of force to settle the dispute. It was with the prospect of a "peaceful settlement" in mind that the withdrawal of US forces from Taiwan was stated as a final objective.

• The Japanese cabinet decided to permit the use of Export-Import Bank of Japan credits to facilitate plant equipments exports to China "on the same footing" as those to other countries. However, China made it clear that it would never apply for such credits until the "Yoshida letter" of March 1964 had been officially nullifed by the Japanese government.

March 3   Japanese Foreign Minister Fukuda presented the Diet with a "unified view" on the status of Taiwan. He stated that, "The Japanese Government is not in a position to speak of the territorial status of Taiwan. But it can fully understand the PRC's claims that Taiwan is part of its territory. With this recognition in mind, the Government will make positive efforts to normalize relations with China." The statement was ridiculed by the People's Daily commentator on March 3 as revealing Fukuda's "two-Chinas plot."

March 4   The Rumanian Scientific and Technical Delegation, led by Gheorghe Pacosts, arrived in Beijing for a twelve-day visit. A protocol of the Fourteenth Session of the Sino-Rumanian Joint Commission on Scientific and Technical Cooperation was signed on March 14.

March 6   Carlos Altamirano, general secretary of the Socialist party of Chile, and Arnold Camu, member of the political bureau of the party, arrived in Beijing for a ten-day visit. Premier Zhou Enlai met them on March 14.

March 7   The Chinese Government Trade Delegation, led by
Bai Xiangguo, left Beijing for Cairo on a fourteen-day
visit.   The 1972 Sino-Egyptian trade protocol was
signed on March 18.   President Anwar Sadat met the
delegation on March 20.
• Many provinces reported the reopening of universities and colleges.   The worker-peasant-soldier students had been recommended by the mass and had
gained at least two years' practical experience at work.

March 8   In a letter to the UN Committee on Decolonization,
Huang Hua wrote: "The Chinese Government had consistently held that the question of Hong Kong and
Macao should be settled when conditions were right,
and the UN had no right to discuss the question."   He
asked that the "erroneous" categorization of Hong Kong
and Macao as "colonial territories" should be immediately removed from all UN documents.

March 9   In Shanghai, Prince Norodom Sihanouk disclosed
that Premier Zhou Enlai had briefed North Vietnamese
leaders in Hanoi, March 3-4, during his talks with
President Nixon, and assured them of Beijing's support
in the Indo-Chinese struggle.   Prince Sihanouk further
said that Premier Zhou had informed him that President
Nixon had been told in the Beijing summit talks that
China would not mediate the Indo-China war by acting
as an intermediary between Washington and the Indo-
Chinese resistance.

March 10   The PRC Ministry of Foreign Affairs issued a
statement condemning the intensified American bombing
raids on North Vietnam.
• It was announced that regular diplomatic contact
would be established between the American and Chinese ambassadors in Paris to discuss the development
of cultural exchange and trade, though contacts would
not be limited to this channel.
• China refuted the Japanese representative's claim
for Japanese sovereignty over Diaoyu and other islands
at the meeting of the UN Committee on the Peaceful
Uses of the Seabed and Ocean Floor Beyond the Limits
of National Jurisdiction.   Japan called China's remarks
"surprising" and "irrelevant."   To Chinese claims to
the Nanxiao and other islands, the Philippine delegate

said that Manila was on record as having "reservations" on China's claim.

March 11   The Polish Government Trade Delegation, led by
Harian Dmochowski, arrived in Beijing for a seven-day
visit.   The 1972 Sino-Polish agreement on the exchange
of goods and payments was signed on March 14.
   • The Hungarian Government Trade Delegation, led
by Tordai Jano, arrived in Beijing for a nine-day visit.
The 1972 Sino-Hungarian agreement on the exchange
of goods and payments was signed on March 14.

March 13   The PRC and Britain signed a joint communiqué
in Beijing on the exchange of ambassadors between the
two nations.   In the communiqué, Britain "acknowledged the position of the Chinese Government that
Taiwan is a province of the PRC," and decided to remove their official representation in Taiwan on this
date.
   • The American and Chinese ambassadors to France
met in Paris for the first time in what was believed to
be a projected series of private discussions on matters
of interest to the two nations.
   • The fourteenth regular meeting of the Sino-Vietnamese boundary through railway traffic was held in
Kunming.   A protocol of the meeting was signed on
March 20.

March 14   Letters on economic cooperation were exchanged
in Katmandu between the PRC and Nepal.

March 18   China conducted a nuclear explosion in the atmosphere at the Lop Nor test site in northwestern China.
The US Atomic Energy Commission, which announced
the test, said the explosion had the force of 20,200
kilotons, the equivalent of 20,000 tons of TNT.
   • Foreign Minister Ji Pengfei met the ambassadors
to China of Syria, Egypt, the Sudan, the Arab Republic of Yemen and Algeria, the chargé d'affaires of Iraq,
the People's Democratic Republic of Yemen and Morocco, and the head of the Mission of the Palestine Liberation Organization in Beijing.   Ji exposed the plot of
King Hussein of Jordan to set up a "United Arab Kingdom" and reiterated China's support for the Palestine
people and other Arab peoples in their struggle against
"US-Israeli aggression."

March 20   The leader of the Soviet delegation on the Sino-
           Soviet border talks, Ilyichev, returned to Beijing,
           having been away since December. On the following
           day, NCNA announced that the Seventeenth Session
           of the Sino-Soviet Commission for Navigation on Bound-
           ary Rivers had come to an end in Moscow without
           agreement.
             • The Chinese Civil Aviation Technical Group, led
           by Ma Renhui, left Beijing to visit Pakistan, Albania,
           Rumania, and Yugoslavia from March 20-April 14.   A
           Sino-Albanian agreement on civil air transport was
           signed on March 18. A Sino-Rumanian agreement on
           civil air transport was signed on April 7. A Sino-
           Yugoslav agreement on civil air transport was signed
           on April 14.

March 21   The Egyptian Government Delegation, led by Mah-
           moud Riad, arrived in Shanghai on the way to Beijing
           for a ten-day visit. Premier Zhou Enlai met the dele-
           gation on March 23.
             • In Sanaa, the PRC and the Arab Republic of
           Yemen signed minutes of talks between the two gov-
           ernments on building the Taiz Hospital for the Arab
           Repubic of Yemen.

March 23   A Chinese film entitled The Red Detachment of
           Women was shown at the 1972 Vienna Film Festival.

March 24   The PRC and Pakistan reached an agreement on
           the supply of general commodities from China to Pak-
           istan under the loan.

March 25   Xie Fuzhi, vice premier and minister of Public
           Security, first secretary of CCP Beijing Municipal
           Committee, chairman of the Beijing Municipal Revolu-
           tionary Committee, and first political commissar of the
           Beijing Garrison, died of cancer of the stomach in
           Beijing at the age of sixty-three after long-term medi-
           cal treatment. A memorial ceremony, held in Beijing,
           was presided over by Li Xiannian.
             • Mrs. Lois Wheeler Snow, widow of the late Edgar
           Snow, her sister Kashin Wheeler and her son Chris-
           topher Snow arrived in Beijing for an eight-day visit
           at the invitation of the Chinese People's Association
           for Friendship with Foreign Countries. Premier Zhou

Enlai and Deng Yingchao called on Mrs. Snow on March 27; Vice Chairman Song Qingling called on her on April 2.

March 28 NCNA reported the discovery of stone implements, probably dating back between 200,000 and 300,000 years, in Hubei province.

March 29 The ninth meeting of the Administrative Council of the Sino-Albanian Joint Stock Shipping Company was held in Tirana from March 29 to April 18. A protocol of the meeting was signed on April 9.
   • The Chinese Government Trade Delegation, led by Chen Jie, left Beijing to visit Afghanistan, Iran, Bulgaria and East Germany. A Sino-Afghan protocol on exchange of goods was signed on April 4. A Sino-Bulgarian agreement on exchange of goods and payments for 1972 was signed on April 26. The delegation returned to Beijing on April 28.

March 30 The Delegation of the Palestine Liberation Organization, headed by Abu Nidal, arrived in Beijing for a twelve-day visit. Premier Zhou Enlai met the delegation on March 31 and again on April 10.

March 31 The Government Delegation of Rwanda arrived in Beijing, headed by Pierre Damien, for a twelve-day visit. Premier Zhou Enlai met the delegation on April 1.
   • By the end of March, all provinces had reported the reopening of colleges and institutes of further education except for Inner Mongolia, which was sending its students to neighboring provinces.

April 1 The subject of language reform was discussed at length, for the first time since the Cultural Revolution, in a letter entitled "How to Regard the Simplified Characters Newly Current Among the Masses" by Guo Moruo, published in the Red Flag. Guo explained that simplified characters were only "the product of a transitional period" and that the main objective was phoneticization.
   • Prime Minister Don Mintoff of Malta led the government delegation to visit China from April 1-8. The delegation was greeted at the Beijing airport by Pre-

mier Zhou Enlai and a crowd of 100,000 persons. In welcoming Prime Minister Mintoff on April 2, Premier Zhou referred to the opposition of "many Mediterranean countries" to the increasing tension created by the two superpowers contending for hegemony in the Mediterranean Sea. On April 8, the People's Daily published an article condemning "the superpowers' scramble for hegemony in the Mediterranean." An agreement on a long-term and interest-free loan by China to Malta was signed on April 8.

• The ten-member delegation of the Japanese Democratic Socialist Party, led by Ikko Kasuga, arrived in Beijing for a fourteen-day visit. Premier Zhou Enlai met the delegation on April 12.

April 2 A regular Sino-American diplomatic contact, as envisaged by the Shanghai communiqué, was held in Paris.

April 5 UN Secretary General Kurt Waldheim appointed Dang Mingzhao as under secretary general for Political Affairs and Decolonization.

• Sino-Korean mutual aid and cooperation agreement for fisheries was signed in Beijing.

• Premier Zhou Enlai met British writer Felix Greene. Premier Zhou told Mr. Greene that the tension in the Far East would continue until the US withdrew its forces and its support from the Saigon regime.

April 8 The Albanian Government Delegation, led by Pico Dodbida, arrived in Beijing for a ten-day visit. A Sino-Albanian agreement on farm machinery loan was signed on April 11. Premier Zhou Enlai met the delegation on April 13.

• The PRC Government Shipping Delegation, led by Ma Ziqing, left Beijing for Ceylon for a twenty-one-day visit. A Sino-Ceylonese shipping service agreement was signed on April 22.

April 10 The First Session of the Sino-Italian Joint Committee was held in Beijing in accordance with the provision of the Sino-Italian Trade and Payments Agreement. The PRC Ministry of Foreign Affairs issued a strong statement supporting Hanoi's spring offensive in Vietnam (which began on March 30).

April 11 Mauritian Prime Minister Sir Seewoosagur Ramgoolam
and Lady Ramgoolam and other distinguished guests
from Mauritius arrived in Shanghai for an official visit
to China from April 11-15. Premier Zhou Enlai met the
delegation on April 12 and 13 in Beijing. The delegation visited the Chinese Export Commodities Fair in
Guangzhou on April 14. A joint communiqué on establishment of diplomatic relations between the two nations
was issued on April 15.

April 14 Chairman Mao Zedong and Premier Zhou Enlai sent
greetings to Premier Kim Il Sung on his sixtieth birthday.
        • Consuelo Gonzales de Velasco, wife of the presi-
dent of Peru, and sixteen other guests from Peru arrived in Guangzhou on the way to Beijing for a seven-
day visit. Premier Zhou Enlai gave a grand welcoming
banquet on April 16.

April 15 Takeo Miki, adviser to the Japanese Liberal Democratic Party, arrived in Beijing for a seven-day visit.
Premier Zhou Enlai met him on April 17 and 21. On
his return, Miki stated that he was confident diplomatic
relations could be established at an early date.

April 16 An article in the Wen Hui Bao and the Liberation
Army Daily called for further efforts to produce popular literature and drama. Various provinces reported
that their professional artists were going down to the
basic levels to cooperate with amateur literary and art
workers, producing large numbers of popular works.

April 17 Afghan Minister of Foreign Affairs Mohammed
Musse Shafiq and his party arrived in Beijing for a
seven-day visit. Ji Pengfei held talks with the delegation on April 17 and 18.

April 18 US Senate Democratic Leader Mike Mansfield and
Mrs. Mansfield and Republican Leader Hugh Scott and
Mrs. Scott and their party arrived in Beijing for a
visit from April 18 to May 3. Premier Zhou Enlai met
the delegation on April 20.

April 19 A Moscow economic weekly, Ekonomicheskaya Gazeta,
announced that trade between the Soviet Union and
China in 1971 had totaled about $153 million.

April 20   The People's Daily published a short commentary
            advocating "the principle of 'walking on two legs' in
            order to make five-year primary education universal
            in the countryside as quickly as possible."
              • Two giant pandas presented by the Beijing Muni-
            cipal Revolutionary Committee to the American people
            were handed over at a ceremony in the US National
            Zoological Park, Washington, DC.

April 21   The Iranian Civil Aviation Delegation, led by Ho-
            shang Arbabi, arrived in Beijing at the invitation of
            the Chinese government for a seven-day visit.

April 23   The Chinese Government Military Delegation, led
            by Chen Xilian, left Beijing for Pyongyang to attend
            celebrations of the fortieth anniversary of the founding
            of the Korean People's Revolutionary Army. The dele-
            gation returned to Beijing on April 30.

April 24   A People's Daily editorial advocated the policy of
            'unity-criticism-unity' in dealing with cadres. Only an
            extremely small number of incorrigible cadres should be
            dismissed, while the rest should be educated, said the
            article.

April 26   The Chinese Workers' Delegation, led by Wang
            Xiuzhen, secretary of CCP Shanghai Municipal Com-
            mittee, left Beijing for Tirana to attend the Seventh
            Congress of the Albania Trade Union and the May Day
            celebrations. The delegation returned to Beijing on
            May 16.

April 27   Premier Zhou Enlai and Zhang Chunqiao met Le
            Duc Tho and other Vietnamese visitors in Beijing.
            They left Beijing for Paris on April 29.
              • The Chinese Border Trade Delegation, led by Zhao
            Yougun, member of Xinjiang Revolutionary Committee,
            left Beijing for Pakistan for a ten-day visit. The 1972
            Sino-Pakistan border trade agreement was reached on
            May 7.

April 29   The Rumanian Government Military Delegation, led
            by Emil Bodnaras, arrived in Beijing from Pyongyang
            for a five-day visit. Premier Zhou Enlai met the dele-
            gation on April 29 and May 3.

- The Ballet Troupe of the Opera Theater of Albania, led by Manthe Bala, arrived in Beijing for a performance tour of China from April 29 to July 3.

April 30 Mrs. Gladys Yang, a British citizen who worked as a translator for the Foreign Language Press and had been detained since 1967 in Beijing, was released from custody.

May 1 No May Day parade was held in Beijing, but NCNA released reports on gala parties held in parks throughout Beijing, and other cities to celebrate the occasion.

May 2 In its review of world military developments for 1971, the Institute for Strategic Studies in London said that more than a quarter of the Russian Army was now deployed along the Sino-Soviet border. The number of Soviet divisions in the area was reported to have risen from 33 to 44 in 1971. The Chinese had some twenty missiles in place in northeastern and northwestern China with F-9 fighters in operation in 1971.

May 4 News of the restoration of the Chinese Young Communist League (CYCL) was reported widely in articles commemorating the May 4th movement. From Yunnan, for example, it was reported that eighty-five percent of CYCL branches in the province had been reestablished. Over 180,000 young people had joined the league and over 30,000 league members had joined the party.

    • NCNA announced the publication of a four-volume Chinese edition of The Selected Works of Marx and Engels.

    • An inaugural meeting of the Asian Table Tennis Union was held in Beijing from May 5-7. A communiqué adopted at the closing session of the meeting was released on May 7. Premier Zhou Enlai met the delegations to the meeting of various countries on May 7.

May 5 Writer Han Suyin arrived in Beijing for a visit from May 5 to July 2.

    • The Tanzanian Military Delegation, led by Geoffrey Oscar Mhagama, arrived in Beijing for a fifteen-day visit. Ye Jianying, minister of Defense, met the delegation on May 19.

• The Shanghai Dance-Drama Troupe of China led
by Xu Jingxian left Beijing for Pyongyang for a performance tour in Korea from May 5 to June 10.

May 9 President Nixon's announcement on May 8 of the mining of North Vietnamese harbors was met on the following day by a strong Chinese protest. The PRC Ministry of Foreign Affairs issued a statement protesting
against the American bombings of two Chinese merchant
ships off the coast of North Vietnam.
    • The Chinese Government Trade Delegation, led by
Chen Jie, left Beijing for a nine-day visit to Kuwait.
    • The Delegation of the China Council for the Pro-
motion of International Trade left Beijing for a twenty-
one-day visit to Mexico.
    • The Mongolian Government Trade Delegation, led
by D. Tserensamga, arrived in Beijing for a ten-day
visit. The 1972, Sino-Mongolian protocol on mutual
supply of goods was signed on May 12.

May 10 The Hungarian Scientific and Technical Delegation,
led by Szili Geza, arrived in Beijing for a seven-day
visit. A Sino-Hungarian scientific-technical cooperation protocol was signed on May 16.

May 11 China's Permanent Representative Huang Hua sent a
letter to the secretary general to protest the further
American escalation of the Vietnam War. According to
Le Monde, the Chinese had been given advance notice
through diplomatic channels of the decision to mine
North Vietnam's harbors.

May 12 The Mauritanian Government Trade Delegation, led
by Ahmedou Ould Abdallah, arrived in Beijing for a
five-day visit. A supplement to the Sino-Mauritanian
trade agreement was signed on May 17.

May 13 The Delegation of the Tanzanian Ministry of Home
Affairs, led by Saidi Ali Maswanya, arrived in Beijing
for a fourteen-day visit. Premier Zhou Enlai met the
delegation on May 14.
    • President Mohamed Siad Barre of the Supreme
Revolutionary Council of Somalia arrived in Shanghai
on the way to Beijing for a five-day visit. Premier
Zhou Enlai held talks with the delegation on May 14,

15, and 17 in Beijing. The delegation left Beijing for Pyongyang on May 18.

• Premier Zhou Enlai met Vietnamese "comrades," Xuan Thuy, Ly Ban, Ngo Thuyen, and Nguyen Van Quang.

May 16 At the Fifty-second Session of the UN Economic and Social Council, Wang Runsheng gave an account of China's control of narcotic drugs in his speech.

• In Beijing, China and the Netherlands signed a joint communiqué raising the status of their diplomatic relations to the ambassadorial level.

• The Tunisian Government Trade Delegation, led by Mohamed Jomaa, arrived in Beijing for a five-day visit. A Sino-Tunis protocol on a supplement to the trade agreement was signed on May 20.

May 17 The Burmese Government Economic Delegation arrived in Beijing for an eighteen-day visit. Vice Premier Li Xiannian met the delegation on May 26.

May 18 A regular Sino-American diplomatic contact was held in Paris. The exchange of doctors between the two countries was reported to be under consideration.

May 19 The Chinese Government Delegation, headed by Bai Xiangguo, left Beijing for Khartoum to take part in the celebrations of the third anniversary of the Sudanese revolution. The 1972 Sino-Sudanese trade protocol was signed on May 27. The delegation returned to Beijing on May 30.

• An agreement on mutual cooperation between the New China News Agency and the News Agency of Burma was signed in Rangoon.

• The Chilean Government Economic Delegation arrived in Beijing for a twenty-day visit. Premier Zhou Enlai met the delegation on June 8. Economic and trade agreements between the two nations were signed on June 8.

May 20 A US Congressional report predicted that China faced a population explosion in the next two decades that would put a tremendous strain on its limited economic resources and diminish any "serious military danger" to the US. The report forecast that China's population would increase to no less than 1,201,260,000 by 1990 and might go as high as 1,333,128,000.

May 21   The Syrian Government Delegaiton, led by Abdel Halim Khaddam, arrived in Beijing for a seven-day visit. Premier Zhou Enlai met the delegation on May 24. A Sino-Syrian agreement on economic and technical cooperation was signed on May 24.

May 23   The People's Daily, the Red Flag, and the Liberation Army Daily carried a joint editorial entitled "Adherence to Chairman Mao's Revolutionary Line Means Victory," in honor of the thirtieth anniversary of Mao's "Talks at the Yanan Forum on Literature and Art."

May 24   Professor John K. Fairbank of Harvard University, and his wife arrived in Beijing for a visit. Premier Zhou Enlai gave a banquet in honor of them with other American visitors (Dr. and Mrs. Jeremy Stone, Dr. Jerome A. Cohen, Mr. and Mrs. Harrison Salisbury, and Mr. and Mrs. Richard Dudman) on June 16. The Fairbanks left Beijing for Shanghai on June 30.

May 25   The Red Flag carried an article entitled "Make Greater Efforts to Develop Amateur Literature and Art Creation by Workers, Peasants and Soldiers," to call for further efforts to produce popular literature and drama.
• Washington diplomatic sources reported that China had rejected a Soviet request to permit twelve of its freighters to enter Chinese ports to unload arms for North Vietnam. The Chinese were said to have informed the Russians that if they were determined to deliver military material to North Vietnam by ship, they should "clear the mines" planted by the US.

May 27   A new campaign was signaled in an editorial published jointly by the People's Daily, the Red Flag, and the Liberation Army Daily to open a drive to "remold" writers and artists to create more "revolutionary" works of art. The article stated that all revolutionary writers and artists must mingle with workers, peasants and soldiers "for a long period of time unreservedly and wholeheartedly."
• The Chinese Table Tennis Delegation, led by

Zhuang Zedong, left Beijing to visit Canada (March 30-April 13), the USA (April 13-30), and Mexico (April 30-May 17). President Nixon received the delegation at the White House on April 18.

May 30   A large delegation, led by Dang Ge, left Beijing to attend the UN Conference on the Human Environment held in Stockholm from June 8-16. At the plenary session on June 8, China successfully proposed that the draft declaration, written by the conference's Preparatory Committee, should be referred for further review to a special working group. During discussion by this group, China argued that one of the greatest threats to the environment was the aggressive policies of imperialism, especially in Vietnam, and that the conference should not remain indifferent to these atrocities. However, this view was not included in the final "Declaration on the Human Environment."

June 2   The Delegation of the China Council for the Promotion of International Trade, led by Wang Wenlin, left Beijing for a visit to Austria, the Netherlands, and Belgium. The delegation left Belgium for home on July 5.

June 5   A joint communiqué was signed by Chinese and Greek ambassadors in Tirana to establish diplomatic relations between the two nations at the ambassadorial level.
    • A report by the party committee of Daqing oilfield, published by the People's Daily, described the way in which "the extreme left trend of thought" toward cadres and technical personnel had been overcome, by distinguishing between those who had made mistakes and the very small minority of class enemies.

June 7   Prince Norodom Sihanouk, in an interview with Harrison Salisbury in Beijing, said that he, the Vietnamese, and the Pathet Lao opposed a new Geneva-type conference on Indo-China, and that he had asked China to do the same. He also revealed that Premier Zhou Enlai had attempted to arrange a meeting between Sihanouk and Nixon during the latter's visit to Beijing, but Nixon had declined.

June 10   The Soviet Government Trade Delegation, led by
Ivan Grishin, arrived in Beijing for an eight-day visit.
A Sino-Soviet goods exchange and payment agreement
was signed on June 13.
   • The Swiss Government Civil Aviation Delegation,
led by Wener Guldimann, arrived in Beijing for an
eight-day visit. Vice Premier Li Xiannian met the
delegation on June 11.

June 12   The PRC Ministry of Foreign Affairs issued a statement condemning the US expansion of the sphere of
bombing up to the areas close to the Sino-Vietnamese
borders, thus threatening the security of China.

June 18   Premier Zhou Enlai met Le Duc Tho at the Guest
House in Beijing.
   • The tenth anniversary of Chairman Mao's instruc-
tion on military building, "Further Promote Militia
Work Organizationally, Politically and Militarily," re-
ceived wide publicity in the mass media.

June 19   Henry Kissinger and his party of eleven members
arrived in Beijing on a five-day visit for concrete
consultations with Chinese leaders to further the normalization of relations between the two nations. Premier Zhou Enlai gave a welcoming banquet on June 20.

June 21   The Trade Delegation from Rwanda, led by Augus-
tin Muniyaneza, arrived in Shanghai on their way to
Beijing for a three-day visit. Vice Premier Li Xiannian met the delegation on June 23. The Sino-Rwanda
trade agreement was signed on June 23.
   • The Chinese Government Trade Delegation, led
by Bai Xiangguo, left Beijing for Pakistan. The 1972
trade protocol between the two nations was signed on
June 23. The delegation left Pakistan for home on
June 28.

June 24   On his return to Washington, Henry Kissinger expressed his hopes of progress on bilateral issues such
as trade and cultural exchanges with China and said
he had been received with "extraordinary courtesy."
   • Madame Sirimavo Bandaranaike, prime minister of
the Republic of Sri Lanka, arrived in Shanghai for a
ten-day state visit to China. Premier Zhou Enlai gave

a grand banquet in Beijing on June 25. Song Qingling
met her on June 26; Chairman Mao met her on June
28. The two nations signed an agreement on economic
and technical cooperation and an agreement on the construction of a cotton spinning, weaving, printing, and
dying mill on June 29. After touring Beijing, Shenyang, Luta, and Shanghai, Premier Zhou Enlai and
Prime Minister Bandaranaike signed a joint communiqué
on July 5 in Shanghai.

June 26 The Chinese People's Institute of Foreign Affairs
gave a welcoming banquet in Beijing for Hale Boggs,
Democratic leader of the US House of Representatives,
and Mrs. Boggs, and Gerald Ford, Republican leader
of the House, and Mrs. Ford. Premier Zhou Enlai met
the leaders on June 28. After touring other parts of
China, the leaders left Guangzhou for home on July 5.

June 27 China and Guyana signed, in London, a joint communiqué to establish diplomatic relations at the ambassadorial level.

June 28 A Sino-Vietnamese agreement on China's supplementary economic and military aid to Vietnam for 1972 was
signed in Beijing.

June 30 The eight-member Chinese delegation, led by Du
Xingyuan, arrived in Pyongyang to attend the 1972
regular meeting of the Board of Directors of the China-
Korea Yalu River Hydro-Electric Power Company. The
delegation left Pyongyang for home on July 29.
    • The Chinese Agricultural Delegation, led by Sha
Feng, left Beijing to visit Albania (July 1-25) and
Rumania (July 25 to August 6).
    • The Chinese Government and Military Delegation,
led by Li Shuiqing, left Beijing to attend the celebrations of the tenth anniversary of the independence of
Algeria. The delegation left Algeria for home on July
9.

July 1 A Red Flag article entitled "Learn Some Political
Economy," stressed the need to match theory with
practice, to use labor and resources sensibly without
making exaggerated plans which could not be fulfilled,
and not to impair the current system of rural organiza-

tion in which the production team was the basic level
unit.

July 4   The Shanghai Dance-Drama Troupe of China, led by
Sun Pinghua, left Beijing for a performance tour of
Japan.   The troupe returned to Beijing on August 16.

July 5   In a press conference after his election, Prime Minister Tanaka Kakuei said that the time was now ripe
for establishing relations with Beijing.
   • According to the New York Times, the Nixon Administration had granted the Boeing Company a $150
million export license covering the proposed sale of
ten Boeing 707 jet airliners to China.   Talks for the
deal, which had been under way since April, were
successfully concluded later in the summer.
   • Government sources in Washington reported that
China might send engineer battalions to North Vietnam
to help with railroad reconstruction as it had done
from 1965-68.

July 6   The French Government Delegation, led by Foreign
Minister Maurice Schumann, arrived in Beijing for a
five-day visit.   On July 10, he was received by Chairman Mao at short notice and unaccompanied by other
French officials.   At this meeting, Mao discussed the
downfall of Lin Biao and his complicity in the plot
against the chairman's life.   Schumann held three
rounds of talks with Ji Pengfei, who described them
as "friendly, fruitful and satisfactory."   He also met
Premier Zhou Enlai on July 10.   It was reported that
the Chinese had expressed great interest in the view
of the enlarged economic community.

July 7   Premier Zhou Enlai met Xuan Thuy, Ly Ban, Ngo
Thuyen, and Nguyen Van Quang.

July 8   The Government Delegation of the People's Democratic Republic of Yemen, led by Abdul Fattah, arrived in Shanghai on their way to Beijing for a ten-
day visit.   Premier Zhou Enlai met the delegation on
July 8, 9, and 12.   At a banquet held on July 9, Premier Zhou Enlai welcomed Japan's new attitude toward
normalization of relations between China and Japan.   A
Sino-Yemen agreement on economic and technical co-

operation was signed on July 12. A joint communiqué
was signed on July 17.

July 9   The progress of the talks between North and South
Korea was regularly reported in the Chinese press,
and on July 9, the People's Daily published an editorial
hailing the joint North-South statement of July 4 as "a
good beginning."

July 10   On their return from Beijing, the Democratic and
Republican leaders of the House of Representatives,
Hale Boggs and Gerald Ford, claimed they had been
told by high officials of their concern at "the possibility of continued Soviet armament and American disarmament." The officials, said Ford, "don't want the
US to withdraw from the Pacific or other points. They
believe our presence is important for the stability of
the world now and in the future." These statements
were "categorically denied" by reliable Chinese sources
in Beijing, according to Agence France-Presse.

July 12   Premier Zhou Enlai met Le Duc Tho, Ngo Thuyen,
Ly Ban, and Nguyen Van Quang.

July 14   Nixon's terms for a Vietnam settlement and his continued Vietnamization of the war were described by the
New China News Agency as a threat which would only
"arouse the Chinese people and the people of the world
to greater sympathy for the Vietnamese people and to
support them to the end."
    • The six-member Chinese Public Health and Friend-
ship Delegation, led by Zhu Zhao, left Beijing to visit
Algeria (July 15-August 2), and Mauritania (August 3-
20).

July 15   The eighteen-member Chinese Agricultural and
Peasant Delegation, led by Hao Zhungshi, left Beijing
to visit Japan from July 18 to August 18.
    • Chinese People's Institute of Foreign Affairs gave
a banquet in Beijing to welcome Gerhard Schroeder,
Chairman of the Foreign Political Committee of the
Bundestag of the Federal Republic of Germany. Premier Zhou Enlai met him on July 19. At the end of
his visit, Schroeder told reporters that he now "knew
the way" toward the opening of diplomatic relations,

and would inform Chancellor Brandt and Foreign Minister Scheel to that effect. Schroeder left Shanghai for home on July 28.

July 16   The Government Delegation of the Arab Republic of Yemen, led by Prime Minister Ahmed Ali Aini, arrived in Beijing on an official visit from July 16–28. Premier Zhou Enlai gave a grand banquet on July 17. An agreement between the two nations on economic and technical cooperation was signed on July 21.   A communiqué on the visit was issued on July 28.

July 17   Chinese hydroelectric survey team, led by Li Shu, arrived in Rangoon, Burma.

July 18   In a statement, the Tanaka cabinet accepted the "three principles" as a precondition for talks to normalize relations between China and Japan.
 • The Chinese Government Civil Aviation Delegation, led by Ma Renhui, left Beijing for Afghanistan for an eight-day visit. A civil air transportation agreement between the two nations was signed on July 26.

July 24   The People's Daily advocated short investigation reports and newspaper articles and criticized verbosity.
 • A preliminary agreement under which China would buy two supersonic Concord jets was signed in Paris by Henri Ziegler, president of Aerospatiale, the French cobuilder of the Concorde, and Wang Yaxiang, head of the Chinese machinery import delegation. Ziegler said delivery would take place in late 1976 and early 1977. The sale price was not disclosed.

July 25   China and Afghanistan signed and exchanged instruments on the gratuitous construction (by China) of a hospital of 200–500 beds for Afghanistan in Beijing.
 • Yoshikatdu Takeiri, chairman of the Central Executive Committee of the Japanese Komeito, together with his colleagues, arrived in Beijing for a six-day visit. Premier Zhou Enlai met the group on July 27, 28, and 29.

July 26   Premier Tanaka decided that the Japan Export-

Import Bank would finance a $150 million synthetic
fiber (vinylon) manufacturing plant in China. The
plant would be sold by Kuraray Co., one of Japan's
larger manufacturers of textile production equipment.

July 27   At the Unesco meeting, on the question of Tibetan
refugees and Chinese refugees in Hong Kong and Macao, Wang Rongsheng demanded that the high commissioner's office "immediately stop all illegal activities on
the question of so-called Tibetan refugees and Chinese
refugees in Hong Kong and Macao, abolish the organs
for these illegal activities, and delete all the related
parts from the report."

July 28   Wang Hairong, assistant foreign minister, told
James Pringle, a correspondent for the Reuters News
Agency, that Lin Biao had been killed on September
12, 1971, after his plan to seize power had failed.
Wang was confirming a statement issued earlier on
July 28 by the Chinese Embassy in Algeria and published there in the government-owned newspaper El
Mondjahid.
     • According to the International Herald Tribune,
Chairman Mao confirmed the death of Lin Biao in his
conversations in July with Mrs. Bandaranaike and
Maurice Schumann. Mao was reported to have said
that Lin had plotted to assassinate him as part of a
conspiracy designed to replace the civilian leadership
with military men, and had died in an air crash while
fleeing the country. Lin, according to Mao, had opposed the moves to rebuild the Communist party apparatus after the Cultural Revolution, and had also
opposed the decision to normalize relations with the
United States. The actual conspiracy was dated by
Mao as beginning in December 1970, after he had decided to throw his authority behind Zhou Enlai in order to counter Lin's attempt to manipulate the Central
Committee.

July 30   China and Ethiopia signed a civil air transport
agreement in Beijing.

July 31   Several purged Chinese Army leaders, such as
Chen Zaidao, Zhong Hanhua, Yang Yun and Cheng
Yun, reappeared in public at a party reception to

mark the forty-fifth anniversary of the PLA.
  • Foreign Minister Ji Pengfei informed the director
general of the UN office at Geneva of the Chinese
government's decision to set up a permanent mission
of the PRC in the UN office in Geneva.
  • The People's Daily, the Red Flag, and the Liberation Army Daily carried a joint editorial to mark the
forty-fifth anniversary of the founding of the PLA,
and to "Carry the Glorious Tradition Forward."
  • Important new archaeological finds continued to
be reported. These included the discovery of a tomb
containing a female corpse, wooden coffins, and burial
accessories from the early Western Han Dynasty at
Mawantui on the outskirts of Changsha, Hunan province.

August 1 In an important article in the Red Flag, the first
    theoretical account was given of the contradictions
    which had led to the downfall of Lin Biao in September
    1971. The article entitled "Grasp the Laws of Class
    Struggle in the Socialist Era" claimed that class ene-
    mies had emerged within the Party every few years
    and that this pattern would continue.
      • The Chinese Government Trade Delegation, led
    by Bai Xiangguo, left Beijing to visit Peru (August 4-
    10), Chile (August 10-14), and Canada (August 15-24).
    A Sino-Peruvian trade agreement was signed on Au-
    gust 9.

August 2 An article published in the People's Daily on Army
    Day described the "criminal scheme" of Liu Shaoqi and
    other "swindlers" to lead the PLA onto "the road of
    isolation from the masses and turn them into a tool for
    a handful of careerists." This scheme had failed, ac-
    cording to the article.

August 6 The Ivo Lola Ribar Song and Dance Ensemble from
    Belgrade, Yugoslavia, led by Nikola Radas, arrived in
    Beijing for a performance tour in Beijing, Tianjin, and
    Shenyang. The ensemble left Shenyang for home on
    August 27.

August 7 Prime Minister Tanaka announced that he would
    visit Beijing in September for talks to normalize dip-
    lomatic relations between China and Japan.

August 9   China and Mauritius signed an agreement on eco-
            nomic and technical cooperation and a protocol of the
            agreement in Port Louis, Mauritius.

August 10   During the Security Council proceedings China
             strongly opposed the application of Bangladesh to join
             the United Nations and exercised its first veto.

August 11   UN Secretary General Kurt Waldheim visited
             China from August 11-15. At a banquet on August
             12, he called for an end to the arms race.

August 12   Foreign Minister Ji Pengfei announced that Pre-
             mier Zhou Enlai welcomed and invited Prime Minister
             Tanaka to visit China.
               • Jiang Qing and Yao Wenyuan met American writer
             and associate professor of history Roxane H. Witke.
               • The Nigerian Government Economic and Trade
             Mission, led by Adebayo Adedeji, arrived in Beijing
             for a ten-day visit. Premier Zhou Enlai met the dele-
             gation on August 16.
               • The Cameroon Government Delegation, led by
             Vincent Efon, arrived in Beijing for an eight-day visit.
             Premier Zhou Enlai met the delegation on August 15.
             An economic and technical cooperation between the
             two nations and a trade agreement were signed on
             August 17.

August 15   Canadian Secretary of State for External Affairs
             Mitchell Sharp and his party arrived in Guangzhou on
             their way to Beijing for an eight-day visit. Premier
             Zhou Enlai met the delegation on August 19.   The
             delegation opened the Canadian Trade Exposition in
             Beijing on August 21.

August 16   Japan Airlines and All-Nippon Airways began air
             services between Shanghai and Tokyo. The aircrafts
             brought home the members of the Shanghai Dance-
             Drama Troup of China.
               • China and Mongolia exchanged notes on the pro-
             longation of the 1952 agreement of economic and cul-
             tural cooperation in Ulan Bator.

August 17   China and Mauritania signed, in Nouakochott, a
             new protocol on the dispatch of a Chinese medical team
             to Mauritania.

August 20   The Tanzanian Goodwill Delegation, led by John S. Malecela, arrived in Beijing for a five-day visit. Premier Zhou Enlai met the delegation on August 21.

August 22   China declined an invitation from the president of the Twentieth Olympic Games Organizing Committee to send an observer delegation to Munich, because of the presence of Taiwan in the games.

   • A cable of congratulations on the twenty-eight anniversary of the liberation of Rumania was sent by Chairman Mao Zedong, Dong Biwu, and Zhou Enlai. The cable expressed admiration for Rumania's opposition to "hegemony and power politics."

   • The Tunisian Government Delegation, led by Foreign Minister Mohammed Masmoudi, arrived in Shanghai on their way to Beijing for a six-day visit. Premier Zhou Enlai met the delegation on August 27. An agreement on economic and technical cooperation was signed on August 27.

August 24   The Chinese Ministry of Foreign Affairs issued a statement protesting the US bombing of the lifeboat of a Chinese merchant ship near an island off the North Vietnamese coast on August 22, which killed five crew members.

   • A People's Daily editorial note stressed having faith in the "socialist enthusiasm of the masses of commune members and basic-level cadres." The note said: "Some cadres encroach upon the right to self-determination of production teams by setting up impractical requirements and rules for them to follow even when they have fulfilled their state plans, and by blindly demanding unified action."

August 25   China cast its first veto in the Security Council to bar Bangladesh from membership in the UN (11-1-4). Before the final vote, China introduced a resolution to delay consideration of the Bangladesh application until POW's were repatriated and all foreign soldiers taken out of Bangladesh.

August 26   The Chinese Government Delegation, led by Li Shuiqing, left Beijing to visit Sweden (August 29 to September 9), Norway (September 9-15), and Finland (September 15-22).

August 27 The Executive Committee of the Asian Table
          Tennis Union decided to invite the Taiwan Table Ten-
          nis Team to participate in the activities of the ATTU
          "in the name of the Taiwan provincial team of the
          PRC." The invitation was rejected by the Olympic
          Committee of Nationalist China.
            • The three-member group of Chinese cancerolo-
          gists, led by Li Mingxin of the Chinese Academy of
          Medical Sciences, attended the First International
          Symposium on Cancer Etiology in Primosten, Yugo-
          slavia from August 27 to September 2.

August 28 Qiao Guanhua arrived in Rawalpindi, Pakistan,
          for a three-day visit. On his arrival, Qiao declared
          that China hoped "all countries in the subcontinent
          will live together in peace and friendship and seek
          among themselves fair and reasonable solutions to their
          mutual problems." At the banquet, Mr. Bhutto said
          that Pakistan wished to have good relations with all
          its neighbors but not at the cost of friendship with
          China.

August 29 Washington reported that a Chinese minesweeper
          had appeared in Hai Phong harbor, and that Soviet
          tankers were now unloading petroleum productions in
          Chinese ports.

August 31 The Japanese advance party arrived in Beijing
          to make preparation for Prime Minister Tanaka's visit
          to China. The party left Beijing for home on Septem-
          ber 5.

September 2 The People's Daily carried an editorial entitled
          "Promote Friendship, Strengthen Unity," to congratu-
          late the opening of the First Asian Table Tennis
          Championships, held in Beijing from September 2-13.
            • The Chinese Government Civil Aviation Delegation,
          led by Ma Renhui, left Beijing for a fourteen-day
          visit to Turkey. A civil air transport agreement be-
          tween the two nations was signed on September 16.

September 4 In a Reuters interview, Prince Norodom Sihanouk
          confirmed "a new agreement between China and the
          Soviet Union to allow more trains to cross China carry-
          ing heavy weapons for the Indo-Chinese battlefield."

He also said that "a new network" of secret trails and new pipelines underground had been constructed to convey supplies through Vietnam despite American bombardment.

September 5 The Pravda published a lengthy and extremely critical article in which two points were stressed. First, that it was a "fable" for the Chinese to seek to link Lin Biao's alleged plot with the Soviet Union. Second, that the new look in Chinese foreign policy was only a tactical adjustment while Beijing's basic "hegemonistic, great-power chauvinistic aspirations" remained unchanged.

September 8 The Ghana Government Trade and Goodwill Mission, led by Major Kodjo Barney Agbo, arrived in Beijing for a ten-day visit. Premier Zhou Enlai met the delegation on September 14. A trade and payment agreement was signed on September 14.

September 9 China signed a contract to purchase ten American Boeing 707s worth $61 million with a provision for the training of crews and spare parts.
 • The Chinese Friendship Group, led by Wang Chendang, left Beijing to visit Albania (September 12-29), Rumania (September 29 to October 13), and Yugoslavia (October 13-27).
 • The CCP Party Workers Delegation, led by Yang Zhunfu, left Beijing for Bucharest, Rumania on a seventeen-day visit.

September 10 NCNA reported that since the beginning of the year, 400,000 young people had gone to settle in the rural areas to take part in "the motherland's socialist revolution and construction."
 • A meeting of the Preparatory Committee for the Asian-African-Latin American Table Tennis Friendship Invitational Tournament was held in Beijing.
 • The New York Times reported that the Soviet Union had recently moved three mechanized divisions to the border area near China, bringing the number of divisions known to be in the region to forty-nine.

September 12 The Chinese Petroleum Study Group, led by Dang Ge, left Beijing to visit Canada (September 16 to October 28), and France (October 29 to November 23). In Canada, Dang Ge said that China now produced thirty million metric tons of oil a year, and was nearly self-sufficient in oil.

September 15 The Togolese Goodwill Mission, led by Joachim Hunlede, arrived in Beijing for a five-day visit. Premier Zhou Enlai met the delegation on September 18. An agreement on economic and technical cooperation between the two nations was signed on September 19. On the same day, a joint communiqué was issued to establish diplomatic relations at the ambassadorial level.

September 16 A loan agreement on providing a cargo ship by China to Sri Lanka was signed in Beijing.

September 17 The Zambian Goodwill Mission, led by Vice President M. Mainza Chona, arrived in Beijing for an eight-day visit. At the grand banquet, Premier Zhou stated that "China was determined to develop friendly relations with all independent African states and support the national-liberation struggles of all those African peoples who are still under colonial rule." In reply Vice President Chona described the construction of the Tanzanian-Zambian Railway as "a symbol of China's commitment to the elimination of poverty and oppression in the world."

September 18 Premier Zhou Enlai met the delegation of the Japanese Liberal Democratic Party, headed by Zentaro Kosaka, chairman of the party's Council for the Normalization of Japan-China Relations.
   • The 1972 regular meeting of the Sino-Mongolian Boundary Through Railway Traffic was held in Ulan Bator.
   • Her Imperial Majesty Parah Pahlavi, Shabanou of Iran, arrived in Beijing for a ten-day visit. Dong Biwu, Zhou Enlai, Jiang Qing and Li Xiannian met her Majesty on September 19.

September 20 The Chinese Government Delegation, led by Guo Lu, left Beijing for the Arab Republic of Yemen to attend celebrations of the tenth anniversary of the founding of the Republic. The delegation left Aden for home on October 21.

September 21   NCNA announced that Prime Minister Kakuei
      Tanaka of Japan would visit China from September 25-
      30.

September 22   At the General Committee of the General As-
      sembly, Chen Chu opposed inclusion on the agenda
      discussion of "measures to prevent terrorism." He
      said that "in discussing the questions of violence, one
      should distinguish between military aggression and op-
      pression on the one hand, and the struggle of re-
      sistance by the victims of aggression and oppression
      on the other." The proposed item failed to make this
      distinction, he said.

September 25   Educational revolution at Beijing University
      was described in an NCNA report. More than sixty
      disciplines were represented by the teaching staff of
      2,000 in the departments of Chinese, history, philos-
      ophy, foreign languages, physics, chemistry, and
      eleven other fields. Since August, 1970, the univer-
      sity had admitted more than 4,000 students from work-
      er, peasant, and soldier backgrounds. Most students
      were around twenty years old. They had at least two
      (in some cases as much as eight) years' practical ex-
      perience. Students in the department of natural sci-
      ences spent a quarter of every year in factories re-
      lated to their specialities. Those in the department of
      arts went to factories and the countryside for about
      two months every year.
         • Prime Minister Kakuei Tanaka of Japan arrived in
      Beijing for a five-day visit. Premier Zhou Enlai held
      talks with him on September 25, 26, 27, and 28.
      Chairman Mao Zedong met him on September 27. Prime
      Minister Tanaka left Beijing for Shanghai in the com-
      pany of Premier Zhou on September 29 and left Shang-
      hai for home on the following day. A joint communiqué
      was issued on September 29. Foreign Minister Ohira,
      on the same day, stated that the treaty between his
      government and the Nationalist regime on Taiwan had
      "lost the meaning of its existence and was declared to
      be terminated." A People's Daily editorial on Septem-
      ber 30 welcomed the agreement to establish relations
      as the result of "the efforts jointly made by the Chi-
      nese and Japanese peoples over a long period of time."

September 27   A meeting protocol of the Sino-Korean Border
        Railway Joint Committee was signed in Pyongyang.
            • John Cass, Chairman of the Australian Wheat
        Board, announced that the sale of one million tons of
        wheat was worth about $72 million to China.   The sale,
        reportedly Australia's first to Beijing since 1969, was
        negotiated in China by a four-member wheat delegation.

September 29   It was announced that talks to establish dip-
        lomatic relations between the PRC and West Germany
        had been successfully concluded in Bonn.   It was also
        announced that Foreign Minister Scheel would visit
        China from October 10–14.

September 30   The US Agricultural Department announced
        that China had purchased about fifteen million bushels
        of American wheat.
            • A ceremony was held in Changsha to mark the
        opening to traffic of a highway bridge over the Xiang
        River.
            • The Chinese Foreign Ministry gave a grand Na-
        tional Day reception in Beijing in honor of the foreign
        guests in Beijing, foreign experts and diplomatic en-
        voys, military attaches, and other diplomatic officials
        of various countries to China.

October 1   For the second year in succession, there was no
        parade on October 1.   The joint National Day editorial
        by the People's Daily, the Red Flag, and the Libera-
        tion Daily Army devoted almost two-thirds of its space
        to foreign affairs.   There was a striking contrast to
        the 1970 editorial in the treatment accorded to the con-
        cept of "Mao Zedong thought."   While the 1970 editorial
        had mentioned it fifteen times with great emphasis,
        this year's editorial, in keeping with the general de-
        creasing emphasis on Chairman Mao as an individual,
        mentioned it only once and then in the combination of
        "Marxism-Leninism-Mao Zedong thought."
            • The Soviet message to Beijing congratulated the
        Chinese people on their National Day anniversary, but
        accused Mao of "theoretical incompetence" in taking
        China away from the path of Marxism-Leninism.
            • The New York Times reported China had resettled
        nearly a half-million high school and college graduates
        from the cities to rural areas and frontier regions

since the start of 1972.
  • The Beijing Man Exhibition Center at Zhoukoudian (hebei) was opened to the public.
  • A ceremony was held to mark the opening to traffic of the longest highway bridge over the Yellow River (1394 meters long) at Beizhen, Shandong.

October 3 The Shipping Delegation, led by Yu Wei, left Beijing for Warsaw to attend the Eleventh Session of the Shareholders' Meeting of the Sino-Polish Ship Broker's Company, held from October 6-17. A protocol of the meeting was signed on October 17.
  • Qiao Guanhua spoke at the plenary meeting of the Twenty-seventh Session of the UN General Assembly. He set out China's position on a wide variety of international issues, giving the ending of the Indo-Chinese War as the first priority.

October 4 China offered to increase its contribution to the UN budget from four to seven percent of the total over the next five years. The new figure would make China the third largest contributor after the US and the Soviet Union. At the same time, the Chinese delegation said, indirectly, that they recognized no obligation to pay the debt of $16.6 million owed by Taiwan, and directly, that China would not help finance the UN presence in Korea, the Office of the High Commissioner for Refugees dealing with refugees from Tibet or other parts of China, or the UN bond issue for peacekeeping in the Middle East.

October 5 The San Marino Government Delegation, led by Foreign Minister Giancarlo Chironzi, arrived in Beijing for an eight-day visit. Premier Zhou Enlai met the delegation on October 8.

October 6 Premier Zhou Enlai met Taiwan "compatriots," overseas Chinese from Japan and the US and American-Chinese descendants, who had come to China for a tour.
  • China and Sierra Leone signed, in Freetown, a protocol on sending a Chinese medical team to work in Sierra Leone.
  • The Chinese Government Civil Aviation Delegation, led by Ma Renhui, left Beijing for a seven-day visit

to Canada.   A Sino-Canadian Civil Air Transport
Agreement was signed on October 13.

• The Delegation of Chinese Scientists left Beijing
for a visit to Britain (October 7-19), Sweden (October
20 to November 2), Canada (November 3-19), and the
US (November 20 to December 16).

• The Chinese Government Friendship Delegation,
led by Fang Yi, left Beijing to visit Congo (October
10-21), Cameroon (October 26 to November 1), and
Nigeria (November 1-11), and returned to Beijing on
November 15.   A Sino-Congo economic and technical
cooperation agreement was signed on October 19.   A
supplementary protocol between China and Equatorial
Guinea on economic and technical cooperation was
signed on October 26.   A Sino-Nigerian trade, economic, and technical cooperation was signed on November 3.

October 7   The Delegation of the People's Bank of China,
led by Qiao Beixin, left Beijing to visit Albania (October 10-18), and Rumania (October 19-29).

October 9   The Chinese Bridge Construction Survey Team,
led by Ma Jiangda, arrived in Rangoon for a twenty-
day visit.

• China and Italy signed a maritime transport agreement in Beijing.

• In an interview with Warren H. Phillips, editorial
director of the Wall Street Journal, Premier Zhou Enlai
made the following remarks: (1) China expected its
1972 grain output to exceed 250 million metric tons
despite the drought; (2) China was opposed to joint
ventures with US industrial companies similar to those
negotiated with Eastern Europe.

October 10   Foreign Minister Walter Scheel of the Federal
Republic of Germany arrived in Beijing for a five-day
visit.   A joint communiqué was issued on October 11
to establish diplomatic relations between the two countries.   Premier Zhou Enlai met him on October 12.

• The Albanian Government Trade Delegation, led
by Kico Ngjela, arrived in Beijing for a month-long
visit.   Premier Zhou Enlai met the delegation on November 7.   The 1973 Sino-Albania goods exchange and
payment protocol was signed on November 9.

• The Medical Delegation of the Chinese Medical
Association, led by Wu Weiran, left Beijing for visits
to the US (October 12 to November 1), Canada (November 1-15), and France (November 16-25), and returned to Beijing on November 30. President Nixon
received the delegation in the White House on October
14.

October 11   The first official detailed Chinese account of the
flight and death of Lin Biao was given by Premier
Zhou Enlai in an article published by the Philadelphia
Bulletin. Premier Zhou's remarks were made in an interview with Bulletin editor, William E. Dickinson, and
other members of the American Society of Newspaper
Editors who were visiting China.
• China and Rwanda signed, in Kigali, a protocol
on the agreement of economic and technical cooperation.

October 13   Two brothers of British nationality detained by
Chinese authorities since September 21, 1967 were deported to Hong Kong. The two men, Frederick and
Percival Farmer, had been arrested in connection with
the Cultural Revolution. They were born of an English father and a Chinese mother and had lived in
China all their lives. The Chinese Foreign Ministry
informed the British Embassy in Beijing that the two
had been arrested for violating laws.

October 14   China and the Republic of Maldives signed, in
Sri Lanka, a joint communiqué to establish diplomatic
relations at the ambassadorial level.

October 15   Premier Zhou Enlai met Le Duc Tho and Ly Ban.

October 22   Henry Kissinger told a news conference in Washington that he believed "peace is at hand" in all of
Indo-China. He said that a final agreement on a truce
and a political settlement could be worked out in one
more conference with the North Vietnamese "lasting no
more than three or four days."

October 23   The Delegation of the Japan-China Memorandum
Trade Office of Japan, led by Kaheita Okazaki, arrived
in Beijing for a seven-day visit. An agreement on
China-Japan Memorandum Trade for 1973 was signed on
October 29.

October 24   At the UN First Committee on Disarmament,
        Chen Chu urged nuclear nations to make a declaration
        neither to be the first to use nuclear weapons nor to
        use them against a nonnuclear country.

October 26   Western journalists were taken on a tour of Bei-
        jing's bomb shelters and were told by a Chinese gov-
        ernment guide that they would provide protection for
        up to ninety percent of the city's population.   Similar
        tunnel complexes were said by the guide to have been
        constructed in other large and medium sized cities.
        A civil defense official said that the shelters were ef-
        fective against nuclear blast and heat, but not against
        radiation.

October 29   British Foreign Secretary Alec Douglas-Home and
        his wife arrived in Beijing for a five-day visit.   Pre-
        mier Zhou Enlai met them on November 1.   No formal
        agreement was announced but it became evident that
        Britain had agreed to provide language training facil-
        ities for some 200 Chinese students; the first group
        arrived in December.

October 30   The Austrian Government Delegation, led by
        Josef Staribacher, arrived in Beijing for a five-day
        visit.   Premier Zhou Enlai met the delegation on No-
        vember 1.   A Sino-Austrian trade and payment agree-
        ment was signed on November 2.

October 31   The Ministry of Foreign Affairs issued a state-
        ment, saying that "The US Government should faith-
        fully keep its word and sign as soon as possible with
        the DRVN the agreement which has already been
        reached."
          • The Algerian Government Delegation, led by Lay-
        achi Yaker, arrived in Beijing for a twelve-day visit.
        Premier Zhou Enlai met the delegation on November 5.
          • The 1973 Sino-Algerian trade protocol was signed
        on November 6.
          • The Guyana Government Economic and Trade
        Delegation, led by Kenneth King, arrived in Beijing
        for an eight-day visit.   Premier Zhou Enlai met the
        delegation on November 8.   A Sino-Guyana protocol to
        economic and technical cooperation agreement and com-
        modies import and export agreement were signed on
        November 8.

November 3 The Malagasy Delegation, led by Foreign Minister Didier Patsiraka, arrived in Beijing for an eight-
day visit. Premier Zhou Enlai met the delegation on
November 6. A joint communiqué was issued on the
same day to establish diplomatic relations at the ambassadorial level.

November 4 The Chinese Postal Delegation, led by Qiao
Weizhong, left Beijing for Switzerland to attend the
annual meeting of the Consultative Council for Postal
Studies of the Universal Postal Union. The delegation
returned to Beijing on December 4.

November 6 The Standing Committee of the National People's
Congress and State Council greeted the fifty-fifth anniversary of the October Socialist Revolution.
• Japanese Foreign Minister Ohira Masayoshi announced that Japan and Nationalist China had agreed
to establish a liaison office in Tokyo to maintain trade
and other nondiplomatic ties. According to Foreign
Minister Ohira, Beijing had given its tacit approval by
saying "neither yes nor no on the matter."
• The Albanian Friendship Military Delegation, led
by Bequir Balluku, arrived in Beijing for a visit from
November 6 to December 9. Premier Zhou Enlai met
the delegation in Beijing on November 7 and December 1.

November 7 The Mauritanian Government Delegation, led by
Mohamed Ould Cheikh, arrived in Beijing for a four-
teen-day visit. Premier Zhou Enlai met the delegation
on November 14.
• The eleven-member Chinese Delegation left Beijing
for Geneva to attend the fifth plenary session of the
International Telegraph and Telephone Consultative
Committee of the International Telecommunication Union.
The delegation returned to Beijing on January 8, 1973.

November 9 According to a US government official announcement, China had a "handful" of 3,500 mile-range liquid
fuel missiles with three-megaton warheads which were
capable of reaching Moscow. In addition, China had
deployed about twenty other missiles with a range of
1,000 and 2,500 miles.

November 10 According to Stockholm Radio, Premier Zhou

Enlai told a group of Scandinavian journalists that the
harvest was four percent or ten million tons below that
of the previous year, when the total had been 250
million tons. Consequently, he said, China needed to
import more grain than previously.

  • The Chinese Government Trade Delegation, led
by Bai Xiangguo, left Beijing to visit Hungary (November 13–16), Yugoslavia (November 16–23), and Rumania
(November 23–28). A Sino-Rumanian goods exchange
and payment protocol for 1973 was signed on November
28.

November 12 The Venezuela Trade Delegation, led by Leopoldo Diaz Bruzual, arrived in Beijing for a seven-day
visit. Vice Premier Li Xiannian met the delegation on
November 16.

November 14 In reply to a note from the Mexican Ambassador
in Beijing on the nuclear issue, the Chinese Foreign
Ministry stated: "China will never use or threaten to
use nuclear weapons against non-nuclear Latin American
countries and the Latin American nuclear-weapon-free-
zone, nor will China test, manufacture, produce,
stockpile, install, or deploy nuclear weapons in these
countries or in this zone, or send her means of transportation and delivery carrying nuclear weapons to
traverse the territory, territorial sea, or territorial air
space of Latin American countries."

  • Nepalese Prime Minister Kirti Nidhi Bista, his wife,
and his party arrived in Kunming on their way to Beijing for a ten-day visit. Premier Zhou Enlai held talks
with the party on November 15 and 16. Chairman Mao
Zedong met Prime Minister Bista on November 17. A
Sino-Nepalese agreement on economic and technical cooperation was signed on November 18.

  • Qiao Guanhua was in London on an official visit
from November 14–17, and in Paris from November 17–
20. He left Paris for home via Rumania on November
20.

November 15 The DRVN Government Economic Delegation,
led by Le Thanh Nghi, arrived in Beijing for a twelve-
day visit. Premier Zhou Enlai met the delegation on
November 17. The 1973 agreement on China's gratuitous
economic and military materials assistance to Vietnam,

and a protocol on China's gratuitous supply of military equipment and materials to Vietnam in 1973 were signed on November 26. The 1973 mutual supply of goods and payment agreement was signed on December 27, after the delegation went touring in European countries and on their way home via Beijing.

November 16   China and Luxembourg signed a joint communiqué to establish diplomatic relations at the ambassadorial level.
    • China and Malta signed, in Valletta, a protocol on the development of projects and technical assistance from China to Malta.

November 17   The Shenyang Acrobatic Troup of China, led by Zhang Yingwu, left Beijing for performance tours in Canada (November 18 to December 15), the US (December 16 to January 13), Chile (January 14 to February 6), Peru (February 6-20), and Mexico (February 20 to March 10), and returned to Beijing on March 12. President Nixon received the troup on January 13 in the White House.
    • The six-member Chinese Delegation, led by Guo Baozhong, left Beijing for Pyongyang to attend the twelfth meeting of the Sino-Korean Committee for Cooperation in River Transport. A protocol of the meeting was signed on January 19, 1973.

November 18   China and Iran signed a civil air transport agreement in Beijing.

November 19   China and Zaire signed a joint communiqué to establish diplomatic relations at the ambassadorial level in Paris.

November 21   China and Jamaica signed in Ottawa a joint communiqué to establish diplomatic relations at the ambassadorial level.
    • China and Sri Lanka signed in Colombo a loan agreement for China to provide a cargo ship to Sri Lanka.

November 22   The twenty-two-year old restriction on travel to China by US ships and aircraft was lifted by President Nixon.

• According to the International Herald Tribune, in October, 300,000 tons of corn were sold to China by the US, while 400,000 tons of wheat had been sold in September.

November 23 The Delegation of Chinese Scientists and technicians, led by Jiang Shengjie, left Beijing for Pakistan to attend the inaugural ceremony of the Karachi Nuclear Power Station. The delegation returned to Beijing on December 25. The twelve-member Chinese medical group, led by Zhang Runxu, left Beijing to study the health work in North Vietnam. The delegation returned to Beijing on December 25.

November 24 The Lebanese Government Delegation, led by Foreign Minister S.E. Khalyl, arrived in Beijing for a twelve-day visit. Premier Zhou Enlai met the delegation on November 28. A trade agreement between the two nations was signed on November 29.

November 25 The China Water Conservation Delegation, led by Jian Zhengying, left Beijing for Sri Lanka on a visit from November 28 to December 14.

November 27 Chairman Mao Zedong, Dong Biwu, Zhu De, and Zhou Enlai greeted the sixtieth anniversary of the independence of Albania and the twenty-eighth anniversary of her liberation.

November 28 China and Chad signed a joint communiqué to establish diplomatic relations at the ambassadorial level.

November 30 At the plenary meeting of the UN General Assembly, Huang Hua criticized Soviet disarmament proposals and added that the Russians should withdraw troops and bases from Mongolia to demonstrate their willingness to renounce the use of all force in international relations.

December 1 NCNA reported the excavation of numerous valuable ancient relics in Gansu, including over 340 well-preserved bronzes of the early Western Zhou Dynasty in September 1967.
  • NCNA reported that over 130 square kilometers of an old Yellow River bed in Dangshan county, Anhui

province, had been transformed to arable land on which trees, grain, and fruits could be grown.

December 2   The Kuwait Government Trade and Economic Delegation, led by Khalid Sulaiman Al-Adsani, arrived in Beijing for a seven-day visit. Premier Zhou Enlai met the delegation on December 5.

December 5   Huang Hua spoke to the UN General Assembly on the Middle East, roundly criticizing Israel for occupying Arab territory, the United States for supporting it and "the other superpower" for hegemonistic ambitions.
  • China and Korea signed, in Pyongyang, an agreement on plant inspection and combat against insect pests.

December 7   China and Korea signed, in Pyongyang, the 1972-73 executive plan for cooperation in public health between the two nations.

December 9   The Guinean Government Delegation, led by Prime Minister Lansana Beauvogui, arrived in Beijing for a seven-day visit. Premier Zhou Enlai met the delegation on December 12. An agreement on China providing a financial credit to Guinea and an agreement on China providing credit in commodities to Guinea were signed on December 13.

December 10   The thirteenth session of Sino-Korean Committee for Scientific and Technical Cooperation was held in Beijing from December 10-23. A protocol of the meeting was signed on December 23.
  • The Chinese Government Trade Delegation, led by Bai Xiangguo, left Beijing to visit Burma (December 11-16), and Sri Lanka (December 17-23). A Sino-Sri Lanka trade and payment agreement was signed on December 19, and a Sino-Sri Lanka agreement on commodity exchange for 1973 was signed on December 23.

December 14   Soviet Ambassador to China V.S. Tolstikov gave a reception in Beijing to mark the fiftieth anniversary of the founding of the Union of Soviet Socialist Republic.

December 20   The Chinese Ministry of Foreign Affairs issued
a statement denouncing US bombing of Hanoi, Haiphong and other extensive areas of North Vietnam.
   • China and Iraq signed a protocol on development
of economic and technical cooperation in Baghdad.

December 21   Joint communiqués on the establishment of diplomatic relations at the ambassadorial level were signed
by Australia and China in Paris, and by New Zealand
and China in New York.

December 22   Foreign Minister Ji Pengfei left Beijing for
Pyongyang for a three-day visit.   Premier Kim Il Sung
held talks with him on December 23.   A press communiqué on the visit was issued on December 25.

December 23   China and DRVN signed in Hanoi a protocol on
the 1973 scientific and technical cooperation plan.

December 26   The Dahomey Government Delegation, led by
Foreign Minister Michel Alladaye, arrived in Beijing
for a seven-day visit.   Premier Zhou Enlai met the
delegation on December 29.   A joint communiqué on
resumption of diplomatic relations was signed on December 29.   Agreements on economic and technical cooperation and in trade and payments between the two
nations were signed on December 30.

December 27   Foreign Minister Nguyen Thi Binh of the Pro-
visional Revolutionary Government of the Republic of
South Vietnam and her party arrived in Beijing for a
six-day visit.   Premier Zhou Enlai met her on December 28; Chairman Mao met her on December 29.   Beijing
held a mass rally voicing firm support for the Vietnamese people's struggle against "US aggression and
for national salvation" on December 29.   A joint communiqué on her visit was issued on January 1, 1973.

December 29   China signed a contract with Japan's Tokyo
Engineering Company for the purchase of an ethylene
manufacturing plant, the first of a series of imports
by China.

December 31   The letter written by Chairman Mao to Jiang
Qing, dated on July 8, 1966, was fully translated into

English by the Nationalist Chinese in Taiwan and appeared in the Issues and Studies, Volume IX, No. 4, January 1973. The letter implied that Mao had disagreed with Lin Biao about the extreme popularization of the "Little Red Book" of his quotations.

Chapter IV

1973

THE INCREASING POWER OF THE LEFTISTS

The Tenth Congress of the Chinese Communist party was held on August 24-28. It was attended by 1,249 delegates, representing a party membership of 28 million. The Congress received no advance publicity, and it lasted for an unusually short period. These crucial circumstances might be attributed to the desire of the leadership to avoid open wrangling and rifts that might arise from factional rivalries. The primary objective of the Congress was to reconstruct the party framework that had been shattered first by the Cultural Revolution of 1966-69 and then, in 1971, by the purge of Lin Biao, Chairman Mao's designated successor. The task was a formidable one, for the rivalries among the moderates, the radicals, the senior leaders, and the military were severe and extensive.

After much jockeying and manipulation, the Congress finally elected 195 full members and 124 alternates to the Central Committee. The new committee was said to combine the old, the middle-aged, and the young. Elected to the Central Committee were many high-ranking leaders purged during the Cultural Revolution. Notable among them was Deng Xiaoping, former general secretary of the party. At the first plenary session on August 30, the party's Central Committee elected five vice-chairmen; Premier Zhou Enlai was named first among the five, and Wang Hongwen second. Others named were Kang Sheng, an elder of the party, who was believed to have been in charge of security affairs; Ye Jianying, executive vice-chairman of the party's Military Affairs Commission; and Li Desheng, chief political commissar of the Army.

The Central Committee also elected twenty-one full

131

members and four alternates to the politburo, the highest ruling body in China. The politburo, in turn, appointed a standing committee of nine to rule when the politburo was not in session. Included in this smaller committee were Chairman Mao, the five vice-chairmen of the Central Committee, and three others: Dong Biwu, acting president of China; Zhang Chunqiao, chairman of the Shanghai Revolutionary Committee; and Zhu De, the old marshal who had led the Red Army to victory in 1949.

The various elections and appointments confirmed Zhou Enlai as second in command after Mao Zedong, and the moderates who followed Zhou gained ground in the new power alignment. But the radical group that formerly led the Cultural Revolution was not ignored. Though Jiang Qing, Mao's wife, and Yao Wenyuan, her protégé, were not elected to the Standing Committee, they remained members of the politburo. Zhang Chunqiao, another close associate of Jiang Qing, was not only appointed to the Standing Committee but also served as secretary general of the party Congress. Of greatest significance was the spectacular rise of Wang Hongwen, who apparently was in third position in the party hierarchy after Mao and Zhou. Wang, a thirty-eight-year-old former textile mill worker, had been a militant leader during the Cultural Revolution. He later became a vice-chairman of the Shanghai Revolutionary Committee and was generally regarded as a protégé of Zhang Chunqiao. The composition of the newly elected Central Committee reflected a careful balancing of the multiplicity of forces on the Chinese political landscape. There was a balance between military (thirty-two percent, down from forty-four percent), party and government cadres (twenty-eight percent, nearly unchanged from twenty-seven percent on the Ninth Central Committee), and representatives of the revolutionary masses (probably forty percent as opposed to twenty-nine percent previously). The military suffered a relative diminution of its power, although in the party's "three-in-one combination" formula, it still remained the most numerous element. Nearly all of the important central and regional military leaders were included in the new Central Committee, as were almost all provincial party committee heads, most of the province-level trade union leaders, and a relatively large number of women (forty-one, or thirteen percent, of the new, as opposed to twenty-three, or eight percent, of the old Central Committee).

In his report to the Congress, Premier Zhou denounced the late Defense Minister Lin Biao and recounted
the events leading up to his death. Zhou told the Congress
that Lin Biao plotted two coups d'état--the first at a plenary
session of the Ninth Central Committee in August 1970 and
the second on September 9, 1971, when an attempt was made
to assassinate Mao and set up a rival Central Committee. On
September 13, after his conspiracy had collapsed, Lin "sur-
reptitiously boarded a plane, fled as a defector to the Soviet
revisionists in betrayal of the party and country, and died
in a crash at Undur Khan in Mongolia." Zhou castigated
Lin Biao as a "bourgeois careerist, conspirator, double-
dealer, renegade, and traitor."

The Congress adopted a new party constitution that
deleted all reference to Lin Biao, designated in the previous
constitution as Chairman Mao's successor. The new constitution named no successor, and the omission prompted speculation that after Mao's death China would be ruled by a collective leadership, including the five vice-chairmen of the
Central Committee.

Wang Hongwen, in his report on the new constitution,
told the Congress that China would undergo revolutions like
the 1966-69 Cultural Revolution many times in the future.
Though the new constitution called on all organizations to
accept the centralized leadership of the party, it maintained
that the masses must have the freedom to speak out against
erroneous political views without fear of retaliation. In 1973,
there were several ideological campaigns of interest. The
first was a switch in the labeling of Lin Biao and his alleged
policies from ultraleftist to ultrarightist. It soon became
clear that the switch was actually the beginning of a new
campaign to defend and develop the victorious fruits of the
Cultural Revolution. Apparently, the leftists within the
party were fearful that the political pendulum had swung
too far to the "right," and that the rejection of Lin Biao
might lead to a rejection of their hard-won gains of 1966-69.

The second campaign concerned the debate over college enrollments. It soon became clear that the debate over
the Zhang Tiesheng case led to the more fundamental issue
of whether or not "going against the tide is a Marxist-
Leninist principle." By handing in a blank paper, the leftists said, Zhang "adopted the attitude of going against the

tide," an attitude that required ability and courage. Both
Zhou and Wang picked up this theme in their congressional
speeches, but their emphasis was different. Zhou sought
to direct it toward past struggles against Liu Shaoqi and
Lin Biao and toward the international struggle against the
Soviet Union, and by describing Mao as one who dared to
oppose the reactionary mainstream. But Wang spoke of resisting erroneous line tendencies in the present and in the
future.

The second half of the year saw a resurgence of ideological fervor, at least in the press, and there were some
indications that the campaign against Confucius was in fact
directed against Zhou Enlai. The People's Daily on October
31 carried a continuation of the anti-Confucian series that
praised Qin Shihuangdi for dismissing Premier Lu Buwei.
The premier was also accused of advising the emperor to
"gracefully abdicate" and to pick as his successor "a person
of excellent virtues," i.e., himself. Thus, the question
boiled down to whether the Qin monarchy should "continue
the adverse political course pushed by Lu Buwei, thus letting all the achievements of feudal reform carried out by
Shang Yang go down the drain and letting history reverse
itself," or whether the monarchy "should stop the interrup-
tion of Lu Buwei's clique, carry out the struggle for wiping
out the slavery system to the end, and push the wheel of
history forward?" Through a careful reading of the debate
over the nature of Confucianism, it is possible to draw links
to what seemed to be major policy differences in the leadership.

In line with its policy of political normalization, China
took steps to restore the labor unions that had been dis-
solved during the Cultural Revolution. In those days, the
labor unions were regarded as political strongholds of Liu
Shaoqi. In April 1973, the labor unions in Beijing and
Shanghai were reestablished, setting examples for other
cities to follow in reorganizing labor. The Federation of
Women, which ceased functioning during the Cultural Revolution, was also restored. At a women's congress held in Wuhan, delegates were urged to oppose the old idea of male
superiority and to promote equality of the sexes. The Communist Youth League, also shattered during the Cultural
Revolution, was reestablished in the various provinces and
regions. The purpose of the reconstruction of the youth

apparatus was to give the party leadership more effective control over young people and to encourage them to take part in supervised political activities at an early age. Those admitted to the league would have some special status, but none would be exempt from a period of compulsory labor in rural areas.

In 1973, some two million graduates from colleges and middle schools were sent to the countryside to work with the farmers. Many were dispatched to remote border regions to settle there. Compulsory rural assignments caused widespread discontent among the youth. Not only did they find rural life uncongenial, but they were often unable to support themselves. They earned less work points than the farmers, and they received no extra income from sideline activities such as raising chickens and growing vegetables.

On June 27, China conducted its fifteenth nuclear test. The hydrogen bomb, set off in the atmosphere at the Lop Nor test site in the remote Xinjiang region, was estimated by the US Atomic Energy Commission to be in the two- to three-megaton range. While China continued making advances in the development of nuclear warheads, the development of delivery missiles was slower than expected. In 1972, China deployed some 1,000-mile medium-range missiles and probably had begun deploying a 1,500-mile intermediate-range missile, capable of striking Soviet targets in Siberia and American targets in the Western Pacific. But her multistage missile, with a capability range of more than 3,000 miles, reaching all targets in the Soviet Union, was not expected to be ready for deployment until 1974.

Industrial production for the first half of 1973 surpassed the planned targets in eighty major industries, including steel, machine tools, and textiles. In some cases the targets were exceeded by as much as fifty percent. A remarkable advance was made in the electronics industry. In the first five months of 1973, production of radios and TV sets increased, respectively, by eighty-nine and ninety-three percent over the same period in 1972. China's major industrial concern was the renovation and modernization of her production facilities. Many factories were old, and their equipment was antiquated. To remedy this situation, China began to purchase high-technology manufactured products from the West and to send technical missions abroad to ac-

quire advanced industrial knowledge. Agriculture suffered
a reverse in the first half of 1973. Drought hit twelve
provinces and regions in northern China, and heavy rains
did extensive damage to crops in the south. To offset the
effects of these natural disasters, rural authorities were
permitted to shift manpower and capital from industry to
agriculture. In the north, extensive well-drilling programs
were undertaken to irrigate arid land. Results indicated
that a record harvest of approximately 256 million metric
tons of grain was taken in, due to heightened per acre
yields, and a greater amount of land was under cultivation.
Even so, China was estimated to have imported close to $1
billion worth of grain during 1973, of which about $650 mil-
lion worth was purchased from the US alone.

Parallel with its efforts to normalize foreign relations,
Beijing began expanding its trade with the West. To finance
imports of Western capital goods, China now began to purchase on credit. Beijing also agreed to pay foreign royalties
and to grant licenses to foreign patent-holders. To earn
more foreign exchange for imports, China raised the price
of its exports--sharply in some cases. Chinese export expansion, however, was likely to remain minimal for some time,
since there were several obstacles to be overcome. Not only
did China have limited agricultural production, but its manufactured goods had yet to develop markets abroad, and product adjustments had to be made to meet standards acceptable
in the West.

Beijing continued its rapprochement with Washington
in 1973. On February 22, after extensive talks in Beijing
between Chinese leaders and Henry A. Kissinger, President
Nixon's foreign affairs adviser before he became secretary
of state, a joint communiqué was announced which said that
China and the US would establish respective liaison offices
in Washington and Beijing. The move was hailed as a significant diplomatic breakthrough after more than two decades
of mutual isolation. In November, Secretary of State Kissinger visited Beijing again for four days of talks with
Chairman Mao and Premier Zhou. In the joint communiqué
issued on November 14, the United States reaffirmed the
"one-China" principle, which was regarded by Beijing as
essential to normalizing relations. The two sides agreed to
expand their liaison offices and to increase trade and cultural exchanges.

The value of Sino-American trade exceeded $500 million by August 1973, and it was expected that the total for the year would approach $1 billion. China's largest commodity purchase from the US was grain, but China also bought cotton, fertilizer, and tobacco. However, rapid expansion of Sino-American trade was impeded by two factors: blocked accounts and the failure so far by the US to grant most-favored-nation status to China. In 1950, the American government froze Chinese assets in the United States amounting to about $78 million, and the Chinese Communists expropriated American properties in China valued at about $250 million. Claims regarding these money matters had to be settled before China would receive US government-backed credits and most-favored-nation tariff treatment. Beijing and Washington initiated talks on these claims and were expected to reach an early settlement. Cultural exchanges between China and the US increased notably after the Zhou-Kissinger meeting in February. Chinese visitors to the US in 1973 included groups of journalists, water-conservation experts, high-energy physicists, librarians, and a gymnastics team. Among Americans invited to visit China were a medical group, a scientific group, a group of elementary and high school teachers, amateur basketball and swimming teams, and the Philadelphia Orchestra.

On October 10, Prime Minister Pierre Elliot Trudeau of Canada arrived in China for a six-day visit. Upon becoming prime minister in 1968, Trudeau had set about normalizing relations with China, and Canada had recognized Beijing in 1970. Prime Minister and Mrs. Trudeau were warmly welcomed by Premier Zhou and several thousand cheering children at the Beijing airport. Trudeau had a series of long talks with Zhou and conferred for two hours with Chairman Mao, who was reported to be alert and keen, asking many questions about the economy and social problems of Canada. On October 13, Zhou and Trudeau signed a trade agreement that stressed long-term commercial contracts, especially in regard to aluminum, wood pulp, nickel, sulfur, and potash. Agreements were also reached on the establishment of consular relations and on the exchange of cultural, medical, and scientific missions. In an earlier accord, signed on October 5, China agreed to purchase up to 224 million bushels of wheat from Canada at an estimated cost of $1 billion. The wheat was to be shipped over a three-year period, beginning in January 1974. Canada's trade with China, totaling about $300 million in 1973, was expected to grow rapidly.

In 1973, China made diligent efforts to cultivate relations with countries in Western Europe. In May, Beijing
sent a valuable collection of archaeological objects for exhibits in Paris and London. In June, Foreign Minister Ji
Pengfei went to Britain and France and invited British Prime
Minister Edward Heath and French President Georges Pompidou
to visit China. The French president arrived in Beijing on
September 11 to confer with Chairman Mao and Premier Zhou.
While they did not agree on all world problems, their views
converged on many points. China supported French efforts
to affirm a European identity and develop European unity,
but it objected to the establishment of an East-West detente
in Europe. In a joint communiqué issued on September 17,
the two sides declared that they were against "all hegemony,"
but they named no nation striving for such a position.
China's active diplomacy in Europe was motivated largely by
the desire to curb Soviet influence in the West. In China's
view, a détente in Europe would allow the Soviet Union to
concentrate more troops on the Chinese-Soviet border. Consequently, Beijing's support of the European Common Market
(EEC) and its attack on the Soviet-inspired European security conference was directed toward encouraging Western
European unity against the Soviet Union.

China's relations with the Soviet Union remained
strained in 1973. No progress was reported regarding the
Sino-Soviet border negotiations, for Moscow had no intention
of giving up territory that Beijing claimed was seized by
czarist Russia. The Soviet Union concentrated from forty-
five to forty-eight divisions along the Chinese border during
the year and accelerated the settlement of Russian farmers
in the disputed area. To strengthen its claim to former
Chinese territories, the Soviet government changed the names
of towns in eastern Siberia from Chinese to Russian. Both
China and Soviet Union launched violent verbal attacks
against each other. One of the most severe attacks against
the Soviet Union was delivered by Premier Zhou Enlai in his
report to the Tenth Party Congress. "The Soviet revisionist ruling clique, from Khrushchev to Brezhnev," Zhou said,
"has made a socialist country degenerate into a social-imperialist country." He denounced the Soviet leadership as
"the new czar" and likened Soviet criticism of China to "an
old trick of Hitler's." Zhou also called on the Chinese people to prepare for a surprise attack on China by Soviet
forces. In spite of such vilification, however, there was no

evidence of serious military threats along the border by either country.

In March, pursuant to an agreement reached in 1972, China and Japan exchanged envoys for the first time. In establishing diplomatic relations with Tokyo, Beijing hoped that Japan would cooperate in curbing Soviet influence in the Far East. The Chinese government publicly supported Japan's claim to four islands north of Hokkaido that had been occupied by the Soviet Union since the end of World War II. On the other hand, China opposed Japan's participation in the proposed joint Soviet-Japanese development of oil and gas resources in eastern Siberia. In April, to influence Japanese public opinion, Beijing sent a Chinese mission to Japan, headed by Friendship Association. The fifty-member group visited various places in Japan, including Hokkaido, where there was strong feeling for return of the four Soviet-held islands.

In April, China and Japan agreed in principle to laying an underseas cable between the two countries by 1975. But Sino-Japanese negotiations for establishing intercountry air service met with difficulties as Tokyo stood firm against Chinese demands that flights between Japan and Taiwan be discontinued. Beijing breathed a sigh of relief when the Tanaka-Brezhnev talks in October did not lead to a settlement of territorial or economic issue between Japan and the Soviet Union.

China played an important role in bringing about the Vietnam ceasefire accord in January. It pushed for a settlement, not only to avoid straining relations with the United States, but also to check Soviet influence in Indo-China. In an agreement reached in Hanoi in June, Beijing promised substantial economic aid for the reconstruction of North Vietnam. In other developments, China strongly criticized the US for bombing raids against Cambodian Communist positions in the summer of 1973. Also China was building two roads from Yunnan province to northeastern Laos, in a determined effort to increase its influence in Indo-China. China was as glad as the US to see the Vietnam cease-fire go into effect in January, and it sent a top-level delegation, headed by Foreign Minister Ji Pengfei, to the International Conference on Vietnam in Paris in February. China moved to ameliorate relations with Thailand, especially after the September student demonstration in Bangkok.

China adopted a pose as the champion of the interests of the Third World in its struggle against the domination of the "superpowers." Speaking before the UN Security Council on June 14, Huang Hua, the Chinese representative, blamed the Soviet Union and the United States for tensions in the Middle East, calling them "the two superpowers which have today taken the place of former imperialist powers as the principal rivals for hegemony." When the Arab-Israeli War broke out in October, Beijing accused Israel of aggression and declared support for the Arabs. The Chinese delegates at the UN declined to support the American-Soviet resolution calling for a cease-fire in the Middle East. Beijing assailed the Soviet Union for "betraying" the Arabs by not giving them sufficient support to attain their objectives.

To maintain buffer zones between both the Soviet Union and India, China cultivated the friendship of Iran and strengthened its relations with Pakistan. The Chinese government reiterated its support for the "common struggle of the African peoples against imperialism and neocolonialism," and, in regard to Latin America, it made efforts to strengthen its ties with Argentina after the leftist regime of President Juan D. Perón returned to power.

January 1   The emphasis in the New Year's joint editorial by the People's Daily, the Red Flag, and the Liberation Army Daily was on domestic issues. The editorial included a new instruction from Chairman Mao: "Dig Tunnels, Store Grain Everywhere and Never Seek Hegemony."
   • NCNA reported that China's grain production in 1972 was 240 million metric tons compared with 250 million metric tons in 1971. The decline was attributed to drought in the north, and to floods and windstorms in the south. China's steel production in 1972 totaled 23 million tons, a 9.5 percent increase over 1971.

January 3   Premier Zhou Enlai met Le Duc Tho and other Vietnamese "Comrades."

January 5   The Italian Government Air Delegation arrived in Beijing for a six-day visit. Premier Zhou Enlai met the delegation on January 9. Sino-Italian civil air transport agreement was signed on January 8.

• Sino-Soviet Commission for Navigation on Boundary Rivers held its eighteenth regular meeting in Heihe, Heilongjiang province from January 5 to March 5, but ended with no agreement.

January 6 Italian Foreign Minister Giuseppe Medici and his party arrived in Beijing for a seven-day visit. Premier Zhou Enlai met the party on January 9. A reciprocal agreement for trademark registration was signed on January 10.

January 9 Huang Hua sent a letter to Secretary General Kurt Waldheim saying that China would not take part in the work of the UN Special Committee on world disarmament.

January 10 Lieutenant General Mobutu Sese Seko, president of the Republic of Zaire, arrived in Beijing for a ten-day visit. Premier Zhou Enlai held a welcome banquet on January 11, and Chairman Mao met him on January 13. Economic, technical cooperation, and trade agreements were signed on January 14. A press communiqué was issued on January 20. On his return to Zaire, President Mobutu said that China had granted Zaire an interest-free loan of 100 million yuan, and that Chinese agronomists and doctors would be coming to work in Zaire.

January 12 The Chinese Government Trade Delegation, led by Bai Xiangguo, left Beijing to visit Britain (January 13-17), and the Netherlands (January 18-25).

January 13 China and Cambodia signed, in Beijing, agreements on China's gratuitous supply of military equipment and material to Cambodia and China's economic aid to Cambodia.

January 16 An Australian journalist, Francis James, who had disappeared during a visit to China in November 1969, was released after having served three years in prison. No official statement was made about his release, which was attributed by many to the personal intervention of the new Australian prime minister.

• Takeo Kimura, Liberal Democratic party member

of the House of Representatives of Japan, arrived in Beijing for a seven-day visit. Premier Zhou Enlai met him on January 17 and 20.

• The Chinese Government Maritime Transport Delegation, led by Yu Wei, left Beijing to visit Chile from January 20-27. A Sino-Chilean maritime agreement was signed on January 26.

• A Chinese journalist group, led by Li Yannian, visited Jamaica (January 16-30), Venezuela (January 30 to February 15), Guyana (February 15 to March 1), Panama (March 1-19), Costa Rica (March 20-27), El Salvador (March 28 to April 5), Colombia (April 6-30), and Ecuador (May 1-10). The group returned to Beijing on June 7.

January 17 The Yashuhiro Nakasone Mission arrived in Beijing for a five-day visit. Premier Zhou Enlai met the mission on January 19. According to Japanese news reports, Premier Zhou was reported as having said that there was no question of joint Japan-China exploitation of oil resources on China's continental shelf. At the same time, Premier Zhou was also reported as having said informally to a visiting leader of the Liberal Democratic party, Takeo Kimura, that the Japanese-American security treaty seemed, at the time, "necessary" for Japan.

• E.F. Hill, chairman of the Australian Communist party (Marxist-Leninist), arrived in Beijing for a visit from January 18 to February 9 as a guest of the CCP Central Committee. Premier Zhou Enlai met him on February 5.

• China granted Madagascar an interest-free loan of 2,000 million Malagasy francs, and Madagascar bought 40,000 tons of rice from China.

January 19 China and Rumania signed, in Beijing, a protocol on China providing complete plants and technical assistance to Rumania.

January 20 Air service between Pakistan and China was inaugurated. Pakistan International Airlines was to operate twice-weekly flights from Karachi and Ismamalad to Beijing.

January 22 Prince Norodom Sihanouk said that China pro-

vided him with an additional $10 million in American
notes every year to enable his forces in Cambodia to
buy arms and equipment clandestinely.

January 24   An article in the People's Daily entitled "Supplies Can Only Be Ensured If the Economy Is Developed,"
emphasized the importance of sideline products in the
communes.

January 25   In Khartoum, China and Sudan signed notes on
the talks for the construction of an ice factory, fishing
boats, a net repair factory, and cold storage facility.
   • The 1973 Sino-Afghan protocol for goods exchange
was signed in Kabul.
   • The People's Daily published the cease-fire agreement to end the war in Indo-China as the front-page
headline news.   The full texts of the agreement were
published by the People's Daily January 26-28.

January 26   The British Embassy in Beijing announced that
David Crook, Elsie Epstein, and Michael Shapiro--the
last three British subjects detained in China--would be
released.

January 27   The Chilean Government Delegation led by Foreign Minister Clodomiro Almeyda Medina, arrived in
Beijing for a six-day visit.   Premier Zhou Enlai met the
delegation on January 30.
   • The Tanzanian Delegation, led by Defense Minister
E.M. Sokoine, arrived in Beijing for a fourteen-day
visit.   Premier Zhou Enlai met the delegation on February 8.
   • Tomotej Dubrovay, general manager of the Czechoslovak Trade Bank, and Vladislav Bejcek, manager of
the foreign contracts department of the bank, arrived
in Beijing for a seven-day visit.   A protocol on the
banking formalities for settling the acocunts of goods
exchange and payments between the two nations was
signed on February 2.

January 28   The People's Daily published an editorial welcoming the formal signing of the agreement to end the
war in Vietnam.

January 29   Chairman Mao Zedong, Dong Biwu, Zhu De, and

Zhou Enlai congratulated the party and state leaders of
DRVN, SVNFL, and PRGRSVN on the formal signing in
Paris of the agreement ending the war and restoring
peace in Vietnam. A formal message of congratulation
was sent to the leaders of DRVN, SVNFL, and PRG-
RSVN in the names of these four persons.

January 30 The Wuhan Acrobatic Troupe of China left Beijing on performance tours to Sri Lanka (January 31 to
February 17), Pakistan (February 17 to March 6),
Afghanistan (March 6-21), Burma (March 21 to April 5),
and Nepal (April 5-24).

January 31 Le Duc Tho and his party arrived in Beijing on
their way home from Paris. They were greeted at the
guest house by Premier Zhou Enlai. Chairman Mao
Zedong met the delegation on February 1. A grand
rally was held with 10,000 people celebrating the signing of the Paris Accords on February 2. The delegation
left Beijing for home on February 3.

February 6 An earthquake of 7.9 magnitude struck the
Ganzi Tibetan autonomous district (Sichuan), causing
considerable damage and some loss of life. Aftershocks
occurred on February 7 and 8.

February 9 The Korean Government Delegation, led by
Foreign Minister Ho Dam, arrived in Beijing for a five-
day visit. Premier Zhou Enlai met the delegation on
February 10. The press communiqué said that China
supported the North Korean view on the independent
and peaceful reunification of the fatherland and believed that US forces "using the signboard of the UN"
should be withdrawn from South Korea.

February 12 The Shanghai Municipal Congress of the Communist Youth League of China was held from February
12-19--the first at this level since the Cultural Revolution.

February 14 The annual edition of the UN Demographic
Yearbook, for the first time listed Shanghai as the
world's most populous city with a population of
10,820,000, and Beijing as the fourth with a population
of 6,757,500.

February 15   Henry Kissinger and his party of seventeen
members arrived in Beijing for a five-day visit.   Premier Zhou Enlai held talks with him on February 15,
16, 17.   Chairman Mao met him on February 17.   In a
joint communiqué, which was released on February 22,
the two nations agreed to establish liaison offices in
the other's capital.   After his return from Beijing,
Kissinger said that discussions would be held in Paris
in March on the settlement of $250 million of private
American claims against China and $78 million of blocked
Chinese assets in the US, he also said that China would
soon release two US pilots, Lt. Comdr. Robert J. Flynn,
and Maj. Philip E. Smith, and would review the life
sentence given in 1954 to John Downey.   The pilots
were released on March 15 and Downey on March 12.

February 16   China and Guinea signed, in Conakry, the 1973
trade agreement.
      • Chinese Government Trade Delegation, led by Beng
Jinbo, left Beijing to visit Finland from February 16 to
March 7.   The 1973 Sino-Finn trade agreement was
signed on March 3.

February 17   The Bulgarian Government Trade Delegation,
led by A. Kozmov, arrived in Beijing for a five-day
visit.   The 1973 Sino-Bulgarian trade agreement was
signed on February 19.

February 18   The Cable and Wireless Company of Hongkong
announced that it had signed an agreement with China
to establish a coaxial telephone cable link between
Hongkong and Guangdong.

February 20   China and Ethiopia signed, in Addis Ababa, a
protocol on economic and technical cooperation.

February 21   Senator Edward M. Kennedy introduced, in
the US Senate, a resolution calling for "prompt establishment of full diplomatic relations" with the People's
Republic of China.   He said the US should end its
diplomatic recognition of the Nationalist Government on
Taiwan and announce a unilateral guarantee for Taiwan
security.
      • The cease-fire agreement in Laos, which was for-
mally signed in Vientiane on February 21, was welcomed

in a People's Daily editorial two days later which emphasized that the United States "must scrupulously
carry out and observe the 1962 Geneva Agreement."
The full text of the agreement was published in the
People's Daily on February 22.

February 22 The air service between Ethiopia and China
was inaugurated. The Shanghai Municipal Revolutionary
Committee gave a reception to mark the inaugural flight
of the Ethiopia Airlines from Addis Ababa to Shanghai.

February 23 Colonel V.I. Ivanov, military attaché of the
Soviet Embassy in Beijing, gave a reception to mark
the fiftieth anniversary of the founding of the Soviet
Army and Navy.

February 24 The Chinese Delegation, led by Foreign Minister Ji Pengfei, left Beijing for Paris to attend the International Conference on Vietnam, held from February
25 to March 2.

February 26 Nepal and China exchanged, in Katmandu, letters on technical assistance.

February 27 The Chinese Government Trade Delegation, led
by Zhou Huamin, left Beijing to visit Mongolia (February
27 to March 5), Hungary (March 6-15), Czechoslovakia
(March 16-20), and Poland (March 21-30). The 1973
Sino-Mongolian protocol on goods exchange was signed
on March 7; the 1973 Sino-Czechoslovak goods exchange
and payment agreement was signed on March 20; the
1973 Sino-Polish goods exchange and payment agreement
was signed on March 23.

February 28 CPPCC National Committee held a symposium in
Beijing to mark the twenty-sixth anniversary of the
"February 28" uprising of the people of Taiwan province. The meeting was presided over by Fu Zuoyi,
who suggested talks with the people on Taiwan to solve
the Taiwan problem.

March 1 China filed its acceptance of the Inter-Governmental
Maritime Consultative Organization with the UN Secre-
tary General.
  • The minutes of the talks between China and Af-

ghanistan for the expansion of the Bagrami Textile
Mill were signed in Kabul.

March 3   Song Weibin, former commercial attaché of the Nationalist Chinese Embassy in Australia, arrived in Beijing with his wife and two children.
   • The Government Trade Delegation of the German
Democratic Republic, led by Dr. Fensk, arrived in Beijing for a seven-day visit. The 1973 Sino-German
goods exchange and payment agreement was signed on
March 5.

March 5   The Fifth Liaoning Provincial Congress of the Communist Youth League of China was held in Shenyang,
the first at the provincial level since the Cultural Revolution.

March 9   China and Spain signed a joint communiqué in
Paris to establish full diplomatic relations at the ambassadorial level.

March 10   The Cuban Government Trade Delegation, led by
Herminio García Lazo, arrived in Beijing for a fourteen-
day visit. The 1973 Sino-Cuban protocol on trade was
signed on March 23.
   • The Rumanian Cultural Delegation, led by Dumitru
Popescu, arrived in Beijing for a fourteen-day visit.
Ye Jianying and Jiang Qing met the delegation on March
12. Yao Wenyuan held talks with the delegation on
March 22.

March 12   Egyptian Foreign Minister Mohamed Hassan El-
Zayyat arrived in Beijing for a four-day visit. Ji
Pengfei held talks with him on March 13 and 14.

March 15   President Nixon announced that the US would
open its liaison office in Beijing around May 1, and
Ambassador David Bruce would be the chief of the office, with Alfred Jenkins and John Holdridge as his
top assistants.
   • The Foreign Ministry issued a statement protesting
against oil drilling off the Korean coast, with the per-
mission of the South Korean government, by a ship
chartered by an American oil company.

March 17   The London Philharmonic Orchestra arrived in
      Beijing for a ten-day performance tour of China.

March 19   China was admitted to the UN Food and Agricul-
      ture Organization (FAO).
          • The Chinese Journalist Delegation, led by Pan
      Fei, left Beijing to visit Britain (March 21 to April 24),
      the Federal Republic of Germany (April 24 to May 15),
      and Italy (May 15 to June 5); it returned to Beijing on
      June 7.

March 20   A summary of the talks between Nepal and China
      on the construction of a ringroad in Katmandu was
      signed in Katmandu.

March 24   V.G. Wilcox, general secretary of the Communist
      party of New Zealand, and his party arrived in Beijing
      for a thirteen-day visit. Premier Zhou Enlai met the
      delegation on March 30.

March 25   The Shanghai Acrobatic Troupe, led by Yuan
      Donglin, left Beijing for performance tours in Albania
      (March 26 to April 16), Rumania (April 17 to May 8),
      and France (May 8-31).
          • El Hadj Ahmadou Ahidjo, president of the United
      Republic of Cameroon, and Mrs. Ahidjo arrived in Bei-
      jing for an eight-day visit. Premier Zhou Enlai held
      talks with them on March 25. Chairman Mao met them
      on March 26. A press communiqué was issued on April
      2. A Sino-Cameroon economic and technical cooperation
      agreement was signed on April 2.

March 26   Minutes of the talks between Nepal and China on
      the construction of the Katmandu-Rhaktapur trolley-bus
      service project were signed in Katmandu.

March 27   The New Zealand Government Ministerial Mission,
      led by Joseph A. Walding, arrived in Beijing for an
      eight-day visit. Premier Zhou Enlai met the delegation
      on March 31.

March 28   The Sixth Beijing Municipal Congress of the Com-
      munist Youth League of China was held from March 28
      to March 31.
          • The Delegation of the Chinese Academy of Sci-

ences, led by Ye Zhijiang, left Beijing for Rumania on a seventeen-day visit. The Sino-Rumanian scientific cooperation plan for 1973-74 was signed on April 1.

• The Sixth Jiangsu Provincial Congress of the Communist Youth League of China was held from March 28-31.

March 30   Huang Zhen was appointed chief of the liaison office of the PRC in the US and Han Xu, deputy chief of the office.

April 2   A Sino-Austrian trade and payment agreement was signed in Vienna.

April 3   The Iranian Economic Delegation, led by Houshang Ansari, arrived in Beijing for an eight-day visit. Premier Zhou Enlai met the delegation on April 8. A Sino-Iranian trade and payment agreement was signed on April 8.

April 4   A protocol on China's sending a medical team to Mali was signed in Bamako.

April 5   At the UN Seabed Committee, Zhuang Yan strongly criticized the Russian view that territorial sea limits should be twelve nautical miles. The Chinese believed that coastal states were "entitled to determine reasonably the limits of their territorial seas according to their specific natural conditions, taking into account the needs of their security and national economic development."

April 6   A Chinese delegation left Beijing for Rome to attend the Second Sino-Italian Amalgamated Committee, held April 8-12.

April 10   Nguyen Thi Binh, foreign minister of the PRG-RSVN, and its party arrived in Beijing for a three-day visit. Premier Zhou Enlai met the party on April 11.

April 11   Hen Trutz Ritter Von Xylander, a thirty-eight-year-old West German technician who had been in a Chinese prison for over five years, was released by the Chinese authorities.

• The Vienna Philharmonic Orchestra gave a première in Beijing.   The Orchestra left Beijing for home on April 16.

• Deng Xiaoping, the former secretary general of the CCP, who was accused of being the "number two capitalist roader" during the Cultural Revolution, first reappeared as a vice premier at a dinner banquet given by Premier Zhou Enlai in honor of Prince Norodom Sihanouk, who arrived in Beijing from Hanoi after an inspection tour of the liberated zone of Cambodia and official visit to DRVN.

• The National People's Congress Standing Committee and State Council sent a letter of support to DPRK government and Supreme People's Assembly Standing Committee, expressing resolute support and solidarity for the new effort of the DPRK government to promote the independent and peaceful reunification of Korea.

April 14   The Chinese authorities notified the Japanese government of the release of five Japanese businessmen because of their "good conduct in prison and in consideration of Sino-Japanese relations."

• The Somai Trade Delegation arrived in Guangzhou on their way to Beijing for a fourteen-day visit.   Premier Zhou Enlai met the delegation on April 28.

• The Czechoslovak Scientific and Technical Delegation arrived in Beijing for a seven-day visit.   A protocol of the joint commission session was signed on April 20.

April 15   A large delegation, led by Liao Zhengzhi, president of the China-Japan Friendship Association, visited Japan from April to May 18.   The delegation traveled widely in Japan and by all accounts, the visit was a considerable publicity success for China.

April 16   Both Beijing and Shanghai held municipal trade union congresses from April 16-21.   Wang Hongwen was elected chairman of the Shanghai Union.   Ni Zhifu was elected chairman of the Beijing Union.

• At the Security Council meeting, Huang Hua condemned "the aggression by Israeli Zionists" in Lebanon, and the connivance and encouragement of the two superpowers, adding that the Soviet proposal for the nonuse of force in international relations was a "downright fraud."

• At the UN Economic Commission for Asia and the Far East, Ji Long spoke on the population question. Drawing up a population policy, he said, was an internal affair of a state, and China's experience had shown that growth in population was not an obstacle to economic development. The Chinese population had grown from "more than 500 million to over 700 million" in the past twenty-four years but while the annual rate of increase in the population had been "about 2%, that of grain was nearly 4% and for the last decade about 5%." China's policy, he said, was to adopt different measures according to different circumstances.

April 17 Tianjin, Anhui, and Shanxi provinces held Communist Youth League Congresses from April 17-26.
• Western Union International Inc. announced it had reached an agreement with China to set up a direct satellite telegraph line between Beijing and New York. The service would use a station being built for China by RCA Global Communications, and would include telex, data, and leased channels.

April 18 A ten-member advance party of Chinese officials arrived in Washington to make preparations for the opening of the first liaison office of the PRC in the US.
• Former Major and Flight Safety Officer of Taiwan's China Airlines, Zhao Mingzhe, crossed over and returned to Beijing.

April 19 Mexican President Luis Echeverria Alvarez arrived in Beijing for a six-day visit. Premier Zhou Enlai gave a grand welcoming banquet on April 19, and held talks with the president on April 20 and 21. Chairman Mao met the president on April 20. A trade agreement between the two nations was signed on April 22, and the press communiqué on the visit was issued on April 24.
• The Chinese Archaeological Group, led by Xia Nai, left Beijing to visit Peru (April 23 to May 15) and Mexico (May 16 to June 5). The delegation returned to Beijing on June 7.
• A Sino-Bulgarian agreement on scientific and technical cooperation was extended.

April 21 In explanation of a vote in the Security Council,

Huang Hua stated that China was abstaining in the vote on the Mideast resolution because it "failed to draw a distinction" between the actions of the aggressors and those of the victims of aggression.

April 24 Hebie, Shaanxi, Gansu, and Guizhou provinces held Communist Youth League Congresses from April 24 to May 4.

April 25 Nigerian Foreign Minister Okoi Arikpo arrived in Beijing for a six-day visit. Premier Zhou Enlai met him on April 28.
• According to Kyodo, a small but significant agreement was reached in April for the export of Chinese oil to Japan. The first contract was for one million tons of crude oil at the "prevailing international price" to be shipped from Luta in North China in Japanese tankers.

April 29 The Delegation of Japan-China Agricultural and Peasant Exchange Association arrived in Beijing for a ten-day visit. Hua Guofeng met the delegation on May 7.

May 1 Beijing held celebrations and gala parties to mark May Day.
• A Chinese delegation, led by Haung Shuze, left Beijing to attend the Twenty-sixth World Health Assembly session in Geneva to be held from May 7 to June 1. Zhang Weixun was appointed assistant director general of the World Health Organization (WHO) on June 1.

May 3 The Pakistan National Dance Ensemble gave its first performance in Beijing.
• NCNA announced that more than 400 rare historical relics excavated by new China since 1949 would be exhibited in France on May 6, and later in England and other countries.

May 4 Hubei, Jilin, Heilongjiang, Hunan, Yunnan, Henan provinces held Communist Youth League Congresses from May 4-12. Shandong, Inner Mongolia, Zhejiang, Fujian and Guangxi provinces held Communist Youth League Congresses from May 14-23.

- A Chinese delegation, led by Wang Yequi, left
Beijing for Paris to attend the opening ceremony of the
Unearthed Relics Exhibition in France. The exhibition
was held from May 8 to July 31.
  - China and Algeria signed an insurance agreement
in Algiers.
  - A Sino-Japanese agreement on seabed cables was
signed in Beijing.
  - Gaston Thorn, foreign minister of Luxembourg,
and his party arrived in Beijing for a seven-day visit.
Premier Zhou Enlai met the delegation on May 6.

May 8 Prince and Madam Norodom Sihanouk left Beijing for
African and European tours. Deng Xiaoping appeared
in a higher position among the Chinese officials to see
them off at the Beijing airport.
  - A governmental air transport agreement between
China and Norway, Denmark, and Sweden was initiated
by a joint Scandinavian negotiating team.
  - Norwegian Foreign Minister Dagfinn Vaavik arrived
in Beijing for an eight-day visit. Premier Zhou Enlai
met him on May 12. A Sino-Norwegian air transport
agreement was signed on May 12.
  - Mrs. Perón, wife of former Argentine President
Juan Domingo Perón, arrived in Beijing for a nine-day
visit. Premier Zhou Enlai met her on May 13.

May 12 Two African lion cubs, a gift from his Imperial Majesty Haile Selassie I, emperor of Ethiopia, were presented to the Chinese government and people at a ceremony at the Beijing zoo.

May 13 The Australian Trade Mission, led by J.P. Cairns,
arrived in Beijing for a sixteen-day visit. Premier
Zhou Enlai met the delegation on May 17.
  - The Delegation of the Rumanian Register of Shipping, led by Savu Emil, arrived in Beijing for a twelve-
day visit. A Sino-Rumanian ship survey agreement was
signed on May 23.

May 14 David Bruce, newly appointed chief of the US liaison
office in China, arrived in Beijing.
  - The Chinese Journalists' Delegation, led by Zhu
Muzhi, left Beijing to visit the US (May 17 to June 15)
and Canada (June 16 to July 1). The delegation returned to Beijing on July 4.

May 15 Danish Foreign Minister and Mrs. R.B. Anderson arrived in Beijing for an eight-day visit. Premier Zhou Enlai met them on May 18. A Sino-Danish civil transport agreement was signed on May 18.

May 16 A Chinese delegation, led by Sun Xiaofeng, attended the Thirteenth Session of the Sino-Rumanian Joint Commission on Scientific and Technical Cooperation. A protocol of the meeting was signed on May 31.

May 17 Premier Zhou Enlai met Dr. Yang Zhenning, Chinese-American Nobel Prize winner (1957), in Beijing on May 17 and again on July 18. Chairman Mao Zedong met him on July 17.

• The US Scientific Delegation, led by Dr. Emil Smith, arrived in Beijing for a twenty-six-day visit. Premier Zhou Enlai met the delegation on May 27.

May 18 Premier Zhou Enlai met David Bruce, chief of the US liaison office in China. At the Security Council meeting, Huang Hua stated that China supported strict sanctions against Southern Rhodesia.

May 19 Shirley MacLaine, the leader of the Friendship Delegation of American Women, and a noted American film actress, left Beijing for home via Guangzhou. The delegation came to China on April 2 to visit Guangzhou, Shanghai, Hangzhou, Xian, Yanan, and Beijing.

May 20 M. Nikolaos Macarezos, deputy prime minister of the Kingdom of Greece, his wife, and his party arrived in Beijing for an eight-day official visit. Premier Zhou Enlai met the delegation on May 22. In the communiqué (issued on May 27), Vice Premier Li Xiannian accepted, with pleasure, an invitation to visit Greece. Three agreements between the two nations were signed on May 23: an agreement on civil transport, a trade and payment agreement, and an agreement on maritime transport.

• The People's Daily carried an editorial entitled "A Law of History," to explain the law of history expounded by Chairman Mao in his May 20, 1970 statement.

May 22 The Chinese Government Delegation, led by Guo Lu, left Beijing to visit Zambia (May 24 to June 8) and Tanzania (June 12 to June 19).

May 23   The Chinese Scientific and Technical Cooperation Delegation, led by Ma Yi, left Beijing for Budapest, Hungary to attend the Twelfth Session of the Sino-Hungarian Commission for Scientific and Technical Cooperation. A protocol of the meeting was signed on June 3.

May 24   A Sino-Congolese economic and technical cooperation protocol was signed in Brazzaville.
    • Mauritius Foreign Minister Charles Gaetan Duval arrived in Beijing for an eight-day visit. Premier Zhou Enlai met the delegation on May 27.
    • Premier Zhou Enlai sent a message to extend congratulations on the tenth anniversary of the founding of the OAU and the convocation of the Tenth Session of the Assembly of the Heads of State and Government of the OAU.

May 25   Speaking at a banquet for a visiting group from Hong Kong sporting groups, table tennis champion Zhuang Zedong invited table tennis players and coaches in Taiwan province as well as enthusiasts of the sport among the overseas Chinese from Taiwan province to take part in the Asian-African-Latin American Table Tennis Friendship Invitation Tournament to be held in Beijing in late August.

May 26   Tianjin held the Tenth Trade Union Congress from May 26-31.

May 27   The British-Chinese Air Service Agreement Negotiating Team arrived in Beijing for a ten-day visit. An air flight agreement between the two nations was signed on June 13.

May 29   Swedish Foreign Minister Krister Wickman and his party arrived in Beijing for an eight-day visit. Premier Zhou Enlai met the delegation on June 1. A Sino-Swedish civil air transport agreement was signed on June 1.
    • A protocol between China and Equatorial Guinea on sending a Chinese medical team was signed in Santa Isabel.

May 30   President Nixon met Huang Zhen, chief of the Chinese liaison office in the United States.

June 1 Xian Radio gave the most prominent line of criticism
of Lin Biao without referring to his name. It said that
his faults had been those of "ultra-rightism" and not,
as previously been suggested, "ultra-leftism" or even
"left in form but right in essence."

• Former French Prime Minister Jacques Chaban-
Delmas and his wife arrived in Beijing for a fifteen-day
visit. Premier Zhou Enlai met them on June 4.

June 4 The Vietnam Workers' Party and the government of
the DRVN, led by Le Duan and Pham Van Dong, arrived in Beijing for a seven-day visit. Premier Zhou
Enlai gave a welcoming banquet on June 4. Chairman
Mao met the delegation on June 5. The joint communiqué stressed "the great victory won by the Vietnamese people against US aggression." Both sides demanded genuine respect for the Paris agreement on
Laos as well as Prince Sihanouk's position in Cambodia.

June 5 A protocol on sending a Chinese medical team to
Tunisia was signed in Tunis.

• The 1973-74 executive plan for the agreement of
public health cooperation between China and Vietnam was
signed in Beijing.

June 6 Foreign Minister Ji Pengfei left Beijing to visit Britain (June 6-10), France (June 10-14), Iran (June 14-
16), and Pakistan (June 16-19); he returned to Beijing
on June 19.

• The minutes of the talks between China and
Rwanda on roads, sugar refinery, and rice cultivation
were signed in Kigali, Rwanda.

June 7 Guangdong, Qinghai, Ningxia, Jiangxi, and Tibet
held Communist Youth League Congresses from June 7-
28.

June 8 The Chinese Medical Delegation, led by Dr. Zai
Paoxian, left Beijing to visit Mexico (June 11 to July
4), Chile (July 5-19) and Peru (July 19 to August 14).

• An agreement on China's gratuitous economic and
military assistance to Vietnam for 1974 was signed in
Beijing.

• An exhibition of Unearthed Relics of the People's
Republic of China began in the Tokyo National Museum
under the joint sponsorship of Japan-China Cultural

Exchange Association, the Tokyo National Museum and the Asahi Simbun.

June 11   China and Canada signed a civil air transport agreement and a relevant technical protocol in Ottawa.
• Liaoning province held the Third Trade Union Congress from June 11-14.

June 13   Foreign Minister Ji Pengfei met Henry Kissinger in Paris.
• An agreement was signed in Beijing under which the British Overseas Airways Corporation would offer regular airline services between London and Beijing, while the Chinese state airline would offer reciprocal services between the two capitals.

June 14   At the Security Council debate, Huang Hua spoke strongly against the policy of the "Israeli Zionists." The theory of so-called "secure boundaries" which they had been advertising was, he said, "a typical theory for expansion." He also said that China was "not opposed to the Jewish nation and the people of Israel" but it opposed "the Israeli Zionists' policies of aggression and expansion."
• The Ethiopian Economic and Trade Delegation, led by Ketema Yifru, arrived in Beijing for a seven-day visit. Premier Zhou Enlai met the delegation on June 18.

June 15   The Korean Government Economic Delegation, led by Choe Jae U, arrived in Beijing for a five-day visit. A Sino-Korean agreement and protocol for economic and technical cooperation were signed on June 18.
• The Chinese Scientific Group, led by Liu Ruiyou, left Beijing for Mexico to attend the Continental Conference on Science and Mankind, held in Mexico City from June 20 to July 4.

June 20   Colonel Moussa Traore, president of Mali, arrived in Beijing for a seven-day visit. Premier Zhou Enlai met him on June 21. Cambodian Prince Sihanouk met him on June 21. Chairman Mao met him on June 22. An economic and technical cooperation agreement between the two nations was signed on June 24.
• The Chinese Friendship Visiting Group, led by

Yue Daiheng, left Beijing to visit Australia (June 23 to
July 15) and New Zealand (July 15–31).

June 21 NCNA announced that the Sino-Japanese Nongovernmental Fishery Agreement would be operative for
another year after the expiration date of June 22, 1973.
  • An economic and trade exhibition of the People's
Republic of China opened in Belgrade, Yugoslavia; it
closed on July 5.

June 22 In the Security Council, China supported the rec-
ommendation that the German Democratic Republic and
the Federal Republic of Germany should both be admitted to the United Nations membership.

June 23 Guangdong, Hebei, Gansu, Shandong, Heilongjiang,
Jiangsu and Inner Mongolia held Trade Union Congresses from June 23 to July 3.

June 24 Premier Zhou Enlai declared China's firm support
for Korean President Kim Il Sung's new line and five
propositions for independent and peaceful reunification
of Korea.
  • The Shanghai Acrobatic Troupe of China, led by
Yuan Donglin, left Beijing to visit Malta (June 26–28)
and Britain (June 30 to July 15).

June 26 China and Egypt signed minutes of talks on building a sandbrick factory in Cairo.

June 27 Qiao Guanhua met David Rockefeller, chairman of
Chase Manhattan Bank, his wife, and members of his
party in Beijing.
  • Tianjin held the Sixth Women's Congress from June
27 to July 1.
  • A hydrogen bomb test was carried out at the Lop
Nor test site in Xinjiang. According to the US Atomic
Energy Commission, the test was in the two- to three-
megaton range. The test was officially announced in
Beijing shortly after it had taken place and the announcement was coupled with a statement that China
would "at no time and under no circumstances be the
first to use nuclear weapons" and the government would
continue to work for the "complete prohibition and
thorough destruction of nuclear weapons."

June 29   Guangxi Zhuang autonomous region, Yunnan, and
          Hubei held Trade Union Congresses from June 29 to
          July 1.
              • Guangdong, Qinghai, Jiangxi, Ningxia Hui autono-
          mous region, and Tibet held Communist Youth League
          Congresses from June 29 to July 4.

June 30   The Sudanese Government Economic and Trade
          Delegation, led by Ibrahim Monsour, arrived in Beijing
          for a ten-day visit. Premier Zhou Enlai met the dele-
          gation on July 3. The 1973 Sino-Sudanese trade proto-
          col was signed on July 4.

July 2   China and Britain signed an agreement for the Chi-
          nese Exhibition of Archeological Finds in London to be
          held from September 20, 1973 to January 23, 1974.
              • The fourteen-member Delegation of American High-
          Energy Physicists, led by Professor Marvin Goldberger,
          arrived in Beijing for a fifteen-day visit. Guo Moruo
          met the delegation on July 8.

July 3   Zhejiang, Ningxia and Fujian held Trade Union Con-
          gresses from July 3-22.
              • The US Congressional Group, led by Senator War-
          ren G. Magnuson, arrived in Beijing for a fourteen-day
          visit. Premier Zhou Enlai met the delegation on July 6.

July 4   David Bruce, chief of the US liaison office in China,
          and his wife gave a reception in Beijing to mark the
          Independence Day of the United States.
              • The chairman of the Chase Manhattan Bank, David
          Rockefeller, announced the conclusion of a correspondent
          bank agreement with the Bank of China.

July 5   China and the Federal Republic of Germany signed
          a trade and payment agreement in Bonn.
              • Prince Norodom Sihanouk and his wife arrived in
          Beijing after visiting eleven African and European
          countries. Premier Zhou Enlai gave him a grand ban-
          quet on July 6 congratulating him on his successful
          visits.
              • It was announced in Washington that Henry Kis-
          singer would visit Beijing in August, and it was thought
          that he would try to reach an understanding about
          Cambodia and give an account of Brezhnev's visit to the

US in June. Prince Sihanouk, however, made it clear
that he, personally, would not be prepared to meet
Kissinger.
 • The Korean Delegation, led by Ko Tae Un, arrived
in Beijing to attend the Council Meeting of the Sino-
Korean Yalu River Hydro-Electric Power Corporation.
The delegation left Beijing for home on August 1.

July 6 President Nixon met Huang Zhen, chief of the Chinese liaison office in the US, at the Western White
House in San Clemente, California.
 • An exhibition of old and contemporary Chinese
prints opened at the Museum of Art and History of Fribourg in the city of Fribourg, Switzerland. The exhibition closed on October 7.

July 7 The Chinese Military Friendship Delegation, led by
Xu Xiangjian, left Beijing for a seven-day tour of Albania.

July 10 Premier Zhou Enlai sent a message to Prime Minister
Lynden O. Pindling of the Bahamas congratulating him
on the independence of the Bahamas and informing him
of the Chinese government's decision to recognize the
Bahamas.

July 13 Her Royal Highness Princess Shobha Shahi of Nepal
and Kumar Mohan Bahadur Shahi arrived in Beijing for
a fourteen-day visit. Vice Premier Li Xiannian met
them on July 17.

July 15 The Beijing Venue of the 1973 Sports Meet of the
Chinese People's Liberation Army took place at the
Capital Indoor Stadium from July 15 to July 29.

July 16 Guangxi, Guangdong, Gansu, Tibet, Heilongjiang,
and Fujian held Women's Congresses between July 16
and August 4.
 • China and Canada exchanged notes on registration
of trademarks.

July 19 The Liaoning Daily published a letter, from a student named Zhang Tiesheng, denouncing "bookworms"
as being against practical knowledge. The People's
Daily reprinted the letter in a prominent position on

August 10.
  • The Chinese Government Trade Delegation, led by
Bai Xiangguo, left Beijing to visit Australia (July 21-
27) and New Zealand (July 27 to August 3). A Sino-
Australian trade agreement was signed on July 24.
  • China and the PRGRSVN signed an agreement on
China providing emergency supplementary free economic
aid to the PRGRSVN in 1973.

July 26 In the Security Council debate on the Mideast,
    Huang Hua stated that China had not participated in the
    voting on the draft resolution because it did not accord
    with China's view. China supported the Arab and Pal-
    estinian people in their struggle for national independ-
    ence against Israeli "aggression" and the superpower
    fight for spheres of influence in the Mideast, he said.

July 27 Major Marien N'Gouabi, president of the People's
    Republic of Congo, and his wife arrived in Beijing for
    a five-day visit. Premier Zhou Enlai held talks with
    them on July 28, 29, and 30. Chairman Mao Zedong
    met them on July 29. An agreement on a loan from
    China to Congo was signed on July 31.

July 28 The Chinese Government Trade Delegation, led by
    Zai Shufan, left Beijing for Moscow on a ten-day visit.
    The 1973 Sino-Soviet goods exchange and payment
    agreement was signed on August 1.

July 31 The Ministry of National Defense gave a grand re-
    ception at the Great Hall of the People in Beijing to
    celebrate the fortieth anniversary of the founding of
    the Chinese People's Liberation Army.

August 1 Jiangsu, Ningxia, and Sichuan held Women's Con-
    gresses between August 1-12.

August 2 Chairman Mao Zedong met Chinese-American doctor
    Chen Bianli and his wife Han Jindong at Zhongnanhai
    in Beijing.

August 3 Miao Yundai, former member of the Executive
    Yuan Council (Minister without Portofolio) of the Guo-
    mindang government, and his party arrived in Beijing
    for a forty-day visit. Premier Zhou Enlai met the party

on August 3. Zhu De met the party on August 6. The part left Guangzhou for the US on September 10.

• China and Sierra Leone signed the minutes of talks on the project to construct a national stadium with Chinese assistance in Freetown.

August 6 A ceremony was held at the Guangji Monastery in Beijing to give the first strike to the Bronze Bell presented by Kyoto Mayor Motoki Funahashi to the China-Japan Friendship Association.

August 7 Vice Premier Li Xiannian and Guo Moruo went to the Embassy of the German Democratic Republic in Beijing to express condolences on the death of Chairman Walter Ulbricht. The Standing Committee of the National People's Congress also sent a message of condolence to the Council of State of the German Democratic Republic on the death of Chairman Walter Ulbricht.

• The People's Daily carried an article entitled "Confucius--the Thinker Who Stubbornly Defends the System of Slavery," by Yang Rongguo, professor of philosophy. This article became the effective launching point of the campaign to criticize Lin Biao and Confucius.

August 10 The People's Daily carried a letter written by Zhang Tiesheng, together with an editorial note by the Liaoning Daily praising it. The People's Daily posed a question of whether book knowledge or the ability to learn should be the academic criterion for university entrance. The subject was also dealt with in an article in a September issue of the Red Flag, with all the comments implying that the reimposition of purely academic criteria for entrance had already gone too far and that the balance needed redressing toward practical experience and political commitment.

August 12 Hunan held the Seventh Trade Union Congress from August 12-16.

• Zhejiang held the Fifth Women's Congress from August 12-17.

August 14 The Chinese Government Delegation, led by Xi Yesheng, left Beijing for Tokyo to negotiate a Sino-Japanese trade accord. According to the New York Times, China rejected a full trade commerce and navigation treaty with Japan in negotiations held between August 17 and 30. China instead approved a three-year trade pact with Japan providing for mutual exchange of most-favored-nation treatment in tariff and custom clearance. The conference also approved establishment of a joint committee that would meet annually to discuss trade between the two countries. It was disclosed that Japan and China had agreed in May to construction of an $18.8 million underseas communication cable that would carry 480 circuits between Tokyo and Beijing by 1976.

August 15 Liaoning held the Second Women's Congress from August 15-19.
 • Yunnan held the Third Women's Congress from August 15-21.
 • Prince Norodom Sihanouk arrived in Tianjin for a rest after taking a trip to Pyongyang. He openly denounced Soviet interference in Cambodian internal affairs.
 • China voted in favor of the Security Council resolution which contained no condemnation of Israeli action against a civil aircraft in Lebanon.

August 16 The Chinese Government Economic Delegation, led by Han Zongzheng, left Beijing to visit Malta from August 18 to September 20.

August 18 The Parliamentary Delegation from the Netherlands, led by A. Vondeling, arrived in Beijing for a seven-day visit. Premier Zhou Enlai met the delegation on August 21.
 • The Journalists' Delegation from Nigeria, led by R.C. Nwokedi, arrived in Beijing for a twelve-day visit. Deng Xiaoping met the delegation on August 28.
 • Five pairs of flamingoes, a gift presented to the Chinese people by Tatsuo Miyazaki, mayor of Kobe city of Japan, were shipped to Beijing on August 13 and were put on display at the Beijing zoo on August 18.

August 20 Shaanxi held the Fourth Women's Congress from August 20-24.

August 21 An interesting and vividly detailed account of Lin Biao's plot, flight and death was contained in an article by Wilfred Burchett in the Far Eastern Economic Review.

• China signed an additional protocol to the Treaty for the Prohibition of Nuclear Weapons in Latin America at a ceremony in Mexico City.

August 24 The Tibet Autonomous Region held the Second Trade Union Congress from August 24-27.

• The Tenth National Congress of the CCP was held in Beijing from August 24-28. On August 24, Zhou Enlai delivered his report to the Congress giving the official version of the Lin Biao affairs. He also put the CCP's membership at 28 million. On the same day, Wang Hongwen gave a report on the revision of the party constitution. He stated that under the draft constitution, cultural revolutions would be a recurring phenomenon. The Congress adopted, on August 28, Zhou Enlai's and Wang Hongwen's reports, and a new CCP constitution, under which the CCP "takes Marxism-Leninism-Mao Zedong Thought as the theoretical basis guiding its thinking." The Congress elected a new Central Committee, consisting of 195 full and 124 alternate members.

August 25 The Asian-African-Latin American Table Tennis Friendship Invitational Tournament was held in Beijing from August 25 to September 6.

August 26 Xinjiang Uighur Autonomous Region held the Third Trade Union Congress and the Third Women's Congress from August 26 to September 5.

August 27 Jiangxi held the Fifth Women's Congress from August 27 to September 1.

• A Sino-Korean border railway transportation meeting was held in Jilin from August 27 to September 10.

August 28 Qinghai held the Fourth Women's Congress from August 28 to September 1.

August 30 The First Plenum of the Tenth CCP Central Committee elected Mao Zedong as chairman, and Zhou Enlai, Wang Hongwen, Kang Sheng, Ye Jianying and Li Desheng as deputy chairmen. It elected, in addition to these, the following to the politburo: Wei

Guoqing, Liu Bocheng, Jiang Qing, Zhu De, Xi Shiyou, Hua Guofeng, Ji Dengjui, Wu De, Chen Xilian, Li Xiannian, Zhang Chunqiao, Yao Wenyuan, and Dong Biwu. Of these, nine were elected to the Standing Committee: Mao, Wang, Ye, Zhu, Li Desheng, Zhang, Zhou, Kang, and Dong.
  • China captured both men's and women's team titles at the AAA Table Tennis Tournament.

August 31 Roy Harris Jenkins, a Labor party member of the British Parliament and former Minister, and his wife arrived in Beijing for a five-day visit. Deng Xiaoping met them on September 4.

September 1 Zhuang Zedong, China's former world men's single table tennis champion from 1961 to 1965, was awarded a replica of the St. Bride Vase at a ceremony held by the International Table Tennis Federation in Beijing.

September 3 Premier Zhou Enlai sent a message of congratulations to the Fourth Conference of the Heads of State and Government of Non-Aligned Countries.

September 5 Prince Gholam Reza Pahlavi of Iran, his wife, Princess Manijeh Pahlavi and their party arrived in Beijing for a ten-day visit. Premier Zhou Enlai met them on September 9.

September 6 According to the Kyodo report, the Japanese Foreign Ministry estimated China's total foreign trade for 1972 at $5,706 million (exports being $2,929 million and imports $2,777 million) which represented an increase of 24.7 percent over 1971. The estimate calculated that seventy-seven percent of China's foreign trade was with non-Communist countries; and that Japan with a total trade of $1,100.2 million was China's leading partner, followed by Hong Kong, Canada, West Germany, the Soviet Union, Britain, France, Singapore, and Italy.

September 8 The Chinese Government Delegation, led by Li Desheng, left Beijing for Pyongyang on a twelve-day visit to attend the celebration of the twenty-fifth anniversary of the founding of the DPRK.

September 11 The thirty-three member Chinese Economic
and Trade Friendship Delegation, led by Liu Xiwen,
arrived in Tokyo for a tour in Japan. Prime Minister
Kakuei Tanaka met the delegation on September 14.
After touring Osaka, Kansai, Okinawa, Nagoya, and
Hakkaido, the delegation left Tokyo for home on October 10.
• French President Georges Pompidou arrived in Beijing for a seven-day visit. This was the first visit to
China by a Western European head of the state since
1949. Premier Zhou Enlai gave a grand welcoming banquet in his honor on September 11. Chairman Mao met
him on September 12 for two hours. He left Beijing to
tour Dadong, Hangzhou, and Shanghai in the company
of Premier Zhou Enlai. At the press conference in Beijing (September 14), President Pompidou reaffirmed
France's determination to seek détente with the Soviet
Union in Europe and emphasized that his trip was
"against no one," including the Soviet Union. The
joint communiqué issued on September 17 said both
China and France were opposed to "all hegemony" but
made no reference to any specific party or to the
"superpowers." Both sides agreed to study possibilities
of developing their economic and technical exchanges
and to conclude a maritime accord and strengthen civil
aviation cooperation.

September 12 The Chinese Scientific and Technical Cooperation Delegation led by Yang Ligong, left Beijing for
Bulgaria on a ten-day visit to attend the Eleventh Session of the Sino-Bulgarian Commission for Scientific and
Technical Cooperation. A protocol of the meeting was
signed on September 22.
• The Philadelphia Orchestra of the United States,
with 130 people in the party, led by its conductor Eugene Ormandy, arrived in Beijing for a performance
tour in Beijing and Shanghai. The orchestra left
Shanghai for home on September 22.

September 14 Premier Zhou Enlai sent a telegram to Mrs.
Hortensia Bussi de Allende and other family members
of the late Chilean president, expressing profound sympathy with them on the death of Salvador Allende as a
martyr at his post.
• The Government Delegation of Chad, led by Addou-

laye Djonuma, arrived in Beijing for an eight-day visit.
Premier Zhou Enlai met the delegation on September 20.
The economic and technical cooperation and trade agreements between the two nations were signed on September
20.

• The Delegation of the Council of the Austrian-
China Research Institute, led by Hermann Whithalm,
former vice chancellor of Austria, arrived in Beijing for
an eight-day visit. Deng Xiaoping met the delegation
on September 19.

September 15 Beijing held the Sixth Women's Congress from
September 15-20.

• NCNA released a joint communiqué issued by China
and Upper Volta to establish diplomatic relations at the
ambassadorial level and to join in economic and technical cooperation. The Friendship Delegation from Upper
Volta, led by Foreign Minister Joseph Conombo, arrived
in Beijing on September 6 for a three-day visit at the
invitaiton of the Chinese government. Premier Zhou
Enlai met the delegation on September 7.

• The eleven-member delegation of the China Council
for the Promotion of International Trade, led by Wang
Yaoding, left Beijing to visit Britain (September 15-26),
France (September 26 to October 6), and Switzerland
(October 6-16).

September 16 Michael Kolokassidea, minister of Commerce
and Industry of Cyprus, his wife, and his assistant
arrived in Beijing for a five-day visit. Deng Xiaoping
met the delegation on September 20. A trade and payment agreement between the two nations was signed on
September 19.

September 17 Shanghai held the Sixth Women's Congress
from September 17-22.

• The large Chinese oil tanker "Renhu" loaded with
crude oil from Daqing arrived in Kashima, Ibaraki prefecture, on her first voyage to Japan.

September 18 Deng Xiaoping called at the residence of Arne
Bjorberg, Swedish ambassador to China, to express his
condolences on the death of King Gustav VI Adolf of
Sweden.

• The Executive Committee of the Asian Games Federation (AGF) voted for the admission of All-China Sports Federal of the People's Republic of China to the AGF and ousted the Taiwan sports organization.

• Nepalese Minister of Foreign Affairs and Finance Gyanendra Bahadur arrived in Beijing for a three-day visit. Premier Zhou Enlai met him on September 19.

September 19   China and Malta signed a protocol on the development projects and technical assistance to be provided by China to Malta in Valletta.

September 21   The Inner Mongolian Autonomous Region held the Fourth Women's Congress from September 21-26.

• Egyptian Vice President Hussein El Shafei and his party arrived in Beijing for a three-day visit on their way to Korea. Premier Zhou Enlai held talks with the delegation on September 21, 22, and 23. Chairman Mao met the delegation on September 23. In the welcoming banquet (September 21), Premier Zhou Enlai expressed China's support for "the Egyptian, Palestinian and other Arab peoples in their just struggles for the recovery of lost territories and Palestinian national rights."

September 23   Henan held the Seventh Trade Union Congress from September 23-25.

• Hunan held the Fourth Women's Congress from September 23-27.

September 25   The ten-member Chinese Librarians' Delegation, led by Liu Jiping, curator of the Beijing Library, left Beijing for a specialized study tour of the United States. Secretary of State Henry Kissinger met the delegation on September 29 in the White House.

September 27   China and Yugoslavia signed an agreement on technical cooperation of shipping registration.

• Lois Snow, widow of late Edgar Snow, and her daughter Sian Snow arrived in Beijing with a portion of Mr. Snow's ashes for interment in China, according to his will.

September 28   British Prime Minister Edward Heath presided over the opening ceremony of "the Unearthed Relics of the People's Republic of China" exhibition at the Royal Academy in London.

September 29   Premier Zhou Enlai and Prime Minister Tanaka
sent messages to each other on the anniversary of
normalization of relations between China and Japan.
Secretary of State Henry Kissinger met Huang Zhen,
chief of the Chinese liaison office in Washington.
   • The Tanzanian Health Delegation, led by A.H.
Mwinyi, arrived in Beijing for a twenty-three-day visit.
Deng Xiaoping met the delegation on October 4.
   • Representatives of one million worker militiamen in
Beijing held a grand meeting in commemoration of the
fifteenth anniversary of the issuing of Chairman Mao's
call to "Organize Contingents of the People's Militia
on a Big Scale." A joint editorial in the People's Daily
and the Liberation Army Daily called for the further
building up of militia forces.

September 30   Premier Zhou Enlai hailed the founding of the
Republic of Guinea-Bissau.
   • Foreign Minister Ji Pengfei informed the Republic
of Guinea-Bissau of China's decision to recognize it.
   • The Delegation of the Mexican Ministry of Public
Health, led by Gloria Ruiz de Bravo Ahaja, arrived in
Beijing for a fourteen-day visit. Deng Xiaoping met the
delegation on October 5.

October 1   China held the National Day celebrations, the
twenty-fourth anniversary of the founding of the People's Republic of China. The once-traditional parade
was replaced by an informal gathering in the city parks
which were attended by the senior leadership and foreign guests. The joint National Day editorial by the
People's Daily, the Red Flag, and the Liberation Army
Daily took the documents of the Tenth Party Congress
as its theme, coupled with the idea that there was a
basic continuity between the line adopted by the Tenth
Party Congress and that previously adopted by the
Ninth Party Congress four years ago. The Chinese
People's Association for Friendship with Foreign Countries gave a National Day reception in the Great Hall
of the People in Beijing for friends and well-known
personages from friendly organizations and cultural,
art, sports and trade circles of various countries.
   • According to the account of a press interview in
Algiers (in early September) published in the Far Eastern Economic Review, Prince Sihanouk made scathing

remarks about the extent to which he was continuing
to receive support from China. He said, "China remains faithful to us but China is playing a big-power
game with America now and so cannot help us as much
as it would like."

October 2   Qiao Guanhua spoke at the plenary session of the
UN General Assembly to give China's view of the world
situation and to outline China's policy on issues such
as disarmament in Cambodia, Korea, and Palestine.

October 4   The New Zealand Trade Mission, led by J.A.
Ealding, arrived in Beijing for a ten-day visit.   Vice
Premier Li Xiannian met the delegation on October 10.
A trade agreement between the two nations was signed
on October 9.
    • The Nippon Steel Corporation and the Kawasaki
Steel Corporation announced, in Tokyo, an urgent plan
to build and deliver a $380 million steel plant to China
by 1975.   China would finance the project with loans
from Japan's Export-Import Bank.

October 5   Canada announced that China had agreed to a
three-year purchase of 179-224 million bushels of wheat,
at a potential price of over $1 billion.
    • A protocol on China's gratuitous supply of military
equipment and materials to Vietnam in 1974 was signed
in Beijing.

October 6   Premier Zhou Enlai met Xu Yiqiao, former adviser
to the Nationalist Government Mission in Japan, and his
wife Su Kuizhen in Beijing.
    • The Chinese Ocean Shipping Delegation, led by
Zhou Qiuyan, left Beijing for Colombo to attend the
First Session of the Sino-Sri Lanka Joint Shipping Service Commission.   The delegation left Colombo on October 16.

October 7   The Korean Railway Delegation, led by Kang
Bong Kun, arrived in Beijing for a visit.   A Sino-
Korean transport agreement was signed on October 9.

October 8   In the Security Council debate on the situation
in the Mideast, Huang Hua condemned Israel for launching the military attacks on October 6 and supported the

Egyptians, Syrians, and Palestinians. The Arab people were right "to raise in resistance" against Israel.

- In Cairo, President Anwar Sadat received Zhai Zemin, Chinese ambassador to Egypt.
- In Beijing, the People's Daily editorial supported Egypt and Syria in their resistance to the Israeli military "aggression." Foreign Minister Ji Pengfei strongly condemned Israeli "aggression" and voiced firm support for the Arab and Palestinian people.

October 9 An eight-member Japanese Dietmen group, led by Katsushi Fujii, arrived in Beijing for a five-day visit. Deng Xiaoping met the group on October 13.

October 10 Canadian Prime Minister Pierre Elliott Trudeau and Mrs. Trudeau arrived in Beijing for a seven-day visit. Premier Zhou Enlai gave a grand welcoming banquet on October 11 and held talks with him on October 11, 12 and 13. Chairman Mao Zedong met him on October 13. Prime Minister Trudeau held his press conference in Beijing on the same day. A Sino-Canadian trade agreement was signed on October 13. Further arrangements were made for an exchange of medical and educational personnel and for the exhibition of Chinese archaeology in Europe to visit Canada. Arrangements were also made for the two sides to set up consulate generals in each other's country.

October 11 Premier Zhou Enlai met Egyptian Ambassador to China Salah El-Abd and Syrian Ambassador Jabr Al Ttrache on separate occasions in Beijing.

October 12 An anti-Confucius campaign article in the People's Daily on August 7 by Yang Rongguo was translated in the Beijing Review.

October 16 A long article published in the Pravda argued that the Chinese Tenth Party Congress had failed to produce any new policies, while the secrecy with which it had been held "pointed to the widening gap between the present-day Beijing leadership and the masses of the people and the distrust felt by the latter."

October 18 The Chinese Scientific and Technical Cooperation Delegation left Beijing for Pyongyang on a nineteen-day visit, and attended the Fourteenth Session of the Sino-Korean Committee for Scientific and Technical Cooperation. A protocol of the session was signed on November 6.

• President Anwar E. Sadat of Egypt sent a message to Premier Zhou Enlai, expressing heartfelt thanks for the stand taken by the Chinese government and the Chinese people in support of the Arab people in their battle against aggression.

October 19 A ceremony of the interment of the ashes of Edgar Snow was held at Beijing University. (He died on February 15, 1972 in Switzerland.)

• In Beijing, China and Vietnam signed the 1974 mutual supply of goods and payment agreement, a protocol on China supplying Vietnam with general goods in 1974, and a protocol on China providing Vietnam with aid in the form of complete projects.

October 21 The Government Trade Delegation from Guyana, led by George King, arrived in Beijing for a five-day visit. Deng Xiaoping met the delegation on October 24. In the United Nations, China supported the unsuccessful attempt to have Prince Sihanouk's government replaced that was led by Lon Nol.

• The Red Flag carried an article praising the actions of the first emperor of Qin (Qin Shihuang). The article maintained that Qin Shihuang had carried through a large number of progressive measures including the "centralization of authority" by a "system of prefectives and counties" in place of the "system of conferment of titles."

October 22 Minister of Education Klaus Von Dohmany of the Federal Republic of Germany, his wife, and accompanying experts arrived in Beijing for a twelve-day visit. Deng Xiaoping met the delegation on October 25.

• The fifth anniversary of the publication in the People's Daily of Chairman Mao's Xia-Xiang directive for the educated youth to go to the countryside was marked by a number of articles in the national and provincial press to describe the success of the subsequent campaign. NCNA claimed that during the previous five years, as many as eight million educated youth had gone to the countryside "to fight for building a new socialist countryside."

October 24 NCNA announced the postponement of Henry
    Kissinger's visit to Beijing.

October 25 In the UN Security Council, Huang Hua ex-
    plained his vote on the resolution put forward by non-
    aligned countries of the Mideast. He said: "China has
    always been opposed to the dispatch of the so-called
    peacekeeping forces, but, because of the appeals re-
    ceived from the Arabs, China would not veto but would
    again not participate in the vote."
        • The Chinese Government Delegation, led by Sha
    Feng, left Beijing for Ankara, Turkey on a seven-day
    visit and attended the celebration of the fiftieth anni-
    versary of the founding of the Republic of Turkey.

October 26 Premier Zhou Enlai met American columnist Cyrus
    Leo Sulzberger of the New York Times, and his wife in
    Beijing.
        • A regular meeting of the Sino-Mongolian boundary
    through railway traffic was held in Huhehot, Inner
    Mongolia.
        • The Sudanese Friendship Delegation, led by For-
    eign Minister Mansour Khalid, arrived in Beijing for a
    five-day visit. Premier Zhou Enlai met the delegation
    on October 28.

October 28 The Chinese Government Civil Aviation Delega-
    tion, led by Chen Zhifang, left Beijing for Switzerland
    on a fifteen-day visit. A Sino-Swiss civil air transport
    agreement was signed on November 12.

October 29 The Fifth Committee of the UN General Assembly
    unanimously favored inclusion of Chinese among UN
    working languages.

October 30 According to the International Herald Tribune,
    Premier Zhou Enlai said to the New York Times column-
    ist C.L. Sulzberger, that Watergate had no adverse ef-
    fect on relations between China and the US.

October 31 Australian Prime Minister Edward G. Whitlam
    and his wife arrived in Beijing for a five-day visit after
    an official visit to Japan. Premier Zhou Enlai held talks
    with him on October 31, November 1, and November 3.
    Chairman Mao met him on November 2. Prime Minister

Whitlam held a press conference in Beijing on November
4. A joint communiqué was issued on November 4, emphasizing the development of economic and cultural ties
but also expressing joint opposition to any "seeking of
hegemony" in the Asian-Pacific region by "an country
or group of countries." It also included an interesting
reference to "An understanding in principle between the
two sides on travel from China to Australia by relatives
of Australian citizens of Chinese descent and Chinese
citizens residing in Australia." Furthermore, an agreement had been reached on a long-term contract for the
sale to China of three million tons of Australian sugar
annually worth $50 million. It was announced on No-
vember 6 that the contract would last three to five
years, beginning in 1975.

November 1 The Delegation of the Albanian Academy of Science, led by Aleks Taqi Buda, arrived in Beijing for a
two-day visit. A Sino-Albanian scientific and technical
cooperation agreement was signed on November 21.

November 6 President Siaka Stevens of Sierra Leone and his
party arrived in Beijing for a nine-day visit. Chairman
Mao met the delegation on November 7. Premier Zhou
Enlai held talks with the delegation on November 7, 8,
and 9. President Stevens gave a press conference in
Beijing on November 10. A protocol and summary of
talks were signed on November 10. A supplementary
protocol to the agreement on economic and technical cooperation was also signed on November 10.

November 7 Soviet Ambassador to China V.S. Tolstikov and
his wife gave a reception in the Embassy in Beijing to
celebrate the fifty-sixth anniversary of the October
Socialist Revolution.

November 10 The Chinese Delegation of the Academy of Science, led by Yue Zhijian, left Beijing for Hanoi on a
twenty-two-day visit. The 1973-74 executive plan for
cooperation in science between the two nations was
signed on November 30.
    • Henry Kissinger, secretary of state and assistant
to the president for national security affairs, arrived
in Beijing from the Mideast for a five-day visit. Premier Zhou Enlai held talks with him on November 12,

13, and 14. Chairman Mao Zedong met him for nearly
three hours on November 12. A joint communiqué was
issued before his departure to Tokyo. The communiqué
said that "both sides agreed that the scope of the functions of the liaison office should continue to expand."

November 12 The seven-member Chinese Medical Delegation,
led by Guo Guanghua, left Beijing for Burma for a
twenty-day visit.

November 14 Henry Kissinger said pointedly in a farewell
banquet speech in Beijing: "No matter what happens
in the United States in the future, friendship with
China is one constant factor of American foreign policy."
  • The Rumanian Government Delegation, led by Ion
Patan, arrived in Beijing for a ten-day visit. Sino-
Rumanian goods exchange and payment protocol were
signed on November 23.

November 16 The Council of the Asian Games Federation admitted China's membership and ousted Taiwan.
  • The Senegal Government Delegation, led by Ous-
mane Seck, arrived in Beijing for a six-day visit. Premier Zhou Enlai met the delegation on November 23. A
Sino-Senegalese agreement on economic and technical cooperation, and a trade agreement between the two nations were signed on November 23.

November 18 The PRGRSVN Delegation, led by President
Nguyen Huu Tho, arrived in Beijing for a five-day
visit. Chairman Mao met the delegation on November
19. Premier Zhou Enlai held talks with the delegation
on November 18, 19 and 20. An agreement on China's
gratuitous economic assistance was signed on November
23. The joint communiqué condemned "the acts in con-
travention and violation of the Paris agreement committed by the Saigon administration with the support
and connivance of the United States."
  • France sold thirty Super-Frelon helicopters to Beijing. According to the Paris report, the contract was
delayed because some parts of the Super-Frelon were
made in the United States and came under the US embargo on exports of strategic material to Beijing.

November 19 A pamphlet outlining Beijing's nuclear weapons

capacity in mid-1973 was published by the International
Institute for Strategic Studies. It suggested that Beijing probably possessed several hundred nuclear devices
and adequate nuclear material for the present weapons
program. As for the delivery systems, Beijing had
some 200 I128 old strike aircraft which might still be
useful for short-range operations, 300 tactical nuclear
strike aircraft, and 100 to 140 TU 16 medium bombers
with a range of approximately 1,650 miles.

November 20   The Chinese Government Maritime Shipping
Delegation, led by Yu Mei, left Beijing for France on a
twelve-day visit to discuss a maritime shipping agreement with France.
   • The Government Delegation from Zaire led by Foreign Minister Nguza Karl I'Bond, arrived in Beijing for
a five-day visit. Premier Zhou Enlai met the delegation
on November 22.

November 21   A ceremony was held in Kabul to mark the
signing of notes of the talks on China's gratuitous construction of a 250-bed hospital for Afghanistan.

November 23   The Chinese Delegation, led by Chen Gang,
left Beijing for an eighteen-day tour to the liberated
areas of Laos.
   • The Chinese Trade Delegation, led by Wang Yaoding, arrived in Manila for a ten-day visit.

November 24   The People's Daily, in an editorial, welcomed
the behind-the-scenes agreement in the United Nations
to disband the UN Commission for the Unification and
Rehabilitation of Korea. According to reports emanating
from Seoul, the UN compromise declaration, which was
not put to a vote, was a result of an agreement between
Kissinger and Zhou Enlai during the former's visit to
Beijing.
   • The Chinese Delegation of Scientific and Technical
Cooperation, led by Chen Weiqi, left Beijing for Albania
on a twenty-day visit and attended the fifteenth ses-
sion of the Joint Committee for Scientific and Technical
Cooperation. A protocol of the session was signed on
December 7.

November 25   Iraq and China signed minutes of the talks on
building the Mosul Bridge in Baghdad.

November 30   Guizhou held the Third Women's Congress
from November 30 to December 4.

December 1   The Canadian Trade Delegation, led by R.E.
Latimer, arrived in Beijing for a seven-day visit.   Li
Jiang met the delegation on December 7.
   • The seventeen-member trade group of the Chinese
Ministry of Foreign Trade, led by Wang Mingzhun, left
Beijing for Canada.

December 2   Beijing attacked the newly signed Soviet-India
agreement by quoting Indian newspaper articles as
charging that Soviet aid projects so far had worked to
India's disadvantage, turning it into a Russian append-
age.

December 3   China and Upper Volta signed an agreement on
economic and technical cooperation in Ouagadougou.
   • The tenth plenary session of the Asian Broadcast-
ing Union in Djakarta announced its decision to admit
China as a full member.
   • The Delegation of the Angolan National Liberation
Front led by President Holden Roberto of the Front,
arrived in Beijing for a fifteen-day visit.   Vice Premier
Li Xiannian met the delegation on December 18.

December 4   The Soviet Union made a call for concrete deeds
for normalizing relations with China in the reply to
China's message of greeting on the Soviet Union's National Day.
   • The People's Daily defended Beijing's economic
policy, attributing shortages of goods to planning requirements and rising expectation.

December 5   Overseas Trade Minister of Australia James
Cairns announced the sale of three million tons of Australian iron ore to China over a three-year period for
about $20 million.

December 6   The 113-member French Delegation, led by Mrs.
Pierre Messmer, wife of the French Prime Minister, left
Paris for Beijing to mark the establishment of Air
France's service between Paris and Beijing.   Deng
Xiaoping met the delegation on December 8.   The dele-
gation left Shanghai for home on December 11.

December 7   Their Majesties King Birendra Bir Birkram Shah
Dev and Queen Aishwarya Rajya Laxmi Devi Shah of
Nepal and their entourage arrived in Beijing for a
seven-day visit. Premier Zhou Enlai gave a grand banquet on December 8. Chairman Mao met the King and
the Queen on December 9. A joint communiqué was issued on December 14.

December 8   A pair of pandas of the giant variety, a gift of
the Chinese government to President Georges Pompidou
of France and the French people, were flown to Paris.

December 11   China began weekly flights from Beijing to
Moscow.

December 12   A Sino-Japanese trade agreement was initialed
in Beijing, the first such agreement since the establishment of diplomatic relations in 1972. It included arrangements for most-favored nation treatment and for a
joint trade committee of officials from both governments.

December 15   The Czechoslovak Government Trade Delegation, led by M. Bursa, arrived in Beijing for a seven-
day visit. The 1974 Sino-Czechoslovak goods exchange,
payment agreements were signed on December 17.
    • The Sri Lanka Government Trade Delegation, led
by Tikiri Illanagarathe, arrived in Beijing for a seven-
day visit. The 1974 Sino-Sri Lanka commodity exchange
protocol was signed on December 22.

December 16   The five-member Korean Delegation, led by
Choe Chong Pil, arrived in Beijing to attend the thirteenth meeting of Sino-Korean Committee for Cooperation
in Border Transport. A protocol of the meeting was
signed on December 31.

December 18   China agreed to buy three million tons of wheat
and maize from Argentina over the next three years.
The agreement was initialed in Beijing.

December 19   Guizhou held the Fifth Trade Union Congress
from December 19-28.

December 21   The Thai Trade Delegation, led by Chatichai
Choonhavan, arrived in Beijing for a six-day visit.

Premier Zhou Enlai met the delegation on December 26.
  • An agreement for Thailand to purchase more than
50,000 tons of diesel oil from China was signed on December 26.

December 26 The first 50,000-kw low-water-head turbo-
generating set, designed and built in China went into
regular operation at the Sanmen Gorge power station.

December 28 An agreement on mutual exemption of visa was
reached between China and the PRGRSVN.

December 31 NCNA reported that during 1973, the first
calendar year since the establishment of diplomatic relations, more than 10,000 Japanese had visited China in
some 200 groups; 5,000 Japanese had visited the Guangzhou Trade Fair.

Chapter V

1974

THE CAMPAIGN TO CRITICIZE LIN BIAO AND CONFUCIUS

The ideological debate intensified and escalated in a way almost resembling the early stages which had led up to the Cultural Revolution in 1965. Most aspects of the domestic scene were focused on the campaign to criticize Lin Biao and Confucius. For instance, it came as no surprise that the rallies to celebrate International Women's Day on March 8 should seek to link the struggle for the emancipation of women with struggle against Confucianism and against Lin Biao's espousal of Confucian tenets.

Outside China, speculation focused on the position of Premier Zhou Enlai, whose absence at functions attended by President Senghor of Senegal on May 9 and Premier Bhutto of Pakistan on May 12 gave rise to further speculations as to his health and political position. The fact that Zhou Enlai had been ill and was still receiving treatment was confirmed when he received US Senator and Mrs. Henry Jackson in the hospital in Beijing on July 5, and it was later reported unofficially that he had a heart condition. Zhou Enlai's partial withdrawal from the political scene brought Deng Xiaoping once more to the forefront of political affairs, notably in the role of chairman of the Chinese Delegation to the Sixth Special Session of the United Nations General Assembly in April and as host to foreign visitors during Premier Zhou's indisposition.

The active force behind the campaign to discredit Confucius and Lin Biao was the radical faction of the party, which had played a dominant role in the Cultural Revolution of 1966–69. In 1974, its leader, Jiang Qing, the wife of Chairman Mao, was given increasing publicity as a national

figure. In July, the <u>People's Daily</u> published two articles to
commemorate the tenth anniversary of her 1964 speech on
the reformation of the Beijing Opera.

Although campaign polemics appeared in the Chinese
press throughout the year, there were two periods of a
fairly clear-cut upsurge in the pace of the campaign. The
first of these began with the publication in the <u>Red Flag</u>
on February 1 of an editorial calling for a more active and
militant campaign. However, a <u>People's Daily</u>'s editorial on
February 20 took what appeared to be a much more moderate
tone. Here the earlier emphasis on class struggle and "going against the tide" was replaced by an emphasis on study
of "combining theory with practice." Much of the anti-Zhou
material had been removed from the newsstands, and were
not to reappear.

Two months later, however, a second upsurge in the
campaign began, this one heralded not by editorials and articles, but by the appearance of wall posters in Beijing criticizing not only the errors of local industrial managers and
political leaders, but also those of offenders in the provinces.
Although the Central Committee was reported to have approved on June 13 the use of wall posters to criticize local
offenders, the posting of criticism of provincial and local
cadres in Beijing was regarded as illegitimate, and posters
containing such criticism were regularly moved, only to be
replaced the following day. Although the discussion of Confucius and Lin Biao continued to dominate the press in the
latter half of the year, the tone of the campaign was characterized by the enjoinder in the National Day editorial to
direct attention to study and criticism within individual organizations.

The assault on Confucian values was accompanied by
a denunciation of foreign influences. Western music was assailed in the Chinese press, which scorned Beethoven as a
capitalist composer and Schubert as a <u>petit bourgeois</u>. The
attack was the most significant since it came only a few
months after the visit of three Western orchestras which had
been given glowing reviews at the time of their performances. Similarly, Michelangelo Antonioni, the Italian film
director who had been welcomed to China to make a documentary in 1971, was now accused by the government of "de-
ception and forgery" with intent to "smear" the Chinese
Revolution.

The beginning of 1974 saw a sweeping reshuffling of military posts in the various strategic regions. Of the ten military regions in China, only the commands of the Chengdu, Kunming, and Xinjiang regions remained definitely unchanged. The situation in Tibet was unclear. Of greatest significance were the transfer of Chen Xilian, commander of the Shenyang military region in Manchuria, to the command of the Beijing region; of Xu Shiyou, commander of the Nanjing region, to the command of the Guangdong region; and of Li Desheng, director of the political department of the armed forces, to the command of the Shenyang region. The shifts were attributed to the desire of the party to exert its authority over military leaders who had been too-long entrenched in certain areas.

Economic growth appeared to slow down in the first half of the year. The growth rate in Shanghai during this period was reported to be six percent, compared with nine percent for the corresponding months of the previous year. In Shanxi province, the growth rate was five percent, compared with twelve percent a year earlier. Some observers attributed the slowing down to the ideological drive, which had brought about disruptions in industrial centers. The need for labor discipline was said to be the reason why the ideological campaign tapered off in the summer.

Despite famine reported in some northern provinces, Beijing announced a good summer harvest. Nevertheless China imported seven million tons of wheat in 1974, including three million tons from Canada, 1.1 million tons from Australia, and one million tons from Argentina. The United States had contracted to deliver 1.5 million tons, but China rejected three American shipments because the wheat contained fungus.

The surge in Chinese-American trade placed the United States as China's third-largest trading partner, after Japan and Hong Kong. This trade was expected to reach $1.25 billion in 1974, an increase of $500 million over the year before. The United States enjoyed an advantage of ten to one in the balance of trade because of China's large importation of American agricultural goods, such as wheat, cotton, corn, and soybeans.

The worldwide energy crisis stimulated China's oil trade

in the Far East. Beijing was prepared to triple its crude oil exports to Japan in 1974. It also promised diesel oil to Thailand, with which it had no diplomatic relations. China's oil production was moderate--fifty million tons in 1973, according to a statement by Premier Zhou Enlai. But reserves were said to be vast--20 billion barrels onshore and more than that offshore, according to one "conservative" estimate. To develop its resources, Beijing purchased exploitation equipment from Denmark, Rumania, and Japan. American companies were taking steps to tap the growing Chinese market for these goods.

Regarding foreign relations, Sino-American relations, which had greatly improved since President Nixon's visit to Beijing in 1972, cooled off in 1974. David K.E. Bruce, head of the US liaison office in Beijing, flew home in January and did not return to China until March. His Chinese counterpart, Huang Zhen, stayed away from Washington for an even longer time. Beijing was dissatisfied with the continued US support for Taiwan and was particularly unhappy about the appointment of Leonard Unger, a well-known career diplomat, as American ambassador to Nationalist China.

If there was no progress in Sino-American relations, there were no signs of deterioration either. Contacts between the two countries continued. In May, a group of American state governors was cordially welcomed by the Chinese Ministry of Foreign Affairs. When Senator Henry M. Jackson visited Beijing, he was received by Zhou Enlai in the hospital where the premier was recuperating. As a showing of good will, the Chinese government promptly released Gerald E. Kosh, a US defense department employee who was captured by Chinese forces in fighting with South Vietnamese troops on the Paracel Islands in the South China Sea.

A congressional delegation, led by Senator J. William Fulbright, visited China in September. The Chinese took the occasion to reiterate the full normalization of relations between the two countries depended on the United States severing relations with Nationalist China. On September 4, George Bush, national chairman of the Republican party, was appointed head of the US liaison office in Beijing to succeed David Bruce. The move was seen as an effort by President Ford to promote friendly relations with China.

No substantial progress toward the normalization of Sino-American relations was achieved during Kissinger's visit to Beijing in late November. There was no progress on the settlement of outstanding American claims against China or on China's frozen assets in the US (the former amounting to some $200 million, the latter to some $75 million). The only positive accomplishment seemed to have been the invitation to President Ford to visit China in the later half of the following year, an invitation which was quickly accepted.

The long-awaited civil aviation agreement between China and Japan was eventually signed on April 20. The negotiations had been long and tough, but the eventual agreement facilitated negotiations on other bilateral matters including fishery, shipping, and a treaty of peace and friendship. The aviation agreement was specifically linked with the joint recognition statement of September 29, 1972. For China, it opened up the prospect of regular air services to the North American continent. The inaugural flight of the civil aviation route between Tokyo and Beijing duly took place on September 29, the second anniversary of the establishment of diplomatic relations between the two countries. After strenuous negotiations, the shipping agreement was initialled on November 2 in Beijing, and on November 13, it was formally signed in Tokyo. The main significance of these agreements was political. It represented a setback to Japanese Conservatives and provided further momentum to the development of Sino-Japanese relations.

Antagonism between China and the Soviet Union continued, but no border clashes occurred. In a speech before the UN General Assembly on April 1, Vice Premier Deng Xiaoping, head of the Chinese delegation, denounced the Soviets as the worst kind of imperialists, "vicious and unscrupulous" in subverting other countries. Two incidents in 1974 added to the tension in relations between the two countries. On January 19, Beijing expelled five members of the Soviet Embassy on charges of spying. In reprisal, the Soviet Union ordered the expulsion of a Chinese diplomat on similar charges. Then, on March 14, a Soviet army helicopter, which had crossed the Chinese border and landed in Xinjiang, was captured by Chinese forces. The Chinese charged that the crew of the reconnaissance plane had been on a spying mission. They dismissed as "lies" the Soviet protest that the plane, assigned to evacuate a sick soldier, had been blown off course in a storm and had made a forced landing.

Sino-Soviet border talks in Beijing showed no progress, although the Soviet representative returned to the negotiation table from time to time. On May 23, the Soviet Union announced that unless China recognized Soviet sovereignty over a disputed island at the confluence of the two border rivers, the Amur and the Ussuri, Chinese ships would be excluded from using "Soviet island waterways." In November, the Soviet government took a moderate stand toward China, when it stressed "peace and friendship" along the Soviet-Chinese border. But when China expressed interest in a nonaggression pact with a withdrawal of forces along the border, the Soviet Union rejected the Chinese proposal.

After two days of fighting between Chinese and South Vietnamese armed forces, China took possession of the disputed Paracel Islands on January 20. These islands, situated in the South China Sea, had attracted the attention of Beijing and Saigon because of possible offshore oil deposits.

Malaysia established diplomatic relations with China on May 31. In a joint communiqué issued in Beijing, China declared that it considered all Malaysian citizens of Chinese origin to have renounced their Chinese nationality and expected them to abide by Malaysian laws and regulations. The Malaysian move was expected to pave the way for the other Southeast Asian nations to recognize Beijing. An informal trade agreement was concluded between China and the Philippines in September when Imelda Marcos, wife of the Philippine president, visited Beijing.

China made vigorous efforts in 1974 to win over the Third World--essentially the developing countries of Asia, Africa, and Latin America. Beijing called for the unity of the Third World against Soviet and US "imperialism." On July 2, at the UN Conference on the Law of the Sea held in Caracas, Venezuela, China supported the position for 200-nautical mile maritime rights advanced by the Third World countries. During the year China also upheld the Arab nations' use of oil as a political weapon against "imperialist exploitation."

January 1 The joint <u>People's Daily</u>, <u>Red Flag</u>, and <u>Liberation Army Daily</u> New Year's editorial stated that "criticizing Confucius is a component part of the Criticism of Lin Biao." The point was well taken and greatly expanded over the following months as the Campaign to Criticize Lin Biao and Confucius became a mass movement. The editorial said that all should continue to "firmly grasp education in the ideological and political line, and adhere to the three principles: Practice Marxism, and not revisionism; unite, and don't split; be open and aboveboard, and don't intrigue and conspire."

• The Chinese Medical Association Replantation Delegation, led by Chen Zhungwei, left Beijing to visit Canada (January 1-12), and the United States (January 12-27).

• NCNA identified important changes in the commanders of China's military regions. In the Guangzhou military region, Xu Shiyou replaced Ding Sheng; in the Fuzhou, Pi Dingjun replaced Han Xianchu; in the Lanzhou, Han Xianchu replaced Pi Dingjun; in the Nanjing, Ding Sheng replaced Xu Shiyou; in the Shenyang, Li Desheng replaced Chen Xilian; in the Jinan, Zeng Siyu replaced Yang Dezhi; and in the Wuhan, Yang Dezhi replaced Zeng Siyu; Chen Xilian was moved to the Beijing military region. Jin Zhiwei was moved to the Zhengdu military region. Yang Yong was newly appointed as the new commander in the Xinjiang military region.

January 3 Japanese Foreign Minister Ohira Masayoshi and his party arrived in Beijing for a three-day visit at the invitation of the Chinese government. Premier Zhou Enlai met Mr. Ohira on January 4 and 5; Chairman Mao Zedong met him on January 5.

• A Sino-Japanese trade agreement was signed on January 5 for a three-year period, including the most-favored-nation clause.

• The Chinese Government Trade Delegation, led by Yao Yilin, left Beijing for a six-day visit to Pyongyang. The 1974 protocol on goods exchange between the two nations was signed on January 5.

January 8 The Chinese Delegation, led by Li Suwen, left Beijing for New York to attend the Twenty-fifth Session

of the US Commission on the Status of Women. The
session was held from January 12 to February 1. The
delegation returned to Beijing on February 8. At the
session on January 14, Li Suwen said that in China,
the government had given women "special labor protection" and equal pay, provided canteens, nurseries and
health centers, promoted planned parenthood and encouraged men to share domestic chores.

January 11   The Chinese Ministry of Foreign Affairs issued
a statement criticizing the Saigon administration for a
recent "brazen announcement" which sought to incor-
porate more than ten of the Nansha Islands under the
administration of Phuoc Tinh province. This was described as "a wanton infringement on China's territorial
integrity."
   • Progress was reported in the negotiations for the
conclusion of the Sino-Japanese civil aviation agreement.
China accepted the Japanese position that their government had neither the jurisdiction nor the diplomatic relations to persuade the Taiwan authorities to remove
their flag from the tail of their aircraft.
   • The Red Flag published an article entitled "Communists Must Strengthen Their Sense of Discipline,"
strongly warning some members against the dangers of
"sectarianism" and "secessionism."

January 12   The Chinese Government Trade Delegation, led
by Li Qiang, left Beijing for Albania on an eight-day
visit. The 1974 protocol on goods exchange and payments between the two nations were signed on January
16.

January 13   China and Thailand signed a trade agreement in
Hong Kong in which 50,000 tons of diesel oil were sold
at a very reasonable price.

January 14   The Malagasy Government Delegation, led by
Didier Ratsiraka, arrived in Beijing for a six-day visit.
Premier Zhou Enlai met the delegation on January 18.
Economic and technical cooperation and trade agreements
between the two nations were signed on January 18.
   • Citing examples from the works of Beethoven and
Schubert, a People's Daily article claimed that European
"absolute" music of the eighteenth and nineteenth cen-

turies was the product of the European capitalist society in the service of the capitalist system and therefore incompatible with the socialist system. The article
praised modern Chinese compositions such as The Sun
Rises.

January 15   The Chinese authorities claimed to have captured,
red-handed, five personnel from the Soviet Union Embassy engaged in exchanging espionage material with one
of their agents (Li Hongshu) under a bridge in the
outskirts of Beijing. The Soviet Union denied the espionage charges and on January 19, arrested and expelled a Chinese diplomat because of alleged espionage
which the Chinese indignantly denied.
    • Deng Xiaoping's position in the leadership gave
rise to comment when his name appeared in a list of
those attending ceremonies among members of the Political Bureau. A Tanyug report, quoting official Chinese sources, claimed he had been promoted to the
politburo.

January 17   Chinese was accepted as a working language of
the UN Security Council.

January 18   The People's Daily reported a fully documented
example of a student (Zhong Zhiming) who had gained
"back-door" entry to a university.

January 19   The Chinese Ministry of Foreign Affairs handed
a note to the Soviet Embassy, expelling five of its members from China for espionage.
    • NCNA reported that a series of clashes took place
between Chinese and South Vietnamese forces in the
Xisha Islands, ending in Chinese victory.

January 22   The six-member Chinese Medical Delegation, led
by Jian Xinzhong, left Beijing for Rumania on a twenty-
day visit. A Sino-Rumanian health cooperation agreement was signed on February 9.

January 25   The Japan-China Memorandum Trade office in
Tokyo was officially closed.

January 29   NCNA announced Chinese government's decision
to repatriate captured personnel of Saigon troops in
batches.

January 30   China inaugurated direct Beijing-Moscow flights
under the terms of the July 1973 aviation agreement.
  • The People's Daily carried an article entitled "A
Vicious Motive, Despicable Tricks," condemning the
anti-China film China by the Italian director M. Antonioni. The article accused him of failing to reflect the
new things, new spirit and new appearance of China,
and instead, using the camera to slander the Cultural
Revolution, insult people, and attack the leadership.

February 1   The Finnish Government Trade Delegation, led
by Jon Groop, arrived in Beijing for a twelve-day visit.
The 1974 Sino-Finnish trade agreement was signed on
February 12.

February 2   In a People's Daily article entitled "Carry the
Struggle to Criticize Lin Biao and Confucius Through
to the End," Lin Biao was referred to as a bourgeois
careerist, conspirator, double-dealer, renegade and
traitor, an out-and-out disciple of Confucius.

February 4   The Chinese Foreign Ministry issued a statement
saying that China could not accept the January 30
Seoul-Tokyo agreement on the exploration and exploitation of the continental shelf because it infringed on
Chinese sovereignty.
  • The Chinese Foreign Ministry issued a statement
saying that China would "definitely not tolerate infringement" on China's territorial integrity in Nansha
Island by the Saigon authorities.

February 5   The nineteenth regular meeting of the Sino-
Soviet Joint Commission for Navigation on Boundary
Rivers was held in Blagoveshchensk (Hailanbao) from
February 5 to March 21. A summary of the meeting
was signed at the end of the meeting.

February 7   The Guinean Government Trade Delegation, led
by Camara Moussa Sanguiana, arrived in Beijing for a
ten-day visit. Premier Zhou Enlai met the delegation
on February 15. The 1974 Sino-Guinean trade protocol
and commodity loans agreements were signed on February
15.
  • The fourteen-member delegation of the Olympic
Committee of Thailand, led by Dawee Chullasapya, ar-

rived in Beijing for a seven-day visit. Premier Zhou
Enlai and Vice Premier Deng Xiaoping met the delegation
on February 12. On his return, Dawee Chullasapya
said that he was assured by Premier Zhou that China's
support for the Thai rebels "was a thing of the past,"
and that China had "stopped giving arms to Communist
countries in this region."

February 8 Premier Zhou Enlai hailed Grenada's independence, and stated that the Chinese government had decided to recognize Grenada.

February 11 The Iraqi Economic Delegation, led by Abdul
Fatah Al-Yaseen, arrived in Beijing for a ten-day visit.
Vice Premier Li Xiannian met the delegation on February
16.
    • China and Jamaica signed an agreement on eco-
nomic and technical cooperation in Kingston.

February 13 The Chinese Government Trade Delegation, led
by Chen Jie, left Beijing to visit Bulgaria (February
13-16) and the German Democratic Republic (February
16-22). The 1974 Sino-Bulgarian goods exchange and
payment agreement was signed on February 15. The
1974 Sino-German goods exchange and payment agreement was signed on February 21.

February 15 The Wuhan Acrobatic Troupe of China, led by
Shen Jian, left Beijing for a performance tour of Latin
American countries including Guyana (February 16-27),
Jamaica (February 28 to March 12), and Argentina
(March 13 to April 1). The troupe returned to Beijing
on April 5.

February 21 Zambian President and Mrs. Kenneth D.
Kaunda, and their party arrived in Beijing for a nine-
day visit. Premier Zhou Enlai gave a grand banquet
on February 21, and held talks with them on February
21, 22, 23, and 24. Chairman Mao Zedong met them on
February 22. An agreement on economic and technical
cooperation between the two nations was signed on February 24.

February 25 President Boumedienne of Algeria left Lahore,
Pakistan for Beijing on a five-day visit to China.

Chairman Mao Zedong met him on February 25, and
Premier Zhou Enlai held talks with him on February 25,
26 and 27. The visit was described in the communiqué
as "a new and significant contribution to the strengthening of the Third World's cause of unity against imperialism."

• The Zimbabwe African National Union Delegation,
led by H.W. Chitepo, arrived in Beijing for a twenty-
one-day visit. Vice Premier Deng Xiaoping met the
delegation on March 14.

February 28   NCNA reported the completion of the first
stage of a large and important water-control project
near Danjiangkou (Henan) on the upper reaches of the
Han.

• The People's Daily denounced the Shanxi opera
Going Up to Peach Three Times, which had been performed in Beijing during the North China Theatrical
Festival. The opera was criticized on the grounds
that it advocated the "Dao Yuan Spirit" to oppose the
movement to learn from Dazhai. The article marked
the beginning of an intense campaign to label the opera
as a political plot to negate class struggle.

• In the UN Security Council, Huang Hua spoke on
the Iraqi-Iran frontier incidents. He said that China
"stood for settlement of such question through friendly
consultations on an equal footing between the two parties in dispute." Therefore, China did not favor UN
involvement in any form in a boundary dispute between
the two countries.

March 4   Chairman E.F. Hill and Vice Chairman N. Gallagher
of the Australian Communist Party (Marxist-Leninist)
arrived in Beijing for a fourteen-day visit at the invitation of the Central Committee of the CCP. Premier
Zhou Enlai met them on March 17.

March 8   International Working Women's Day was celebrated,
with attacks on Confucius and Mencius because of their
"contempt for women."

• A photo exhibition of the new archaeological discoveries in China opened at the Grand Hall of the Royal
Art and Historical Museum in Brussels under the joint
sponsorship of the museum and the Belgium-China Association. The exhibition was scheduled to last over
one month.

March 9   The Polish Government Trade Delegation, led by
           T. Nestorowicz, arrived in Beijing for a six-day visit.
           The 1974 Sino-Polish goods exchange and payment
           agreement was signed on March 11.
           • Khalid Salih Al-Ghuneim, the speaker of the Na-
           tional Assembly of Kuwait, his wife, and two other mem-
           bers of his party arrived in Beijing for a five-day visit.
           Premier Zhou Enlai met the party on March 10.

March 11   At the UN Population Commission, Xu Lizhang said
           that China's population had increased from about 500
           million to more than 700 million in the last two decades.
           He also said that the Chinese government was pursuing
           a step-by-step policy of planned population growth.

March 12   China announced its support for Algeria's proposal
           for the convening of a special session of the UN Gen-
           eral Assembly to discuss problems of raw materials and
           development.

March 14   Sri Lanka Foreign Trade Minister Tikiri Banda
           Illangaratne and his party arrived in Beijing for a
           five-day visit. Premier Zhou Enlai met the delegation
           on March 18.

March 15   The Soviet Union Foreign Ministry announced
           that one of their helicopters had strayed accidentally
           across the Xinjiang border while on a first-aid mission.
           The Chinese protested strongly on March 23 that the
           helicopter, an MI-4 armed reconnaissance type, had in-
           truded deep into Xinjiang. The protest-note disclosed
           that since January 1973 there had been as many as
           sixty-one Soviet air intrusions in China's Xinjiang re-
           gion. On March 28, the Soviet Union Foreign Ministry
           handed the Chinese Embassy in Moscow a note demand-
           ing the return of the helicopter.

March 20   China and Guinea-Bissau signed a joint commu-
           niqué in Conakry to establish diplomatic relations at
           the ambassadorial level.

March 22   David Bruce, Head of the US liaison office in
           China, returned to Beijing after an eight-week absence.

March 23   Tanzanian President Julius K. Nyerere visited

China for the third time (the previous occasions being
in 1965 and 1968) from March 23-31. He received a
warm welcome from Chairman Mao on March 25. On
March 29, Premier Zhou Enlai gave a grand banquet in
his honor, and an economic and technical cooperation
agreement was signed.
 • The 1973-74 China-DRVN protocol on scientific and
technological cooperation plan was signed in Beijing.
 • The Hungarian Government Trade Delegation, led
by Tordai Jeno, arrived in Beijing for an eight-day
visit. The 1974 Sino-Hungarian goods exchange and
payment agreement was signed on March 25.

March 26   Reports from Manila stated that President Marcos
had sent Foreign Minister Romulo to Beijing as a special envoy to conduct negotiations to establish diplomatic
relations.
 • The People's Daily published an editorial entitled
"Reasonable Proposal for Solving the Internal Problems
of South Vietnam," to support the PRGRSVN six-point
proposal of March 22.

April 1   Khieu Samphan, head of the Cambodian delegation,
arrived in Beijing on April 1. He finally left Beijing
on May 27, after having, in the meantime, visited
North Korea (April 5-8), and eight countries in Europe,
Africa and Asia. He was treated by the Chinese as a
very high-ranking fellow Marxist-Leninist revolutionary
and, in the words of a welcoming editorial printed in
the People's Daily on April 1, as leading the "first important delegation to China from the interior part of
Cambodia." On April 2, he met Chairman Mao in an
atmosphere of "warmth, cordiality, friendship and
militant solidarity." On May 26, Samphan and Li Xiannian signed an agreement on China's gratis provision
of military equipment and supplies to Cambodia in 1974.

April 2   At the Second Asian Table Tennis Championships
held in Yokohama, Japan, China won the men's team
event, the women's doubles, and the girls' singles.
 • At the UN Economic Commission for Asia and the
Far East (ECAFE) in Colombo, Huang Mingda reiterated
that attempts to survey China's seabed resources by
superpowers and oil monopolists were an infringement
on China's sovereignty.

April 3   According to the New York Times, Sino-American
          trade in 1974 was expected to grow to $1,250 million as
          opposed to $800 million in 1973. The China trade ac-
          counts were, however, badly imbalanced. In 1973,
          China imported about $750 million worth of goods and
          exported only $64 million. In 1974, imports were ex-
          pected to value $1,150 million against an export value
          of $100 million.
          • An exhibition of Unearthed Relics of the People's
          Republic of China was held in Belgrade, Yugoslavia
          from April 3 to June 2.
          • Premier Zhou Enlai sent a message to Madame
          Georges Pompidou expressing, on behalf of Chairman
          Mao Zedong, deep condolences on the death of the late
          President Georges Pompidou.

April 4   The Austrian Delegation, led by Foreign Minister
          Rudolf Kirchschlaeger, arrived in Beijing for a four-
          teen-day visit. Premier Zhou Enlai met the delegation
          on April 6. The visit coincided with the Austrian In-
          dustrial Exhibition in Beijing, held from March 29 to
          April 11.

April 6   The Chinese Delegation to the Sixth Special UN
          Session, headed by Vice Premier Deng Xiaoping, left
          Beijing for New York. On April 10, Deng made an
          important speech in which he declared that the two
          superpowers were "vainly seeking world hegemony" but
          that "the international situation was most favourable to
          the developing countries." He also said that China was
          a socialist country and a developing country as well,
          and that China belonged to the Third World. Deng
          Xiaoping left New York on April 16.
          • Premier Zhou Enlai sent a message of congratula-
          tions to Souvanna Phouma on his assumption of the of-
          fice of premier of the Provisional National Union govern-
          ment of Laos.

April 10 The largest railway station in South China, the
          Guangzhou Railway Passenger Station, was ready for
          use.

April 18 In his stopover in Paris on his way home from New
          York, Deng Xiaoping had talks with the French Prime
          Minister M. Messmer.

April 20   In Libreville, China and Gabon signed a joint communiqué establishing diplomatic relations at the ambassadorial level.
   • The Sino-Japanese civil aviation agreement was
signed in Beijing. For China it opened up the prospect
of regular air services to the North American continent.

April 21   The 1974 Sino-Afghan trade and payment agreement, and the protocol on the exchange of goods between the two nations were signed in Kabul.
   • The Joint China-Vietnam Boundary Railway Commission signed a protocol on joint transport in Nanning.

April 24   Zhuang Yan told the UN Security Council in its
debate on the Mideast that China would not participate
in the vote on a resolution condemning all violence, because the Arabs and Palestinians were fighting for their
lost territories and against aggression, which was justified violence.
   • The thirteen-member delegation of the Sino-British
Trade Mission, led by Lord Nelson, arrived in Beijing
for a seven-day visit. Vice Premier Li Xiannian met
the Mission on April 29.

April 26   Vice Premier Deng Xiaoping called at the Austrian
Embassy in Beijing and extended his condolences over
the death of President Franz Jonas.
   • China and Mongolia signed a protocol on mutual
supply of goods in Beijing.

April 28   Vice Premier Deng Xiaoping suggested, in his
talks with a visiting West German Youth Delegation,
that the Soviet Union's strategic forces in Europe meant
that a war there was "possible and indeed probable."
   • The eleven-member delegation of the Consultative
Assembly of the Yemen Arab Republic, led by the
Speaker Abdulla Ben Hussein Al Almar, arrived in Beijing for a nineteen-day visit. Vice Premier Deng Xiaoping met the delegation on April 30.

April 30   Zhuang Yan told the Sixth Special Session of the
UN General Assembly that China did not recognize the
credentials of the "Lon Nol clique" and South Africa.
China did not think that Portugal had the right to rep-
resent Guinea-Bissau, Angola, and Mozambique.

May 1 A nationwide film festival of ten color films of model
revolutionary theatrical works took place from May 1-23.
  • New uniforms were introduced into the People's
Liberation Army.
  • On International Labor Day, the Wen Huibao and
the Liberation Army Daily carried a portrait of Mao
Zedong on their front pages with these slogans: "Practice Marxism and not revisionism; unite and don't split;
be open and above-board and don't conspire."
  • The biggest road bridge across the Wu River in
Pengshui county, Sichuan province (271 meters long,
50 meters high and 7 meters wide with two lanes and
a footpath 1 meter wide each side) was opened.
  • Huang Hua, at the Sixth Special Session of the UN
General Assembly, said that China supported the Declaration on the Establishment of a New International Economic Order and the Program of Action. He condemned
the World Bank and the IMF for exerting economic pressure on some Third World countries and for refusing to
expel the Chinese Nationalists. China would not participate in these organizations, he said.

May 4 A protocol of the Twenty-fourth Session of the Joint
Standing Commission of the Sino-Polish Shipping Company was signed in Warsaw.
  • Eleven crew-members of a wrecked trawler from
Taiwan, who were rescued by a Yandai fishing team,
left Shanghai for Taiwan.
  • The fifty-fifth anniversary of the May Fourth
Movement was marked by what appeared to be an unprecedented number of meetings and rallies, notably
those held nationwide by the Communist Youth League
and Red Guards. The People's Daily editorial, entitled
"Commemorate the 55th Anniversary of the May 4 Movement," noted that "The current movement to criticize
Lin Biao and Confucius is a continuation of the protracted struggle waged by CCP and the masses of
revolutionary people under its leadership against domestic and foreign enemies since May 4, 1919."

May 6 Senegalese President Senghor and his party arrived
in Beijing for a twelve-day visit. Chairman Mao met
the president on May 7. Premier Zhou Enlai gave a
banquet on May 6. A joint communiqué on the visit
was issued on May 18.

May 7   President F.E. Marcos of the Philippines received all
        members of the Chinese National Men's Basketball Dele-
        gation in Manila.

May 11   Pakistan Prime Minister Zulfikar Ali Bhutto, Mrs.
        Bhutto, and their entourage arrived in Beijing for a
        four-day visit. Chairman Mao Zedong met them on May
        11. Premier Zhou Enlai held talks with them on May
        12. Vice Premier Deng Xiaoping hosted a banquet and
        held talks with them on May 12, 13, and 14. A joint
        communique was issued on May 14.
          • The Soviet Government Trade Delegation, led by
        I.T. Grishin, arrived in Beijing for a twelve-day visit.
        The 1974 Sino-Soviet goods exchange and payment
        agreement was signed on May 15.
          • A strong earthquake occurred in the Zhaotong area
        in Yunnan province and the Liangshan Yi Autonomous
        Zhou in Sichuan province; aftershocks occurred on May
        12.

May 17   President Makarios of Cyprus and his party ar-
        rived in Beijing for an eight-day visit. Chairman Mao
        met him on May 18. Premier Zhou Enlai held talks with
        him on May 18. Vice Premier Deng Xiaoping hosted a
        banquet and held talks on May 18. The two leaders
        continued their talks on May 19 and 20.

May 20   It was announced that Malaysia and China agreed to
        establish diplomatic relations. At China's invitation the
        Malaysian Prime Minister Tun Abdul Razah visited China
        from May 28 to June 2. Chairman Mao Zedong received
        him on May 31. Premier Zhou Enlai met him on May 29.
        Zhou Enlai and Razah signed a joint communiqué on
        May 31 establishing diplomatic relations at the ambassa-
        dorial level between China and Malaysia. Zhou Enlai
        said China "considers anyone of Chinese origin who has
        taken up of his own will or acquired Malaysian national-
        ity as automatically forfeiting Chinese nationality," and
        enjoined those in Malaysia who have retained Chinese
        nationality to abide by Malaysian laws. It was an-
        nounced in Kuala Lumpur that the Malaysian government
        had closed all its existing consular relations with Tai-
        wan. On his return, Razah stated that Chairman Mao
        and Premier Zhou had categorically assured him that
        they regarded the remnant terrorists in Malaysia as in-
        ternal affairs for Malaysia to deal with.

May 22 The French Industrial, Scientific, and Technical
Exhibition was held at the Beijing Exhibition Hall from
May 22 to June 7.
  • The Chinese Government Trade Delegation, led by
Sun Suozhang, left Beijing to visit Sweden (May 23-31),
Austria (June 1-8), and the Federal Republic of Ger-
many (June 9-18).

May 23 Tass published a Soviet note suggesting a joint
project to widen a channel near the confluence of the
Amur and Ussuri rivers. Meanwhile, passage of Chinese vessels through Soviet internal waterways would
be possible, provided Soviet rights and territorial integrity were respected. The Chinese Ministry of Foreign Affairs rejected the Soviet note as hypocritical and
as an attempt to "blackmail" China.
  • The People's Daily carried an article entitled "Keep
to the Correct Orientation and Uphold the Philosophy of
Struggle," to mark the thirty-second anniversary of the
publication of the "Talks at the Yanan Forum on Literature and Art." It linked the talks to the current situation.

May 24 The leader of the Conservative party and former
British Prime Minister Edward Heath was given a rap-
turous welcome on his visit to China from May 24 to
June 2. On May 25, within 24 hours of his arrival, Mr.
Heath was received by Chairman Mao. Premier Zhou
Enlai met him on May 27. Vice Premier Deng Xiaoping
hosted a banquet and held talks with him on May 25.

May 26 The Chinese Government Trade Delegation, led by
Chen Jie, left Beijing for Nepal on a nine-day visit.
A new Sino-Nepalese trade and payment agreement was
signed on June 1.

May 29 The Chinese Government Maritime Navigation Delegation left Beijing for Bulgaria on a seven-day visit.
Sino-Bulgarian maritime transport agreement was signed
on June 4. The Chinese Scientists' Delegation, led by
Zhou Peiyuan, left Beijing to visit the Federal Republic
of Germany (May 30 to June 16), Switzerland (June 17-
27), and France (June 27 to July 14).

May 30 Chairman Mao Zedong met Chinese-American physicist

Dr. Li Zhengdao, who came to China to visit his relatives. Zhou Enlai, Wang Hongwen, Zhang Chunqiao,
Jiang Qing, Yao Wenyuan, Deng Xiaoping, Guo Moruo
met him on May 24. He left Guangzhou for the US on
June 6.

• Premier Zhou Enlai sent a message to the Palestine
National Council, congratulating it on the convocation
of the Conference of the Palestine National Council.

• Twenty-two fishermen of Taiwan, who had been
rescued from shipwrecks, left Zhejiang for Taiwan.

May 31 On the Syrian-Israeli disengagement agreement, an
NCNA editorial noted that the Soviet Union had lost
ground as a result of Kissinger's energetic diplomacy.

June 1 Acting Chairman Dong Biwu and Premier Zhou Enlai
sent a message to Jigme Singye Wangchuck, the new
king of Bhutan, congratulating him on his coronation.

June 3 Secretary of State Henry Kissinger, at a dinner
given by the National Council for US-China Trade,
the National Committee on US-China Relations, and the
Committee on Scholarly Communication with the People's
Republic of China, affirmed the commitment of the administration to the "constant improvement of relations
with the PRC."

• In Beijing, the Nippon Steel Corporation of Japan
signed a contract with China to build a giant steel
plant in Wuhan, capable of an annual production of
three million tons of hot rollings and 70,000 tons of
silicon steel. The Chinese were expected to finance
the plant on a deferred basis with the assistance of
Japanese banks.

• The Chinese Wushu (traditional Chinese boxing
and sword play) Delegation, led by Guo Lei, left Beijing to visit Mexico (June 4-21), and the US (June 22
to July 15).

June 6 The Pictorial Exhibition of Archaeological Finds in
New China, sponsored by the Finland-China Society,
was held in Helsinki from June 6-23.

• The Ghanian Government Agricultural Friendship
Delegation, led by F.G. Bernasko, arrived in Beijing
for a nineteen-day visit. Vice Premier Li Xiannian met
the delegation on June 24.

June 11 Yao Guang, Chinese ambassador to Mexico, delivered to the Mexican government the depository letter of the "Treaty for the Prohibition of Nuclear Weapons
in Latin America," an Instrument of Ratification of Additional Protocol II.
    • Zhuang Yan told the UN Security Council that
China considered Bangladesh eligible for membership in
the UN.

June 12 The People's Daily carried an article entitled "A
Good Example" to describe what a valuable precedent
was set by the resettlement of 2,000 educated young
people from the new industrial city of Zhuzhou to support agricultural stations established by factory-run
schools throughout the country.

June 13 Posters attacking the Beijing Municipal Revolutionary Committee were placed outside its committee office,
signalling a new phase of the Campaign to Criticize
Lin Biao and Confucius.

June 14 The decision to train more Marxist theorists was
conveyed in a short commentary in the Red Flag entitled "Strengthen the Ranks of Marxist Theorists," coin-
ciding with a number of reports from provincial radio
stations describing their training.
    • The Chadian Trade Mission, led by Mahamat Gab-
dou, arrived in Beijing for a twenty-day visit.

June 17 China conducted another nuclear test in Xinjiang.

June 20 In New York, China and Trinidad and Tobago
signed a joint communiqué to establish diplomatic relations at the ambassadorial level.

June 24 NCNA reported that the ten-year-old project to
harness north China's biggest waterway system, the
Haihe, "had changed the temperament of this formerly
rampant river. It is now made to serve the people according to their will."

June 26 The Soviet Deputy Foreign Minister Leonid Ilyichev
was sent to Beijing for border negotiations.

June 28 In Caracas, China and Venezuela signed a joint

communiqué to establish diplomatic relations at the ambassadorial level.

• Chinese party and state leaders Wang Hongwen,
Ye Jianying, Zhang Chunqiao, Deng Xiaoping, and Guo
Moruo met American physicist, Dr. Yang Zhenning, who
came to China to visit his relatives. On the same day,
Dr. Yang also met and dined with Jiang Qing, Chen
Xilian, and Qi Denggui.

June 29 The six-member delegation of Chinese Workers,
Youth and Women, led by Wang Zhaozhu, left Beijing
for Tanzania to take part in the celebrations of the
twentieth anniversary of the Tanganyika African National Union. The delegation returned to Beijing on
July 15.

• The Chinese Military Goodwill Mission, led by Li
Da, left Beijing for Tanzania to take part in the tenth
anniversary celebrations of the founding of the Tanzanian People's Defense Forces. The delegation returned to Beijing on July 15.

July 1 US Democratic Senator Henry M. Jackson arrived in
Beijing for a seven-day visit. Vice Premier Deng
Xiaoping met him on July 4; Premier Zhou Enlai met
him in the hospital on July 5. Upon his return, he
urged the reversal of the American diplomatic ties between Beijing and Taipei with the Embassy to be transferred to the former and the liaison office to the latter.

• A festival was held beginning July 1; it comprised
a series of documentaries on Daqing oilfield and Dazhai
production brigade. The aim was to advance the mass
movement to learn from Dazhai and Daqing still further.

• The celebration of the fifty-third anniversary of
the party on July 1 was accompanied by an explicit
editorial in the People's Daily entitled "The Party Exer-
cises Overall Leadership." It stressed the party's position as the core of leadership of the entire population.

• The Red Flag carried an article entitled "The
Revolutionary Struggle Requires a Contingent of Marxist Theorists," to describe the relationship of workers-
peasants-soldiers theorists to professional theorists, and
their role "to strengthen the ties of these contingents
so that they can overcome their own weakness of learning from each other's strong points."

July 2 At the general debate at the Third Conference on
the Law of the Sea in Caracas, China welcomed the
conference as a successful achievement of the small and
medium-sized countries in their struggle for maritime
rights against the two superpowers, who, under the
terminology "freedom of the high seas" sought a "mon-
opoly of the high seas."

July 3 Acting Chairman Dong Biwu and Premier Zhou Enlai
sent a message to Madam María Estela Martínez de
Perón, president of the Republic of Argentina, expressing deep condolences on the death of the late
President Juan Perón.

July 4 David K.E. Bruce, chief of the US liaison office in
China, gave a reception in Beijing to mark Independence
Day.
    • Vice Foreign Minister Zhai Shufan arrived in Hav-
ana for a seven-day visit. The 1974 Sino-Cuban trade
protocol was signed on July 11.
    • The Chinese Government Maritime Transport Dele-
gation, led by Dong Huamin, visited Japan at the invitation of the Japanese government from July 4 to
August 2. The talks on the signing of the Sino-
Japanese maritime transport agreement were suspended
at the end of July because they had reached an impasse
on the issue of calls at Japanese ports by vessels from
Taiwan.

July 9 The Soviet Union claimed that as long ago as 1964,
it had agreed to relocate the border along the "fairway"
of navigation rivers and along the middle of nonnavi-
gable waterways. Had this been accepted, Chenbao
Island would have become Chinese, but the proposal
had been rejected without discussion.

July 10 The Delegation of the China Council for the Promotion of International Trade, led by Wang Yaoding, left
Beijing for Osaka, Japan, to preside over the opening
of the Chinese Exhibition which was held from July 13
to August 11.
    • The Philippine Oil Mission, led by Geronimo Vel-
asco, arrived in Beijing for an eight-day visit. Vice
Premier Li Xiannian met the mission on July 15.

July 12   The Chinese Archeological Finds Exhibition was held
at the Museum of the Eastern Antiquities in Stockholm,
Sweden, from July 12 to July 16.

    • In Colombo, China and Sri Lanka signed a protocol
on the building of the Jin Gang (River) controlling project and related documents.

    • Tunisian Foreign Minister and Mrs. Habib Chatti,
and their entourage arrived in Beijing for a five-day
visit.   Vice Premier Deng Xiaoping met them on July
14.   A protocol to the agreement of economic and technical cooperation was signed on July 14.

July 13   The Rumanian Friendship Group, led by Ion Stans-
scu, arrived in Beijing for a twenty-six-day visit.   Hua
Guofeng met the group on July 15.

July 14   The Turkish Government Delegation, led by Foreign
Minister Turan Gunnes, arrived in Beijing for a seven-
day visit.   A Sino-Turkish trade agreement was signed
on July 16.   Vice Premier Deng Xiaoping met the delegation on July 17.

July 16   Hua Guofeng had a talk in Beijing with all members
of the Cameroon Government Agricultural Delegation,
led by Felix Tonye.

July 18   The Niger Government Delegation, led by Vice
President Sido, arrived in Beijing for a ten-day visit.
Vice Premier Deng Xiaoping held talks with him on July
18, 19 and 20.   Premier Zhou Enlai met him on July 20.
The joint communiqué was signed to establish diplomatic
relations at the ambassadorial level on July 20.   A Sino-
Niger economic and technical cooperation agreement was
signed on July 20.

July 20   Zhuang Yan told the UN Security Council that China
recognized Archbishop Makarios as the legitimate head
of state of Cyprus.   China had voted in favor of the
resolution on Cyprus calling for the withdrawal of all
foreign military personnel other than those under the
authority of international agreements, although China
had reservations on the question of dispatching the UN
force to Cyprus.

    • The Chinese Medical Team, led by Fang Qi, arrived
in Vientiane, Laos, for a twelve-day visit and gave medical treatment to Prince Souvanna Phouma.

July 25 The Pakistan Government Trade Mission, led by
Ejaz Ahmad Naik, arrived in Beijing for a nine-day
visit. Sino-Pakistan trade protocol was signed on July
27.

July 30 Abdel Rahim Bouabid, Special Envoy of Moulay Hassan III, king of Morocco, and his party arrived in Beijing for a four-day visit. Vice Premier Li Xiannian met
the party on August 1.

July 31 The Chinese Ministry of National Defense gave a
grand reception in Beijing marking the forty-seventh
anniversary of the founding of the Chinese People's
Liberation Army. Premier Zhou Enlai made his first
public appearance at the reception after a period of indisposition which necessitated hospital treatment in late
May, soon after the conclusion of the agreement to
normalize relations with Malaysia.

August 1 The People's Daily carried an article stressing the
party's role as the core of leadership of the entire
population. It also urged the country to learn from
the Army, and the Army from the people, to grasp
revolution, promote production and preparedness for
war.
   • The Chinese Government Delegation, led by Su
Jie, left Beijing to visit Zambia (August 2-20), and
Tanzania (August 21 to September 10) and attended the
sixth round of the talks on the Tanzania-Zambia railway.
   • The DRVN Government Economic Delegation, led
by Vice Premier Le Thanh Nghi, arrived in Beijing for
a nine-day visit. Vice Premier Li Xiannian met the
delegation on August 2.

August 2 The Sino-Norwegian maritime transport agreement
was officially signed in Beijing.
   • Huang Hua told the UN Security Council that China
supported the people of Guinea-Bissau in their application for membership in the United Nations and in their
struggle for liberation.
   • Jiang Qing's speech at the July 1964 forum was
described in a Red Flag article as being full of the
Marxist spirit of going against the tide, and laying a
firm foundation for proletarian literature and art.

August 3   The Chinese Trade Delegation, led by Chen Jie,
     left Beijing for a fourteen-day visit to Brazil.   On Au-
     gust 15, a joint communiqué was issued to establish
     diplomatic relations at the ambassadorial level.   The
     minutes of trade talks were also signed on August 17.
        • NCNA reported that the Tibetan language was a
     major subject taught at more than 3,000 schools in the
     Tibet autonomous region.   The Tibet Nationalities Insti-
     tute had a Tibet language faculty which trained lin-
     guists and translators.   The Tibet People's Publishing
     House put out 1.5 million copies of books in Tibetan.
     The circulation of the Tibetan edition of the Tibet
     Daily rose from 2,000 in 1956 to some 25,000 in 1974.
     As a result of local political, economic, and cultural de-
     velopment, the vocabulary of the Tibetan language had
     been constantly enlarged.   Some 100,000 new words and
     phrases had been introduced since 1956.

August 4   A People's Daily article claimed the modern revo-
     lutionary opera Song of Yuan Ding was an attempt to
     oppose the policies of the Cultural Revolution in educa-
     tion and the arts, because the opera advocated the
     Confucius slogan "to restrain oneself and restore the
     rites" and pushed ideas such as "the teacher must be
     respected" and "knowledge comes first."
        • Rumanian Foreign Minister George Macovescu, his
     wife, and their party arrived in Beijing for a six-day
     visit.   Prince Norodom Sihanouk met the party on Au-
     gust 8; Vice Premier Li Xiannian met them on August 9.
        • The Chinese Archaeological Finds Exhibition Group,
     led by Liu Yangzhao, left Beijing to attend the opening
     ceremony of the Exhibition of Archaeological Finds of
     the People's Republic of China in Toronto, Canada.
     The exhibition was held from August 8 to November 17.

August 7   The Swiss Industrial Technology Exhibition was
     held in Beijing from August 7-20.   NCNA reported that
     China's crude oil output shot up by 21.3 percent in the
     first six months of this year compared with the corres-
     ponding period of last year.

August 9   The People's Daily reported the resignation of
     President Richard M. Nixon and his replacement by
     President Gerald Ford without comment.   President Ford
     met Huang Zhen, chief of the liaison office of China in

the United States, at the White House at the former's
request after he was sworn in.

    • The Equatorial Guinean Government Delegation, led
by Vice President Don Miguel Eyegue, arrived in Beijing
for a thirteen-day visit. Vice Premier Deng Xiaoping
held talks with the delegation on August 10, 11, and
12.

August 10 The Chinese Delegation, led by Huang Shuze,
left Beijing to attend the UN World Population Conference held in Bucharest, Rumania, from August 19-30.
At the conference, he criticized the theory of the population explosion as a fallacy peddled by the superpowers. He also said that China's population policy varied
in different parts of the country.

    • Vice Foreign Minister Qiao Gunghua met, in Bei-
jing, Leopoldo Benites, president of the Twenty-eighth
Session of the UN General Assembly, and Ecuador's
permanent representative to the UN; Vice Premier Deng
Xiaoping met them on August 12.

August 12 An important one-month theatrical festival was
held in Beijing from August 12 to September 11 under
the auspices of the cultural group of the State Council.
The festival brought together theatrical productions
from Shanghai, Guangxi, Hunan, and Liaoning.

August 16 The Malian Government Trade Delegation, led by
Assim Diawara, arrived in Beijing for a twelve-day
visit. Vice Premier Deng Xiaoping met the delegation
on August 27.

August 17 A large-ramped earth platform and a heap of
slave skulls dating back 3,500 years were unearthed
from the site of city walls of the Shang Dynasty (sixteenth century to eleventh century BC) in Zhengzhou
by archaeological workers in Henan province.

August 19 NCNA began daily releases of the Bank of
China's exchange rates for the people's currency (renminbi) against convertible currencies.

August 20 The Sports Delegation of the People's Republic
of China to the Seventh Asian Games left Beijing for
Teheran by a special plane. Party and state leaders,

Deng Xiaoping and Hua Guofeng bade farewell to the delegation at the airport. The Seventh Asian Games were held from September 1-16.

August 21   The Chinese Party and Government Delegation, led by Vice Premier Li Xiannian, left Beijing for Bucharest on a five-day visit and attended the celebrations of the thirtieth anniversary of the liberation of Rumania. President Nicolae Ceausescu held talks with the party on August 25.

August 22   Rwanda Foreign Minister Nsekalije Aloys and his party arrived in Beijing for a six-day visit. Vice Premier Deng Xiaoping met the party on August 27.

August 27   A civil air transport agreement between China and Laos was signed in Beijing.

August 30   China ratified the second protocol of the treaty for the prohibition of nuclear weapons to Latin America (the Treaty of Tateloco).
    • At the World Population Conference, Li Dingzhuan said that China welcomed the part of the world population plan of action which stated that "the formulation and implementation of the population policy was the sovereign right of each country." Li, however, regretted the reference to a target for restricting population growth.

September 2   Togolese President Gnassigbe Eyadema, Madame Eyadema and their entourage arrived in Beijing for a six-day visit. The president had extensive talks with Vice Premier Deng Xiaoping. On September 4, he met Chairman Mao Zedong. An agreement on economic and technical cooperation between the two nations was signed on September 5. For the first time Premier Zhou Enlai did not see a foreign head of state visiting Beijing.
    • A five-nation conference attended by China, Vietnam, Korea, Mongolia, and the Soviet Union to coordinate time schedules of international passenger trains was held from September 2-7 in Beijing.
    • The US Congressional Delegation, led by Senator James W. Fulbright, arrived in Beijing for a thirteen-day visit. Vice Premier Deng Xiaoping met the delegation on September 5.

September 3 The People's Daily commentator strongly denounced the Indian government for incorporating Sikkim
as an "associate state" of the Indian Union.
  • The West German Christian Democratic Union leader
H. Kohl visited China from September 3-7. He had extensive talks with Vice Premier Deng Xiaoping.

September 6 In Washington, Secretary of State Kissinger
expressed his satisfaction with the progress of Sino-
American ties and dismissed the significance of the appointment of Ambassador Unger to Taiwan and of Taiwan's opening of two new consulates in the United
States as nothing more than "bureaucratic snafus."
  • Premier Zhou Enlai sent a message of congratulations to Guinea-Bissau leaders when the peace agreement between Portugal and Guinea-Bissau was signed.

September 7 The Chinese Government Trade Delegation, led
by Zhai Shufan, left Beijing to visit Iraq (September
10-15), and Syria (September 16-22) at the invitation
of the respective governments of the two nations.

September 8 General Yakubu Gowen, head of the Military
Government of Nigeria, made a state visit to China
from September 8-15. He met Chairman Mao Zedong on
September 10. The communiqué was issued on September 15.

September 11 The Ministry of Foreign Affairs issued a statement denouncing India's constitutional amendment (ratified by India's Upper House on September 7) making
Sikkim an associate state as "outright expansionism."

September 14 NCNA reported the completion of the Danjiang
canal project in the region of Xiangyang (hubei), part
of the Danjiangkou water-control project.
  • The exhibition of arts and crafts of the Ming and
Qing Dynasties was held in Beijing from September 14
to October 10.

September 15 The Chinese Scientific and Technical Coopera-
tion Delegation, led by Sun Yuyu, left Beijing for
Czechoslovakia for a ten-day visit and attended the
Sixteenth Session of the Joint Committee of Sino-
Czechoslovakia Scientific and Technical Cooperation. A
protocol of the session was signed on September 24.

September 16 Premier Zhou Enlai sent a personal message
    to President of the Mozambique Liberation Front Samora
    Moises Machel, extending warm congratulations to "the
    heroic Mozambique people on their victory in the strug-
    gle against imperialism and colonialism for national in-
    dependence."

September 17 President Moktar Ould Daddah of Mauritania
    arrived in Beijing for a ten-day state visit. The pres-
    ident had extensive talks with Vice Premier Deng
    Xiaoping, but unsuccessfully sought public Chinese
    support for Mauritania's claims to Spanish Sahara.
    Chairman Mao Zedong met him on September 19. Pre-
    mier Zhou Enlai met him on September 26. An eco-
    nomic and technical cooperation agreement between the
    two nations was signed on September 19. The Chinese
    Economic and Trade Exhibition was held in Wellington,
    New Zealand, from September 17-29.

September 20 At the invitation of Premier Zhou Enlai, Madam
    Imelda Romualdez Marcos, wife of the Philippines presi-
    dent, arrived in Beijing for a ten-day visit. Premier
    Zhou Enlai met her in a hospital in Beijing on September
    20. She also met Jiang Qing and Li Xiannian on the
    same day. Chairman Mao met her on September 27. A
    trade agreement between the two nations was signed on
    September 29.

September 21 A protocol on the Twelfth Session of the Sino-
    Bulgarian Commission for Scientific and Technical Co-
    operation was signed in Beijing.

September 23 An exhibition of modern Chinese graphic art
    was held in London from September 23 to October 12
    under the joint sponsorship of the Society for Anglo-
    Chinese Understanding and the Polytechnical of Central
    London.
        • A People's Daily article entitled "Mutual Support
    and Sincere Cooperation," outlined China's main prin-
    ciples for the granting of aid. China's aid was given
    in accordance with principles of sovereignty and equal-
    ity.

September 25 David K. E. Bruce, chief of the liaison office
    of the US in China, left Beijing for home.

September 26   The Hunan-Guizhou railway from Zhuzhou (Hunan) to Guiyang (Guizhou) was formally opened to traffic.

September 27   The Laotian Government Economic Delegation, led by Thao Soth Phetrasy, arrived in Beijing for an eight-day visit. A Sino-Laotian agreement on economic and technical cooperation was signed on October 3.

September 29   The inaugural flight of the civil aviation route between Tokyo and Beijing took place on September 29, marking the second anniversary of the establishment of diplomatic relations between the two nations.

September 30   Premier Zhou Enlai gave a grand reception in the Great Hall of the People in Beijing marking the twenty-fifth anniversary of the founding of the People's Republic of China.
   • China and Albania signed a protocol on goods exchange and payment agreement for 1975 in Beijing.

October 1   The joint National Day editorial by the People's Daily, the Red Flag and the Liberation Army Daily entitled "Forward Along the Great Road of Socialism," summed up the period optimistically: "We have in the main completed the socialist transformation of the ownership of the means of production." The editorial also stated that the movement to criticize Lin Biao and Confucius should be broadened and deepened in the future for a considerable length of time.
   • The Soviet Union Presidium, the Supreme Soviet, and the Council of Minister sent their greetings to the Chinese people. The message stressed that normalization and restoration of friendship should be achieved through a nonaggression treaty.

October 2   In his speech at the general debate in the UN General Assembly, Qiao Guanhua said that China supported the people in Mozambique, Angola, Zimbabwe, Namibia, Azania (South Africa) and Spanish Sahara in their "liberation struggles."

October 3   Vice Premier Deng Xiaoping told Japanese visitors in Beijing that a peace treaty should be speedily concluded and added that China was willing in this connection "to shelve the territorial problem involving the disputed Senkaku Island." Japanese visitors were from the Japan-China Friendship Association (Orthodox) Delegation, led by Hisao Kuroda, and the Delegation of the Japan-China Cultural Exchange Association, led by Kenzoo Nakajima.

October 4   The president of Gabon, El Hadj Omar Bongo, his wife, and their party arrived in Beijing for a six-day visit. Vice Premier Deng Xiaoping, on behalf of Premier Zhou Enlai, gave a grant banquet on October 4. Chairman Mao met the President on October 5, and Premier Zhou Enlai met him on the following day in a hospital. Agreements on economic and technical cooperation, and on trade were signed on October 6.

October 5   The Economic and Trade Exhibition of the People's Republic of China was held in Georgetown, Guyana from October 5 to November 20.
   • A regular meeting of Sino-Korean border railway transport was held in Korea's Sariwon city from October 5-22. A protocol of the meeting was signed on October 22.

October 7   The Chinese government presented a tapestry depicting the Great Wall and an ivory carving depicting China's Chengdu-Kunming Railway to the United Nations Headquarters.
   • The Burmese Trade Delegation, led by U San Win, arrived in Beijing for a ten-day visit. Vice Premier Li Xiannian met the delegation on October 9.

October 8   The Chinese Art and Craft Exhibition was held at the National Art Museum in Lima, Peru, from October 8-25.
   • The Australian Government Delegation, led by James Cairns, arrived in Beijing for an eight-day visit and opened the Australian Exhibition in Beijing on October 11. The exhibition closed on October 23.

October 9   Vice Foreign Minister Qiao Guanhua visited Bonn at the invitation of the government of the Federal Republic of Germany from October 9-11. Chancellor Helmut Schmidt received him on October 10. It was announced that Chancellor Schmidt would visit China in

1975, and that Herr Strauss would visit China during the next year.

October 10   Former Guomindang President Chief of Staff and Guomindang Emissary to Tokyo Mt. Shang Chen visited China during October and was received by Ye Jianying on October 10.

October 11   Mokolo Wa Mpombo, chief adviser to the president of Zaire, arrived in Beijing for a twelve-day visit. Vice Premier Li Xiannian met him on October 17.
   • The Argentine Congressional Group, led by Italo Luder, arrived in Beijing for a ten-day visit.   Vice Premier Li Xiannian met the group on October 14.
   • The Venezuela Congressional Delegation, led by Gonzalo Barrios, arrived in Beijing for a five-day visit. Vice Premier Deng Xiaoping met the delegation on October 14.
   • The Tanzanian Shipping Delegation led by Sepeky Foum, arrived in Beijing for a six-day visit, and attended the eighth meeting of the Board of Directors of the Sino-Tanzanian Joint Shipping Company.

October 13   The Federal Diet Delegation of the Federal Republic of Germany, led by Richard Jaeger, arrived in Beijing for a seven-day visit.   Zhu De, Li Xiannian met the delegation on October 14; Vice Premier Deng Xiaoping met it on October 15.   According to the West German News Agency, the DPA, Deng told the delegation that a Third World War was a distinct possibility because of the superpowers' hegemonism.

October 14   Minister of Agriculture and Forest Sha Feng left Beijing for Sydney, Australia for a twelve-day visit. He opened the Chinese Economic and Trade Exhibition in Sydney on October 18.   The exhibition was held until October 27.   Sha Feng met Prime Minister Whitlam on October 25.

October 15   The People's Daily carried an article entitled "Typify Contradictions and Struggles in Everyday Life," criticizing the theories of "inspiration," "truthful writing," and "no conflict" in literary writings and artistic creations.

October 16   The People's Daily carried an article criticizing
    "bourgeois and revisionist views" in the studies of the
    eighteenth-century Chinese classical novel The Dream
    of the Red Chambers. The article, written by Liang
    Xiao, was entitled "Criticize the Bourgeoisie Without
    Respite."
        • NCNA reported that in the past twenty-five years,
    the Chinese people had mastered the sciences of nuclear
    energy, jet propulsion, electronics, computing, automa-
    tion and laser techniques, besides successfully testing
    an atomic bomb, a hydrogen bomb, guided missiles with
    nuclear warheads, and an artificial satellite.

October 17   A People's Daily article entitled "Maintain Inde-
    pendence and Keep the Initiative in Our Own Hands and
    Rely on Our Own Efforts in Developing Foreign Trade,"
    discussed the achievements made in China's foreign trade
    over the past twenty-five years. The volume of China's
    imports and exports in 1973 was 5.66 times what it was
    in 1952 and 2.59 times that of 1965. China had estab-
    lished trade relations with over 150 countries and re-
    gions and signed trade agreement or protocols at govern-
    ment level with more than fifty countries. China's Ex-
    port Commodities Fair was inaugurated in 1957 and was
    held twice a year in Guangzhou thereafter. At the first
    occasion, China played host to only a little over 1,200
    people and regions. But in recent years the number at
    each fair had exceeded 20,000 from more than 100 coun-
    tries and regions.

October 18   Prime Minister Poul Hartling of Denmark, his
    wife, and their party arrived in Beijing for a nine-day
    visit. Premier Zhou Enlai met him in a hospital on Octo-
    ber 19, and Vice Premier Deng Xiaoping hosted a grand
    banquet on behalf of Premier Zhou Enlai on the same
    day. Chairman Mao met him on October 20. On October
    21, an agreement on maritime transport between the two
    nations and the letters on the establishment of a joint
    committee to promote trade and economic relations be-
    tween the two nations were signed.
        • The Chinese Government Delegation, led by Fang
    Yi, and the Chinese Military Goodwill Delegation, led by
    Zhang Zaijian left Beijing for Lusaka on a ten-day visit
    and attended the celebration of the tenth anniversary
    of the independence of the Republic of Zambia.

October 19   The Hungarian Scientific and Technical Delegation arrived in Beijing for a nine-day visit, and attended the Thirteenth Meeting of the Joint Commission.
A protocol of the meeting was signed on October 26.

October 20   China and Laos signed a postal and telecommunication agreement in Beijing.

October 21   George H.W. Bush, the newly appointed head of
the liaison office, arrived in Beijing, and held talks
with Vice Premier Deng Xiaoping on November 2.
  • The 1974 regular meeting of the Sino-Mongolian
Boundary Through Railway Traffic was held in Ulan
Bator from November 21-26.

October 22   The Polish Delegation, led by E. Wisniewski,
arrived in Beijing for an eight-day visit and took part
in the twelfth session of the shareholders' meeting of
the Chinese-Polish Ship Broker's Company.

October 23   Chinese Ambassador Song Zhuguang, on behalf
of the Chinese government, officially presented a pair
of giant pandas, a gift from the Chinese government to
the British people, at a ceremony held at the London
Zoo.

October 24   The 1975-76 plan for the execution of the China-
Vietnam public health cooperation agreement was signed
in Hanoi.

October 25   The DRVN Economic Delegation, led by Vice
Premier Le Thanh-Nghi, arrived in Beijing for a four-
day visit.   The 1975 agreement on China's military and
economic aid to Hanoi, and mutual trace pact were
signed on October 26.   Premier Zhou Enlai met the
delegation in the hospital on October 27; Prince Sihanouk met it in Beijing.

October 26   The Chinese Beijing Opera Troupe, led by Yu
Huiyung, left Beijing for Algeria to attend the celebrations of the twentieth anniversary of the founding of
the Democratic People's Republic of Algeria for home on
November 27.

October 28   The Chinese Government Delegation, led by Sha

Feng, left Australia for New Zealand for a seven-day visit.

October 29   Huang Hua spoke to the Security Council in support of South Africa's expulsion from the United Nations.

October 30   The Ugandan Friendship Trade Delegation, led by E.L. Athiyo, arrived in Beijing for a twelve-day visit.   Vice Premier Li Xiannian met the delegation on November 10.
  • The first airliner of the Civil Aviation Administration of China (CAAC) on the Beijing-Karachi-Paris International Air Service carrying a Chinese goodwill delegation arrived at the Karachi airport at 0310 hours and continued its flight to Paris.

October 31   The Chinese Government Trade Delegation, led by Chen Jie, left Beijing to visit Zambia (October 31 to November 9), Tanzania (November 9-16), and Madgascar (November 17-23).

November 1   At the UN General Assembly, Huang Hua spoke against the idea of sending a "special mission" to Cyprus.   He said that the problem could be solved only by Cyprus' people, who had made a good beginning in their talks.   China voted in favor of the resolution on Cyprus.

November 2   After strenuous negotiations, the shipping agreement between China and Japan was initialed in Beijing, and formally signed on November 13 in Tokyo. The two countries also agreed to establish consulates in Shanghai and Osaka in 1975.

November 3   The Cambodian Economic and Financial Delegation, led by Ieng Sary, arrived in Beijing for a visit from November 3 to December 4.   Vice Premier Li Xiannian held talks with Ieng Sary on November 4.   Premier Zhou Enlai met Ieng Sary in a hospital in Beijing on November 24.

November 4   China and Korea signed the 1975-76 plan for scientific cooperation in Pyongyang.

November 5   Trinidadian Prime Minister Eric Williams arrived
in Beijing for a six-day visit. He visited Premier Zhou
Enlai in the hospital on November 5, and held talks
with Jiang Qing, Li Xiannian and met Chairman Mao on
November 6. In a speech in Beijing, he praised the
Trinidadian Chinese, and spoke of the possibility of
selling Trinidadian sugar and fertilizer to China.
   • E.F. Hill, chairman of the Australian Communist
party (M-L) and Mrs. Hill arrived in Beijing for a visit
from November 5 to January 4, 1975.
   • The DRVN and China signed an agreement on broad-
casting and television cooperation in Beijing.
   • The Chinese Goodwill Delegation, led by Zhai Shu-
fan, left Beijing for Paris by a scheduled flight of the
CAAC to take part in the celebrations of the official in-
auguration of the Beijing-Karachi-Paris air service.
   • The Yugoslav Government Scientific, Cultural,
Educational and Technical Delegation, led by Krasto
Bulasic, arrived in Beijing for a ten-day visit. Vice
Premier Li Xiannian met the delegation on November 12.
An agreement on scientific and technical cooperation be-
tween the two nations was signed on November 12.

November 6   Soviet Ambassador to China V.S. Tolstikov and
his wife gave a reception in the Embassy in Beijing to
celebrate the twenty-seventh anniversary of the October
Socialist Revolution. Radio Beijing broadcast in its
Russian service, a message from the National People's
Congress and the State Council to the Presidium and
the Council of Ministers of the Soviet Union for the occasion. The message called for an agreement on mutual
nonaggression and on military withdrawal from the disputed areas. On November 26, Mr. Brezhnev, at a rally
in Ulan Bator, decisively rejected these proposals.
   • The protocol of the Fifteenth Session of the Sino-
Korean Committee for Scientific and Technical Cooperation was signed in Beijing. Hua Guofeng held talks with
the Korean Scientific and Technical Cooperation Delegation.

November 7   At the UN World Food Conference in Rome, Hao
Zhongshi said that China had imported more than $2
billion worth of food grain between 1972 and 1974 but
had also exported grain, chiefly rice, of the same value.
   • The Philippine Trade and Economic Mission, led by

Vicente Paterno, arrived in Beijing. Minister of Foreign Trade Li Jiang held talks with the delegation and
the delegation met Vice Premier Li Xiannian on November
12. On November 17, the ten members of the Philippine Chamber of Commerce, led by David S. Sycip,
arrived in Beijing as the guest of the China Council
for the Promotion of International Trade. Five contracts for the sale of Philippine coconut oil, logs, ply-
wood, copper concentrate and raw sugar were signed
under the terms of an agreement which had been
reached between Mr. Paterno and Li Jiang.

• The French Goodwill Delegation, led by Robert
Galley and Madam Chirac, left Paris for Beijing by a
CAAC plane to attend the celebrations of the official
inauguration of the Paris-Karachi-Beijing air service.

November 8 China and Norway exchanged letters of agreement on the reciprocal registration of trademarks.

November 10 The Chairman of the Presidential Council of
the People's Democratic Republic of Yemen, Salim
Rubayya Ali, arrived in Beijing for a nine-day visit.
He met Premier Zhou Enlai in the hospital on November
10, and Chairman Mao on November 12. An agreement
for economic and technical cooperation between the two
nations was signed on November 13.

November 12 Vice Minister of Foreign Affairs Han Xianlong
left Beijing for Japan to sign a Sino-Japanese maritime
transport agreement (on November 13) and make a
friendly visit at the invitation of the Japanese government. During his visit from November 12-19, he called
on Prime Minister Kakuei Tanaka and gave him a letter
from Premier Zhou Enlai. The Prime Minister urged
his visitor to make an early conclusion of the peace
treaty.

November 14 The appointment of Qiao Guanhua to replace
Ji Pengfei as minister of Foreign Affairs was announced
in Beijing.

• Lin Fang spoke to the UN First Committee on disarmament proposals. He said that the draft resolution
to stop nuclear tests was unacceptable to China unless
it was linked with measures to prohibit and destroy
existing nuclear weapons.

November 18 Huang Hua spoke to the UN General Assembly, welcoming the participation of the Palestine Liberation Organization (PLO) in the debate on the Mideast. He argued the essence of the Palestine problem was "Zionist aggression" and the superpower struggle for hegemony in the area.

November 20 China's pavilion and exhibits at the Chinese Economic and Trade Exhibition recently held in Georgetown, Guyana, were presented to the Guyana government.

November 21 Prince Abdor Reza Pahlavi, younger brother of the shahanshah of Iran, arrived in Beijing for a three-day visit. Vice Premier Li Xiannian met him on November 21, and Foreign Minister Qiao Guanhua hosted a banquet in his honor on the same day.

November 22 China and Upper Volta signed a protocol on agricultural cooperation projects in Ougadougou, capital of Upper Volta.

November 23 NCNA reported that 600,000 educated young people from Beijing, Tianjin, and nine provinces had gone to the countryside in the past few months to participate in socialist construction.

November 25 Secretary of State Henry A. Kissinger arrived in Beijing directly from the summit with the Soviet leaders at Vladivostok. Kissinger met Premier Zhou Enlai in the hospital, accompanied by Vice Premier Deng Xiaoping, on November 25. During the following three days, Kissinger held lengthy talks with Deng Xiaoping and Qiao Guanhua. In the joint communiqué, issued on November 29, they affirmed their commitment to the principles of the Shanghai communiqué. The two governments agreed that President Ford would visit China in 1975.
  • The Chinese Delegation, led by Du Xingyuan, left Beijing for Pyongyang to attend the twenty-seventh meeting of the Council of the Sino-Korean Yalu Hydroelectric Power Corporation. The protocol of the meeting was signed on December 27.

November 26 A People's Daily article entitled "Rifle Must Al-

ways Be in the Hands of Party and People," denounced
Lin Biao for opposing absolute party leadership over
the Army.   The article stated that Chairman Mao's
teaching that "The Party commands the gun," was an
unalterable principle of Marxism.
    • The Chinese Government and Party Delegation, led
by Yao Wenyuan left Beijing for Tirana to take part in
the celebrations of the thirtieth anniversary of the liberation of Albania.   President Enver Hoxha received the
delegation on November 28; the delegation left Tirana
for home on December 1.
    • The Algerian Trade Delegation, led by A. Cheref,
arrived in Beijing for a four-day visit.   The 1975 Sino-
Algerian trade protocol was signed on November 29.
    • Huang Hua spoke in the UN General Assembly in
support of the draft resolution cosponsored by China
with thirty-six other countries to have Cambodia's seat
in the UN occupied by representatives of Prince Sihanouk's government instead of the "Lon Nol clique."

November 27   The new Beijing-Teheran-Bucharest-Tirana air
    service run by the General Administration of Civil Avi-
    ation of China was formally inaugurated.   The Chinese
    Goodwill Delegation arrived in Teheran, Bucharest, and
    Tirana to take part in the celebration of the formal in-
    auguration.
        • The Chinese Government Trade Delegation, led by
    Li Qiang, left Beijing to visit Iran (November 27 to
    December 6), and Rumania (December 7-14).   The 1975
    Sino-Rumanian goods exchange and payment protocol
    was signed on December 14.   NCNA reported that al-
    most every people's commune now had a credit coopera-
    tive and one-third of the production brigades had credit
    service centers.

November 28   The People's Daily denounced the latest Amer-
    ican-Russian SALT agreement as simply "new emulation
    rules for their next round of nuclear arms race."   NCNA
    reported that 200,000 builders from Hebei province ar-
    rived at the construction sites of the Haihe River har-
    nessing project, initiating the second decade in the
    campaign to tame the historically unruly river.

November 29   A six-member Chinese delegation led by Ma
    Beide, left Shenyang for Sinuiju city in Korea to attend

the fourteenth meeting of the Sino-Korean Committee for Cooperation in Border River Transport. The protocol of the meeting was signed on December 26.

December 4   An exhibition of Chinese archaeological finds was held at the National Museum of the Netherlands in Amsterdam from December 4, 1974 to January 28, 1975.

December 5   Premier Zhou Enlai met Le Duc Tho and Xuan Thuy in a hospital in Beijing. Mr. Ikeda Daisaku, president of the Japanese Buddhist organization, Sokagakkai, visited Premier Zhou Enlai in the hospital in Beijing. The Chinese Premier sent his greetings to Mr. Miki (Japanese Prime Minister) and expressed a hope that the peace treaty could be concluded at an early date.
   • The Chinese Government Trade Delegation, led by Sun Suozhang left Beijing for Finland on a fifteen-day visit. The 1975 Sino-Finnish trade agreement was signed on December 20.

December 6   Mohammad Naim, the special envoy of Afghan President Mohammad Daoud, arrived in Beijing for a six-day visit. Premier Zhou Enlai met him in the hospital on December 7. A Sino-Afghan economic and technical cooperation agreement was signed on December 12.

December 7   China and Tunisia signed the exchange notes for local expenditure of the agreement on economic and technical cooperation in Tunis.

December 9   The US Senate Democratic leader Mike Mansfield, his wife, and his party arrived in Beijing for a six-day visit at the invitation of the Chinese People's Institute of Foreign Affairs. Premier Zhou Enlai met Senator and Mrs. Mansfield in the hospital. Vice Premier Deng Xiaoping held talks with the delegation.
   • China and Malagasy signed a protocol for sending a Chinese medical team to Malagasy in Tananarive.
   • The Chinese Economic and Trade Exhibition was held at the Venezuela Square in Caracas from December 9-22.

December 10   The American National Gallery of Art in Wash-

ington gave a reception prior to the opening of the
Chinese Archaeological Finds Exhibition in Washington.

December 11   China and Guinea signed a protocol, in Conakry, on China's sending a medical team to Guinea.

December 12   Premier Zhou Enlai met Pakistan Foreign Minister Aziz Ahmed in the hospital.

December 13   The Chinese Archaeological Finds Exhibition
opened to the public at the American National Gallery of
Art in Washington.

December 14   China and Gambia issued a joint communiqué
to establish diplomatic relations at the ambassadorial
level, following a visit by the head of the Chinese Mission in Mauritania Lin Bingnan.

December 16   President Mobutu Sese Seko of Zaire and his
party arrived in Beijing for a seven-day visit.   Premier Zhou Enlai met the delegation in the hospital on
December 16.   Vice Premier Deng Xiaoping hosted a
banquet on December 16.   Chairman Mao met the delegation on December 17.   Prince Norodom Sihanouk also
met the delegation on December 18.

December 17   Huang Hua spoke on the Korean question at a
plenary meeting of the UN General Assembly.   He said:
"In order to facilitate the independent and peaceful reunification of Korea, it is imperative to eliminate the
interference by outside force and have all the US
troops withdrawn from South Korea."
   • China and Finland signed a civil air transport
agreement in Beijing.

December 18   According to a Kyodo report, Japanese im-
porters had to cancel arrangements to take delivery of
the remaining 900,000 tons of the 4.9 million tons of
Chinese crude oil they had originally contracted for
1974.   The Japanese economic recession had reduced
demand for oil and furthermore, Chinese oil was being
imported at $13.50 a barrel compared with $12.60 for
Indonesia's equally good mina crude.   Price revision
talks were to be held in January 1975.
   • The Chinese Government Trade Delegation, led by

Chen Jie, left Beijing for Czechoslovakia on a seven-
day visit. The 1975 goods exchange and payment
agreement between the two nations was signed on December 20.

• A ceremony was held in Beijing for the handover
of a pair of white rhinoceroses presented by London
Zoo to the Beijing Zoo.

• NCNA reported that in 1974, China built a number
of large and medium-sized water conservancy projects
with state funds and many small ones financed by people's communes and production brigades. Involving
over six billion cubic meters of earth and stone work,
these projects had expanded irrigated acreage by two
million hectares and freed 1,660,000 hectares from
waterlogging.

December 19 The Korean Government Trade Delegation, led
by Li Tae Baek, arrived in Beijing for a nine-day visit.
The 1975 goods exchange protocol between the two nations was signed on December 21.

December 20 NCNA reported the completion of the Liujia
Gorge hydropower station in Gansu, China's largest
hydropower station.

• NCNA reported that China achieved initial success
in renovating the big hydraulic project on Yellow River.
With initial success, the Sanmen Gorge Dam (Henan)
now played a positive role in flood and ice-flow control, irrigation and power generation.

• The 1975 trade agreement between China and Finland was signed in Helsinki.

• The 1975 trade agreement between China and
Switzerland was signed in Berne.

• The Rumanian Scientific and Technical Cooperation
Delegation arrived in Beijing for a four-day visit and
attended the Sixteenth Session of the Joint Commission
of the two nations. The protocol of the meeting was
signed on December 21.

December 21 NCNA reported that in the first eleven months
of 1974, Shanghai produced fourteen percent more
watches and forty-one percent more cameras than in
the corresponding 1973 period while the output of bicycles and sewing machines reached all-time records.

December 23   China and Senegal signed a protocol in Dakar
on sending a Chinese medical team to Senegal.

December 25   Chinese and foreign Moslems in Beijing held
service at the Donggazu Mosque to mark the Annual
Corban Festival.

December 27   NCNA reported that China completed a 1,152
km oil pipeline, leading from Daqing to the North China
port of Qinhuangdao, with a parallel line in the northern section terminating at Dieling in Liaoning province.
   • The nine-member Chinese Government Economic
and Technical Delegation, led by Yang Rongiie, left
Beijing to visit Laos from December 27 to January 18,
1975.
   • The DRVN Economic Delegation, led by Nguyen
Van Hieu, arrived in Beijing for a five-day visit.
Vice Premier Li Xiannian met the delegation on December 28.   The 1975 agreement on China providing gratuitous economic aid to Vietnam was signed on December 28.

Chapter VI

1975

AN ANOMALOUS YEAR

The year began with the convention of the long-heralded Fourth National People's Congress at Beijing from January 13-18. Three major tasks faced the Congress: the revision of the constitution that had practically been suspended since the 1966 Cultural Revolution, the setting forth of basic policies--internal and external, and the reconstruction of the government leadership. The leadership had been badly decimated by the Cultural Revolution and the subsequent purges. All of these motions were first approved by the Central Committee of the Chinese Communist party in a meeting held January 8-10. The action by the Congress, although a mere formality, was necessary to put into effect the Central Committee's decisions that were concerned with the structure of policies of the government.

The revised constitution abolished the post of the chief of the state, which had been left vacant since its last incumbent, Liu Shaoqi, was purged at an early stage of the Cultural Revolution. The functions of the chief of the state were to be assumed by the Standing Committee of the Congress, whose new chairman was Zhu De, the former marshal who had led the Red Army to victory over the Nationalists in 1949. Although the Congress remained "the highest organ of state power," the constitution stipulated that it was to function under the leadership of the Communist party.

It was made clear by Zhang Chunqiao that the document aimed at "strengthening the party's centralized leadership of the structure of the state." He called attention to the provision that the chairman of the Central Committee of the Communist party (Mao Zedong) "commands the country's armed forces." In general the new constitution embodied the basic precepts of Chairman Mao. It held that "class contradictions" and "class struggle" must persist in a socialist society. It enjoined the state personnel to study earnestly the thought of Mao Zedong and "firmly put proletarian politics in command."

A significant feature of the new constitution was its enunciation on international politics. "China," the document said, "will never be a superpower." It would oppose "the imperialist and socialist imperialist policies of aggression and war and the hegemonism of the superpowers."

The Congress featured the appearance--perhaps the last major public appearance--of Premier Zhou Enlai. Although his appearances at some forty subsequent occasions during the year were given publicity in the press, they were, for the most part, short meetings with foreign visitors conducted in the hospital where, with the exception of brief periods, he had been a patient for the last eighteen months. The illness which kept him thus confined was not publicly diagnosed; the rumored diagnoses varied from heart disease to stomach cancer. Premier Zhou Enlai set forth the basic policies of the government when he presented the political report to the Congress. Citing Mao Zedong extensively, the Premier envisaged the economic development of China in two stages. The first stage was to build "an independent and relatively comprehensive industrial and economic system" before the year 1980. The second stage was to achieve the "comprehensive modernization" of agriculture, industry, national defense, and science and technology before the end of the century. The priorities for developing the national economy were agriculture, then light industry, and finally heavy industry.

In international affairs, Premier Zhou saw the contention for world hegemony between the two superpowers, the United States and the Soviet Union, growing more and more intense. Their struggle, said Zhou, "has extended to every corner of the world" and "is bound to lead to world war someday." While describing Sino-American relations as having improved since 1972, he pointed out that the relations between China and the Soviet Union had worsened because of the hostile actions on the part of the Soviet leadership. He called for vigilance and preparedness for war.

The new state of governmental ministers, as approved by the Congress, was headed by Premier Zhou Enlai. Under him were twelve deputy premiers, with Deng Xiaoping as the first deputy premier and Zhang Chunqiao as the second. Deng, the former secretary general of the Communist party, had been purged during the Cultural Revolution. He was rehabilitated in 1973 and since then had rapidly risen to a prominent position. In 1975, in addition to being the first deputy premier, he was named chief of the army staff, thus holding a key position in the political-military power structure. Besides the post of deputy premier, Zhang Chunqiao was also appointed chief political commissioner of the army. The post of minister of defense, which had been left vacant since Lin Biao's fall in 1971, was given to Ye Jianying. Since Ye was seventy-six years of age, he was generally regarded as devoid of political ambitions.

If the "moderates" were dominant in the central government, the "radicals" led by Jiang Qing (Chairman Mao's wife) and Zhang Chunqiao had a strong voice at the high levels of the party hierarchy, particularly the Standing Committee of the politburo. The leadership alignment appeared to be based on a compromise between the moderate and the radicals. It was, in fact, a transitional arrangement pending the final successions to Chairman Mao and Premier Zhou. Zhou was reported to be very ill in October when he failed to attend the celebrations for the twentieth anniversary of the People's Republic of China. Although Mao was absent from the Tenth Central Committee's Second Plenum and the Fourth National People's Congress in January, he did seem to be taking a more active role in the receiving of important state visitors than he had in the recent past, sitting in, as it were, for the ailing Zhou, and giving weight to the negotiations conducted, in Zhou's absence, by Vice Premier Deng Xiaoping.

In line with Premier Zhou's program to transform China into a "powerful modern socialist country" in twenty years, workers throughout the country were urged to make the utmost effort to raise production. Not all workers cooperated, however. In July, the government found it necessary to send 10,000 troops into thirteen factories in the city of Hangzhou, Zhejiang province, to help with production, which was stalled because of "disturbances from bourgeois factionalism." The situation was soon brought under control. The

principal mass movement of the previous year against Confucius and Lin Biao was transformed in the early months of
1975 into the paradox of a mobilizational campaign for production. The precise implications of the implementation of
Premier Zhou's program became clearer as the documents
were published in late October from a conference on the use
of the Dazhai model in agricultural planning. The conference
opened in Xiyang County, Shanxi province on September 15
and closed in Beijing on October 19. Vice Premier Hua
Guofeng delivered the summary report at the conference and
there he stressed the importance of developing "Dazhai-type
counties" throughout the country.

Statistics from various provinces indicated an industrial growth of nine to eleven percent for the first half of
1975. China had a good harvest for the year, as a record
wheat crop was reported for the summer.

China had large trade deficits amounting to $1.3 billion
in 1974. To improve the trade balance, Beijing took vigorous steps to increase its oil production. It was expected
that China's export would rise sharply in 1975. China was
believed to have extensive deposits of oil, ranking it possibly with Saudi Arabia. Its 1975 production was estimated
by Western experts to be around 1.3 million barrels a day
with expansion proceeding at an annual growth rate of twenty-five percent or more. Beijing used oil exports not only
to earn foreign exchange but also as an instrument to realize
its diplomatic aims. A contract signed in March to export
fifty-eight million barrels of crude oil to Japan, with the
hint that China could export more to meet Japanese needs,
was plainly intended to deter Japan from cooperating with
the Soviet Union in the huge project to develop oil production in eastern Siberia. Beijing's oil diplomacy was also extended to other parts of Asia, particularly Thailand, Hong
Kong, North Korea, and the Philippines.

Beijing was displeased at the United States' continued
maintenance of diplomatic relations with Taiwan and its repeated declarations to honor its mutual defense treaty with
Nationalist China. However, Chinese leaders indicated to
US congressmen and reporters that Beijing would like the
United States to maintain armed forces in Asia as a deterrent
to Soviet expansion. Secretary of State Henry A. Kissinger
arrived in Beijing on October 19 for a four-day visit. He

talked with Chairman Mao Zedong and held a series of conferences with Vice Premier Deng Xiaoping. China opposed
Washington's détente with Moscow, but Secretary Kissinger
deemed it necessary to avoid "needless confrontation" with
the Soviet Union.

China became the United States' largest grain customer
in 1974, buying three million tons of US wheat. But the
situation drastically changed in 1975 when Beijing canceled
two orders of wheat for a total of 983,000 tons. No official
reasons were given for these cancellations, but economic observers found several reasons for the Chinese action. These
included China's foreign exchange shortages, improved
weather conditions early in the year, a decline in wheat
prices in the world market, and the traces of smut, a plant
disease, found in the US wheat imported in 1974. On the
other hand, Beijing showed a renewed interest in purchasing
high-technology equipment from the United States. In December, President Ford visited Beijing for further negotiations. Again, neither side was convinced by the logic of the
arguments of the other on an American policy of détente with
Moscow.

Beijing did its best to embarrass the post-Jiang Jieshi
leadership in Taipei by releasing, with considerable publicity,
two groups of Guomindang prisoners and permitting those
among them who wished to leave the mainland to return to
Taiwan. This left the Guomindang government with the difficult decision of whether or not to accept the repatriation
of its own erstwhile partisans. The first group who chose
to return were ten former Guomindang senior officers who
arrived in Hong Kong in mid-April, freed by an amnesty
granted war criminals by the NPC at Mao's instruction.
They were denied entry by the government in Taiwan and
two months later one of the ten committed suicide in Hong
Kong out of frustration over his situation. In September,
144 alleged former Guomindang agents were released, sixty
of which sought to return to Taiwan and were accepted via
receiving stations on the offshore islands still held by the
Taiwan government.

Although Sino-Soviet relations had deteriorated over
the course of the year, there was actually rather little direct interaction. The Soviet border negotiating team, headed
by Leonid Ilyichev, returned to Beijing once again early in

February, sent off with a major Pravda editorial calling on China to take "really constructive steps" in the negotiations. The team returned to Moscow three months later, giving no indication that progress in the negotiations had been made. Two months later the Chinese denounced the European security conference in Helsinki and accusing the Soviet leaders of "following Hitler's beaten track" by publicly calling for peace and privately pursuing expansionist aims. The Soviet reply was a lengthy article in Kommnist calling for unity among Communist party in opposing to Maoist leadership of the CCP.

Beijing supported a united Western Europe and formally recognized the European Economic Community on May 8, believing that it would help restrain the Soviet Union. On May 12, Chinese Deputy Premier Deng Xiaoping arrived in Paris for a six-day state visit. He had several meetings with French President Valery Giscard d'Estaing and Premier Jacques Chirac and invited them both to visit China in 1976. The two nations agreed to hold regular political consultations and to set up a joint economic commission to promote commercial exchanges.

Beijing pressured Japan to sign a treaty of peace and friendship which would assure that both countries would oppose attempts of any third nation to establish hegemony in Asia. The Japanese government, under Premier Takeo Miki, desired closer relations with Beijing, for Japan saw no threat from China but was not sure about the Soviet Union. Japan, however, did not deem it advisable to be dragged into the Sino-Soviet conflict, and therefore the treaty negotiations continued with no sign of immediate conclusion.

President Kim Il Sung of North Korea arrived in Beijing for an official visit on April 18. The purpose of his visit was not made known but if President Kim was seeking China's military support for a new Korean War, he might have been disappointed. It seemed that Beijing had cautioned North Korean against military adventures. In any case, at a banquet given by President Kim in honor of the Chinese leaders on April 26, Chinese Deputy Premier Deng Xiaoping stressed China's support of a "peaceful unification" of Korea. Beijing, however, backed the North Korean position that the United States should withdraw its troops from South Korea and negotiate directly with North Korea.

With the US withdrawal from Indo-China, Beijing was faced not only with the danger of Soviet penetration, but also with the possibility of Vietnamese hegemony in Southeast Asia. A unified state from a consolidation of North and South Vietnam could first gain ascendency over Laos and Cambodia and then extend its political influence to the rest of Southeast Asia. Furthermore, North Vietnam leaned much closer to Moscow than to Beijing.

China had maintained closer relations with the Cambodian insurgents, however. A delegation of Cambodian Communist leaders visiting Beijing on August 15 was given a warm welcome by the Chinese. An agreement on economic and technical cooperation between the two countries was signed on August 18. The Cambodian Communists seemed responsive to the Chinese efforts at having Prince Norodom Sihanouk, the former Cambodian head of state who had lived in Beijing since his overthrow in 1970, restored to some nominal position in the new government.

China established diplomatic relations with the Philippines on June 9 and with Thailand on July 1. The winning over of two formerly anti-Communist countries further extended China's influence in Southeast Asia. Chinese and Indian troops clashed on October 20 in the disputed territory of Arunachal Pradesh along the eastern border between the two countries. Four Indian soldiers were killed. India protested, but China claimed that it was the Indian troops that crossed the Chinese border. Meanwhile Beijing recognized the new government in Bangladesh in late August, just two weeks after the assassination of Mujibur Rahman, and continued to engage in cooperative development projects with Pakistan, which to date had involved more than $330 million in Chinese loans and grants to the Dacca government.

Strengthening its public identity with the Third World and improving its relations with Third-World nations were projects to which Beijing devoted considerable attention during the course of the year. More than half of China's nearly fifty state visitors in 1975 were from Third-World nations, several of which established diplomatic relations with China pursuant to these visits. A modest program of Chinese foreign aid and technical assistance continued, with the model project in this program, the Tanzanian-Zambian Railway, opening in October, a year ahead of schedule.

January 1   The People's Daily, the Red Flag and the Liberation Army Daily carried the New Year's Day joint editorial entitled "New Year Message," to call upon the
people to grasp revolution and promote production, and
the party committees at all levels to adhere to the principles: "practice Marxism, and not revisionism; unite,
and don't split; be open and aboveboard, and don't intrigue and conspire."
  • All Beijing newspapers gave front-page prominence
to a large photograph of Chairman Mao Zedong.

January 2   China and Dahomey signed a protocol on an agricultural project and letters of exchange on related local
expenses.

January 3   Dutch Foreign Minister M. van der Stoel arrived
in Beijing for a six-day visit. He met Premier Zhou
Enlai in the hospital on January 4, and held talks with
Vice Premier Deng Xiaoping.

January 5   The Thai Visiting Delegation, led by Chatichai
Choonhavan, arrived in Beijing for a five-day visit at
the invitation of the Chinese Committee for the Promotion of International Trade. Premier Zhou Enlai met the
delegation on January 8.

January 6   In New York, China and Botswana signed a joint
communiqué to establish diplomatic relations at the ambassadorial level.

January 7   Prime Minister Dominic Mintoff of Malta arrived
in Beijing for a three-day visit. Premier Zhou Enlai
met him in hospital on January 7, and Chairman Mao
met him on January 9. In his banquet speech, he said
that his visit was primarily the development of commerce
with China.

January 8   The Tenth Central Committee of the CCP held
its Second Plenary Session from January 8-10 to discuss
the preparatory work for the forthcoming National People's Congress. At the same time, it was confirmed
that the plenum had elected Deng Xiaoping to be vice
chairman of the Central Committee of the CCP and a
member of the Standing Committee of the politburo.

January 9 Li Fuchun, member of the Tenth Central Committee of the CCP and vice premier of the State Council,
died of illness in Beijing at the age of seventy-five.
A solemn ceremony was held in Beijing to pay respect
to him on January 15. Premier Zhou Enlai presided
the ceremony, and Vice Premier Deng Xiaoping delivered a memorial speech.

January 12 Mr. Franz Joseph Strauss, chairman of the
Christian Socialist Union of West Germany, arrived in
Beijing for a six-day visit at the invitation of the Chinese People's Institute for Foreign Affairs. Chairman
Mao met him on January 16, and Premier Zhou Enlai
met him in the hospital for an hour in the afternoon
on the same day. During his visit, he watched a combat exercise of the 196th infantry division outside Tianjin. The reception at the German Embassy was cancelled because of an alleged threat by German students
at the Foreign Language Institute in Beijing to kill the
"reactionary" visitor.

January 13 The First Session of the Fourth National People's
Congress took place in Beijing from January 13-17. On
the last day it adopted: (1) a new PRC constitution,
which differed from that of 1954, with no position for
the PRC chairman; (2) Zhang Chunqiao's report on the
revision of the constitution; and (3) Zhou Enlai's report
on the work of the government. Both reports were delivered on January 13.
    • The delegation of the Japan-China Economic Asso-
ciation, led by Inayama Yoshihira, arrived in Beijing for
a five-day visit. Premier Zhou Enlai met the delegation
in the hospital on January 16, and Vice Premier Li
Xiannian held talks with the delegation on long-term
coal and oil imports and on future technological cooperation between the two nations.

January 16 The preliminary negotiations for the peace treaty
were resumed in Tokyo by Vice Foreign Minister Togo
Fumihiko and Ambassador Chen Chu.

January 17 In Ventiane, China and Laos signed minutes of
talks on building a highway from upper Laos to Luang
Prabang city and dwellings for 500 people in the same
city, as well as a protocol on the working conditions

and living standards of Chinese engineering and technical personnel in Laos. It was further reported in
Ventiane that China was extending interest-free loans
to build the Nam Bak-Luang Prabang highway, a meeting hall, official living quarters and the headquarters
and living quarters of the joint police and a hospital in
Luang Prabang.

• The First Session of the Fourth National People's
Congress elected Zhu De as Chairman, and Dong Biwu,
Song Qingling, Kang Sheng, Liu Bocheng, Wu De, Wei
Guoqing, Saifudin, Guo Moruo, Tan Zhenlin, Li Jing-
quan, Ulanfu, Ngapo Ngawang Jigme and others as
deputy Chairmen of the NPC's Standing Committee. The
NPC appointed the following members of the State Coun-
cil: Premier, Zhou Enlai; Vice Premiers, Deng Xiao-
ping, Zhang Chunqiao, Li Xiannian, Chen Xilian, Ji
Dengkui, Hua Guofeng, Chen Yonggui, Wu Guixian,
Wang Zhen, Yu Qiuli, Gu Mu, and Sun Jian; Minister
of Foreign Affairs, Qiao Guanhua; Minister of National
Defense, Ye Jianying; Minister of Public Security, Hua
Guofeng, and other ministers.

January 18   China and Sweden signed an agreement on maritime transport in Beijing.

January 19   Kazimierz Mijal, general secretary of the Communist party of Poland, arrived in Beijing for a visit
to China at the invitation of the Central Committee of
the CCP. He left Beijing for home on March 16. During his stay, he met Yao Wenyuan and Wang Hongwen.

January 20   The Standing Committee of the Fourth NPC held
its first session. Jiang Hua was appointed president
of the Supreme People's Court, and Ji Pengfei, secretary general of the Standing Committee of the Fourth
NPC.

• Mr. Hori Shigeru, a senior member of the Liberal
Democratic party, met Vice Premier Deng Xiaoping in
Beijing, and visited Premier Zhou Enlai in the hospital.
Premier Zhou told Mr. Hori that he highly valued the
stand which had been taken by Mr. Miyazawa in Moscow,
rejecting Gromyko's proposal to bypass the question of
the four northern islands and conclude a treaty of
friendship and goodwill.

January 22 Amadou Mahtar M'Bow, director general of the United Nations Educational, Scientific, and Cultural Organization (Unesco), and his party arrived in Beijing for a seven-day visit. He met Vice Premier Deng Xiaoping on January 27, and Premier Zhou Enlai in the hospital on January 28.

January 24 The Chinese Agricultural Science Delegation, led by Liang Zhangwu, visited Albania from January 24 to February 9.
  • The Chinese Government Trade Delegation, led by Li Jiang, visited Pakistan (January 24–30), and Sri Lanka (January 31 to February 7). The 1975 Sino–Sri Lanka trade protocol was signed on February 7.
  • The Government Trade Delegation of the GDR, led by Kurt Fenske, arrived in Beijing for a four-day visit. The 1975 Sino-German agreement on goods exchange and payment was signed on January 25.

January 27 The Chinese Government Economic Delegation, led by Dao Qi, left Beijing for a twelve-day visit to Nepal. An agreement was signed on February 2 by which China would provide the finance and technical aid for the construction of a 407 km highway between Pokhara and Surkhet, costing more than 800 million rupees.

January 28 According to the New York Times, China, in two successive measures, cancelled all her outstanding orders for American wheat for the crop year beginning July 1, 1975. This still left fifty-three million bushels on order to be delivered before June 30, 1975.

January 29 The Sino-Italian Amalgamated Committee to Promote and Develop the Trade and Economic Relations between the two nations was formed in Beijing.
  • President Gerald R. Ford sent a letter to Premier Zhou Enlai, congratulating him on his appointment as Premier of the State Council.

January 30 Foreign Minister Alieu Badara N'Jie of Gambia arrived in Beijing for a seven-day visit. He met Premier Zhou Enlai in the hospital on January 31, and held talks with Vice Premier Deng Xiaoping on February 2. The two nations signed an economic and technical cooperation agreement on February 2. He also lunched with Prince Norodom Sihanouk during his visit.

January 31 Prime Minister Eric Williams of Trinidad and Tobago arrived in Beijing for a seven-day visit. He met Premier Zhou Enlai in the hospital on February 1, and held talks with Vice Premier Deng Xiaoping. An agreement was signed on February 3 to establish embassies in the two nations' capitals.

• Minister of Defense Sir Albert Maori Kiki from Papua-New Guinea arrived in Beijing for a fourteen-day visit. He met Vice Premier Li Xiannian on February 7. Sir Albert subsequently stated that China was interested in buying tea, coffee, cocoa, copra, palm oil, timber and copper from Papua-New Guinea in exchange for Chinese oil and rice.

February 2 The State Council and the Military Commission of the Central Committee of the CCP issued a joint spring festival circular. It called on the people to launch a movement to support the Army and give preferential treatment to the families of the army men, and the army units to launch a movement to support the government and cherish the people, in accordance with Chairman Mao's consistent teachings.

February 4 A serious earthquake of 7.3 magnitude occurred in the Yingkou-Haicheng area of Liaoning province, causing damage of varying degrees in the epicentral region. Losses and casualties were minimized as a result of precautions taken in following observations by seismologists.

• NCNA reported that on December 28, 1974, the Nanjing Purple Mountain Observatory of the Chinese Academy of Sciences spotted a faint celestial body at right ascension on three hours 4.3 minutes and declination plus eighteen degree thirteen minutes. It moved rapidly in a north by west direction with an angular velocity of more than half a degree per day.

• The Liuqiaxia hydroelectric power station, the biggest in China, went into operation in the upper reaches of the Yellow River. With a total capacity of 1,225,000 kw, the station generated 5,700 million kwhr of electricity a year.

February 5   NCNA reported that a Beijing power plant succeeded in using an electronic computer to replace man-
ual labor in controlling the operation of a 100,000 kw
coal-burning steam turbine generating set.
   • China agreed to conduct some of its trade with
Japan in American dollars, including the oil trade.
The way was thus clear for the signing of new oil contracts in March.
   • A Sino-Laotian trade agreement was signed in Beijing.   In the agreement, China agreed to grant loans
to Laos for the purchase from China of medicine, lor-
ries, canned food, textiles, building materials and oil.

February 6   China participated in the Thirty-third World
Table Tennis Championship held in Calcutta, India from
February 6–11.

February 9   The People's Daily carried an editorial entitled
"Study Well the Theory of the Dictatorship of the Proletariat."   The article initiated a fresh campaign for the
nation to study a new "important instruction" by Chairman Mao.

February 11   A festival of theatrical works from the Xinjiang
Uighur autonomous region, Shaanxi, Heilongjiang and
Sichuan opened in Beijing.   From March 20 on, the
areas of origin of the works in the continuing festival
were provinces of Guangdong, Hubei, Henan, Yunnan,
Jilin and Gansu.

February 12   Leonid Ilyichev arrived in Beijing to head the
Soviet delegation for border talks.   The first round
of the talks was held on February 15.
   • It was reported that work was about to start on
the first French petrochemical complex to be built in
China, at a cost of 1–3 billion francs.   According to
Radio Paris, about 500 Frenchmen and their families
were to spend three years at the site, 800 km northeast of Beijing, during the construction of their plant.

February 15   The Preparatory Committee for the Third National Games of the PRC issued a circular to physical
culture workers and sportsmen in Taiwan province and
those among Taiwan-born overseas Chinese, warmly welcoming them to form a sports delegation for the Third

National Games to be held in Beijing from September 7-27, 1975.

February 16   New Zealand Minister of Agriculture and Fisheries Colin James Moyle and his party arrived in Beijing for an eight-day visit.   He met Hua Guofeng on February 20.
  • The Chinese Government Delegation, led by Jiang Huilian, arrived in Banjul, Gambia for a seven-day visit and attended the celebrations of the tenth anniversary of Gambian independence.

February 18   An exhibition of archaeological finds of the PRC was held at the Palace Fine Arts in Brussels from February 18 to April 14.

February 20   The Mozambique Friendship Delegation, led by Samora Moises Machel, arrived in Beijing for a ten-day visit at the invitation of the Chinese government.   He met Premier Zhou Enlai in hospital on February 20.
  • NCNA reported that Palace foundations dating back 3,400 to 3,500 years, and a tomb containing skeletons of slaves killed as human sacrifices, had been unearthed at the site of city walls of the Shang Dynasty (sixteenth century B.C. to eleventh century B.C.) in the ancient city of Banlong in Huangbi county, Hubei province.

February 22   The People's Daily published a list of quotations from Marx, Engels and Lenin on the dictatorship of the proletariat to support the campaign of implementing Chairman Mao's instruction.
  • Vice Premier Chen Xilian left Beijing for Katmandu, Nepal for a six-day visit and attended the coronation of His Majesty King Birendra Bir Birkram Shah Dev.

February 24   Premier Zhou Enlai met Prince Norodom Sihanouk in the hospital in Beijing and gave his support for the Cambodian revolutionaries.   Both leaders were critical of American backing for the Lon Nol regime.

February 27   The Chinese Economic and Trade Exhibition was held in Kingston, Jamaica from February 27 to March 11.
  • President Henri Lopez of the People's Republic of

the Congo arrived in Beijing for a ten-day visit. He
met Premier Zhou Enlai in the hospital on February 28
and was entertained by Prince Norodom Sihanouk on
March 2. An economic and technical cooperation agreement between the two nations was signed on March 2.

February 28 The Chinese Military Delegation, led by Yang
Yong, visited Hanoi from February 28 to March 17 at
the invitation of the DRVN.
  • Royal Lao Airlines inaugurated services between
Vientiane and Guangzhou.

March 1 The fishery negotiations between China and Japan
were formally resumed in Tokyo. Foreign Minister
Miyazawa told the press on the following day that Chinese military alert zones on the high seas were blocking the conclusion of a fishery agreement.

March 2 The Red Flag carried an article entitled "On the
Social Basis of the Lin Biao Anti-Party Clique" by Yao
Wenyuan. The essay was a well-argued, essentially
realistic (rather than simply radical) approach to the
problems facing China in the transition from socialism
to communism.

March 3 The Sino-Hungarian goods exchange and payment
agreement was signed in Budapest.

March 4 Premier Zhou Enlai met Ieng Sary, special adviser
to the deputy prime minister of the Royal Government
of National Unity of Cambodia, in the hospital in Beijing.
  • The fourth round of peace treaty negotiations was
held in Tokyo without any progress. The Chinese reportedly insisted that opposition to the third-country
hegemony was an "important principle," and therefore
wished to translate paragraph seven of the 1972 joint
statement by Premiers Kakuei Tanaka and Zhou Enlai
into express provision of the treaty. The Japanese
position was that such a reference to the third-country
hegemony was not proper in a bilateral treaty, and
clearly the Japanese were unwilling to put their name
to a treaty with wording which would be taken as a
clear and hostile reference to the Soviet Union.

March 7 NCNA carried the March 7 statement of Prince

Sihanouk, warning the Americans to stop interfering in Cambodian affairs.

March 8   Foreign Minister Vernon Mwaanga of Zambia arrived in Beijing for a four-day visit at the invitation of the Chinese government. Premier Zhou Enlai met him in the hospital on March 10, and Prince Sihanouk met him on March 11. At the banquet, he said that Zambia preferred to achieve the independence of Zimbabwe (Rhodesia) "around the conference table."

March 11   The 1975 Sino-Bulgarian goods exchange and payment agreement was signed in Beijing.
   • The 1975 Sino-Polish goods exchange and payment agreement was signed in Warsaw.
   • China and Guinea signed the 1975 trade protocol and an agreement on the provision of commodity loan by China to Guinea in Conakry.

March 12   Guyanese Prime Minister L.F.S. Burnham, his wife, and his party arrived in Beijing for a six-day visit at the invitation of Premier Zhou Enlai. He visited Premier Zhou Enlai in the hospital on March 12. An agreement on economic and technical cooperation between the two nations was signed on March 14. The Tanjug reported that China was understood to have granted Guyana credit totalling twenty million RMB (renminbi), the equivalent of $10 million.
   • Foreign Minister S. Rajarratnam of Singapore arrived in Beijing for a ten-day visit at the invitation of Foreign Minister Qiao Guanhua. Premier Zhou Enlai met Mr. Rajarratnam in the hospital on March 16. At the end of his visit he said that the two sides had agreed to intensify their economic, cultural and social exchanges. However, an early exchange of ambassadors was not thought likely.

March 15   Iraqi Foreign Minister Ahmad al-Iraqi arrived in Beijing for a seven-day visit. Premier Zhou Enlai met him in the hospital on March 17. The two nations signed a long-term trade agreement, sports agreement, and medical protocol on March 19.

March 17   The Standing Committee of the Fourth National People's Congress decided at its second session to grant a special amnesty to, and to release, all war criminals in custody. In the report, Hua Guofeng said that those released would enjoy citizens' rights, be given suitable jobs if able to work and if not, a proper livelihood; those who were ill would get free medical care. Those who wished to return to Taiwan would be free to do so and facilities would be provided for travel. If they subsequently wished to return they would be welcome.

March 19 The Supreme People's Court granted a special amnesty to all war criminals in custody and released them in accordance with instructions given by Chairman Mao and the Central Committee of the CCP, and the decision adopted by the Second Session of the Standing Committee of the Fourth NPC. The war criminals released by special amnesty this time numbered 293.
  • Parliamentary Under Secretary for Trade E.P. Deakins arrived in Beijing for a nine-day visit and opened the British Machine Tool and Scientific Instruments Exhibition in Shanghai on March 25. He met Li Jiang in Beijing on March 22.

March 20 NCNA reported that China made her first precision phase laser geodimeter in geodetic survey. The geodimeter had proved effective in field work over the past year under a variety of topographical and climatic conditions.
  • NCNA reported that the preparatory groups for the Ninth All-China Trade Union Congress, the Tenth Congress of the Communist Youth League of China, and the Fourth National Women's Congress held their first meetings in Beijing from February 26 to March 20.

March 21 An oil mission, led by Geronimo Velasco, president of the Philippine National Oil Company, arrived in Beijing for a six-day visit. During its stay in Beijing, the mission concluded an agreement with the China National Chemical Import and Export Corporation.

March 23 Chinese party and state leaders Ye Jianying, Hua Guofeng, Wu De, and Jiang Hua received all the personnel recently released by special amnesty.

March 27 Vice Premier Chen Yonggui arrived in Mexico for a ten-day visit. President and Mrs. Luis Echeverria

met him on March 28.   He made a stopover in Bucharest,
Rumania on his way home from Mexico on April 6.

March 28   A previously arranged visit by a Chinese drama
group was cancelled by the US State Department after
the Chinese had refused to delete the phrase "We are
determined to liberate Taiwan" from a song in its program.   Beijing protested vigorously at what was described as a violation of the Shanghai communiqué of
1972.
    • Speaker Carl Albert and John Rhodes of the US
House of Representatives arrived in Beijing for a ten-
day visit.   Vice Premier Deng Xiaoping met them on
April 1.

April 1   Tunisian Prime Minister Hadi Nuwayrah arrived in
Beijing for an eight-day visit at the invitation of Premier Zhou Enlai.   Premier Zhou Enlai met him in the
hospital on April 3.   It was reported by Tunisian Radio
that two projects had been agreed upon, to be financed
under the 17-million dinar five-year loan from China,
namely the construction of the Sidi Salem-Cap-Bon Dam
and 1,000 Chinese railway-wagons to carry phosphate.
    • The Lanqiang road bridge in Lanqi county on the
upper reaches of the Jiandong River was opened to
traffic.   It was 1,041 meters long and eleven meters
wide, making it the longest road bridge in the province.
    • A fairly well-preserved Chinese seaboat of the
Song Dynasty (960-1270 A.D.) was unearthed in
Zhuanzhou Bay, Fujian province.   Chinese archaeological workers also found valuable relics in the boat.   Also unearthed were pottery and porcelain, copper and
iron wares, articles made of bamboo, wood and rattan,
Chinese chess pieces, bones of edible animals and fruit
kernels.
    • The Red Flag carried an article entitled "On Exer-
cising All-Round Dictatorship Over the Bourgeoisie" by
Zhang Chunqiao.

April 2   Dong Biwu, acting head of the state and vice chairman of the Standing Committee of the Fourth NPC, died
in Beijing at age eighty-nine.   A solemn ceremony was
held in Beijing on April 7 to pay last respects to him.
Vice Chairman Wang Hongwen presided over the ceremony, and Vice Chairman Ye Jianying delivered a memorial speech.

April 4   Vice Premier Li Xiannian paid a visit to Iran from
          April 4-10 and was received by the shah and by Prime
          Minister Hoveyda. In his speech of April 5, Li praised
          the successful policies of the Iranian government which,
          under the leadership of the shah, had raised national
          prosperity.

April 5   Jiang Jieshi (Chiang Kai-shek) died as the result
          of an illness in Taiwan, at the age of eighty-seven.
          He was succeeded by Vice President Yan Jiagan.

April 6   The Belgian Government Economic Delegation, led
          by Prince Albert, arrived in Beijing for a ten-day visit
          and opened the Belgian Industrial Exhibition, held in
          Beijing from April 8-19.

April 7   Swissair inaugurated its Zurich-Geneva-Athens-
          Bombay-Beijing-Shanghai air service. The Swiss Good-
          will Delegation, led by Bundersrar Willy Ritschard, ar-
          rived in Beijing to celebration the occasion. The dele-
          gation left Beijing for home on April 15.

April 10 China reached an agreement with Belgium, the
          Netherlands and Luxembourg on reciprocal registration
          of trademarks, and notes were exchanged to this effect.

April 11 A settlement of the Shang Dynasty (sixteenth cen-
          tury to eleventh century B.C.), the first one found
          south of the Yangzi River, was uncovered in Jiangxi
          province. The discovery was made in Wuzheng village
          of Shanqi People's Commune in Qiangjiang county.
          Archaeological excavations over an area of 1,000 square
          meters were carried out on three occasions in a year
          beginning winter 1973. Significant discoveries on the
          large numbers of production implements and household
          utensils, including Chinese characters and pot marks
          carved on pottery, provided fresh data for the study
          of the origin and evolution of the Chinese written lan-
          guage.
             • The Chinese Technical Group of Fresh Water Fish
          Breeding, led by Zang Hongdao, made a study tour to
          Mexico in accordance with the provisions in the exchange
          of notes on cultural, scientific, and technological ex-
          change between the two nations.

April 13 Ten of the war criminals released under the March

17 decision left Beijing for Taiwan via Hong Kong,
where they arrived on April 14.

April 16   Thai Foreign Minister, Mr. Chatichai Choonhavan,
said the 350,000 Chinese in Thailand with Taiwan pass-
ports would have to either change them to PRC pass-
ports, take up Thai citizenship, or become stateless.
He added that the Chinese language study program in
Thailand would also have to be modified.
   • The Chinese Government Trade Delegation, led by
Chen Jie, left Beijing for Mongolia for a six-day visit.
The 1975 Sino-Mongolian protocol on the mutual supply
of goods was signed on April 20.

April 17   The Chinese leadership greeted the victory of the
Khmers Rouge on the liberation of Phnom Penh with
messages, public meetings and commentaries. The high
point of the celebrations was the call which Vice Premier Deng Xiaoping made at the mansion of Prince
Sihanouk in Beijing, bringing a copy of the message
dated April 17 from Chairman Mao, Premier Zhou Enlai,
and Zhu De.
   • President Kim Il-sung, the state and party leader
of the Democratic People's Republic of Korea, visited
China from April 17-26. He met Chairman Mao in the
afternoon of his arrival in Beijing, and Premier Zhou
Enlai in the hospital on April 19. He held talks mainly
with Vice Premier Deng Xiaoping. A joint communiqué
was issued on April 26 in which China specified their
support for a peaceful reunification of Korea and demands for the withdrawal of American troops from South
Korea.
   • According to the China-Japan trade agreement, the
First Session of the China-Japan Joint Trade Committee
was held in Beijing from April 18-22.

April 18   Letters providing for mutual exemption from income
and other taxes on freight earnings by vessels of China
and Sri Lanka in their ports were exchanged at a ceremony in Colombo.

April 19   The protocol of the seventeenth meeting of the
China-Vietnam Border Railway was signed in Hanoi.
   • Belgian Prime Minister Leo Tindemans arrived in
Beijing for a nine-day visit. He met Chairman Mao on

April 20 for thirty-five minutes. He also met Premier
Zhou Enlai in the hospital on the same day. A Belgian
Radio report said that it had been agreed that Belgium
would supply a coal-fuelled power station to China, and
that shipping and air agreements had also been concluded.
   • China and Greece reached an agreement on the
reigstration of trademarks on a reciprocal basis.

April 20 Vice Premier Li Xiannian visited Pakistan from April
20-25. During the visit he declared China's main policies in South Asia were to render resolute support to
the people of South Asia in their struggle against hegemony and expansionism. It was announced that China
had offered to supply Pakistan with a wide range of
textile machinery and a cement making plant on extremely good terms.

April 23 An acupuncture class for foreign doctors was in-
augurated at the Beijing Traditional Chinese Medicine
Research Institute, sponsored by the Ministry of Public
Health, UNDP, and WHO.

April 24 NPC Chairman Zhu De and Premier Zhou Enlai
greeted the fifth anniversary of summit conference of
Indo-Chinese peoples.
   • The Yemen Arab Public Delegation, led by Lt. Col.
Mujahed Abou Shawareb, arrived in Beijing for a nine-
day visit. Premier Zhou Enlai met the delegation in the
hospital on April 30.

April 26 Shandong province held its Sixth Women's Congress.
   • Chinese Ambassador to Sri Lanka Huang Mingda,
visited the Maldives from April 26-30. While in the
Maldives he signed a communiqué formally handing over
telecommunications equipment as a gift of the Chinese
government.

April 28 Vice Premiers Deng Xiaoping and Chen Xilian
called at the mansion of the Cambodian head of state
and paid last respects to the remains of Queen Sisowath
Kossamak of Cambodia in Beijing. Zhu De and Zhou
Enlai sent a message to Prince Sihanouk, expressing
deep condolences on her death. The remains were
cremated at a ceremony in Beijing on May 4.

April 29   The Chinese government issued a strong statement
           condemning the Indian government's action in Sikkim.
             • The Ministry of Foreign Affairs issued a statement,
           expressing firm support for the statement of April 26
           and 27, 1975 respectively made by DRVN and PRG-
           RSVN.   The statements reiterated that the US must
           strictly implement the Paris agreement.
             • NCNA reported that China had made rapid ad-
           vances in its postal and telecommunications services.
           Compared with the liberation year of 1949, the number
           of post and telegraph offices had increased more than
           600 percent, that of rural post offices 6,190 percent
           and the total mileage of mail routes, 570 percent.
           China now maintained postal and telecommunications con-
           nections with some 100 countries and regions in differ-
           ent parts of the world.

April 30   Mao Zedong, Zhu De, and Zhou Enlai greeted lib-
           eration of Saigon.   The message stated that "We Chi-
           nese people have always regarded the Vietnamese peo-
           ple's struggle as our own struggle and their victory as
           our own victory."   Vice Premier Deng Xiaoping extended
           his warm congratulations at RSVN and DRVN Embassies
           in Beijing to hand over the copies of this message of
           greeting from the three Chinese leaders on May 1.

May 1   Party and state leaders joined the people in Beijing
         in celebrating May 1, International Labor Day.   A large
         photograph of Chairman Mao was printed on the front
         page of the People's Daily and all other papers in the
         capital in celebration of the occasion.

May 2   More than 10,000 people in Beijing gathered at a
         grand rally in the Great Hall of the People to celebrate
         the liberation of Saigon and the entire South Vietnam.
         Ye Jianying spoke at the rally.   He described the vic-
         tory as a blow against "imperialism, colonialism, and
         hegemonism."

May 3   According to the People's Daily (October 25, 1976),
         a politburo meeting took place at which Mao Zedong
         warned Jiang Qing, Wang Hongwen, Zhang Chunqiao
         and Yao Wenyuan against "functioning as a gang of
         four" and told them "Don't do it anymore."

May 4 Sir Christopher Soames, the EEC commissioner for
external affairs, visited Beijing at the invitation of the
Chinese People's Institute for Foreign Affairs from May
4-11. He met Vice Premier Li Xiannian on May 8, and
Premier Zhou Enlai in the hospital on the same day.
An agreement was reached on the establishment of official relations between China and the community, and on
the accreditation of the Chinese representative to the
EEC.

May 5 Ilyichev left China after a sojourn which had lasted
since February 12. Kankovsky, the deputy head, stayed
in Beijing. Mr. Ilyichev's return to Moscow was said
to be temporary, and did not signify a break in the
border talks.

May 7 China and Cameroon signed a protocol on sending a
Chinese medical team in Yaounde.

May 8 The 1975 Sino-Cuban trade protocol was signed in
Beijing.
• A ceremony for exchanging notes on the construc-
tion of the Shihr-Sayhur Road in Democratic Yemen with
Chinese assistance was held in Aden.

May 10 The 1975 Sino-Afghan protocol on the exchange of
goods was signed in Kabul.

May 11 Two Chinese freighters arrived at Da Nang, South
Vietnam, loaded with rice, textiles, medicines and other
goods from the Chinese to aid the Vietnamese people.

May 12 A signing ceremony for the joint statement of the
China-Japan Friendship Association and Japanese Social-
ist party (JSP) was held in Beijing. The Japanese So-
cialist Party Delegation visited Beijing from May 5-12.
On May 9, Mr. Tomomi Narita said in Beijing that the
JSP gave "basic consent" to the Chinese stand on hege-
mony, but that this did not mean hostility to the Soviet
Union.
• At the invitation of the French government, Vice
Premier Deng Xiaoping and Foreign Minister Qiao Guan-
hua made an official visit to France from May 12-18.
Vice Premier Deng Xiaoping was treated with the protocol
normally reserved for a head of state. He had several

meetings with President Giscard d'Estaing, and Prime Minister Chirac. Although no formal communiqué was issued, a number of significant agreements were made: regular Sino-French consultations would be held at the foreign ministerial level; a joint economic commission would be established to promote Sino-French bilateral trade; the French president and prime minister accepted Deng's invitation to visit China the following year.

May 13 The Chinese Government Trade Delegation, led by Chen Jie, left Beijing for Accra on an eight-day visit. The 1975 Sino-Ghana trade protocol was signed on May 20.

May 15 In commemoration of the thirty-third anniversary of Chairman Mao's "Talks at the Yanan Forum on Literature and Art," a number of theatrical works selected by the Ministry of Culture were being staged in Beijing, including Xinjian's Uighur opera The Red Lantern, and Hubei's Han opera The Red Detachment of Women.

May 19 Foreign Minister J.R.L. Kotsokoane of the Kingdom of Lesotho visited China at the invitation of the Chinese government from May 19-29. He met Premier Zhou Enlai in the hospital on May 21.
    • Princess Ashraf Pahlavi, sister of His Imperial Majesty Mohammed Reza Pahlavi, the shahanshah of Iran, arrived in Beijing from North Korea for a three-day visit at the invitation of the Chinese government. She met Premier Zhou Enlai in the hospital on May 19.

May 23 On the occasion of the thirty-third anniversary of Chairman Mao's "Talks at the Yanan Forum on Literature and Art," the People's Daily gave prominent coverage to articles by Chinese writers and photos reflect the art troupes' service to the workers, peasants and soldiers.

May 25 The Rumanian Government Delegation, led by Deputy Prime Minister Paul Ciulescu, arrived in Beijing for a six-day visit and officiated at the opening ceremony of the Rumanian Industrial Exhibition in Beijing on May 29. Premier Zhou Enlai met the delegation in the hospital on May 27.

May 27 Nine members of the Chinese mountaineering expedition (eight Tibetans, of whom one was a woman, and one male Han) were reported as having reached the summit of Mt. Everest (Chomolungma), the second Chinese expedition to do so (the first was in 1960).

May 28 Zhuan Yan said in the UN Security Council that China had not participated in the vote on the Mideast resolution because of China's view on the dispatch of United Nations forces.

May 30 The Beijing Review published on its first page the message sent by the CCP Central Committee to the Central Committee of the Burmese Communist party expressing condolences on the death in action of Thakin Zin and Thakin Chit.

May 31 China and Egypt exchanged letters in Beijing for the extension of the period of validity of the trade agreement and payment agreement between the two nations from January 1, 1974 to December 31, 1976. The 1975 protocol of the trade agreement between the two nations was signed at the same time.
    • China and Rumania signed a postal and telecommunication agreement in Bucharest.
    • The Chinese phonetic alphabet (pinyin) would be used to transliterate Chinese names into Roman script as from September 1 according to an NCNA announcement.

June 1 A bridge, described as a reinforced concrete road bridge, 162 meters long, spanning the Hei River in southwest Yunnan province, was opened for traffic.

June 3 Vice Premier Deng Xiaoping met the delegation of the American Society of Newspaper Editors led by Eugene C. Patterson, editor of the St. Patterson Times. Vice Premier Deng was reported to have told the group that China acknowledged the difficulty for the US to pull out of Taiwan.

June 6 Foreign Minister Donald Willesee of Australia arrived in Beijing for a seven-day visit at the invitation of the Chinese government. Premier Zhou Enlai met him in the hospital on June 7. Mr. Willesee was said to have pro-

tested against Chinese nuclear tests and to have discussed the proposed agreement for a Chinese family reunion in Australia.

June 7   President Ferdinand E. Marcos of the Philippines
made an official visit to China from June 7-11 at the
invitation of Zhu De, Chairman of the NPC Standing
Committee, and Premier Zhou Enlai. President Marcos
met Chairman Mao for one-and-a-half hours soon after
his arrival in Beijing, and was photographed with Zhu
De, Deng Xiaoping, Jiang Qing, Hua Guofeng, and
other Chinese leaders. Premier Zhou Enlai and President Marcos signed a joint communiqué on June 9 to
establish diplomatic relations at the ambassadorial level.
The Philippines "fully understands and respects"
China's claim to Taiwan, according to the communiqué.
A trade agreement was also signed on June 9.

June 8   The Thai National Assembly Delegation, led by Pra-
sit Kanchanawat, speaker of the House of Representatives, arrived in Beijing for a nine-day visit at the invitation of the Chinese People's Institute of Foreign Affairs. Vice Premier Deng Xiaoping met the delegation
on June 16.
  • More than 30,000 people of various nationalities in
Lhasa, Tibet, held a mass rally at the Working People's
Palace of Culture Plaza to celebrate the second successful ascent of the Chomolungma (Mt. Everest) by a
Chinese mountaineering expedition group.

June 9   The Philippine Government issued an announcement
to terminate all existing diplomatic relations with Taiwan.

June 11   Gambian President Dawda Kairaba Jawara and his
party arrived in Beijing for a seven-day visit. Premier
Zhou Enlai met him in the hospital on June 11, together
with Zhu De and Ulanfu. Chairman Mao met him on
June 12.
  • New Zealand Minister of Trade and Industry Warren W. Freer, Mrs. Freer, and their party arrived in
Beijing for a ten-day visit. A China-New Zealand
agreement on reciprocal registration of trademarks was
signed on June 18.
  • A water-supply project, built in Dodoma region
with Chinese aid, was handed over to Tanzania. The

project was started in 1973 and was completed in the
second quarter of this year in accordance with an
agreement between the two nations.

June 12   Premier Zhou Enlai met, in the hospital, Aiichiro
Fujiyama, president of the Japanese Association for the
Promotion of International Trade.   Japanese reports indicated that the Japanese government was disappointed
and pessimistic about the peace treaty negotiations.

June 13   The Exhibition of the People's Republic of China
was held in Cologne, West Germany from June 13-25.
   • Since a resolution in the UN Security Council was
mostly concerned with the peacekeeping force in Cyprus, China did not participate in the vote on it.

June 15   The Albanian Government Economic Delegation, led
by Adil Carcani, arrived in Beijing for a thirty-four
day visit at the invitation of the Chinese government.
Premier Zhou Enlai met the delegation in the hospital
on June 15.   The two nations signed agreements on
July 3rd, on a long-term interest-free Chinese loan to
Albania, on a goods exchange, and on payments for
1976-80.

June 16   The Mixed Chinese-Danish Trade Commission held
its first meeting in Copenhagen from June 16-20.
   • In Urumchi, Xinjiang, China and Pakistan exchanged letters on border trade for 1975 between the
two nations.

June 17   According to Vientiane Radio in Laos, China agreed
to supply 4,000 tons of rice free of charge and sell a
further 6,000 tons on a commercial basis, and to sell
5,700 bicycles, 500 ploughs and an unspecified number
of water pumps.

June 19   The Theatrical Festival, sponsored by the Ministry
of Culture, began in Beijing.   Following two similar
ones held early this year, the current festival drew
plays from Qinghai, Shandong, Anhui, and Fujian provinces.

June 22   Premier Zhou Enlai sent a message to President
Samora Moises Machel, greeting the founding of the

People's Republic of Mozambique. The Chinese Government Delegation, led by Ye Fei, arrived in Lourenco Marques to attend the celebrations of the Independence of Mozambique at the invitation of the Mozambique Liberation Front. The Chinese Wushu delegation gave a performance in the Mozambique capital on June 26. An agreement on economic and technical cooperation between the two nations was signed on July 3. The Chinese Government Delegation left Lourenco Marques for home on July 3.

June 23   Li Suwen, head of the Chinese delegation at the World Women's Conference in Mexico City, said that in China "countless women are doing the work formerly considered suitable for men only and more and more are filling leading posts at all levels."

June 26   The People's Daily carried an editorial marking the tenth anniversary of Chairman Mao's directive on medical and health work, entitled "Profound Revolution in the Field of Public Health."

June 27   President Omar Bongo of Gabon visited China from June 27-29. Premier Zhou Enlai met him in the hospital on June 28, and Vice Premier Zhang Chunqiao held talks with him.

June 28   Ye Jianying met all members of the Korean People's Army Friendship Visiting Group in Beijing.
   • Ye Jianying and Wu De met the delegation of the French Marxist-Leninist Communists, led by Jacques Jurquet.
   • 18,000 Chinese workers, peasants, and soldiers gathered at the capital indoor stadium in Beijing to warmly welcome the triumphant return of the Chinese mountaineering expedition, from its second ascent of the Chomolungma from the north face.

June 29   The General Administration of Civil Aviation of China gave a reception in Beijing to celebrate the inauguration of the Iran air flight to China.

June 30   The Economic and Trade Exhibition of the People's Republic of China was held at the Sports Palace in Quito, Ecuador, from June 30 to July 14.

• Prime Minister Kukrit Pramoj arrived in Beijing
for a seven-day visit at the invitation of Premier Zhou
Enlai. Three Vice Premiers, Deng Xiaoping, Chen
Xilian and Hua Guofeng met him at the airport on his
arrival. He met Premier Zhou Enlai in the hospital on
June 30, and Chairman Mao on July 1. A joint communiqué was issued on July 1 to establish diplomatic relations at the ambassadorial level. On July 2, at his
press conference in Beijing, the Thai Prime Minister
said that he had discussed the Communist party of
Thailand with Chairman Mao. The Chinese leader observed that "since it is small, it should not be dangerous." In the communiqué, China enjoined Chinese residents in Thailand who elected to retain Chinese nationality to "abide by the law" of Thailand, "respect the
customs and habits of the Thai people, and live in
amity with them." Thailand "acknowledges" China's
claim to Taiwan, according to the communiqué.
• An oil pipeline from Beijing to Qinhuangdao (Hebei)
came into operation, completing the 1507 km pipeline
from Daqing (Heilongjiang) to Beijing.

July 1   The People's Daily carried an editorial entitled
"Study the Theory of the Dictatorship of the Proletariat,
Strengthen Party Building," marking the fifty-fourth
anniversary of the founding of the CCP. It noted that
some party members became so engrossed in daily rou-
tines that they neglected theory study and so made
mistakes.
• The 676 km Baoji (Shaanxi)-Chengdu (Sichuan)
Railway was opened to traffic; it was China's first
electric railway.

July 2   The Red Flag published an article entitled "Bring
the Vanguard Role of the Party Organization of Leading
Groups into Full Play," to emphasize the role of the
leadership core of the party committee.
• A ceremony was held at the Beijing zoo for the
presentation of a gift elephant from Premier Pham Van
Dong of the DRVN.

July 3   George Bush, chief of the liaison office of the US in
China, gave a reception in Beijing to mark the 199th
anniversary of the Independence Day of the US.
• The Guinea-Bissau Government Delegation, led by

Foreign Minister Victor Saud Maria, arrived in Beijing
for a seven-day visit. Premier Zhou Enlai met the
delegation in the hospital on July 6. An agreement on
economic and technical cooperation between the two nations was signed on July 9.
  • NCNA reported that more than 200,000 women workers, cadres, and peasants in the Beijing area since
1973 received checkups, free of charge, for possible
cancer or tumors. This was followed up by prompt
treatment when necessary.

July 4 Premier Zhou Enlai sent a message to Aristides Pereira, general secretary of the African Party for the Independence of Guinea and Cape Verde, greeting the
proclamation of the Independence of the Cape Verde.
  • The Iraqi Government Delegation, led by Vice
President Taha Muhyiddin Marouf, arrived in Beijing
for a four-day visit. He was received by Chairman Mao
and Premier Zhou Enlai in the hospital on July 6. He
held talks with Vice Premier Deng Xiaoping. A protocol
on developing trade and economic and technical cooperation was signed on July 6.

July 5 Agricultural machines and implements as well as other
materials were presented to Gabon as gifts from China
at a ceremony held in Libreville.

July 8 NCNA reported that a new oil pipeline, running from
the North China port of Qinghuangdao to Beijing had
been completed. The 355 km pipeline formed a part of
the 1,507 km underground artery linking the Daqing
oil field in Northeast China to North China. Crude oil
from Daqing reached Dongfanghong Oil Refinery of Beijing's general petrochemical works through the pipeline
on June 23. The pipeline ran through thirteen counties and cities in Hebei province and Tianjin and Beijing
municipalities, intersecting rivers, railways and highways at more than 100 junctures. Many heating and
booster stations were built along the line to ensure a
steady flow of crude oil.

July 10 China and Ecuador signed a trade agreement and
an agreement to establish commercial offices in Beijing.

July 12 Premier Zhou Enlai sent a message to Manuel Pinto

da Costa, president of the Democratic party of São
Tomé and Principe, congratulating him on the proclamation of independence of São Tomé and Principe. A
joint communiqué to establish diplomatic relations at the
ambassadorial level in São Tomé was signed.

July 14 A big, electricity powered irrigation project went
into operation in Pingyin county, Shandong province,
in the lower reaches of the Yellow River. The project
included the supply of drinking water for 60,000 hill
dwellers. The people made use of the fertile silt carried by the river to improve 1,860 hectres of low-lying
fields.

July 15 France and China reached an agreement on registration of trademarks on a reciprocal basis.

July 18 NCNA reported that communications would be enhanced by a number of projects including a new railway
station at Taiyuan, the reconstruction of an 818-meter
three-deck bridge at Jinan, the construction of a
bridge, 776 meters long and twelve meters wide, over
the Jialing River in Nanzhong (Sichuan), and the expansion of the Jilin bridge over the Songhua River to
accommodate four lanes of traffic and pavement on both
sides.

July 19 Beginning on July 19, PLA units led by their commanders had gone to "participate in labor on the front-
line of industrial production." Factories mentioned in
this context included the Hangzhou combined printing
and dyeing factory, and the Hangzhou No. 2 cotton
textile factory.

July 21 A valuable collection of relics and a fairly well-
preserved male corpse, buried 2,140 years ago, were
unearthed in a tomb dating from the early period of
the Western Han Dynasty (206 B.C. to A.D. 24). The
tomb was excavated on Fenghuangshan (Phoenix Hill)
in the town of Qinanzheng in Jiangling county, Hubei
province.
  • Vice Premier Deng Xiaoping explained to the Japanese journalists group, led by Takeo Arai, that China
would never compromise on the hegemony clause but
would wait until Japan accepted it as the US had in

the Shanghai communiqué. Mr. Deng also confirmed that China did not object to the resumption of air services between Japan and Taiwan.

July 22   NCNA reported that nineteen out of twenty-four summer grain-producing provinces, municipalities and autonomous regions recorded increased in many cases, varying from ten to twenty percent.

July 23   The Malagasy Government Economic Delegation, led by Lt. Col. Joel Rakotomalala, arrived in Beijing for a six-day visit. Vice Premier Deng Xiaoping met the delegation on July 25. An agreement on economic and technical cooperation between the two nations was signed on July 28.
   • A ceremony for the handing over of a rice paddy project built with Chinese aid to Rwanda was held in Kigali, the capital of Rwanda.

July 24   Chinese surveyors and cartographers determined the exact height of the Chomolungma--the highest peak in the world--to be 8,848.13 meters.
   • The 1975 Sino-Soviet trade and payment agreement was signed in Moscow. Trade both ways rose by five percent in 1975 compared to the previous year. Chinese exports rose by four percent to $141 million and Soviet exports rose by six percent to reach $143 million. Textiles and related products represented almost half of China's exports, while three quarters of the Soviet shipments were machinery.

July 26   Another satellite was sent into orbit on July 26 with the following parameters: It makes one complete orbit around the earth in ninety-one minutes, along a trajectory the perigee of 186 km and the apogee of 464 km, with an angle of orbit to the equator plane of sixty-nine degrees.

July 31   A ceremony for presenting the "July 31" hospital and a water-supply project at Owando built with Chinese aid was held at Owando in Northern Congo.
   • Luo Ruiqing, seventy-one year-old former chief of the Chinese Communist Army's general staff, reappeared for the first time in almost a decade at an Army Day reception in Beijing.

• NCNA's transmission of a report identified Wang Hongwen as vice chairman of the CCP Central Committee, and vice chairman of the Military Commision of the CCP Central Committee.

August 2 The Beijing International Swimming and Diving Friendship Invitational Meet was held in the Capital Indoor Stadium from August 2-11.

August 6 Another theatrical festival, sponsored by the Ministry of Culture, began in Beijing. Participating in the current festival were from Ningxia Hui autonomous region, Zhejiang, Jiangxi, and Guizhou provinces and the Tibet autonomous region.
• US Senators Charles H. Percy, Jacob K. Javits, Clairborne Pell, and Adlai Stevenson and Congresspeople Paul Finley, Margaret Heckler, and Paul N. McCloskey Jr. visited China from August 6-16. They held talks with Vice Premier Deng Xiaoping. The Korean situation was among the issues discussed by them. The Chinese side seemed to share the American view that war should and could be avoided in Korea. The Americans were given the impression that China accepted and attached importance to the role of America as a Pacific power, and would not favor its further withdrawal from the region in the near future, with the exception of Taiwan.

August 7 China sponsored a resolution in the UN Security Council calling for membership of the two Vietnam states, and submitted a draft resolution with thirty-four other states for the General Assembly on the withdrawal of UN troops from Korea.
• During the night, torrential rains in Zhumadian (Henan) caused floods which affected 5,490,000 people and swept away numerous homes.

August 8 Liu Xianming spoke to the UNCTAD Board against the alleged economic aspects of disarmament. He favored real disarmament by those countries incurring astronomical military expenditures, but not by the Third-World countries whose defense capabilities were limited.
• The Burmese Foreign Minister, U Hla Phone, visited China from August 8-13. He held several talks with Foreign Minister Qiao Guanhua, and met Vice Premier Deng Xiaoping on August 11. In a public pro-

nouncement, both nations expressed satisfaction with having improved mutual understanding.

• China and the Federal Republic of Germany concluded a reciprocal agreement for trademark registration by an exchange of letters.

August 11 When the US vetoed the draft resolution in the UN Security Council, Huang Hua strongly criticized it for calling for a "package deal" linking the admission of South Korea with the admission of the two parts of Vietnam.

August 12 A group of twenty-five culture workers and competitors of Taiwan province origin residing in Japan and led by Huang Wenjin, arrived in Beijing to take part in the Third National Games of the PRC.

• The DRVN Economic Delegation, led by Vice Premier Ly Thanh Nghi, arrived in Beijing for a six-day visit. He held talks with Vice Premier Li Xiannian and met Premier Zhou Enlai in the hospital on August 16.

August 13 A report in the Washington Post said that Chairman Mao had invited former president Richard Nixon to visit China again, but that Mr. Nixon had not accepted because he wished to complete his memoirs.

August 14 China and the Netherlands signed a maritime transport agreement in Beijing.

August 15 China and Japan signed a fishery agreement in Tokyo. On the same day, Foreign Minister Qiao Guanhua and Ambassador Ogawa exchanged notes in Beijing on the mutual establishment of consulates-general in Osaka and Shanghai.

• The New Cambodian Government Delegation, led by Deputy Premiers Khieu Samphan and Ieng Sary, visited Beijing from August 15-19. Khieu met Premier Zhou Enlai in the hospital on August 18. An agreement on economic and technical cooperation was signed by Vice Premier Deng Xiaoping and Khieu Samphan on August 18. Before the Cambodians left Beijing for North Korea under the leadership of Premier Penn Nouth, a joint communiqué was issued on August 18.

August 17 The Thai Trade Mission, led by Thongyod

Chittiwira, arrived in Beijing for a five-day visit.
Vice Premier Li Xiannian met the delegation on August
20.

  • The Tianjin Acrobatic Troupe of China, led by
Zhang Jiyuan, left Beijing to visit Finland (August 17-
31), Sweden (September 1-14), Norway (September 15-
27), Denmark (September 28 to October 16), Iceland,
and Spain.

August 20   A 10,000-word editorial in the CPSU theoretical
    journal, Komminist, launched an all-out attack on what
    it identified as "Maoism." "In our days," the editorial
    claimed, "Maoism carries a danger for the people of all
    states, regardless of their social system." The edi-
    torial also made it clear that no reconciliation was pos-
    sible with a regime headed by Mao.

    • US Representatives John B. Anderson, John M.
    Slack and Edward J. Derwinski, and Senators Robert
    C. Byrd, James B. Pearson, and Sam Nunn visited
    China from August 29–29. Vice Premier Deng Xiaoping
    met the delegation on August 23. The Chinese leader-
    ship was said to be disassociated from the Communist
    drive for power in Portugal, and puzzled by the dis-
    agreements between the congressmen on fundamental
    issues.

August 21   In Korea, the arrangements for Prince Sihanouk's
    return to Cambodia were evidently agreed upon, and
    the prince returned to Beijing with the Government
    Delegation led by Premier Penn Nouth on August 23.
    Sihanouk and Khieu went to see Premier Zhou Enlai in
    the hospital on August 26 and were received by Chair-
    man Mao Zedong on the following day, together with
    Premier Penn Nouth. On September 6, the same three
    leaders had a formal meeting with a group of Chinese
    leaders including Zhu De, Deng Xiaoping, Zhang Chun-
    qiao, Jiang Qing, Yao Wenyuan and Li Xiannian, before
    being toasted at a farewell banquet given by Deng
    Xiaoping, at which Sihanouk thanked the Chinese gov-
    ernment for its hospitality.

August 22   Just before the declaration of independence by
    the new state of Papua-New Guinea, the Chinese Trade
    Delegation, led by Sun Suozhang, visited the country

from August 22 to September 3; it was the first mission from China and the first trade delegation from any foreign country. A trade agreement was signed covering cocoa, copper ore and other commodities.

August 24 NCNA reported that a new 150,000 kw hydroelectric power station went into full operation in Anhui province, situated on the upper reaches of the Jingyi River, a tributary of the Yangze. The station has three power generating units.

August 28 The Exhibition of Archaeological Finds of the PRC closed in San Francisco, after an eight-month display of exhibits in the United States. The exhibitions began in Washington DC the previous December 13. It moved to Kansas City later and then to San Francisco.

August 29 The Third National Games Preparatory Committee gave a banquet in Beijing to welcome the Taiwan Provincial Sports Delegation. Present at the banquet was Vice Premier Hua Guofeng. The Third National Games were held from September 2-28.
    • The Chinese Foreign Ministry decided not to allow a special Soviet delegation to enter China to take part in the thirtieth anniversary celebrations of the victory of war against Japan.

August 30 The Central Delegation, headed by Vice Premier Hua Guofeng, left Beijing for Tibet to attend the tenth anniversary celebrations for the founding of the Tibet autonomous region. The delegation arrived in Lhasa on September 5.

August 31 The theory-study movement was further complemented by the publications of a series of articles on the popular novel Shuihu Zhuang (Water Margin). Launched under Mao's instructions, the "discussion" began with the publication in the People's Daily on August 31 of an article entitled "Attach Importance to the Commentary on Water Margin," which appeared together with Lu Xun's original commentary on the novel and five articles in the September issue of the Red Flag. The discussion focussed on the theme of class capitulationism or class reconciliation portrayed by a main character, Song Jiang.

Discussion of the book was being promoted because it
was intended to serve as teaching material.

• Premier Zhou Enlai sent a message recognizing the
new government of the People's Republic of Bangladesh,
and on the same day it was announced that China would
buy 4,000 metric tons of jute from Bangladesh.

• The Chinese Party and Government Delegation,
led by Vice Premier Chen Xilian, arrived in Hanoi for
a five-day visit and participated in the celebrations of
the thirtieth anniversary of the founding of the DRVN.
Chinese leaders Mao Zedong, Zhu De, and Zhou Enlai
greeted the Vietnamese leaders on the occasion.

September 1 It was announced that China had agreed to
     sell more than 500,000 tons of crude oil in exchange
     for 200,000 tons of Thai rice.

September 2 Speaking to the UN General Assembly on the
     establishment of a new international economic order, Li
     Qiang said that China wanted international economic af-
     fairs and the international monetary system to be jointly
     administered by all countries of the world on equal
     terms.

• NCNA reported that Beijing astronomical observatory of the Chinese Academy of Sciences discovered a
new star on August 30, at twenty-two hours forty-five
minutes Beijing time. A new star, the Nova, was in
the Swan (Cygnus) constellation. Its right ascension
was twenty-one hours ten minutes, its declination,
forty-eight degrees one minute, its visual magnitude
was about two. Spectrophotographic observation
showed wide and strong emission bands. It was the
brightest new star since the outburst of the Nova in
the Puppis constellation in 1942.

September 3 Special amnesty releases Zhang Haishang,
     Yang Nanzun, and Zhao Yixue returned to Beijing from
     Hong Kong, after their wish to go to Taiwan was not
     granted.

• West German Minister of Economics Hans Friderichs
visited China from September 3-8 and opened the German exhibition in Beijing under the name Technogerma-
75. The exhibition was held from September 5-18.

September 4 The People's Daily carried a front-page edi-

torial entitled "Criticism of Water Margin." The article
stated: "At present, our country is in an important
period of historical development. We must adhere to
the Party's basic line and policies, and we must uphold
the principles advanced by Chairman Mao--'practice
Marxism, and not revisionism; unite, and don't split;
be open and aboveboard, and don't intrigue and conspire,' unite with all the forces that can be united
with, criticize revisionism and push the socialist revolution and construction forward."

September 5 China and Niger signed two protocols in Niamey, capital of Niger, one on projects of agricultural
cooperation and the other on the dispatch of a Chinese
medical team to Niger.

September 6 Chinese Party and State leaders Deng Xiaoping,
Zhang Chunqiao, Chen Xilian, and Wu Guixian met all
members of the Taiwan Provincial Sports Delegation to
the Third National Games.

September 7 NCNA reported that China established trade
relations with more than 150 countries and regions,
and signed trade agreements and protocols at the
governmental level with more than sixty of them. The
total volume of China's imports and exports in 1974
was 7.5 times the figure for the early postliberation
year of 1952.

September 8 A large group of clay sculptures, "The Wrath
of Serfs," was put on display at the Tibet Museum of
Revolution in Lhasa to celebrate the tenth anniversary
of the founding of the Tibet autonomous region.
   • A new air service between Lanzhou and Lhasa was
inaugurated.
   • President Gerald R. Ford met the delegation of the
China Council for the Promotion of International Trade,
led by Li Qiang, at the White House.
   • Foreign Minister Nsekalije Aloys of Rwanda and
his party arrived in Beijing for a five-day visit at the
invitation of the Chinese government. Vice Premier
Deng Xiaoping met the delegation on September 9.

September 9 The tenth anniversary of the founding of the
Tibet autonomous region was celebrated in Lhasa. Hua

Guofeng led a central delegation to attend the celebrations. Texts of speeches and articles marking the anniversary drew attention to the Region's 1974 statistics,
indicating that the value of industrial output was nearly
four times greater than that of 1965.

• China and Mexico signed a scientific and technical
cooperation agreement in Mexico City.

• Tens of thousand of Beijing people gathered in
Tiananmen Square and at the airport to see off Prince
Norodom Sihanouk, Madam Sihanouk, Penn Nouth, and
Madam Penn Nouth.

September 10 China and Mauritius signed letters of exchange
on agricultural and technical cooperation in Port Louis,
capital of Mauritius.

• A pair of giant pandas, gifts from China to Mexico,
were airlifted to Mexico by a special plane.

September 11 The railway link to the main Shanghai-Hang-
zhou line was opened to traffic.

September 12 The Friendship Delegations from Zambia and
Tanzania arrived in Beijing for a ten-day visit at the
invitation of the Chinese government. Vice Premier
Li Xiannian met the two delegations on September 18.
The minutes of the Seventh Round of Talks on the
Tanzanian-Zambian Railway, and three protocols were
signed on September 18.

September 15 China formally recognized the EEC when Mr.
Li Lianbi, who was concurrently ambassador to Belgium,
presented his credentials to the president of the EEC
Council of Ministers, Mr. Mariano Rumor.

• Premier Zhou Enlai sent a message to the government of Papua-New Guinea, congratulating it on its independence and extending diplomatic recognition.

• West German Opposition party leader, Franz Josef
Strauss, arrived in Beijing for a five-day visit at the
invitation of the China Committee for the Promotion of
International Trade. Vice Premier Deng Xiaoping met
him on September 18.

• The First National Conference on Learning from
Dazhai in Agriculture was held from September 15 to
October 19 in Xiyang (Shanxi). Attended by over
7,000 people, including major leaders, such as Deng

Xiaoping, Jiang Qing, Yao Wenyuan, Chen Xilian, Hua Guofeng, Chen Yonggui, Wu Guixian, it discussed how "basically" to fulfill the task of mechanization of agriculture by 1980 and to increase the growth rate in agriculture. Jiang Qing was reported as having made an "important speech" during the opening session.

September 16   A visit to China by the group of fourteen American mayors was cancelled at the last moment. The difficulty was the inclusion among the fourteen mayors of Mr. Carlos Romero Barcelo, mayor of San Juan, Puerto Rico.
  • The thirty members of the Thai Royal Family Delegation, led by Prince Siriratua Diskul, went to Beijing in the middle of September at the invitation of the Chinese People's Institute for Foreign Affairs. Vice Chairman of the NPC Standing Committee, Tan Chenlin, gave a dinner for them on September 16.

September 19   Mr. Edward Heath, former prime minister of Great Britain visited China September 19-21. He had a meeting on September 20 with Vice Premier Deng Xiaoping, and the next day he had a one-hour meeting with Chairman Mao Zedong.
  • Cambodian Deputy Prime Minister Ieng Sary arrived in Beijing for an eight-day visit. Vice Premier Deng Xiaoping met him on September 19.

September 21   The Chinese Party Delegation, led by Zhang Chunqiao, visited North Korea from September 21-27. The delegation was given an audience by President Kim Il-sung on September 24 and 25. In a speech in Pyongyang on September 26, Zhang made reference to revisionism and hegemonism.

September 22   Chinese judicial organs decided to release the ninety-five armed special agents and forty-nine crew members of armed agents carrying vessels of the Chinese Nationalists in custody.
  • China and Syria signed an agreement on broadcasting and television operation in Beijing.
  • The three-year private-level protocol on safe fishing operations, based on the intergovernmental pact, was signed in Beijing by the Fishery Association of China and the Japan-China Fishery Association of Japan.

• The Vietnamese Workers' Party and the government delegation led by Le Duan, arrived in Beijing for
a seven-day visit at the invitation of the Chinese party
and government. The delegation was received by
Chairman Mao on September 24. The two Vice Premiers, Le Thanh Nghi and Li Xiannian, signed the
agreement on an interest-free loan on September 25,
and at the same time, a protocol was signed about the
supply of goods by China during 1976.

September 23   The fourteen-member delegation of the Scientific and Technical Association of China, led by Professor Zhou Peiyuan, left Beijing to visit the US at the
invitation of the Committee of Scholarly Communication
with the People's Republic of China. President Gerald
R. Ford met the delegation at the White House on
September 27.
• The Australian Landscape Painting Exhibition was
held at the Jiangsu Provincial Art Gallery in Nanjing
from September 23 to October 7.
• NCNA reported that an electric pumping project
which made use of Yellow River water to irrigate 20,000
hectares of land had been completed in the arid central
Gansu province.

September 24   A ceremony was held in Sanaa, the capital of
the Yemen Arab Republic, to sign an agreement for
China to hand over the Sanaa Industrial Technical
School to the YAR.

September 25   Guo Fenglian, secretary of the Dazhai Brigade's Communist party branch, made a speech at the
National Conference on Learning form Dazhai. She
described how the Dazhai Brigade kept advancing on
the socialist road in the midst of stormy class struggle
and the battle against nature in the last two decades.
The Dazhai Brigade comprised eighty-three peasant
households with over 450 people who farmed 56.4 hectares of land.

September 26   In a key speech to the UN General Assembly,
Foreign Minister Qiao Guanhua presented a general survey of international affairs as seen form China and
gave the Chinese views on a number of major problems
including the SALT, Helsinki agreements, the Korean

problem, the Mideast, and the question of revising the UN Charter.

September 27 Foreign Minister Qiao Guanhua rejected the proposal which Dr. Henry Kissinger made on September 22 for a conference between China, the US and the two Koreas to preserve the armistice after the dissolution of the UN command in South Korea.
  • China praised the decision to raise the world oil price ten percent at the meeting of OPEC nations in Vienna.

September 28 China and France signed a maritime agreement in Beijing.
  • Prince Norodom Sihanouk returned to China to attend the National Day celebraiton in Beijing. Vice Premier Deng Xiaoping met him at the airport on his arrival and gave a banquet in his honor on September 28.
  • A central delegation, headed by Chen Xilian, arrived in Urumchi, Xinjiang by a special plane to attend the celebrations of the twentieth anniversary of the founding of the Xinjiang Uighur autonomous region.

September 29 NCNA reported that total retail sales of consumer goods in China showed an 8.4 percent rise in the first half of this year over the same period last year.
  • Sixty-five of the US-Jiang armed agents and crew members of agent-carrying vessels recently released by Chinese judicial organs applied to return to Taiwan for reunion with their families. Their applications were approved by the government.
  • In Urumchi, Chen Xilian declared that "we must never forget that the Soviet revisionists have not renounced their intention to subjugate our country. We must heighten our vigilance and be prepared to fight."

September 30 The Standing Committee of the NPC and the State Council cabled a message to the Revolutionary Committee of the Xinjiang Uighur autonomous region, greeting the twentieth anniversary of the founding of the Xinjiang Uighur autonomous region.
  • NCNA reported that in the first eight months of 1975, total value of industrial output was 17.3 percent higher than in the corresponding period of last year.

October 1 The twenty-sixth anniversary of the founding of
the People's Republic of China was formally marked in
Beijing by a "grand reception" held on the eve of National Day in the Great Hall of the People. Given by
Vice Premier Deng Xiaoping on behalf of Premier Zhou
Enlai, the reception was attended by over 4,000 people
including Chinese leaders, leading members of the departments of the party, government, and the PLA; also
attending were representatives of all fronts in Beijing,
the National Conference on Learning from Dazhai in
Agriculture, the Third National Games, as well as foreign guests, party and state leaders.

• On the National Day, all Beijing papers carried a
large front-page portrait of Chairman Mao, quotations
concerning the need to rule the bourgeoisie by dictatorship, to practice Marxism, to grasp revolution, and to
unite to win still greater victories. In place of a National Day editorial, the People's Daily printed an editorial marking the twentieth anniversary of the founding of the Xinjiang Uighur autonomous region.

• The nine-member Petroleum Delegation, led by
Zhang Wenbin, left Beijing for Norway on a twenty-day
tour at the invitation of the Norwegian government.

October 2 China and Japan signed a civil aviation agreement in Beijing to cover mutual landing and transit
rights.

October 3 A Chinese Wushu delegation, led by Bai Bing,
left Beijing to visit Egypt (October 5-16), Turkey
(October 17-30), Tunisia (November 6-9), Morocco
(November 10-20), Algeria (November 21 to December
2), and Mauritania (December 3-10).

October 4 China and Bangladesh signed a joint communiqué
in New York City to establish diplomatic relations at
the ambassadorial level.

October 5 NCNA reported that all ten counties and eighty
percent of the communes in the hilly Dujia and Miao
autonomous prefecture in Hunan province were now
linked by motor roads.

October 6 President Dzemal Bijedic of Yugoslavia visited
China at the invitation of Premier Zhou Enlai from Oc-

tober 6-12. He met Chairman Mao on October 8. At
the welcoming banquet, the president said that Yugoslavia had always advocated a policy of détente. During Vice Premier Deng Xiaoping's speech, the ambassadors of the Soviet Union, Mongolia and the four bloc
countries of Eastern Europe walked out.

October 7 The official Soviet message on China's National
Day asserted that the Soviet government "stands for
the normalization of relations with China and the reestablishment of friendship and cooperation between
the two countries."

October 8 NCNA reported that sixty recently released "US-
Jiang" armed agents and crew members of vessels left
Xiamen (Fujian) by boat for Quemoy to return to
Taiwan. Five others left Shenzhun for Taiwan via
Hong Kong.

October 11 NCNA reported that the Beijing Scientific Instrument Factory, under the Chinese Academy of Sciences, had successfully trial manufactured a high-
resolution electronic scanner microscope. This microscope had a resolving power of 100 angstrom units and
magnification from twenty to 100,000 times. It could
produce a three-dimensional image and directly examine
a metal in uneven cross-section, the surface of a cata-
lyst, and a whole spore—something other microscopes
could not do. The electronic scanner microscope could
directly observe the object in its natural form. It
could also be equipped with auxiliary devices such as
x-ray microscopic spot analysis and electronic diffrac-
tion for analyzing chemical compositions and crystal
structures of an object as well as the workings of their
semi-conductor elements and integrated circuits for
faults.

October 13 The Chinese liaison office in Washington had
asked the US State Department that the "Office of
Tibet" in New York be closed, and that a proposed
tour by a Tibetan song-and-dance ensemble be cancelled. The Chinese statement claimed that the American refusal of these requests constituted undisguised
interference in China's internal affairs.

October 15   The National Conference on Learning from Daz-
       hai held the plenary closing session at the Great Hall
       of the People in Beijing.   Hua Guofeng made a summary
       report at the session, saying, "Get the Whole Party
       Mobilized, Go All Out to Develop Agriculture and Strive
       to Build Up Dazhai-Type Counties Everywhere."   Party
       and state leaders who attended the session included
       Ye Jianying, Deng Xiaoping, Zhang Chunqiao, Yao
       Wenyuan, Li Xiannian, Chen Xilian, Qi Denggui, and
       Hua Fuofeng.

October 16   China and Albania signed a protocol of the Six-
       teenth Session of the Joint Committee of Technology
       and Technical Science Cooperation in Beijing.

October 18   The 1975 Sino-Guinea trade protocol was signed
       in Beijing.
            • The People's Daily and the Liberation Army Daily
       published a joint editorial entitled "In Commemoration
       of the 40th Anniversary of the Victory of the Long
       March," to mark the occasion.   The editorial said that
       the Long March had proved the truth of Mao's thesis
       that "when the Party line is correct we have every-
       thing; if the line is incorrect, we will lose what we al-
       ready have."
            • China and Czechoslovakia signed a protocol of the
       Seventeenth Session of the Joint Commission for Scien-
       tific and Technical Cooperation in Beijing.

October 19   Chairman Mao Zedong received Madam Mariam
       Traore, wife of the president of Mali.
            • The National Conference on Learning from Dazhai
       came to the end with the closing speech by Chen Yong-
       gui.   He said that the conference would bring about
       the modernization of industry, national defense, and
       science and technology to support agriculture.
            • Henry Kissinger and his wife arrived in Beijing
       for a five-day visit.   He had a series of talks with
       Vice Premier Deng Xiaoping.   Chairman Mao met them
       on October 21.   Secretary Kissinger told his hosts
       that the US would resist hegemony, but it would also
       make every effort to avoid needless confrontations when
       it could do so without threatening the security of a
       third country.

October 20   Lai Yali condemned South Africa's policy of
     apartheid in the UN Special Political Committee.   Lai
     did not believe that the policy of détente proclaimed
     by South Africa was genuine; it was an attempt to un-
     dermine the unity of the African states.   The only
     solution in South Africa was for the people to over-
     throw the authorities.

October 23   Nepalese Princes Gyanendra and Dhirendra and
     their wives arrived in Beijing for an eight-day visit.
     Zhu De, chairman of the NPC Standing Committee, met
     them on October 23, and Vice Premier Chen Xilian
     gave a banquet on the same day.   China and Guyana
     signed an agreement on import and export commodities
     in Beijing.

October 25   The 1976 Sino-DRVN mutual supply of goods
     and payment agreement was signed in Beijing.
        • The 1976 Sino-Pakistan trade protocol was signed
     in Rawalpindi.
        • The People's Daily and the Liberation Army Daily
     published a joint editorial marking the twenty-fifth
     anniversary of the Chinese entry into the Korean War.
     It said that "No matter how violent a storm may break
     out in the world hereafter, the Chinese people will al-
     ways unite and fight together with their Korean com-
     rades-in-arms."

October 27   China successfully conducted an underground
     nuclear test.

October 28   Lhasa Radio reported that 1.3 million Tibetans
     were living in Tibet, and another 1.7 million in neigh-
     boring Chinese provinces.
        • Wei Guoqing attended the meeting to convey the
     spirit of the National Conference on Learning from Daz-
     hai in Guangzhou in the capacity of the first secretary
     of Guangdong Provincial Party Committee, chairman of
     the Provincial Revolutionary Committee and the first
     commissar of the PLA Guangdong Units.

October 29   West German Chancellor Helmut Schmidt visited
     China from October 29 to November 2.   He was wel-
     comed at the airport by Vice Premier Deng Xiaoping
     and met Chairman Mao on October 30.   Agreements on
     maritime transport and civil aviation were signed dur-

ing the visit and letters were exchanged on the establishment of a mixed committee to promote economic and
trade relations.

October 30   Prince Sihanouk of Cambodia returned from
   North Korea to Beijing and was greeted at the airport
   by Vice Premier Li Xiannian.
      • The Ministry of Coal Industry held a conference
   of coal mining team leaders in Beijing from October 30
   to November 11. The conference was attended by more
   than 5,000 people, including leaders of members of ex-
   traction, tunnelling, mechanical and electrical engineering, geological prospecting teams, and other grass root
   units from China's major coal mines.

November 1   The Indian government spokesman said that
   four Indians had been killed when a patrol party was
   ambushed by Chinese troops within Indian territory on
   the northern border on October 20.
      • Three new airlines went into operation in China,
   while five existing ones were extended and seventy
   regular flights added each week. According to the new
   flight schedule, China would increase its domestic lines
   to 115 with 344 flights a week.

November 3   China and Korea signed the 1975 protocol on
   border railway transport in Shenyang.
      • The Chinese Foreign Ministry issued a statement
   saying that Indian troops had crossed the "line of actual control of November 7, 1959" at Dulong Pass in
   the eastern sector of the Sino-Indian border, intruding
   into Tibet. China had fired back in self-defense. The
   Ministry had handed a protest to the Indian Embassy
   on October 22 offering to return the bodies of the four
   Indians. On October 28, the Indian authorities had
   collected the bodies at Dulong.

November 5   In Canberra, China and Fuji signed a joint
   communiqué to establish diplomatic relations at the ambassadorial level.
      • China and Bulgaria signed a protocol of the Thir-
   teenth Meeting of the Commission of Scientific and
   Technical Cooperation in Sofia.
      • China and Gambia signed a trade agreement in
   Beijing.
      • China and Hungary signed a protocol of the Four-

teenth Meeting of the Commission of Scientific and
Technical Cooperation in Budapest.

November 6 Soviet Ambassador V.S. Tolstikov and his wife
gave a reception in the Embassy in Beijing marking the
fifty-eight anniversary of the October Socialist Revolution.
    • In Apia, China and West Samoa signed a joint com-
muniqué to establish diplomatic relations at the ambassadorial level.

November 7 Chinese diplomats attending the Moscow Red
Square ceremony to mark the fifty-eighth anniversary
of the October Socialist Revolution walked out when
Soviet Defense Minister Andrei Gechko denounced the
"provocative policies of the Chinese leaders."

November 9 Newsweek reported that when Chairman Mao
met with foreign visitors, he had to use lip-reading
assistants. Mao, who was no longer able to conduct a
normal conversation, had three women assistants who
read his lips when he said something to a foreign
visitor. They then conferred on what he said. If he
nodded in agreement, senior interpreter Nancy Dong
translated for the visitor.
    • NCNA reported that about one million cadres and
one hundred million commune members had been working together in an unprecedented drive to improve
farming conditions since last winter, in step with the
deepening movement to learn from Dazhai. Among the
results were: (1) four million hectares of cropland
provided with new or improved irrigation facilities; (2)
two million hectares protected from waterlogging; (3)
5.33 million hectares of rolling fields levelled; (4) 1.13
million hectares of hill slopes terraced; (5) 1.2 million
hectares of low-yield fields improved; (6) 400,000 hectares of wasteland reclaimed. In addition, more than
260,000 pump wells had been put into operation in
northern China during this period.

November 10 Writer Han Suyin told reporters in Hong Kong
that she had just spent ten days in Tibet and had
learned that the Panchen Lama was studying in Beijing.

November 11 China and Syria signed a civil air transport
agreement in Damascus.
    • Huang Hua outlined China's position on disarma-
ment to the UN First Committee. He said that China

supported the establishment of nuclear-free zones in
Latin America, South Asia, the Middle East, Africa and
the Indian Ocean. China opposed the Soviet idea of
calling a disarmament conference.

• President Ne Win of Burma visited China from November 11-15 at the invitation of Zhu De and Zhou
Enlai. He was greeted at the airport by Vice Premiers
Deng Xiaoping and Zhang Chunqiao. He met Chairman
Mao on November 13. In a joint communiqué, the two
sides agreed "not to carry out acts of aggression
against each other." They also expressed their opposition "to the attempt of any country or group of countries to establish hegemony and spheres of influence
in any part of the world."

November 13   In New York, China and Comoros signed a
joint communiqué to establish diplomatic relations at the
ambassadorial level.

November 14   China and the Philippines signed an oil trade
agreement in Manila.

• A new hydroelectric power station went into operation at Papanxia in Gansu province on the upper
reaches of the Yellow River. Three generating units
with a combined capacity of 108,000 kw had so far been
commissioned at the new station. Two more would soon
be installed to bring the total to 180,000 kw.

November 15   Minister for International Trade and Industry
Komoto Toshio arrived in Beijing to open the Japanese
industrial and technical exhibition. The exhibition was
held in Beijing from November 18 to December 2.
Mr. Toshio left Beijing on November 19 and told reporters in Tokyo that Japan would be able to conclude
a long-term crude oil import agreement with China by
the spring, since the Chinese had shown a "flexible"
attitude toward it.

• The Chinese Foreign Ministry issued a statement
hailing Angolan independence from Portugal (November
11), but continued to denounce the Soviet Union for
interference and stirring up civil war.

November 18   NCNA reported that a big coal mine with an
annual capacity of 900,000 tons had been recently built
and put into operation in Guizhou province.

• Huang Hua welcomed the adoption in the General

Assembly of Resolution 3390 B (XXX) dissolving the UN command and withdrawing troops stationed in Korea under the UN flag. Huang said the United States could not legitimately claim some forces in South Korea in accordance with the "US-ROK Bilateral Defense Treaty" when they went out as UN forces, and when the armistice agreement prevented the introduction of reinforcing military personnel in Korea.

November 19   French Foreign Minister Jean Sauvagnargues visited Beijing from November 19–24 at the invitation of the Chinese government. He met Premiers Li Xiannian and Deng Xiaoping. On his return to Paris, he said that France was still a privileged partner of China, the only difference between them being on détente and especially on the Helsinki Conference.

November 21   Zhu De, Chairman of the NPC Standing Committee, sent a message of condolence to the Spanish Regency Council, mourning the death of the Spanish Chief of State Franco. On February 23, 1976, Zhu De congratulated King Juan Carlos on being proclaimed as king.

The People's Daily carried an article entitled "Water Margin and Peasant Revolution," to seek to demolish the views that "Water Margin" was an epic of peasant revolution, a textbook for peasant revolution and a classic on peasant revolution. The article concluded that it was instrumental in disintegrating such revolutions in Ming Qing times.

November 24   The Guangming Daily carried an article entitled "South China Sea Islands, Chinese Territory Since Ancient Times," spelling out China's claims in detail. The article presented detailed historical evidence in support of China's claim to sovereignty over the islands of the South China Sea (Nansha, Xisha, Dongsha and Zhongsha).

• NCNA reported that a fairly well-preserved skeleton of a stegodon was recently discovered in a mountain cave in Shuizheng county, Guizhou province. The stegodon is a long extinct genus of mammals that are intermediate between elephants and mastodons. The stegodon lived between twelve million years and some 100,000 years ago. The age of the fossils of stegodon dates back probably half a million years.

November 25 Premier Zhou Enlai sent a message of congratu-
lations on the independence of Surinam and declared
China's recognition. Ambassador Wang Zhanyuan in
Guyana attended the independence celebration.

November 30 NCNA reported that China produced over
twenty percent more crude oil in the first ten months
of this year than in the same 1974 period and topped
the state plan. The refining quota was also surpassed,
showing a thirteen percent increase over the corresponding 1974 period.

December 1 NCNA reported that a 200,000 kw thermal power
station was completed in the western suburbs of Beijing.
   • An article in the Red Flag on the criticism of Beijing and Qinghua Universities revealed a major contro-
versy over education policy. Some wished to retain
the Cultural Revolution policy, including the selection
of students with worker-peasant-soldier backgrounds
and practical experience, and the placing of major emphasis on revolutionary ideology. Opponents of the
policies claimed they produced bad academic standards.
   • China and Iraq signed a protocol to amend the
trade agreement in Beijing.
   • The 1975-76 Sino-DRVN protocol of the Executive
Organization for Scientific and Technical Cooperation
was signed in Hanoi.
   • President Gerald Ford arrived in Beijing for a
six-day visit at Premier Zhou Enlai's invitation. Vice
Premiers Deng Xiaoping and Li Xiannian met the president at the airport. Later, the president met Zhu De
and Jiang Qing. Although no joint communiqué was issued and no obvious results ensued, the president's
visit took place in a cordial atmosphere. On December
2, President Ford met Chairman Mao for a talk which
he afterwards described as "wide-ranging" and "friendly, candid, substantial and constructive." In his final
address at the banquet, the president reaffirmed the
American commitment to complete normalization of relations on the basis of the Shanghai Communiqué.

December 2 China launched its fourth earth satellite on
November 26 and, in a brief report on December 2,
stated that it had "returned to earth as scheduled after
orbiting the earth normally."

December 3   China and Sri Lanka signed a commodity ex-
        change protocol in Beijing.

December 5   Mao Zedong, Zhu De, and Zhou Enlai sent a
        message of congratulations to the founding of the Peo-
        ple's Democratic Republic of Laos to the new president
        and the new premier.
            • The 1976 Sino-Finnish trade agreement was signed
        in Beijing.

December 6   Vice Premier Deng Xiaoping met George Bush,
        chief of the liaison office of the United States in China,
        and his wife.   Ambassador Bush would soon leave his
        post to head the CIA.

December 9   The People's Daily carried an article to support
        the East Timor people's struggle for national liberation
        and independence, adding the hope that the problems
        would be solved by peaceful means.
            • In a long article in the People's Daily entitled "A
        Great Revolution to Combat and Prevent Revisionism,"
        Liang Xiao noted that not everyone had understood the
        essence, significance and necessity of the Cultural
        Revolution and the movement to criticize Lin Biao and
        Confucius, and not everyone had made a correct ap-
        praisal of the movement's major and minor aspects.
        Referring to the education front, he said that the
        present "absurd" arguments to the effect that there had
        been no construction after destruction indicated that the
        main danger at present was still revisionism.

December 11   Li Yi, former lieutenant general of the Guomin-
        dang Army, returned to the mainland from Taiwan.

December 13   An agreement worth $100 million was signed
        between Rolls-Royce and the China National Technical
        Import Corporation for the supply and construction in
        China of Spey jet engines.   One of the conditions in-
        sisted on by the Chinese was that the engine should
        work efficiently in forty degrees of frost, thus making
        it viable for operation in China's northern winters.

December 15   China and Iran reached an agreement on re-
        ciprocal trademark registration in Beijing.

December 16   Kang Sheng, member of the political bureau
of the CPC, died of prolonged illness at the age of
seventy-seven. A memorial ceremony was held in Beijing on December 21. Ye Jianying delivered a memorial
speech.
   • China successfully launched another man-made
earth satellite.
   • Huang Hua, speaking at the Security Council, welcomed the independence of East Timor. He called on
the Security Council to ask for the immediate withdrawal of Indonesian troops, and to respect the independence, sovereignty, and territorial integrity of East
Timor in accordance with the principles of the United
Nations charter.

December 20   Foreign newsmen visiting Qinghua University
saw large-character posters attacking university authorities as well as the Minister of Education Zhou Rongxin,
as opponents of revolution.
   • China and Cameroon signed two documents on the
construction of the Lagod Hydro-Electric Power Station
and a Cultural Palace in Yaounde.
   • The 1976 Sino-German goods exchange and payment agreement was signed in Berlin.

December 21   China and Somalia signed the minutes of talks
on well-drilling and water supply works in Baidoa.
The minutes were signed in Mogadishu.
   • President Manuel Pinto de Costa of São Tomé and
Principe arrived in Beijing for a five-day visit at the
invitation of the Chinese government. He was greeted
at the airport by Vice Premier Li Xiannian, and he met
Zhu De and Chairman Mao Zedong on December 22 and
23 respectively. The two nations signed agreements on
economic and technical cooperation and on trade on December 25, the final day of the visit.

December 22   Japan and China exchanged instruments of
ratification of the fishery agreement.

December 23   A further amnesty for former Guomindang officials was announced on December 23, affecting all
former Guomindang party, government, military and
special agency personnel at or above county or regi-
mental level being held in custody. Appropriate ar-

rangements would be made for their jobs. Those who
wished to return to Taiwan could do so.
  • NCNA reported that a 753 km railway trunk line
linking Qiaozuo (Henan) and Qizheng (Hubei) was completed in eight months. It ran parallel to the middle
section of the Beijing-Guangzhou Railway.

December 26 The People's Daily published an article entitled "Train Workers with Socialist Consciousness and
Culture in the Course of the Three Great Revolutionary
Movements," by the Qinghua University Party Committee to describe progress in the revolution in education
at Qinghua University. The article also gave a forceful
refutation of the right wing of reversing decisions already made and of the fallacious and absurd arguments
existing in education.

December 27 China and Korea signed the 1976-77 public
health cooperation plan in Pyongyang.
  • The Chinese government informed the Soviet Union
that the Public Security authorities had released the
Russian helicopter and three crew members detained
since March 1974 after penetrating more than seventy
km into the territory of Xinjiang. It was stated that
after investigations the crew members' explanation that
their flight over Chinese territory had been uninten-
tional was now considered credible. At the time of the
penetration these explanations had been dismissed as
"lies."

December 29 The Government Delegation of the Democratic
Republic of East Timor arrived in Beijing to have talks
with officials of the Chinese Foreign Ministry and Ministry of National Defense. Foreign Minister Qiao Guanhua said that the Chinese government and people strongly condemned the Indonesian government's annexation
of East Timor as an act of "aggression."

December 31 From an end of the year NCNA report, it was
deduced that the average annual earnings of workers
in industrial and other enterprises were about $360.

Chapter VII

1976

A YEAR OF TRANSITION

The year 1976 was the most turbulent since the establishment of the People's Republic of China in 1949. On January 8, Premier Zhou Enlai died, after having spent most of the last twenty months of his life in a hospital. Although the overwhelming majority of observers agreed that Vice Premier Deng Xiaoping would succeed him in the premiership, the New China News Agency, on February 7, stunned the world by listing the Minister of Public Security, Hua Guofeng, as "Acting Premier." A few days later, the Chinese media started to launch attacks against Deng. Deng was accused of having leashed, between July and September 1975, a "rightist storm of verdict reversal" against the party center.

The next surprise came in early April. Hundreds of thousands of people went to the Tiananmen Square on April 4 to commemorate the late Premier Zhou Enlai. The ceremony had become a notable mass demonstration in support of his political heritage and by implication, of Deng Xiaoping. On the following day, several thousand people gathered at the National People's Congress building to protest against the removal by the police of the numerous wreaths and placards. During this protest, there were clashes between the police and the masses. On April 7, two resolutions of the CCP Central Committee were released, the first appointing Hua Guofeng first vice-chairman of the Central Committee and premier of the State Council, the second dismissing Deng Xiaoping from all posts both inside and outside the party and government. Simultaneously, a nationwide campaign to criticize Deng set the tone in domestic politics.

On June 15, a Foreign Ministry spokesman announced

that Chairman Mao would no longer receive foreign visitors,
thus giving the first hints of the imminent departure of the
party leader. On July 6, the old Marshal Zhu De, chairman
of the National People's Congress' Standing Committee,
passed away. His death was followed by a devastating
earthquake which virtually wiped out the city of Tangshan
on July 28. Then, on September 9, Chairman Mao died.
Factional disputes that had raged up to the eve of Mao's
death now took an abrupt turn. On October 6, Jiang Qing,
Mao's widow, and three other leftist leaders--Wang Hongwen,
Zhang Chunqiao, and Yao Wenyuan, the party's chief propa-
gandist--were arrested. Six days later, Beijing announced
that Premier Hua Guofeng had been elected chairman of the
Chinese Communist party. He was acclaimed the leader of
the nation at a rally of one million people in Beijing on October 24, thus affirming the victory of the moderates over
the leftists in the bitter struggle for power. The arrest of
the four leftists was officially confirmed on October 22, when
Beijing announced that the party Central Committee, under
the leadership of Hua Guofeng, had "shattered" an attempt
by the "anti-party clique" to "usurp party and state power."

Hua Guofeng was a relatively little-known leader. He
had been chief of the Communist party branch in Chairman
Mao's home district in Hunan province. He was generally
regarded as a moderate and appeared at that time to be a
compromise candidate chosen for his lack of strong factional
involvement. The new leadership shake-up put Hua Guofeng
at the top of the party hierarchy. He was named not only
chairman of the party, succeeding Mao Zedong, but also
chairman of the Military Commission. He was apparently
supported by moderate senior party leaders and army commanders to carry out the program of economic development
set forth by the late Premier Zhou Enlai--widespread modernization that would bring forth a powerful, modern, socialist
China by the end of the twentieth century.

China's economy showed signs of slowdown in 1976.
Figures for the year indicated an industrial growth of seven
percent, compared with an average ten percent annual
growth in the preceding fifteen years. The slowdown was
partly attributable to factional quarrels over the policy of
economic development. The pragmatists, such as Deng
Xiaoping, emphasized professionalism and modern technology
for developing a comprehensive economic system, but the

leftists adhered to Chairman Mao's principles of hard work, self-reliance, and mass enthusiasm. As the struggle mounted against Deng Xiaoping, the economic plans prepared under him necessarily lacked vigorous support for implementation.

Foreign trade registered a decrease in the year, ending a two-year expansion. Beijing canceled all orders for American wheat and corn and cut its purchase of Japanese steel by seventy-five percent. Exports of oil to Japan and the Philippines were also reduced. China's move was attributable to the anti-rightist campaign, which certainly unnerved the economic planners. But bona fide economic factors also played a role. The buying spree during the two previous years, 1974-75, had resulted in a deficit of $730 million in trade with Japan, China's largest partner, and $145 million with the United States. This was incompatible with China's standing policy of maintaining an even balance of trade and Chairman's call for self-reliance rather than dependence on the purchase of foreign technology. The new emphasis on economic development, however, was expected to change the situation. On October 27 Beijing announced resumption of large-scale foreign trade in 1978.

On February 21, after repeated Chinese invitations, former US President Richard Nixon arrived in Beijing for a second visit. Though no longer president, Nixon was treated by the Chinese as a head of state. He had three long sessions with Premier Hua Guofeng and a friendly talk with Chairman Mao Zedong. In Beijing, Nixon supported the Chinese position against Soviet expansionism. The reason for Beijing's eagerness to have Nixon revisit China were complex. The Chinese were not pleased with the US policy of détente with the Soviet Union, and the continued recognition of Taiwan was a disappointment to them. Inviting Nixon to China had been a symbol of building a great bridge between the two countries. The Chinese government hoped that this might impress on the US the importance of Sino-American relations and make clear to future Chinese leaders Mao's basic policy of normalizing relations with the US.

At a news conference on September 9, Secretary of State Henry A. Kissinger said that he did not think Chairman Mao's death would set Sino-American relations back.

He added that the United States, for its part, would continue to strengthen the ties with Beijing in accordance with
the Shanghai communiqué issued at the end of former President Nixon's visit, which called for normalization of relations. On October 15, Kissinger further stated that the US
would consider it "a grave matter" if China were threatened
by an outside power. This was a strong enunciation of US
interest in China's security, and it was intended as a reas-
surance to the new Chinese leadership. The statement was
followed by a Washington announcement that President Ford
had approved the sale to Beijing of a computer system capable of defense as well as industrial uses.

Sino-Soviet relations showed no signs of improvement
in 1976. In February, Beijing reported an armed clash between Chinese militia and Soviet troops along the Xinjiang
border in the northwest. The Chinese accused the Soviet
troops of intrusions, but Moscow denied any such clash.
On September 14, Beijing rejected messages of condolences
from the Soviet and East European Communist parties on the
death of Chairman Mao. A Chinese spokesman said that the
messages were unacceptable because the Chinese Communist
party did not have relations with its counterparts in Eastern
Europe. China's nuclear test on September 26, only two and
a half weeks after Chairman Mao's death, showed that Beijing
would continue to strengthen its defense against any Soviet
military threat. At a UN meeting on October 5, Chinese
Foreign Minister Qiao Guanhua spurned Soviet attempts to
normalize relations. He denounced Soviet imperialism as "the
biggest peace swindler and the most dangerous source of war
today."

Beijing intensified its efforts to expand trade in Western Europe, welcoming the visits of West German and French
officials to hold trade conferences in China. Though actual
trade between the two areas was relatively small, Chinese
purchase of Western European merchandise was clearly on the
rise. Special attention was given to West Germany, where
the Chinese did not hesitate to mix business with politics.
They encouraged Bonn to work for an economic and military
union of Europe to balance the Soviet power.

For some time China had been negotiating a peace
treaty with Japan to bring a formal end to World War II.
One of the demands made by Beijing was that the treaty

should include a provision stating that both countries opposed the efforts of any third nation to achieve hegemony in
Asia. Asserting that the provision was aimed at the Soviet
Union, in 1976, Moscow warned that it would be forced to
"reconsider" its relations with Japan if Tokyo acceded to the
Chinese demand. Although Japanese Premier Takeo Miki
declared on January 13 that Japan would agree to the Chinese request on the subject of "hegemony," Sino-Japanese
negotiation showed little progress.

Beijing gave Premier Kaysone Phomvihan of Laos an
enthusiastic welcome when he visited China in March. He
was received by Chairman Mao. An agreement on economic
and technical cooperation was concluded, under which China
gave Laos an interest-free loan. In April, Beijing agreed to
India's proposal that the two countries exchange ambassadors. Since the border dispute in 1961, each had sent the
other a charge d'affaires rather than an ambassador. Beijing's efforts to curb Soviet expansion appeared to be a
major factor in the shift of its India policy. Beijing signed
a military protocol with Egypt on April 21, a month after
Cairo abrogated its friendship treaty with the Soviet Union.
It was reported that Beijing was to supply spare parts to
Egypt for its Soviet-made MIG fighters. The conclusion of
the treaty was regarded as a significant success for China.

January 1   The New Year's Day People's Daily, Red Flag,
        and Liberation Army Daily editorial signalled a cam-
        paign against the restoration of capitalism and a re-
        newed emphasis on continuing the Cultural Revolution.
        It carried a recent new instruction of Mao Zedong:
        "Stability and unity do not mean writing off class
        struggle; class struggle is the key and everything else
        hangs on it."
            • Two poems written by Chairman Mao Zedong in
        1965 were reprinted in the People's Daily, the Red Flag,
        and other Beijing newspapers on New Year's Day. They
        were: Chongshang Jinggangshan (Jianggang Mountains
        Revisited), and Niaoer wenda (Two Birds: A Dia-
        logue). The poems were also published in the January,
        1976 issue of the Journal of Poetry which resumed pub-
        lication on New Year's Day.
            • On New Year's Eve, Chairman Mao met Julie Nixon

Eisenhower and her husband David Eisenhower. Vice
Premier Deng Xiaoping met them on New Year's Day.
  • NCNA reported that more than 6,000 workers' and
peasants' colleges with 460,000 students had been established in factories, mines, and rural areas throughout the country. The new colleges differed from
China's old universities and colleges in objectives, type
of students enrolled, curriculum, teaching materials
and methods, and examinations.

January 2 Vice Premier Deng Xiaoping met the delegation
    of American Congressmen, led by Representatives Mar-
    garet M. Heckler and Patsy P. Mink.

January 3 A ceremony was held in Beijing marking the for-
    mal opening of the China-Korea Friendship Oil Pipeline.
      • The 1976 Sino-Bulgarian goods exchange and pay-
    ment agreement was signed in Sofia.
      • China began to build an oil storage depot in Hong
    Kong under an agreement for an unprecedented purchase
    of land for this purpose from the British Administra-
    tion.

January 8 The death of Premier Zhou Enlai on January 8
    was announced by NCNA on January 9. Zhou Enlai
    died of cancer in Beijing at the age of seventy-eight.
    The NCNA transmitted the list of names of the funeral
    committee which was headed by Chairman Mao, and an
    announcement that the funeral would be held on Janu-
    ary 15. It added that in accordance with Chinese cus-
    tom and protocol, no foreign representatives were to
    be invited to the funeral. Meanwhile, mourning cere-
    monies were to be held on January 12, 13, and 14.
    The memorial ceremony, prior to the scattering of the
    late Premier's ashes in the river and on the land of the
    motherland in accordance with his wishes, took place in
    Beijing on January 15. The memorial speech was de-
    livered by Vice Premier Deng Xiaoping.

January 9 NCNA reported that universal five-year primary
    school education had been achieved in the main through-
    out the vast countryside of China. By the end of
    1975, well over ninety-five percent of school-age chil-
    dren in the country had been enrolled compared to 84.7
    percent in 1966, and primary school attendance had in-
    creased by thirty percent.

January 13   The Soviet Foreign Minister Andrei Gromyko
warned the Japanese in Tokyo that the Soviet Union
might have to review its relationship with Japan if it
submitted to Chinese insistence on including a clause
about hegemony in the peace treaty.

January 14   China and Korea signed a protocol of the Fifteenth Meeting of the Joint Committee for Cooperation
in Border River Transport in Shenyang.
   • Soviet First Deputy Premier Mazurov led the
Government Delegation to sign the condolences book
at the Chinese Embassy in Moscow for the death of
Premier Zhou Enlai.

January 16   A US Bureau of Mines forecast by K.P. Wang
suggested that oil output in China could reach 4.4
million barrels per day by the 1980s, with exports
reaching 362 million barrels per day in the early 1980s
and double that level by 1985, by which time China
would have joined the US, USSR, Saudi Arabia and
Iraq as one of the world's "big five" producers.

January 17   The Communist Party Committee of Qinghua
University summed up its experience in the revolution
in education over the past few years in an article entitled "Bring Up Workers with Socialist Consciousness
and Culture in Their Great Revolutionary Movements."

January 18   General Vo Nguyen Giap visited Beijing on his
way home from his visits to Moscow and other countries.   He had talks with Defense Minister Ye Jianying.
It was the first high-level Vietnamese visit since that
of Secretary General Le Duan, in September, 1975.

January 19   The 1976 Sino-Polish goods exchange and payment agreement was signed in Beijing.

January 20   In Tokyo, Prime Minister Miki laid down four
conditions for the acceptance of a hegemony clause as
follows: (1) Anti-hegemonism should not be aimed at
any third country, such as the Soviet Union; (2) The
clause should not oblige Japan or China to take any
joint action; (3) The clause should oppose the hege-
monic ambition of any nation anywhere in the world,
not merely in Asia; (4) The clause should be inter-

preted as the expression of a universal principle of
peace in consonance with the United Nations charter.
These conditions were accepted by China.

January 23   China successfully conducted its eighteenth nuclear test.   It was a low-yield atmosphere test which
took place at Lop Nor.
• Beijing–Phnom Penh air service was officially inaugurated.
• The State Council and the Military Commission of
the Central Committee of the CCP issued a circular to
call on the Army and people throughout the country to
make a conscientious study of the two poems by Chairman Mao and the New Year's Day editorial, "Nothing is
hard in this world if you dare to scale the heights."
The circular also called for further repudiating of the
counterrevolutionary revisionist line of Liu Shaoqi and
Lin Biao, safeguarding and developing the victories of
the Cultural Revolution, and giving warm support to
the "new socialist things."

January 25   The Rumanian Government Trade Delegation, led
by Deputy Prime Minister Ion Patan, arrived in Beijing
for a six-day visit.   The delegation was greeted at the
airport by Vice Premier Hua Guofeng.   The Sino–Rumanian long-term trade agreement and the 1976 goods exchange and payment protocol were signed on January
29.

January 26   Huang Hua told the Security Council that China
had decided not to participate in the vote on the Middle
East draft resolution because the words in the draft
resolution could be used by Israel as a pretext for its
policy of "aggression and expansion."

January 27   Vice Premier Hua Guofeng met the Maltese Delegation, led by Joseph Cassar, minister of education and
culture.

January 28   China and Sri Lanka signed an agreement in
Colombo for an interest-free loan of about 22.9 million
rupees in convertible currency in two installments in
the first half of 1976.   The loan was repayable over
five years, including a two-year grace period, by way
of export of Sri Lankan goods or convertible currency.

• Three Guomindang men, two US-Jiang armed special agents and one crew member of an armed agent-
carrying vessel who had been released recently were
scheduled to take a boat from the Fujian coast and return to Taiwan.

January 31   Further clarification of the struggle over education policy was provided in a detailed article in the
Red Flag.   Entitled "Repulse the right deviationist wind
in science and technical circles to reverse correct verdicts," the article claimed that the opposition had deliberately confused "science and technology" with "the
science and technology front."

February 3   The Central Committee of the CCP appointed
Hua Guofeng as acting premier of the State Council.

February 4   A major editorial in the People's Daily accused
the Soviet Union of having ulterior economic designs
on Angola and other parts of Southern Africa and also
of harboring deeper strategic aims as part of the Soviet
contention with the United States.   The editorial went
on to warn that "if the Soviet revisionists are allowed
to do evils in Angola and realize their designs, it is
hard to say that there will not be a second or even a
third Angola."

February 6   The Government of the People's Republic of
China extended an invitation to former President Richard M. Nixon and Mrs. Nixon to revisit China on February 21, 1976, the fourth anniversary of their first
visit.   They accepted the invitation.
• The People's Daily carried an article entitled "The
Continuation and Deepening of the Great Proletarian
Cultural Revolution: Gratified to See the Mass Debate
on Education at Qinghua University Advancing Against
the Waves," echoing some of the accusations made
against Deng Xiaoping during the Cultural Revolution.

February 7   The People's Daily published an announcement
that Hua Guofeng, hitherto minister of Public Security,
had, in his new capacity as acting premier of the State
Council, met the Venezuelan ambassador.

February 8   The 1976 Sino-Albanian protocol on goods ex-

change and payment was signed in Tirana. A protocol
on the use of China's loans by Albania for 1976 was also signed.

February 9 The 1976 Sino-Korean protocol on the mutual
supply of goods was signed in Pyongyang.

February 10 A wall-poster campaign began at Beijing University attacking "a capitalist roader" readily identifi-
able as Deng Xiaoping. The criticism grew more intense as time passed.

February 11 The delegation from the Federal Republic of
Germany, led by Alfred Dregger, arrived in Beijing
for a visit. Foreign Minister Qiao Guanhua met the
delegation on February 13, and Zhang Chunqiao met
the delegation on the following day. Acting Premier
Hua Guofeng met the delegation on February 19.

February 13 A rally of some 1,800 people took place in
Shanghai. Sponsored by the Municipal Revolutionary
Committee, the purpose was to denounce Deng Xiaoping.

February 14 The People's Daily published a front-page
article by Li Zheng entitled "It is necessary to go on
criticizing Confucius." The article employed most of
the quotations from the anti-Confucius campaign in
early 1974.
    • The Zaire Government Delegation, led by Engulu
Baangampongo Bakolele Lokanga, visited China from
February 14-19. Acting Premier Hua Guofeng had a
talk with the delegation on February 18. In a speech
at the banquet, the leader of the Zaire delegation asserted that "so long as the Russians and Cubans continue their aggression against Angola, we will never
admit and recognize the Movement of the People's Liberation of Angola."

February 16 Acting Premier Hua Guofeng met special envoy
of Mauritanian President Moktar Ould Daddah, Maloum
Ould Braham, who arrived in Beijing on February 14
for a three-day visit.

February 17 The Chinese People's Insurance Company Delegation, led by Feng Tianshun, visited North and South

Vietnam from February 17 to March 3.

• On its front page, the People's Daily published an article entitled "The Crux of Taking 'Three Instructions' as the Key to Restore Capitalism: Teachers, Students, Staff and Workers of Beijing University Criticizing the Revisionist Programme with 'Three Instructions' as the Key Link." The article claimed that the capitalist roader distorted Chairman Mao's instructions by placing two other instructions on the same footing with that of studying the theory of the dictatorship of the proletariat.

February 18   The People's Daily printed on the front page an article entitled "Zhaoyang Agricultural College on Fundamental Differences Between Two Education Lines." The article discussed ten aspects of the fundamental differences between the two lines in education, gave warm praises of Chairman Mao's policy on education, and criticized the "revisionist" educational system.

February 20   A Sino-Moroccon protocol on the building of a sports complex in Morocco was signed in Rabat.

February 21   At the invitation of the Chinese government, former President Richard M. Nixon and his wife visited China from February 21-29. The visit was timed to coincide with the fourth anniversary of the signing of the Shanghai communiqué. As it turned out, the former president became the first Western leader to spend much time with the new acting premier. Including the 100-minute meeting with Chairman Mao on February 23, Mr. Nixon spent a total of about eight hours in discussion with Hua Guofeng. Few details of the talks were released.

February 22   The People's Daily carried an article entitled "Develop New Things and Restrict Bourgeois Rights" by Liang Xiao. The article accused the capitalist roaders of being bitterly opposed to the three-in-one combination of the old, middle-aged, and young, and in particular to young cadres participating in leading bodies at various levels.

February 24   At the Twenty-fifth Congress of the Communist Party of the Soviet Union (February 24 to March 5),

the general secretary L. Brezhnev said that Maoism
would continue to be opposed but that the Soviet Union
was willing to improve relations on the basis of peaceful
coexistence. He identified Maoism as a source of war.

February 25 In Beijing, Wang Hongwen, Zhang Chunqiao
and Qi Denggui had a talk with E.F. Hill, chairman of
the Australian Communist party (M-L), and his wife
along with Albert Edward Bull, vice-chairman of the
party, and his wife. They visited China from February
9-26.

February 28 More than 100 people, including personalities
from various circles and Taiwan "compatriots" in Beijing,
met in the Taiwan Hall of the Great Hall of the People
to mark the twenty-ninth anniversary of the February
28 Uprising of the people in Taiwan. Liao Zhengzhi
spoke at the meeting and reiterated the strong determination of the Chinese people to liberate Taiwan.

March 2 The London Times suggested that Jiang Qing was
behind the current campaign against Deng Xiaoping.

March 3 China and Ghana signed, in Accra, the 1976 trade
protocol.

March 5 The Chinese Economic and Trade Delegation, led
by Li Qiang, visited Cambodia at the invitation of the
Cambodian government from March 5-12. The 1976
Sino-Cambodian economic cooperation agreement was
signed on March 10.

March 6 The Sino-Hungarian agreement on goods exchange
and payment for 1976 was signed in Beijing.

March 8 The Hong Kong newspapers reported that the posters in Guangzhou criticized Jiang Qing for giving a
visiting American professor, Roxane Witke, details of
her personal affairs, embarrassing to Chairman Mao.
  • The West German Delegation, led by Hans Matt-
hoefer, arrived in Beijing for a ten-day visit. On
March 8, the two nations agreed to exchange delegations
on coal, steel, and oil and natural gas.

March 10 NCNA reported that China took part for the first

time in the exhibition of daily necessities (over 1,500 articles) in London under the sponsorship of the British paper, Daily Mail.
  • The People's Daily carried an editorial entitled "Reversing Correct Verdicts Goes Against the Will of the People," to indicate that the current debate had isolated the capitalist roaders in the party. The editorial included another new Mao quotation: "You are making the socialist revolution, and yet don't know where the bourgeoisie is. It is right in the Communist Party—those in power taking the capitalist road. The capitalist roaders are still on the capitalist road."

March 13 NCNA reported that the newly Latinized form of the written Uighur and Kazakh languages was now popular in the Xinjiang Uighur autonomous region.

March 15 China welcomed the abrogation of the Soviet Friendship and Cooperation Treaty by Egypt. This "signified the bankruptcy of Soviet hegemonism in Egypt."
  • The Laotian Party and Government Delegation, led by Premier Kaysone Phomvihan, arrived in Beijing for a visit from March 15-24. The delegation was greeted at the airport by Acting Premier Hua Guofeng, Yao Wenyuan and Wu De. The delegation met Zhu De, held talks with Acting Premier Hua Guofeng and Yao Wenyuan, and was received by Chairman Mao on March 17. On March 18, an economic and technical cooperation agreement was signed. Kaysone announced that China would continue to give interest-free loans. The visit was a diplomatic breakthrough for both sides, since Laos had earlier been regarded by most observers as a Vietnamese and Soviet reserve.

March 17 Huang Hua spoke in the Security Council in support of the imposition of sanctions by Mozambique on Southern Rhodesia. He condemned the Rhodesian incursion into Mozambique under the pretext of pursuing guerrillas.

March 19 The People's Daily carried an article entitled "It is necessary to continue to criticize Confucius" by Li Zheng. The article said that the essentials of the revisionist line that opposed Chairman Mao's proletarian revolutionary line were to change the party's basic line of taking class struggle as the key link, to negate the great proletarian revolution and to restore capitalism in China.   The doctrines of Confucius and Mencius were precisely an important ideological origin of revisionism.

March 20   The first issues of five Chinese art journals became available today.   They were People's Theatre, People's Cinema, People's Music, Dance, and Fine Art.
   • Surprise was recorded over the absence of Chairman Mao's usual interpreters, Wang Hairong, Tang Wensheng, and Zhang Hanzhi, from his meeting with the visiting Laotian leaders on March 17.
   • Mr. Thomas Gates, a banker who had served as defense secretary in the Eisenhower Administration, was appointed head of the US liaison office in China to succeed George Bush.

March 22   Acting Premier Hua Guofeng met the Ethiopian Official Goodwill Delegation in Beijing.   The delegation arrived in Beijing on March 20 for a fourteen-day visit. An agreement on economic and technical cooperation between the two nations was signed on March 22.

March 23   The Anshan Iron and Steel Company, China's biggest, held a grand meeting to commemorate the sixteenth anniversary of "The Charter of the Anshan Iron and Steel Company," which was approved by Chairman Mao personally.   According to the Daily Telegraph (London), steel production at Anshan was said to have dropped to 5.6 million tons in 1975.

March 26   It was reported by the official Middle East News Agency in Cairo that China had provided the Egyptian Air Force with 30 MIG engines and spare parts, free of charge.

March 27   NCNA reported that some 1,000 bamboo slips, most of them recording laws and documents dating back about 2,200 years, were found in one of the twelve tombs recently excavated in Yunmen county, Hubei province.   They dated from the late years of the Warrings States period (221 B.C.) to the Qin Dynasty (221 B.C. to 207 B.C.).

March 28   The People's Daily published an editorial entitled

"Beat Back Right Deviationist Attempt to Reverse Correct Verdicts, Promote Industrial Production." It said:
"In criticizing the reactionary theory of the productive
forces, they should more effectively grasp class struggle as the key link, adhere to the principle of grasping revolution and promoting production, use revolution to command production and push it forward."

March 31 Huang Hua spoke in the Security Council in explanation of China's nonparticipation in voting on the
resolution on Angola. He said China had given military
assistance to the three liberation movements until January 1975 when the date of independence was fixed with
Portugal. Leading members of the three liberation
movements had visited China since then, each asking
for military assistance. China, however, had not responded to their request, rather it had urged them to
solve their differences peacefully. Huang said China
would not participate in voting on the draft resolution
because the wording in the draft resolution would be
used by the USSR to justify its intervention in Angola.

April 3 The People's Daily carried an article by the mass
criticism group of Beijing and Qinghua Universities entitled "An Admission of the Reversing Verdicts and
Seeking Restoration--a Criticism of an Article Dished
Up After a Hint Had Been Given by That Unrepentant
Capitalist Roader Within the Party." The authors offered an analysis of an article written last year, at the
behest of Deng, entitled "On the General Programme
for All Work of the Whole Party and the Whole Country,"
seeking to demonstrate the purposeful and programmatic
way in which he set about "reversing verdicts and
seeking restoration." The original article was intended,
it is claimed, as an attack on the Cultural Revolution,
Chairman Mao's revolutionary line and on the cadres
and masses implementing that line.

April 4 Many thousands of people mourned the late Premier
Zhou Enlai in Tiananmen Square, central Beijing, and
placed wreaths and placards in his honor. The ceremony had become a "notable mass demonstration" in
support of his political heritage, and by implication,
Deng Xiaoping.

April 5   Several thousand people gathered at the National People's Congress building to protest against the removal by the police of the numerous wreaths and placards.   During this protest, there were "sporadic" clashes between the police and the masses.   Police arrested many demonstrators.   Several cars were burned and a building ransacked and set on fire.   Placards supporting Deng Xiaoping and others criticizing Jiang Qing had been seen on the Heroes Monument.   Wu De made a broadcast speech to disperse the onlookers and the masses at Tiananmen Square.

April 6   Incidents similar to those in Beijing on April 4-5 took place in Zhengzhou (Henan).   At about the same time, similar happenings occurred in Kunming, Changchun, Shijiazhuang, Nanjing, Wuhan, Huhehot, Shanghai, Guangzhou, Taiyuan and other places.
   • The People's Daily carried an editorial entitled "Firmly Keep to the General Orientation of Struggle" which, significantly, did not deal with the Tiananmen incident, but concluded with a passage on the need for vigilance in the face of resistance to the campaign.
   • Huang Hua told the Security Council that China supported the imposition of sanctions against the Southern Rhodesian authorities and the enforcement of those sanctions by the Security Council, adding that to be effective, sanctions should be expanded to cover South Africa and the US should stop importing Rhodesian chrome and nickel.

April 7   The 1976 Sino-Sudan trade protocol was signed in Khartoum.
   • NCNA carried the official account of the Tiananmen Square incident as follows: "a handful of class enemies, under the guise of commemorating the late Premier Zhou Enlai, ... engineered an organized, premeditated and planned counterrevolutionary political incident in Tiananmen Square in the capital."   NCNA also released the full text of Wu De's broadcast appeal on April 5 in the Tiananmen Square.
   • NCNA released two resolutions of the CCP Central Committee: the first appointing Hua Guofeng first vice chairman of the Central Committee and premier of the State Council, and the second dismissing Deng Xiaoping from all posts both inside and outside the party.   The

two resolutions were proposed by Chairman Mao and the political bureau of the Central Committee unanimously adopted them.

April 8   The Sudanese Press Delegation, led by Ahmed Tigani El Tayeb, arrived in Beijing for a visit from April 8 to May 3.   The delegation met Premier Hua Guofeng on April 21, and Yao Wenyuan on April 29.

   • A Sino-Rumanian shipping agreement was signed in Beijing.

   • The resolutions of the Central Committee were signals for the mobilization of large numbers of people, initially in the capital and then in the provinces, to acclaim the resolutions, to express condemnation of Deng Xiaoping and those who, in regarding him as championing their cause, took part in the disturbances, and to show support for the Central Committee.   The proliferation of rallies and demonstrations throughout China was accompanied by the publication of a number of significant articles aimed at reinforcing the official interpretation of the disturbances and indicating the themes to be taken up at all levels.

April 9   Mass rallies were held in Henan, Shanghai, Anhui, Hunan, Gansu, Hubei, Heilonjiang, Shandong, Shanxi, Guangdong, Jiangsu, Sichuan, Guizhou to support Central Committee resolutions and denounce "Deng Xiaoping's crimes."

April 10   The People's Daily carried an editorial entitled "A Great Victory" which, besides summing up the case against Deng Xiaoping, made clear the view that he had been both "saved" by Chairman Mao, and, once his recidivism was evident, brought down by him.

   • Rallies and demonstrations were held in Liaoning, Hebei, Tibet, Ningxia, Xinjiang, Inner Mongolia, Hunan, Fujian, Anhui, Henan to hail the two resolutions adopted by the Central Committee of the CCP on April 7.

April 11   Rallies and demonstrations were held in Shanxi, Shaanxi, Yunnan, Shandong, Guangxi, Zhejiang to hail the two resolutions adopted by the Central Committee of the CCP on April 7.

April 13   The Red Flag carried an article entitled "Commu-

nists Must Work for the Interests of the Vast Majority
of the People." It pointed out that Deng Xiaoping had
completely betrayed the highest interests of the workers, the poor and lower-middle peasants and other labor-
ing masses, who constitute the overwhelming majority
of the Chinese population, to serve as a bourgeois representative in the party.

April 14 Mohamed Boucettu, special envoy of Moulay Hassan
II, king of Morocco, arrived in Beijing for a three-day
visit. Vice Premier Li Xiannian met him on April 15.
   • Chairman of the Standing Committee of the NPC
Zhu De and Premier Hua Guofeng sent a message to
President Khieu Samphan, Prime Minister Pol Pot, and
Chairman Nuon Chea, extending warm congratulations,
on behalf of Chairman Mao Zedong and the Chinese
government and people, on their assumption of the high
posts of president of the state, prime minister of the
government, and chairman of the permanent committee
of the People's Congress of Democratic Kampuchea, respectively.

April 15 The Chinese Ambassador to Guinea Bissau, Mr.
Jia Huaiqi, visited the Republic of Cape Verde and
signed a joint communiqué to establish diplomatic relations at the ambassadorial level as from April 25.

April 16 Chairman Mao Zedong, Zhu De, and Premier Hua
Guofeng sent a message to President Khieu Samphan,
Prime Minister Pol Pot, and Chairman Nuon Chea, extending, on behalf of the Chinese Communist party,
government, and people, the warmest congratulations
on the occasion of the first anniversary of the National
Independence Day of Democratic Kampuchea.

April 17 Premier Hua Guofeng met American physicist Dr.
Yang Zhenning. Dr. Yang visited China from March
27 to April 8.
   • China issued a statement indicating that the Swed-
ish and Philippines consortium for exploring oil in the
Nansha group was an encroachment on Chinese territory.

April 18 Egyptian Vice President Hosni Mubarak arrived in
Beijing for a seven-day visit. He was greeted at the
airport by Premier Hua Guofeng and Ulanfu. Premier

Hua Guofeng held talks with the delegation. Zhu De met the delegation on April 19, and Chairman Mao did so on April 20. A military cooperation agreement between the two nations was signed. No details were released.

• The People's Daily carried an editorial entitled "What Does the Incident at Tiananmen Square Show?" First, it showed the presence of the bourgeoisie within the CCP and the existence of the two-line intraparty struggle between the proletariat and the bourgeoisie; second, there really were counterrevolutionaries whose activities were linked to schemes for restoration and retrogression; and third, counterrevolution was short-lived.

• A comprehensive Han-Uighur dictionary which contained 47,000 words and phrases was published by the Xinjiang People's Publishing House.

April 22 Huang Hua told the UN Security Council that China had voted in favor of the resolution on East Timor although it maintained its reservations about the appointment of the secretary general's special representative.

April 26 The Red Flag carried an article by Chi Heng entitled "Great Victory for Dictatorship of the Proletariat," to state that the counterrevolutionary riot at Tiananmen was promptly smashed by heavy blows from the "iron fist" of the dictatorship of the proletariat.

April 28 Prime Minister Robert Muldoon of New Zealand arrived in Beijing for an eight-day visit. He met Chairman Mao on April 30, and held a series of talks with Premier Hua Guofeng and Foreign Minister Qiao Guanhua. Letters on mutual granting of most-favored-nation treatment in shipping were exchanged at a ceremony on May 1.

April 29 An explosion outside the Soviet Embassy occurred, killing two Soviet soldiers and injuring at least one Chinese. The Soviet Union lodged an official protest.

April 30 The Sino-Albanian protocol of the Eleventh Session of the Board of Directors of the Joint Stock Shipping Company was signed in Tirana.

• A ceremony was held in Katmandu for the exchange

of letters on the extension of the validity of the agreement between China and Nepal on trade, intercourse and related questions between Tibet and Nepal.

May 3 The new British Foreign Secretary Anthony Crosland, visited China from May 3-9. He had talks with Premier Hua Guofeng, Foreign Minister Qiao Guanhua, and Foreign Minister Li Jiang. No specific achievement was reached. Mr. Crosland told reporters in Tokyo that the Chinese leaders had assured him repeatedly that there would be no change in China's foreign policy following the dismissal of Deng Xiaoping.

• The minutes of talks between China and Equatorial Guinea were signed in Malabo for the building of a Bicomo hydroelectric power station and a high-tension power transformer and transmission line between Bicomo and Bata.

May 4 The fifty-seventh anniversary of the May 4th Movement was marked by Red Guard and CYL rallies and meetings. The People's Daily carried a front-page article entitled "Take the Road of Integrating with the Workers and Peasants, Be Vanguards in Combating and Preventing Revisionism," to praise the role of the educated young people going to the countryside, a "socialist new thing" opposed by Deng Xiaoping.

May 6 Premier Hua Guofeng met former Nepalese prime minister and his wife.

May 7 To commemorate the tenth anniversary of Chairman Mao's "May 7th Directive," the People's Daily carried a front-page article entitled, "The Fighters in Criticizing the Bourgeoisie," recapturing the basic spirit of the directive to criticize revisionism and bourgeoisie, and to restrict bourgeois Right.

May 10 Prime Minister Lee Kuan Yew of Singapore visited China from May 10-23. He met Chairman Mao on May 12, and held talks with Premier Hua Guofeng. He left China on May 23 without any communiqué or reference to any kind of agreement.

May 11 China's Beijing Opera Troupe from Shanghai left Shanghai for a performance tour in Japan from May 12

to June 26. The troupe gave its premiere in Tokyo on
May 13.

May 12 A protocol was signed in Bissau between China and
Guinea-Bissau on the dispatch of a Chinese medical team
to Guinea-Bissau.

May 13 The Red Flag carried an article entitled "Criticize
the Revisionist Fallacies on the Industrial and Transport
Front," to denounce Deng Xiaoping. The article said,
"Deng Xiaoping pushed a revisionist programme and line
and took the lead in stirring up the right deviationist
attempt to reverse the correct decisions of the Great
Proletarian Cultural Revolution."

May 14 Premier Hua Guofeng met the new Guyanese Ambassador to China, John Carter.
    • NCNA reported that a microwave communications
trunk line, linking Beijing with more than twenty provinces, municipalities and autonomous regions throughout
China, had been completed. The line was equipped
with a 960-channel transistorized and a 600-channel
electron tube microwave signalling system, designed
and made in China.

May 15 The People's Daily, the Red Flag, and the Liberation Army Daily published a joint editorial entitled "The
Great Cultural Revolution Will Shine Forever," to mark
the tenth anniversary of the May Sixteenth CCP Central Committee Circular, drawn up under Chairman Mao's
personal guidance. The article sought to show that
Deng Xiaoping's acts after he resumed work constituted
continuation and development of the "February Outline
Report" which Chairman Mao criticized in the circular.

May 16 Sri Lanka Deputy Minister of Defense and Foreign
Affairs Lakshman Jayakody arrived in Beijing for a five-
day visit. Premier Hua Guofeng met him on May 20.

May 20 The Chinese Government Delegation, led by Fang
Yi, left Beijing for Sudan to take part in the celebrations of the May 25 Revolution anniversary. The delegation stayed in Sudan till June 1.

May 21 The 1976 Sino-Soviet agreement on goods exchange
and payment was signed in Beijing.

May 23   NCNA reported that a large, up-to-date battery of
sixty-five coke ovens had been completed and put into
operation at the Benxi Iron and Steel Company in
Liaoning province.
   • In commemorating the thirty-fourth anniversary of
Chairman Mao's "Talks at the Yanan Forum on Literature and Art," the People's Daily published an article
entitled "Deepen the Criticism of Deng Xiaoping, Persevere in the Revolution in Literature and Art--Study
'Talks at the Yanan Forum on Literature and Art,'" to
accuse Deng of attempting to reverse the reforms in
literature and art, of attempting to oust the new leadership in literature and art.

May 26   Prime Minister Z.A. Bhutto of Pakistan arrived in
Beijing for a five-day visit. He met Chairman Mao on
May 27, becoming the last distinguished foreign guest
to do so, and held talks with Premier Hua Guofeng.
A joint communiqué was issued at the end of the visit.
China expressed support for the new changes in the
diplomatic patterns in South Asia including Pakistan's
normalization of relations with India. The two nations
signed an agreement on scientific and technical cooperation, and the protocol to the agreement on May 30.

May 28   In New York, China and Surinam signed a joint
communiqué to establish diplomatic relations at the ambassadorial level.

May 29   Two strong earthquakes, with magnitudes of 7.5
and 7.6, struck the Longling-Luxi area of Yunnan
province.
   • NCNA reported that China had completed a new
crude oil wharf of the 100,000-ton class in Dalian.
Two tankers, one 100,000 tons and another 50,000
tons, were recently filled at the wharf.

May 31   According to a broadcast commentary by Lu Da, a
report which appeared in the People's Daily on May 31
said that a set of "rules" for industrial management
were drawn under Deng Xiaoping's orders and entitled
"Certain Problems in Speeding Up Industrial Development." The "rules" advocated running factories by
experts, putting technology in command, the omnipo-
tence of rules and regulations, material incentives, the

direct and exclusive control of enterprises by the Ministry concerned, and the "slavish comprador philosophy." By means of the "rules," Deng denied the commanding role of proletarian policies over economics, but sought to reinstate the most experienced, to put technical expertise in command, and to rely on experts to run factories.

June 2 Vice Premier Zhang Chunqiao met the Comoros Government Delegation, led by Salim Himidt. The delegation arrived in Beijing on May 31 for a ten-day visit. A Sino-Comoros economic, technical cooperation agreement was signed on June 10.

• Nepalese King Birendra, at the invitation of Chairman Zhu De, the Standing Committee of the NPC, and Premier Hua Guofeng, visited Sichuan and Tibet (the first foreign leader to visit the autonomous region) from June 2-9. He was met at Chengdu airport by Premier Hua Guofeng, and Ngapo Ngawang Jigme. The Nepalese Foreign Minister K.R. Aryal said, after returning to Katmandu on June 9, that Premier Hua and Foreign Minister Qiao Guanhua would visit Nepal "at a time convenient to both Nepal and China."

June 3 General Guy Mery of France visited China from June 3-13. He had "wide ranging and friendly" talks with Premier Hua Guofeng, and conferred with Defense Minister Ye Jianying. He visited a Chinese seaborne unit in Shanghai and toured naval facilities in Dalian.

June 5 The 1976 Sino-Afghan protocol on the exchange of goods was signed in Beijing.

June 6 The 1976 Sino-Egyptian protocol on the trade agreement was signed in Cairo.

June 10 Premier Hua Guofeng met Thomas S. Gates, Jr., the new chief of the liaison office of the United States in China.

June 11 President Ratsiraka of Madagascar visited China from June 11-15. He was greeted at the airport by Premier Hua Guofeng, and held talks with him during the visit. China and Cuba signed a trade agreement, a payment agreement, and the 1976 trade protocol in Havana.

• Chinese vessels were thought to have seized two South Korean fishing boats on June 11 and June 13. Seoul announced their seizure by unidentified vessels on the high seas in the East China Sea, 110 miles southwest of Sohukasando Island. This followed official Chinese warnings to South Korean trawlers to stop fishing in China's territorial waters where they had been openly fishing since April.

June 15   The foreign press was told by a government spokesman, "Chairman Mao is well advanced in years and is still very busy with his work. The Central Committee of our Party has decided not to arrange for Chairman Mao to meet foreign distinguished visitors."
• Indian Foreign Minister Chavan stated in the Lok Sabha that Mr. K.R. Narayanan, a career diplomat, would be sent to China in two months time and then China would be expected to reciprocate, thus restoring full diplomatic relations.

June 16   Yao Wenyuan met the Yugoslav broadcasting and television delegation, led by Ismail Bajra.

June 18   The Sino-Iranian Joint Trade Committee reached an agreement on 1976 trade arrangements between the two nations and signed a memorandum in Beijing.
• Lai Yali called on the Security Council, condemned South Africa for the Soweton atrocities, and asked all states and people to give active support to the struggle of the Azanian people against racism.

June 20   Australian Prime Minister Malcolm Fraser and his party arrived in Beijing for an eight-day visit. He was greeted at the airport by Premier Hua Guofeng. He held talks with Premier Hua Guofeng, Zhu De, and other party and state leaders.
• An agreement on China's relics exhibition, to be held in Australia, was signed on June 23. At a banquet in Beijing on June 23, Mr. Fraser described the areas of agreement as "very broad and more important" than the areas of disagreement.

June 23   Lai Yali told the Security Council that China would not participate in the vote on Angola's application for UN membership. Although Angola had won independence

from Portugal, Lai said, its independence was not complete because of the continued armed intervention by
forces of "Soviet-imperialism."
  • NCNA reported that China's first all-transistor
radio-telemetering automatic weather stations had been
successfully built by the Institute of Radio Research
in Jiangsu province. The stations were to be installed
to replace the meteorologists in recording weather
changes in such inhospitable places as high mountains,
rugged sea islands and deserts.

June 28 NCNA reported that four big electric-powered irrigation stations had been completed in the central plain
of Jilin province, an important grain producer in Northeast China. The four stations, with a total of 115
groups of electric motors and pumps, were able to lift
fifty cubic meters of water per second.

June 29 A ceremony was held to mark the formal opening
of the road section of the double decker road-rail
bridge across the Huangpu River, linking the main city
of Shanghai with the general petrochemical complex then
under construction. The railway deck was opened on
September 11, 1975.
  • NCNA reported that a supplementary 291.5 km railway line between Shanghai and Nanjing was formally
opened to traffic. The second track of the Tianjin-Shang-
hai railway totalling 1,300 km was also opened to traffic.
  • NCNA reported that the 716 km Yunnan-Tibet
Highway leading to Lhasa was now opened to traffic.

June 30 China and the Seychelles signed a joint communiqué
to establish diplomatic relations at the ambassadorial
level.

July 1 A Sino-Ethiopian trade agreement and the 1976-77
protocol to the agreement were signed in Beijing.
  • The People's Daily, the Red Flag, and the Liberation Army Daily published a joint editorial to mark the
fifty-fifth anniversary of the founding of the CCP. In
one passage, it quoted Mao's statement that the bourgeoisie existed "right in the Communist Party" and went
on to elaborate the point in a long quotation from a
1964 directive by Mao concerning the Socialist Education
Movement.

- China and Malaysia signed an agreement for China to purchase 18,000 tons of rubber valued at more than $50 million in Kuala Lumpur.

July 3 Mao Zedong, Zhu De and Hua Guofeng sent a message to President Ton Duc Thang and other leaders of DRVN on its unification, proclaimed on the same day.

July 5 The eighth round of talks on the Tanzanian-Zambian Railway took place in Lusaka between the governments of Zambia, Tanzania and China from July 5-8. The minutes of the talks, a protocol on railway technical cooperation, and three other protocols were signed on July 8.

July 6 An obituary notice, issued by the CCP Central Committee, the NPC Standing Committee, and the State Council, reported the death of Zhu De age ninety, in Beijing at 3:01 PM. At the time of his death, Zhu De was a member of the Standing Committee of the politburo and chairman of the Standing Committee of the NPC. Last respects were paid to his remains at Beijing Hospital on July 8, and mourning ceremonies were held at the Working People's Palace of Culture July 9-10, followed by a memorial meeting on July 11 at the Great Hall of the People, presided over by Wang Hongwen, at which the memorial speech was delivered by Hua Guofeng.

- The People's Daily published an editorial to praise the summit conference of the Organization for African Unity. It said that the Soviet Union had become "the primary threat to the independence and security of the African countries."

July 7 K.R. Narayanan, the first Indian ambassador to China in fifteen years, arrived in Beijing, presenting his credentials on July 24.

July 9 In the Security Council, Lai Yali said that China "disapproved adventurist acts of terrorism, and assassination, kidnapping and hijacking of aircraft," but this was no excuse for Israel's "act of aggression committed against a sovereign state." China condemned Israel's action at Entebbe over the hijacked plane.

July 10   Hugh Scott, the US Senate Republican minority
leader visited China for two weeks from July 10.   He
had separate talks with Qiao Guanhua and Zhang Chunqiao.   He was quoted as saying that there would be no
change in the American China policy before the new administration took office in January 1977.
  • Chairman Mao Zedong and Premier Hua Guofeng
sent a message of greeting to President Kim Il-sung
marking the fifteenth anniversary of the signing of the
Sino-Korean Treaty of Friendship, Cooperation and Mutual Assistance.

July 11   The Red Flag carried an article entitled "Inner-
Party Struggle and Party Development," to mark the
fifty-fifth anniversary of the founding of the CCP.
The article quoted Chairman Mao as saying, "Will there
be need for revolution a hundred years from now?
There is always need for revolution."

July 12   China and Aden signed the minutes of talks on
building the Aden Friendship Hospital.

July 14   A ceremony in Kapiri Mposhi, Zambia was held to
mark the formal handing over by China and opening to
traffic of the PRC's largest aid project, the 1860 km
Tanzanian-Zambian Railway, from Dar-es-Salaam, Tanzania to Kapiri Mposhi.
  • Premier Hua Guofeng met Juan Jose Bremer Mar-
tino, under-secretary of the presidency of Mexico.

July 15   President Mathieu Kerekon of Benin arrived in Bei-
jing for a six-day official visit at the invitation of the
Chinese government.   He was greeted at the airport by
Premier Hua Guofeng.

July 16   NCNA reported that a total of 117 novels were published in China between 1972 and 1975.   Notable among
these were Surging Waves, On the Eve, Shipbuilders,
On the March, Barefoot Doctor Hong-yu, The Bright
Golden Road, and The Sparkling Red Star.
  • Hundreds of thousands of workers, peasants, soldiers and young people throughout China took part in
grand swimming galas in celebration of the tenth anniversary of Chairman Mao's swim in the Yangtze River.

July 19   China lodged an official protest against the July 12
statement by Japanese Foreign Minister Miyazawa on an
early normalization of US-China relations. He was
charged with interfering in China's internal affairs
and for departing from the 1972 Sino-Japanese joint
statement which acknowledged that Taiwan was a part
of China.

July 21   Princess Ashraf Pahlavi, sister of His Imperial Majesty Shahanshah of Iran, arrived in Beijing for a
twelve-day visit at the invitation of the Chinese government. Premier Hua Guofeng met her on July 23. After
visiting Tibet, she left Beijing for home on August 1.

July 23   The Radio Beijing began its Hungarian language
program.

July 26   President Seretae Khama of Botswana made an official visit, at the invitation of Chinese government, from
July 26 to August 9. He was greeted at the Beijing
airport by Premier Hua Guofeng. The two nations
signed an agreement on economic and technical cooperation on August 8.
   • Premier Hua Guofeng met Edward Gough Whitlam,
former Australian Prime Minister and the leader of Labor party, and Mrs. Whitlam.
   • NCNA reported that over 100 ancient ape-teeth
fossils, a fairly complete lower jaw bone (mandiblex),
and fragments of a deformed upper jaw bone, had been
discovered in Lingnite Seams in Lufeng county, Yunnan
province. Preliminary analyses dated the beds of the
recent discovery to the Pliocene period, three to twelve
million years ago.

July 28   A strong earthquake occurred in the Tangshan-
Fengnan area in Hebei province, North China, at 03:42
hours on July 28. Comparatively strong shocks were
felt in Beijing and Tianjin. Figures released by the
country's network of seismological observatories specified the magnitude of the principal shock to be 7.4,
with the epicenter at 39.4 degrees north latitude, 118.1
degrees east longitude. Damage of varying degrees
was reported in the epicentral region.

July 29   The scale of damage and loss of life in the Tang-

shan-Fengnan area was assessed to some degree from
the statistics released concerning the massive rescue
and reconstruction operation that was mounted. Twenty-four provinces, municipalities and regions sent medical and rescue teams including, for example, fifty-six
medical teams consisting of 870 personnel that arrived
from Shanghai on July 29, followed by a further 3,000
medical personnel, a 100-strong relief team from Shaanxi,
and similar teams from Jiangxi (700), Liaoning (3,000),
Inner Mongolia (490), Gaungxi (150), Zhejiang (800),
and Shandong (800).

   • The CCP Central Committee cabled a message of
sympathy to the earthquake-striken area. The Central
Committee called on the Communist party members "to
conscientiously study Chairman Mao's important instructions, take class struggle as the key link, deepen the
great struggle to criticize Deng Xiaoping's counterrevolutionary revisionist line and repulse the right deviationist attempt at reversing correct verdicts, and unite
to fight against the serious natural calamity."

July 30 The 670-meter railway bridge across the Luan River
in the Beijing-Tangshan line was reopened by teams
from Shenyang working alongside PLA teams.

   • NCNA reported the dispatch of a high-powered
central delegation by the CCP Central Committee and
the State Council, led by Premier Hua Guofeng, the
three subdivisions of which visited factories, mines,
villages, army camps, offices, schools and hospitals in
Tangshan, Tianjin and Beijing on July 30. Premier
Hua Guofeng visited the Kailuan Coal Mine, and Tangshan Iron and Steel Company.

July 31 NCNA reported that a huge outlet tunnel one meter
high, 2.9 meters wide, and 711 km long, the largest in
Beijing thus far, was completed in five years and eight
months by commune peasants of Yanqing county, outside the Great Wall on the outskirts of Beijing. When
the auxiliary project was completed, over eighty percent of the county's farmland or 26,000 hectares had
gravitational irrigation, carrying river water into the
Guandeng reservoir.

August 1 The People's Literary Publishing House published
Lu Xun Shuxin Ji (Collection of Lu Xun's Letters) in

two volumes, among several of Lu Xun's works published to commemorate the fortieth anniversary of his
death.

• The People's Daily carried an editorial entitled
"Forever Adhere to Chairman Mao's Line on Army Building," to mark the forty-ninth anniversary of the founding of the PLA. The article said that Deng Xiaoping
had used the need to prepare for war to promote the
view that weapons decide everything, thus reversing
the relationship between people and things, and policies
and military affairs.

August 6   Premier Hua Guofeng met Ieng Sary, Deputy
Prime Minister in charge of foreign affairs of Democratic Kampuchea.

August 7   The Beijing-Shanhaiguang railway, damaged by
the strong earthquake in Tangshan-Fengnan area, was
reopened to traffic at 19:40 hours on August 7.

August 8   NCNA reported that the antiquated written scripts
of the Uighur and Kazakh Nationalities were officially
replaced by new Romanized scripts throughout the
Xinjiang Uighur autonomous region on August 1, 1976.
Based on the Chinese phonetic system, the new scripts
have been adopted for use in all fields. The old
scripts of the two languages, treasured as cultural
legacies, will be used as vehicles for the study of historical relics and data.

August 11   In Beijing, China and Gambia signed a protocol
on dispatching a Chinese medical team to work in Gambia.

August 15   Premier Hua Guofeng sent a message to the Fifth
Conference of the Heads of States and Governments of
Non-aligned Countries, extending congratulations on
behalf of Chinese government. The conference was
held in Colombo, Sri Lanka, from August 16-18.

August 16   An earthquake hit the Songpan-Pingwu area in
northern Sichuan on August 16. The magnitude of the
Sichuan earthquake was 7.2, its epicenter being at
latitude 32.7 north and longitude 104.1 east.

August 17   Rallies and forums were held by the youth in
Beijing, Shanghai, and Tianjin to mark the tenth anni-
versary of Chairman Mao's first meeting with the Red
Guards on August 18, 1966.

August 20   The Chinese Ambassador to Zaire, Gong Dafei,
called on President Bokassa of the Central African Republic during a visit to Bangui. It was agreed on August 20 that diplomatic relations (broken off by the
Central African Republic in 1966) would be normalized
at the ambassadorial level.
   • The song-and-dance ensemble of Xinjiang Uighur
autonomous region was on performance tour in West
Asia from August 20 to October 12, including Afghanistan, the People's Republic of Yemen, the Yemen Arab
Republic, Syria, Iraq, and Kuwait.

August 23   The People's Daily editorial entitled "Grasp Crucial Point and Deepen the Criticism of Deng Xiaoping"
pointed to the struggle being deepened and advanced
by the distribution of three documents of negative example, namely, "On the General Programme for All
Work of the Party and the Country," "Some Problems
Concerning the Work of Science and Technology" (An
Outline Report), and "Some Problems in Accelerating
Industrial Development" (Regulations for Industry).
These documents were said to have been worked out
on instructions by Deng Xiaoping and constituted a
concentrated demonstration of the ultra-rightist essence
of his counterrevolutionary line and a systematic expression of his revisionist viewpoint.

August 24   The Chinese Song and Dance Ensemble left Beijing for friendly visits to Mozambique, Kenya, Madagascar, and Ethiopia from August 24 to October 25.
   • The recovery operation in the Tangshan-Fengnan
area was given much publicity in the media. NCNA reported that the first coal had been mined again at the
Kailuan coalfield.

August 27   The Red Flag carried an article entitled "Adhere
Forever to Chairman Mao's Line in Army Building,"
criticizing "the arch unrepentant party capitalist-roader
Deng Xiaoping's revisionist fallacies concerning army
building." It wrote "Victory in a future war against

aggression depends chiefly not on the most advanced
weapons, but on the masses of the people who are armed
with Mao Zedong thought, on Chairman Mao's concept
of people's war and, on the correct political and military
lines Chairman Mao has formulated for our Party and
army."

August 28   China and Kampuchea signed a protocol on the
implementation of the economic cooperation agreement in
Phnom Penh.

August 29   NCNA reported that the first China-designed and
built oceangoing oil tanker of the 50,000-ton class was
launched at the Dalian Hongqi shipyard.   Construction
of the hull of the tanker "Xihu" took only 135 days,
marking a new level for China's shipbuilding industry.
• China, Chad, and Cameroon signed a protocol on
the construction of a highway bridge over the Chari
River linking Ndjamena of Chad and Kousseri in Cameroon.

August 30   The sixth earth satellite was launched.

August 31   NCNA reported that surveys made by Chinese
archaeologists of historical relics on the Xisha Islands
had yielded excellent results, including many important
discoveries, such as three pieces of celedon-glazed pottery of China's Southern Dynasties (A.D. 420-589), a
number of copper coins of the Song and Ming Dynasties
(1368-1644).

September 1   NCNA reported that 43 of the local factories
and mines in the Tangshan-Fengnan area had resumed
production and all 409 primary and middle schools had
started the new term on September 1.

September 2   The Western Samoan head of the state, Malietoa
Tanumafili, visited China from September 2-9.   The
delegation was greeted at the airport by Premier Hua
Guofeng.   An agreement on economic and technical cooperation between the two nations was signed on September 8.

September 4   A ceremony was held in Kabul to mark the
signing of the letters exchanged between China and

Afghanistan concerning the building of a 25,000-spindle
cotton textile, printing and dyeing mill and a paper mill
with a daily capacity of eight tons. These mills were
to be built with Chinese assistance.

September 6   Former US Secretary of Defense James Schlesinger arrived in Beijing for a visit from September 6-
29 at the invitation of the Chinese People's Institute of
Foreign Affairs. Members of his party were told that
the invitation came from Chairman Mao. He had talks
with many of Chinese leaders, and visited defense installations and military forces throughout China, including Xinjiang and Inner Mongolia. Premier Hua Guofeng
met him on September 28. Before leaving for Tokyo,
Schlesinger was reported from Beijing as having criticized China's military equipment as not being of sufficient quality to pierce Soviet armor or to down contemporary Soviet aircraft. In his opinion it was entirely feasible for the Soviet Union to thrust deep into
Xinjiang and Inner Mongolia, detach areas and hold
them successfully against any Chinese counterattacks.

September 8   The Red Flag published an article entitled
"The Reactionary Nature of the Practice" for its adverse
political effect but also for its being a tactic to bring
about capitulationism and national betrayal through a
"grand policy" involving the signing of long-term contracts with foreign countries for the import of technology and equipment in return for the export of China's
mineral resources.

September 9   The announcement of Chairman Mao Zedong's
death, at the age of eighty-two, was in the form of a
message to the whole country from the Party Central
Committee, the Standing Committee of the National People's Congress, the State Council, and the Military
Commission of the Party Central Committee. The message read in part as follows: "Comrade Mao Zedong
passed away at 00:10 hours September 9, 1976 in Beijing as a result of the worsening of his illness and despite of all treatment, although meticulous medical care
was given him in every way after he fell ill." A later
announcement carried details of mourning services to
be held from September 11-18 at the Great Hall of the
People during the late Chairman's lying in state, of a

memorial rally to be held in Tiananmen Square at 15:00
hours Beijing time on September 18, of arrangements
for mourning throughout China and in representative
bodies abroad, of the nationwide tribute to be observed
at the time of the memorial service, of the decision not
to invite foreign governments and organizations to send
representatives.

September 10   Huang Hua spoke to the UN Security Council,
thanking members for their condolences on the death of
Mao Zedong and for their high appraisal of Mao's
achievements.   He said that the Chinese people would
continue to follow "Mao's revolutionary line and policies
in foreign affairs."

September 11   Beginning at 10:00 hours, party and state
leaders stood before the catafalque to pay their respects and to keep vigil.   During the next seven-day
mourning period, other members of the funeral committee, provincial leaders, representatives of workers,
peasants, soldiers and Red Guards also took turns
standing vigil.   The wreath presented by Jiang Qing
was made of sunflowers, ears of wheat, maize and flowers
of xanthoceras sorbifolia.   The wreath bore the inscription "Deeply mourn the esteemed great teacher, Chairman Mao Zedong" from "your students and comrades-in-
arms, Jiang Qing and Mao Anqing, Li Min, Li Na, Mao
Yuanjin and Mao Yuanshin."

September 14   Premier Hua Guofeng led party and state
leaders attending the mourning ceremony.   Diplomatic
envoys, representatives of foreign Marxist-Leninist
parties and organizations who took part in the mourning ceremony were received by Premier Hua Guofeng.
   • NCNA reported that US government officials and
personages from various circles called at the liaison
office of the People's Republic of China to express condolences on the passing away of Chairman Mao.   Pay-
ing condolence calls were Brent Scowcroft, assistant to
the president for National Security Affairs (representing President Ford), Secretary of State Henry A. Kissinger, Senate Democratic party leader Mike Mansfield,
and Senate Republican party leader Hugh Scott.
   • The People's Daily carried an article entitled
"Chairman Mao, we will remember you always," written

by the 8341 unit of the PLA, saying, "We vow to live
up to your expectations. We determined to turn our
grief into strength, carry on the cause you left behind
and persist in taking class struggle as the key link,
keep to the party's basic line and persevere in continuing the revolution under the dictatorship of the
proletariat."

September 15 The death of Chairman Mao elicited a telegram
from the Communist party of the Soviet Union to the
Communist party of China. This, along with similar
messages from Poland, East Germany, Bulgaria, Czechoslovakia and Mongolia were rejected by the Chinese.
The Foreign Ministry spokesman stated the following:
"We have no party-to-party relations with them and we
have rejected their messages." The death of Chairman
Mao was widely noted throughout the world. Almost all
the heads of state or government of the nearly 150
countries in the world sent messages of condolence to
Beijing. Many governments, especially in the Third
World, declared official periods of mourning, some of
them for several days.

September 16 The joint editorial by the People's Daily, the
Red Flag, and the Liberation Army Daily entitled
"Chairman Mao Will Live Forever in Our Hearts," reaf-
firmed why Chairman Mao would never be forgotten.
As for the future, it said "Chairman Mao adjured us:
'Act according to the principles laid down'."

September 18 The mass memorial meeting, attended by one
million people and transmitted live throughout China,
was held from 15:00 to 15:30 hours in Tiananmen
Square. It was presided over by Wang Hongwen, and
the memorial speech was delivered by Hua Guofeng.
After the Beijing meeting, similar memorial meetings
were held by leading organs of all localities at and
above county level. In the memorial speech, Premier
Hua Guofeng said, "The whole Party, the whole army
and the people of all nationalities throughout the country must respond to the call of the Party Central Committee actively, turn grief into strength, carry on the
cause left behind by Chairman Mao, 'practice Marxism,
and not revisionism; unite, and don't split; be open
and aboveboard, and don't intrigue and conspire', and,

under the leadership of the Party Central Committee, carry through to the end the cause of the proletarian revolution in China which Chairman Mao pioneered."

September 21   Huang Hua told the UN General Assembly that the Chinese Government Delegation was "deeply moved" by the condolences expressed on the death of Mao Zedong in numerous United Nations bodies and by the large number of condolence calls at the Chinese mission.
    • US Democratic leader Mike Mansfield and Mrs. Mansfield, and Senator John G. Glenn, Jr. and Mrs. Glenn arrived in Beijing for a visit at the invitation of the Chinese People's Institute of Foreign Affairs from September 21 to October 11. Vice Premier Li Xiannian met the delegation on October 9.
    • Premier Hua Guofeng entrusted the Chinese Embassy in Korea to lay a wreath in the mourning hall for the late Vice President Choi Young Kun.

September 23   The Jamaica Delegation, led by Deputy Prime Minister David Coore, arrived in Beijing for a seven-day visit. Premier Hua Guofeng met the delegation on September 24. A Sino-Jamaican trade and economic cooperation agreement, and protocols of the agreement were signed on September 26.

September 24   NCNA reported that state leaders or their representatives and government representatives of 105 countries had made condolence calls at Chinese embassies, 169 cables or letters of condolence from 123 heads of state or government had been sent to China, besides which there had been condolences from Marxist-Leninist parties and organizations of many countries in the five continents.

September 25   The Red Flag carried an article entitled "Mao Zedong Thought Will Forever Guide Us Forward," saying, "Chairman Mao adjured us to 'act according to the principles laid down' which means to act according to Chairman Mao's proletarian revolutionary line and policies."

September 26   China successfully conducted a new nuclear test.

September 29   At a meeting of the politburo, Hua Guofeng
    and Jiang Qing exchanged serious words over the use
    of the adjuration and also the succession question.   At
    this meeting, Jiang Qing formally proposed to the polit-
    buro and particularly to Hua, that she be supported as
    head of the Central Committee of the party.   Jiang
    Qing told Hua that he was "incompetent" to lead the
    party, where upon he answered that he was "competent"
    and "[knew] how to solve problems."

September 30   The People's Daily published an article enti-
    tled "Turn Grief into Strength," to support the adjura-
    tion.   Identifying the adjuration as a component of
    Chairman Mao's proletarian revolutionary line, turning
    grief into strength meant "defying death" in defending
    his policies, waging "resolute struggle" against all class
    enemies, tempering oneself in "violent storms," encour-
    aging the "growth of newly emerging forces" and daring
    to "go against the tide."

October 1   The Pravda carried an important article signed
    by I. Alexandrov to survey Sino-Soviet relations in a
    nonpolemic tone.   It claimed that the deterioration of
    mutual relations at the beginning of the 1960's was
    through no fault of the Soviet side.   The article out-
    lined a number of major steps taken by the CPSU
    aimed at the improvement of Sino-Soviet relations.   It
    concluded that "We believe, therefore, that there are
    no problems in the relations between our states that
    cannot be resolved, given mutual desire and a spirit of
    good neighbour-liness, mutual benefit and consideration
    for each other's interest."   The article expressed the
    Soviet willingness to repair relations with China.
        • The public screening of forty-seven recently com-
    pleted films began.   It included feature films, film ver-
    sions of operas, documentaries, and science and educa-
    tional films.   Among these, Lu Xun Zhandou de Yisheng
    (The Militant Life of Lu Xun) was included to mark the
    fortieth anniversary of his death.
        • The National Day's editorial in the People's Daily
    entitled "Study Mao Zedong Thought, Carry Out Chair-
    man Mao's Behests," urged the cadres at all levels to
    "act according to the principles laid down," and to
    "practice Marxism, and not revisionism; unite, and don't
    split; be open and aboveboard, and don't intrigue and

conspire."

   • The twenty-seventh anniversary of the founding
of the People's Republic of China was marked in Beijing
by a forum attended by the party and state leaders,
and over 400 representatives of workers, peasants,
soldiers, teachers, students, and commercial workers,
including Hua Guofeng, Wang Hongwen, Ye Jianying,
Zhang Chunqiao, Jiang Qing, Yao Wenyuan, and Li
Xiannian. The forum reaffirmed the intention to continue the campaign against Deng Xiaoping and to follow
the late Chairman's adjuration to "act according to the
principles laid down."

October 2 Japan made an official protest against China's
   nuclear test of September 26, because the test led to
   an increase in the levels of radioactivity in Japan.
      • A draft of the speech, to be delivered to the UN
   General Assembly on October 5 by Qiao Guanhua was
   sent to Premier Hua Guofeng for his approval. Upon
   discovering that the adjuration was included, he struck
   it out, because "three of the characters were wrong
   compared with the original in Chairman's handwriting."

October 4 Liang Xiao (a homonym for two universities,
   Beijing and Qinghua) published an article, entitled
   "Forever act according to the principles laid down," in
   the People's Daily.

October 5 Qiao Guanhua spoke to the UN General Assembly
   to reiterate China's view of the international situation.
   He said that China was determined never to seek to be
   a superpower.

October 6 On the evening of October 6, or in the early
   morning hours of October 7, less than a month after
   Chairman Mao's death, a coalition led by Hua Guofeng,
   Ye Jianying, and Wang Dongxing arrested nearly thirty
   high-ranking party and government officials, including
   four politburo members; Wang Hongwen, Zhang Chunqiao, Jiang Qing, and Yao Wenyuan. These four were
   to become known collectively as the "Gang of Four."
   An official confirmation came at a rally held in Beijing
   on October 21.

October 7 The CCP Central Committee appointed Hua Guo-

feng as its chairman and as chairman of its Military Affairs Commission in succession to Mao Zedong.
  • Huang Hua told the UN Security Council to adopt a resolution condemning South Africa for refusing to implement Security Council resolution 385 (1976) and calling on it to terminate its illegal occupation of Nambia immediately and to release all political prisoners.

October 8 The CCP Central Committee, State Council, the Standing Committee of NPC, and Military Affairs Commission of the CCP Central Committee decided to build a memorial hall in Beijing for Mao Zedong and to place Mao's coffin in it "so that the broad masses of the people will be able to pay their respects to his remains." The CCP Central Committee also decided to publish Mao Zedong Quanji (Collected Works of Mao Zedong) under the "direct leadership" of the politburo headed by Hua Guofeng, and Volume V of Mao Zedong Xuanji (Selected Works of Mao Zedong).

October 9 The whole party, the whole Army and the people of all nationalities throughout China expressed warm support for the two decisions of the CCP Central Committee on October 8, 1976 and declared their firm determination to carry out Chairman Mao's behests, uphold Marxism-Leninism-Mao Zedong thought, adhere to the Chairman's proletarian revolutionary line, "practice Marxism, and not revisionism; unite, and don't split; be open and aboveboard, and don't intrigue and conspire."

October 10 The People's Daily published an article, "Resolutely Combat Soviet Modern Revisionism: to make it clear that the arrest of the Gang of Four did not change China's policy toward the Soviet Union.
  • The joint editorial of the People's Daily, the Red Flag and the Liberation Army Daily endorsed the two decisions as "Common Aspirations of Hundreds of Millions of People." Echoing the texts of the decisions, the editorial also described them as being of tremendous historical significance.

October 11 Prime Minister Michael Somare of Papua New Guinea visited China from October 11-17. He met Premier Hua Guofeng on October 12 and signed a joint communiqué to establish diplomatic relations at the ambassadorial level.

October 15 Wall posters appeared in Beijing and Qinghua Universities, and in Shanghai denouncing the Gang of Four by name.

October 17 China successfully conducted another underground nuclear test.

October 18 Two million Shanghai industrial workers firmly supported two important decisions by the CCP Central Committee and pledged to obey all orders issued by the Party Central Committee headed by Hua Guofeng.

October 21 To commemorate the fortieth anniversary of the passing away of Lu Xun, the People's Daily carried an article entitled "An Out-and-Out Capitulationalist," praising his revolutionary stand and correct proposition which aroused the discontent and hatred of the "four villains."
  • The official confirmation of the arrest of the Gang of Four came at the rally held in Beijing on October 21. Radio Beijing reported that army men and people had mounted a mammoth demonstration to celebrate Hua Guofeng's being made chairman of the CCP Central Committee and its Military Affairs Commission and to hail the victory of the CCP Central Committee headed by Chairman Hua in shattering the scheme of the anti-party clique of Wang Hongwen, Zhang Chunqiao, Jiang Qing, and Yao Wenyuan. Similar demonstrations were reported throughout China during the period of October 21-25.

October 23 The Sino-Hungarian protocol of the Fifteenth Meeting of the Commission for Scientific and Technical Cooperation was signed in Beijing.

October 24 An official account of the circumstances leading to Chairman Hua's assumption of office and the attempted takeover by the Gang of Four was given in Wu De's speech at a celebration rally in Beijing on October 24. The rally took place at Tiananmen Square and was attended by one million people, together with party and state leaders including Chairman Hua. Wu De began his speech by stating that the rally was being held to celebrate Comrade Hua Guofeng's assumption of the two posts and to celebrate victory over the antiparty clique's attempt to usurp party and state power. He went on to say, "On April 30, Chairman Mao wrote to Comrade Hua Guofeng in his own handwriting, 'With you in charge, I'm at ease', which expressed his boundless trust in Comrade Hua Guofeng." The Gang of Four had challenged the appointments. Wu De attacked the Gang of Four for trying to split the CCP and seize power.

October 25   Ceremonies in Tokyo and Beijing marked the inauguration of the new China-Japan seabed cable.
    • The joint editorial of the People's Daily, the Red Flag, and the Liberation Army Daily, entitled "Great Historic Victory," explained that Hua Guofeng's appointment as chairman was made in accordance with the October 8 resolution of the CCP Central Committee. This was also in accordance with the arrangements Chairman Mao had made before he passed away.

October 27   NCNA announced that the CCP Central Committee had decided to appoint Su Zhenhua concurrently as first secretary of the Shanghai Municipal Committee of the CCP and chairman of the Municipal Revolutionary Committee. It also decided to dismiss Zhang Chunqiao, Yao Wenyuan, and Wang Hongwen from all posts inside and outside the party in Shanghai.

October 29   The Liberation Army Daily published an article entitled "Comrade Hua Guofeng Is Our Party's Worthy Leader," praising Chairman Hua for his appointments. Reiterating that he was Mao's choice, it referred to his tenure as first vice-chairman and premier as the most difficult period since the founding of the People's Republic of China because of the natural disasters and the "four pests" which were rampant.

October 30   Chairman Hua Guofeng sent a formal message of greeting to mark the convocation of the Seventh Congress of the Albanian Party of Labour.

November 1   The People's Daily reiterated the economic slogan "grasp revolution, promote production." It accused the Gang of Four of distorting and opposing this principle and of sabotaging production.

November 2 One hundred thousand Shanghai militiamen held a grand rally to pledge to obey the Party Central Committee headed by Chairman Hua Guofeng, and fight the antiparty Gang of Four to the finish.

    • The CCP Central Committee, NPC Standing Committee, State Council, and Military Affairs Commission of the CCP Central Committee made an announcement that Mao Zedong's domestic and foreign policies would be retained. The announcement contained no phrase criticizing Deng Xiaoping.

November 5 A People's Daily article gave the first major sign of cultural policy after the Gang of Four. It revealed a directive by Chairman Mao Zedong of July 25, 1975, on behalf of the film Chuangye (Pioneers), about Daqing, and against "nit-picking" in judging works of art. The article attacked the Gang of Four's regime strongly by saying "what they enforced in literary and art circles was an out-and-out bourgeois dictatorship, a fascist dictatorship," and thus signaled a more liberal policy. It also revived the slogan "let a hundred flowers blossom, let a hundred schools of thought contend."

November 7 NCNA reported that since 1966, archaeological workers had found fifteen ancient sites, excavated ten historical sites and cemeteries (including 341 ancient tombs), and unearthed a large number of relics.

    • China sent a message to the Soviet Union, marking the fifty-ninth anniversary of the Bolshevik Revolution. It said that the Chinese people "always [hold] dear its revolutionary friendship with the Soviet people."

    • China and Iraq signed the minutes of their joint talks on the construction of the Baghdad sports hall.

    • The CPC Central Committee sent a message to the Albanian party, marking the thirty-fifth anniversary of the founding of the Albanian party.

November 8 Premier Hua Guofeng greeted Enver Hoxha on his reelection as the leader of the Albanian party.

    • The Liberation Army Daily carried an article entitled "Comrade Hua Guofeng as Leader of Our Party is Chairman Mao's Wise Decision," to embellish Chairman

Hua's image. It said "In taking the decision to shatter
the scheme of the Gang of Four, he had lived up to
Chairman Mao's expectations.

November 11   A Sino-Mongolian trade protocol was signed in
Beijing.

November 12   Huang Hua told the Security Council that
China supported Vietnam's application for membership
in the United Nations. Hua said that China welcomed
the Vietnamese achievement of independence, liberation
and reunification.

November 13   Vice Premier Li Xiannian predicted that China's
foreign trade would be "flourishing in three years from
now." In his talks with the visiting French delegation
he said that China wanted petrochemical technology, oil
and mineral exploration equipment, steel-making and
power-generating equipment. He went on, however, to
make the pertinent comment, "One needs foreign currency to buy all these things."

November 14   The NPC Delegation, led by Ulanfu, left Beijing to visit Iraq and Kuwait by the invitations of these
nations from November 14-29.
     • A front-page article in the People's Daily exposed
and condemned the Gang of Four antiparty clique for
its crimes in sabotaging the efforts to grasp revolution
and promote production. The article said, "The 'gang
of four' asserted that production will go up automatically
when revolution is carried out well." By this they
meant to negate party leadership and throw production
into chaos so that the "socialist economy would autono-
matically fall into an anarchist state and capitalism would
be restored."

November 15   Another earthquake struck the Tangshan area
of Hebei province.
     • President Salah Addin Ahmed Bokassa of the Cen-
tral African Republic and his party visited China from
November 15-22. He met Chairman Hua Guofeng on
November 16. The two nations signed agreements on
economic and technical cooperation and on trade on
November 16. In the communiqué, both sides "unanimously condemn[ed] the acts of aggression by social

imperialism in indulging in armed intervention in Angola."

• China and Somalia signed a certificate handing over a highway section between Belet Uen and Galcaio in Somalia. This was the first stage of the construction work of the Belet Uen-Burao Highway in Somalia being built with Chinese aid.

November 16 The People's Daily carried an article entitled "A Plot of the 'Gang of Four' to Usurp Party and State Power," to expose the crimes of the Gang of Four in directing "the spearhead of struggle against Chairman Mao, Premier Zhou Enlai, and a large number of leading cadres of central and local party, government and army organs who adhere to Chairman Mao's revolutionary line."

• A veteran Guomindang official, former member of the Executive Yuan, Miao Yundai, visited China from the US from November 16 to December 25. He was received by Wu De on November 16.

November 17 China successfully conducted a new hydrogen bomb test.

November 18 Chairman Hua Guofeng met Thakin Ba Thein Tin and Thakin Pe Tint, chairman and vice-chairman of the Central Committee of the Communist party of Burma.

November 19 The People's Daily printed on the front page an important article entitled "A Sinister Programme of the 'Gang of Four' for Usurping Party and State Power," that first appeared in the Liberation Army Daily on November 15, which criticized the "Gang of Four" antiparty clique for its counterrevolutionary crime of making opposition to empiricism the "key link."

November 20 The protocol of the Fourteenth Session of the Sino-Bulgarian Commission for Scientific and Technical Cooperation was signed in Beijing.

November 21 A People's Daily article by the Research Institute of Lu Xun exposed Jiang Qing as an actress who capitulated to the Guomindang reactionaries in the 1930's, not a "progressive artist" as she styled herself.

November 22 The Liberation Army Daily published an article
    entitled "Obey the Party Central Committee Headed by
    Chairman Hua in All Our Actions," to stress the neces-
    sity for revolutionary authority. The article stated
    that, in April 1976, Chairman Mao had issued an explicit
    instruction that it was necessary to publicize Hua Guo-
    feng to make him known to the people step-by-step but
    the antiparty clique controlling the media had prevented
    its implementation.

November 23 Following a visit to China, Senator Mansfield
    said that "further delay in dealing with the Taiwain
    problem may well strengthen the hand of the elements
    in the Chinese leadership seeking to restore greater
    comity with the Soviet Union even at the expense of the
    US relationship."
      • Six US Senators, led by Senator Curtis, having
    also completed a visit, said that during their meeting
    with Vice Premier Li Xiannian it had been made clear
    to them that the Soviet threat had priority over the
    Taiwan issue.

November 24 Wu Xiaoda spoke to the General Assembly in
    explanation of China's vote in favor of the resolution
    on the question of Palestine. He said China accepted
    the report of the Committee on the Exercise of the In-
    alienable Rights of the Palestine people, agreeing that
    Israel should withdraw from all the Arab territories it
    had occupied and that the Palestinian people should re-
    gain their national rights. Wu said, however, that if
    the realization of peace in the Middle East "in accord-
    ance with all relevant resolutions" was interpreted as
    covering Security Council Resolutions 242 (1967) and
    338 (1973), China wished to record the reservations it
    had expressed earlier on these two resolutions.
      • The solemn ceremony of laying the cornerstone
    for the Memorial Hall for Chairman Mao Zedong was held
    at Tiananmen Square in Beijing. Chairman Hua Guofeng
    attended the ceremony, at which he made a speech and
    filled in earth around the cornerstone for the Memorial
    Hall. In his speech, Chairman Hua had no criticism
    against Deng Xiaoping.

November 25 The protocol of the Eighteenth Session of the
    Sino-Czechoslovak Joint Commission for Scientific and
    Technical Cooperation was signed in Prague.

November 26 NCNA reported that the fossilized right parietal (roof of the skull) bone of a child dating back about 100,000 years was recently found at the well-known paleoanthropological site of Dingzun in Shanxi province. "Dingzun Man," a type of homo between the ape-man and the modern man, was first discovered at the site in 1954.

November 28 The head of the Soviet Government Delegation at the Sino-Soviet border talks, Deputy Foreign Minister Ilyichev, arrived in Beijing to resume the border talks. There were indications that no substantive change had occurred in the positions of either side.

November 29 Huang Hua, China's ambassador and permanent representative at the United Nations, was recalled to become the new foreign minister.

November 30 The Third Session of the Standing Committee of the Fourth National People's Congress was held in Beijing from November 30 to December 2. Song Qingling presided over the meeting. The agenda included a resolution on the nomination of Deng Yingchao (Zhou Enlai's widow) as vice-chairman of the NPC Standing Committee (which was approved), and an explanatory statement by Li Xiannian on the appointments and removals proposed by Chairman Hua Guofeng. Apart from the decision to appoint Huang Hua to replace Qiao Guanhua as foreign minister, no other details were given. Wu De spoke at the session to stress the continuation of criticism of Deng Xiaoping and repulsion of right deviationist attempt to reverse correct verdicts. He said that "we have got rid of sabotage and interference by the 'gang of four,' we should, and certainly can, do our jobs better." However, Song Qingling in her statement mentioned no Deng Xiaoping. The session praised Chairman Hua Guofeng as the most reliable successor Chairman Mao himself chose.

December 1 Premier Hua Guofeng sent a message of greetings to President Souphanouvong on the occasion of the first anniversary of the founding of the People's Democratic Republic of Laos.
  • The Standing Committee of the National Committee of the Chinese People's Political Consultative Conference

(CPPCC) attended the Third Session of the Standing Committee of the Fourth NPC as observers unanimously expressed wholehearted support for Comrade Hua Guofeng as chairman of the Central Committee of CCP and chairman of its Military Commission, warmly hailed "the great victory of the Central Committee headed by Chairman Hua Guofeng in smashing at one blow the plot of the 'gang of four' to usurp party and state power, and indignantly exposed and denounced the towering crimes of the 'gang of four'."

December 2   The Party Central Committee, the Standing Committee of the NPC, the State Council, and the Military Commission of the Central Committee of the CCP issued a special "Announcement" to state the principles of government and party foreign policies. It declared, "We will continue to implement unswervingly Chairman Mao's revolutionary line and policies in foreign affairs, and adhere to proletarian internationalism. We will never seek hegemony or be a superpower.... We will unswervingly establish or develop relations with all countries on the basis of the Five Principles of Peaceful Co-existence."

December 5   Premier Hua Guofeng met the delegation of Marxist-Leninist Communists of France led by Jacques Jurquet.

December 6   Premier Hua Guofeng met Vice Premier Do Muoi of DRVN on his way home from Moscow.

December 7   China used its veto in the first vote proposing Waldheim for a second term of office as UN secretary general. The veto was changed to a vote in favor in the second vote, allegedly because China found the Third-World countries favored Waldheim continuing in office.
     • China successfully launched another man-made earth satellite. It was returned to earth with precision according to plan on December 10.

December 8   The Tanzanian Government Delegation, led by First Vice President Aboud Jumbe, visited China from December 8-15. Premier Hua Guofeng met the delegation on December 10. In his speeches in China, the vice

president praised China's role in their bilateral relations and indeed China's pattern of relations with other
countries in Africa.

　• The People's Daily devoted its second page to the
commemoration of the martyr Yang Kaihui, Chairman
Mao's second wife.　She was arrested by the Guomindang and died a heroine on November 24, 1930.　The
forty-sixth anniversary of the death of the martyr
Yang Kaihui was commemorated at the mausoleum in
Changsha county, Hunan province by a mass meeting.

December 9　Chairman Hua Guofeng and other leading comrades of central organs received trainees and staffs of
Military and Political Academy, totalling more than
1,500, at the Great Hall of the People.

December 10　The Second National Conference on Learning
from Dazhai in Agriculture was held between December
10-27 in Beijing and attended by 5,000 representatives.
Chairman Hua Guofeng made an important speech.　He
reviewed the events of 1976 and looked forward to 1977
as a year in which the Gang of Four would be smashed
completely and China would go towards great order, a
year of united struggle and triumphant advance.　There
was no mention of Deng Xiaoping in his entire speech.
He called for the achievement of the modernization of
agriculture, industry, national defense, and science
and technology by the end of the century.

December 13　The Central Committee of the CCP sent a message to the Fourth Congress of the Vietnam Workers'
Party extending warmest greetings.

December 14　NCNA reported that the Institute of Computing
Technology under the Academy of Science of China recently built a general, large, high-speed electronic
computer with integrated circuits.

　• Chairman Hua Guofeng met E.F. Hill, chairman of
the Australian Communist party (M-L) and his wife,
J.A. Hill.

December 15　NCNA reported that the open-hearth furnace
No. 1 of the steel plant of Thai Nguyen iron and steel
complex in Vietnam was completed with Chinese help and
began tapping molten steel on December 15.　The com-

plex was heavily damaged during the war.

• A People's Daily article pointed out that Chairman Mao's important directive on the novel Water Margin (Shuihu Zhuan) was a sharp criticism of the capitulationism practiced by the Gang of Four.

December 16 A People's Daily article entitled "Maggots Undermining Socialism from Within," attacked the Gang of Four for disrupting national economy. The article said, "Out of their counterrevolutionary needs, the gang of four intentionally blurred the distinction between socialist accumulation and 'outing profit in command'."

December 17 Premier Hua Guofeng met the Rumanian Party and Government Delegation, led by Leorghu Ogren.

• Chairman Hua Guofeng and other leading party and and state leaders received in the Great Hall of the People more than 1,800 representatives attending the preparatory meeting for the National Conference on Learning from Daqing in Industry.

• The People's Daily published an article entitled "A Desperate Move Before Destruction Ended," to accuse the Gang of Four of forging Chairman Mao's last words. It stated that they had fabricated and used the phrase, "Act according to the principles laid down" to create confusion and to replace Chairman Mao's instruction "Act in line with past principles." The article traced the course of events from the time when Mao responded to a report delivered by Hua Guofeng on April 30, 1976, in which he referred to things not going so well in a few provinces, to the crisis that developed in early October. On April 30, 1976, Mao told Hua to "Take your time, don't be anxious. Act in line with past principles. With you in charge, I am at ease."

December 19 The 1977-78 Sino-Korean scientific cooperation plan was signed in Beijing.

December 20 The People's Daily carried a report from a Baoding delegate at the National Conference on Learning from Dazhai in Agriculture which said that armed clashes took place in the city because of the Gang of Four's attempt to seize power there.

December 21 Chairman Hua Guofeng sent a message to Le

Duan marking his election as secretary general of the Vietnamese Workers' Party.

December 22   The Yemen Arab Republic Government Delegation, led by Lt. Col. I.M. Al-Hamdi, visited China from December 22-26.   Premier Hua Guofeng met the delegation on December 22.   An agreement on economic and technical cooperation between the two nations was signed on December 23.
   • China and Finland signed the 1977 trade agreement in Helsinki.

December 23   Sichuan radio reported that the Gang of Four had conspired to organize a counterrevolutionary armed riot in Yibin (Sichuan), causing serious loss of life and property.
   • The eighty-third anniversary of Chairman Mao Zedong's birthday was commemorated by the release of a full-length, color documentary Eternal Glory to the Great Leader and Teacher Chairman Mao Zedong.   It not only recorded scenes of last summer's mourning but also included shots from old films showing his revolutionary activities.

December 25   Guizhou radio reported that the Gang of Four and their supporters had caused serious trouble in the provinces by "dragging out and struggling against leadership cadres at all levels."
   • China and Kampuchea signed a trade protocol and an agreement on economic and technical cooperation in Phnom Penh.
   • The People's Daily published Mao Zedong's Lun Shida Guanxi (On the Ten Great Relations) to handle contradictions correctly.

December 26   The large Shandong tractor plant went into production in Yanzhou (Shandong).

December 30   Those close to the incoming President Jimmy Carter were reported to be in favor of normalizing diplomatic relations with Beijing without "abandoning" Taiwan.

Chapter VIII

1977

BEGINNING OF THE HUA ERA

The sudden arrest of the Gang of Four in October, 1976, showed Chairman Hua Quofeng's alertness and his ability to decide and act swiftly. He moved quickly to consolidate his power, but he was beset with difficulties, since he lacked extensive relationships with party veterans and military leaders. As a result, there were serious disturbances in the provinces of Sichuan, Jiangxi, and Fujian, as well as the cities of Wuhan, Hangzhou, and even Baoding, only ninety miles south of Beijing. Troops were sent into these areas to prevent the seizure of power by supporters of the Gang of Four, and changes in military and administrative leadership were ordered in Heilongjiang, Zhejiang, Jiangsu, Guizhou, and four other provinces. The speedy rise of military power was significant.

Demands for the return to power of Deng Xiaoping added to the unrest. Deng was first purged as a rightist during the 1966 Cultural Revolution. With the assistance of Premier Zhou Enlai, he was later rehabilitated and in 1975 named first deputy premier. He was expected to succeed Premier Zhou, who was in poor health, and to arrest the trends of radicalism by means of moderate pragmatism and economic development. Considering him a menace to their continuing revolution, the leftists purged him for the second time in April 1976. With the arrest of the Gang of Four, however, the tide again turned in his favor. Early in 1977, wall posters appeared in Beijing calling for his return, and demonstrations were held to stress similar demands.

Deng was backed by a powerful force, represented in the capital by Ye Jianying and in the South by influential generals, such as Xu Shiyou and Wei Guoqing. In July, the

Central Committee of the party finally restored Deng Xiaoping to his posts as member of the politburo and its Standing Committee, vice-chairman of the Central Committee, vice-chairman of the Military Commission of the party, deputy premier, and chief of the General Staff of the Army. Tough and blunt, he was regarded as one of the most capable administrators in China. He seemed likely to dominate the party center and deviate further from Mao's radical party line.

In August, the Eleventh Congress of the Chinese Communist party met in Beijing. It confirmed the party leadership, composed of Chairman Hua Guofeng, Minister of Defense Ye Jianying, and Deputy Premier Deng Xiaoping. The Congress elected a new Central Committee of 201 regular and 132 alternate members. There were seventy-six (37.8 percent) who had been purged as "capitalist roaders" and "anti-party elements" during the Cultural Revolution, and had been rehabilitated since 1972. Their rehabilitation confirmed the end of leftist radicalism.

The new Central Committee met on August 21 and elected twenty-three members to the politburo, to be headed by Hua Guofeng. The Standing Committee of the politburo was composed of Chairman Hua and four deputy chairmen: Ye Jianying, Deng Xiaoping, Li Xiannian, and Wang Dongxing. Of the politburo members, eleven had military backgrounds, reflecting Beijing's stress on order and discipline. This was indeed a group of mainly old and experienced generals and cadres. The twenty-three full members of the Politburo averaged sixty-eight years of age, ten of them were over seventy. Of the twenty-three, twenty joined the party between 1921 and 1935, two between 1936 and 1949, and only one after the establishment of the PRC in 1949.

Among these 201 members of the Central Committee, 110 (54.7 percent) were reelected from the full members of the Tenth Central Committee, twenty (ten percent) were promoted from alternate to full-member status, and seventy-one (35.3 percent) were new members. In terms of party seniority, 19.1 percent of those members of the Tenth Central Committee who joined the party by 1935 and 39.3 percent of those who joined the party between 1936 and 1949 did not reappear, as opposed to 71.8 percent of those who joined the party after 1949. Hence, the purge of the Cultural Revolutionary Left hit mainly the Central Committee

members with low party seniority and representatives of mass
organizations. The Eleventh Central Committee presented itself as a more civilian, more cadre-oriented, and more veteran leadership group with a tendency towards a slightly
stronger representation of the central machine than its two
predecessors.

The Eleventh Congress adopted a new party constitution which allowed more discussion within the party. The
Communist party stated that the constitution should create a
situation in which there would be "both unity of will and
personal ease of mind and liveliness." Party members should
have the right to criticize party organizations and officials
and carry their appeals to the highest authority. On the
other hand, party agencies should be responsible for check-
ing up on the observance of discipline.

Under the new leadership, Mao's rigorous revolutionary
line was replaced by a set of liberal policies that promoted
"political liveliness and economic prosperity." In January
1977, official newspapers revived the liberal slogan of the
1950's that called for the contention of a hundred schools of
thought and the blooming of a hundred flowers in science
and culture. Beijing now stressed the importance of a "revolutionary united front" that would include not only workers
and peasants but also intellectuals and "patriotic democratic
parties." The new leadership declared that it would continue to "raise high" the thought of Mao Zedong, but subtly
cited from Mao only those statements that lent support to the
new policies.

Education underwent a major change under Beijing's
new leadership. To provide a basis for China's rapid modernization, it was found necessary to reverse Mao's educational policy, which was oriented toward class struggle rather
than technical learning. Emphasis was put on quality rather
than the political background of the students. Examinations
were reinstituted, and authority to discipline students was
restored. High school graduates, particularly those in natural sciences, could enter college directly, without having
to spend years working in the countryside. Special attention
was given to science and technology. Large funds were
promised to universities and technical institutes for scientific
research. Scientists were given more time and freedom to do
their work.

In February 1977, Beijing convened four national conferences on military affairs to discuss modernization of the
defense establishment, especially air defense and arms production. There was a keen recognition by military leaders
of the need for modern, sophisticated weapons, which were
deemed absolutely necessary to deal with a possible surprise
attack by the Soviet Union. Parallel to the emphasis on advanced weapons was the demand for a smaller, more efficient
army, trained to use modern weapons. The large army of
three million men, backed by an armed militia of several millions, was the pride of Mao Zedong, who believed in the
"human sea" of troops that would "drown" foreign invaders.
Beijing now backed away from Mao's precept that men were
more important than weapons. The new leadership was prepared to import foreign arms if necessary.

In 1977, economic development was given high priority
by Beijing not only because it was indispensable to making
China a modern, powerful nation, but also because of the
slow economic growth, attributable to political strife, in the
previous year. At the beginning of the year, a series of
conferences was held to discuss various economic problems.
In a major economic review, issued in September, Beijing
called for centralized control of industry, higher production
and profits, and introduction of foreign technology, "Revolution," the leadership declared, "can never be substituted for
production."

In October, the State Planning Commission announced
that industrial production was on the increase after a period
of stagnation. The grain harvest was "fairly good," in spite
of a drought in the spring. Petroleum output for the first
six months of 1977 rose 10.6 percent over the same period a
year earlier. The increase, however, represented a sharp
decline when compared with the annual rise of about twenty
percent in the past decade. In line with the policy of foster-
ing economic prosperity, Beijing announced, in October,
wage raises for factory workers and government officials.
About fifty to sixty percent of the urban work force would
be covered by the increases. In addition, the government
would offer urban residents better housing, food, and welfare benefits, while peasants were to receive higher incomes
and more consumer goods. To ensure sufficient food supply,
Beijing increased its purchases of foreign grain in 1977.
The total purchase of wheat for the year added up to more
than five million tons, the largest since 1973.

The new Carter administration reaffirmed its interest
in normalizing ties with China. But because of public opposition to abandoning Taiwan, President Carter had to look
for a formula that would improve relations without "the appearance" of forsaking Taiwan. In pursuit of this policy,
Secretary of State, Cyrus R. Vance, visited Beijing during
August 22-26. He was received at the airport by Huang
Hua, Chinese minister of foreign affairs, but the Chinese
reception was notably less enthusiastic than that accorded
former Secretary Henry A. Kissinger during his several
visits to China. For two days, Secretary Vance talked with
Huang Hua. Finally, on August 25, he had a long discussion with Deng Xiaoping. The talks were cordial, but there
was no progress on the improvement of relations; Vance was
unable to find a formula to satisfy Beijing. The Beijing conditions for normalization remained unchanged, namely, that
the United States withdraw its remaining military personnel
from Taiwan, that diplomatic relations with Nationalist China
be severed, and the 1954 security treaty with it be abrogated. Beijing was not interested in any formula that would
enable the United States to give Taiwan some form of guarantee in place of the security treaty. Nor would Beijing consider the possibility that upon severing diplomatic relations
with the Nationalist regime, the United States might establish
a liaison office in Taipei. More important, Beijing rejected
any suggestion that it would not use force against Taiwan.

On August 27, upon the return of Secretary Vance,
President Carter lauded his China trip as a "major step"
toward normalizing relations with Beijing. But the Chinese
leaders disagreed. On September 6, in a manner unusual
in diplomatic circles, Deputy Premier Deng Xiaoping told the
executives of the Associated Press that China's efforts to
establish diplomatic relations with the United States had
"suffered a setback" during the visit of Secretary Vance.
He called Vance's discussions in Beijing a retreat from proposals made by former President Gerald R. Ford and former
Secretary Henry Kissinger. According to Deng, President
Ford in December 1975 had promised that if he was reelected
he would sever diplomatic ties with Taiwan and establish relations with Beijing.

The purge of the Jiang Qing group did not result in
any change in Beijing's anti-Soviet policy. In an interview
with a visiting German delegation on September 25, Deputy

Premier Deng Xiaoping said that the "warming up" of Sino-
Soviet relations was out of the question not only for this
generation, but even for the next. On October 7, a limited
agreement was concluded between China and the Soviet Union
concerning navigation on the Ussuri River on their disputed
border. It was provided that at times of low water, Chinese
ships could use a channel near Khabarovsk, at the junction
of the Amur and Ussuri rivers. The agreement had no im-
pact on the dispute over regions along the border.

There were increasing contacts between China and
Western Europe. A Chinese delegation was sent to France
to visit defense industries for possible armaments purchases.
In April, Margaret Thatcher, the British Conservative party
leader, was invited to visit China. She was given a banquet
by Deputy Premier Li Xiannian, who did not miss the opportunity to discuss the menace of Soviet power. In Eastern
Europe, Beijing continued its efforts to isolate the Soviet
Union whenever possible. When President Tito of Yugoslavia
visited China on August 30, he was given a regal reception--
in sharp contrast to the time when Mao Zedong considered
him among the worst of renegades.

Beijing constantly reminded Japan that the Soviet
troops stationed in eastern Siberia were directed not only
against China but more against the United States and Japan.
To divert Tokyo from helping develop oil and gas resources
in Soviet Siberia, China was willing to increase its oil exports to Japan. Friendly relations were maintained with
North Korea, which had adopted a detached attitude toward
the Soviet Union. Beijing pledged support for North Korea's
struggle for an "independent and peaceful unification" of
Korea. Sino-Indian relations improved after the exchange
of ambassadors in 1976. Indian ships were admitted to Chinese ports and trade ties were revived. But the Tibetan
question continued to be a thorny issue between the two
countries. Beijing accused India of supporting refugees for
Tibet's secession from China.

Finally, many heads of state visited Beijing in 1977,
including President Ne Win of Burma, President Francisco
Macias Nguema of Equatorial Guinea, Lt. Col. Sebyi Kountche,
the chief of state of Niger, and President Ahmadou Ahidjo
of Cameroon. Beijing granted small amounts of aid to Equatorial Guinea and Niger during the visits of their chief
executives.

January 1   The joint <u>People's Daily</u>, <u>Red Flag</u>, and <u>Libera-</u>
<u>tion Army Daily</u> editorial on New Year's Day looked
towards the creating of "a completely new situation in
which there are political liveliness and economic prosperity, and in which a hundred schools of thought
contend and a hundred flowers blossom in science and
culture, and the people's livelihoods steadily improves
on the basis of the development of production," together with the fulfillment of the plans for comprehensive modernization before the end of the century.

January 2   China's longest highway bridge, the 3500-meter
bridge over the Yellow River at Luoyang (Henan), was
opened to traffic.
    • NCNA published a report entitled "How Chairman
Mao Ascended Jinggangshan Again," as an addition to
the two poems by Chairman Mao which were published
on January 1, 1976.
    • Major General Ziaur Rahman, the chief martial law
administrator and chief of army staff from Bangladesh,
visited China from January 2-6. Premier Hua Guofeng
met him on January 4. An economic and technical cooperation agreement and a trade and payment agreement
were signed on January 4.

January 3   NCNA reported on new projects completed in
1976. In water conservancy, 4,200 million cubic meters
of earth and stone work were done, 440,000 hectares
of terraced fields and new farmland built and 3.66
million hectares of waterlogging-prone farmland leveled
or improved. Twelve small nitrogen fertilizer plants
were built in the Guangxi Zhuan autonomous region
and nineteen in Hebie province. Three big and
medium-sized tractor plants in Heilongjiang, Shandong,
and Liaoning provinces went into production. More
than fifty new coal shafts completed in 1976, and six
of the eight collieries of the Kailuan coal mines which
were wrecked by the earthquake had partially or fully
resumed production. An oil pipeline network in Northeast China has been virtually completed and those in
North and East China were being laid at high speed.
After completing the first stage of installing two
100,000 generating units at high speed and with good
quality, the Xintian Power Plant in Shandong province
in 1976 installed two new 200,000 kw generating units.

The second 300,000 kw generating unit was put into
operation in the Wangding Power Plant near Shanghai.
A water-supply channel of the Baishan hydroelectric
power station in Jilin was completed. The whole length
of Shanghai-Nanjing double track was opened to traffic
in 1976. The oil supplying installation capable of handling 300,000 tons of oil yearly at the Qinghuangdao
harbor was put into operation and three tanker berths
were completed at the Qinghuangdao oil terminal, with
a combined yearly loading and unloading capacity of
ten million tons. The China-Japan cable and a carrier
communications trunk line linking Beijing with Shanghai
and Hangzhou were successfully completed.

January 4 NCNA announced that three geological maps,
edited by the Chinese Academy of Geological Science,
would soon be on sale in China and abroad. They were
the Tectonic System Map of the People's Republic of
China, the Geological Map of the People's Republic of
China, and the Geological Map of Asia.
    • Fifty-nine theatrical programs in a rich variety
of art forms were staged in the Chinese capital during
the New Year Festival. Seven mobile troups made the
rounds of factories, villages and army barracks at the
same time.

January 6 A color documentary entitled Eternal Glory to the
Esteemed and Beloved Premier Zhou Enlai was put on
the screen in commemoration of the first anniversary
of the passing away of Premier Zhou Enlai. In the
sequence showing the lying in state and the memorial
service, there were no shots of the Gang of Four or
Deng Xiaoping. The latter's funeral oration was replaced by a narration.

January 7 The People's Daily carried an article to condemn
the Gang of Four in interfering with and suppressing
reports of the nationwide mourning after Premier
Zhou's death. Yao Wenyuan, in particular, was singled
out for having killed an NCNA report for a front-page
article on the educational revolution at Qinghua in the
People's Daily on January 14, 1976, the eve of the
memorial meeting.

January 8 The first anniversary of the death of the late

Premier Zhou Enlai was marked by commemoration meetings both in Beijing and other parts of the country,
and publication of articles extolling his virtues and
condemning the activities of the Gang of Four in opposing, persecuting, framing, and harassing him.

January 9   A poster appeared in Beijing calling for Deng
Xiaoping's appointment as Premier of State Council.

January 10   Chairman Hua Guofeng met the delegation of the
Central Committee of the Marxist-Leninist Communist
party of Honduras.
   • The National Conference of the Coal Industry to
Learn from Daqing and Catch Up with Kailuan was held
in Beijing from January 10-25.

January 11   The longest highway bridge in Fujian province
opened to traffic.   The bridge across the Minjiang
River is 733.7 meters long and 11.5 meters wide with
foot paths on both sides.
   • Another thirteen letters by Lu Xun had recently
been discovered after the publication of the Collected
Letters of Lu Xun in 1976.
   • The Liberian Goodwill Delegation, led by Adolphus
Benedict Tolbert, arrived in Beijing for an eight-day
visit.   The delegation met Huang Hua, Li Xiannian,
and Chairman Hua Guofeng on January 14.

January 14   The iron weight of a steelyard and a dozen
towns dating more than 2,000 years back had recently
been unearthed in Weizhang county of Hebei province,
500 km north of the Great Wall.   The weight belonged
to the Qin Dynasty (221-207 B.C.) and towns to the
Yan and Qin states of the Warring States period (476-
22 B.C.).
   • Foreign Minister Huang Hua met David Rockefeller,
president of the board of the Chase Manhattan Bank
of the United States and his party.   Huang Hua reportedly told Rockefeller that China wished to settle
the outstanding dispute concerning the frozen Chinese
assets in the US (valued unofficially at $76.5 million)
and the private and corporate American claims regarding property seized in 1949 (valued at $196.9 million).

January 15   For the first time, a quotation of Hua Guofeng

replaced the traditional Mao Zedong quotation of the
day on the front page of the People's Daily.

January 18   China and Thailand exchanged notes in Beijing
confirming the reaching of an agreement on reciprocal
registration of trademark.
• NCNA reported that a high precision digitized
seismological instrument, the component nuclear procession magnetometer, had been devised and manufactured by a radio factory in Anhui province. This
automatic instrument modernized China's earthquake
observation and forecasting. Based on the principle
of nuclear procession, the instrument could measure
and record the intensity of the earth's magnetic field
continuously. When the geomagnetic field of the rock
formations showed abnormal variation before the oc-
currence of an earthquake, the magnetometer could
measure the variations with fair accuracy and provide
reliable geomagnetic data for earthquake observation
and forecasting.

January 19   Premier Hua Guofeng sent a message to President Tito of Yugoslavia, expressing condolences on the
death of Dzemal Bijedic, president of the Yugoslav
Federal Executive Council.

January 22   A protocol of the Sixteenth Meeting of the Korea-
China Border River Navigation Cooperation Committee
was signed in Pyongyang.
• Chairman Hua Guofeng met Yoshikatsu Takeiri,
chairman of the Central Executive Committee of the
Japanese Komeito.

January 23   Chairman Hua Guofeng and other central leading
leaders received at the Great Hall of the People more
than 3,000 representatives attending the National Conference of Coal Industry on Learning from Daqing and
Catching Up with Kailuan.

January 25   The 1977 Sino-Rumanian protocol on goods exchange and payment was signed in Bucharest.

January 28   Sino-Finnish agreement on maritime transport
was signed in Helsinki.
• The People's Daily printed a front-page article

entitled "The 'Gang of Four' and the Trotskites." It said, "Our present serious struggle against the 'gang of four' has a striking resemblance to that waged by the Bolsheviks against the Trotskyites more than 50 years ago."

January 29   The 1977 Sino-Pakistan protocol on scientific and technical cooperation program was signed in Islamabad.

January 31   An article in the Xinhua Daily reported that in Jiangsu the Gang of Four had incited and abetted militiamen to attack party and government organs, to seize public security departments by force and to carry on beatings, smashing and looting.   During a visit by a foreign head of state to Nanjing in August 1976, they interfered with the motorcade of the state guests, distributing handbills and blocking traffic, attempting to cause an incident involving a foreign country and then make charges against the provincial CCP committee.

February 1   Two protocols for 1977 were signed in Beijing between China and Albania involving the exchange of goods and payments, and the use of the Chinese loans to Albania.
• NCNA reported that a large clansmen's cemetery dating back to the late period of primitive society was excavated along with 30,000 stone artifacts and other relics in Lodu county on Qinghai province in the upper reaches of the Yellow River.   Using the isotope carbon 14 dating technique, archaeologists verified the age of the cemetery to be 4,000 years old.

February 2   China and Argentina signed a trade agreement in Beijing.

February 3   The Government Delegation of the People's Democratic Republic of Yemen, led by Foreign Minister Mohammad Saleh Mutie, arrived in Beijing for a six-day visit at the invitation of the Chinese government.   The delegation met Vice Premier Li Xiannian on February 5, and left Beijing for Vietnam on February 8.

February 4   The minutes of the meeting on China's assistance

to Mali in building four water conservancy projects of
a state farm "office of Niger" was signed in Bamako.

February 5   Deng Yingchao, vice-chairman of the National
People's Congress Standing Committee, visited Burma
from February 5-11 at the Burmese government's in-
vitation.
   • The protocol of the Seventeenth Meeting of the
Scientific and Technical Committee between China and
Korea was signed in Beijing.
   • Chairman Hua Guofeng and other central leaders
received at the Great Hall of the People more than 800
representatives attending the National Conference on
People's Air Defense Work, the meeting of leading
cadres of the enterprises under the Third Ministry of
Machine Building, and two meetings called by the Science and Technology Commission for National Defense
of the Chinese People's Liberation Army.

February 7   A joint editorial by the People's Daily, the Red
Flag, and the Liberation Army Daily called on party
committees at all levels to mobilize the masses to study
two important documents: Chairman Mao's work "On
the Ten Great Relationships," and Chairman Hua Guofeng's speech at the Second National Conference on
Learning from Dazhai in Agriculture, and to make a
thorough exposure and criticism of the Gang of Four.

February 8   The protocol of the twenty-ninth meeting of the
Board of Directors of the Sino-Korean Yalu River
Hydro-Electric Power Company was signed in Pyong-
yang.
   • President Jimmy Carter received Huang Chen,
the head of the Chinese liaison office in Washington.

February 10   The Pravda printed an article hostile to China,
resuming polemics for the first time since the death of
Mao Zedong.   The article concluded, "Our country will
never take the road of aggression, will never raise
the sword against other peoples, China included."

February 12   Chairman Hua Guofeng met the delegation of
the Norwegian Workers' Communist Party (M-L), headed
by Paul Steigan, chairman of the party.   The delegation
arrived in Beijing on January 26 for a twenty-one day
visit.

February 13   Premier Hua Guofeng sent a message of condolence to Mrs. Indira Gandhi, offering deep condolences
on the death of the Indian President Fakruddin Ali
Ahmed.

February 15   The Geju (opera) Baimao Nü (The White-haired
Girl) was repremiered on the Beijing stage after over
a decade of suppression by the Gang of Four. It was
one of numerous cultural items to be revived about this
time.

    • NCNA reported that more than 50,000 criticism
and denunciation meetings of the Gang of Four had
been held in Beijing in recent months with a total at-
tendance of over twenty-five million. Wall posters,
exhibitions, broadcasts, poetry recitals and every other effective means had been employed to denounce
their crimes in plotting against the party and the
government.

February 17   In Monrovia, China and Liberia signed a joint
communiqué to establish diplomatic relations at the
ambassadorial level.

    • Premier Hua Guofeng sent a message to Mohammad
Daoud, president and prime minister of Afghanistan,
warmly congratulating him on his election as the first
president of the republic.

    • NCNA reported that more than a thousand people
from Yunnan province and Kunming city held a meeting to welcome Duan Liuzhang, "a former secret agent
of the Jiang gang who had crossed over to the motherland."

February 21   Chairman Hua Guofeng and the leading central
leaders received the representatives at the national
conference on railway work.

    • In Monrovia, China and Liberia signed an agree-
ment on economic and technical cooperation between
the two nations.

February 26   A ceremony for the exchange of letters concerning the additional credit accorded by China to
Tunisia for the Medjerdah-Cape Bon Canal project was
held in Tunis.

February 28   A meeting was held in Beijing in commemoration of the thirtieth anniversary of the February 28 Uprising waged by the people in Taiwan province. Liao Zhengzhi said: "The behests of Chairman Mao and Premier Zhou on liberating Taiwan and reunifying our motherland will surely be carried out under the leadership of the Party Central Committee headed by Chairman Hua."

March 1 The chief Soviet delegate to border talks with China, Leonid Ilyichev, left Beijing after the failure of three months' negotiations on boundary problems.
  • The 1977 Sino-Sudanese trade protocol was signed in Khartoum.
  • NCNA announced that two well-preserved fossil teeth of ape-men had recently been discovered by Chinese archaeological workers in Yunxi county in Hubei province. Judging by fossilization, tint and size of the teeth, and the degree of wear and tear of the tooth tips, both teeth probably belonged to one middle-aged ape-man.

March 3 NCNA reported that a large shipbuilding site, dating back about 2,200 years, was recently found in the city of Guangzhou. It belonged to the Qin Dynasty (246 B.C.-207 B.C.), and the Western Han Dynasty (206 B.C.-24 A.D.).

March 4 The Second Session of the China-Japan Joint Trade Committee was held in Tokyo from March 2-4.

March 5 The People's Daily, the Red Flag, and the Liberation Army Daily carried a joint editorial entitled "Learn from Comrade Lei Feng," marking the fourteenth anniversary of the publication of Chairman Mao's inscription--"Learn from Comrade Lei Feng." It said, "We must be like Comrade Lei Feng, and persist in putting proletarian politics in command."

March 6 Premier Hua Guofeng sent a message of congratulations, on the occasion of the convocation of the first Afro-Arab summit conference, to the heads-of-state at the conference.

March 9 Several observers concluded that a major two-week meeting of senior party, government, and army leaders

was held in China during the latter half of March.
The key issue was believed to have been the return
to office of the former Deputy Premier Deng Xiaoping.
Between March 9 and March 24 none of the senior
party and military officials in the Chinese provinces
made any public appearances.

• Australia announced that it would deliver two million metric tons of wheat during the eight months ending 1978 to China under the 1977 contract. The cost
was estimated at about $500 million, the highest since
1974.

• A poem, written by Ye Jianying, "Yanan Re-
visited," and a poem written by Zhu De, "Mourning
the Death of Comrade Chen Yi," were both carried in
the January issue of the Chinese Journal Poetry.
Nearly forty writers had their poems published in this
issue, including the twenty-six poems commemorating
Premier Zhou Enlai, and a poem in memory of Yang
Kaihui.

• The Tangshan-Fengnan earthquake of last July
took a heavy toll of people's lives and property because the Gang of Four and their henchmen in the
Chinese Academy of Science paid no heed to warnings
from professional seismological observatories and amateur observation posts. This was revealed in a front-
page report in the People's Daily.

March 11 Chinese astronomers in Beijing discovered a ring
system round the planet Uranus, similar to Saturn's.

March 12 China and Korea signed a long-term trade agreement (1977-81), and the annual protocol for 1977 in
Beijing.

• Premier Hua Guofeng sent a message to Yasir
Arafat warmly congratulating him on the convocation
of the Thirteenth Palestine National Council Conference.

• Premier Hua Guofeng sent a message to Mozambican President Samora Moises Machel expressing profound sympathy and solicitude on the recent flood in
southern Mozambique.

March 14 Zhang Diesheng was arrested at a criticism rally
held in Shenyang on March 14. He was accused of
being a counterrevolutionary who had attacked Chair-

man Mao, Premier Zhou Enlai, and Chairman Hua, and who had been harbored by the diehard of the Gang of Four and his few cohorts in Liaoning.

March 15   China and Bulgaria signed the 1977 goods exchange and payment agreement in Beijing.

March 16   The entire People's Daily front page was devoted to an article entitled "Complete Reversal of Relations Between the Enemy and Ourselves," criticizing the Gang of Four for distorting Chairman Mao's instruction on the bourgeoisie being "right in the Communist Party."

March 17   The Western Samoa Parliamentary Delegation, led by Leota Leuluaiali Ituau Ali, arrived in Beijing for a fourteen-day visit. Premier Hua Guofeng met the delegation on March 17.

March 18   The Soviet decree establishing a 200-mile economic zone from March 1 as a temporary fishery measure was sharply criticized by the People's Daily as a "fraud."

March 19   A People's Daily article entitled "Invasion of Zaire by Soviet-Paid Mercenaries Is Intolerable," denounced the Soviet Union as the "boss of the mercenary troops" from Angola, and pledged to support "the just struggle of the Zairian armed forces and people in resisting foreign aggression."
   • China and DRVN signed the 1977 mutual supply of goods and payment agreement in Beijing.
   • The hydroagricultural project repaired with Chinese assistance on the Guinean Island of Kaback was handed over to Guinea at a ceremony held in Conakry.
   • The People's Daily reported the 1977 spring drought to be the worst since 1949. The report that the State Council had held an emergency telephone conference on March 19 to arrange programs to protect wheat, combat drought, and ensure that spring sowing was carried out, underlined the seriousness of the spring drought. The report spoke of the drought being very serious in the Yellow River and Huai River basins in northern China, the major wheat producing areas in the north being the worst affected.

March 20   The Chinese Military Goodwill Delegation, led by Yang Zhengwu, left Beijing to attend the celebrations of Pakistan's National Day at the invitation of General Ziaul Haq, chief of staff of the Pakistan Army. The delegation left Pakistan for home on March 31.

March 21   China and Egypt signed a long-term trade agreement which would remain in force from January 1, 1977 to December 31, 1980. A trade protocol between the two nations for 1977 was also signed in Beijing.

March 22   Premier Hua Guofeng sent a message to Louis Sylvain Goma, prime minister of the People's Republic of the Congo, expressing deep condolences on the tragic assassination of President Marien Ngouabi.

March 24   Lai Yali, speaking in the Security Council, accused the South African authorities of a policy of brutal racial oppression and an attempt to perpetuate apartheid by establishing "puppet governments" and reserves for Africans in arid areas. He said the Security Council should take immediate action to implement an arms embargo and economic sanctions against South Africa. He also accused the USSR of using mercenaries to invade Zaire.

March 26   NCNA reported the recent excavation of a bronze chariot and horse, about 2,000 years old, in Xingyi county in Guizhou province.

March 27   In an interview, Vice Premier Li Xiannian told Denis Hamilton, the editor-in-chief of the Times, that "We adhere to one of Chairman Mao's principles: We will not attack others unless we are attacked. We will not fire the first shot. Even if Russia occupied half of China we would go on fighting. Should the Russians put one step on Chinese territory she would find herself in a swamp." The interview article was published in the Sunday Times in London.

March 28   Chinese dance-drama troupes left Shanghai to visit France (March 28-May 1), and Canada (May 2-15).

March 29   Premier Hua Guofeng sent a message to Mohammed Reza Pahlavi, Shahanshah of Iran, extending deep

sympathy and solicitude on the strong earthquake in southern Iran.
• NCNA reported the discovery of a large coalfield in Suxian in Anhui province.

March 30 Premier Hua Guofeng sent a message to Morarji Desai, congratulating him on his assumption of the office of the prime minister of the Republic of India.
• The National Conference on Forestry and Fishery sponsored by the Chinese Ministry of Agriculture and Forestry was held in Beijing from March 12-30.

March 31 An agreement on the building of a stadium in Ndjamena with Chinese assistance was signed in the capital of Chad, Ndjamena.
• The People's Daily article entitled "Chairman Hua Is a Brilliant Example of Studying and Putting Mao Zedong Thought into Practice," identified Qiaozheng county in Shanxi province as the native place of Chairman Hua Guofeng.

April 2 Chairman Hua Guofeng and Vice Premier Li Xiannian met Toshio Doko, president of the Federation of Economic Organizations of Japan and the delegation led by him.

April 3 Chairman Hua Guofeng met Hans Filbinger, vice-chairman of the Christian Democratic Union and premier of Baden-Wurttemberg.

April 4 China and Austria concluded a reciprocal agreement for trademark registration.
• Chairman Hua Guofeng gave a banquet in honor of Ronald Petterson, chairman of the Communist party of Sweden. The delegation arrived in Beijing for a twenty-day visit on March 17.

April 5 The State Council issued a circular on the launching of a nationwide health campaign. The circular urged the people to "wage a people's war to eliminate pests and diseases, strive to wipe out the 'four pests'-- rats, bed bugs, flies and mosquitoes, and eliminate the most serious diseases that endanger people's lives."
• Li Zhenshu and Liang Geliang captured the men's doubles title at the Thirty-fourth World Table Tennis Championship in Birmingham, England.

April 6 Mauritanian President and Mrs. Moktar Ould Daddah
visited China from April 6-10 (their third visit).
Premier Hua Guofeng met them at the airport and held
talks with them on April 8.
- The People's Daily gave front-page prominence to
a facsimile of a copy made by Chairman Mao in his own
handwriting of Ye Jianying's poem "Looking Afar."
Chairman Mao copied the poem for his son Mao Anqing
and daughter-in-law Shao Hua when they called on him
toward the end of 1965 on the occasion of his seventy-
second birthday. The poem was first published in the
Guangming Daily on October 16, 1965.

April 7 NCNA reported that the National Conference on Finance and Banking was held in Daqing to strive to
increase production and practice economy so as to increase socialist accumulation for faster development of
industrial and agricultural production. Vice Premier
Yu Qiuli addressed the conference.
- Mrs. Margaret Thatcher visited China from April
7-13 at the invitation of the Chinese government.
She met Chairman Hua Guofeng, Li Xiannian, Deng
Yingchao, Huang Hua, and Li Qiang. In Beijing, she
said, "We in Britain believe strongly in our traditional
parliamentary democracy, and in an economic system
which had brought prosperity to our people. We do
not seek to impose our ideas on others, but we are
always eager to discuss and defend them in public and
in private."
- The CCP Central Committee called for a mass
movement to study Volume V of the Selected Works of
Mao Zedong, which was to be published by the People's
Publishing House on April 15. The volume covered
the period September 1949-1957, and contained seventy
articles, forty-six of which had not previously been
published. The compilation and publication of the volume had been carried out by the Committee for Editing
and Publishing Chairman Mao Zedong's Works under the
CCP Central Committee headed by Chairman Hua Guofeng.

April 10 The Stuttgart Chamber Orchestra of West Germany
gave concerts of Bach, Beethoven and other classical
Western composers in Beijing and Shanghai from April
10-14.

April 11   A People's Daily editorial, following Hua Guofeng, declared that "the key link in running the country well" was "to achieve stability and unity, consolidate the dictatorship of the proletariat and attain great order across the country in the acute struggle between the two classes."

   • NCNA reported that a National Conference on Communications Work was held recently in Beijing to make concerted efforts to go on tapping production potentials and raising efficiency through technical innovation and technical revolution.

April 13   Chairman Hua Guofeng met Roy Jack, speaker of the House of Representatives of New Zealand and his party.

   • The People's Daily carried an editorial article entitled "Hold High Great Red Banner of Mao Zedong Thought and Deepen the Exposure and Criticism of the Gang of Four," to stress the repudiation of the ultra-rightist essence of the counterrevolutionary revisionist line of the Gang of Four and its manifestations in various spheres, and to denounce and discredit them thoroughly in terms of theory in the fields of philosophy, political economy, and scientific socialism.

April 14   China and Jordan announced their decision simultaneously in their respective capitals to establish diplomatic relations at the ambassadorial level. The joint communiqué was signed in Washington on April 7.

April 15   The joint editorial by the People's Daily, the Red Flag and the Liberation Army Daily marked the occasion of Volume V of the Selected Works of Mao Zedong, and launched a mass study movement.

April 17   Deng Yingchao, vice-chairman of the National People's Congress Standing Committee, visited Sri Lanka from April 17-22.

   • NCNA reported the recent discovery in Lufeng (Yunnan province) of an almost complete lower jaw of an ape living some 8,000,000 years ago.

April 18   China and Cuba signed the 1977 trade protocol in Beijing.

• President Raymond Arthur Chung of Guyana visited China from April 18-30. Chairman Hua Guofeng met him on April 21.

April 20 Shanghai-Hangzhou-Changsha-Guilin airline was opened to traffic, following the opening of the Shanghai-Lanzhou-Urumchi airline on April 15. With the opening of this new line, it now took less than four hours to travel from Shanghai to Guilin instead of more than one day via Guangzhou.

• The National Conference on Learning from Daqing in Industry opened at the Daqing oilfield on April 20. The opening session was presided over by Chairman Hua Guofeng. The conference moved to Beijing on April 27, where it closed on May 13. Attended by 7,000 representatives from industrial enterprises throughout China, it was the biggest of its kind ever held. The People's Daily carried an article entitled "Grasp the Key Link in Running the Country Well and Promote a New Leap Forward in the National Economy," to advance prescriptions for straightening the enterprises ideologically, politically and organizationally. On May 9, Chairman Hua Guofeng made a speech, noting that Daqing was convincing proof of China's ability to complete the "Four Modernizations" in the remaining years of this century.

April 21 China and Hungary signed the 1977 agreement on goods exchange and payment agreement in Beijing.

• Mme. Lucette Cabral, wife of Luis Cabral, president of the Republic of Guinea-Bissau, and Mme. Carmen Pereira, vice president of the National People's Assembly of Guinea-Bissau, arrived in Beijing for a fourteen-day visit at the invitation of the Chinese government. Chairman Hua Guofeng met them on April 30.

April 23 The Chinese charge d'affaires walked out of a rally commemorating the anniversary of Lenin's death when the secretary of the Central Committee, Zinyatin, criticized China's policies as running counter "to the vital interests of all people." It should be noted that this was the first public attack by a prominent Soviet leader since the death of Mao Zedong.

April 25   A study course in acupuncture for foreign doctors,
sponsored by the UNDP and WHO, was inaugurated at
Jiangsu College of New Medicine in Nanjing. Medical
workers from Botswana, Cameroon, Ethiopia, Nigeria,
Somalia, and Zambia attended.

April 26   China and Guinea signed the 1977 trade protocol
in Conakry.
   • China and Rumania signed the 1977-80 executive
plan agreement on health cooperation in Beijing.
   • The People's Daily reprinted on the front page an
important article by Chairman Hua Guofeng under the
headline "It Is of Great Value to Give Rein to Drive."
An accompanying editor's note said that the article,
written by Chairman Hua Guofeng on April 2, 1963,
was a "brilliant example in studying and applying
Marxism-Leninism-Mao Zedong Thought."

April 27   The commentators of the People's Daily, the Red
Flag, and the Liberation Army Daily declared that "it
has now been established, supported by an enormous
amount of conclusive evidence, that Zhang Chunqiao
was a Guomingdang agent; Jiang Qing, a renegade;
Yao Wenyuan, an alien class element; and Wang Hongwen, a new-born bourgeois element."
   • President Ne Win of Burma visited China from
April 27 to May 10. Chairman Hua Guofeng met him
at the Beijing airport. This was President Ne Win's
ninth visit to China.
   • NCNA reported that the 250 pits containing slaves
killed as human sacrifices dating back more than 3,000
years were discovered near Wuguan village in Anyang
city, Henan province by the Institute of Archaeology
of the Chinese Academy of Sciences last summer. The
sacrificial pits discovered this time, covering an area
of 5,000 square meters, were in the eastern part of
the Royal Tombs of the Yin-Shang Dynasty. In the
200 or so pits already excavated, most of the 1,000
skeletons had their heads chopped off. The skeletons
found in the pits were mostly young men between
twenty and thirty years of age.

April 28   Chairman Hua Guofeng inspected the Daqing oil
wells between April 17 and 19. He mounted the der-
rick platforms, entered workshops and warehouses,

visited worker-peasant villages, walked into workers'
dormitories and mess halls, and inquired after the
workers, cadres, technicians and their families.

April 29 NCNA reported that the National Conference of
Directors of Supply and Marketing Cooperatives had
been held in Beijing recently.
   • Premier Hua Guofeng sent a message to Major
General Ziaur Rahman, warmly greeting his assumption
of the office of president of the People's Republic of
Bangladesh.

May 1 The People's Daily carried a long article by Chairman
Hua Guofeng entitled "Continue the Revolution Under
the Dictatorship of the Proletariat to the End: A
Study of Volume V of the Selected Works of Mao Zedong." He related the overthrow of the Gang of Four
to Chairman Mao's theory of continuing revolution, and
emphasize the need to remain loyal to and to defend
Chairman Mao's banner.
   • Five new documentaries, two feature films, and
five scientific and educational films were shown on
May Day. The five documentaries were: On the Publication of Volume V, Victory of October, On Daqing,
On Dazhai, and Shanghai Turn to Chairman Hua. The
two feature films were: Our Motherland and A Long
Journey of Ten Thousand Li. The educational films
were: The System of Personal Responsibility at Daqing, and The Universe.
   • China and Germany signed, in Hamburg, an agreement to enhance the friendly cooperation between the
two sides in technical surveys and classification of
ships.
   • Chairman Hua Guofeng, party and state leaders
joined representatives to the National Conference on
Learning from Daqing in Industry and the working
people in Beijing at gala garden parties in celebrating
International Labor Day.

May 3 President El Hadj Omar Bongo of Gabon visited China
from May 3-5. Chairman Hua Guofeng met him on
May 4.
   • China and the German Democratic Republic signed
the 1977 goods exchange and payment agreement in
Beijing.

May 4   Shaikh Sabah Al-Ahmad Al-Jaber, Kuwait Minister
        of Foreign Affairs, and his party visited China from
        May 4-8.   Chairman Hua Guofeng met the delegation
        on May 5.
            • The "Learn From Lei Feng" exhibition began in
        Beijing.

May 5   An NPA delegation, led by Saifudian, deputy chair-
        man of the NPC Standing Committee, visited Rumania
        for seven days at the invitation of Rumanian Grand
        National Assembly, proceeded to Yugoslavia (May 11-
        21), and arriving back in Urumchi on May 21.
            • NCNA announced that a large-size purifying in-
        stallation, using activated carbon absorption to treat
        waste water discharged in oil refining (the first of its
        kind designed and made by China) had gone into op-
        eration in a refinery in Hunan province.
            • NCNA announced that Chairman Hua Guofeng
        made an inspection tour of Heilongjiang, Jilin, and
        Liaoning provinces from April 21-25 after presiding
        over the opening ceremony of the National Conference
        on Learning from Dazhai in Agriculture.
            • More than 1,000 workers, peasants, and soldiers
        in Guangzhou area met to mark the fifty-first anniver-
        sary of the former National Institute of Peasant Move-
        ment established by Chairman Mao Zedong and of the
        publication of his article "Analysis of the Classes in
        Chinese Society."

May 6   China renewed $62 million credit for the purchase by
        Chile of industrial equipment and technical assistance
        for mining copper.
            • Princess Beatrix of the Netherlands met Chairman
        Hua Guofeng in Beijing.   She came to China for a
        twelve-day tour, including Inner Mongolia.
            • China's new permanent representative to the
        United Nations, Chen Chu, arrived in New York to
        assume his duty.
            • NCNA reported that Chairman Hua Guofeng in-
        spected Tangshan city in the afternoon of April 26,
        and delivered a speech to praise the workers of the
        Kailuan coal mines for their revolutionary spirit in the
        struggle to restore production.

May 7   China and Congo signed, in Brazzaville, the minutes
        of talks on the construction of a "People's Palace" in

Brazzaville with Chinese assistance.

• Chairman Hua Guofeng sent a message to Nicolae Ceausescu, general secretary of the Rumania Communist party, expressing the warmest congratulations on the centenary of the national independence of Rumania.

May 8 Thomas S. Gates, Jr., chief of the liaison office of the US in China, left his post for home.

May 10 NCNA reported that China's Tianjin Song and Dance Ensemble staged performances in Tokyo (May 4-7), in Kobe (May 8-12), in Nagoya (May 12-18), in Nagano (May 19-24), in Niigata, Akita, Hirosaki, Hachirobe, and Aomori (May 27 to June 3), in Hokkaido (June 3-10), in Fukushima, Sendai, Iwaki, in Tohoku area and Yokohama, Takasaki and Omita in Kwanto area (June 11-21), and returned to China on June 24.

May 11 A protocol of the dispatch of a Chinese medical team to Mali was signed in Bamako.

• NCNA announced that a well-preserved tomb of the Yin Dynasty (the end of the thirteenth century B.C. to the beginning of the twelfth century B.C.) was excavated, starting last year, by members of the Institute of Archaeology of the Chinese Academy of Science in Anyang city in Henan province. A two-character inscription ("Lady Hao") and a three-character inscription ("Mother Queen Xin") found on utensils suggested that this was the tomb of a spouse of King Wu Ding, whose reign was the longest of the Yin Dynasty.

May 12 The population of mainland China was estimated at 850 million, according to the Washington Population Reference Bureau report. The bureau reported that the estimated birth rate on the Chinese mainland was twenty-seven per 1,000 people and the death rate, ten per 1,000 people.

• An earthquake with the strength of 6.6 on the Richter scale rocked Northeast China. The quake had its epicenter at Ninghe, near the industrial city of Tangshan.

May 13 A ceremony for handing over to Togo a rice-growing center built with Chinese aid was held in Lomé. A related document was also signed.

May 18   The National Exhibition on Learning from Daqing in Industry began in Beijing. Chairman Hua Guofeng met Jusuf Adjitorop and his Communist Party of Indonesia Central Committee Delegation.

May 19   Letters on 1977-78 trade between China and Iraq were signed and exchanged in Baghdad.
* China and Czechoslovakia signed a goods exchange and payment agreement for 1977 in Prague.

May 20   Trade between India and China was resumed after a break of fifteen years. The first deal, signed at the Guangzhou Trade Fair amounted to a modest $1.7 million.

May 23   China and Poland signed the 1977 goods exchange and payment agreement in Warsaw.
* The People's Daily carried an editorial entitled "Hold Still Higher Great Banner of Chairman Mao's Revolutionary Line in Literature and Art," to commemorate the thirty-fifth anniversary of his talks at the Yanan forum. A fine arts exhibition for the occasion began at the China Art Gallery in Beijing.

May 24   The Memorial Hall was completed on May 24, six months after the laying of the cornerstone by Chairman Hua on November 24, 1976. Located in Tiananmen Square, the Hall was 105 square meters and 33.6 meters high, its surroundings landscaped with pines, cypresses and flowers. During the construction, over 700,000 people from all over China took part in voluntary labor. Work in progress included completing interior decoration, sculpturing a statue of the late chairman, and installing the crystal sarcophagus.
* Chairman Hua Guofeng sent a message to President Tito of Yugoslavia, warmly greeting the president's eighty-fifth birthday.

May 25   China and Gambia signed the minutes of talks on the construction of a stadium and a sportsmen's hotel in Banjul with Chinese assistance.
* The forty-five-member Zhungqing Acrobatic Troupe of China left Beijing to visit Western Samoa, Fiji, Papua New Guinea, and the Philippines by invitation.

- Soviet bloc ambassadors walked out of a Beijing reception celebrating "African Liberation Day," when Foreign Minister Huang Hua said, "The recent intrusion of foreign mercenaries into Zaire is a fresh crime committed single-handedly by a superpower against a sovereign African state and its people."

May 26 Deng Xiaoping had written two letters to Chairman Hua Guofeng, praising him and saying he was willing to return to work at any position, the Chinese-language newspaper Ming Bao reported in Hong Kong.

May 27 In terms of manpower, the Chinese Navy was the world's third largest but in terms of ships, it remained "a miniscule mix" of aging oceangoing craft, submarines, and patrol boats, the Far Eastern Economic Review said. Manpower was put at 170,000 officers and men, including a naval air force with 25,000 personnel and 28,000 marines.

May 28 Chairman Hua Guofeng met the delegation of the Central Committee of the Portuguese Communist party (M-L), led by its General Secretary Heduino Vilar.

May 30 In New York, China and the Barbados Republic signed a joint communiqué to establish diplomatic relations at the ambassadorial level.

May 31 China and Equatorial Guinea signed, in Malabo, a protocol on the dispatch of a new Chinese medical team to Equatorial Guinea.

June 1 The National Toy Exhibition, which opened in Beijing today, added new color to the celebration of International Children's Day in the capital. The five big halls displayed over 4,000 toys made of metal, wood, plastic and fabrics. Included were folk toys, educational toys, children's games, and many others.

June 2 General Vo Nguyen Giap, the defense minister of DRVN, visited China June 2-20. He met Chairman Hua Guofeng and Deng Yingchao on June 3. During the visit, Premier Phan Van Dong and Vice Premier Vo Chi Cong made a stopover in Beijing on their way home from abroad. They met Chairman Hua Guofeng and Deng Yingchao on June 8.

June 3 The People's Daily carried an article entitled "Wang
Hongwen--A Typical New Bourgeoisie," which mainly
showed how Wang Hongwen camouflaged his counterrevolutionary features during the Cultural Revolution.
   • Chairman Hua Guofeng met the Congolese Military
Committee Friendship Delegation, led by Major Fran-
çois-Xavier Katali, minister of the interior.

June 4 The People's Daily reported that, to commemorate
the thirty-fifth anniversary of Mao Zedong's Talks at
the Yanan Forum, the historical Beijing opera Bishang
Liangshan (Driven Up Mt. Liang), based on the novel
Shuihu Zhuan (Water Margin), had been restaged.
This signaled the return of public performances of
classical Beijing opera for the first time since 1966.
   • China and Yugoslavia signed the 1977-78 scientific
and technical cooperation agreement in Beijing.
   • Premier Hua Guofeng met the Cape Verde Government Delegation, led by Abilie Duarte, minister of foreign affairs.

June 5 NCNA reported that China had made a new breakthrough in drilling technology with the successful
manufacture of synthetic diamond drilling bits.
   • The People's Daily and all other Beijing papers
gave front-page prominence to the inscription written
by Chairman Hua Guofeng: "Learn from the hard-bone
Sixth Company and strive to accelerate the revolutionization of our army."

June 6 President Gaafar Mohamed Nimeri of Sudan visited
China from June 6-16, and was greeted at the airport
by Chairman Hua Guofeng. He held talks with Vice
Premier Li Xiannian. An economic and technical cooperation between the two nations was signed on June 9.

June 7 It was announced that Secretary of State Cyrus
Vance would visit China from August 22-26 for what
was described initially as a "very, very difficult round
of talks." Later it was announced that he would spend
four days in China "to further our communications in
the light of the Shanghai communiqué."

June 10 Chairman Hua Guofeng met Luis Echeverría Alvarez,
former president of Mexico, Mrs. Echeverria, and their
party.

- China and Spain reached an accord on a trademark registration and protection agreement in Beijing.
- China and Guinea-Bissau signed the minutes of a meeting on the construction of water conservancy project on River Udunduma with Chinese assistance.

June 11   China and Rwanda signed, in Kigali, the minutes of a meeting on cooperation in developing a rice cultivation project in Rubindi of Rwanda.

June 12   The protocol of the Nineteenth Railway Conference between China and Vietnam for 1977 was signed in Hanoi.
- Italian Foreign Minister Arnaldo Forlani visited China from June 12-17. He held talks with Huang Hua. He said later that China was anxious to negotiate a full-scale trade agreement with the EEC.

June 13   Fang Yi gave a banquet in honor of the delegation of the US Committee on Scholarly Communication with the People's Republic of China headed by biochemist Philip Handler, president of the US National Academy of Sciences in Beijing.
- The PRC Ministry of Foreign Affairs in Beijing protested to the Japanese government against the alleged infringement on Chinese sovereignty caused by the Japanese Diet's approval of the agreement between Japan and South Korea on the development of the continental shelf.

June 16   Prime Minister L.S. Goma of Congo visited China from June 16-21, and was greeted at the airport by Chairman Hua Guofeng. He held talks with Chairman Hua Guofeng on June 18. An economic and technical cooperation agreement between the two nations was signed on June 18.

June 18   Prime Minister Kaysone Phomvihan of Laos visited China from June 18-20. He held talks with Vice Premier Li Xiannian on June 19, and met Chairman Hua Guofeng on the same day.
- China and Mongolia signed a goods supply protocol for 1977 in Ulan Bator.
- China and Ethiopia signed minutes of talks on opening Chinese air services between Beijing and African countries via Addis Ababa.

June 19   The Yi people, a minority nationality in Southeast
China, recently adopted a "draft for the standard Yi
language," which was based on the "draft for alpha-
betic Yi language" introduced in 1956.

• The Liberation Army Daily carried an editorial to
mark the fifteenth anniversary of the publication of
Chairman Mao's instruction on the militia. It stressed
the militia's role as an aid to and reserve for the PLA
and urged the emulation of Lei Feng and the hard-
bone Sixth Company in order to learn from the PLA.

June 20   Robert Mugabe, general secretary of the Zimbawe
African National Union, visited China from June 20-30.
At the banquet on June 24, Vice Premier Li Xiannian
said that China had "no political contacts, no economic
trade or any other dealings" with the Vorster or Smith
regimes.   The Rhodesians met Chairman Hua Guofeng
on June 28.

June 21   NCNA reported that Dang Aoqing, professor of
chemistry at Jilin University, had developed a new
theory associated with the principle of conservation of
molecular orbital symmetry and a new approach to
molecular orbital calculation.

• The Somalian Government Delegation, led by Vice
President Ismail Ali Abokor, visited China June 21-29.
Chairman Hua Guofeng met the delegation on June 22.
A protocol on the aid agreement was signed on June
23.

June 23   The 1,500-year old Yungang caves, gems of ancient Chinese architecture and sculpture, were restored to their former splendor with the completion of
large-scale repair and renovation work which began
three years ago at Premier Zhou Enlai's suggestion.

June 25   Kaihara Osamu, former secretary general of the
Japan National Defence Council, met Chinese Deputy
Chief of General Staff Zhang Zaijian in Beijing.

• NCNA reported that since 1974, China's tea garden acreage had increased annually by an average of
67,000 hectares, and tea output by 17,500 tons a year.

June 28   China and Morocco signed minutes of the joint trade
committee meeting in Rabat.

June 29 Chairman Hua Guofeng met the Palestine Liberation
Front Delegation and declared emphatically, "The Chinese resolutely side with the Palestinian and Arab
people."
   • The US Secretary of State Cyrus Vance declared
in a speech at the Asian Society "The US is and will
remain in Asia as a Pacific power." He went on to
say that the Carter administration "[placed] importance
on the peaceful settlement for the Taiwan issue by the
Chinese themselves." In a press conference the following day, President Carter himself confirmed his intention to live up to the Shanghai communiqué, but he
was evasive regarding the question of abandoning the
defense commitment to Taiwan.

June 30 China and Ethiopia signed the 1977-78 trade protocol.
   • In Mouakchott, China and Mauritania signed the
minutes of the meeting for building a port in Mouakchott with Chinese assistance.
   • The People's Daily published the long explanation
of the struggle over the "Outline Report on the Work
of the Chinese Academy of Sciences." The article appeared to indicate a shift in policy towards intellectuals
which corresponded to recent adjustments to various
sectors of the economy. The praise for the "Outline
Report" could also be construed as a vindication of
Deng Xiaoping.

July 1 The Beijing opera Dielian Hua (Butterflies' Attach-
ment to Flowers) dealing with Mao Zedong's former
wife, Yang Kaihui, was premiered in Beijing.
   • Premier Hua Guofeng sent a greeting message to
the Fourteenth Session of the Organization of African
Unity (OAU) Assembly.
   • The National Conference of Geological Departments
on Learning from Daqing was held in Beijing from July
1-14. Chairman Hua Guofeng and other party and
state leaders received the participants (over 2,600)
on July 3.
   • The Delegation of the Chinese People's Institute
of Foreign Affairs was received by Vice President
Walter Mondale in Washington. The delegation left
Los Angeles for home on July 22 after touring Washington, Williamsburg, New York, Chicago, Des Moines
and San Francisco.

July 2 The National Conference on cancer work attended
        by 300 people engaged in cancer research, barefoot
        doctors and medical personnel from basic units in all
        parts of China closed in Beijing on July 2. The re-
        port on the meeting noted the scale and scope of re-
        search since 1966 and indicated that the conference
        had mapped out a plan for 1977-80.
            • Sister Jiang, a Chinese opera banned by the
        Gang of Four for a dozen years, was restaged in the
        capital city (Beijing) to wide acclaim.

July 3 Chairman Hua Guofeng, Ye Jianying, Li Xiannian
        and Wang Dongxing met foreign experts who took
        part in translating Volume V of the Selected Works of
        Mao Zedong. Between May 12 and July 3, the Liber-
        ation Army Daily carried ten commentators' articles
        focusing on questions related to accelerating the "revo-
        lutionization and modernization" of the PLA. Written
        on the instructions of Chairman Hua Guofeng, they
        dealt with what was referred to as ten "shoulds and
        should nots," summarizing the essential points for
        bringing about the "revolutionization and moderniza-
        tion" of the Army, and for relating criticism of the
        Gang of Four to actual conditions in the Army.

July 5 Vice Premier Li Xiannian said that Sino-American
        bilateral relations could continue to be improved, pro-
        vided both sides seriously implemented the principles
        laid down in the Shanghai communiqué. He reiterated
        the three conditions required of the US government
        for normalization, namely, (1) the severance of diplo-
        matic relations with the regime in Taiwan, (2) the
        total withdrawal of American troops and military in-
        stallations, and (3) the abrogation of the mutual se-
        curity treaty. He added that none of the three could
        be dispensed with. He totally rejected any idea by
        which China's sovereign claims over the island could
        be diluted by, for example, pledging to a foreign
        power how this internal problem would be solved. He
        concluded, "As to when in what way the Chinese peo-
        ple are to liberate their sacred territory of Taiwan,
        that is entirely China's internal affair, which brooks
        no interference from other countries."

July 6 The Farmland Capital Construction Conference attended by 1,140 delegates, which was held initially in Xiyang county and subsequently in Beijing from July 6 to August 5, determined to ensure the average availability of one mu of stable high-yield land for each person in the rural areas by 1980.

- NCNA reported that the 7001 drilling team under the Sichuan province Petroleum Administrative Bureau recently completed a 7,058 meter-deep well, the deepest so far in China.

July 7 The Chinese Academy of Sciences' Work Conference was held in Beijing from June 20 to July 7 to map out a draft program for advancing China's scientific research.

- The Albanian Zeri I Popullit (Voice of the People), official organ of the Albanian Party of Labour, indirectly criticized China, by attacking the theory of the three worlds. Even though China itself was not mentioned by name, it signalled an open ideological break with China. The editorial directly attacked some of the more cherished principles of China's foreign policy. The view that the Third World constituted a revolutionary motive force in world affairs was dismissed as a "flagrant violation of the teachings of Marxism-Leninism."

- Radio Havana, in a commentary, attacked China's alliance with neocolonial regimes and her moving away from the Third World interests, especially in Africa. As an example of this it mentioned the equipping of Mobutu against the Shaba rebels, the invitation to President Bongo of Gabon in spite of his participation in the reported mercenary attack on Benin, and the hosting of President Nimeri of Sudan who was seeking the overthrow of the Ethiopian Revolutionary Government.

July 9 The anniversary of the Albanian Army Day was duly marked in Beijing.

July 11 The EEC delegation, led by Ronald de Kergolay, visited China in July to begin the detailed negotiations of a commercial agreement between China and the EEC. Li Qiang met the delegation on July 11.

July 14 The National Conference on Foreign Trade and on

Exchanging Experiences in Learning from Daqing and Dazhai was held in Beijing July 14-28. The conference was attended by 1,400 delegates. Referring to the concept of self-reliance, Vice Premier Yu Qiuli said it had nothing in common with a "closed-door" policy, that it did not mean refusing to learn from good things from other countries, that it was very detrimental to indiscriminately reject foreign science, technology and culture. In economic and foreign trade work, he added the policy should be to rely on one's own efforts while making external assistance subsidiary and to combine study with self-creation.

July 16 The Third Plenary Session of the Tenth Central Committee of the CCP was held in Beijing from July 16-21. It unanimously adopted three resolutions. The first confirmed the appointment of Hua Guofeng as chairman of the Party Central Committee and the Military Commission. The second restored Deng Xiaoping to all posts held in April 1976. The third expelled the members of the Gang of Four from the party and dismissed them from all posts inside and outside it. In addition, the Plenum decided to convene the Eleventh National Party Congress at an appropriate time this year.

July 20 Chairman Hua Guofeng met the delegation of the Central Committee of Communist party of the US led by Michael Klonsky.
• Chen Chu told the Security Council that China recommended Vietnam's membership in the United Nations and believed that Vietnam would make positive contributions to the realization of principles in the UN charter. China thought Vietnam was qualified for membership in 1976 and the objection raised by a permanent member (the US) was unreasonable.

July 21 China and the Soviet Union signed the 1977 goods exchange and payment agreement.

July 23 The joint editorial by the People's Daily, the Red Flag, and the Liberation Army Daily, entitled "An Historic Meeting," indicated that Hua Guofeng had recommended to a central working conference held in March 1977 the repudiation of the slanders and unfounded charges made by the Gang of Four against Deng Xiaoping. His reinstatement, it said, conformed to the wishes of the people and was proof that the Central Committee headed by Chairman Hua was of one heart with the masses. The joint editorial also drew attention to the composition and qualities of the present leading group and indicated that the verdict delivered on the Gang of Four was justified.

July 24 NCNA reported that the State Council had recently promulgated the "Regulations for the Administration of Measurements of the PRC (tentative)." It was a decree to improve the administration of metrological work following its "Order on the Unification of the System of Measurements" of 1959.

July 25 The Chinese response to the Albanian criticism consisted largely of the republication of statements by foreign Marxist-Leninists supporting the Three Worlds theory. On July 25, Petros Stagod, a leader of the Greek Revolutionary Communist Movement, was quoted inter alia as saying that Chairman Mao's concept had dealt a heavy blow to "revisionism, dogmatism, splittism and opportunism which may be leftist in words."

July 26 The three-volume illustrated encyclopedia of medicinal herbs and animal products on the Qinghai-Tibet plateau was now available in China. The encyclopedia had illustrations and descriptions of 455 kinds of drugs, their names in Tibetan, Han and Latin, the names of the families they belong to, their habitat, the methods of collecting and processing them, and their properties, taste, and function.

July 27 The spokesman of the Chinese Ministry of Foreign Affairs said, "China has not stopped its assistance to Albania. Neither has China received the notification concerning the expulsion of the Chinese experts described in foreign newspaper reports."

July 28 The People's Daily carried an article to describe the history of the "August 1 Nanchang Uprising of 1927" in celebration of the 50th anniversary of the founding of the China PLA.

July 29 NCNA reported that on July 25, two women and eight men plus a cameraman on the Chinese mountaineering Expedition for the first time ascended Pobeda Peak, rising 7,443.8 meters above sea level, at 15:31 Beijing time. This mountain was the highest peak of the Tianshan mountain range.

July 30 The People's Daily and other Beijing papers prominently printed on their front pages a letter written by Chairman Mao to the Jiangxi Communist Labour University on July 30, 1961.
 • The 1977 Beijing International Friendship Invitational Football Tournament closed at the Workers' Stadium in Beijing. Attending the closing ceremony and watching the tournament final were Deng Xiaoping, Wu De, Chen Yonggui, Wu Guixian, and Su Zhenhua. When Vice-Chairman Deng Xiaoping and other leaders appeared on the rostrum, the 80,000 spectators gave them a prolonged, thunderous, standing ovation.

July 31 The CCP Central Committee, the State Council, and the Military Commission jointly held a meeting to mark the fiftieth anniversary of the founding of the PLA. It was presided over by Chairman Hua Guofeng who mounted the rostrum together with Ye Jianying and Deng Xiaoping in army uniform.
 • The People's Daily carried an editorial entitled "Build Inner Mongolia into an Impregnable Wall Against Imperialism and Revisionism" to greet the thirtieth anniversary of the founding of the Inner Mongolian autonomous region. Chen Xilian, who headed the Central Delegation to the celebrations of the occasion, addressed a 5,000-strong rally held in Huhehot.

August 1 A joint editorial by the People's Daily, the Red Flag, and the Liberation Army Daily, entitled "Accelerate the Modernization of National Defense," marked the fiftieth anniversary of the founding of the Chinese PLA. The editorial reiterated and expanded the call for the revolutionization and modernization of the PLA, linking the tasks to the strengthening of the economy as a whole. The Ministry of National Defense gave a reception to celebrate the occasion. Attending the reception were Hua Guofeng, Ye Jianying, Deng Xiaoping, and other party and state leaders. Ye Jianying made

a speech at the reception. He declared, "We must ensure that the gun remains firmly in the hands of the
Party," and "we must speed up the revolutionization
and modernization of our army."

August 4 UN Secretary General Kurt Waldheim visited China
August 4-11. He met Foreign Minister Huang Hua on
August 4 and Chairman Hua Guofeng on August 6.
 • NCNA reported that Chairman Hua Guofeng, Vice-
Chairmen Ye Jianying, Deng Xiaoping, and other party
and state leaders had received the delegates to these
conferences: Conference on Foreign Trade, Conference on National Farmland Improvement Construction,
the Second National Conference of Posts and Telecommunications Departments Learning from Daqing, the
National Conference of Public Health Bureau Directors,
the National Conference of Cereals and Oil Industry,
and the Forum on the National Programme for Combining Traditional Chinese and Western Medicine.

August 5 Chairman Hua Guofeng sent a message to Spylos
Kyprianou, acting president of the Republic of Cyprus,
expressing deep condolences on the death of President
Makarios.

August 6 The People's Daily published an article by Su Yu
entitled "Great Victory for Chairman Mao's Guideline
on War." While stressing the need to modernize the
PLA, the article claimed that advantages in moral, social, political and economic conditions and geographic
factors compensated for shortage in equipment.

August 8 Chairman Hua Guofeng met Fernand Lefebvre,
first secretary of the Marxist-Leninist Communist par-
ty of Belgium.
 • Chairman Hua Guofeng met the delegation of the
Central Committee of Communist Workers' Party of
Denmark, led by Chairman Benito Scocozza.

August 10 The People's Daily gave front-page prominence
to the facsimile of a classical style poem entitled
"Reading 'On Protracted' Once Again" written by Ye
Jianying on September 4, 1965. In this poem Ye expressed his boundless esteem for Chairman Mao and
infinite loyalty to Mao Zedong thought.

August 11   NCNA reported that the 125,000 kw generating
         unit at the Douhe Power Station in the Tangshan area
         was back in operation as part of the Beijing-Tianjin-
         Tangshan power grid.

August 12   Vice Premier Chen Yonggui met a visiting Al-
         banian agricultural delegation.
             • The Eleventh National Congress of the CCP took
         place in Beijing August 12-18. On the previous day,
         the preparatory meeting was held to elect a presidium
         of 223 delegates with Hua Guofeng as chairman, Ye
         Jianying, Deng Xiaoping, Li Xiannian, and Wang Dong-
         xing as vice-chairmen. The Congress was attended
         by 1,510 delegates, representing over thirty-five mil-
         lion party members. The press communiqué underlined
         the broad generational and qualification base formed
         by the delegates among whom 72.4 percent were work-
         ers, peasants, and soldiers and other working people,
         6.7 percent were revolutionary intellectuals, and 20.9
         percent were revolutionary cadres. Women party mem-
         bers made up nineteen percent, minority 9.3 percent
         and middle-aged and young party members 73.8 per-
         cent of the delegates. The communiqué added that
         Taiwanese party members had also elected delegates.
         Chairman Hua delivered the political report to the
         First Plenum of the Congress on August 12. It con-
         tained over 32,000 characters and took some four hours
         to deliver. Ye Jianying delivered the report on the
         revision of the constitution of the CCP at the second
         plenum of the Congress on August 13. The third
         plenum was held on August 18 when delegates elected
         the Eleventh CCP Central Committee of 201 members
         and 132 alternate members by secret ballots, adopted
         a resolution on the political report, and the new con-
         stitution of the CCP. The Congress closed with a
         short address by Deng Xiaoping.

August 13   China and Cape Verde signed an economic and
         technical cooperation agreement in Praia.

August 15   NCNA reported that a big tomb with a wooden
         outer-coffin and more than 1,000 burial objects dating
         back about 2,100 years was recently discovered in
         Ruobowan in Guixian county in Guangxi Zhuang auton-
         omous region. The burial articles included bronzes,

ironware, lacquered wooden utensils, pottery, jade
and stone vessels as well as plant seeds. Also found
was a wooden slip inscribed with more than 300 characters in the Li Shu (clerical) script, a traditional
style of writing for official documents introduced in
the Qin Dynasty (221-207 B.C.).

August 17 On the eve of the departure of Secretary of
State Cyrus Vance and his party to Beijing, the State
Department spokesman described the forthcoming talks
as "exploratory" and he indicated that Vance would be
talking about a number of possible options ranging
from an explicit pledge by Beijing to unite with Taiwan
peacefully to a unilateral statement by the US that it
expects China to avoid the use of military force in
area.

August 19 The Eleventh Central Committee of the CCP held
its first plenum on August 19 to elect the politburo
and its Standing Committee. The new politburo in-
herited all thirteen old members and admitted ten new
ones--two of them were former alternate members.
The five members constituting its Standing Committee
were, Hua Guofeng, Ye Jianying, Deng Xiaoping, Li
Xiannian, and Wang Dongxing.

August 20 As Secretary of State Cyrus Vance prepared to
leave for Tokyo, the State Department made it clear
that no major progress was anticipated and the Carter
administration, having taken into account congressional
and public opinion, would refuse normalization even if
that should mean giving merely the appearance of
abandoning Taiwan.
    • Armymen and civilians in Beijing held huge pa-
rades and demonstrations to celebrate the successful
convocation of the Eleventh National Congress of the
CCP. The People's Daily published an article dealing
with the importance of running state farms well. The
article urged the need to reduce the numbers of non-
productive personnel, and emphasized socialist accumulation to expand reproduction and improve people's
livelihood.

August 21 A joint editorial by the People's Daily, the Red
Flag, and the Liberation Army Daily, entitled "A Great

Milestone," warmly acclaimed the triumphant close of
the 11th Party Congress.

August 22 US Secretary of State Cyrus Vance and his party visited China August 22-26. Vance's reception in
Beijing was described by American reporters as "low-
key." Vance held a talk with Vice Premier Deng
Xiaoping at the Summer Palace on August 24. On August 25, Chairman Hua met Vance for an hour. Vance
described the talks as "candid and serious." At a
press conference on the eve of his departure from
Beijing, Vance would not be drawn into describing
this talk as anything more than "useful."

August 24 The Albanian leader, Enver Hoxha sent a message to Chairman Hua greeting the convention of the
Eleventh Party Congress.

August 29 Chairman Hua Guofeng met the DRVN National
Assembly Delegation, headed by Truong Chinh, on its
way home from Mongolia.
• President Carter said that normalization was un-
doubtedly going "to be well into the future," but described Vance's visit as a "very important step"
towards the end. Vance himself described the visit
as "exploratory," but said that he found it "very encouraging."

August 30 The regular meeting of the Sino-Mongolian Border
Railway Joint Commission was held in Huhehot from
August 22-30. The protocol of the meeting was signed
on August 30.
• President Tito of Yugoslavia arrived in Beijing to
one of the most rapturous welcomes ever accorded a
foreign statesman. He was met at the airport by
Chairman Hua Guofeng, Vice Chairmen Deng Xiaoping,
Li Xiannian as well as other Chinese leaders. One
hundred thousand people in the capital lined the
streets and Tiananmen Square, through which the
motorcade passed, was officially likened to "a sea of
flowers" as "the people performed dances to the shouts
of welcome and music." The welcoming editorial in the
People's Daily declared that the visit would "promote
the development of the just united struggle against
hegemonism waged by various people and the progres-

sive cause of national liberation and social emancipation in various countries. It will have a far-reaching
influence internationally." Chairman Hua gave a banquet in President Tito's honor on the evening of the
30th and together with Deng Xiaoping and Li Xiannian,
he held talks with the Yugoslav visitors on August 31
and September 1. The leaders were described as having had an exchange of views on matters of common
interest. The talks proceeded in a cordial and friendly atmosphere. President Tito also paid his respects
at Chairman Mao's Memorial Hall and visited the Great
Wall on September 2. On September 3, accompanied
by Li Xiannian, he and his party left Beijing for
Hangzhou, Shanghai and Urumchi, from which he left
for home on September 8. No official communiqué was
issued. However, President Tito went on to reveal
that Chairman Hua had accepted an invitation to visit
Yugoslavia "at an appropriate date."

September 1   The Memorial Hall for Chairman Mao Zedong, a
solemn and magnificent edifice, was completed in Beijing. Rising 33.6 meters, the Memorial Hall stood
south of the monument to the People's Heroes in the
southern part of Tiananmen Square, with its main entrance opening on the north. The Hall is located between Tiananmen and Qianmen on the north-south axis
of the city. It is flanked by the Great Hall of the
People on the west and the Museum of the Chinese
Revolution and the Museum of Chinese History on the
east.

September 2   The Delegation of the Chinese People's Asso-
ciation for Friendship with Foreign Countries, led by
Wang Pingnan, left Beijing to visit Iran, Somalia and
Iraq.

September 6   Vice Premier Deng Xiaoping gave an interview
to a visiting Associated Press delegation. Dismissing
American-inspired reports of progress resulting from
the Vance trip as incorrect, Deng stated bluntly that
efforts towards normalization had suffered a setback.
Vance's discussions were a retreat from the proposals
previously advanced by former President Ford and
former Secretary of State Kissinger. The reaction in
Washington was decidedly cool.

September 7   The Chinese Government Agricultural Delega-
        tion, led by Sha Feng, left Beijing to visit Yugo-
        slavia and Algeria at the invitation of these two gov-
        ernments.

September 8   On the eve of the first anniversary of the
        death of Chairman Mao Zedong, the People's Daily
        carried a significant article by the theory group of
        the CCP Central Committee's General Office.   The
        article, entitled "Forever Bear Chairman Mao's Teach-
        ings in Mind and Persevere in Continuing the Revo-
        lution Under the Dictatorship of the Proletariat," re-
        called how the Gang of Four tried to have their sup-
        porters appointed as deputy directors of the General
        Office and Political Commissar to Unit 8341.   Regard-
        ing the action subsequently taken by Unit 8341
        against the Gang of Four, the article stated that it
        acted under the direct command of Chairman Hua and
        Vice Chairman Ye.   The article was also interesting
        for the account it provided of the late Chairman's
        relying on the unit and his members of staff to in-
        vestigate the operation and implementation of rural
        policies in 1955, the Socialist Education Movement and
        the Cultural Revolution in Beijing.
          • NCNA reported that China's printing workers had
        completed printing two hundred million copies of Volume
        V of the Selected Works of Mao Zedong to commemorate
        the first anniversary of the death of Mao Zedong.   The
        occasion was also marked by the publication of a num-
        ber of important articles, including the chairman's
        "On the Question of Whether Imperialism and All Reac-
        tionaries Are Real Tigers" (dated Wuohang, December
        1, 1958), and an innerparty directive (dated December
        13, 1963) entitled "Strive to Learn form Each Other
        and Don't Stick to the Beaten Track and Be Compla-
        cent."

September 9   The principal event to commemorate the death
        of Chairman Mao was a rally held in Beijing during
        which the recently completed Memorial Hall was opened.
        Chairman Hua's speech included reference to the mo-
        mentous victories won in the struggle against the Gang
        of Four and to China's adhering to the strategic Three
        Worlds concept in foreign affairs.   Those attending in-
        cluded party and state leaders and the late Chairman's

relatives, Mao Anqing, Shao Hua, Li Min, and Gong Linghua. Other events included a soirée, exhibitions, memorial meetings and the broadcast of a recording of Mao's reading of the epitaph on the Monument to the Heroes of the People.

September 10   In Tunis, China and Tunisia signed a contract on the building of the Medjerda-Cape Bob Canal for Tunisia.

• In a two-hour meeting with Japanese parliamentarians, Vice Premier Deng Xiaoping complained "the United States was playing with two cards" (China and Taiwan). He said that China could not tolerate such an approach by the Carter administration in working out full diplomatic relations.

• Ambassador from Taipei James C.H. Shen, met Secretary Vance. It was the first time for several years that the ambassador had had official talks with the secretary of state.

• A joint editorial by the People's Daily, the Red Flag, and the Liberation Army Daily, entitled "Mao Zedong Thought Will Shine Forever," marked the first anniversary of the death of Mao Zedong. The editorial stressed the comprehensive nature of Mao Zedong thought and stated that it could not be curtailed, distorted, or doctored. It emphasized the need to use Mao's thought as a guide to action, not as a dogma, and warned against the mechanical application of quotations in disregard of time, place and circumstances. Urging the systematic study of Mao's thought to enhance the party's understanding of it, the editorial stressed the importance of mastering its stand, viewpoint, and method.

September 12   The People's Daily published an article entitled "Great Guiding Principle for Socialist Construction," by the State Planning Commission, to describe Mao's major contribution to China's economic construction. The article said that Mao's contribution to Marxist theory was the identification of the main contradiction in the period of socialism--the struggle between the proletariat and the bourgeoisie and between the socialist and the capitalist roads.

September 14   The eight-member delegation of the Chinese

People's Association for Friendship with Foreign Countries, led by Ding Xuesong, left Beijing to visit Iceland, Sweden, Norway, Finland, and Denmark.

September 15   Chairman Hua Guofeng met the Mozambique
Government Delegation, led by Marcelino Dos Santos,
minister of Development and Economic Planning.

September 16   President Ne Win of Burma visited China from
September 16–20 on his way to Pyongyang, Korea.
Chairman Hua Guofeng met him at the airport.   He
visited Mao's mausoleum and held talks with Chairman
Hua Guofeng and Vice Premier Deng Xiaoping on
September 17.

September 17   China conducted a nuclear test.
   • The Chinese Goodwill Military Delegation, led by
Yang Zhengwu, left Beijing to visit France and Ru-
mania.

September 18   Premier Hua Guofeng sent a message to Kirti
Nidhi Bista, warmly congratulating him on his assumption of the office of prime minister of Nepal.
   • The CCP Central Committee issued a circular to
announce that a national conference on science would
be held in the spring of 1978.   The circular reaffirmed China's current economic policy, outlined the
steps being taken to plan the conference, announced
the setting up of a state scientific and technological
commission.   Referring to the recent maltreatment of
scientists and intellectuals under policies implemented
by the Gang of Four, the circular stated that they
should be restored to relevant professional work to
which they would devote five-sixths of their time, and
enjoy both responsibility and status.
   • President Senyi Kountche of Niger visited China
from September 18–23.   He held talks with Vice Premier Li Xiannian, and met Chairman Hua Guofeng on
September 21.   The Sino-Niger protocol on economic
and technical cooperation was signed on September 21.

September 19   The Chinese song-and-dance ensemble from
Zhejiang province left Beijing for performance tours to
Somalia, Egypt, Tunisia, Algeria, Senegal, and Moroc-
co.

September 20   President Macias Nguema of Equatorial Guinea
     visited China September 20-27. He was greeted at the
     airport by Chairman Hua Guofeng. At a banquet in
     his honor, Vice Premier Li Xiannian inveighed against
     Soviet interference in Africa, upon which eight diplo-
     mats representing Soviet bloc countries walked out.
     He held talks with Chairman Hua Guofeng on Septem-
     ber 23.

September 21   Xu Xiangjian, in his People's Daily article en-
     titled "Always Adhere to the Principle that the Party
     Commands the Gun," said that it was imperative to
     hold high the banner of Chairman Mao, implement the
     party's correct line, adhere to the system of collective
     leadership by the party committee and organizational
     discipline, preserve party unity, be open and above-
     board, and guard against any double-dealing acts.
       • Premier Hua Guofeng sent a message to Premier
     Pham Van Dong, warmly extending congratulations for
     Vietnam's entry into the United Nations.
       • A protocol of the economic and technical coopera-
     tion agreement between China and Mozambique was
     signed in Beijing.

September 24   The protocol on handing over the new build-
     ing for the Rumanian Embassy in the People's Republic
     of China was signed in Beijing.

September 25   The Ministry of Education held a national
     work conference in Beijing on the enrollment of stu-
     dents in institutes of higher learning. Chairman Hua
     Guofeng and the four vice-chairmen received the par-
     ticipants on September 25, along with the representa-
     tives attending the preparatory meeting for the Na-
     tional Conference on Science, in the Great Hall of the
     People.
       • Vice Premier Deng Xiaoping averred to the chair-
     man of the Defense Committee of the West German
     Parliament that a Sino-Soviet rapprochement was "out
     of the question for the next generation." Deng
     thought war was inevitable in the long run, but he
     said China was not eager for it and indeed the war
     could be postponed as the result of efforts by all
     people.

September 26   The premier and secretary of the Communist
          party of Kampuchea Central Committee, Pol Pot,
          visited China at the head of the government and party
          delegation from September 26 to October 4, accom-
          panied by the two deputy premiers in charge of for-
          eign and economic affairs, Ieng Sary and Vorn Vet,
          respectively. The delegation began talks with Chair-
          man Hua Guofeng, Vice Premiers Deng Xiaoping, and
          Li Xiannian on September 29, and continued to the
          30th. Apart from a brief visit to North Korea from
          October 4-8, Pol Pot did not leave China until October
          22.
             • NCNA reported that better management of finan-
          cial and bank work was the main topic of the recent
          National Conference on Bank Work held in Beijing.
          The conference called for certain unification of bank
          work, implementation of bank rules and regulations,
          enforcement of financial discipline and the proper con-
          centration of money and material to ensure fulfillment
          of the country's national economic plan and completion
          of key construction projects.
             • The delegation of the China Council for the Pro-
          motion of International Trade, headed by Wang Yao-
          ding, ended its visit to the United States. Since its
          arrival in Seattle on September 6, the delegation had
          toured Washington, New York, Cleveland, Chicago,
          New Orleans, Los Angeles and San Francisco, where
          it visited factories and other enterprises and made
          contacts with industrial and business circles.
             • The Philippine Delegation, led by General Remeo
          C. Espino, arrived in Beijing for a short visit. Vice
          Premier Deng Xiaoping met the delegation on Septem-
          ber 28.

September 27   Vice Premier Deng Xiaoping met George H.W.
          Bush, former chief of the US liaison office in China,
          Mrs. Bush and his party.
             • NCNA reported that a 220,000 volt high-tension
          power transmission and transforming project had been
          completed in Hubei province recently. This was the
          fourth Danjiang-Wuhan transmission and transforming
          project.

September 28   The new Chinese Embassy Building was in-
          augurated in Islamabad, Pakistan.

September 29   Foreign Minister Huang Hua made a speech
        on the Chinese domestic situation and foreign policy
        to the UN General Assembly. He said, "The factors
        for war are visibly growing and social-imperialism is
        the most dangerous source of war."
          • Chen Chu said in the UN Security Council that
        China could not support the draft resolution, put for-
        ward by the UK, asking the secretary general to ap-
        point a representative to participate in discussion on
        Zimbabwe (Rhodesia), but out of consideration for the
        position of African states concerned, China would not
        participate in the vote.
          • Vice Premier Deng Xiaoping addressed more than
        800 "Taiwan compatriots residing in foreign countries,
        compatriots from Hong Kong and Macao, overseas Chi-
        nese and Chinese who have naturalized in foreign
        countries," who had come in twenty-seven groups to
        attend the October 1st celebrations.
          • Chairman Hua Guofeng met the Rumanian People's
        Friendship Delegation, led by Paul Niculescu.

September 30   Chairman Hua Guofeng gave a grand recep-
        tion in the Great Hall of the People, marking the
        twenty-eight anniversary of the founding of the PRC.
        All four Vice Chairmen, Party and State leaders, and
        more than 3,000 Chinese and foreign guests attended
        this reception, including Pol Pot, Aiichiro Fujiyama,
        William P. Rogers, and Mrs. Rogers. In a toast re-
        mark, Chairman Hua pointed out that "it is expected
        that the national economic plan for 1977 will be ful-
        filled successfully or overfulfilled."

October 1   The twenty-eighth anniversary of the founding
        of the People's Republic of China was celebrated with
        galas attended by over 600,000 in Beijing's six main
        parks. The joint editorial of the People's Daily, the
        Red Flag, and the Liberation Army Daily called for
        less empty talk and more hard work if the tasks of
        modernizing agriculture, industry, national defense,
        science and technology were to be accomplished.

October 2   Author William H. Hinton left Beijing for home.
        Since his arrival on June 22 in China, he had visited
        communes, farms, factories and schools in Beijing,
        Shanxi and Heilongjiang.

October 3 The ESCAP Delegation, invited by the Chinese Foreign Ministry and led by Executive Secretary J.S. Maramis, visited China from October 3-15. Maramis said afterwards that the Chinese government had told him that it would pursue a "more active approach" to the activities of ESCAP.

October 4 Foreign Minister Huang Hua visited Canada from October 4-6, and was received by Prime Minister Trudeau on October 5.
 • President Ahmadou Ahidjo of Cameroon visited China from October 4-10. He was greeted at the airport by Chairman Hua Guofeng. An economic and technical cooperation agreement between the two nations was signed on October 7.

October 5 Vice Premier Li Xiannian, in an interview with the Asian Wall Street Journal stated, "Chairman Mao told Mr. Kissinger there are such a heap of counter-revolutionaries in Taiwan that it cannot be managed without a fight. Whether the fight takes place in five years, ten years, or even longer, that is another matter." Li went on to reaffirm China's three-point stand for the American withdrawal from Taiwan. He further said that it would be "inappropriate" for the US or any other country or private company to supply arms to the Nationalists once diplomatic ties are established between the US and China.
 • NCNA released the text of the CCP Central Committee's decision on Party education, entitled "On Running Well Party Schools at Various Levels." Referring to the seriousness of the disruption caused to the party organization and the damage caused to the party's tradition and style of work by both the Lin Biao and Gang of Four episodes, the decision emphasized the need for extensive lecturing, within the party and among the people, on the party's nature, organizational principles, discipline, and tradition and style of work.

October 6 A joint editorial by the People's Daily, the Red Flag, and the Liberation Army Daily marked the first anniversary of the "smashing" of the Gang of Four. Noting the significance of the victory over the opposition, the editorial emphasized the need for the investigative work to be carried out thoroughly.

• NCNA announced that China and the Soviet Union discussed specific issues relating to navigation channels that exist on such rivers along the Sino-Soviet boundary as the Heilong and Wusuli rivers and reached agreement on a number of issues.

October 7 The Chinese Government Delegation, led by Ye Fei, minister of communications, left Beijing to visit the People's Democratic Republic of Yemen and the Yemen Arab Republic.

• Foreign Minister Huang Hua arrived in Paris from Canada to visit France at the invitation of the French government. He was received by President Giscard d'Estaing on October 7.

• NCNA released the text of the State Council circular on its decision to hold the Third National Conference on Farm Mechanization; its tasks would include a review of progress and of future plans towards implementing the policy of achieving basic farm mechanization by 1980.

October 9 An article in the People's Daily by Luo Ruiqing catalogued the misdeeds of Lin Biao from 1935, linked him with the Gang of Four during the Cultural Revolution, and stated that the Gang of Four had creatively applied his tricks more skillfully than he.

• The inauguration ceremony for the Central Party School was attended by Chairman Hua Guofeng who became the school's president, Vice Chairmen Ye Jianying, Deng Xiaoping, and Wang Dongxing, and other leaders, including Hu Yaobang, a member of the CCP Central Committee, and a Vice President of the school. In his speech, Chairman Hua Guofeng emphasized the importance of grasping all facets of the basic principles of Marxism-Leninism-Mao Zedong Thought, not bits and pieces, and of grasping them concretely and not abstractly.

October 11 Ex-Premier Kukrit Pramoj of Thailand visited China from October 11-19, and met Chairman Hua Guofeng on October 13.

October 12 NCNA reported that China had discovered another site containing 100,000-year-old paleoanthropologic fossils. A large part of well-preserved right

parietal bone, the biggest paleoanthropologic fossil
found in China in the past decade, was unearthed.
The site was a cliff on the west bank of a deep ravine
between the Xuqiaoyao brigade in Yanggao county,
Shanxi province, and the Houqiaoyao brigade in Yang-
yuan county, Hebei province in North China.
  • West German Foreign Minister Hans-Dietrich
Genscher visited China from October 12-15. Chairman
Hua Guofeng met him on October 14.

October 13 Premier Hua Guofeng sent a message to Ahmed
      Hussein Al Ghashmi, chairman of the Command Coun-
      cil of the Yemen Arab Republic, expressing deep con-
      dolences on the untimely death of Chairman Ibrahim
      Mohammed Al-Hamdi.

October 14 Vice Premier Deng Xiaoping told a visiting Japan-
      ese ruling party leader (Susumi Nikaido, former chief
      cabinet secretary) that China was considering a 200-
      mile fishery zone, but would not take "unreasonable"
      measures against Japan.

October 16 NCNA announced that works of important Chi-
      nese writers since May 4, 1919, including those by
      Guo Moruo, Mao Dun, Pa Jin, the late works of Lu
      Xun would be republished. The complete annotated
      works of Lu Xun would be issued volume by volume
      and the music of Nie Er, Xian Xinghai, Ma Ge and Ho
      Luding, and reproductions of paintings by Xu Bei-
      hong, Ji Baishi, and Qiao Sudi would be printed. At
      the same time, works of classical literature, painting
      and music, together with foreign literature including
      Greek mythology, works by Shakespeare, Heine, Gogol,
      Balzac and Hugo, piano compositions by Beethoven,
      Chopin and Bach, and drawings by Rembrandt would
      be issued in line with the principle of making the past
      serve the present and foreign things serve China.
      Among other developments announced were the stage
      revivals of the Beijing opera Driven to Join the Liang-
      shan Mountain Rebels and, the first modern opera
      based on folk music, The White-haired Girl.

October 18 An interregional training seminar on food fore-
      casting, sponsored by China on behalf of the World
      Meteorological Organization (WMO) and UNDP, opened in
      Nanjing.

October 20   NCNA reported that a recent national work conference held by the Ministry of Education had decided
to change enrollment policy for students of high education in the interests of modernization, including the
reintroduction of examinations to test the academic
level of potential students.
   • Chairman Hua Guofeng met former British Prime
Minister Edward Heath and his party. Hua said, "We
hope to see a united and strong Europe. We believe
that Europe, on its part, hopes to see a strong China,
too."
   • NCNA announced that 15,000 oracle tortoise shells
and bones dating back about 3,000 years were recently
found in the area of Zhouyuan in Shaanxi province.

October 21   NCNA announced that the Shanghai Literature
and Art, a journal mainly devoted to new literary
works, was founded in Shanghai recently. The first
issue had twenty-eight contributors and included fic-
tion, essays, reports, poems, and literary criticism.
   • A certificate for handing over the highway between Galcaio and Garowe in Somalia was signed in
Mogadishu. The 228 km Galcaio-Garowe Highway was
the second section of the 970 km Belet Uen-Burao
Highway being built at this time with the Chinese aid.
The first section of 362 km was transferred to Somalia
on November 15, 1976.

October 22   The Seventeenth Meeting of the Joint China-
Albania Committee for Scientific and Technical Cooperation was held in Tirana from October 22-November
4.   The protocol of the meeting was signed on November 4.

October 23   The Fourth Session of the Standing Committee
of the Fourth National People's Congress was held from
October 23-24 and it was decided to hold the Fifth
NPC in spring 1978. Chairman Hua Guofeng addressed
the plenary session of the meeting on October 23. He
said that the convoking of the Fifth NPC would be
preceded by the convoking of new People's Congresses
in the provinces, municipalities, and autonomous regions to ensure the success of the election of deputies
to the Fifth NPC. Vice Premier Yu Qiuli delivered a
report on the development of the national economy to

the plenary session on October 23. He announced that
on the basis of the gradual improvement in the economy, about forty-six percent of the total number of
workers and staff were to have their wages raised
beginning October 1.

• The decision concerning enrollment was accompanied by a series of articles and reports, most of
which sought to explain why it was imperative to re-
introduce examinations and the practice of direct admission to college from school. The fall in standards
was graphically illustrated in an October article in the
People's Daily, entitled "Scholastic Examinations Are
Very Necessary," where it was pointed out that in
recent tests among graduates in Shanghai, many had
performed very poorly, sixty-eight percent failing
mathematics, seventy percent failing physics, and
seventy-six percent failing chemistry, with some unable to answer a single question in their own special-
ity.

October 24 In an interview with AFP, Vice Premier Deng
Xiaoping said that China "would not like to see the
Communist Parties of France, Italy and Spain come to
power or even to participate in government." They
would carry out "a policy of appeasement" towards
the Soviet Union.

October 25 To avoid giving offense to the Chinese government, the Carter administration quietly refused per-
mission for the proposed visit to America by the Dalai
Lama.

• Foreign Minister B.E. Talboys of New Zealand
visited China from October 25-November 2. He met
Chairman Hua Guofeng on October 28. The two nations declared a common view regarding the international situation in the Pacific region.

October 26 Vice Premier Deng Xiaoping told French newspaper editors visiting Beijing that terrorism, cut off
as it was from the masses, had nothing to do with
revolution, and he "categorically condemned terrorism
as anti-revolutionary and anti-Marxist-Leninist."

October 28 Wu De came under criticism on large-character
posters put up at Beijing University. He was accused

of "not having respected democracy" in elections of delegates to the upcoming Municipal People's Congress.

October 29 The Chinese Telecommunications Delegation arrived in Cambodia for a fourteen-day visit. The protocol on the opening of telecommunications links between the two countries was signed on November 10.

October 31 NCNA claimed that locust plague, once a contributing factor to terrible famines, had been brought completely under control.

November 1 The People's Daily carried a 35,000 word article, "Chairman Mao's Theory of the Differentiation of the Three Worlds Is a Major Contribution to Marxism-Leninism," to demonstrate how the theory reflected and explained the underlying forces at work in the world today. In the theory, which Mao proposed in February 1974, the US and USSR were the first world; Japan, Europe, and Canada were the second, Asia, Africa and Latin America were the third.
    • China and Iran signed the 1977-78 goods exchange agreement and a trade memorandum.

November 2 The New York Times reported that although China had refused to accept foreign loans or direct investment, its expensive imports through deferred payments had led to a debt of $1.3 billion, including long-term deferred payments for purchases of plants between 1973 and 1975 and short-term credits for imports of grain. That amounted to twenty-three percent of total hard currency earnings with the non-Communist world of $5.75 billion last year. This gave China a debt-service ratio, of twenty-three percent, just under the warning mark of twenty-five percent.
    • Premier Don Mintoff of Malta visited China from November 3-7 and was welcomed by Chairman Hua Guofeng at the airport. He met formally with Chairman Hua Guofeng on November 5. The protocol on economic and technical cooperation between the two nations was signed on November 6.

November 5 Vice Premier Wang Chen openly told a visiting

British trade mission that China would like to purchase British Harrier vertical take-off aircraft.

November 6   The Standing Committee of the NPC and the State Council sent a message to the Presidium of the Supreme Soviet and the Council of Ministers of the USSR, marking the sixtieth anniversary of the October Socialist Revolution.

November 7   V.S. Tolstikov, Soviet ambassador to China, and his wife gave a reception in Beijing to mark the sixtieth anniversary of the October Socialist Revolution.   Among guests at the reception were Huang Hua and Yu Chan.
  • A ceremony to hand over 2,000 tons of wheat and other materials from China to Cape Verde was held on a Chinese cargo ship at port Mindelo.

November 8   NCNA announced that the first digital satellite communication ground station designed and built by China had been put into operation with satisfactory results.   The new station would be used to transmit the format of the People's Daily, radio and television programs, and other messages from Beijing to far-off areas.

November 11   The five-man trade mission from the Indonesian Chamber of Commerce and Industry visited the Guangzhou Fair at the invitation of the Chinese side, for the first time since 1965.

November 13   The certificate for handing over the Chinese-aided Mogadishu stadium was signed in Mogadishu, Somalia.   The stadium, with a capacity of 30,000 seats, covered a building area of more than 23,000 square meters.
  • Vice Premier Gu Mu told Japanese Dietmen visiting Beijing that China would be able to export more than ten million tons of oil a year to Japan by 1982.

November 16   The Guardian reported that China ordered several executive jet aircraft and crop dusting planes from Grumman Aircraft.   Any such purchase would require the approval of CoCom and the consent of Washington, because the Harrier contained some US-based components for which the US export licenses would have to be issued.

November 18   Yang Hushan told the UN First Committee that China wished to disassociate itself from the consensus in favor of the World Disarmament Conference and the calling of a Special Session of the General Assembly for this. He said that China wanted the complete prohibition and thorough destruction of nuclear weapons.

November 20   The National Meteorological Conference was held between November 20–December 2 in Beijing to set tasks in the coming year.

• Le Duan, general secretary of the Vietnamese Communist party, led a delegation to Beijing at the invitation of the CCP and government for a visit from November 20–25. He was greeted at the airport by Chairman Hua Guofeng. Hua reiterated at the opening banquet that China would "ally with all countries subjected to imperialist and social-imperialist aggression, subversion, interference, control or bullying to form the broadest possible united front against superpower hegemonism." This passage was omitted in the Vietnamese press report. Le Duan, for his part, declared that "we are determined not to allow any imperialist and reactionary force whatsoever to encroach upon our independence and freedom." He thanked the Chinese for their aid, but added "I also wish to sincerely thank the Soviet Union and the other socialist countries for their warm support and great and valuable assistance."

November 24   Chen Chu told the Security Council that China would vote in favor of the resolution condemning the use of mercenaries against Benin in January 1977. Chen particularly blamed one of the superpowers for using mercenaries against African states and said that the resolution adopted by the Organization of African Unity (OAU) against mercenaries was significant.

• The First Session of the Seventh Beijing Municipal People's Congress was held from November 24–December 3. Chairman Hua Guofeng was elected as a deputy to the Fifth NPC, and Wu De was elected chairman of the committee.

November 26   Vice Chairman of the Standing Committee of
          the NPC Deng Yingchao visited Iran from November
          26 to December 2, and met the shah on December 1.
              • The protocol of the Fifteenth Session of the
          Joint Sino-Bulgarian Committee for Scientific and
          Technical Cooperation was signed in Sofia.
              • The protocol of the Sixteenth Session of the Sino-
          Hungarian Commission for Scientific and Technical Co-
          operation was signed in Beijing.
              • Premier Hua Guofeng sent a message to Argentine
          President Jorge Rafael Videla, extending his deep
          sympathy and solicitude in connection with the strong
          earthquake in the country.

November 27   China quietly indicated its support for Presi-
          dent Sadat's initiative. NCNA reported without com-
          ment his visit to Jerusalem and his meetings with Is-
          raeli leaders.
              • Chairman Hua Guofeng, Li Xiannian, and Wang
          Dongxing and other central leaders joined the workers
          in reinforcing the main dam of the Miyun reservoir and
          inspected this hydraulic project on the northeastern
          outskirts of Beijing at a time when the winter farm-
          land improvement campaign was sweeping the whole
          country.

November 28   Chairman Hua Guofeng sent a message to
          President Josip Broz Tito, marking the National Day
          of Yugoslavia.
              • A delegation, led by Li Qiang, visited Britain
          from November 28 to December 5. They met Prime
          Minister James Callaghan, as well as Conservative
          party leader, Mrs. Thatcher. They toured British
          industrial and technological establishments. It was
          the first such visit in almost five years.
              • NCNA announced that the 150 km Leap Forward
          Canal, carved out along the precipices of the Taihang
          Mountains, was completed recently in Anyang county,
          Henan province.

November 29   Chen Chu, speaking in the UN General As-
          sembly, praised the armed struggle of the Palestinians
          in the Middle East and condemned Israeli measures to
          impose its laws and settle its people in occupied ter-
          ritories. He also blamed superpower interference in

the area to gain control and welcomed the expulsion
of Russians from Egypt, the Sudan, and Somalia.

November 30 There was an agreement in principle on an
eight-year trade pact under which Japan proposed to
import 6.8 million tons of oil a year in the first year,
rising to fifteen million tons after five years, as well
as coal at the rate of 150,000 tons in the first year
but rising to one million tons after five years. The
total value of Japanese imports from China over the
eight years was estimated at $10 billion.

December 1 The People's Daily carried a long article by the
theoretical group of the office of the PLA General
Political Department and the Liberation Army Daily,
published on November 30 by the Liberation Army
Daily, entitled "Whoever Attempts to Destroy Our
Great Wall Courts His Own Ruins--Settle Accounts
with Zhang Chunqiao for the Counter-Revolutionary
Crimes He Committed in the General Political Department," cataloging and criticizing Zhang Chunqiao's
activities during his twenty-one months as director
of the General Political Department of the PLA. During that period he was said to have transmitted no instructions from Chairman Mao, nor did he meet the
masses of the department, or submit any constructive
opinion about the army's political works.

December 3 Vice Premier Chen Yonggui had an extensive
tour in Cambodia from December 3-15. Chen began
by going to the south, and then, accompanied for the
rest of his tour by Pol Pot himself, to the center,
north, northwest and finally--with Ieng Sary and Vorn
Vet joining the entourage--to the west and southwest.

December 4 Premier Hua Guofeng sent a message to Morarji
Desai, prime minister of India, expressing deep sympathy and solicitude over the suffering caused by
cyclones in India's southern coasts.

December 5 Li Qiang visited France from December 5-14.
He toured French corporations and industrial estab-
lishments, and met Prime Minister Raymond Barre.
    • Wu Xiaoda, speaking in the UN Sixth Committee,
said that China opposed "terrorist acts" by individuals

or groups of individuals who were isolated in their
political struggle.

December 6   Premier Hua Guofeng sent a message of greetings to Mobutu Sese Seko on his reelection as president of the Republic of Zaire.

December 8   New Zealand announced the first butter sale
to China, worth NZ $2.5 million.

December 10   China carried off the title at the Ninth Asian
Men's Basketball Championships in Kuala Lumpur by
beating South Korea 61 to 58.

December 11   A Sino-Mongolian protocol on talks in meteorological communications was signed in Ulan Bator.

December 14   General Ziaul Haq, the chief marshal law administrator, visited China from December 14-19.   He
met Premier Hua Guofeng and Vice Premier Deng
Xiaoping.   Vice Premier Deng expressed satisfaction
that relations between the South Asian countries had
gradually improved.   General Ziaul appreciated China's
support for the establishment of a nuclear weapon-
free zone in South Asia.
    • Maltese Prime Minister Don Mintoff attended a
ceremony for launching of the first oil tanker ordered
by China.   The oil tanker, "Daqing 216," was built
at a Maltese drydock constructed with the cooperation
of the two countries.

December 15   China and Rumania signed the 1977-78 scientific
cooperation plan in Bucharest.
    • NCNA released the text of a State Council cir-
cular on the convocation of the National Conference on
Learning from Daqing and Dazhai in Urban and Rural
Commerce in 1978.   Among the tasks of the conference
were exchanging experience, commending the advanced
planning, and organizing emulation drives, besides encouraging the emulation of Daqing and Dazhai.

December 17   China and Czechoslovakia signed the 1978
goods exchange and payment agreement in Beijing.
    • Premier Hua Guofeng sent a message to Kim Il-
sung, extending congratulations on his reelection as

president of the Democratic People's Republic of Korea, and a message of congratulations to Li Jong Ok on his election as premier.

• NCNA announced that a fairly well-preserved skeleton of an adult mammoth (an extinct elephant that lived tens of thousands of years ago) was discovered in Mingshui county, Heilongjiang province in October. It was approximately three meters tall and five meters long.

December 18   China and Czechoslovakia signed the protocol of the Nineteenth Session of the Joint Commission for Scientific and Technical Cooperation in Beijing.

December 19   China and Ghana signed a long-term trade and payment agreement and a trade protocol for 1978 in Beijing.

December 20   NCNA announced, and the People's Daily and other papers published, the second draft scheme for simplifying Chinese characters.   Prepared by the Committee of the Reform of the Chinese Written Language, with the approval of the State Council, the scheme listed 853 simplified characters, 248 of which were already in wide use in personal communications. The other 605 were to be discussed in forums throughout the country.   The report noted that the first scheme was published, section by section, beginning in 1956 and during the ensuing twenty-year period, 2,238 characters were simplified.

December 21   China and Rumania signed the 1978 protocol on goods exchange and payment in Beijing.   Chairman Hua Guofeng met Ion Patan, deputy prime minister, who led the delegation.

December 22   Premier Hua Guofeng and other central party and state leaders received, at the Great Hall of the People, Taiwan "compatriots" attending the consultation conference on electing deputies of Taiwan province to the Fifth NPC.

• China and Iran agreed to jointly scale the Chomolungma in the next two years.   The two sides agreed to form a joint mountaineering team according to the principle of equality, with the task of reaching the peak of Chomolungma at 8,848 meters above sea level by the route taken by the Chinese expedition in 1960 and 1975 from the northern slope.

December 24 On the eve of the opening of the Third National Conference of Farm Mechanization, Chairman Hua Guofeng, Deng Xiaoping, Li Xiannian, and Wang Dongxing visited the farm mechanization exhibition and attended a farm machinery demonstration at the Beijing Agricultural Exhibition Center.

• Premier Hua Guofeng sent a message to the shahanshah of Iran, expressing deep sympathy and solicitude for the damage caused by earthquake in Iran.

December 26 A formal soirée was held in the Great Hall of the People to mark the eighty-fourth anniversary of the birth of Chairman Mao Zedong.

• NCNA reported that of the country's eighty major industrial products, thirty-two completed annual state quotas by the end of November. The total industrial output value of the first eleven months was up by 13.7 percent, compared with the corresponding period of 1976. It was estimated that it would be over fourteen percent by year's end.

• Vice Premier Deng Xiaoping met E.F. Hill and Mrs. Hill, chairman of the Australian Communist party (M-L).

December 27 Chairman Hua Guofeng met the internationally known Dutch film director Joris Ivens and French film worker Marceline Loridam.

December 28 In a review of exposure and criticism of the Gang of Four in China in 1977, NCNA reported that there were three campaigns. The first campaign was launched last winter and lasted through spring. It concentrated on exposing the crimes of this handful of careerists in splitting the party and plotting to usurp the supreme leadership of the party and the state. Stress was put on their conspiracies at the time when Chairman Mao was seriously ill and after he passed away, and on their plot for armed rebellion. The second campaign, which started in March, fully exposed the reactionary histories of the Gang of Four

and their armies in destroying this criminal evidence.
The third campaign, now in full swing, was a decisive
one to win complete victory, by making a fundamental
distinction between Chairman Mao's revolutionary line
and the Gang of Four's revisionist line, clarifying
people's thinking which the Gang of Four confused,
and liquidating their poisonous influence.

December 29 The Seventh Session of the Standing Committee
of the Fourth National Committee of the Chinese People's Political Consultative Conference was held in
Beijing December 27-29.

December 30 An official report at the end of the year said
that the 1977 grain harvest was no bigger than that
of 1976, following one of the worst years for drought
and other natural disasters since 1949. The American
estimate was that about 283 million tons would be har-
vested.

December 31 It was announced that a trial postal code system, based in six digits, with the first two representing the province or autonomous region, the third the
postal district, the fourth the county or municipality
and the last two the post office delivering the mail,
would be introduced in Shanghai, Jiangsu and Liaoning
provinces on January 1, 1978.
    • Pich Cheang, Kampuchean ambassador in China,
issued a statement saying that the Vietnamese Army,
since September 1977, had "launched systematic and
large-scale aggressive acts of invasion against Democratic Kampuchea." The same day the Vietnamese
Embassy in China issued a statement proposing negotiations to solve the border issue between Vietnam and
Kampuchea.

Chapter IX

1978

THE FOUR MODERNIZATIONS ON THE MARCH

A new, pragmatic approach to domestic affairs, characterized by a plan called the Four Modernizations (of agriculture, industry, national defense, science and technology) received primary attention in virtually every aspect of life in China. China, separated so long from the outer world by an instinctive xenophobia and a mixture of reclusive Maoism, in 1978 began its Great Leap Outward, or what Beijing's propagandists call the "New Long March."

In turning toward modernization, the new leadership took immediate steps to reshape the party line. They had completed the delicate task of desanctifying Mao's legacy without besmirching it completely. They put forth the line that Mao's philosophy was basically correct, but that it was distorted and misapplied by his onetime heir apparent Lin Biao and the Gang of Four. Mao's sponsorship of the Cultural Revolution was excused on the grounds that he was aged, infirm, and confused. In subtle ways they promoted a flexible interpretation of the thought of Mao Zedong. The basic principles of Mao, said Deng Xiaoping, were integrated with reality. "If we just copied past documents word for word, we wouldn't be solving any problem, let alone solving any problem correctly." They did not completely reject Mao's teachings, but did deny any religious reverence for his ideology.

The Fifth People's Congress, China's nominal legislature, was convened on February 26 to act on the CCP proposal. It reappointed Premier Hua Guofeng. Ye Jianying, the aging marshal, was elected chairman of the Standing Committee of the People's Congress to carry out the ceremonial functions of the head of state. Xu Xiangqian, who

had stressed professionalism and discipline in the Army, replaced Ye as minister of defense.   The People's Congress
reconfirmed China's political structure without clarifying
the power relationship among the top leaders.   Hua Guofeng
remained the highest ranking official, but Deng Xiaoping
seemed to hold more executive power.   After his appointment as deputy premier and vice-chairman of the party in
1977, Deng steadily consolidated his power and took steps
to remove his adversaries, especially those who had played
important roles in the Cultural Revolution.

The new Chinese constitution, approved by the People's Congress in March, restored to the people the right to
a trial defense and to lodge complaints against government
officials.   It also provided that ethnic minorities had the
right to preserve or reform their customs.   In June, China
reportedly set free 110,000 political prisoners detained since
the "anti-rightist" campaign in the 1950's.   In addition,
thousands of party cadres and intellectuals, purged during
and after the Cultural Revolution, were put in rehabilitation
programs.   In late November, wall posters indirectly critical
of Mao began to appear in Beijing and other cities.   The
posters seemed a part of a public campaign for democracy
and civil liberties.   The emphasis upon the political guarantees of the new constitution provided a liveliness and rich-
ness to the texture of Chinese politics.

Progress in agriculture was probably the highest
priority of the Four Modernizations.   It is also the most difficult.   The Beijing leadership set a goal of producing 400
million tons of wheat, rice and other grains by 1985 and for
achieving substantial agricultural mechanization by 1980.
Both goals seemed too ambitious.   Though land in China
was intensively cultivated and Chinese farmers were known
for their innovation and diligence, yields lagged far behind
those of other countries.   Beijing conferred with foreign
farm experts, including US Secretary of Agriculture Bob
Bergland, about new seed varieties, the use of insecticides,
and the exchange of specialists.   While the Chinese had
made some progress toward mechanization, they needed more
than one million additional tractors, 320,000 trucks, at least
three million combine harvesters, new drainage and irrigation machinery, and 700,000 technicians for machinery repair and maintenance.   The hardware would be difficult to
get, since farm equipment was normally bought with surplus

capital, which China ordinarily had to use to purchase grain from abroad. The result was that China, in 1978, remained a net importer of grain, and the rationing of edible oils and other staples continued.

Comprehensive economic growth, with a rapid modernization of the industrial sector, was a goal set in 1978. Toward that end, Beijing ended its economic isolation and broadened its dealings with foreign capitalist countries. For the first time in its history, the leadership made policy changes that would allow foreign loans and joint ventures, Chinese banks were to receive deposits from foreign traders and international loans could be arranged. Beijing expressed interest in setting up joint manufacturing facilities with foreign firms in China, Hong Kong, and Macao. Five American oil companies--Union, Exxon, Pennzoil, Gulf, and Phillips-- sent delegations to China to discuss offshore oil exploration. In late November, the Coastal State Gas Corporation announced an agreement to import 3.6 million barrels of crude oil from China; it was the first US company to do so since the regime came to power. On November 4, US Energy Secretary James Schlesinger announced in Beijing that the Chinese had agreed on a tentative list of cooperative energy development projects. China's foreign trade rose sharply in the first half of 1978. Exports increased by twenty-nine percent and imports by sixty percent, compared with the same period in 1977. Total 1978 trade exceeded $20 billion.

In education, the leadership made broad changes that reversed the policy of Mao Zedong. Speaking at the National Conference on Education in April, Deng Xiaoping declared that examinations were imperative to schools. High standards and rigid discipline had to be enforced if China was to become a modern industrial power by the end of the century, he said. Nationwide examinations for admission to universities were not only reinstated, but became rigorous and uniform. Elite schools were established and provided the best teachers and facilities. Among teachers, ranks and titles were restored. Salary increases were restored and other prerequisites were adopted. A far-reaching program of scientific and technological advancement was launched in 1978. A conference held in Beijing March 18-31 was attended by 6,000 delegates to discuss their role in modernization. Two programs were revealed: a three-year plan to speed up research and development in such technical fields as

genetic engineering, laser technology, and computer technology; and an eight-year plan to lay the foundation for over-
taking more advanced Western countries in a broad stratum
of science and technology by the year 2000. Beijing planned
to send thousands of students to study in foreign countries,
including the United States.

Although China had the world's largest standing army
(about 3.5 million), China's military machine was primitive--
at least twenty years behind those of the superpowers.
China's most potent bomber was the antiquated TU-16 of
1954. The People's Liberation Army had no antitank missiles, no armored helicopters and no modern battle tanks.
Its nuclear warheads were mounted on intermediate-range
missiles. Although China's Navy was the world's third
largest (in terms of manpower, not ships), it was also out-
dated; its two nuclear-powered submarines, for example,
carried no missiles. By 1978, the need for military modernization was recognized. "It is foolish to think," declared
the Commission on Science and Technology for National Defense, "that it would be possible to use old weapons to
fight an enemy equipped with missiles and nuclear weapons."
Beijing therefore decided to improve its weapons to whatever
extent possible, given its financial means. Chinese representatives were sent to France and West Germany to examine
advanced weapons for possible purchase. In May, a Chinese
military delegation visited France to discuss purchase of
long-range, wire-guided antitank missiles. In November,
Britain reportedly sold China diesel engines for use in naval
vessels.

Six years after the 1972 Shanghai communiqué called
for normalization of relations between China and the United
States, that goal was finally reached. On January 1, 1979,
the two nations officially established diplomatic relations.
It was announced simultaneously in Washington and Beijing,
on December 15, that Deng Xiaoping was to visit the United
States on January 29 and embassies were to be established
on March 1. The agreement was the result of months of
secret negotiations in which the United States finally agreed
to sever ties with Taiwan. China had insisted that this was
the prerequisite of normalization with Washington.

For most of the year, the Carter administration sought
to improve relations with China without granting full recogni-

tion. By expanding trade, exchanging technology, and approving allied arms shipments, Carter hoped to induce Beijing to soften its stand on Taiwan. That was the thinking that Zbigniew Brzezinski, President Carter's national security adviser, took to Beijing on May 20. Brzezinski and Chinese leaders discussed global strategy, emphasizing their mutual concern over Soviet domination in various parts of the world. Beijing was pleased by Brzezinski's emphasis on the "congruence of fundamental interests" between China and the United States. It was receptive to signs that Washington was moving away from détente with the Soviet Union in favor of closer Sino-American relations. Although no agreement was reached on Taiwan, the two countries did agree to step up trade and continue to share technological capabilities. In a reversal of policy, Washington agreed to sell China an airborne geological exploration system with an infrared scanning system. That device, used primarily for oil exploration, also had potential military uses.

In July, a delegation of US scientists headed by Frank Press, President Carter's science adviser, visited China. Beijing, interested in promoting basic and applied science, suggested cooperation in the form of student exchanges, seminars, and joint research projects. Beijing bought 3.9 million metric tons of wheat from the United States in 1978, its first purchases in four years. This augured well for the expansion of grain trade and perhaps the sale of other farm products to China. In November, China signed a $500 million contract with Pan American World Airways to build and operate a chain of hotels in Beijing, Shanghai, and other cities. In late December, the Coca-Cola Company announced that it would begin sales in China in January. Coke would become the first consumer product to be sold in China since the regime came to power.

The antagonism between China and the Soviet Union turned into an intensive diplomatic war. Containing Soviet influence was the overriding idea in Chinese foreign policy. When Moscow offered to hold talks to improve relations, China dismissed the gesture as propaganda. Sino-Soviet relations were exacerbated by a border incident on May 9. Beijing charged that thirty Soviet troops, supported by a helicopter and navy boats, crossed the Ussuri River into the Hulin area of Heilongjiang province. The troops allegedly shot at Chinese inhabitants, wounding a number of

them.   The Soviet Union expressed regret over the incident,
but denied that its troops had shot or beaten Chinese citizens.

On May 29, at the UN General Assembly Special Session on Disarmament, Chinese Foreign Minister Huang Hua
called the Soviet Union "the most dangerous source of a new
world war."   Huang added that Moscow was "increasing its
military threat to Western Europe, striving to expand its
influence in the Middle East, and carrying out a series of
military adventures in Africa."   On September 6, China announced that by April 29, 1980 it would terminate the 1950
Sino-Soviet treaty of mutual defense.   The pact was intended
as a defense measure against Japan and its allies, including
the United States.

On April 3, China signed its first trade agreement
with the European Community, not only to bring itself closer
to the industrial strength of Western Europe, but also, in
the words of Beijing, "to support its struggle against hegemony (Soviet domination)."   During the year, Europeans
flocked to Beijing to arrange business deals.   West German
firms signed a $4 billion contract to build and equip seven
coal mines.   Danish and Dutch concerns concluded agreements to expand harbors.   British and West German companies submitted bids for the building of a $14 billion inte-
grated steel mill in Hebei province, while the French were
negotiating a $12 billion loan for the purchase of French
power-generating equipment.

It was in Eastern Europe, the backyard of the Soviet
Union, that the Chinese launched the boldest assault on the
Soviet diplomatic frontier.   On August 16, Chairman Hua
Guofeng arrived in Rumania for a five-day visit.   The first
ruler in China's history to visit an Eastern European nation,
he was given a boisterous reception, with half a million
Rumanians lining up the streets of Bucharest to cheer him.
Hua toured major industrial plants and held lengthy talks
with President Nicolae Ceausescu.   At a state dinner, Hua
took the opportunity to declare that those who sought to
rule the world would eventually be crushed under the iron
blows of the people.   It was plain that the remark was directed against the Kremlin.

Hua left Bucharest for Yugoslavia on August 21.   He

was warmly welcomed in Belgrade. In a statement referring to possible Soviet intervention, he observed that "Yugoslovia is ready at all times to repel the enemy." China's friendship with Yugoslavia and rapprochement with capitalist nations led to a rift with Albania, once an ideological ally.

Another great economic power that Beijing was particularly eager to align with in its scheme against the Soviet Union was Japan. A significant step toward that end was the signing of a peace and friendship treaty between the two countries on August 12. Negotiations for the treaty had been suspended in 1975 because Japan was unwilling to accept the Chinese proposal that the treaty should provide against "hegemony" by a third country. Moscow raised strong objections to the hegemony clause, maintaining that it was aimed at the Soviet Union. Apparently encouraged by the United States, Japan brushed aside fears of Soviet retaliation and dispatched Foreign Minister Sunao Sonoda to Beijing to sign the treaty. Under it, Japan agreed to oppose efforts by any country to establish hegemony in the Asia-Pacific region or anywhere else. Another step taken toward closer Sino-Japanese relations was the signing of a $20 billion eight-year agreement between Beijing and a Japanese trade group on February 16. China undertook to export oil and coal to Japan in exchange for Japanese plants and technology.

On May 4, Chairman Hua Guofeng visited North Korea. He appeared successful in drawing Pyongyang away from the USSR.

China's relations with Vietnam, once a closer ally, had badly deteriorated since the end of the Vietnam War in 1975. Vietnam's war with Cambodia gave rise to the Chinese apprehension that Hanoi, backed by Moscow, was aiming to dominate Indo-China. In March, Hanoi ordered a crackdown on private commerce. Ethnic Chinese in southern Vietnam in particular were given harsh treatment. Their stores were closed, their property confiscated, and many of them were forced to move to uninhabited forests. By the middle of July, 140,000 ethnic Chinese had fled into China. Beijing demanded that Vietnam immediately stop its policy of persecuting the Chinese. On July 3, China announced the termination of all economic aid to Vietnam. Border clashes took place on August 25 and November 1. In the latter,

six Chinese were killed. Beijing lodged a protest with Vietnam, warning that the Vietnamese must bear responsibility
if they continued their armed intrusions at the Chinese border. The Soviet Union and Vietnam signed a friendship
treaty on November 2. The parties agreed to consult each
other with a view toward eliminating attacks or threats of
attack to either country. The Chinese denounced the treaty
as a "military pact" that threatened world peace. China and
India, hostile to each other since their border war in 1962,
showed signs of reconciliation in 1978.

By the end of 1978, the carefully devised theory of
the three worlds, set up as China's blueprint for foreign
policy, had evolved into an "Us versus Them" strategy of
China, and whatever countries could be persuaded to join
Beijing against the Soviet Union. Chinese fear of Soviet influence in Vietnam had sustained tension on the China-
Vietnam border, and set Beijing up as an ambivalent ally of
bloodthirsty Cambodian regime, a relationship that created
no little embarrassment to the Beijing leadership.

January 1 The joint editorial by the People's Daily, the Red
    Flag, and the Liberation Army Daily said that in 1978
    the Fifth NPC, the Fifth CPPCC, and the National
    Science Conference would be major events in the politi-
    cal and cultural life of Chinese people.
    • NCNA announced that China's biggest blast fur-
    nace was put into operation in the Anshan Iron Steel
    Company. With a volume of 2,580 cubic meters, the
    new blast furnace could turn out 1,500,000 tons of
    pig iron operation.
    • The arranged classical Beijing opera Yangmen
    Nüjiang (Women Generals of the Yang Family) was re-
    staged for the first time since the Cultural Revolution.
    • Premier Hua Guofeng sent a message to amir of
    the state of Kuwait Sheikh Jaber Al-Ahmed Al-Sabah,
    expressing condolences on the death of Amir Sheikh
    Sabah Al Salem Al Sabah.
    • Chairman Hua Guofeng visited the workers and
    cadres of Tangshan on January 1 and 2 to congratu-
    late them on their achievements in overcoming the
    serious damage caused by an earthquake.

January 2 Vice Premier Deng Xiaoping met Senator Edward
Kennedy, Mrs. Kennedy and their party in Beijing.
  • The Third National Conference on Agricultural
Mechanization was held in Beijing from January 4-26.
In his speech, Chen Yonggui set forth the main tasks
for the conference: deepening the exposure and criticism of the crimes of the Gang of Four in sabotaging
China's agricultural mechanization, and eradicating
their poisonous influence; working out a program for
the basic completion of agricultural mechanization by
1980; and discussing outlines for the further development of farm mechanization in the period of the sixth
five-year plan (1981-1985).
  • Liao Zhengzhi wrote in the People's Daily that
China should make it easier for overseas Chinese to
come to China and for their families to leave China in
order to visit them abroad. Correspondence and ex-
pedited exchange of visits were, he said, both normal
and desirable, and would help to liberate Taiwan.
Overseas Chinese should not accept dual nationality,
but on the other hand they should not be forced to
choose, and would remain kinfolk even if they were
to become foreign nationals.

January 5 NCNA announced that Chairman Mao Zedong's
former residence in the town of Zhasi on the route of
the Long March in southwest China's Yunnan province,
and the site of the Zhasi meeting called by him were
recently opened to the public in commemoration of his
eighty-fourth birthday.

January 6 The delegation of the China Council for the Promotion of International Trade, led by Wang Yaoding
left Beijing to visit the United Arab Emirates, Bahrain,
and Kuwait, and held an opening ceremony of the
economic and trade exhibition of the PRC in Dubai.

January 7 Chairman Hua Guofeng met E.F. Hill, chairman
of the Australian Communist party (M-L), and his
wife, J.A. Hill in Beijing.
  • China and Brazil signed a trade agreement in
Beijing.

January 10 China and Vietnam signed the 1978 mutual supply of goods and payment agreement in Beijing.

January 12   Chairman Hua Guofeng, Vice Chairmen Ye Jianying, Deng Xiaoping, and Wang Dongxing, and other party and state leaders received representatives at the National Learn-From-Daqing Conference in the Metallurgical Industry, the Third National Conference on Agricultural Mechanization, and other meetings.

January 14   Premier Hua Guofeng sent a message to His Highness Sheikh Jaber Al-Ahmed Al-Sabah, extending congratulations on his accession to the emirate of the State of Kuwait.

January 15   The National Conference on Exchanging Experience on Technical Innovations in Industry and Communications was held by the State Planning Commission in Yantai (Shandong province) from January 15-22.
    • China and Bulgaria signed the 1978 goods exchange and payment agreement in Beijing.
    • NCNA announced that nineteen new deep-water berths for vessels of 10,000 tons and upward were put to use along China's seacoast in 1977. Emphasis was laid on the improvement of the three major seaports--Shanghai, Tianjin, and Guangzhou.
    • Chinese players won six out of the seven titles at the Norwich Union International Table Tennis Championships which closed in Brighton, England on January 5.

January 18   Vice Chairman of the Standing Committee of the NPC Deng Yingchao visited Cambodia from January 18-21. She said that all countries, including socialist countries, must abide by the five principles of peaceful coexistence. The Cambodian people's cause of safeguarding their territorial integrity was a just one.

January 19   Prime Minister Raymond Barre of France visited China from January 19-24. He was greeted at the airport by Premier Hua Guofeng. Towards the end of his visit, Barre declared French readiness to help China build nuclear power stations on the condition that Beijing accept "normal international safeguards." It was announced that Premier Hua and President Giscard d'Estaing had accepted mutual invitations to visit each other's countries at some future mutually convenient

dates. On January 23, China and France signed a
scientific and technical "framework" agreement which
was the first of its kind between China and a Western
country. The agreement dealt with joint studies and
projects in animal genetics, pharmacology, computer
technology, telecommunications, and geological exploration.

January 20   The Bank of China began issuing traveller's
checks in Renminbi in two demonominations, fifty and
one hundred yuan.

January 21   China and Laos signed two protocols providing
for China to supply complete sets of equipment to
Laos.
    • The People's Daily carried an article accusing the
Soviet Union of "stirring up trouble and adding fuel
to the conflict" between Cambodia and Vietnam.

January 22   Premier Hua Guofeng sent a message to Bulent
Ecevit, congratulating him on his assumption of the
office of Prime Minister of the Republic of Turkey.

January 25   Chairman Hua Guofeng sent a message to Rumanian President Nicolae Ceausescu, greeting him on
his sixtieth birthday.
    • China and Bangladesh signed a trade protocol in
Dacca.

January 26   The Ministry of Education issued a circular on
its decision, ratified by the State Council, to set up
specially staffed and funded "key" primary and sec-
ondary schools.
    • China successfully launched another earth satel-
lite which functioned normally after fulfilling the set
task of scientific experimentation.
    • NCNA reported that twenty old tombs, dating from
2,000 years ago, had recently been excavated in
Guangdong province. They belong to the Warring
States period (475-221 B.C.).
    • NCNA reported that the National Conference on
State Farm discussed how to accelerate the expansion
of state farms and give scope to their role as pace-
setters in speeding up China's agricultural development. China had more than 2,000 state farms, which
owned more than four million hectares of land.

January 27   Chairman Hua Guofeng met Burundi Foreign
             Minister Albert Muganga and his party.
                • China and Korea signed a protocol of the Seven-
             teenth Meeting of the China-Korea Border River Navi-
             gation Cooperation Committee in Shenyang.

January 29   Chairman Hua Guofeng, Vice Chairmen Ye
             Jianying, Li Xiannian, Wang Dongxing and other party
             and state leaders received personages from press and
             film circles in Hong Kong and Macao, more than 3,000
             representatives at National Conference of Labor Heroes
             in Coal Industries, and other conferences.
                • Canadian Secretary for External Affairs Donald
             Jamieson visited China from January 29-31.   He met
             Chairman Hua Guofeng on January 31.

February 1   China's first Chinese-English Dictionary was in
             print.   The new dictionary was medium-sized, com-
             pact and handy, but included some features of the
             encyclopedia.   There were 6,000 Chinese characters
             and some 60,000 entries, totalling four million words.

February 3   China and Poland signed the 1978 goods ex-
             change and payment agreement in Beijing.
                • China and the EEC initialled a nonpreferential
             trade agreement for five years in Brussels.
                • Vice Premier Deng Xiaoping visited Nepal from
             February 3-6.   Among other things, he talked with
             his hosts about regional cooperation in harnessing
             water resources (although this was conceded to be a
             complex problem), and he agreed that China would
             study the possibility of promoting international tourism
             in Tibet via Nepal.

February 4   Chairman Hua Guofeng met President Sadat's
             special envoy, Hassan al-Tohamy, and he publicly af-
             firmed China's support for Sadat's peace initiative
             with Israel.
                • China and Yugoslavia signed, in Belgrade, a
             protocol on the opening of a Beijing-Belgrade airline
             and beginning of regular flights between the two
             capitals.

February 7   The Chinese Delegation of Import and Export
             Corporations, led by Liu Qing, left Beijing for India.

China agreed to import more pig iron from India.

• Chairman Hua Guofeng went to the Capital Iron and Steel Company to encourage workers to do an even better job. He said that the first eight years were crucial to China's goal of accomplishing the Four Modernizations in twenty-three years, and that concentrated efforts must be made in these eight years to push forward iron and steel production.

February 12   The National Conference on mass culture work, convened by the Ministry of Culture, was held in Xiyang (Shanxi province) January 12-23.

• Premier Hua Guofeng sent a message to R. Premadasa, congratulating him on his assumption of the post as the prime minister of Sri Lanka.

February 13   The Ministry of Education announced a nationwide plan for a standardized five-year primary school, beginning at age six, three-year junior school and two-year senior middle school. The new system would gradually replace the old nine-year school system in use in most rural areas.

February 14   Foreign Minister Huang Hua met US Senator Henry Jackson and his party in Beijing.

February 16   In Beijing, China and Japan signed a long-term trade agreement valid 1978-1985, under which China would export petroleum and coal, Japan technology, complete plants, and building materials; exports from each side would total $10,000 million in value.

February 17   Premier Hua Guofeng sent a message to Sheikh Saad Al-Abdullah Al-Salem, congratulating him on his nominations heir apparent and appointment as prime minister of the State of Kuwait.

February 18   The Standing Committee of the Fourth NPC issued a notice: The First Session of the Fifth NPC was scheduled to be convened in Beijing on February 26. The Eighth Session of the Standing Committee of the Fourth National Committee of the CPPCC decided to hold the first session of the Fifth National Committee of the CPPCC on February 24 in Beijing.

• The Second Plenum of the Eleventh CCP Central

Committee was held in Beijing from February 18-23 to complete the political, ideological and organizational preparations for the successful convocation of the Fifth NPC.

• NCNA reported the completion of the first Chinese-designed-and-built dry dock for 50,000-ton ships at Shanhaiguan (Hebei province).

February 19 The journal Economic Research, suspended for years, resumed publication and the first 1978 issue came off the press. The current issue carried an editorial and four articles by economists, repudiating the specious economic theories of the Gang of Four.

February 20 China and Ethiopia signed, in Addis Ababa, the minutes of their talks on the construction of Addis Ababa gymnasium with Chinese assistance.

• The delegation of the Chinese People's Association for Friendship with Foreign Countries, led by Wang Bingnan, left Beijing to visit Pakistan, Bangladesh, and India. In India, Foreign Minister Vajpayee accepted an invitation from Wang to visit China at a time convenient to himself. Wang also had meetings with Prime Minister Morarji Desai (March 12), and with Mrs. Gandhi.

February 22 Chairman Hua Guofeng met Vice President Berislav Sefer of Yugoslavia.

• The Japan External Trade Organization (JETRO) estimated that China's world trade in 1977, based on transactions with forty-five major countries, had reached $14,290 million, almost reaching the 1975 record of $14,575 million. The estimates suggested that imports had risen by 7.3 percent to reach $6,450 million while exports rose by 8.2 percent to reach $7,840 million.

February 24 The First Session of the Fifth National Committee of the CPPCC was held from February 24 to March 8 in Beijing. Deng Xiaoping, executive chairman of the National Committee of the Fifth CPPCC were released on February 25. It adopted the "Constitution of the CPPCC," approved the resolution on the first session of the Fifth National Committee of the CPPCC, and elected Deng Xiaoping chairman of the

Fifth National Committee of the CPPCC. The session
also elected twenty-two vice-chairmen of the Fifth National Committee of the CPPCC, and a 243-member
Standing Committee of the Fifth National Committee of
the CPPCC. A letter, addressed to the Standing
Committee of the NPC, from the presidium of the Supreme Soviet was delivered to the Chinese Embassy in
Moscow. It suggested that the two countries should
issue a joint statement on their bilateral relations.

February 25   China and the Philippines exchanged notes to
further trade development between the two nations.
• The preliminary meeting of the first session of
the Fifth National People's Congress was held in Beijing
to adopt the name list of the 254-member presidium
headed by Hua Guofeng and the nomination of Li
Xiannian as secretary-general.

February 26   The First Session of the Fifth National People's
Congress was held in the Great Hall of the People from
February 26 to March 5. A total of 3,456 deputies
attended the meeting. In his capacity as premier,
Hua Guofeng delivered a three-and-a-half hour report
on the work of the government. Ye Jianying delivered
the report on the revision of the state constitution.
The meeting adopted the constitution of the PRC, and
approved the report on the work of the government,
electing Ye Jianying chairman of the Standing Committee of the NPC, and the twenty vice-chairmen and the
secretary general together with the 175 members of the
Standing Committee. Approving the proposal of the
CCP Central Committee, it also decided on Hua Guofeng
as premier of the State Council, elected Jiang Hua
president of the Supreme People's Procuratorate, and
decided on the choices of the thirteen vice premiers
of the State Council, and the appointments of ministers
heading the commissions.
• In his report to the NPC, Hua Guofeng referred
obliquely to the Vietnam-Cambodia conflict, and urged
its resolution through negotiation. He was careful,
however, to avoid endorsing the Vietnamese terms of
February 5 or the very stiff preliminary conditions.
• The Fifth NPC and the CPPCC were widely hailed
in an editorial written jointly by the People's Daily,
the Red Flag, and the Liberation Army Daily. It said,

the session was "of great importance and charged with a great historic mission, namely, to hold high the great banner of Chairman Mao, implement the party line formulated at its Eleventh National Congress, and further eradicate the pernicious influence of the Gang of Four."

February 27 China and Hungary signed a goods exchange and payment agreement in Beijing.

February 28 The National Committee of the CPPCC held a meeting at the Taiwan Hall of the Great Hall of the People in Beijing in commemoration of the thirty-first anniversary of the February 28th Uprising by the people in Taiwan. Liao Zhengzhi addressed the meeting.
   • The political department of the PLA Fujian Front Headquarters issued notices on rules governing awards to Taiwan airforce and naval personnel who crossed over with aircraft or vessels, together with detailed instructions as to navigational courses and identification procedures. The HQ also issued an order on guarantees to officers and men who surrendered with PLA passes of safe conduct or who voluntarily laid down their arms on the battlefield.

March 1 The Ministry of Education decided to list eighty-eight higher institutions as the first group of key or pilot universities and colleges for the whole country.
   • China and Mongolia signed the 1978 protocol on mutual supply of goods in Beijing.

March 4 The Chinese Railway and Foreign Trade Delegation, led by Xing Beichun, visited Cambodia from March 4 to April 1.

March 5 Xu Xianjian's article entitled, "Life of Service, Pillar of Strength" was published in the People's Daily and the Liberation Army Daily to mark the eightieth anniversary of Zhou Enlai's birth. He wrote that the late premier was known as a pillar of strength, with unmatched energy and the highest integrity.

March 6 The People's Daily, the Red Flag, and the Liberation Army Daily in a joint editorial entitled "Transform

China in the Spirit of the Foolish Old Man Who Removed the Mountains," hailed the successful First Session of the Fifth NPC.

• Chairman Hua Guofeng and other party and state leaders received the deputies to the First Session of the Fifth NPC at the Great Hall of the People.

March 7   The First Session of the Standing Committee of the Fifth NPC met and endorsed the system of military services, submitted by Su Yu. From 1978, according to reports, conscripts would serve three years in the Army, four years in the Air Force, land-based units of the Navy and specialized technical units of the Army, and five years in the Navy and Marines. In general, the term for volunteers was fifteen to twenty years, with a maximum age limit of forty.

March 9   The People's Daily, the Red Flag, and the Liberation Army Daily carried a joint editorial to hail the successful conclusion of the First Session of the Fifth National Committee of the CPPCC.

• Chairman Hua Guofeng and other party and state leaders received members attending the First Session of the First National Committee of the CPPCC.

• China and Liberia signed a protocol in Monrovia to build the Barreke sugar project.

• The Ministry of Foreign Affairs delivered a reply to the Soviet ambassador in Beijing (to the letter of February 24) rejecting the proposal and declaring that the Soviet Union had refused to take "minimum actions" under the 1969 understanding between the then Premiers Zhou Enlai and Kosygin.

March 10   China and Somalia signed agreements for radio, television and press cooperation in Beijing.

March 11   The CCP Central Committee, in a notice, announced that the National Science Conference would convene on March 18.

March 12   Vice Premier Li Xiannian visited the Philippines from March 12-16, and was welcomed at the airport by President and Mme. Marcos. He visited the International Rice Institute, and signed a pact on scientific and technical cooperation between the two countries

on March 14. President Marcos announced that he had
reached an agreement with Li that their conflicting
sovereign claims to islands in the Spratly (Nan Sha)
Group could be resolved by negotiation.

March 13 Vice Premier Deng Xiaoping met the Somali press
delegation, led by Abdul Kassim Salad Hassan in Beijing.

March 14 Vice Premier Deng Xiaoping met the sixth delegation of the Japanese Komeito, headed by Junya Yano.
   • NCNA announced that over 10,000 victims of the
Gang of Four had been rehabilitated by the Shanghai
Municipal Committee of the CCP. Rehabilitation measures included cancelling wrong verdicts, stopping unjust punishment, and adjusting improper work assignments.
   • Albert Einstein's works were compiled, translated,
and published by the Commercial Press. Printed in
three volumes the edition ran to one million three-
hundred-thirty thousand words.
   • A ceremony was held in Lomé to hand over to
Togo two rice-growing centers and to sign a related
protocol on the establishment of stations from which
information concerning rice production and agricultural technology could be disseminated.

March 15 China conducted a successful nuclear test in the
atmosphere at Lop Nor test site.
   • Chairman Hua Guofeng and other party and state
leaders received the cadres, fighters, staff members,
and workers of the Academy of Military Science and
extended their warm greetings on the twentieth anniversary of the founding of the academy.
   • All Beijing papers carried on their front pages
an article entitled "Develop the Advanced Military Science of the Chinese Proletariat," by Ye Jianying, to
mark the twentieth anniversary of the founding of the
Academy of Military Science. The article pointed out
that "In order to build a modernized national defense,
it is very important for us to develop advanced military technique and improve our arms and equipment.
It is also extremely important and urgent to study
military science and military theory."
   • NCNA announced that skulls and other human

bones believed to have belonged to descendants of the
Beijing man, who lived between 400,000 and 500,000
years ago, had been found by Chinese paleontologists
near Dadong in northern Shanxi province. The homo
erectus represented by these finds was named Xuqiayao
Man, since the fossils were dug up near the village of
Xuqiayao. The site was one of the largest and rich-
est sources of paleolithic culture discovered so far in
China.

March 17   China and Guinea signed the 1978 trade protocol.

March 18   Vice Premier Li Xiannian visited Bangladesh at the
invitation of its government from March 18-21. During
his visit, a five-year science and technology cooperation agreement and an economic and technical cooperation
agreement were signed.

    • The State Council approved the restoration of ti-
tles to teachers in schools of higher education. There
were four titles: Professor, Associate Professor,
Lecturer, and Assistant.

    • The National Science Conference was held in the
Great Hall of the People in Beijing March 18-31, attended by 6,000 delegates from all over China. Chairman Hua opened the meeting and major speeches were
made by Vice Premiers Deng Xiaoping and Fang Yi.
Deng Xiaoping reiterated that science was part of the
productive forces, but admitted the very big gap between Chinese science and technology and advanced
world levels. He added that "at least 5/6 time" of the
work time of scientists and technicians should be left
free for scientific and technical work.

    • The People's Daily, the Red Flag, and the Libera-
tion Army Daily in a joint editorial, hailed the opening
of the National Science Conference. It stated: "If
we fail to develop new scientific techniques vigorously
including atomic energy, different kinds of satellites,
lasers, genetic engineering, and especially integrated
circuits and electronic computers, and if we fail
earnestly to step up theoretical research in such basic
subjects as modern mathematics, high-energy physics,
and molecular biology, it is inevitable that the talk
about modernization of agriculture, industry, and national defense will end in nothing."

March 21   China and Afghanistan signed the 1978 protocol
of goods exchange.

March 22   Norwegian Foreign Minister Knut Frydenlung,
Mrs. Frydenlung, and their party arrived in Beijing
for a seven-day visit.

March 23   Vice Premier Deng Xiaoping met Mr. and Mrs.
Friedrich Zimmermann, first vice-chairman of the
Christian Democratic Union of West Germany.

March 26   The 1978 Sino-Egyptian trade protocol was signed
in Cairo.
   • Vice Premier Deng Xiaoping met the Japanese Socialist party's Eighth Delegation, led by Ichio Asukata.

March 27   The Chinese Biological Products Study Group,
led by Li Zhizhong, left Beijing for Geneva in response to an invitation from the WHO to see the WHO
research centers in Switzerland, Britain, France,
Belgium, the Netherlands and Denmark.

March 29   Prime Minister Kriangsak Chamanan of Thailand
visited China from March 29 to April 4.   A trade
agreement and a science and technology cooperation
agreement were signed on March 31.   At the welcoming banquet on March 29, Vice Premier Deng Xiaoping
placed great stress in the Thai government's contribution to stability in the region.

March 31   NCNA announced that the CAAC inaugurated a
Beijing-Karachi-Addis Ababa air service.

April 1   Vice Premier Deng Xiaoping met Nepalese National
Panchayat Delegation, led by Gunjeswari Prasad Singh.

April 2   Chairman Hua Guofeng and other party and state
leaders received about 6,000 representatives attending
the National Science Conference in the Great Hall of
the People.
   • A contract on two purchases of rice by Malaysia
from China was signed in Kuala Lumpur.
   • The No. 2 Jianghan (Wuhan) bridge, 566.2 meters
long, 25.5 meters (6 lanes) wide, and capable of bearing 150-tone trailer trucks, was opened to traffic.

The Lingling road bridge over the Xiang in Hunan
province and the Qingzhushan Bridge in Lengshui-
Jiang over the Zi (369m long, 16m wide) were also
opened to traffic.
  • The renewal of party-to-party relations between
China and Yugoslavia was confirmed by a visit to Belgrade by a special Chinese Communist party delegation. It was led by Li Yimen and was received by
S. Dolanc, secretary of the Executive Committee of
the Presidency of the League of Communists of Yugoslavia.

April 3 China and the EEC signed a trade agreement in
Brussels.

April 4 Li Qiang visited West Germany April 4-10. He met
Chancellor Helmut Schmidt on April 6. The Chinese
displayed special interest in cooperation in the energy
and raw material fields.

April 5 A People's Daily article refuted Soviet "slander"
against overseas Chinese. The article regarded Soviet
accusations as an "obvious attempt" to disrupt China's
international prestige and to isolate her so as to gain
supremacy in Asia and the rest of the world.

April 6 The Chinese Navy commander gave a banquet in
Beijing for the captain and crew of a French destroy-
er, Dugnay-Trouin, the first warship from a western
country to pay a goodwill visit to China.

April 7 The Ministry of Education decided to have the 1978
college entrance examination standardized throughout
the country. The Ministry also edited a review syllabus for all applicants to fill out their basic knowledge. The syllabus covered political studies, Chinese, mathematics, physics, chemistry, history, geog-
raphy, and foreign languages.

April 8 China formally handed over the 286 km Na Sang-
Boun Hai road in upper Lao after four and a half
years of work. It was named the Lao-Chinese Friendship Highway Number One.
  • NCNA announced that at the site of Hemudu in
the lower reaches of the Yangtze River, archaeologists

excavated nearly 7,000 fairly well-preserved stone artifacts (pottery utensils, bone objects, and wood-work). All items were carbon 14 dated about 7,000 years old.

• Complementary minutes of talks on a Chinese-aided well-sinking project in Senegal were signed in Dakar.

• Chairman Hua Guofeng and the CCP Central Committee approved revival of the Central Patriotic Sanitation Campaign Committee. Points for emphasis included better environmental protection, popularization of sanitation knowledge, and improved rural sanitation. The State Council issued a circular to conduct a nationwide public health campaign to eradicate, before May Day, pests that outlived the winter, carry through major urban and rural sanitation reforms, and fight contagious disease.

April 9 A People's Daily editorial entitled "Integrating Moral Encouragement with Material Reward" endorsed the recent shift of emphasis towards more material incentives.

• I.T. Grishin led the Soviet Trade Delegation to China for a visit April 9–19.

• The 1978 Sino-Soviet goods exchange agreement was signed on April 17.

April 10 Chairman Hua Guofeng met the delegation of the Central Committee of the Argentine Communist party (M-L), led by General Secretary Guillermo Juarez.

• Chairman Hua Guofeng met Rear Admiral Joy Kobla Amedume and other distinguished Ghanaian guests.

April 11 The US Department of Agriculture announced a sale of 600,000 tons of wheat to China, the first since 1974, for delivery in the marketing year beginning on June 1.

April 12 The instruments of agreement on the utilization of the symphonic system for communication transmission experiments were exchanged at a ceremony held in Beijing between China, West Germany, and France.

• Mongolia informed Beijing that Soviet troops were stationed there by invitation and that they would stay as long as a "Chinese threat" continued.

• A maritime incident, involving about one hundred Chinese fishing boats which were seen in and around the territorial waters off the northwest of the Diao-yu or Senkaku Islands, occurred on April 12. Some of the boats carried placards claiming Chinese sovereignty over the islands. The Japanese protested on the following day, and within four days the ships had all moved out.

April 13   China and Vietnam signed a protocol of the Twentieth Railway Joint Committee meeting in Nanning.
• President Carter reaffirmed the American commitment to normalizing relations, but, significantly, made it clear that rapid progress would not be made in that regard.
• It was announced that twenty-six Chinese universities would be opened to Hong Kong and Macao postgraduates who supported the Communist party, and that examinations would be held for this purpose in Guangzhou in the middle of May.

April 14   President Mohamed Siad Barre of Somalia visited China at the invitation of the Chinese government from April 14-18.   Chairman Hua Guofeng greeted him at the airport.   The two nations signed an economic and technical cooperation agreement on April 18.
• The Standing Committee of the Fifth NPC held its first session in Beijing from April 14-15 to hear reports from He Ying and Fang Yi.

April 15   The Third Asian Badminton Invitation Championships were held in Beijing April 15-21.   China won the men's singles and double, the women's singles, and the boys' singles.
• President Hua Guofeng sent a message to Mozambican President Samora Moises Machel, extending profound sympathy and solicitude to the flood-afflicted people in central Mozambique.
• The National Railway Conference was held in Beijing April 15-23 to map out the objectives to be achieved in the next eight years in modernizing the railway.

April 16   The Sixth Enlarged Session of the Third Executive Committee of the All-China Women's Federation met in

Beijing April 16–21 and decided to call the Fourth
National Women's Congress in Beijing next September.

April 17   Chairman Hua Guofeng and Vice Chairman Ye
Jianying, in a message (marking the third anniversary
of the founding of Democratic Kampuchea) to Phnom
Penh, praised the "correct" Cambodian leadership.

April 18   A further Chinese purchase of 400,000 tons of
wheat was announced by the US Department of Agriculture.

April 20   The Third Session of the Sino-Rumanian Joint
Commission for Foreign Trade was held in Bucharest
from April 20–25.

April 21   The Portuguese governor of Macao, Colonel Garcia
Leanfro, visited China from April 21 to May 8.   It was
the first such visit to China by any governor of
Macao.

April 22   The National Conference on Education Work, convened by the Ministry of Education, was held in Beijing from April 22 to May 16.   In his speech on the
opening day, Vice Premier Deng Xiaoping called for
better academic standards and greater respect for
teachers among students.   The conference adopted a
draft outline program for education from 1978–85, including doubling the 1965 number of university students.
   • The All-China Federation of Trade Unions held
its executive meeting April 22–24, and decided to hold
the Ninth National TUC next October.

April 23   Radio France and the British Broadcasting Corporation transmitted the stereophonic broadcast of a
concert, given by the Chinese Central Philharmonic
Society, live by satellite.   This was China's first live
concert broadcast to Europe.

April 24   The National Conference on Judicial Work was held
in Beijing from April 24 to May 22.   The conference
discussed inter alia the new constitution, the specialist legal system, and judicial work in the new period.
   • Prime Minister Nasir Muhammad of the People's

Democratic Republic of Yemen visited China April 24–
28. He was greeted at the airport by Chairman Hua
Guofeng. The two nations signed an economic and
technical cooperation agreement on April 20.

April 27 The State Council called an emergency antidrought
telephone conference on the evening of April 27 to
make arrangements to protect winter wheat and sow
the spring fields in the areas affected by a serious
drought.
• The All-Army Conference on Political Work was
held from April 27 to June 6 in Beijing, at which
speeches were made by Hua Guofeng and Ye Jianying
referring to strengthening political work under new
historical conditions, accelerating the revolutionization
and modernization of the PLA, raising its control effectiveness and fulfilling the general task for the new
period. Deng Xiaoping spoke at the conference on
June 2 and focussed his comments on the theme "seeking truth from facts." The chief of the Defense Staff,
Sir Neil Cameron of England, visited China from April
27 to May 3, and met Chairman Hua Guofeng on April
30.

April 28 China and Bangladesh signed an agreement for cooperation to exchange news.
• President France Albert Rene of Seychelles
visited China from April 28 to May 4, and met Chairman Hua Guofeng on May 4.
• The National Conference on Medical Science,
Pharmacology and Health Work was held in Beijing
from April 28 to June 12.

April 29 NCNA reported that a new highway bridge had
opened to traffic in Wuhan city. The highway was
divided into three sections by the Yangtze and its
tributary, the Han River.
• Vice Premier Deng Xiaoping met the Friendship
Delegation of Yugoslav Socialist Alliance of Working
People.

April 30 Liao Zhengzhi indicated that many Chinese residents had recently returned from Vietnam and that
China was concerned.

May 1 The People's Daily editorial took socialist labor emulation as its main theme, linking it with the revival of
trade union activity, rebutting the opposition's views
by quoting Lenin and Mao, and emphasizing the importance of cost, quality, and safety when seeking
accelerated economic development. The role of party
leadership, the balance between moral encouragement
and material reward, and the role of trade unions was
also stressed.

• Gala theatrical performances were held at the indoor capital stadium to celebrate May 1, International
Labor Day. Chairman Hua Guofeng, Vice Chairmen
Deng Xiaoping, Li Xiannian, and Wang Donxing and
other party and state leaders attended the gala.

May 2 Vice Premier Gu Mu left Beijing to visit France and
other European countries (Switzerland, Belgium, Denmark, and West Germany) from May 2 to June 7.

• Vice Premier Deng Xiaoping met the delegation of
the editorial staff of the newspaper Call, organ of the
Central Committee of the Communist party of the USA
(M-L), led by Daniel Leon Burstein.

• Chairman Hua Guofeng met Abdallar Farhat, Tunisian minister of defense, Mrs. Farhat, and his party.

• The 1978 Sino-Korean protocol of goods exchange
was signed in Beijing.

• The National Conference of Transport Departments, in which four million people were engaged in
maritime transport, inland navigation, and road transport, was held in Daqing from May 2-11.

May 3 Chairman Hua Guofeng, Vice Chairmen Deng Xiaoping,
Li Xiannian, and Wang Dongxing, and other state and
party leaders received delegates to the conference on
political work of the PLA and the national meeting of
model workers.

May 4 Xuan Thuy, secretary of the Vietnam Communist
party's Central Committee, stated that some Chinese
residents had suddenly crossed illegally into China.

• The CCP Central Committee issued a circular, marking the fifty-ninth anniversary of the May Fourth movement, which announced that the Tenth CYL Congress
would be held in Beijing in October 1978,. It also
announced the decision to hold a meeting of the Fifth

Committee of the All-China Youth Federation and the Nineteenth Congress of the All-China Students Federation at an appropriate time next year.

• NCNA reported that the State Planning Commission recently held a national conference on practicing economy. The delegates exchanged experiences, reported on their 1977 achievements, studied the present major methods for economy, and worked out plans for 1977-80 to save more fuel.

• NCNA reported that three primary school teachers had recently been designated as "teachers of a special grade" in Beijing. China practiced an eleven-grade pay scale for primary school teachers, based on teaching proficiency, attitude toward work, and political quality. Grade one was the highest.

May 5 CAAC inaugurated a Beijing-Urumchi-Belgrade-Zurich air service. It was scheduled to fly once a week on this route.

• The Chinese Economic Delegation visited Britain from May 5-26.

• Chairman Hua Guofeng visited North Korea from May 5-10, accompanied by Vice Premier Geng Biao. He held talks with President Kim Il-sung. There was no indication of the issues covered in the talks, although Hua called, in very strong terms, for a total and rapid withdrawal of American troops from the South.

May 7 NCNA reported that China's first oil manufacturing installation, with a 1,200 atmospheric pressure capacity, had been turned out by the Lanzhou General Machinery Plant. The installation was specially made for acidizing and manufacturing treatment of oil (gas) wells and was made to meet the needs of the growing oil industry.

• NCNA reported that around two thousand students from the city's (Beijing) 507 middle schools participated in a mathematics contest. Contestants were required to complete two tests in three hours. The first one, consisting of eight problems, was primarily a test of speed, with a time limit of one hour; the second asked students to solve five more difficult problems in two hours.

May 8   Vice Premier Deng Xiaoping met General Felix Galvan
        Lopes, the Mexican secretary for defense and his par-
        ty.
            • Vice Premier Deng Xiaoping met Milojko Drulovic,
        the outgoing Yugoslav ambassador to China.

May 9   A Soviet helicopter crossed the Wusuli (Ussuri) River
        into Heilongjaing province, and eighteen military boats
        also crossed the river to four km into Chinese terri-
        tories "shooting continually," seizing fourteen Chinese
        inhabitants, and dragging them back to the river be-
        fore giving up their efforts on May 9.   The Chinese
        Foreign Ministry issued a note demanding an apology
        from Moscow.

May 10 NCNA announced that the eighteenth-century tomb
        of Emperor Qian Long in Zunhua county in Hebei pro-
        vince was recently opened to the public.   The tomb,
        known as Yu Ling, was located about 100 km east of
        Beijing.

May 11 Vice Foreign Minister Yu Chan said that the Sino-
        Indian border issue need not prevent progress being
        made in other aspects of their relations.
            • The National Textile Conference began on May 11
        in Tianjin.   The industry employed 2.8 million work-
        ers.
            • The Red Flag published an article entitled "China's
        New Constitution Marks the Beginning of a New Period
        in the Development of the Country's Socialist Legal
        System," written by Jiang Hua, the president of the
        Supreme People's Court.   He wrote, "In handling a
        case, stress must be laid on the weight of evidence,
        on investigation and study; the practice of obtaining
        confessions by compulsion and then giving them cre-
        dence is strictly forbidden."

May 12 NCNA reported that the popular classical novel, A
        Dream of Red Mansion, had been translated into the
        Uighur language and published by the Xinjiang Pub-
        lishing House.
            • The Ministry of Education reported that the
        5,700,000 youth who took the college entrance exam-
        inations at the end of 1977, 278,000 were admitted.
            • China and Bulgaria confirmed the further exten-

sion of the March 23, 1955 agreement on scientific and technical cooperation.

• On the May 9th Incident, a Soviet note of May 12th explained that the incident was one of inadvertent trespass, and that the Soviet troops had been chasing a dangerous armed criminal, but the Chinese rejected this explanation on the 17th.

• The East German News Agency reported from Hanoi that China had warned Vietnam on May 12 that it would withdraw Chinese specialists from twenty projects being built in Vietnam under assistance agreements. The decision came into effect on May 19, and the Chinese had said that the funds set aside for the projects would be used instead to provide food for the Chinese expelled from Vietnam.

May 14 His Majesty King Birendra Bir Birkram Shah Dev and Her Majesty Queen Aishwarya Laxmi Devi Shah of Nepal arrived in Beijing for an unofficial visit at the invitation of the Chinese government on their way to Japan. Premier Hua Guofeng held a banquet to welcome them.

May 15 The Ministry of Education announced that in the autumn semester, all Chinese primary and middle schools on the full-day ten-year system would try out new standard textbooks. The fifty-four new teaching materials edited by the Ministry of Education included: teaching programs for various subjects, the first volumes of various new textbooks and reference works. Altogether, 112 books were planned.

• President Nicolae Ceausescu of Rumania visited China from May 15-20. He was welcomed at the airport by Chairman Hua, Vice Chairmen Deng Xiaoping, Li Xiannian and Wang Dongxing. At the official banquet to welcome the president on the day of his arrival, Chairman Hua said, "We believe that a new world war can be postponed so long as the people of the world maintain their unity and persist in struggle." The two leaders signed a long-term agreement on economic and technical cooperation on May 19.

May 16 According to the Financial Times, Li Qiang, minister of foreign trade, stated that the Chinese import and export corporations had restored and adopted in-

ternational practices on export orders and forms of
payment.

May 17 Foreign Minister Huang Hua told the Zairean ambassador in Beijing that China supported Zaire's struggle
"to repulse the Soviet-Cuban mercenaries that [had]
invaded the Shaba region." Cuba, he said, was not
acting as a nonaligned state, but was acting for the
Soviet Union.

• Indications that the current rehabilitation of
cadres would be extended to include an estimated
100,000 people purged in 1957 were reported by Kyodo
(Japanese News Agency), which noted sources close
to the authorities.

May 19 Vice Premier Deng Xiaoping met the delegation of
UPI, led by Roderick Beaton, and answered their
questions on Sino-American relations and the international situation.

• A new punctuated and revised edition of The
Twenty-Four Histories, a comprehensive general history of China and perhaps the most complete national
history in the world, came off the press after twenty
years. Running to some forty million Chinese characters in 3,249 volumes, the series comprised twenty-
four history books which covered a period of several
thousand years from the earliest records to the fall of
the Ming Dynasty in 1644.

May 20 Zbigniew Brzezinski visited China May 20-23. He
was greeted at the airport by Foreign Minister Huang
Hua and the newly appointed chief of the Chinese
liaison office in Washington, Cai Zemin. Speaking at
a banquet in his honor on May 20, Huang Hua said
that "Social-imperialism was preparing for war with the
aim of seizing world hegemony, and the people of the
world should not be lulled by illusions of peace." In
reply, Brzezinski declared that the American commitment to friendship with China was based on a "long-
term strategic view," and was not "a tactical expedi-
ent." On May 23 he had a cordial conversation with
Chairman Hua Guofeng on the question of common interests and presented to the Chinese leader gifts from
President Carter to the Chinese people. These gifts
included a flag of the People's Republic which American

astronauts had taken to the moon and a piece of moon rock.

May 21   Premier Hua Guofeng sent a message to Veselin Diuranovic, expressing most sincere congratulations on his reelection as president of the Executive Council of the Socialist Federal Republic of Yugoslavia.
• Robert Mugabe, president of the Zimbabwe African Union, visited China May 21-23. He met Vice Premier Geng Biao.

May 22   Vice Premier Deng Xiaoping met the Italian Post and Telecommunications Delegation, led by Vittoing Colombo, minister of Transport and Merchant Navy.

May 23   The Second Session of the Standing Committee of the Fifth NPC was held in Beijing May 23-24 to hear the report on Chairman Hua's visit to North Korea, and discuss measures for workers and cadres retirement and the procuracy.
• Nippon Steel Corporation signed a contract in Beijing for the construction of an integrated steel works in Baoshan, in the suburbs of Shanghai, with an eventual production capacity of six million tons of crude steel a year. The equipment was said to be worth 400 billion yuan.

May 24   China and Kenya signed a trade agreement in Nairobi.
• President Joachim Yhombi-Dpango of Congo met Chairman Hua Guofeng in Beijing in the course of a three-day stopover en route to North Korea.
• The Chinese spokesman complained of the "Vietnamese practice of compelling the Chinese residents to become naturalized, which violates the agreement between the two sides and runs counter to general principles of international law."

May 25   In London, China and Oman signed a joint communiqué to establish diplomatic relations at the ambassadorial level.
• President Sambra Machel of Mozambique visited China from May 25-31. Chairman Hua Guofeng met him at the airport. President Machel thanked China for the arms, equipment, and instructors which had

been given to Mozambique during the liberation war. The two nations signed a protocol of economic and technical cooperation agreement.

May 26 The Chinese government spokesman said that it would send ships to Vietnam to bring home the "persecuted Chinese," whom a Chinese report put at 89,700 on the following day.

May 27 A Foreign Ministry Spokesman in Hanoi stated that the Chinese (Hoa) in Vietnam would be "gradually turned into Vietnamese citizens" in accordance with the agreement of the two nations. The Chinese ambassador in Hanoi gave the Vietnamese government a note from Beijing on the "persecuted Chinese," but Hanoi dismissed the persecution reports as fabricated, and gave a note from the Vietnamese side two days later asking for a meeting as soon as possible to discuss matters.

• The China Federation of Literature and Art Circles held an enlarged national committee meeting in Beijing from May 27 to June 5, after an interval of twelve years, and marked the thirty-sixth anniversary of Chairman Mao's talks at the Yanan Forum on Literature and Art.

May 28 One hundred and three bronzes dating back about 3,000 years were unearthed by Chinese archaeologists in Fufeng county, Shanxi province. They belonged to the Western Zhou Dynasty (around eleventh-century 771 B.C.).

May 29 Foreign Minister Huang Hua spoke in the Tenth Special Session of the General Assembly Plenary meeting, saying that China was willing to discuss disarmament and hoped that the session would make a positive contribution to world peace. He said that China supported the complete prohibition and destruction of nuclear weapons and that the US and the USSR should first destroy most of their nuclear weapons. Nuclear-free zones should also be supported, but not proposals for nonproliferation and nuclear test bans, he said.

May 30 The first session of the Sino-Nepalese Joint Boundary Inspection Committee was held in Katmandu from

May 17-28. The agreement of the meeting was signed
on May 28. The Chinese delegation left Katmandu for
home on May 30.
  • China and Argentina signed the minutes on the
exchange of instruments enforcing the trade agreement
between the two nations.

May 31 Ambassador Sato from Japan officially proposed to
the Chinese Ministry of Foreign Affairs that the peace
treaty talks should be resumed.
  • NCNA reported that construction began in Beijing
on the preliminary study of the engineering work for
China's first 30 BeV-50BeV proton synchrotron to be
completed in 1982.

June 1 The railway from Xiangfan (Hebei) to Chongqing
(Sichuan) was opened to traffic.

June 2 The National Conference on Light Industry was held
in Beijing from June 2-10.

June 3 Foreign Minister Huang Hua visited Zaire June 3-7,
met President Mobutu in the capital of Shaba province,
Lumumbashi on July 4, and congratulated him on his
victory over the Soviet-Cuban hired mercenaries.
  • Cambodian Deputy Premier Ieng Sary, visited
China on his way to the UN Disarmament Conference
and again on his way back. He met Vice Premier
Deng Xiaoping on June 3, and was received by Chairman Hua Guofeng on his return visit on July 14. On
the following day he met the former foreign minister
of Thailand, Chatichai Choonhavan, who was also visiting China with a delegation, through the offices of
Vice Premier Deng Xiaoping. It was understood that
they discussed the Thai-Cambodian border problems.

June 5 The Japanese News Agency quoted Chinese sources
as saying that Sino-Vietnamese relations had begun to
deteriorate in late 1975 after Le Duan had signed a
communiqué in Moscow voting full support for Soviet
foreign policy, i.e. "surrender to hegemonism." Vice
Premier Deng Xiaoping told the Japanese visiting delegation that Chinese aid to Vietnam in the past two
decades had reached twenty billion yuan--more than
Russian aid to Vietnam. The Chinese rejected Viet-

nam's proposal to hold talks, but said that they would send ships to pick up the Chinese residents beginning July 20.

June 6 The protocol of the Eighteenth Session of the Sino-Korean Joint Committee for Scientific and Technical Cooperation was signed in Pyongyang.

June 7 Chairman Hua Guofeng met the Burmese Military Delegation, led by General Kyaw Htin.

June 8 NCNA reported that the National Working Conference on Food Hygiene was held in Beijing under the ten ministers and commissions of the State Council. On the basis of the 300,000 items of data collected by the Health Department in cooperation with other departments, the delegates discussed ways to prevent possible pollution of food by the industrial "three wastes," and worked out some measures to be used.

• China and Spain signed a civil aviation transport agreement in Beijing.

• President Juvenal Habyalimana of Rwanda visited China June 8-14. He held talks with Vice Premier Deng Xiaoping, and met Chairman Hua Guofeng on July 10. The two nations signed an economic and technical cooperation agreement on July 10.

• Foreign Minister Huang Hua visited the Netherlands June 8-11 and met Queen Juliana and Premier Can Agt. At a news conference he stated that China believed Western Europe favored a strong China to cope with the Soviet threat. For its part, China was in favor of the establishment of a partnership on equal footing between Western Europe and the US.

June 9 The Ministry of Foreign Affairs issued a statement repeating earlier claims on the forced expulsion of Chinese from Vietnam, attacking a Vietnamese Ministry of Foreign Affairs statement of May 27 (which attacked China's May 24 statement) and rejecting a proposal in the Vietnamese May 27 statement that "representatives of the two governments meet soon to settle the differences" on the grounds that "such a proposal was made purely out of propaganda needs." The statement urged the Vietnamese side to stop persecution and expulsion of overseas Chinese and refrain from any further acts detrimental to the friendship between the two nations.

June 10 Soviet Ambassador to China V.S. Tolstikov left his post for home.

• The 1978 Sino-Pakistan border trade agreement was signed in Gilgit.

• An "important directive" from Chairman Hua Guofeng and the CCP Central Committee to the Tianjin Municipal Party Committee described Lin Hujia, hitherto secretary of the Shanghai Municipal Party Committee as first secretary of the Tianjin Municipal Party Committee and chairman of the Municipal Revolutionary Committee.

June 11 NCNA announced the decision to set up a Society of Traditional Chinese Medicine and to revive the Chinese Medical Association, the Chinese Pharmaceutical Association, the Chinese Nurses Association, and the Permanent Council of the Chinese anti-TB Association together with the resumed publication of twelve more journals in addition to the five already reactivated within a year.

• Premier Sir Kamimese Mara of Fuji visited China from June 11-16. He held talks with Vice Premier Li Xiannian and met Chairman Hua Guofeng on June 13.

• Foreign Minister Huang Hua visited Turkey June 11-15; the first visit ever to the country by a high-ranking Chinese official.

June 12 The ten-day National Conference on Medical Science, the largest of its kind since 1949, closed in Beijing.

June 13 A People's Daily article envisaged further straightening out of the ranks ideologically, and rectification of work-style to achieve unity in thought and practice.

• The Red Flag published an article entitled "Planned Control of Population Growth," urging CCP organizations at all levels to make efforts to realize the target set by the Fifth National People's Congress of reducing China's annual population growth to less than nine percent within three years.

June 14 Vice Premier Deng Xiaoping met the press delegation from Zaire, led by Mokolo Wa Mpombo.

June 15   Foreign Minister Huang Hua visited Iran June 15–
17, and had talks with the shah and with Premier J.
Amuzegar.

• Vice Premier Deng Xiaoping met a twenty-member
delegation of the Thailand-China Friendship Association, led by former Foreign Minister Chatichai Choonhavan.

• A ten-minute ovation greeted a concert in Beijing
by the Central Philharmonic Society under the baton
of the world-famous Japanese conductor Seiji Ozawa,
music director of the Boston Symphony Orchestra and
conductor of the new Japan Philharmonic Orchestra.
It was the first time a foreigner had conducted a Chinese symphony orchestra since 1949.

June 16   The Chinese government told Vietnam to close its
consulates in Guangzhou, Kunming, and Nanning, al-
leging that the Vietnamese had refused a Chinese
consulate general in Ho Chi Minh City.

• Vice Premier Geng Biao led the Chinese Government Delegation to Pakistan for a visit from June 16–
21.   On June 18, Geng and General Ziaul Haq inaugurated the 500-mile Karakoram Highway, built with Chinese aid, from the Khunjerab border area through
Gilgit to Thakot--coinciding in part with the old "Silk
Road."

• King Juan Carlos of Spain visited China June 16–
20.   He held talks with Vice Premier Deng Xiaoping,
and met Chairman Hua Guofeng.   The two nations
signed a civil aviation agreement on June 8.

June 17   Chairman Hua Guofeng, Vice-Chairmen Ye Jianying,
Deng Xiaoping, Li Xiannian, and Wang Dongxing, and
other party and state leaders called at the Beijing
Hospital to pay their last respects to the remains of
Guo Moruo, an outstanding Chinese "proletarian fight-
er" on the cultural front.   He died on June 12 in
Beijing at the age of eighty-five.   The memorial meet-
ing for Guo Moruo took place on June 18 at the Great
Hall of the People.   Vice Premier Deng Xiaoping deli-
vered a eulogy.

• Vietnam complained that China had cut off most
of its aid, and had further "ceaselessly given all-
round support to the Kampuchean authorities in their
border war of aggression against the Vietnamese people."

• A People's Daily commentator openly accused the
Soviet leadership of being the instigator of the "anti-
China and anti-Chinese campaign in Vietnam," and
placed the ultimate blame for the "campaign of ostraciz-
ing, persecuting, and expelling Chinese residents"
from Vietnam on the Soviet Union.

June 19   President William Tolber of Liberia made a visit to
China June 18-29. He held talks with Vice Premier
Li Xiannian, and met Chairman Hua Guofeng. The
two nations signed an agreement on economic and
technical cooperation on June 28.
        • The National Supplies Conference was held in
Beijing from June 19 to July 4.
        • The CCP Central Committee sent a letter to greet
the convening of the Eleventh Congress of the Yugoslav counterpart.

June 20   The National Finance and Trade Conference on
Learning from Daqing and Dazhai, convened by the
CCP Central Committee, was held in Beijing from June
20 to July 9. It was attended by 5,000 cadres representing twelve million employees in those sectors of
the economy. On July 7, Chairman Hua Guofeng addressed the conference. He emphasized the importance
of carrying out the principle of "developing economy."
        • Foreign Minister Qais Abdul Munim Alzawawi
visited China from June 20-24. He held talks with
Huang Hua, and met Chairman Hua Guofeng on June
23.
        • Vice Premier Deng Xiaoping met Henry Ford II,
chairman of the board of Ford Motor Company.

June 21   Chairman Hua Guofeng met Christian Semler, chairman of the Central Committee of the Communist party
of Germany and his party.

June 22   The Chinese Ministry of Foreign Affairs condemned
the exchange of the ratification instruments between
Japan and South Korea (on June 22) for the continental
shelf agreement.

June 24   NCNA reported that Minghua and the Zhangli, two
ships sent by the Chinese government to bring back
Chinese nationalities from Vietnam, reached the seas

off Vietnam on June 9 near Ho Chi Minh City. However, the two ships were unable to enter the harbors of Ho Chi Minh City and Haiphong City.

• The People's Daily carried an article entitled "One of the Fundamental Principles of Marxism," affirming points made by Vice Premier Deng Xiaoping at the All-Army Political Work Conference. The article said that the criterion for truth in ideology was practice and the relationship between theory and practice was based on theory tested by practice and not practice "tailored" by theory.

June 26 A meeting of the State Council's leading planned parenthood group took place in Beijing June 26-28. It was reported that the population growth rates for Beijing, Shanghai, Tianjin, Sichuan, Liaoning, Shandong, Jiangsu, and Hubei had fallen to less than one percent.

June 28 The Performing Arts Company of the People's Republic of China left Beijing for the United States at the invitation of the National Committee on US-China Relations. It gave its premiere the warm welcome of 4,000 spectators in the Metropolitan Opera House at Lincoln Center in New York on July 5.

• China and Laos signed a civil aviation agreement in Vientiane.

• NCNA announced that a Tibetan-Han dictionary was compiled in Chengdu. It contained over 60,000 entries.

July 1 The Red Flag published the full text of Chairman Mao's work, "Talk at an Enlarged Working Conference Convened by the Central Committee of the CCP," to mark the fifty-fourth anniversary of the founding of the CCP. The speech was delivered originally on January 30, 1962, and printed and distributed within the party in 1966. The speech dealt mainly with the question of democratic centralism and of promoting democracy inside and outside the Party.

• China and Korea signed a hydrological work cooperation agreement along the Yalu and Dumen rivers in Beijing.

July 2 The People's Daily carried an editorial entitled "Con-

scientiously Implement Democratic Centralism," to emphasize the general relevance of the late Chairman
Mao's 1962 message to the present period. It also
stressed the need to resolve contradictions among the
people by democratic methods and not by dictatorship.

July 3 China informed Vietnam that it had been compelled
to recall its experts and stop technical and economic
aid because the Vietnamese had "increased a foul atmosphere of villifying and inciting antagonism against
China and destroyed the minimum conditions required
for the continued stay of Chinese experts in Vietnam."
• Hanoi radio reported that in Cao Lanh province,
"some reactionary elements among the Hoa people" had
incited compatriots of the Yao and Miao nationalities
to go to China. The Japanese News Agency reported
from Ho Chi Minh City that a local official stated that
almost 250,000 of the roughly 800,000 ethnic Chinese
living in Cholon had applied to return to China, but
many of them were now requesting cancellation of their
applications because China would only accept those who
were "persecuted or discriminated against," and only
a few Chinese in the Cholon district considered themselves to be in this category.
• China and Vietnam held a meeting in Hanoi to
discuss the matter on China's dispatch of ships to
bring home victimized Chinese.

July 4 The People's Daily published the newly issued "Draft
Decision of the CCP Central Committee Concerning
Some Problems in Speeding Up the Development in Industry," which had also been referred to as the "30-
Point Decision on Industry."
• NCNA reported an interview with a spokesman of
the Overseas Chinese office of the State Council, in
which he accused the Vietnamese of compelling Chinese
residents to take Vietnamese citizenship. He also
claimed that only one or two percent of the more than
100,000 overseas Chinese forced to leave Vietnam for
China were from the South, so that their persecution
or expulsion could not be explained by the "socialist
transformation" campaign going on in the southern
provinces.

July 7 Cambodian Premier Pol Pot gave a banquet to Chinese

technicians whom he described as having "succeeded in restoring, repairing, and constructiong various facilities which had been seriously damaged during the war with the Americans.

• The Chinese Ministry of Foreign Affairs presented a note to the Albanian Embassy announcing the cessation of its economic and military aid. The note set out the details of the aid programs since 1954. The note also announced the decision to repatriate China's 513 economic and military experts from Albania.

• The US Scientific and Technology Delegation, led by Frank Press, adviser to President Carter, arrived in Beijing for a four-day visit. Vice Premier Deng Xiaoping met the delegation on July 10. Frank Press praised China's plans for the modernization of its science and technology as based on a careful assessment of needs and set towards "realistic priorities."

July 9   Ji Pengfei met Yasir Arafat on July 7, and Syrian President Hafez Assad on July 9 in Damascus. He and his party returned to Urimchi on July 10 after a visit to Venezuela, Mexico, Canada, and Syria.

July 10   The Vietnamese Ministry of Foreign Affairs lodged a strong protest with the Chinese Embassy in Hanoi against the intrusion of Chinese aircraft into Vietnamese air space on July 8. On July 12, the Chinese Ministry of Foreign Affairs denied the intrusion.

July 11   One of the most popular cartoons among Chinese children was reissued after being banned by the Gang of Four for more than a decade. The recent release of 300,000 copies of San-Mao the Vagabond was sold out as soon as it hit the bookshelves.

July 12   Vice Premier Deng Xiaoping met Amadou-Mahtar M'Bow, director general of Unesco, in Beijing.

• NCNA reported that China had developed a new anti-Malarial drug of high efficacy, quick effect and low toxicity.

• Eric Williams, prime minister of Trinidad and Tobago, met Geng Biao in Port of Spain.

July 13   Vice Premier Li Xiannian told the visiting Mitsui delegation that China was willing to induce foreign funds to finance modernization programs, according to a Japanese press report from Beijing.

July 14 A deadlock was reached in the Sino-Vietnamese meetings in Hanoi to resolve the differences over repatriation of Chinese nationals. The Chinese insisted on receiving only Chinese citizens and not Vietnamese citizens of Chinese origin. The Vietnamese aide insisted, "In Vietnam, there are no 'persecuted Chinese residents' but only more than 20,000 Chinese residents who have fled the repression and persecution in Cambodia and taken refuge in Vietnam."

July 16 China and Korea held the 1978 Regular Meeting of Sino-Korean Border Railway Transport Talks from July 16-24. The protocol of the meeting was signed on July 24.

July 17 The Japanese government-owned Japan National Oil Corporation announced that China and Japan had reached agreement on the joint development of oil resources in Bohai Bay.
• Florizel A. Glasspole, governor general of Jamaica, met Vice Premier Geng Biao in Kingston.

July 18 The Daily Telegraph reported that approved immigration from China into Hong Kong reached more than 26,000 up to mid-July, almost as many as came in during the entire preceding year. The increased influx was regarded as putting a severe strain on the Hong Kong economy.

July 19 In a note, China proposed to the Vietnamese government that their vice foreign ministers entered into negotiations on the question of Chinese nationals residing in Vietnam early next month whether in Beijing or Hanoi.

July 20 President Jimmy Carter received all the members of The Performing Arts Company of the PRC in the Rose Garden of the White House.
• NCNA reported that the 1,300-year-old tomb of the second emperor of the Tang Dynasty (618-907) was recently opened to the public as an underground museum. Zhao Ling was one of the most ancient Chi-

nese imperial tombs discovered so far, west of Xian, Shaanxi province, on the ridge of Qiuzong Mountain.

July 21 China and Japan resumed negotiations to conclude the peace and friendship treaty in Beijing.
  • Vice Premier Geng Biao held talks with Ptolemy Reid, general secretary of the National People's Congress and deputy prime minister of Guyana, in Georgetown.

July 22 NCNA reported that eleven Chinese medical journals would resume publication in the third quarter of this year and would be circulated at home and abroad. They included: The Journal of Preventive Medicine, The Journal of Obstetrics and Gynecology, The Chinese Journal of Pediatrics, The Chinese Journal of Radiology, The Chinese Journal of Neuropsychiatry, The Chinese Journal of Tuberculosis and Respiratory Diseases, The Chinese Journal of Laboratory Diagnosis, and Progress in Physiological Sciences.

July 23 Vice Premier Deng Xiaoping met His Royal Highness Prince Gyanendra Bir Birkram Shah of Nepal and his party in Beijing.

July 24 A basic agreement on joint Sino-Japanese exploration for offshore oil in Chinese territorial waters in Bohai Bay was announced. The announcement also indicated that the two nations would study a similar development in the mouth of the Pearl River.
  • NCNA reported that the Chinese Society of Agronomy held a symposium recently at which 706 specialists presented 562 papers ranging from "latest developments in research in photosynthesis" and "gene engineering" two new methods of cultivating hybrid rice.

July 25 Vice Premier Deng Xiaoping met American columnist Marquis William Childs and his wife.

July 26 NCNA reported that in August a new national rail timetable would come into effect. 1,066 freights and eighty-seven passenger services, including fifteen special or direct express services, were to be added. All provincial and autonomous regional capitals with

the exception of Lhasa, and the municipalities of
Shanghai and Tianjin were to be linked with Beijing by
direct express.

• NCNA reported that preliminary excavation on the
remains of a city and tombs dating back over 2,000
years and containing more than 10,000 relics had been
carried out by archaeologists in Pingshan county in
Hebei province. The city site was the capital of
Zhungshan state in the Warring States period (475-
221 B.C.).

• Chairman Hua Guofeng met the Rumanian Government Delegation, led by Gheorghe Oprea, first deputy
prime minister.

July 28 In Beijing, the China National Technical Import
Corporation and the Japanese Hitachi Ltd. and Tokyo
Shibaura Electric Co., signed a protocol and contract
on a complete color television plant for China.

• NCNA reported that a double-edged steel sword,
dating back about 2,500 years, was recently unearthed
in Changsha in Hunan province.

• The Chinese government agreed to start the Sino-
Vietnamese negotiations at the vice-foreign-minister
level on the question of the Chinese nationals residing
in Vietnam on August 8, 1978 in Hanoi.

• NCNA reported that the Chinese ships, Minghua
and Zhangli were instructed to sail home for the time
being pending further instruction. The ships were
sent to Vietnam to bring back victimized Chinese nationals.

July 29 The Chinese Government Delegation, led by Vice
Premier Chen Muhua, left Beijing to visit Somalia,
Gabon and Cameroon.

• The Cambodian Military Delegation, led by Son
Sen, visited China from July 29 to August 5. Vice
Premier Deng Xiaoping met the delegation on July 30.
Chairman Hua Guofeng met the delegation on July 31.

July 30 Chairman Hua Guofeng, Vice-Chairmen Ye Jianying,
Deng Xiaoping, Li Xiannian, and Wang Dongxing, and
other party and state leaders received representatives
attending the National Conference on Capital Construction in Agriculture and other specialized meetings.

• Vice Premier Geng Biao held talks with Dom Mintoff, prime minister of Malta, in Malta.

July 31   The Mali Government Delegation, led by Foreign
Minister S.E.M. Alioune Blondin Beye, visited China
from July 31 to August 5. Chairman Hua Guofeng
met the delegation on August 2.

• Chairman Hua Guofeng met the Korean People's
Army Friendship Delegation, led by Lt. General O
Guk Ryol.

• The Red Flag carried an article accusing the Soviet Union of making Vietnam a "forward post" for its
domination of the Indian Ocean and Pacific region.

• The Chinese Ministry of National Defense gave a
grand reception in Beijing marking the fifty-first anniversary of the founding of the Chinese PLA.

August 1   The Liberation Army Daily carried an editorial
entitled "Promote the Tradition of Seeking Truth from
Facts in Political Work," to stress the need to develop
political work in line with practice.

August 3   Luo Ruiqing, secretary general of the Military
Commission of the CCP Central Committee, died at age
seventy-two. Speaking at the memorial service for
him on August 12, Vice Premier Deng Xiaoping described him as a time-tested, loyal revolutionary
fighter of the proletariat.

August 4   China was admitted to the International Union of
Crystallography at its General Assembly held in Warsaw.

• The Libyan Government Delegation, led by Abd
as-Salam Jallud, visited China August 4-9. The delegation met Vice Premier Deng Xiaoping on August 5,
and Chairman Hua Guofeng on August 8. A joint
communiqué was issued on August 9 to establish diplomatic relations at the ambassadorial level, following
which, Taiwan authorities broke relations with Libya.

• Nie Rongzhen stressed the role of the military in
modern warfare at the National Militia Conference held
in Beijing on August 4. He said, "The militia are indispensable for combat support, troop replacements,
aid to the front and for securing the rear-area."

August 5   Chairman Hua Guofeng, Vice-Chairmen Ye Jianying, Li Xiannian, and Wang Dongxing, and other party and state leaders attended the performance given
by the National Symphony Orchestra of Korea.

August 6 NCNA reported that a city site dating back 3,000
           years had been excavated in Shandong province. It
           was the site of the ancient city of Qufu, the capital
           of the Lu state from the eleventh century B.C. to the
           second century B.C.

August 7 NCNA reported that a rock dating back more than
           3,600 million years was discovered in the Daipingzhai
           area in Hebei province.

August 8 Chairman Hua Guofeng sent a message to Sudan-
           ese President Gaafar Mohamed Nimeri, expressing sym-
           pathy and solicitude to the people of the flood-afflicted
           areas.
              • Vice Foreign Ministers Zhung Xidong and Hoang
           Bich Son began a series of vicious conferences in
           Hanoi on the question of Chinese nationals residing in
           Vietnam.

August 10 The Central League School was reopened on Au-
            gust 10.
               • The CCP Central Committee approved "The Reso-
            lution of the Military Commission of the Central Com-
            mittee of the CCP on Strengthening Political Work in
            the Army" and authorized its issuance.
               • Vice Premier Deng Xiaoping met Japanese Foreign
            Minister Sunao Sonoda.

August 11 The People's Daily carried an article denouncing
            the "reactionary" theory of "like father, like son" in
            politics. It said, "The CCP has always paid attention
            to a person's class or family origins, but has never
            considered it the sole, decisive factor. On the con-
            trary, when the party judges people, it stressed the
            individual's own political showing, rather than his or
            her antecedents. It holds that, while people are not
            free to choose their parents, they can freely deter-
            mine which side they are on."

August 12 In Beijing, Chinese and Japanese Ministers of
            Foreign Affairs Huang Hua and Sonoda Sunao signed
            the Sino-Japanese Treaty of Peace and Friendship.
            Under it, each declared neither party would seek
            hegemony in the Asian-Pacific region or in any other
            region, and both opposed efforts by other countries

to establish such hegemony. However, the treaty would not affect the position of either country regarding its relations with third countries.

• NCNA reported that four American oil firms (Exxon, Union Oil of California, Phillips Petroleum, and Pennzoil) had been invited to study exploration and development of reserves in several Chinese offshore areas.

August 13   Chairman Hua Guofeng, Vice-Chairmen Ye Jianying, Deng Xiaoping, Li Xiannian, and Wang Dongxing, and other state and party leaders received the delegates to the National Conference on Machine Building in Learning from Daqing and delegates to other conferences in the Great Hall of the People.

• A ceremony was held in Colombo, Sri Lanka to hand over the Wallawe fresh-water fish breeding experimental station which was built with Chinese aid.

August 15   China's Third Nuclear Physics Conference was held in Lushan, Jiangxi province, in which 146 papers were submitted; 117 on results in experiments and theoretical research since the Second Nuclear Physics Conference in 1974.

August 16   Chairman Hua Guofeng visited Rumania as the head of a delegation from August 16-21. He proceeded to Yugoslavia (August 21-29), and to Iran (August 29 to September 1), and then returned to Urumchi on September 1 and to Beijing on September 5.

• Chairman Hua Guofeng left Beijing on August 14 and made a stopover at Urumchi on his way to Rumania. He sent a message of greetings from the plane to the leaders of Afghanistan, Turkey, Iran, and Bulgaria. China and Rumania reached several agreements including the establishment of an intergovernmental committee on economic and technological cooperation, a protocol on cooperation in production and technology, an agreement on scientific and technological cooperation, a protocol on the exchange of engineering technicians and students, and the 1979 trade protocol. Further agreements were signed on tourism and quarantine arrangements for animals and plants as well as on the opening of shipping routes.

• The Standing Committee of the Fifth NPC at its

third session approved the long-term agreement on economic and technical cooperation between China and Rumania.

August 18   The Chinese Military Friendship Delegation, led by Su Yu, visited Korea from August 18 to September 1.

August 19   The relationship between "letting a hundred schools of thought contend" and the development of natural science was discussed in a People's Daily signed article. It said, "The principle of 'letting a hundred schools of thought contend' provides favorable conditions for scientific and technological advance and encourages people to help each other through discussion and correcting wrong understanding."

• A People's Daily article said, "The Vietnamese authorities' violation of the 1955 agreement between the Chinese and Vietnamese parties is the root cause of the present dispute between the two countries over the Chinese national issue. The Vietnamese authorities must correct their attitude towards the 1955 agreement before a common language can be found on the current negotiations between the two sides."

August 21   Chairman Hua Guofeng and his party flew to Belgrade from Rumania. During the course of the visit, Yugoslav foreign policy, its economic progress and its achievements in developing its own form of socialism were extensively praised in the Chinese media. An agreement on the establishment of the Sino-Yugoslav Committee on Economic, Scientific and Technological Cooperation, and a long-term agreement on economic, scientific and technological cooperation were signed on August 26.

August 25   Bad feelings between China and Vietnam were further inflamed when an incident took place on August 25 at the Huu Nghi or Youyiguan (Friendship Pass) on the border in Cao Lang province. The Vietnamese complained that hundreds of Chinese, including plain-clothes police and soldiers, crossed the border and attacked Vietnamese cadres and personnel with cutlasses, knives, rods and pointed bamboo stakes.

August 29   The Second Session of the China-Nepal Boundary
Joint Inspection Committee was held in Katmandu from
August 29 to September 17.

• Chairman Hua Guofeng and his party visited Iran
from August 29 to September 1. This was the first
visit by Chinese leader to a nonsocialist country. An
agreement on cultural cooperation was signed during
the visit. No joint communiqué was released after the
conclusion of the visit.

September 2   The Cambodian People's Representative Assembly, led by Nuon Chea, visited China September 2-7.
Chairman Hua Guofeng met the delegation on September
6.

• A People's Daily article refuted Lin Biao's fallacy
that "every sentence is right." It said, "Starting with
this formulation, Lin Biao and the 'gang of four' split
up and dismembered the complete, close-knit and scientific ideological system of Mao Zedong thought into
separate phrases and sentences for the original purpose of distorting and tampering with it."

September 3   Vice Premier Deng Xiaoping greeted with
pleasure the signing of the China-Japan treaty of peace
and friendship when he met more than fifty Japanese
friends visiting Beijing. He said the treaty increased
the "strength of China and Japan in opposing hegemonism and benefit the peace, security and stability
of Asia and the Pacific region."

• Chairman Hua Guofeng made inspection tours of
the Shihezu area of the Xinjiang Uighur autonomous
region, and the Sardapan grasslands in the Tianshan
mountains pastureland.

September 5   Chairman Hua Guofeng and his party returned
to Beijing from Urumchi after successfully ending his
official visits to Rumania, Yugoslavia and Iran. He
was welcomed at the airport by Vice-Chairmen Ye
Jianying, Deng Xiaoping, Li Xiannian, and Wang Dongxing, and other party and state leaders.

September 6   Vice Premier Deng Xiaoping told the visiting
Japanese news commentators that China intended to
terminate its alliance treaty with the Soviet Union before next April, that China supported Japan's main-

tenance of self-defense power, but not nuclear weapons, that China wanted to see Japan remain under the
American nuclear umbrella, and that China would increase oil exports to Japan to forty or fifty million
tons a year in the future.

September 8 Zhang Zaijian visited Japan on his way to
Mexico from September 8-14. He became the first
senior Chinese military leader to do so.
  • Vice Premier Deng Xiaoping visited Pyongyang
from September 8-12. He held talks with President
Kim Il-sung and attended the celebration of the thirtieth anniversary of the founding of the Democratic
People's Republic of Korea.
  • The Fourth National Women's Congress was held
in Beijing from September 8-17. It was attended by
nearly 2,000 delegates. Chairman Hua Guofeng, and
Vice-Chairmen Ye Jianying, Li Xiannian and Wang
Dongxing attended the opening ceremony. Kang Ke-
qing, who delivered the report, was elected chairper-
son of the Executive Committee.

September 9 The second anniversary of the death of Chairman Mao Zedong was marked by the publication of
three hitherto unpublished poems by him on the front
page of the People's Daily and all other papers. The
three poems, which were also printed in facsimiles of
Chairman Mao's handwriting, were "To the Tune of
He Xin Lang, 1923," "Mourning Comrade Luo Rong-
huan--a Lushi, December 1963," and "Reading His-
tories--to the Tune of He Xin Lang, Spring 1964."
To commemorate the occasion, an article by Xu Shiyu,
another by Li Desheng, and a third by the political
department of the PLA 8341 unit, were published to
praise the late Chairman Mao Zedong. A noticeable
event marking the anniversary was the national tele-
vising of the play Yang Kaihui, which portrayed the
late Chairman Mao as a young man in the 1920s.
  • Chairman Hua Guofeng met General S. Potocar,
and Mrs. Potocar and members of the Yugoslav People's Army Delegation.
  • A director of British Rolls-Royce, Sir Peter
Thorton, announced that China had contracted with
Rolls-Royce, to an amount possibly over £80,000,000,
to help modernize China's aeroengine industry.

September 11 Mr. Toshio Komoto and Li Qiang, the two
             ministers of international trade, agreed to expand
             Sino-Japanese trade under the long-term agreement
             signed in February 1978. The period covered by the
             agreement was extended by five years, from 1985 to
             1990. Mr. Komoto met Chairman Hua Guofeng on
             September 14.

September 12 Foreign Minister Myint Maung of Burma held
             talks in Beijing with vice minister of Foreign Affairs,
             Han Nianlong. Vice Premier Li Xiannian met Mr.
             Maung on September 14.
             • Tanzanian Prime Minister Edward Morimge Sokoine
             visited China from September 12-15 at the invitation
             of the Chinese government. He was greeted at the
             airport by Chairman Hua Guofeng. He held talks with
             Vice Premier Li Xiannian, and met Chairman Hua Guofeng
             again on September 14. A protocol on further develop-
             ment of economic and technical cooperation between the
             two nations was signed on September 14.

September 13 Chairman Hua Guofeng met the Yugoslav State
             and Party Delegation, led by Cvijetin Mijatovic.

September 14 Rumanian Prime Minister Manes Manescu ar-
             rived in Beijing from Pyongyang for a visit. He met
             Chairman Hua Guofeng on September 15.
             • NCNA reported that around 200 ancient tombs,
             some dating back 4,200 years, were unearthed in
             Sichuan province. The earliest of them were from
             clan communes ranging in time from latter-day matri-
             archal to early patriarchal society.

September 15 China and the Federal Republic of Germany
             signed an agreement for scientific cooperation.

September 16 The Chinese-Polish Joint-Stock Shipping Com-
             pany held its Fourteenth Session of Shareholders'
             Meeting in Beijing from September 16-26.

September 18 China and Australia signed an agreement to
             establish consulate generals in each other's countries.
             • China and Yugoslavia signed an agreement for
             scientific cooperation in Beijing.

September 19   Ye Jianying, chairman of the Standing Committee of the NPC, and Premier Hua Guofeng sent a
message to General Mohammad Zia-ul-Haq, warmly
congratulating him on his assumption of the presidency
of Pakistan.
  • Premier Hua Guofeng met Jacques Chirac, former
Prime Minister of France, and Mayor of Paris, Mrs.
Chirac and other French guests accompanying him on
the visit.

September 20   President of Chad General Felix Malloum Nga-
koutou Bey-Ndi, arrived in Beijing for a visit from
September 20-27 and held talks with Chairman Hua
Guofeng on September 23.
  • China and Sudan signed the 1978-79 trade proto-
col in Beijing.
  • Foreign Minister Tengku Ahmad Rithauddeen Bin
Tengku Ismail of Malaysia held talks with Foreign Min-
ister Huang Hua in Beijing. He also had talks with
Vice Premier Deng Xiaoping on September 22.

September 21   The foreign ministers of the nine EEC countries met in Brussels and agreed on a special regula-
tion with regard to imports from China (the relaxation
of restrictions for twenty supplementary products).
  • Foreign Minister Huang Hua visited Greece on his
way to the UN General Assembly from September 21-22.
He signed a cultural agreement during the visit.
  • Chairman Hua Guofeng, Vice-Chairmen Ye Jianying, Deng Xiaoping, Li Xiannian, and Wang Dongxing,
and other party and state leaders received the delegates to the Fourth Women's Congress.
  • The Chinese government notified the Japanese
government that it would like to have talks to amend
the Japan-China fishery agreement.

September 22   Vice Premier Deng Xiaoping told the visiting
French Gaullist leader and mayor of Paris, Jacques
Chirac, that China approved of the Camp David accords
agreed to by the leaders of Egypt and Israel under
the auspices of President Carter.
  • The People's Daily carried an article entitled
"Talk on the Question of Abstract Affirmation and
Specific Negation of Marxism-Leninism-Mao Zedong
Thought," which stated that "Thought" embodied basic

principles of universal significance and specific principles and conclusions and, as such, was a theory of
guiding all aspects of work but not a criterion for
testing truth. It went on to cite examples to rebut
the contention that to test truth in practice led to the
abstract affirmation and specific negation of the
"Thought."

• A contract for the supply of equipment and materials for the Jamaican Cotton Polyester Textile Company Limited, to be built with Chinese aid, was signed
in Beijing.

• China and Chad signed a protocol on economic
and technical cooperation in Beijing.

September 23   China and Pakistan signed an agreement on
the purchase and sale of ships in Islamabad.

September 24   NCNA reported that a 5,000-year-old pottery
basin painted with figures of dancers was unearthed
by Chinese archaeologists working in Qinghai province.
The basin dated back to the Neolothic Age.

• The nine-member delegation from the European
Economic Community, led by Wilhelm Haferkamp, ar-
rived in Beijing for a courtesy visit. Chairman Hua
Guofeng met the delegation on September 27.

September 26   China proposed that the Sino-Vietnamese
talks should be adjourned because the Vietnamese
side had rejected China's proposals without submitting
constructive proposals of its own for a comprehensive
settlement on the matter of Chinese nationals. The
Chinese delegation left Hanoi for home on September
27.

September 27   Prime Minister Kirti Nidhi Bista of Nepal arrived in Beijing for an eight-day visit. He met Chairman Hua Guofeng on October 1, and Vice Premier
Deng Xiaoping on September 28. The two nations
signed an agreement to complete construction projects
on October 1.

• Foreign Minister Huang Hua met his Indian counterpart, Atal Bihari Vajpayee, at the United Nations
at the Chinese initiative. It was the first face-to-face
meeting between the two foreign ministers in sixteen
years.

September 28 Foreign Minister Huang Hua, at the Thirty-
    third Session of the UN General Assembly, stressed
    the need for people to be aware of the growing danger
    of war so that they could make preparations to combat
    the aggressor, to deter future wars, and to oppose
    policies of appeasement which augmented the dangers
    of war.
       • Ilya Sergeevich Sherbakov, new Soviet Union
    ambassador to China, presented his credentials to
    Ulanfu, vice-chairman of the Standing Committee of
    the NPC.
       • Chairman Hua Guofeng met the Tanzanian Chama
    Cha Mapinduzi (Revolutionary party) delegation, led
    by Rashidi Mfaume Kawawa.

September 29 China and Congo signed an intergovernmental
    trade agreement in Brazzaville.
       • Japanese Foreign Minister Sonoda told the Diet
    that it would be diplomatically inadvisable to establish
    facilities on the Senkaku Islands to strengthen Japan's
    claim, although it would be natural for Japan to create
    a port of refuge for fishing boats using the islands.

September 30 China and Bulgaria signed the protocol of the
    Sixteenth Meeting of the Commission for Scientific and
    Technical Cooperation between the two nations in Bei-
    jing.
       • Chairman Hua Guofeng met Prince Abdul Reza
    Pahlavi, brother of shahanshah of Iran, and Michel
    Poniatowski, former French minister of state, and his
    wife.
       • Chairman Hua Guofeng held a reception in Beijing
    to mark the twenty-ninth anniversary of the founding
    of the People's Republic of China. Those attending
    included Vice-Chairmen Ye Jianying, Deng Xiaoping,
    Li Xiannian, and Wang Dongxing, together with other
    state and party leaders, and over 3,000 people.

October 1 Besides the need to adopt a correct attitude for
    modernization, the People's Daily National Day editorial
    referred to heated discussions having taken place con-
    cerning the criteria for testing truth, economic laws,
    and business management, the need to implement party
    policy on cadres, intellectuals, rural economic work
    and distribution, and the need to eliminate empty talk

and inaction and to enhance study and unity to achieve modernization.

• To mark National Day, the Red Flag published its own editorial entitled "Emancipate Our Minds and Advance at a Faster Pace," referring inter alia to the need to have both the spirit and the ability to utilize favorable international factors, including the introduction of advanced technology and equipment, the availability of foreign capital, organizational experience and facilities to train personnel, so as to accelerate construction.

October 2   NCNA reported the completed construction of a high-yielding oilfield at Renqiu in Hebei province.

October 3   Vice Premier Geng Biao left Beijing to visit the Congo, Guinea, Mali, Ghana, Nigeria, Rwanda, and Somalia from October to November 6.

• Vice Premier Fang Yi left Beijing to visit the Federal Republic of Germany and France from October 3-22.

October 4   China and Finland signed the 1979 trade agreement in Helsinki.

• China signed a ship's technical survey cooperation agreement with Italy in Rome.

• The British Rail Delegation visited China October 4-18 and helped plan modernization and expansion of China's 33,000-mile rail network.

• In a ceremony in Cairo, China handed over six China-made cine-projectors to Egypt.

October 5   China and Chile signed an agreement to sell copper to China in Santiago for the next three years.

• China and WHO signed a memorandum on technical cooperation in health service.

• An agreement was signed in Hong Kong whereby the Chinese airline would operate charter flights between Guangzhou and Hong Kong, to serve passengers going to the Export Commodities Fair on October 12.

October 6   Foreign Minister Huang Hua visited Rome from October 6-10.   He signed agreements on cultural cooperation and on scientific and technical cooperation.

• China and the Federal Republic of Germany signed

an agreement on television cooperation in Beijing.
  • NCNA reported that a huge oilfield, covering more
than 200,000 square km was discovered in central Qinghai province.

October 7 EEC Commissioner for External Affairs W. Hafer-
    kamp was told in Beijing that China was prepared to
    accept "all the traditional economic means" for the
    purpose of financing European imports except for gov-
    ernment-to-government loans.
      • An intergovernmental trade agreement between
    China and Mali was signed in Bamaco. The new agree-
    ment was to replace the one concluded in 1961.
      • Vice-Chairman Wang Dongxing met Cambodian
    Deputy Prime Minister Ieng Sary and his party, who
    arrived in Beijing on their way to New York to attend
    the UN General Assembly.

October 8 Mr. James Schlesinger, the US energy secretary,
    told reporters in Tokyo, after his three-week tour of
    China, that China had untapped reserves of 100 bil-
    lion barrels of oil, three times the known reserves of
    the US itself.

October 9 China and the Federal Republic of Germany
    signed an agreement on scientific and technical coop-
    eration, and minutes of talks to implement the agree-
    ment in Bonn.
      • NCNA reported that a number of 2,000-year-old
    wooden strips with characters written in Chinese ink
    describing military affairs and a seal of a minority of-
    ficial had been excavated from tombs of the Han Dy-
    nasty (206 B.C.-A.D. 220) by Chinese archaeological
    workers in Qinghai province.

October 10 Chairman Hua Guofeng met the Rumanian Party
    Workers Group and the delegation of the Rumanian
    Journal Era Socialist.
      • Vice Premier Deng Xiaoping met the visiting press
    delegation from the Federal Republic of Germany, led
    by Dr. Georg Negwer.
      • Foreign Minister Huang Hua visited London Octo-
    ber 10-14. He met Prime Minister James Callaghan on
    October 11.

October 11   A ceremony marked the opening of classes at
the Chinese Academy of Social Sciences' Postgraduate
Institute.
• The Ninth National Trade Union Congress was
held in Beijing at the Great Hall of the People from
October 11-22. The Congress was attended by nearly
2,000 delegates, and Chairman Hua Guofeng, Vice-
Chairmen Ye Jianying, Deng Xiaoping, Li Xiannian,
and Wang Dongxing attended the opening ceremony.
Deng Xiaoping addressed the Congress on behalf of the
party Central Committee.

October 13   The appointment of Lin Hujia as mayor of Beijing
to replace Wu De was confirmed by an official Chinese
spokesman. Wu De retained his positions on the politburo and the Central Committee.
• There were numerous further charges by Vietnam
of Chinese violation of the border, including an alleged incident on October 13 in which Chinese border
guards killed two Vietnamese border guards and captured one Vietnamese on duty.

October 14   Ye Jianying sent a message of congratulations
to Daniel Arap Moi on his assumption of the presidency
of the Republic of Kenya.

October 15   Diplomatic sources said that Vice Premier Chen
Xilian was dismissed as commander of the Beijing military garrison.

October 16   The Tenth National Congress of the Communist
Youth League of China was held in Beijing October
16-26; the first since 1964. A work report entitled
"Glorious Mission of the Chinese Youth" was delivered
by Han Ying, who was later elected first secretary of
the CYLCC.

October 17   Chilean Foreign Minister Herman Cubillos Sallato,
his wife, Marcele Sigall, and their party arrived in
Beijing for a friendly visit from October 17-28.
Vice Premier Deng Xiaoping met the delegation on
October 19. The two nations agreed to increase their
bilateral trade and their cultural and scientific exchanges.

October 20   JETRO estimated China's exports to thirty-one
          countries in the first six months of 1978 to be $4.5
          million, an increase of twenty-six percent on 1977,
          and imports to be $4.5 million, an increase of sixty-
          nine percent on 1977, with the US emerging as China's
          number three trading partner. A surplus from trade
          with Hong Kong and ASEAN states helped meet a defi-
          cit in trade with OECD countries. Total trade in 1978
          was expected to reach $20 billion and while there would
          be more deals involving commission processing and
          production sharing, China would move to attract pri-
          vate capital from Western countries.
             • Chairman Hua Guofeng, Vice-Chairmen Ye Jian-
          ying, Deng Xiaoping, Li Xiannian, and Wang Dong-
          xing, and other party and state leaders received the
          delegates to the Ninth National Congress of Trade Un-
          ion and the Tenth National Congress of the Communist
          Youth League of China.
             • Vice-Chairman Deng Xiaoping inspected the new
          housing estates along the five km East-West thorough-
          fare south of the Tiananmen Square.
             • China and France signed a protocol on supple-
          mentary items of scientific and technological exchanges
          in Paris.
             • A summary of talks between China and Burma on
          the construction of a national indoor stadium for Burma
          was signed in Rangoon.
             • China and Sweden signed an agreement on scien-
          tific and technological cooperation.
             • China was restored to its rightful place in the
          International Gymnastic Federation at its Fifty-sixth
          Congress, held in Strassbourg.

October 21   Vietnam, China, Korea, Mongolia, and the Soviet
          Union held a conference in Ulan Bator October 16-21
          to arrange timetables for passenger trains. A protocol
          was signed at the end of the conference.

October 22   Vice Premier Deng Xiaoping visited Japan Octo-
          ber 23-29. On October 23, a ceremony was held to
          exchange the documents of ratification of the China-
          Japan Treaty of Peace and Friendship. The Chinese
          leader invited Prime Minister Fukuda to visit China,
          and Mr. Fukuda invited Chairman Hua Guofeng to visit
          Japan. Both invitations were accepted. On October

23, Deng and his wife, Zhuo Lin, were received by
the Emperor Hirohito at the Imperial Palace. Deng
held two rounds of talks with Fukuda on October 23
and 25.

October 23   The Overseas Chinese University was reopened
in Zhuangzhou in Fujian province.

October 24   The delegation of the Chinese People's Association for Friendship with Foreign Countries, led by
Luo Shigao left Beijing to visit Niger, Upper Volta,
Benin, Mali, the Gambia, Guinea Bissau, Mauritania
and Tunisia.
   • Mexican President José López Portillo and his wife
visited China October 24-30. Chairman Hua Guofeng
greeted them at the airport, had a cordial meeting
with them, and held a welcome banquet in the evening.
The two nations signed a cultural agreement and an
agreement on tourism cooperation on October 27.

October 25   Chairman Hua Guofeng met the Guinean Demo-
cratic Party Delegation, led by Diane Lansana.
   • Vice Premier Deng Xiaoping told Japanese report-
ers that he saw no sign of tension in Korea. As for
Vietnam, he said "People call Vietnam the Cuba in the
East. I agree with this view."

October 26   The Chinese Foreign Ministry lodged a strong
protest against Vietnam's encroachments upon Chinese
territorial integrity and sovereignty and its deliberate
anti-China provocation. The protest note cited alleged
border crossings by Vietnamese troops in which Chinese
personnel were fired on and beaten. (September 20,
24, 29 and 30, and one other occasion.)

October 27   The Committee for Editing and Publishing the
Selected Works of Guo Moruo was formed in Beijing,
headed by Zhou Yang.
   • NCNA accused the Vietnamese of having recently
deliberately stepped up their anti-China campaign.
"Since mid-September the situation has gone from bad
to worse." In addition to border violations and the
infliction of casualties on local residents, thereby
threatening China's security, an atmosphere of military
tension had been created by the Vietnamese authorities

having stepped up their war preparations in the border areas. For more than a month, Moscow openly incited Hanoi and declared that "Vietnam may today as it did yesterday count on the support of the Soviet Union." At the time, the commentary charged that Vietnamese authorities were mobilizing many divisions of their forces for a massive attack on Kampuchea at the onset of the dry season in November.

October 28   Chairman Hua Guofeng inspected the Beijing Vinylon Plant. He was accompanied by Lin Hujia, new mayor of Beijing.

October 29   Vice Premier Deng Xiaoping returned to Beijing from Japan after a successful official visit to Japan. Greeting him at the airport were Chairman Hua Guofeng, and Vice-Chairman Ye Jianying.

• Vice Premier Li Xiannian addressed the National Conference of Representatives of Meteorological Departments. Li called on those working in meteorology to study, learn more about science, and help with the Four Modernizations. The conference was attended by more than 1,300 representatives from meteorological departments all over the country.

October 30   In a special commentator's article, the People's Daily criticized those who "talk of Mao Zedong Thought every day" and yet "go against the fundamental principle of Marxism that practice is the only criterion for judging what is truth, a principle to which Chairman Mao gave strong emphasis."

October 31   A National Work Conference on Intellectual Youth Going to Mountains and Countryside was held in Beijing from October 31 to December 10. Chen Yonggui indicated that the policy would continue for some years but numbers would be reduced as modernization was achieved.

• The People's Daily claimed that recent Vietnamese textbooks had "brazenly" incorporated Chinese territory and territorial water into Vietnam compared with books and maps published in Vietnam in earlier years. Meanwhile, the Vietnamese alleged that China was violating the border in Cao Lang province, notably in Tan Thanh village on October 31 and Bao Lam village on

October 29, as well as on three occasions in Thanh
Loa village on October 26.

November 1   NCNA reported that a 2,000-year-old section
of the Great Wall built by the Yan State, one of the
Warring States in northern China during the period
475 B.C.-221 B.C., was found in Jilin province during the 1975-77 archaeological survey. This section
of the Great Wall measured two to three meters high
and four to six meters wide at its base and extended
intermittently for more than 125 km.

November 2   NCNA reported a serious nationwide drought
in China in 1978, saying that "in length of time,
breadth of scope, and seriousness of extent, it has
surpassed the great droughts of 1934, 1959 and 1966.
The drought in Hubei, Jiangxi, Henan, Xhanxi and
other provinces has been the worst for fifty to seventy
years, in Jiangsu for sixty to a hundred years and
Anhui has suffered from a particularly bad drought not
seen for 122 years."
    • China and WHO cosponsored training classes to
teach the new immunology technique of enzyme-linked
immunoabsorbent assay in Beijing and Shanghai.
    • China and Korea signed an agreement on plant
disease inspection and the prevention and elimination
of crop diseases and pests in Beijing.
    • The Third National People's Air Force Conference
was held in Beijing. Chairman Hua Guofeng, Vice-
Chairmen Ye Jianying, Deng Xiaoping, Wang Dongxing
and other party and state leaders attended the opening session. Ye Jianying delivered a speech.
    • Vice Premier Li Xiannian received Abu al-Hawl,
the special envoy of Chairman Yasir Arafat of the PLO.

November 3   The Soviet-Vietnamese treaty of friendship and
cooperation, signed in Moscow on November 3, was
regarded in China as a military alliance.
    • Chairman Hua Guofeng met Australian Deputy
Prime Minister J.D. Anthony and his wife.
    • Chairman Hua Guofeng sent a message to Prime
Minister Patrick John, expressing warm congratulations on the independence of Dominica.

November 4   A People's Daily articled quoted instructions by

Chairman Hua Guofeng during his tour of Xinjiang
that agricultural combines were to be set up in Xinjiang on the lines of the Belgrade agricultural-indus-
trial combines.

• Chairman Hua Guofeng met James Schlesinger,
the US energy secretary.

• US Secretary of Agriculture Robert Bergland and
his party arrived in Beijing for a visit at the invitation of the Chinese Ministry of Agriculture and Forestry.

• NCNA reported that large numbers of armed personnel were sent by the Vietnamese authorities on
November 1 to intrude into Dinghaoshan area, Jingsi
county, the Guangxi Zhuang autonomous region of
China. The intruders launched a surprise attack on
Chinese commune members and militiamen with machine
guns, submachine guns and rifles, wounding twelve
of them and kidnapping eight others. Six of those
kidnapped were killed by the Vietnamese. Throughout the incident, the Chinese militiamen had exercised
the greatest restraint and never returned a single
shot.

November 5 Vice-Chairman Wang Dongxing and Vice Premier Yu Qiuli led a delegation to visit Cambodia November 5-9 at the invitation of the Central Committee
of the Communist party of Kampuchea and the government of Kampuchea.

• Vice Premier Deng Xiaoping visited Thailand
November 5-9, proceeding to Malaysia (November 9-
12), Singapore (November 12-14), and Burma (November 14), returning to Beijing on the same day. In
Thailand, Mr. and Mrs. Deng were received by the
king and queen shortly after their arrival. Agreements on trade and on scientific and technical cooperation were signed during the visit. At his press conference on November 8, Vice Premier Deng told correspondents that the Vietnamese-Soviet treaty would
enhance Vietnam's role as "the Cuba in the East."
He further said that the treaty was "not only directed
at China, but it also constituted an important component part of the Soviet Union's global strategy in
the Asian-Pacific region." As for China, he said, it
depended on "how far Vietnam will go" in the first instance with regard to Kampuchea. "We will decide

on the way of dealing with it in accordance with the
distance it will go with its policy of hegemonism."

November 6   Vice Premier Wang Chen arrived in London to
inspect the Harrier jump-jet aircraft, see North Sea
oilfields and visit a shipyard.   During his ten-day
visit to Britain, Wang told Secretary of Industry Eric
Varley that he had come "for concrete discussions
with the aim for introducing into China your advanced
technology and equipment in various sectors of industry."   The Sino-British scientific and technological
exchange agreement was signed on November 15.   It
was also agreed in principle that Sino-British trade
should be roughly quadrupled to reach a total of about
$10 billion over the next seven years.   To this end
the British secretary of state for industry would visit
Beijing early in the new year to sign the necessary
accords.   Meanwhile Britain would consider further the
sale of Harrier jump-jets to China.

November 8   Secretary of State Vance said that while Washington would not sell arms to either Moscow or Beijing
it would neither oppose nor approve allied arms sales
to China, provided they were defensive in nature and
did not constitute a threat to Taiwan or contribute to
instability on the Sino-Soviet border.

November 9   The Chinese delegation of the Fourth Machine-
Building Ministry, led by Jian Min, arrived in Paris
for a visit to France.
    • A US Hotel Group, Intercontinental, signed an
agreement with the Chinese government in Beijing to
build up to six hotels in Beijing and other cities.
    • Vice Premier Deng Xiaoping and his party visited
Malaysia from October 9-12.   On November 11, he reiterated that "anyone of Chinese origin who acquired
Malaysian citizenship automatically forfeited Chinese
nationality."   As for those overseas Chinese retaining
Chinese nationality, "we hope they will abide by the
laws of this country."   Malaysian Premier Datuk Hussein Bin Onn explained that Malaysia and other ASEAN
countries did not wish to take sides in the Sino-Vietnamese rivalry.

November 10   An agreement was signed in Beijing between

China and Brazil whereby China would buy at least
1.5 million tons of steel valued at $500 million in re-
turn for oil.

November 12 China and Hungary signed a protocol in Beijing for the Seventeenth Meeting of the Commission
for Scientific and Technical Cooperation.

November 13 The Chinese National People's Congress Delegation, led by Ulanfu, visited Egypt November 14-18.
President Sadat met the delegation on November 16.
The delegation proceeded to visit Sudan (November
18-23), and Turkey (November 24-28).
   • Vice Premier Deng Xiaoping visited Singapore
from November 13-14.

November 14 Vice Premier Deng Xiaoping returned to Beijing
after his tour of Thailand, Malaysia and Singapore and
a surprise stopover in Burma. Chairman Hua Guofeng,
and other party and state leaders greeted him at the
airport.

November 15 NCNA reported a "recent" declaration by the
Beijing Municipal CCP Committee that the Tiananmen
Incident was a "completely revolutionary action."
   • The People's Daily published a front-page com-
mentator's article to stress reversing unjust verdicts
of the Lin Biao-Gang of Four vintage. In this con-
text, the article called for CCP Committees at all levels
to finish such rehabilitation work by mid-1979.
   • The Guangming Daily published an article entitled
"A Criticism of Yao Wenyuan's 'Comments on the New
Historical Play Hai Jui Dismissed from Office'," to make
a detailed rebuttal of the allegations made by Yao.
The article stressed that wrong verdicts must be reversed including the purge on the literary scene
launched by his comments.
   • In Beijing, Vice Premier Deng Xiaoping met with
the Japanese Diet Delegation, led by Shoichi Miyake,
and Mrs. Hori.

November 16 The play Yu Wusheng Chu (Where the Silence
Is) about the Tiananmen Incident (April 5, 1976) was
performed in Beijing for the first time.
   • NCNA reported that a group of twenty-four gov-

ernment and religious leaders were freed from prisons
in Tibet.

• The CCP Central Committee decided to remove the
designation of all the remaining rightists and to in-
struct all local authorities to implement the party's
relevant policies and to assign appropriate jobs to all
those involved including former rightists who had
their labels cancelled.

November 17 China and Rumania signed a protocol of the
Nineteenth Session of their Joint Commission on Scientific and Technical Cooperation in Bucharest.

November 18 Tiananmen shichao (Poems on Tiananmen) was
published by the Second Foreign Language Institute
in Beijing.

• China and Mongolia signed the 1978 annual meeting protocol of their joint commission on the border
railway.

• China and the Philippines signed a postal-parcel
agreement in Beijing.

November 19 A fourteen-page wall poster appeared in Beijing, accusing Mao Zedong of supporting the Gang of
Four and being responsible for removing Deng Xiaoping
in 1976. This was the first batch of numerous posters
on "democracy wall" about this time.

November 20 More wall posters praised the late Zhou Enlai
as the only leader who protected China from becoming
a "fascist" state in the period 1966-1976.

• The State Council decided to use the Chinese
phonetic alphabet to standardize the Romanization of
Chinese names and places from January 1, 1979.

November 21 The People's Daily carried an article entitled
"The Truth About the Tiananmen Events--History
Turned Upside Down Through the People's Daily by
the 'gang of four' Turned Right Side Up," to aim at
setting the record straight. The article described
how the Gang of Four had used the affair to oust
Deng Xiaoping, then in charge of central work, after
he had initiated a struggle against them on Chairman
Mao's instructions. It stated that Deng had nothing
to do with what had happened.

November 24   Vice Premier Li Xiannian met Senator Edmund
    Muskie in Beijing.

November 26   Vice Premier Deng Xiaoping told Sasaki Ryo-
    saku of the Democratic Socialist party of Japan that
    it was "a normal thing" to put up wall posters, and
    showed "the stable situation in our country."
    • China and Mongolia signed the minutes of talks
    on exchange in nontrade payment in Ulan Bator.
    • NCNA reported that a bridge 380 meters long,
    ten meters wide and forty meters high, crossing the
    Hongshui River--the biggest in the Guangxi Zhuang
    autonomous region--was completed and opened to traf-
    fic.
    • A wall poster called for the ousting of Vice
    Chairman Wang Dongxing, formerly Mao Zedong's
    bodyguard, and urged the appointment of Vice Pre-
    mier Deng Xiaoping as premier.

November 27   Vice Premier Deng Xiaoping met American col-
    umnist Robert D. Novak.
    • China and the Netherlands signed a civil air
    transport agreement in The Hague.

November 28   Chairman Hua Guofeng sent a message to
    President Josip Broz Tito of Yugoslavia to warmly
    greet the thirty-fifth anniversary of the founding of
    the Socialist Federal Republic of Yugoslavia.

November 29   China and Bangladesh signed a maritime
    transport agreement in Beijing.
    • The French Exhibition on Petroleum, Natural Gas
    and Petrochemical Technology was held in Beijing from
    November 29 to December 8.

December 1   Chairman Hua Guofeng, Vice-Chairmen Ye Jian-
    ying, Deng Xiaoping, Li Xiannian, and Wang Dong-
    xing, and other party and state leaders received the
    Chinese Sports Delegation to the Eighth Asian Games.

December 2   NCNA announced the adoption of the Chinese
    phonetic scheme for the Romanization of names of Chi-
    nese persons and places from January 1, 1979. It re-
    placed the various old ways of spelling including the
    Wade-Gile system and eliminated long-standing confusion.

December 3 The People's Daily saw the establishment of the
Kampuchean National Front for National Salvation as
a signal for Hanoi to launch a full-scale aggression
against Kampuchea.

December 4 China and France signed a long-term economic
cooperation agreement in Beijing to raise bilateral
trade to FFr 60 billion over the seven-year period
ending in 1985; about eight times the present volume
of trade. The French also won two contracts for the
sale of 900 MW pressurized water nuclear reactors
worth FFr 10 billion. French Minister of Foreign
Trade Jean François Deniau told reporters afterwards
that the main areas for cooperation would be steel,
electricity, mining research, the hotel trade, port
facilities, aeronautics, nonferrous metals, rail and
road transport, vehicles, public works and oil.
• President Omar Bongo of Gabon visited China,
his fourth visit, December 4-6. He was greeted at
the airport by Chairman Hua Guofeng. Chairman Hua
Guofeng and Vice Premier Deng Xiaoping met him
again on December 5.
• The Chinese Foreign Affairs Institute held a banquet to welcome the US Congressional Delegation, led
by Democratic Senator Harrison A. Williams, Jr.

December 5 China and Sweden signed a ten-year agreement
on cooperation in industry, science and technology in
Beijing.
• China and Australia signed minutes of the talks
to exchange ionospheric information in Beijing.

December 6 In London, the Bank of China signed agreements with UK banks for seven separate "deposit facilities" totalling $1.2 billion. NCNA noted that these
would be supported by Britain's Export Credits Guarantee Department.
• NCNA reported that Nippon Steel Company agreed
to provide $2 billion worth of equipment for a steel
mill at Baoshan near Shanghai.
• The People's Daily urged units that had occupied
school buildings during the Cultural Revolution to
carry out the August decision of the State Council and
leave the buildings as soon as possible.
• Ye Jianying, chairman of the Standing Committee

of the NPC, sent a letter of reply to Khieu Samphan, president of Kampuchea, voicing firm support for the Kampuchean people's just struggle against aggression by the Vietnamese expansionists.

December 7 On human rights in China, Huang Guo claimed in her speech at the UN Third Committee, that "the very extensive democratic rights that masses enjoyed in new China were without precedent in her country and constituted a record that imperialist countries were unable to equal."

December 9 China and Japan signed a protocol to settle disputes by arbitration in maritime transportation in Beijing.
　　　• Minister of Foreign Trade Li Qiang and President Marcos of the Philippines agreed in Manila that the Philippines would serve as China's exclusive source of copper concentrates, in exchange for crude oil and other items from China.

December 10 China and Bangladesh signed the 1979 trade protocol in Beijing.
　　　• The circumstances of Tao Zhu's demise were graphically described by his daughter, Tao Suliang, in an article appearing in the People's Daily.

December 11 Chairman Hua Guofeng met Rumanian Deputy Prime Minister Paul Niculescu.
　　　• NCNA reported that 300,000 copies of Tao Zhu's book, Idealism Integrity and Spiritual Life, would soon be reprinted by the China Youth Publishing House.
　　　• Marshal Peng Dehuai, a former defense minister who opposed Chairman Mao Zedong, was rehabilitated, when the novel, Defense of Yanan, reestablished its fame in the Liberation Army Daily after being banned for over a decade.

December 12 The Xian Incident and Comrade Zhou Enlai, a book which recalled Comrade Zhou Enlai's immortal contributions to the settlement of the incident, was published on the occasion of its forty-second anniversary. The book told how Comrade Zhou Enlai carried out Chairman Mao Zedong's decision to work out a peaceful settlement of the incident with the Guomindang, and thus saved China from subjugation by the Japanese aggressors.

December 13   The Chinese Foreign Ministry issued a note lodging a strong protest against "the Vietnamese authorities' incessant encroachments upon Chinese territory or wounding Chinese civilians in the Beibu Gulf along the Chinese-Vietnamese border." Several incidents were cited and the note ended with the warning that should such incidents continue the Vietnamese authorities "must be held responsible for the consequences arising therefrom."
   • The People's Daily carried an article entitled "Father Expected Us to Be Healthy and Make Progress," written by Chairman Mao's son, Mao Anqing and his daughter-in-law, Shao Hua, commemorating the eighty-fifth anniversary of Mao's birth.
   • The People's Daily carried Chairman Mao's speech, "On Conducting Rural Surveys," delivered in Yanan on September 13, 1941 to the women's life investigation group, emphasizing enriching theory through practice.

December 14   NCNA reported that Vietnamese troops occupied territory in the Guangxi border region and opened fire on Chinese frontier guards.
   • China and the Philippines signed an agreement to exchange news by their respective news agencies.
   • China deposited an instrument of accession to the convention on offenses and certain other acts committed on board aircraft known as the Tokyo Convention.

December 15   NCNA reported that a new German-built $325 million addition to the Wuhan Iron and Steel Works, put up by a consortium of eighteen West German companies, went into operation.

December 16   The US and China simultaneously released a joint communiqué on their decision to establish diplomatic relations as of January 1, 1979, and to exchange ambassadors on March 1, 1979. The main terms of the agreement were that the US recognized the PRC as the sole legitimate government of China, that it "acknowledged" the Beijing position that Taiwan was a part of

China and that the US would end all official governmental relations with Taiwan. But at the same time it could maintain and develop its existing socioeconomic relations with Taiwan on a "people-to-people" basis.

• At his press conference in Beijing, Chairman Hua Guofeng said that continued American arms sales to Taiwan "would be detrimental to the peaceful liberation of Taiwan."

• The People's Daily published an editorial entitled "Historical Event," appealing to the Taiwan authorities to make "a sober assessment of the situation, adapt themselves to the demands of the times and refrain from going against the common aspirations of entire Chinese people."

• The Ministry of Foreign Affairs issued a statement condemning Vietnam for producing, on December 3, 1978, a so-called "Kampuchean National United Front for National Salvation" and for calling for the overthrow of the government of Democratic Kampuchea. The statement supported the latter's "just struggle." Vietnam was accused of having deployed more than ten divisions of regular troops along the border and of having "started a new massive military offensive action against Kampuchea." The statement made no specific commitments regarding possible Chinese active response.

• The People's Daily carried an article clarifying Chairman Mao's thesis on innerparty two-line struggle. It said, "The correctness or incorrectness of the line, has to be judged according to whether or not it conforms with reality. We have to test this through practice which is the sole criterion for testing truth. Overemphasis of the thesis in abstract terms will lead to pure idealism."

December 17   Minister of Foreign Trade Li Qiang visited Macao for one day and held talks with Governor García Leandro, covering China's support for Macao's current development projects.

• At his press conference in Beijing, the chief of the US liaison office, Leonard Woodcock, said that during his visit in August 1977, Secretary Vance had successfully sought to recreate the atmosphere which had prevailed in Sino-American relations in 1972 and 1973. But it was after Dr. Brzezinski's visit in May

1978 that the emphasis on normalization got a substantial push and the two sides began a more serious effort in mid-July. Vice Premier Deng Xiaoping joined the negotiations in December, and there were meetings with him which led to the successful conclusion.

December 18   The Eleventh CCP Central Committee held its third plenary session in Beijing from December 18-22. It was attended by 169 members and 112 alternate members of the Central Committee. Chairman Hua Guofeng presided over the session and made a speech. The communique of the session was issued on December 22. The main decisions were to endorse a shift in emphasis on work to socialist modernization, to concentrate on agricultural development, to abrogate erroneous CCP Central Committee documents concerning the movement "to oppose the right-deviationist wind to reverse correct verdicts" and the Tiananmen events. Decisions were also made to correct erroneous conclusions on Peng Dehuai, Tao Zhu, Bo Ibo, Yang Shanggun and others, to elect Chen Yun as additional vice-chairman of the CCP Central Committee, and Deng Yingchao, Hu Yaobang and Wang Chen additional members of the politburo and to elect a 100-member Central Commission for Inspecting Discipline, headed by Chen Yun, to enforce the value and historical significance of the discussion of whether practice is the sole criterion for testing truth, emphatically to affirm Chairman Mao's achievement as a great Marxist and to accept the task of propagating his system of thought so that it could be integrated into the universal principles of Marxism-Leninism-Mao Zedong Thought.

• At a press conference in Hong Kong, Li Qiang said that any loans accepted by China would be based on China's ability to repay, because self-reliance was still China's basic principle in economic construction. Li also said that China welcomed joint investments with foreign firms whose equity shares in such ventures might run up to forty-nine percent with the length of such ownership negotiations.

December 19   Boeing announced in Seattle that China had bought three Boeing 747 airliners.

• In Atlanta, Georgia, Mr. J. Paul Austin, chairman of Coca-Cola Co., announced that it reached an agreement with China, on December 13, to sell Coca-Cola there and to open a bottling plant in Shanghai.

• China and Yemen signed a protocol, in Beijing, to construct an international conference hall in Yemen with Chinese aid.

• Shanghai's Qiaotong University became a sister college to four American universities: the University of Michigan, the University of California at Berkeley, California State University at San Diego, and Washington University, St. Louis. The agreement which ran from 1979 to 1982, included plans to exchange teachers and academic data, and invitations for short conferences.

December 20   China and Yugoslavia signed, in Belgrade, a plan for cooperation in education and culture.

December 21   China and Sri Lanka signed the 1979 trade protocol in Colombo.

• NCNA reported that a nearly complete skeleton of a hornless rhinoceros, an extinct species, and two well-preserved bird fossils were unearthed in the small mountain village of Shanwang in Shandong province. They dated back fifteen million years to the mid-Miocene Epoch of the Tertiary Period.

December 22   General Agreement on the purchase of complete plants from the Nippon Steel Corporation of Japan for the Baoshan Iron Steel Complex was signed in Shanghai. The total cost of all the plants and other expenses under the agreement came to about $2,000 million, and payments were to be made in cash. Under the agreement, the Nippon Steel Corporation supplied the Baoshan Iron and Steel Complex with sixteen units of equipment, including a coking plant, an iron smelting plant, a steel mill, a blooming mill, and a chemical plant. The project was to be carried out in two stages: the first blast furnace system was to be completed before October 1, 1981, and the second was to be ready for operation on January 1, 1983.

December 23   China and Korea signed the 1979 protocol, in Beijing, for a mutual supply of goods.

December 24   The Chinese Foreign Ministry lodged a strong
        protest with the Vietnamese Embassy in Beijing, com-
        plaining about several military incidents and encroach-
        ments upon Chinese territory which had taken place
        December 10-23. The note said that the Vietnamese
        authorities must be held responsible for the conse-
        quences arising therefrom.

December 25   The People's Daily editorial warned that any
        attack from Vietnam would be met with a counterattack.
        • The People's Daily published the text of "Unin-
        terrupted Revolution," written by the late Chairman
        Mao Zedong in January 1958.
        • A memorial meeting was held in Beijing to com-
        memorate the rehabilitated Peng Dehuai and Tao Zhu.
        Vice Premier Deng Xiaoping delivered a eulogy for the
        former, and Vice Chairman Chen Yun delivered a eu-
        logy for the latter.

December 26   Wang Renzhung, age seventy-one, was ap-
        pointed as vice premier.
        • An art exhibition praising the late Chairman Mao
        Zedong was held at the China Art Gallery in Beijing,
        marking the anniversary of his eighty-fifth birthday.
        • NCNA reported that in 1978, China harvested
        roughly 295 million tons of grain, ten million tons more
        than last year. This fell short of the original produc-
        tion target due to a severe drought and to shortcom-
        ings in the work in some areas.
        • Foreign Minister Huang Hua presented a report
        to the Standing Committee of the NPC. He said that
        diplomatic normalization between China and the US
        would curb Soviet influence in the world.

December 27   The Standing Committee of the National Com-
        mittee of the CPPCC endorsed the communiqué of the
        Third Plenum of the Eleventh CCP Central Committee.

December 28   China and Yugoslavia signed the 1979 trade
        agreement to double their bilateral trade to reach a
        total value of $400 million.
        • Ye Jianying, Hua Guofeng, and Deng Xiaoping
        sent a message to Rabah Bitat, interim president of
        Algeria, expressing deep condolences on the death of
        Houari Boumedienne, president of the Republic of Al-
        geria.

• The National Conference on Overseas Chinese Affairs and the Second National Congress of Returned Overseas Chinese were held in Beijing December 22-28.

• The first group of fifty Chinese scholars arrived in Washington for advanced studies in the United States.

December 31   The National Procuratorial Conference closed in Beijing. It was attended by over 250 procurators and other judicial workers in people's procuratorates in various provinces, municipalities and autonomous regions. Hu Yaobang delivered a major speech to the conference. He stressed that judicial workers must seek truth from facts, investigate and study and adhere to the mass line.

Chapter X

1979
APPRAISALS OF THE THIRTIETH ANNIVERSARY

In 1979, although Hua Guofeng remained chairman of the Chinese Communist party and premier of the government, Senior Deputy Premier Deng Xiaoping was clearly the dominant power and final decision-maker. In the interest of domestic stability and of his modernization plans, Deng chose not to purge high-ranking adversaries within the party, and expressed his intention "to add but not subtract" from the nation's leadership. The addition of twelve new members to the Central Committee--all victims of the 1966-69 Cultural Revolution--and the naming of two new politburo members--Zhao Ziyang and Peng Chen--strengthened Deng's power. The expansion of membership in the top levels of the party was matched by the increasing diversification of governmental structures to facilitate the implementation of modernization programs and to direct new ventures. On July 1, the National People's Congress ended its two-week session by appointing three economic experts as deputy premiers. Among them was Chen Yun, who became head of the new State Economic and Finance Commission.

The memory of Mao Zedong continued to be a delicate and far-reaching issue. In late 1979, an intensive campaign was launched to downgrade Mao and discredit his Cultural Revolution. The former chairman was harshly attacked in wall posters appearing throughout the country and was accused of directly supporting the Gang of Four, the radical leaders of the Cultural Revolution. A violent reaction by the Maoists, however, forced Deng Xiaoping to adopt a milder attitude. He stated that Mao's contributions to Chinese society were beyond the power of words to describe, but at the same time, reaffirmed his utilitarian notion that "practice is the sole criterion of truth." The efforts to demythologize

465

Mao's precepts continued. In a speech on September 29, Ye Jianying, senior deputy chairman of the Communist party, repeated the generally held view that Mao was a "great man, not a god," and added that the Cultural Revolution was an "appalling catastrophe suffered by all our people."

Early in 1979, Deng Xiaoping supported the use of large-character posters on the so-called "Democracy Wall" as an appropriate means of expressing individual grievances. As China became more open, the outside world began to learn about the views expressed at this location. In April, four members of an active group named the Human Rights Alliance were arrested for putting up wall posters denouncing China's "bureaucratic system and its monsters." The government ordered the removal of all posters considered antigovernment or anti-Communist.

Of great embarrassment to the government were the groups of petitioners--totaling more than 10,000--who, in the summer, travelled to Beijing seeking redress for a variety of grievances. They complained of unemployment, shortages of housing and food, and injustices dating back to the Cultural Revolution. The government appointed 1,000 officials to investigate their complaints, accompany them back to their home districts, and help resolve their problems. By the year's end, the Democracy Wall had become a liability to the government. An alternative site, some distance away and less publicly accessible, was designated with explicit provisions for posters. In October and November, the trial of China's most famous dissenter, Wei Jingsheng, took place. Accused of both giving a Western correspondent military information about the Vietnamese campaign and slandering the Chinese state, Wei was convicted after a one-day trial and sentenced to fifteen years in prison. This sentence was upheld on appeal.

In July, the National People's Congress adopted a new criminal code and a law of criminal prcedure barring arbitrary prosecutions. The new code restricted political prosecution by defining a counterrevolutionary offense as an act committed, and not just as thoughts harbored, against the dictatorship of the proletariat and the socialist system. It also declared that everyone, regardless of rank, was equal before the law. The new criminal procedure law stated that the family of a detained person must be notified of the arrest within twenty-four hours and that the courts must try the case within six months. Defendants had the right to a lawyer, and the courts were ordered to rely on hard evidence, not just confessions, in reaching a verdict. The new laws were intended to quell fears of prosecution so that intellectuals and professionals could devote themselves more freely to building the country. Since July, television, newspapers, and radio had devoted considerable time to these provisions. They were presented as measures of protection for the individual and as the rights of individuals in the socialist society.

As an attempt to enlist the talents and experience of former industrialists in the nation's modernization plans, the government announced, in late January, that the rights of the business class would be fully restored. Assets and bank accounts confiscated during the Cultural Revolution were to be returned, with interest. Businessmen could return to their requisitioned homes, and their children would not be discriminated against in schools or jobs. Their professional titles would be restored, and those with special talents would be given political advancements. The rights policy was then extended to former landowners and "counterrevolutionaries" whose holdings had been seized during the Cultural Revolution and who had been subjected to continued discrimination. According to reports from Beijing, members of these groups had been reformed and should no longer be treated as part of a subclass.

In 1978, as part of the effort to make China a powerful and prosperous nation by the end of the twentieth century, the government launched the Four Modernizations Program for industry, agriculture, defense, and science and technology. Although rapid economic growth was projected at first, a more moderate approach was adopted during 1979. The war against Vietnam required increases in the military budget, and thus made difficult the vast purchase of imported technologies. There also proved to be an insufficient number of technicians and skilled workers to handle the sophisticated foreign equipment. In May, Chen Yun began readjusting the nation's economic plans and looking toward a more gradual and balanced growth. On June 18, before the National People's Congress, Chairman Hua Guofeng admitted that "some of the measures we adopted were not prudent enough."

The original development program called for the construction of 120 new facilities, including ten steel plants, nine nonferrous metal complexes, ten oil and gas fields, thirty power stations, eight coal mines, six new railways, and five harbors--all to be completed by 1985 at a cost of $75 billion a year. It soon became apparent, however, that although China had an abundant supply of natural resources, the plan was simply too ambitious for a poor country. By mid-1979, Beijing was partaking in a slower development program and concentrating on only the most-needed projects. The construction of steel mills and the development of other heavy industries were reduced substantially. The projected industrial growth for 1979 was revised down from ten to eight percent. The nation's overall budget for 1979 projected total revenues of $70.7 billion, with approximately equal expenditures. However, a deficit was expected.

With seventy-five percent of the Chinese population living on farms, the role of agriculture in economic growth was increasingly recognized. To spur agricultural output, Beijing adopted the following measures: it raised the prices of grains to give peasants twenty percent more money for their produce; it reduced the tax on harvests and the prices of chemical fertilizers and farm equipment; and it encouraged peasants to seek profits from both produce grown on their private land, and sideline activities such as fishing and raising poultry. The government projected a four-percent growth in agricultural output for 1979.

With the population of China increasing at a rate of 1.5 percent a year and reaching 950 million by 1979, Beijing took measures to discourage a further population growth. These measures involved taxation and economic sanctions against couples with more than two children. The government's intention was to reduce population growth to five births per 1,000 people by 1985. Meanwhile, the rapid growth of the population had serious economic repercussions. According to an official estimate, about ten percent of China's population did not have enough food in 1979, and about twenty million workers were unemployed. Despite its primary commitment to industrial growth, the government found it necessary to help raise the standard of living by increasing state investments in agriculture and light industries.

To attract foreign investment, Beijing guaranteed profits to foreign participants in joint-venture enterprises in China. Foreign companies were allowed to repatriate part of their profits and to employ outside managers, engineers, and accountants. In addition, during the June National People's Congress meetings, the Chinese adopted specific legislation called the Law of the People's Republic of China on Joint Ventures Using Chinese and Foreign Investment. This was adopted on July 1, 1979 by the Second Session of the Fifth National People's Congress. This law, together with innovative insurance provisions formed by the Chinese People's Insurance Company against political turmoil, represented efforts by the authorities to give confidence to foreign investors. In addition, special zones for foreign factories were being established. So far, the plans seemed attractive to overseas Chinese investors who were apparently more comfortable in the development of business contracts. While other foreign investors remained cautious, the general consensus was that the law was more promising than many had expected. China's exports for the first seven months of 1979 rose to $4.64 billion, a forty-percent increase over the same period in 1978. Imports increased by seventy percent to a total of $5.6 billion, leaving a trade deficit of nearly $1 billion.

After thirty years of what Deng called the "abnormal state of Sino-US relations," China and the United States established formal diplomatic ties on January 1, 1979. At the same time, the United States severed diplomatic relations with Taiwan and terminated its mutual defense treaty with the Chinese Nationalist government. US President Jimmy Carter acknowledged that Taiwan was part of China but made it clear that normalization with Beijing would not jeopardize the well-being of Taiwan. The United States would maintain commercial, cultural, and other relations with Taiwan through nongovernmental means.

China's decision to speed up normalization with the West was influenced by two considerations: the fear of encirclement by the new Soviet-Vietnamese alliance and the desire to achieve economic modernization by expanded trade with the US. Beijing reduced its opposition to the policy of sending US arms supplies to Taiwan, and although Beijing refused to rule out the use of force in recovering the island, a number of conciliatory gestures in the interest of peaceful

unification were made. It was this subtle change in policy
which at last brought about the normalization sought by
President Richard M. Nixon during his visit to China in
1972.

On January 28, Senior Deputy Premier Deng Xiaoping
arrived in the United States for a nine-day visit to discuss
global problems and cooperation between the two countries.
Deng was given a full-dress welcome on the White House
lawn, honored at a formal state dinner, and made the guest
of honor at a gala performance at Washington's Kennedy
Center. In statements to the media, Deng criticized any
US-Soviet strategic arms agreement that might be signed,
and called for curbs on Soviet expansionism. Although he
was perhaps more moderate in private conferences with
President Carter, Deng made it clear that China differed
considerably from the United States in its perception of Soviet designs. On the whole, Deng's talks with President
Carter were fruitful, and his genial response and pleasant
manner generated much enthusiasm among the American public. In a joint communiqué issued on February 1, the two
governments stated their opposition to efforts by any country to establish "hegemony or domination" over others.
Hegemony is the term commonly used by the Chinese to re-
fer to Soviet expansionism.

On January 31, Carter and Deng signed a series of
agreements on scientific and cultural exchanges. These included an overall pact on cooperation in science and technology, a separate accord on cooperation in the field of high-
energy physics, an agreement on space technology that
would enable China to enlist the aid of the US National Aeronautics and Space Administration (NASA) in launching a
civilian communications satellite, an agreement aimed at increasing cultural contacts in a variety of fields, a scientific
agreement calling for student exchange programs, and an
interim agreement providing for the establishment of American Chinese consulates in Shanghai and Guangdong and for
Chinese consulates in Houston and San Francisco.

Deng left Washington on February 1 for visits to Atlanta, Houston, and Seattle. On February 5, he left Seattle
for China. He issued a statement of warm thanks to the
American people, saying that he looked forward to "everlast-
ing friendship and cooperation" between China and the
United States.

In early May, US Secretary of Commerce Juanita M. Kreps arrived in Beijing to help restore full trade relations between China and the United States. The May 11 negotiators overcame a major obstacle by agreeing on settlements of mutual, preexisting financial claims in both the public and private sectors. On May 14, the two nations reached a trade agreement that would be the foundation of full economic cooperation. China would be granted a most-favored-nation trading status and tariff restrictions on Chinese exports to the United States would be significantly lowered. The amount of Chinese textiles exported to the United States was still to be worked out, however, and the accord required final approval by the US Congress.

To reassure China of continued American friendship and support, Vice President Walter Mondale visited Beijing on August 25. The vice president told the Chinese that "a strong and secure and modernized China" was in the interest of Americans and that the United States was committed to joining China in advancing their "many parallel strategic and bilateral interests." Mondale and Chinese leaders signed a cultural exchange pact and an agreement for the United States to help China develop hydroelectric power.

On October 15, Chairman Hua Guofeng arrived in Paris to begin a twenty-three-day, four-country tour of Western Europe. It was the first visit to Western Europe ever made by a Chinese head of government. At welcoming ceremonies in Paris, Hua noted Europe's "pivotal role in international affairs" and urged that France and China strengthen their cooperation in opposing foreign (Soviet) aggression. Hua's next stop was Bonn, West Germany, where government officials, anxious to improve relations with Moscow, had hoped that Hua would not continue with his anti-Soviet rhetoric. In Munich, however, Hua called on Western Europe to bolster its military strength against hegemony, or Soviet domination. It was in Great Britain, though, where Hua delivered his strongest attack on the Soviets. On October 28, at a dinner with Prime Minister Margaret Thatcher, Hua implicitly compared the USSR to the Nazis and identified it as the major threat to world peace. Arriving in Rome on November 3 for the last leg of his tour, Hua conferred with Prime Minister Francesco Cossiga and then travelled to Venice to visit the house of Marco Polo. Back in Rome he met informally with Enrico Berlinguer, head of the Italian Communist party. Hua returned to China on November 6.

The normalization of relations between the United States and China was a source of deep concern to the Soviet Union. Russia was especially displeased with the joint Sino-American communiqué condemning "hegemony." The Soviet Union loomed large in the background of China's military action against Vietnam. Beijing considered the Soviet-Vietnamese alliance a threat to China's security. When Chinese forces attacked Vietnam in February, Moscow warned Beijing to stop "before it is too late." Although Soviet planes and ships were rushing military supplies to Vietnam, no Soviet military activity was reported along the Chinese border.

Relations between China and Vietnam had been deteriorating since 1978, with Hanoi's harsh treatment of its ethnic-Chinese minority and its invasion of Cambodia, an ally of China. Increasingly frequent border incidents heightened the tension and finally convinced Beijing that Hanoi "must be taught a lesson." On February 17, 1979, China launched a major attack along its 500-mile (805 km) border with Vietnam. Supported by artillery and tanks, Chinese forces invaded four Vietnamese provinces.

On February 21, after a brief pause to renew supplies, the Chinese resumed their advance in the direction of Lang Son in northwest Vietnam. By March 2, the Chinese had penetrated some 25 miles (40 km) into Vietnamese territory, and had taken Lang Son, Cao Bang, and Lao Cai. Having reached its goal, Beijing announced that its forces were withdrawing to Chinese territory. The withdrawal was completed by March 16, when Vietnam offered to hold talks to ensure peace along the border and ultimately to normalize relations. The first two sessions, held in Hanoi in April, immediately arrived at a deadlock. Subsequent meetings during the year also served merely as an opportunity to exchange accusations. The main difficulty in the negotiations involved Hanoi's refusal to consider the Chinese demand that Vietnamese forces be withdrawn completely from Cambodia. The two weeks of action constituted a test for China's largely untested military forces, and there was reason to believe that the performance of the Chinese troops and leadership was not at all what had been expected.

In addition to Soviet, Vietnamese, and American bilateral relations, Sino-Japanese relations showed progress.

Visits between the two countries by large friendship delegations continued. Japanese authorities agreed to organize
and finance the preparation of students in China who were
to study in Japanese universities, and exchanges between
top-ranking officials of both countries continued. The
Chinese encouragement of increased Japanese self-defense
efforts reflected China's concern with the growing Soviet
naval presence in Northeast Asia. Despite a setback early
in the year when Chinese authorities called for renegotia-
tions of arrangements between the two countries, the visit
of Japanese Prime Minister Ohira in December and the economic agreements that grew out of this visit indicated the
success the Japanese had in combining their business and
social concerns. By the end of the year it seemed clear
that Japanese enterprises and the Japanese government had
established a firm foundation for future developments. Japan
awaited a promised visit by Chairman Hua Guofeng.

In 1979, thirty years after the establishment of the
People's Republic of China, the Chinese political scene involved a party hierarchy that was more stable at the top
than it had been at any other time since the overthrow of
the Gang of Four in October 1976. At the same time, resistance to new policies and ideas continued to be strong at
the middle and lower levels. In the field of foreign affairs,
there still remained stresses and strains on Chinese policy.
The costs of the Vietnam incident were high in terms of
men, materials, and international favor, but China had made
the decision to pay the price.

January 1 The People's Daily New Year's Day editorial focussed on the need to shift the emphasis of party work
to socialist modernization, the theme of the recently
held Third Plenum of the Eleventh CCP Central Committee. It drew attention to the disparity in productivity between Chinese levels and those achieved in advanced economies, including such examples as grain
production, in which China's attainments fell far short
of those in the United States, and steel production, in
which a Chinese worker averaged only ten tons output
a year compared with 300 tons by Japanese workers.
It also indicated that on China's railways, steam engines still accounted for eighty percent of the total

number of locomotives, and went on to state that China was between fifteen and twenty years behind in most fields of science and technology. Noting in particular Japan's economic advance, the editorial also reiterated specific points about improving management and systems, and the need to import advanced technology and to utilize foreign funds.

• China and the US formally established diplomatic relations at the ambassadorial level. President Carter, Premier Hua Guofeng, and Vice Premier Deng Xiaoping exchanged messages of mutual congratulations.

• The message from the Standing Committee of the Fifth NPC stated that from January 1, 1979 the PLA was ordered to stop its bombardment of the offshore islands. The message called for an end to the state of military confrontation along the Taiwan Straits to create the conditions in which contact and exchanges could take place to end the artificial separation of Taiwan from the motherland.

• Vice Premier Deng Xiaoping emphasized both themes of the New Year's Day editorial and the message to Taiwan in his speech delivered at the meeting of the National Committee of CPPCC.

• In Taiwan, President Jiang Jingguo called for continued struggle against the Chinese Communists and said, "We will talk with the mainland only when a democratic system is emerging across the Taiwan Straits."

• Vice Premier Deng Xiaoping was named Time magazine's "Man of the Year" for 1978.

• The People's Daily published a letter from Chairman Mao Zedong to Guo Moruo, written in Yanan on November 21, 1944. The publication was regarded as illustrating his modesty in dealing with others, his welcoming criticism and his acknowledgement of his own fallibility.

• According to a decision of the State Council, all Chinese publications and documents in English, French, German, Spanish and other languages published in China, from January 1, 1979 started using the Hanyu Pinyin system of Romanization.

• An archaeological exhibition was opened in Beijing. On display were more than 2,000 exhibits chosen from among 10,000 items unearthed since 1974, mainly from the tombs of two kings of the Zhongshan State during the Warring State period (405–221 B.C.).

January 2 Vice Premier Deng Xiaoping met the US Congressional delegation led by Democratic Representative
Thomas Ludlow Ashley. Deng told them "China would
adopt a realistic attitude toward solving the Taiwan
question."
   • Vice Premier Li Xiannian left Beijing on an official
goodwill tour to Tanzania, Mozambique, Zambia and
Zaire. He returned to Beijing via Pakistan on January
22. In the course of his visits he explained the Chinese position on Indo-China and reaffirmed China's
support for the Patriotic Front and SWAPO in their respective struggles for the liberation of Zimbabwe (Rhodesia) and Namibia. In Mozambique he met Robert
Mugabe on January 11 and was said to have pledged to
send further arms and military advisers to help train
Mugabe's forces so as to step up the guerrilla war.
While in Zambia he met SWAPO representatives, but the
other leader of the Patriotic Front, Mr. Nkomo, was
said to have refused to meet him because of his (Nkomo)
close connections with Cuba and the Soviet Union. At
press conferences in Tanzania on January 7 and 8, he
expressed high admiration for the way the front line
states, including Angola, had supported the struggles
of the people in southern Africa without ever flinching
from national sacrifices called for in the effort. He
called upon Britain and the United States to exert
heavy pressure on South Africa and Rhodesia and to
compel them to make essential concessions so as to
truly meet the demands of the Zimbabwean and Namibian
peoples for national independence. At the same time
he called for the continuation of armed struggle to com-
plement the negotiations. Vice Premier Li continued to
criticize foreign interference in Africa. But he was
pleased to be able to support the moves for the normalization of relations between Angola and Zaire. This
paved the way for Chinese overtures to Angola to normalize their relations and two days later the Angolan
government accepted China's invitation to begin talks
towards this end.

January 3 Hu Yaobang was appointed general secretary of
the CCP Central Committee and took over the duties
of former Propaganda Director Zhang Pinghua, who
was dismissed.
   • Chairman Hua Guofeng met the Bangladesh-China
Friendship Delegation, led by Mirza Guhulam Hafiz.

January 4 The Central Commission for Inspecting Discipline of the CCP held its first plenary session in Beijing January 4-22.

January 5 At a conference in Beijing with American correspondents, Vice Premier Deng Xiaoping called for UN intervention in Cambodia, and expressed his hope that Taiwan would be reunited with China within a year.

• The Ministry of Foreign Affairs sent a note to the Embassy of Vietnam in Beijing, lodging a strong protest with the Vietnamese side against its continual expulsion of inhabitants of Vietnam into China's territory. The note demanded that Vietnam adopt immediately measures to take back these inhabitants.

• Chairman Hua Guofeng met the President of the European Parliament Emilio Colombo. Vice Premier Deng Xiaoping met him on the following day.

January 6 China and Sudan signed a protocol in Khartoum to send a Chinese medical team to Sudan.

• Prince Norodom Sihanouk arrived in Beijing for a short stay en route to New York to attend the Security Council meeting. He and his delegation were met by Vice Premier Deng Xiaoping at the airport. Vice Premier Deng declared: "The Chinese government and people firmly support Kampuchea in its just struggle against Vietnamese aggression." Chairman Hua Guofeng met the delegation on January 8.

January 7 The Chinese government issued a statement denouncing Vietnam's "massive war of aggression" against Cambodia. After the fall of Phnom Penh, NCNA denounced the new "puppet regime" of Heng Samrin.

• The Nippon Light Metal Company signed a contract with two trading firms to supply $150 million worth of aluminum smelting equipment and technology. The plant was to be built in Qiuyang and to be commissioned in March 1987, producing 80,000 tons a year.

• NCNA reported that a Palaeolithic site dating back between 400,000 and 500,000 years was discovered within the boundaries of Shanchengzi people's commune in the foothills of Changbai mountains in Liaoning province.

January 8 Tens of thousand of people took part in a demonstration marking the anniversary of the death of former

Premier Zhou Enlai. The People's Daily published many
articles by the older generation of revolutionaries to
commemorate his death.
   • China and Djibouti established diplomatic relations
at the ambassadorial level.
   • China and Bulgaria signed the 1979 goods exchange
and payment agreement.

January 9 The magazine Tansuo (Explorations), whose editor was Wei Jingsheng, went on sale for the first time.
   The third and last issue was dated March 11, 1979.
   • Vice Premier Deng Xiaoping met the US Senate
   Delegation, headed by Democratic Senator Nunn.
   • Guo Genglian, party secretary of Dazhai Production Brigade in Shanxi province told Xinhua (NCNA)
   that "the brigade was examining its work of past years
   in the light of the newly adopted decision of the CCP
   to shift the focus of work to China's modernization.
   We have to overcome arrogance which has impeded our
   progress."

January 10 The place where Mao Zedong and Zhou Enlai
   lived and worked from November 22, 1947 to March 21,
   1948 in Yangjiagou, Shanxi province, was renovated
   and opened to the public.

January 11 China and Czechoslovakia signed the 1979 goods
   exchange and payment agreement in Prague.
   • Taiwan Premier Y.S. Sun said in Taipei that the
   unification sought must be one that could promote
   peace, advance human welfare, implement democratic
   and constitutional government, safeguard human rights,
   and encourage a free economy and respect for private
   ownership of property.
   • Chen Chu spoke at the Security Council meeting
   which had been called to consider Vietnamese aggression against Democratic Kampuchea. He said that the
   Security Council should declare that Vietnam's aggression constituted a threat to international peace and
   security, call on Vietnamese troops to withdraw and if
   they failed to do so, the Security Council should meet
   again "to consider the adoption of effective measures
   in accordance with the relevant provisions of the United
   Nations Charter."

January 12   Ieng Sary arrived in Beijing and was received
by Vice Premier Deng Xiaoping.
  • On January 14, a government statement reaffirmed
that the Chinese government and people would "do their
utmost to support and aid the Kampuchean people in
every way."

January 13   Vice Premier Deng Xiaoping met Thai Deputy
Prime Minister Sunthorn Hongladarom and his party.
Chairman Hua Guofeng met him on January 15.
  • Two hundred twenty-one pieces of Paleolithic artifacts discovered in Mbeya region of Southwest Tanzania
by the Chinese coalfield exploration team were officially
handed over to Tanzania.
  • The People's Daily reaffirmed that disciplinary action would be taken against anyone who violated party
members' democratic rights or retaliated against critics.

January 14   In Beijing, Chinese and Thai representatives
signed a protocol under which China could supply Thailand with crude oil every year from 1979 to 1983. The
supply would be about 700,000 tons of crude oil in
1979, about 900,000 tons in 1980 and one million tons
a year thereafter.
  • Vice Premier Deng Xiaoping met the Japanese
House of Councilor Delegation, led by Speaker Ken
Yasuri. Chairman Hua Guofeng met the delegation on
the same day.
  • Premier Hua Guofeng sent a message to Yasir Arafat, congratulating him on the convening of the Fourteenth Meeting of the Palestinian National Council held
in Damascus.

January 15   China and France signed a three-year scientific
basic research cooperation agreement in Paris.
  • NCNA reported that a tooth fossil of an ape-man
of approximately the same period as Beijing Man (Homo
Erectus Pekinensis) was recently discovered by archaeologists near Yunyang in Henan province.

January 16   China and Zambia signed an agreement on scientific and technical cooperation in Lusaka.
  • China and Hungary signed the 1979 goods exchange
and payment agreement in Budapest.
  • Special committees were set up to draft a criminal

code, a civil code, and a law on legal procedure to be submitted to the Standing Committee of the NPC for examination, adoption, and promulgation.

• The journal Poetry carried a poem by Mao Zedong written during the Long March in 1935 in praise of Peng Dehuai, and twenty-five poems written by Tao Zhu between 1935 and 1969.

January 17 All Beijing newspapers gave front-page prominence to the revised regulations on awards for inventions. The regulations stipulated that to qualify, an invention must be a new important scientific or technical achievement and fulfill three conditions: (1) no one has done it before; (2) it is advanced; (3) it has been proved in practice to be usable.

• NCNA reported that the China Currency Manufacturing Company would issue 1,500 sets of commemorative gold medals. Each set consisted of four medals, struck in the form of coins, with the designs of four scenic spots in Beijing, namely, the Great Wall, the White Dagoba of the Beihai Park (the Winter Palace), Qi Nian Dian (pavillion of prayer for good harvests) in the Temple of Heaven, and the Summer Palace.

• US Secretary of State Cyrus Vance said that the establishment of US-China relations enhanced "significantly the prospects for stability and peace in Asia and the Pacific," and stressed that normalization of US-China diplomatic relations did not threaten any other country.

January 18 Foreign correspondents in China reported considerable activity regarding wall posters and small-scale newspapers. A "human rights activist," Fu Yuehua, was reported to have been arrested on January 18 and to have gone on a hunger strike in a Beijing prison. She was a municipal worker, closely involved in unofficial campaigns for free speech and democratic reforms.

• China and Cuba signed the 1979 trade protocol in Beijing.

January 19 NCNA reported that some 90,000 tourists came to China in 1978 compared to only 50,000 in the previous year.

• In 1978, People's Daily claimed that since the campaign against China had started, Vietnamese authorities had expelled over 170,000 Chinese residents to China, including Vietnamese citizens of Chinese origin and Vietnamese people.

January 20 Su Yu called for emancipation of thinking and democracy in military studies. He said, "The basic principles of guiding warfare set forth by Comrade Mao Zedong are still applicable to today's objective conditions. But they must be applied flexibly in light of actual conditions. Some principles which no longer fit actual conditions must be changed, and there must be new solutions and new answers about which Comrade Mao Zedong never spoke to questions arising in future wars."

• Foreign Minister Van der Klauw of the Netherlands visited China January 18-25. He met Chairman Hua Guofeng on January 20, and signed a civil aviation agreement on the same day to establish a regular air service between the two nations.

• On his way home from Africa, Vice Premier Li Xiannian visited Karachi, Pakistan January 20-22.

• China and East Germany signed the 1979 goods exchange and payment agreement in Beijing.

• China and Zaire signed a protocol in Kinshasa, Zaire involving China supplying diversified commodities to Zaire.

January 21 Shanghai Municipal Council decided to allow "religious patriotic organizations" to resume their activities.

• The report in the People's Daily described the "five-fixes-and-one-reward" system in the production team in Guangdong province.

January 22 China and Poland signed the 1979 goods exchange and payment agreement.

• The People's Daily printed on the front page an editorial entitled "An Important Decision to Accelerate Agricultural Development" (adopted by the Third Plenum of the Eleventh Central Committee of the CCP). It emphasized the positive roles of private plots, sideline occupations and village fairs.

• The Central Committee of the CCP announced measures to revive the policy toward the national bourgeoisie: (1) all private houses should be returned to their owners; (2) their talents in engineering, technology and management should be brought into play and such professional titles as engineer, technician and technical adviser, be given to those qualified; (3) those who perform their duties well could be commended as advanced producers or advanced individuals; (4) their material benefits should be improved. They should get fifty to seventy percent of their wages while on sick leave as was stipulated; (5) they could collect fixed interest which they should have cashed in before September 1966 but did not; (6) no discrimination was allowed against their children with regard to admission to the party, the Communist Youth League and schools and employment; (7) they would recover huge sums in bank deposits and property confiscated with the approval of Lin Biao and the Gang of Four during the Cultural Revolution.

January 23 Prime Minister Gaston Thorn of Luxembourg visited China from January 23-29. Vice Premier Deng Xiaoping held a welcoming banquet in his honor on January 24. Chairman Hua Guofeng met him on January 25.

January 24 Vice Premier Deng Xiaoping met Hedley Donovan, editor-in-chief of Time magazine and his assistant March Clark, head of the bureau of Time in Hong Kong.
     • China began negotiations in Washington and Brussels on textile export quotas vital to its trade balance projections.
     • On production teams, the People's Daily stated that integrating the right of ownership with those of use, production and distribution and vesting all four rights in the basic accounting unit was conducive to developing the productive forces.

January 25 The Ministry of Foreign Trade explained how direct trade with Taiwan could be expanded in various ways. China could supply special local products such as wine, tea, porcelain, and herbal medicines, while China would purchase Taiwanese industrial and agricultural products such as television sets, tape recorders, sugar, bananas, and pineapples. China would also purchase industrial products from Taiwan manufactured from raw materials imported from China. Payments could be made in mutually acceptable currencies. Residents of Taiwan were invited to the Guangzhou Fair.

January 26   Lai Yali told the UNDP Governing Council in New York that the UNDP should stop giving aid to Vietnam while Vietnam was continuing its policy of aggression against Kampuchea.

January 27   Vice Premier Deng Xiaoping left Beijing to visit the US, the first visit by a Chinese leader to the US since the founding of the PRC in 1949.
   • The former governor of Macao, Pedro García Leandro, declared in Lisbon that Macao was not a national territory, but on the other hand one must also bear in mind that China was not interested in the integration of Macao. He meant that there would be no change in the present status of Macao in the next few years.

January 28   NCNA announced the "recent" CCP Central Committee Decision on the Question on Removing the Designations of Landlords and Rich Peasants and on the Class Status of the Children of Landlords and Rich Peasants, under which all people in the mentioned categories who had remolded themselves should be regarded as normal commune members, and not as bad elements.
   • The Central People's Broadcasting Station broadcasted on January 28 and February 1 a number of songs and pieces of music performed by Taiwan artists. The Taiwan music was chosen from records presented by overseas Chinese over the past few years.
   • The People's Daily printed, on the front page, an editorial stressing the need to pay full attention to providing the peasants with immediate benefits. The specific policies included: (1) keeping state grain purchases stable, and keeping such purchases from being excessive; (2) reducing the difference caused by raising the purchase price for agricultural products and lowering the selling price for industrial products; (3) increasing the state investment in agriculture and providing more loans for rural collectives; (4) giving priority to difficult and backward areas by providing financial, material and other assistance for agriculture.

January 29 Vice Premier Deng Xiaoping visited the US from
        January 29 to February 4. He met President Jimmy
        Carter in the White House on January 29 and told him
        the two nations were "duty bound" to help maintain
        peace and stability in the world. On January 31, he
        signed, with President Carter, a cultural agreement as
        well as an agreement on scientific and technological co-
        operation (covering agriculture, energy, space, health,
        environment, earth sciences, engineering and other
        areas of science and technology), a high-energy phys-
        ics agreement and consular agreement were also signed
        that day. The two countries agreed to set up a joint
        commission on scientific and technical cooperation to
        meet annually in each country alternately. President
        Carter announced that American consulates would be
        opened in Shanghai and Guangzhou, while Chinese con-
        sulates would be opened in Houston and San Francisco.
        Hundreds of students would be exchanged. On Janu-
        ary 31, Deng told American journalists that Vietnam
        had been provoking the Chinese side along its border,
        including making troop movements. He commented,
        "...but as to actions to take, we will have to wait and
        see. I can only say two things: one, that for us
        Chinese, we mean what we say, and the second, we
        Chinese do not act rashly. Deng also assured Amer-
        ican Chinese that they would be allowed to visit their
        families in China, and that those relatives in turn
        could visit them in the US. The joint communiqué is-
        sued on February 1 after Deng's discussion in Washing-
        ton reaffirmed their opposition "to efforts by any coun-
        try or group of countries to establish hegemony or
        domination over others, and that they are determined
        to make a contribution to the maintenance of interna-
        tional peace, security and national independence." In
        addition to the several agreements signed during the
        visit, the two sides agreed to conclude trade, aviation,
        and shipping agreements which were to be discussed
        during the forthcoming visits to China by the Secre-
        taries of Treasury Michael Blumenthal, and of Com-
        merce, Juanita Kreps. President Carter accepted an
        invitation to visit China at a convenient time, and the
        president, in turn, invited Chairman Hua Guofeng to
        visit the United States; this was also accepted. Deng
        visited Atlanta, Houston, and Seattle after leaving
        Washington. In Georgia, he inspected a Ford Motor

plant and in Texas he visited oil corporations as well
as a rodeo. In Seattle, he visited the Boeing aircraft
complex. Deng met former President Richard Nixon on
January 31 in Washington and Prince Norodom Sihanouk
as well.
  • Chairman Hua Guofeng met the Belgrade City
Delegation, led by Zivorad Kovacevic, president of the
Belgrade City Assembly.

January 31 NCNA reported that the first phase of a mining
and ore dressing project for a large tin mine with reserves of 800,000 tons was almost completed. Situated
in a mountainous area in South China's Guangxi Zhuang
autonomous region, the mining area extended some 100
km.

February 1 Wu Han's Hai Rui Baguan (The Dismissal of
Hai Rui) was restaged in Beijing.
  • The importance of collective leadership by the
Party Committee at all levels was stressed in a People's
Daily editorial. The editorial said, "All important questions of the Party's line, principles and policies, pro-
motions, appointments, dismissals or transfers of leading cadres must be brought up for collective discussion
and all Party Committee members present at the meetings should fully voice their opinions before any decisions are made. Decisions should not be left to any
individual."

February 2 Rural areas on the outskirts of major cities
should provide ample and varied supplies of fresh
meat, eggs, poultry, fish, milk, vegetables and fruits
for the urban population, according to an article in the
People's Daily. The article said, "Developing these
areas into non-staple food producing centers will help
achieve a brief market and satisfy the needs of city
consumers while also boosting economy in the rural outskirts and increasing peasants' income."

February 4 The People's Daily published, in full, the late
Premier Zhou Enlai's speech to a forum of writers and
artists and a meeting on scenario writing on June 19,
1961.
  • He was quoted as having said, "Socialist freedom
and ease of mind implies allowing people to voice different opinions based on different circumstances."

February 5 NCNA announced that the last link of the Chi-
nese-built Karakoram Highway in Pakistan was being
constructed.
   • A group of thirty-two scientific workers from
China's Academy of Sciences left Beijing and Shanghai
to study and research in the Federal Republic of Germany for one or two years. They were the first group
to win scholarship from Germany's Alexander Von Hum-
boldt Foundation.

February 6 Vice Premier Deng Xiaoping visited Japan February 6-8 on his way home from the US. On February
7, he spent one-and-one-half hours with Prime Minister
Ohira, discussing Vietnam, Cambodia and Korea, among
other issues. He told Prime Minister Ohira that Vietnam must be punished for its expansionism against
Kampuchea.
   • Ding Xuesong, China's first appointed woman ambassador, left Beijing for her post in the Netherlands.

February 7 NCNA reported that the Bank of China had
established correspondent relations with 828 banks and
their 2,277 branches in 139 foreign countries and regions. A total of seventy-five foreign banks sent
delegations to China in 1978.
   • The protocol of the Eighteenth Meeting of China-
Korea Committee for Cooperation in Border Transport
was signed in Sinuiju.
   • Su Zhenhua, member of the CCP Central Committee,
and member of the CCP political bureau, died of a heart
ailment in Beijing at the age of sixty-seven.

February 8 China and Portugal signed a joint communiqué
in Paris to establish diplomatic relations at the ambassadorial level, and agreed that the status of Macao remained unchanged.
   • Vice Premier Deng Xiaoping was greeted at the
airport by Chairman Hua Guofeng and other party and
state leaders when he returned from his visits to the
US and Japan.
   • Ye Jianying, chairman of the Standing Committee
of the Fifth NPC, sent a message to Ben Jeddid Chadli,
extending warm congratulations on his election to the
presidency of the Democratic People's Republic of Algeria.

• The People's Daily editorial entitled "Hold the Great Banner of the National, Democratic and Patriotic United Front," stated: "The Chinese people firmly stand by the Kampuchean people who are victims of aggression, resolutely oppose the aggression and enslavement of weak and small nations by hegemonists, and will give many-sided support to the Kampuchean people who are fighting hard."

February 10   The Ministry of Finance decided to lower taxes on the rural collectives. The new policy was expected to expedite a total income growth of 1,000 million yuan a year in the rural areas. Beginning in 1979, industrial and commercial units belonging to the people's communes and their subdivisions were to be exempt from income taxes if their net annual profits were less than 3,000 yuan as opposed to the old starting point of 600 yuan. The tax rate remained twenty percent as before.

• Premier Hua Guofeng sent a message to President Ziaul Haq of Pakistan appealing for clemency for Mr. Z.A. Bhutto.

• The Ministry of Foreign Affairs sent a note to the Vietnamese Embassy in Beijing, lodging a strong protest against the Vietnamese authorities' military provocations on Chinese borders.

February 11   Chairman Hua Guofeng and Vice Premier Li Xiannian met the Pakistan Military Goodwill Delegation, led by Defense Secretary Lt. General Ghulam Jilani Khan. In the conversation, Vice Premier Li warned the Vietnamese authorities not to turn a deaf ear to what China had said.

February 12   Indian Foreign Minister A.B. Vajpayee began his delayed visit to China, after illness had caused a postponement last October. On his arrival on February 12, Mr. Vajpayee noted that it was the first visit to China by a cabinet minister from India in twenty years. He met Vice Premier Deng Xiaoping on February 14. The official Chinese report quoted Mr. Deng as saying, "As for the boundary question, we can solve it through peaceful consultations. This question should not prevent us from improving our relations in other fields." He met Chairman Hua Guofeng on February 13. He cut

his visit short and returned to India on February 19
when the Chinese invasion of Vietnam took place.

• For the third time in a week, the People's Daily
stressed the need to uphold public and production order and discipline in labor following the recent disturbances in Shanghai and Yunnan. It printed on the
front page a commentator's article urging the people to
foster unity and stability.

• Chairman Hua Guofeng sent a message to President
Josip Broz Tito of Yugoslavia, expressing deep condolences over the death of Comrade Edvard Kardelj.

February 13   A red-carpet welcome was given to Prince
Norodom Sihanouk on his return to Beijing from the
United States.

February 14   Vice Premier Deng Xiaoping told Indian reporters in Beijing regarding the Vietnam situation, that
China "may have to do something that we do not want
to do, if people deny us the wish to live in a peaceful
environment."

• Hanoi released a memorandum on the question of
the so-called "Hoa" or Chinese people in Vietnam. The
memorandum declared that China, from early 1978, had
"enticed and coerced" hundreds of thousands of Hoa
people to go to China in order to cause disorder in
Vietnam. Of the 170,000 Hoa people who had gone to
China, nearly 100,000 came from Quang Ninh province
bordering on China.

• The memorandum also drew attention to various
Western reports to the effect that large Chinese forces
had built up on the Vietnam border, in numbers ranging from 150,000 to 160,000 Chinese soldiers.

February 15   The People's Daily carried an article entitled
"Do Well in Handling People's Letters and Visits and
Promote Stability and Unity," stating that when excessive demands could not be met, some people had caused
disturbances in the name of exercising democratic
rights. It added that democracy was essential but it
must be tempered by centralism and freedom by discipline; citizen's rights had to be balanced by duties.

• President Suharto of Indonesia raised the question
of settling the citizenship of approximately one million
foreigners in Indonesia with the Executive Board of

BKPKB, an association of citizens of Chinese descent. He asked the BKPKB leaders to help remove traces of exclusivism on the part of foreign citizens, both in their way of life and in business.

February 16   The Chinese Foreign Ministry sent a note to the Vietnamese Embassy in Beijing strongly protesting the Vietnamese authorities' dispatch of armed personnel to encroach upon China's territory, to kill Chinese personnel and to raid Chinese trains, all creating new grave incidents of bloodshed.   The note warned the Vietnamese authorities that they should bear full responsibility for all the consequences arising thereof.

• A ceremony was held at Muong Sai in northern Laos to hand over the Laos-China Friendship Textile Mill.   With Chinese aid, construction had begun in March 1978 and was completed at the end of that year with an annual capacity of 300,000 meters of cloth.

• Chairman Hua Guofeng, Vice-Chairmen Ye Jianying, Deng Xiaoping met Prince Norodom Sihanouk, Madam Sihanouk, Samdech Penn Nouth, and Madam Nouth.

• Chen Chu sent a letter to the president of the UN Security Council, strongly condemning the Vietnamese authorities for their wanton armed provocations along the Sino-Vietnamese borders, gravely threatening the security of the southern border of China.   The letter expressed hopes that the United Nations would uphold justice, exercise its functions and authority and take the necessary measures to halt the Vietnamese authorities' armed incursions and provocations against China, to stop their aggression and military occupation of Kampuchea, withdraw all their forces from Kampuchea and immediately cease all their acts jeopardizing the peace and security of Southeast Asia and the whole world.

February 17   The Sixth Session of the Fifth NPC Standing Committee was held in Beijing February 17-23.   The opening session approved the reports on Deng Xiaoping's visit to the US and Li Xiannian's visit to four African nations and Pakistan.

• Hanoi announced that China had launched, early that morning, "an aggressive war" all along the border, shelling cities and towns and attacking deep into Viet-

namese territory.   NCNA declared, in a statement au-
thorized by the Chinese government, that China's frontier troops had been driven past forebearance by Vietnamese provocations over the previous two years and
had been forced to rise in counterattack. The statement called for negotiations to be held quickly over the
border.

February 18 The first Soviet warning against China's invasion of Vietnam appeared in an official government
statement issued by Tass which assured Hanoi that the
Soviet Union would "honor its obligations." This was
modified, however, by a later statement that the heroic
Vietnamese people were capable of standing up for
themselves this time again, and that they had reliable
friends.

February 19 Vietnamese Premier Pham Van Dong and Kampuchean Chieftain Heng Samrin signed the Vietnamese-
Kampuchean treaty of peace, friendship and cooperation
in Phnom Penh. The treaty was denounced by Beijing
as a concrete step taken by Hanoi "to cover up its
crimes of aggression against Kampuchea and to rig up
the Indochinese Federation."
• The People's Daily editorial called for increased
authority for China's enterprises. The list included
independent accounting, accepting leadership from only
one leading department, the right to reject any assistant when no production conditions were given, and the
right to reject any assignment above the state plan
coming from any leading departments. The editorial
said that a system of contracts must be introduced in
all enterprises to ensure the fulfillment of state quotas
and links among supply, producer and purchase units.
Enterprises which break contracts must give compensation and pay fines, it said.

February 20 The three-month training course (organized by
UNIDO in Shanghai) on diesel engines for foreign technicians from a number of developing countries came to
an end.

February 21 At a press conference held in Hanoi, Vietnamese Vice Foreign Minister Nguyen Co Thach flatly
turned down China's negotiation proposal.
• Mr. Roy Jenkins, president of the EEC Commission,

visited China from February 21 to March 1. He met
Vice Premier Deng Xiaoping on February 23 and Pre-
mier Hua Guofeng on the following day. Mr. Jenkins
told a press conference in Beijing that the joint China-
EEC Trade Committee would hold its first meeting in
Beijing on May 3.

February 22   The Nippon Steel Corporation was told that a
cooperation agreement (signed two months earlier)
could not be implemented because no loan was provided
by Japan to furnish the project. It was also reported
that other negotiations on offshore oil development, a
cement plant and similar projects were stalled because
of the Chinese demand for settlement in US dollars instead of yuan.

February 23   NCNA reported that a large tomb containing a
wooden outer coffin dating back 2,100 years was excavated on the outskirts of Changsha, Hunan province.
   • A government reshuffling involving thirteen new
appointments and the dismissal of some ministers, was
confirmed by the Sixth Session of the Fifth NPC Standing Committee.
   • Former Beijing Mayor Peng Zhen was chosen to
head a newly established legal commission under the
Standing Committee of the NPC.
   • "Regulations of the People's Republic of China
governing the Arrest and Detention of Persons Accused
of Crimes" was unanimously adopted at the Sixth Session of the Standing Committee of the Fifth NPC. The
new regulations superseded those adopted at the Third
NPC on December 20, 1954. The objective of the regulations, it was stated, was "to maintain public order
effectively, to punish criminals, safeguard the socialist
system and protect the people's freedom of person and
their homes from encroachment."
   • Chen Chu told the UN Security Council that China
did not want an inch of Vietnamese territory and said
that the Chinese government was prepared to enter into
concrete negotiations on any constructive measures at
once to ensure peace on the border.

February 24   The People's Daily carried Zhou Yang's speech
text in serial (on February 23 and 24), delivered at the
Guangzhou Forum in December 1978, in which he at-

tempted to draw a line between bourgeois liberalization
and the freedom of creation and discussion.

February 25   British Industry Minister Eric Varley arrived
in Beijing to negotiate a trade agreement. On March 4
the two nations signed an agreement on economic cooperation in which the two countries set themselves the
target of $14 billion worth of trade and exchange be-
tween now and 1985.

   • The Chinese Ministry of Education and Scientific
Association gave a reception in Beijing in honor of the
first group of postgraduate students from the US. The
eight scholars would take one-year or two-year courses
in Chinese history and literature of Chinese language
in Chinese institutions of higher learning.

   • The US Secretary of Treasury W. Michael Blumenthal, Mrs. Blumenthal and his party visited China from
February 24 to March 2. He held talks with Chinese
Minister of Finance Zhang Jingfu and exchanged views
with Chinese leaders in economic and trade circles.
He was kept waiting for forty-five minutes to meet
Chairman Hua Guofeng on February 28 following his
criticism of China's action in Vietnam. In his capacity
as President Carter's special envoy, he attended the
inauguration ceremony of the US Embassy in Beijing
on March 1.

February 26   Vice Premier Deng Xiaoping told Takeji Watanabe, president of the Kyodo News Service, that China
would not make Vietnamese withdrawal from Kampuchea
as a condition of a Chinese withdrawal from Vietnam.
He offered the opinion that the "punitive action" would
end in less than the thirty-three days that had been
needed to settle the border problem.

   • The People's Daily front-page article called for
speeding the rehabilitation of cadres at rural grass-
roots units. Under the people's communes throughout
the country, the article said, there were a total of
680,000 production brigades, which were redivided into
4.8 million production teams.

   • The "February Backlash" or "Counter-Current" of
1967 was actually a struggle to defend Chinese Communist party principles and not a move for capitalist restoration, as then charged. This was revealed in a
12,000-word article in the People's Daily.

- The Sino-Yugoslav Mixed Committee for Economic, Scientific and Technical Cooperation held its first meeting in Beijing from February 26 to March 2.

February 27 Leonard Woodcock, head of the US liaison office in Beijing, was confirmed by the Senate as ambassador, and presented his credentials to Ye Jianying, chairman of the Standing Committee of the NPC, on March 7.
  - NCNA reported that Chinese medical workers had developed an oral contraceptive for men. Gossypol-- a phenolic substance obtained from the root, stem and seeds of cotton. Trial use by over 10,000 healthy men gave an effective rate of up to 99.89 percent.
  - China and Mexico signed a protocol, in Beijing, on the fourth conference of the two nations' scientific and technical cooperation.
  - The Third Session of the Nepal-China Boundary Joint Inspection Committee was held in Katmandu from January 10 to February 27 to discuss matters related to drawing a new Nepal-China topographic boundaries map on the scale of 1:50,000.

February 28 NCNA reported that five new hotels for foreign tourists were being built in Nanjing, Zhengzhou, Xian, Nanning and Kunming, with total accommodation space for 3,200 people. Foreign Minister Huang Hua held talks with Hassan Mohamed Al Tohamy, special envoy of Egyptian President Sadat in Beijing. Vice Premier Deng Xiaoping met him on February 28, and Chairman Hua Guofeng met him on the following day.
  - Vice Premier Deng Xiaoping met Jay Hammond, Governor of Alaska.
  - People of all walks of life in China's Taiwan province would be invited to visit the mainland, and arrangements would be made to organize people of all walks of life on the mainland to visit Taiwan. This announcement was made at the meeting in Beijing commemorating the thirty-second anniversary of the February 28 Uprising in Taiwan.

March 1 China and the US formally opened embassies in each other country's capital. Chai Zemin, the first newly appointed Chinese ambassador to the US, presented his credentials to President Jimmy Carter at the White House.

• Vice President Walter F. Mondale received Dang
Ge, special envoy of the Chinese government and minister for metallurgical industry, at the White House.

• The Chinese Ministry of Foreign Affairs sent a
note to the Vietnamese Embassy in Beijing proposing
"concrete negotiations on ending the current border
conflict at the level of vice-minister of foreign affairs."

• The Revolutionary Committee of Sichuan province
issued a series of measures on family planning. The
measures provided for working parents with only one
child who agreed not to have a second to receive five
yuan a month in child welfare subsidies.

March 2 The Vietnamese Foreign Ministry replied to the
Chinese proposal that it was ready to hold negotiations
once the Chinese "immediately, completely and uncondi-
tionally withdraw their troops across to the other side
of the historical borderline."

• Chairman Hua Guofeng met the Yugoslav Government Delegation, led by Branislav Ikonic, vice president
of the Federal Executive Council. Agreements and a
protocol were signed, including an agreement on scientific and technological cooperation, an agreement on cooperation in veterinary science, and a protocol of the
first meeting of the Sino-Yugoslav Joint Committee for
Economic, Scientific and Technological Cooperation.

• The thirty-year deadlock over mutual "frozen"
claims and assets was settled. Mr. Blumenthal and
Zhang Jingfu initialled an agreement whereby claims by
US citizens and businessmen against China dating back
to 1949 would be settled at forty-one cents per dollar.
China would thus pay $80 million to the US Treasury
to settle American claims totalling $197 million. On
October 1, the United States, for its part, agreed to
release $80 million of Chinese assets that were frozen
during the Korean War.

March 3 Vice Premier Chen Muhua left Beijing to visit Australia, New Zealand, Fiji and West Samoa.

March 4 The CCP Central Committee decided to hold an exhibition in memory of Comrade Zhou Enlai's birthday
at the Museum of the Chinese Revolution in Beijing.

• Chinese troops completed the seizure of Langson
in northern Vietnam. The Chinese government issued a

statement that "having attained the goals set for them"
the Chinese troops in Vietnam would commence withdrawal that same day.
    • Minister of Foreign Trade Li Wiang left Beijing to
visit Thailand, Malaysia, and Singapore.

March 6 The Shanghai Municipal Security Bureau issued a
    notice, approved by the Shanghai Municipal Revolution-
    ary Committee, ordering all those taking part in demon-
    strations to obey the police and preserve order, and
    to abstain from interfering with railway traffic or put-
    ting up posters except in designated places.
    • The Laotian government accused China of making
provocative military moves on the border, sending spies
into Laos to foment division among minority people
there. On the same day NCNA described the complaints
as groundless.

March 9 Premier Hua Guofeng sent a message to Mohamed
    Benahmed Abdelghani, warmly congratulating him on
    his assumption of the office of Algerian prime minister.

March 10 A ceremony was held in Niamey, Niger, to hand
    over the Niger Kolo agricultural project, developed with
    Chinese aid.
    • NCNA reported that a bronze lantern in the shape
of a human figure was among a number of archaeological
finds unearthed from three tombs of the Han Dynasty
(206 B.C.-228 B.C.) in Zhaoping county, Guangxi
Zhuang autonomous region.
    • The Chinese Ministry of Foreign Affairs protested
to the Laotian ambassador to China against the false
charges (March 6). It added that on March 7, the
Laotian government unilaterally ended the agreement
with China under which Chinese experts were helping
to build highways in northern Laos.

March 11 Vice Premier Deng Xiaoping met outgoing Thai
    Ambassador to China Kasem S. Kassemsri.
    • The Secretary of the Chinese Olympic Committee
Song Zhong accepted a proposal of the International
Olympic Committee in Lausanne to talk to the Taiwan
Sport Organization.

March 13 The Fujian province archaeological team found a

wooden coffin in the shape of a boat, dating back more than 2,000 years, at the famous scenic spot of Wuyi mountain in the northwestern part of the province.

• A change in China's present capital investment system from direct government appropriations to contracted loans under supervision by the Bank of Construction was suggested in an article in the People's Daily.

• Vice Premier Li Xiannian met A.W. Clausen, president of the Bank of America, and his party in Beijing.

• The Boston Symphony Orchestra arrived in Beijing on the first leg of a week-long tour of China. The orchestra was scheduled to give one concert in Shanghai and three more in Beijing, plus a number of lectures and training sessions.

• The People's Daily hinted that the rehabilitation of Liu Shaoqi, the state chairman disgraced during the Cultural Revolution, might be carried further.

March 14   A military Trident aircraft was reported to have crashed on a factory in the outskirts of Beijing, killing forty-four people.

March 15   Premier Hua Guofeng met Governor of Tokyo Ryokichi Minobe, and Chairman of the Metropolitan Assembly Ichiro Kono.

• The Chinese Foreign Ministry, in a note to the Laotian Foreign Ministry, expressed immense regret on the unilateral and unreasonable act of the Laotian government which requested that the Chinese side suspend the construction of the highway from M. Nam Bak to Luang Prabang city and withdraw all Chinese engineers and technicians.

• NCNA reported a recent national conference on the study of religion, held in Kunming, Yunnan province. Attended by over 100 scholars, teachers and cadres, the conference included papers on Buddhism, Lamaism, Islam, Taoism and Christianity.

• The Vietnamese Foreign Ministry issued a note to the Chinese Foreign Ministry declaring Vietnam's willingness to begin vice-ministerial negotiations one week after the complete withdrawal of Chinese troops from Vietnam.

March 16   Foreign Minister Huang Hua told Ambassador Wood-

cock in Beijing that the Chinese Government regarded
the bill in Congress (the Taiwan Act) as contravening
the China-US agreement on establishing diplomatic relations.

• Foreign Minister Huang Hua claimed that the frontier forces of the Chinese PLA in Guangxi and Yunnan,
after attaining their set goals in the self-defensive
counterattack against the Vietnamese aggressors, completed their withdrawal from Vietnam and returned to
Chinese territory on March 16.

• The CCP Central Committee had to readjust the
national economy in view of current material and financial resources; it concluded that the capital construction front was too wide and overextended. The decision received support at a national conference on capital construction. Reports from Beijing indicated a re-
assessment of modernization targets.

• Chen Chu explained his vote in favor of the
vetoed resolution in the Security Council on Vietnam's
aggression. He said that in many ways the draft resolution was unsatisfactory, because it did not condemn
Vietnam for its aggression nor did it state that Vietnam
provoked the Sino-Vietnamese border conflict. He
said that China's vote in favor of it was solely because
the draft resolution called for withdrawal of Vietnamese
troops from Kampuchea.

• In a front-page editorial, the People's Daily demanded state farms to set the pace to modernize agriculture. To this end, said the article, state farms
must: (1) break with the small producer's practice of
growing everything for their own consumption and instead introduce specialized production which would
facilitate mechanization; (2) run industrial or commercial enterprises in line with local conditions; (3) improve management and observe economic acocunting.

March 17   American freighter Letitia Lykes arrived at
Shanghai, the first American merchant ship to call at a
Chinese port in thirty years.

• President J.B. Bagaza of Burundi visited China
from March 17-20. Chairman Hua Guofeng met him on
March 19. The two nations signed an economic and
technical cooperation agreement on the same day.

March 19   Japan and China agreed to extend the eight-year

bilateral trade agreement for an additional five years to last up to 1990. The trade target for the extended thirteen-year period was more than doubled, to between $40 billion and $60 billion.

• Vice Premier Deng Xiaoping met Swiss Public Economic Department Head, Mr. Fritz Honegger.

• The Chinese Foreign Ministry sent a note to the Vietnamese Foreign Ministry, proposing that Sino-Vietnamese negotiations at the level of vice-foreign minister start about March 28 and be held in turn in Hanoi and Beijing, with their first round to be held in Hanoi.

March 21 Sichuan's Gonzui Hydroelectric Power Station, the biggest in Southwest China, was completed and the last generating unit put into operation.

• Vice Premier Deng Xiaoping met seventy-eight-year-old British friend, Mr. Malcolm McDonald.

March 23 NCNA reported that hundreds of "overambitious" projects had been scrapped or cut back in a readjustment of economic plans.

• China and Thailand signed a commercial maritime navigation agreement and two supplementary protocols.

• The People's Daily published the text of a memorandum given by Vice Premier Li Xiannian to Premier Pham Van Dong on June 10, 1977 and set out the background of the border dispute as the Chinese saw it. It quoted a Vietnamese vice foreign minister as having told China formally on June 15, 1956 that "from the historical point of view" the Nansha and Xisha islands were Chinese territory. The change of stand came, Mr. Li declared, in 1974 and 1975 when the Vietnamese side, "using the opportunity of the liberation of southern Vietnam, invaded and occupied six of China's Nansha Islands."

March 26 Vice Premier Deng Xiaoping met the US Congressional Delegation, led by Al Ullman, chairman of the Ways and Means Committee of the House of Representatives.

• Sir Murray Macehose, the governor of Hong Kong, visited Beijing March 26–30, at the invitation of Li Qiang, the minister of Foreign Trade. He met Vice Premier Deng Xiaoping on March 29. An agreement was signed in Guangzhou between the China Light and Power

Company, the Hong Kong utility, and the Guangdong Electric Company for the former to supply a million units of electricity a day to Shumzhun.

• The Chinese Foreign Ministry, in a note to the Vietnamese Foreign Ministry, reiterated that all Chinese frontier troops were withdrawn to Chinese territory as of March 16, without leaving a single soldier on Vietnamese territory.

March 27 NCNA reported that Chinese archaeologists had excavated Wangyin site in southern Shandong province, where there were tombs, the remains of house foundations, storage pits, and human skeletons dating back about 6,000 years. It was a Neolithic site of the early period of Dawengou culture.

March 28 NCNA reported that bank loans would gradually replace direct government appropriations for most future capital investment projects.

March 29 Wei Jingsheng, a major activist in the democracy and human rights movement, was arrested as a counter-revolutionary.

• The Beijing Municipal Revolutionary Committee adopted a public notice ordering public gatherings and demonstrations to obey the police, and banning slogans, large-character posters, publications, and photographs which opposed socialism or disclosed classified information.

• China and Bangladesh signed a protocol on scientific and technical cooperation.

March 31 Jialilue (The Life of Galileo), a play by Brecht, premiered in Beijing. The first contemporary foreign play to be staged in China since 1966, it was directed by Huang Zuolin, seventy-three-year-old head of the Shanghai People's Art Theatre, and translated from the 1957 German edition by Ding Yangzhong.

• The Chinese Foreign Ministry, in a note to the Vietnamese Foreign Ministry, pointed out that the Vietnamese side should respond positively to the repeated Chinese proposals by removing the obstacles it had placed in the way of holding the negotiations.

April 1 The Standing Committee of the Fifth NPC met in

Beijing to review the international situation and China's foreign relations.
• NCNA reported that a conference was held in Beijing March 22-31 to adopt the eight-year plan for the study of law. The 1978-85 national program for the study of law covered 100 items, including the theory of jurisprudence, constitution, civic code, criminal code, code of legal procedures, economic law, international law, and history of the legal system.

April 2 Vice Premier Deng Xiaoping met former Argentine Admiral Emilio Eduardo Massera in Beijing.

April 3 The Standing Committee of the Fifth NPC decided not to extend the Treaty of Friendship, Alliance and Mutual Assistance between the USSR and China, due to expire on April 11, 1980. In notifying the Soviet government of this decision, Foreign Minister Huang Hua proposed negotiations "for the solution of outstanding issues and the improvement of relations between the two countries." He told Soviet Ambassador J.S. Shcherbakov that their differences of principle should not hamper the development of "normal state relations on the basis of the five principles of peaceful co-existence."
• Deputy Prime Minister Goh Keng Swee of Singapore arrived in Beijing for a two-week visit. Chairman Hua Guofeng met him on April 4, and Vice Premier Deng Xiaoping met him on April 5.

April 4 In a note, the Vietnamese Foreign Ministry called for negotiations even if it continued to claim presence of Chinese troops on Vietnamese soil.

April 5 Foreign Minister Huang Hua met Somali Foreign Minister Abdurahman Jama Barre in Beijing. Chairman Hua Guofeng met him on April 7.
• Crowds gathered at Tiananmen Square to mark the anniversary of riots there three years ago.
• In Beijing Vice-Chancellor Zhou Peiyuan of Beijing University and Alfred Bowker, chancellor of the University of California, signed an agreement for academic exchange and cooperation between the two universities. The agreement provided for an exchange of teaching programs, outline of courses, academic journals and

other publications, postgraduate students, and professors and lecturers.

• The 497 Chinese engineers and technicians participating in the Chinese-aided highway construction from
Nam Bak to Luang Prabang in Northern Laos were
called home because of a request from the Laotian government.

• The Lyon Orchestra, led by Francisqua Collomb,
mayor of Lyon, arrived in Beijing for a performance-
tour in China. Under the baton of Serge Baudo and
Sylrain Cambrelling, the orchestra gave eight concerts,
four in Beijing and four in Shanghai, featuring French
composers of the nineteenth and twentieth centuries,
the program included Berlioz's Symphonie Fantastique
and Debussy's La Mer. The orchestra left Shanghai
for Japan on April 18.

April 6   The Chinese Foreign Ministry accepted the invitation by the Vietnamese Foreign Ministry (April 4) and
said that a delegation, led by Vice Foreign Minister
Han Nienlong, would arrive in Hanoi on April 14.

April 8   The National People's Congress Delegation, led by
Deng Yingchao, left Beijing for a twelve-day visit to
Japan. She attended the unveiling of a stele en-
graved with a poem by Premier Zhou Enlai in Arashi
Yama city in Kyoto.

April 9   A spokesman of the Foreign Ministry declared,
"Pakistan's former Prime Minister, Mr. Bhutto, was an
old friend of the Chinese people, who did much to promote Sino-Pakistan friendship. Chinese leaders made
several appeals to grant him clemency. We deeply regret his execution."

April 11   The Chinese People's Political Consultative Conference Delegation, led by Rong Yiren (one of China's
most powerful national capitalists before liberation), left
Beijing to visit the Federal Republic of Germany. The
delegation attended the opening ceremony of the annual
Hanover Fair, and visited companies, factories and research centers in Bonn, Hamburg and Munich.

April 14   Chairman Hua Guofeng met Ilija Vakicm, president
of the Federal Chamber of Economy of Yugoslavia.

• The Sino-Vietnamese talks began in Hanoi. Vietnamese Vice-Foreign Minister Phan Hien called for a
settlement of the border and territorial problems on the
basis of respecting the "status quo of the borderline
left by history and delineated by the 1887 and 1895
conventions," along with mutual withdrawal of armed
forces three to five km from the line of actual control
prior to February 17 in order to form a demilitarized
zone.

April 15 High Mass was held in the Church of Immaculate
Conception in Beijing to celebrate Easter Sunday.
About 500 Chinese and foreign Catholics attended.
• Vice Premier Deng Xiaoping met the American physicist Professor Li Zhengdao and his wife. Dr. Li was
in China for a three-month visit and gave lectures at
the invitation of the Chinese Academy of Sciences.
• NCNA reported that China's oceangoing fleet now
comprised several hundred vessels with a carrying
capacity of several million tons. They included general
cargo ships, bulk cargo carriers, oil tankers, and passenger steamers. When the fleet was first set up in
1961, routes were confirmed to thirteen ports in five
Southeast Asian countries. This has been extended to
400 ports in 100 countries and regions.

April 16 Vice Premier Deng Xiaoping met the delegation of
the Armed Service Committee of the House of Representatives of the United States, led by Committee Chairman
Melvin Price.
• China and the Yemen Arab Republic signed a protocol on sending a Chinese medical team to work in
northern Yemen in Sanaa.
• The ten-member delegation of the Chinese Academy
of Social Science, led by Huan Xiang, visited the United
States for a month at the invitation of the US Committee
on Scholarly Communication with the People's Republic
of China.

April 17 Vice Premier Deng Xiaoping met historian He Bing-
di of the University of Chicago.
• Chairman Hua Guofeng sent a message to President
Tito, extending profound sympathy for the bereaved
families and injured people, victims of the recent strong
earthquake in Montenegro.

April 18   The first plenary session of the Sino-Vietnamese
           negotiations was held in Hanoi.
           • Vice Premier Deng Xiaoping met the delegation of
           the US House of Representatives led by Jack Brooks,
           chairman of the Committee of Government Operations.
           • The United States Foreign Relations Committee
           Delegation, headed by Committee Chairman Senator
           Frank Church, arrived in Beijing together with a dele-
           gation of US corporation leaders. The two delegation,
           totalling forty-eight members, were visiting China as
           guests of the Chinese People's Institute of Foreign Af-
           fairs and the China Council for Promotion of Interna-
           tional Trade. Vice Premier Deng Xiaoping met the
           delegations on April 20.

April 19   China and Egypt signed the 1979 trade protocol in
           Beijing.
           • China and Yugoslavia reached an agreement in
           Beijing on mutual exemption of visa and visa charges.

April 21   Premier Hua Guofeng met Nigerian Major-General
           Yar'Adua, Chief of Staff of the Armed Forces.
           • China and Pakistan signed the 1979 trade protocol
           in Beijing.
           • The Delegation of US Congressmen, led by Rep.
           Augustus F. Hawkins, visited China at the invitation
           of the Chinese People's Institute of Foreign Affairs.
           • The nine-member delegation from Zhongshan Uni-
           versity in Guangzhou, headed by its president, Li
           Jiaren, left Beijing to visit the United States at the
           invitation of the University of California at Los Ange-
           les. In January last year, a UCLA delegation visited
           China at the invitation of Zhongshan University and
           they established relations of academic exchanges with
           them.
           • In talks with the US Senate Foreign Relations
           Committee Delegation, headed by Senator Church, Vice
           Premier Deng Xiaoping said that the US should not be
           so concerned about the possibility of a PRC attack on
           Taiwan: first, the PRC would not have the military
           capacity to do so for at least five years; second,
           force would only be used if the total refusal by the
           Taiwan authorities to enter into a dialogue were to
           continue indefinitely or if the Soviet Union were to be-
           come involved.

April 23   The People's Daily reported the discovery of Hei-
longjiang province's worst case of theft of state proper-
ty since 1949.   A group headed by a woman called
Wang Shouxin had embezzled property worth 536,000
yuan since 1972.
   • The Laotian Foreign Ministry wrote to the UN
Secretary General complaining about the massing of
Chinese troops along the Laotian border, and their
occupation of a portion of Laotian territory in Luang
Hamtha province.

April 24   Soviet Foreign Minister Andrei Gromyko presented
the Chinese ambassador in Moscow with a note of the
Soviet government, which drew attention to previous
Soviet proposals for improving their relations on the
basis of agreement as to the principles which should
govern their relationship.

April 25   Foreign Minister Huang Hua held a banquet in
honor of Dr. Henry Kissinger in Beijing.   Kissinger
had talks with Prince Norodom Sihanouk and met Vice
Premier Deng Xiaoping on April 27.

April 26   The second plenary session of the Sino-Vietnamese
negotiations was held in Hanoi.   China put forth its
counterproposals which included a mutual commitment
not to join any military bloc directed against the other
or to provide bases for other countries, and declaring
that pending a settlement on the basis of the Chinese-
French border agreement, both sides should respect
the boundary that existed by common consent in 1957.

April 28   China and the Philippines exchanged letters of the
1979 lists of import and export commodities in Beijing.

April 29   The UN Secretary General Kurt Waldheim, his wife
and officials from the Secretariat visited China from
April 29 to May 2.   Foreign Minister Huang Hua told
Waldheim that the Laotian claims of border incursions
by China were untrue.   Vice Premier Deng Xiaoping
warned Waldheim there would be a second "lesson" for
Vietnam if "border provocations" continued.   Waldheim
met Chairman Hua Guofeng and Prince Norodom Sihanouk before his departure.

April 30   Vice Chairman Wang Dongxing appeared in public
for the first time in a month along with other leaders,
ending rumors of a purge within the politburo.

• The EEC and China postponed the first meeting of
their trade committee which was scheduled to have taken
place in Beijing early in May because the member states
had been unable to agree on the quota limits for Chinese cotton cloth imports.

May 1   The May Day editorial in the People's Daily said that
an important task now facing the Chinese working people was to launch a nationwide movement to increase
production and practice economy.

May 2   China and France signed minutes of talks to undertake scientific and technical cooperation and exchange
in metrology in Beijing.

• Prime Minister Datuk Hussein Onn of Malaysia arrived in Beijing for an eight-day visit. He was greeted
by Chairman Hua Guofeng and other senior officials at
the Beijing airport. He held talks with Chinese leaders
including Premier Hua Guofeng and Vice Premier Deng
Xiaoping, the chief topics being bilateral trade and the
Indo-Chinese crisis.

• A seven-day forum was held in Beijing to mark the
sixtieth anniversary of the May Fourth Movement. It
was sponsored by the Chinese Academy of Social Sciences. In a speech given for the occasion, Zhou Yang
said, "All theories and thoughts, including Marxism-
Leninism-Mao Zedong Thought have to develop and be
enriched through the constant testing in practice.
Whatever proves wrong or not appropriate to the new
conditions should be discarded, and the new discoveries
made in the course of practice should be absorbed. If
these points are followed consciously, the theory of
Marxism will remain ever-green."

May 3   The mausoleum containing the body of Mao Zedong
was reopened after several months' closure "for maintenance."

• In his speech at the meeting in commemoration of
the sixtieth anniversary of the May Fourth Movement,
Chairman Hua Guofeng said, "In socialist modernization, we will again encounter many new situations and
new problems. We should foster the style of study

which entails integrating theory with practice and, under the guidance of the basic principles of Marxism-Leninism-Mao Zedong Thought, proceed from actual conditions, emancipate the mind, study new conditions, and solve new problems."

May 4 The Standing Committee of the Fifth National Committee of the Chinese People's Political Consultative Conference held its third session in Beijing.
   • The third plenary meeting of the Sino-Vietnamese negotiations was held in Hanoi. Referring to the Vietnamese three-point proposal, Han Nianlong pointed out that "the Vietnamese side not only evades fundamental problems, but does not even abide the five principles of peaceful coexistence in deeds."

May 5 Juanita M. Kreps and Richard N. Cooper, secretary of Commerce and under secretary for Economic Affairs at the State Department, visited China May 5-15. A five-year protocol on cooperation in science and technology was signed on May 8, together with protocols on cooperation in atmospheric science and technology, fisheries and marine science, technology, metrology, and standards. Ms. Kreps and Li Qiang initialled, on May 14, an agreement on trade relations with mutual accord of most-favored-nation treatment. An agreement on foreign assets was also signed. Vice Premier Deng Xiaoping met her on May 10.
   • NCNA reported that Vietnam had driven at least 20,000 Chinese nationals and Vietnamese citizens into Guangxi province by land and water in April.
   • In reply to the Soviet note of April 24, a memorandum was handed to the Soviet Embassy in Beijing which called for the holding of talks on a separate basis from those on the border and that these should be aimed at defining their bilateral relations and at eliminating the obstacles to the development of their trade, cultural and other exchanges. China was ready for such talks to be held at any time. The next move, therefore, was up to Moscow.
   • Vice Premier Deng Xiaoping met the 100-member delegation from the French Institute of Higher Learning of National Defense, headed by Lt. General André Marty, president of the Institute.
   • Former US Secretary of State Henry Kissinger said,

at a press conference in Hong Kong, that China's military action against Vietnam was triggered by Vietnam's repeated border provocations and its attempt to dominate the region with Soviet backing. Kissinger flew to Hong Kong on May 3 after visiting China.

May 8 China and the Philippines initialled a civil air transport agreement in Manila.
  • The People's Daily printed, on the front page, an editorial describing importing as an "important and complex task." It said, "At present, priority must be given to items which are urgently needed, and which can yield quick results and more profit at not too high a cost."
  • The first English translation of the complete text of the classical Chinese novel A Dream of Red Mansions (Hong Lou Meng) was published in three volumes by the Foreign Language Press in Beijing.

May 9 Zhang Jie, vice-chairman of the Islamic Association of China, led a delegation to visit Libya at the invitation of the secretary general of the Libyan Association for the Propagation of Islam.
  • The Chilean Government Delegation, led by R.K. Basquez, visited China, and signed a scientific and cultural agreement at the end of the visit. The agreement included a provision for joint research cooperation in Antarctica. Chinese scientists were expected to join with a team in the Chilean sector during the summer expeditionary season of November 1979 to March 1980.

May 10 Foreign Minister Huang Hua held talks with Brian Talboys, New Zealand's deputy prime minister in Beijing, and Premier Hua Guofeng met him on May 12.
  • Liu Xiwen, at the Fifth Session of UNCTAD in Manila, spoke on the urgent need to change existing international economic relations to meet the needs of developing countries. He said China had "decided to become a party to the final and official agreement on the common fund and to undertake the relevant assessed contribution."

May 11 NCNA announced that the Chinese government had decided to release and repatriate the first group of captured Vietnamese armed personnel in the immediate

future and it again proposed that the Red Cross soci-
eties of the two countries meet as soon as possible to
discuss and handle the specific matters concerning the
repatriation of all the captured personnel by the two
sides.

May 12   The fourth plenary session of the Sino-Vietnamese
negotiations was held in Hanoi.
   • Han Nianlong urged Hanoi to study the Chinese
eight-point proposal and make active response so as to
bring the negotiations forward.
   • China and Jordan signed a trade agreement in
Beijing.
   • NCNA reported that the "Lotus" cave, another
limestone cave, was recently discovered near Xingping,
a scenic spot of the Guangxi Zhuang autonomous region.
The cave was 3,000 meters long and endowed with various stalagmites, stalactites, pillars and curtains of
stone.
   • NCNA reported that three pieces of paper which
might date back to between 73 and 49 B.C. were recently found in Fufeng county, Shaanxi province. This
discovery pushed the likely date for the world's first
paper back some 150 years earlier than had been previously assumed.
   • Vice Premier Deng Xiaoping met the Zaire Military
Delegation, led by Brigadier General Eluke Monga Andu.
   • Vice Premier Geng Biao left Beijing to visit Sweden,
Norway, Finland, and Iceland.

May 14   Vice Premier Deng Xiaoping met the Count and
Countess Barcelona, parents of the King Don Juan
Carlos de Borbón of Spain.
   • China and Italy signed a scientific and technologi-
cal cooperation agreement in Beijing.
   • Premier Hua Guofeng met Mohammad Saifur Rah-
man, special envoy of President Ziaur Rahman of Bang-
ladesh.

May 15   Lai Yali, at the First Session of the Disarmament
Commission in New York, stated China's comprehensive
program of disarmament: In the field of nuclear weapons, the ultimate aim should be the complete destruction and prohibition of all nuclear weapons and their
means of delivery. The two nations with the largest

nuclear arsenals should immediately cease to make nuclear weapons and begin to destroy them. In the field of conventional arms, the ultimate aim should be to reduce them to reasonable ratios. As a first step, the two nations with the largest supplies of conventional weapons should renounce military intervention against other states, withdraw their troops stationed abroad, dismantle military bases on foreign soil and greatly reduce conventional weapons and equipment.

May 16 The Ministry of Education announced plans to hold college entrance examinations throughout China July 7-9. Best qualified students would be enrolled in key schools and strict standards would be set for entrance to teachers' training schools.

• Vice Premier Deng Xiaoping met the Jiji press delegation from Japan, led by Director Tadayoshi Ohata, in Beijing.

• NCNA announced that a set of four coins would be issued by the People's Bank of China to mark the thirtieth anniversary of the founding of the PRC. On one side the coins would bear the national emblem of the PRC, while the reverse sides would have four designs; Tiananmen, the Momument to the People's Heroes, the Great Hall of the People, and the Memorial Hall of Chairman Mao Zedong.

May 17 China and Liberia signed a trade agreement in Monrovia.

• China and Tunisia signed a trade agreement in Beijing.

• Premier Hua Guofeng met American physicist Lee Zhengdao, his wife and their sons and daughter-in-law. Professor Lee had been giving lectures at the Chinese universities on science and technologies at the invitation of the Chinese Academy of Sciences.

• The Delegation of the Chinese People's Association for Friendship with Foreign Countries, led by Wang Bingnan, left Beijing to visit the Federal Republic of Germany, Austria, and Italy at the invitation of each nation.

May 18 The fifth session of the Sino-Vietnamese negotiations was held in Hanoi. Han Nianlong proposed that the current round negotiations be concluded.

• The Sino-Rumanian Economic and Technical Cooperation Committee held its first meeting in Beijing May
15-18. The protocol of the meeting was signed on May
22.

• China and Japan signed an agreement in Tokyo
whereby Japanese commercial banks could extend short-
term trade funds and medium-term syndicated loans to
China. This financial support was intended to assist
the smooth implementation of the Sino-Japanese long-
term trade agreement.

• Premier Hua Guofeng met Vice-Chairman Amadou
Baba Diarra of the Malian Military Committeee for National Liberation.

• NCNA reported that Liao Chengzhi led a mission
to Japan on May 18, primarily to reassure the Japanese
that there was no change in China's policy of promoting
economic and trade exchanges with Japan. Su Yu, a
senior adviser in the mission, called on Ganri Yama-
shita, director-general of the Defense Agency, on May
18, and two days later held a political discussion with
retired Japanese officers.

May 19 The Chinese government announced that it would
unilaterally release the first batch of Vietnamese prisoners of war.

• Premier Hua Guofeng met Agha Shahi, adviser for
Foreign Affairs of Pakistan. Vice Premier Deng Xiaoping
met him on May 20.

• China and Algeria signed a long-term trade agreement in Beijing.

May 20 NCNA reported that over 140 foreign professors,
specialists and teachers had been invited to give lectures in Shanghai's institutions of higher learning since
last year. They were from Australia, Belgium, Britain,
Canada, Egypt, France, Italy, Japan, New Zealand,
Peru, United States, and West Germany. Seventy of
them were to lecture there for a period of more than
one year. Lectures covered the fields of computer
programming, automation, systems engineering, lasers,
microwave technology, phototelecommunication, robots,
theoretical physics, automatic physics as well as various modern languages.

May 21 One hundred twenty Vietnamese prisoners were ex-

changed for forty-three Chinese on the border on May
21.   More prisoners were exchanged on May 28 and
June 5.   The final exchange took place on June 29.
The total of 1,636 Vietnamese were exchanged for 238
Chinese.
 • Vice Premier Kang Shien visited Brazil at the in-
vitation of the Brazilian government May 21-27.

May 22   Chairman Hua Guofeng met Vice Premier Paul Niculescu from Rumania.

May 23   The People's Daily printed, on the front page,
Zhao Ziyang's remark in a recent provincial party meeting.   Zhao Ziyang, an alternate member of the political
bureau of the party Central Committee, and First Secretary of the Sichuan Provincial Party Committee, said,
"interference by people promoting the two erroneous
trends of thought currently prevalent within the Communist Party and in society at large must be overcome."
 • NCNA reported that excavations at two sites with
the foundations of palaces, about 100 km west of Xian,
one dating back 3,100 years and the other 2,900 years,
had been in progress for three years.   They were discovered in the spring of 1978 in Qishan and Fufeng
counties.

May 24   Vice Premier Deng Xiaoping met Shoji Sato, the departing Japanese ambassador to China and Mrs. Sato.
 • China and Mali signed an economic and technical
cooperation protocol in Beijing.

May 25   Deng Yingchao, member of the political bureau of
the CCP Central Committee visited Korea from May 25
to June 1 at the invitation of President Kim Il-sung.
She attended a ceremony to unveil the statue of the
late Premier Zhou Enlai and a monument at the square
of the Huangnam fertilizer plant of Hamhung on May 31.

May 26   The twenty-one-member agricultural delegation, led
by Wang Feng, left Beijing for a study tour in the
United States.
 • Qinghua University and the University of California at Berkeley signed an agreement to become affiliated
universities.   Under the agreement, the two universities
would exchange postgraduate students free of tuition as
well as research scholars.

May 27   NCNA reported that the first railway line was completed in southern Xinjian Uighur autonomous region.
  • Vice Premier Xu Xiangqian hosted a banquet to welcome the Goodwill Military Delegation from Somalia. Premier Hua Guofeng met the delegation on June 2.

May 28   Vice Premier Kang Shien visited the United States from May 28 to June 12. President Carter met him on May 29.
  • Ye Jianying, chairman of the Standing Committee of the Fifth NPC, sent a message to Karl Carstens, warmly congratulating him on his election to the presidency of the Federal Republic of Germany.

May 29   Foreign Minister Huang Hua met Ambassador Robert Strauss, the US President's special representative for trade negotiations, in Beijing. Vice Premier Deng Xiaoping met him on May 30.
  • China and Finland signed an agreement on economic, industrial, scientific and technical cooperation between the two nations in Beijing.

May 31   Vice Premier Deng Xiaoping met Zenko Suzuki, liberal democratic member of the House of Representatives of Japan.
  • At the end of the third round of the Sino-American trade talks in Beijing, the United States decided to go ahead and impose quotas unilaterally. Both sides took pains to point out that no animosity or bitterness had developed and that they would meet again in due course to have yet another round of talks.

June 1   A national forum on acupuncture, the largest ever held in China, took place in Beijing from June 1-5 and was attended by over 300 Chinese and 100 foreign specialists.
  • Soviet President Leonid Brezhnev said that the Soviet Union was prepared to hold talks with China but not "at the expense of the interests of third countries."

June 2   NCNA reported that a nine-day symposium on the History of the Taiping Heavenly Kingdom (1851-1864) came to an end in Nanjing, where 210 papers were given by Chinese historians and seven were presented by foreign historians.

June 4   Soviet Foreign Minister Gromyko presented the Chinese ambassador with a memorandum offering to hold
negotiations in July and August this year in Moscow.
"These should be held at the deputy foreign minister
level or by specially empowered representatives." He
said Chairman Hua told visiting Australian Foreign
Minister Andrew Peacock that it was likely that the
talks would take place.

 • China established a string of military camps in
north Pakistan near the Afghan border. Soldiers were
placed at several points along the 537-mile Karakoram
Highway to guard against possible sabotage by Afghan/
Russian agents.

 • The meeting of the Standing Committee of the
Fifth National Committee of the CPPCC endorsed 109
new members to the Fifth National Committee of the
CPPCC, including He Zizhen, the second wife of the
late Chairman Mao Zedong, Wang Guangmei, widow of
Liu Shaoqi, Lu Dingyi, and Yang Xianzhen.

June 5   In a speech marking the fourth anniversary of the
opening of the Suez Canal, President Anwar Sadat announced the conclusion of a military deal with China.
Although he gave no details, Western sources claimed
that it involved the sale of up to sixty Mig-19 aircraft.

 • Doctors from India, Japan, the United States, and
Hong Kong watched four brain operations performed under acupuncture. This was part of the on-the-post
observation at the ongoing National Forum on Acupuncture.

 • Premier Hua Guofeng sent a message to Surya
Bahadur, warmly congratulating him on his assumption
of the post of prime minister of Nepal.

 • Vice Premier Deng Xiaoping met the delegation of
the National Council of US-China Trade, led by Mr. W.
Surrey, in Beijing.

 • The China Council for the Promotion of International Trade gave a reception in Beijing to welcome His
Royal Highness the Duke of Kent. The duke, who was
vice-chairman of the British Overseas Trade Board,
opened the British Energy Exhibition in Beijing.

June 6   Vice Premier Deng Xiaoping met Australian Foreign
Minister Andrew Peacock. The two nations initialled a
scientific and technical cooperation agreement.

June 7 The Bank of China opened a branch in Luxembourg, the first to be set up abroad since 1949.

• Peacock Venom, a famous historical play was staged in Chengdu by the Sichuan People's Theatre, to mark the first anniversary of the death of Guo Moruo, one of China's outstanding men of letters.

June 10 The Second World Badminton Championships took place in Hangzhou (Zhejiang province) June 10-20.

June 11 China and the Federal Republic of Germany signed a scientific and technical cooperation protocol in Beijing.

• The Sino-American Joint High-Energy Physics Committee held its first meeting in Beijing. Vice Premier Deng Xiaoping met the American members of the committee.

June 12 NCNA reported that China was making progress with its plans to build a high-energy physics experimental center housing a 50 BeV (billion electron volts) to be completed in 1985.

• NCNA reported that new petrochemical projects were under construction at the Jilin Chemical Industry Company in Northeast China. The new projects included an installation for synthetic alcohol imported from West Germany which had a yearly output of 100,000 tons. Japanese equipment with an annual production of 80,000 tons of butadiene-styrene rubber, and Japanese equipment producing 50,000 tons of butanol and octanol annually.

• The Eighth Meeting of the Fifth NPC Standing Committee was held in Beijing, where it was decided to hold the Second Session of the Fifth NPC on June 18. The meeting also approved the draft criminal law, the draft criminal prosecution law, a draft law governing joint Chinese and foreign stock enterprises and several other draft laws.

• An annex to the implementation accord between China and the US on cooperation in high-energy physics was signed in Beijing.

June 13 China and Madagascar signed, in Tananarive, the minutes of talks on the construction of the Antalaha hydroelectric station with Chinese aid.

• In Dar Es Salaam, China and Tanzania signed an
agreement under which sixty Chinese doctors would
work at regional or district hospitals and the Muhimbill
Medical Center in Dar Es Salaam.

June 14   Lai Yali said, at the Security Council meeting, that
China had decided not to participate in the vote on the
draft resolution extending the mandate of the United
Nations Interim Force in Lebanon, although it supported
the part condemning Israeli aggression and demanding
Israeli respect of the independence and territorial unity
of Lebanon.

June 15   The Laotian Foreign Ministry sent a note to its
Chinese counterpart, demanding that the Chinese Embassy staff in Laos be limited to twelve and the military
attaché's office be closed.

• Lai Yali spoke in the Security Council to state that
China would not participate in the vote on the Cyprus
resolution draft as it renewed the mandate of the
United Nations peacekeeping force in Cyprus, but, he
said, China supported its "positive element."

• The United Nations adopted the Pinyin Romanization of Chinese names.

• NCNA reported that more than seventy cave tombs,
dating back as far as 2,400 years, had been found on a
hill in Guixi county in Jiangxi province.   They contained funeral objects of the Warring States period
(475–221 B.C.).

• The Second Session of the Fifth National Committee
of the CPPCC was held in Beijing from June 15 to July
2.   It was attended by 1,734 of the 2,015 committee
members.   The opening speech was delivered by Deng
Xiaoping, chairman of the National Committee of the
CPPCC.

June 16   China and Peru signed the minutes of talks in
Lima to strengthen their relations of trade and friendship.

• The Chinese Foreign Ministry statement claimed
that over the previous twelve months more than
230,000 refugees had been driven into China from
Vietnam.

June 17   Vice Premier Li Xiannian held a banquet welcoming

Deputy Prime Minister Dawee Chullasapya of Thailand.
Vice Premier Deng Xiaoping met him on June 18.

• The preliminary meeting of the Second Session
of the Fifth NPC was held to endorse the agenda for
the session. The meeting was presided over by Ye
Jianying, chairman of the NPC Standing Committee.

• At a press conference, Ji Pengfei said that there
would be a changeover from local revolutionary committees to people's governments, and that the new electoral
law would make election at the county level direct
whereas those at the highest level would remain indirect. Elections would continue to be conducted by
secret ballot.

June 18   The Second Session of the Fifth NPC was held in
Beijing from June 18 to July 1. It was attended by
3,279 of a possible total of 3,471 deputies. Chairman
Hua Guofeng delivered a report on the work of government on June 18. Vice Premier Yu Qiuli delivered the
report on the draft of the 1979 national economic plan
on June 21. Zhang Jingfu delivered a report on the
final state accounts for 1978 and the draft state budget
for 1979 on June 21. Peng Zhen delivered his report
explaining the seven draft laws on June 26. The session closed on July 1, after endorsing the policy of readjustment, restructuring, consolidation and improvement of the economy, approving the above reports,
plan, accounts and budget, passing a resolution on
amendments to relevant provisions of the constitution
and adopting the seven laws. Appointments made at
the final plenum included the election of Peng Zhen as
vice-chairman of the NPC Standing Committee, the en-
dorsement of Chairman Hua Guofeng's nomination of
Chen Yun, Bo Yibo, and Yao Yilin as vice premiers of
the State Council, and Fang Yi as president of the
Chinese Academy of Sciences.

June 19   Premier Hua Guofeng sent a message to Jamaican
Prime Minister Michael Manley, expressing sympathy
and solicitude to the Jamaican government and people
for the heavy losses caused by flood.

• A People's Daily article urged the establishment of
a system of defense lawyers to strengthen the socialist
legal system, safeguard the people's democratic rights
and the legal rights of the state--both collective and

individual--and to promote the Four Modernizations in China.

June 21   Vice Premier Deng Xiaoping met the British members of the study group on rural development from Oxford University's Institute of Commonwealth studies and Queen Elizabeth House, led by Neville Maxwell.

June 22   China and Ireland signed a joint communiqué in New York to establish diplomatic relations at the ambassadorial level.
   • NCNA reported that the exchange of prisoners of war with Vietnam was completed.
   • China and the United States signed a protocol on scientific and technical exchanges in medicine and public health in Beijing.
   • China and Chile signed a trade accord in Santiago.
   • China and Tunisia signed a cultural cooperation agreement in Beijing.

June 24   The People's Daily commentator praised the initiative of Guangdong province in developing processing and assembly industries with raw materials and parts supplied by foreign businessmen. About 300 projects in the medium- and small-scale light and textile industries had been set into operation with agreements worth more than $300 million.

June 25   The Vietnamese government delegation, led by Vice Foreign Minister Dinh Nho Liem, arrived in Beijing to take part in the second round of the Sino-Vietnamese negotiations. The negotiations were scheduled to begin on June 28.
   • Chairman Hua Guofeng announced that the ten-year plan adopted in 1978 would be replaced by a five-year plan starting in 1981.

June 26   Premier Hua Guofeng met the Pakistan Labor Delegation, led by Faiz Ali Chisti, minister of Labor and Manpower.

June 27   The State Statistical Bureau of China issued a communique on the fulfillment of the country's 1978 national economic plan. The communiqué announced that in 1978, China's total industrial and agricultural

output value reached 569,000 million yuan, or an increase of 12.3 percent over 1977. The national income
was twelve percent over the 1977 figure which was
eight percent more than 1976. By the end of 1978,
China's population was 975,230,000 (including Taiwan
province), and its natural population growth rate was
twelve per thousand.

June 28 The Central Committee of the CCP invited leading
members of the Democratic parties and nonparty personages to a democratic consultative meeting held in the
Great Hall of the People. Chairman Hua Guofeng, Vice-
Chairmen Ye Jianying and Li Xiannian attended the
meeting. The issues discussed included the election of
additional vice-chairmen to the Standing Committee of
the NPC, vice premiers of the State Council and vice-
chairmen of the National Committee of CPPCC.

• The Standing Committee of the Fifth National Committee of the CPPCC held its sixth session in Beijing.

June 29 NCNA reported that China was to begin joint ventures using foreign capital on the basis of equality and
mutual benefit in an attempt to raise funds for construction, import advanced technology and equipment, improve economic management, and speed up the country's
modernization.

• China and the Belgium-Luxembourg Economic Union
signed, in Beijing, an agreement on the development of
economic, industrial, and scientific cooperation, and two
protocols on economic, industrial, and technological cooperation, and one on scientific and technological cooperation.

• Vice Premier Deng Xiaoping met Mr. Konosuke
Matsushita, chief consultant of the Matsushita Electric
Industrial Company Ltd., Japan.

• Foreign Minister Huang Hua held a banquet to welcome Sri Lankan Foreign Minister A.C.S. Hameed, Mrs.
Hameed, and his party. Chairman Hua Guofeng met
him on July 1.

June 30 The People's Daily published an editorial to mark
the fifty-eighth anniversary of the founding of the
CCP. It emphasized the party's responsibility in leading the modernization program.

July 1   It was announced that the CCP Central Committee
and the State Council had decided to restore the administrative area of the Inner Mongolian region to what
it had been in July 1969.   Consequently, from July 1,
1979, parts of Liaoning, Jilin, Heilongjiang, Gansu,
and Ningxia were restored to the region.

July 2   Chairman Hua Guofeng met the study group of the
League of Communists of Yugoslavia, headed by Execu-
tive Secretary Svetozar Durutovic.
  • Vice Premier Deng Xiaoping met Miao Yuntai and
his wife, Zhao Peiqiang, who returned from the United
States to participate in the Second Session of the Fifth
National Committee of the CPPCC.   Miao Yuntai was
elected a member of the Standing Committee at the
meeting.
  • China sent documents of its accession to the Vi-
enna Convention on Consular Regulations to the United
Nations.

July 3   Clashes between Chinese and foreign students in
Shanghai resulted in injuries to some forty people.
  • The CPC Central Committee issued a circular to
prohibit interference in the state assignment system by
parents in leading positions in party, state and PLA
organizations.

July 4   US Ambassador to China Leonard Woodcock and Mrs.
Woodcock gave a reception in Beijing to mark American
Independence Day.
  • The Organic Law of the Local People's Congresses
and Local People's Government was promulgated by an
order issued by Ye Jianying, chairman of the Standing
Committee of the Fifth NPC.
  • The new electoral law, adopted at the Second Session of the Fifth NPC on July 1, was promulgated by
an order issued by Ye Jianying, chairman of the Standing Committee of the Fifth NPC.   The new law went
into effect on January 1, 1980.   The law stipulated
that deputies to the people's congresses at commune
(town) and county levels were to be elected directly by
the voters.   Deputies to the national and provincial
people's congresses were to be elected indirectly by the
people's congresses of the next lower level.   The law
also stipulated that the number of candidates nominated

for direct elections should be fifty to 100 percent more
than the number of deputies to be elected. The number of candidates nominated for indirect elections
should be twenty to fifty percent more than the number of deputies to be elected. The election of deputies
to all levels of people's congresses should be conducted
by secret ballot.

July 5   The Organic Law of the People's Courts and the
Organic Law of the People's Procurates were promulgated by an order issued by Ye Jianying, chairman
of the Standing Committee of the Fifth NPC.
   • A ceremony was held at the Chinese Embassy in
Brazzaville in Congo to hand over the Bouenza Hydroelectric Power Station and a high-tension transmission
and transformation project in Southern Congo.
   • The Vietnamese Government Delegation, at the
Sino-Vietnamese negotiations (held in Beijing), proposed a draft agreement on five points of antihegemonism, which included items such as not threatening to
punish or teach others lessons, no use of overseas nationals or alliance with imperialists and others against
peace, national independence, democracy and socialism, etc. This was denounced by the Chinese side as
a trick to deceive public opinion and to camouflage
Vietnamese preparations against China, their tightening
of control in Laos, their war in Kampuchea and their
ambitions in Thailand and Southeast Asia.
   • The Chinese Government Delegation, at the Sino-
Vietnamese negotiation (held in Beijing), urged the
Vietnamese authorities to stop persecuting Chinese nationals, Vietnamese citizens of Chinese descent, and
ethnic minorities, driving them to China. It also urged
them to change their policy of creating and exporting
refugees and take back to Vietnam those still drifting
on the sea and those who had not yet been resettled.

July 6   Mme. I. Marcos of the Philippines visited China
July 6-12. Premier Hua Guofeng met her on July 6.
Several agreements were signed, including a long-term
eight-year trade agreement under which China pledged
to sell at least 1.2 million tons of oil per annum at a
very reasonable price. The other agreements included
the building of hotels and air flights. The value of
their two-way trade was projected to reach $2 billion
by 1985.

• The Criminal Law was promulgated by an order
issued by Ye Jianying, chairman of the Standing Committee of the Fifth NPC. The new law was to become
effective on January 1, 1980. The law was divided
into two major parts, general provisions and specific
provisions. It consisted of eight chapters with 192
articles.

July 7 A Sino-American trade agreement was signed in Beijing. American officials estimated that under the three-
year treaty, bilateral trade could double from the 1978
level of $1.1 billion.

• The spokesman quoted in China Youth News cited
progress in absorbing youth into city services, and
urged the development of collectively owned suburban
bases for agriculture in side-line occupations, noting
that collective enterprises accounted for three-quarters
of the nation's industrial enterprises, one third of its
industrial workers and one fifth of the total output
value of industry.

• Over 4.6 million candidates took the college entrance examinations. The examinations lasted three
days. Sixty-seven percent of the candidates were 1979
senior middle school graduates.

July 8 The law of the PRC on joint ventures using Chinese
and foreign investment was promulgated by an order
issued by Ye Jianying, chairman of the Standing Committee of the Fifth NPC. The law provided legal status
for joint ventures in China and protected the rights
and interests of foreign participants. The joint ventures would take the form of limited liability companies.

July 9 An earthquake hit Liyang county, Jiangsu province,
killing eleven people, injuring some 2,000, and destroying many houses. It was magnitude six on the Richter
scale.

• Premier Hua Guofeng sent a message to President
Ieremia Tabai of Kiribati, warmly greeting the proclamation of independence of the Republic of Kiribati and informing him of the Chinese government's decision to
recognize the government of the republic.

• Burmese Premier U Maung Kha visited China July
9-13. Chairman Hua Guofeng met him on July 9, and
Vice Premier Deng Xiaoping met him on July 10. The

two nations signed an economic and technical agreement on July 12.

July 11 The <u>People's Daily</u> pointed out the need to institute a system under which leading officials would personally meet the people at regular intervals and handle their letters. "This will help leaders bear in mind the fact that they are the servants of the people, and leading organizations improve their style of work," the commentary emphasized.

• Foreign Minister Huang Hua supported the North Korean rejection of the American proposals for trilateral talks involving South Korea as "absolutely correct."

July 13 The Chinese Foreign Ministry sent a note to the Vietnamese Foreign Ministry protesting against Hanoi's continued creation of tension along the Sino-Vietnamese border by sending armed personnel into China's Yunnan and Guangxi provinces for spying, reconnaissance and armed provocations, all of which threatened the security of China's border areas.

• China decided to participate in the International Conference on Indo-Chinese Refugees, scheduled to be held in Geneva July 20-21.

• NCNA reported that from January to June inclusive, the total value of imports and exports came to 21,300 million yuan, a 43.2 percent rise compared with the same period the previous year. Exports reached 9,500 million yuan, an increase of 26.8 percent, and imports 11,800 million yuan, an increase of 59.9 percent.

July 15 The delegation from the EEC arrived in Beijing to take part in the first joint commission meeting. The EEC informed China of the decision to extend the general system of preferential tariff to China beginning in 1980.

July 16 The border incident near Dacheng (Xinjiang) resulted in the death of one Chinese and the injury of another. On July 17, the Soviet Foreign Ministry delivered a verbal protest to the Chinese Embassy, which complained of a border violation by four armed personnel who clashed with a Soviet frontier detail. The Chinese Foreign Ministry note of July 24 complained of a Soviet

violation in which two men were ambushed and kidnapped. The Chinese described this as but the latest
of a series of incidents designed to harass Chinese
herdsmen.

• Premier Hua Guofeng sent a message to the Sixteenth Conference of the Heads of State or Government
of the OAU, extending warm greetings on behalf of the
Chinese government and people.

July 17 Vice Premier Geng Biao told the Korean Worker's
Party Delegation in Beijing, "In the future, no matter
what may happen in the world, the CCP and the Chinese people will always join the MWP and the Korean
people in a united struggle and make common progress
together." Premier Hua Guofeng met the delegation on
July 25.

July 18 The Chinese Government Delegation, led by Vice
Foreign Minister Zhang Wenjin, arrived in Geneva to
attend the Indo-Chinese Refugees Conference.

• China decided not to go ahead with the purchase
of two French nuclear reactors. The reason given for
the cancellation of the project was the revision of
China's economic target.

• NCNA reported that surveying was now in full
swing near the Ming Tombs, Zhangping county, Beijing,
for the construction of China's first 50 BeV synchro-
trom.

• NCNA reported that China was allowing foreign
airlines to use an air transit route from Hong Kong to
the Sino-Burmese border, passing over Guangzhou,
Kunming, and Lincang. China also opened Baiyun Airport in Guangzhou as an emergency landing airport for
airliners from other countries.

• The eighty-member Chinese dance study group
left New York for home after a one-month visit to the
United States. The group visited New York and took
part in the first USA International Ballet Competition
in Jackson, Mississippi, and the American Dance Festival in Durham, North Carolina.

July 19 NCNA reported that the total number of refugees
driven into China by the Vietnamese authorities reached
some 251,000, causing the Chinese people great difficulties.

• NCNA announced that China would issue 50,500 gold coins to commemorate the International Year of the Child. The national emblem of the PRC would appear on one side of the coin, and a Chinese boy and girl watering a flower, and the symbols of the International Year of the Child, and of the UN Children's Fund would be on the other.

• The Japan-China Scientific and Technology Exchange Commission held its second annual meeting in Tokyo.

• Ye Jianying and Hua Guofeng sent a message to His Excellency Suddam Hussein, warmly congratulating him on his assumption of the presidency and premiership of the Republic of Iraq.

July 20 A special division to handle economic disputes was set up under the intermediate people's court in Chinqing. The economic division was empowered to sanction those enterprises and organizations that violated the government's economic rules and regulations and to bring to justice those people guilty of serious offences in economic affairs.

• Zhang Wenjin, at the International Conference on the Indo-Chinese Refugees Problem in Geneva, condemned Vietnam for causing the Indo-Chinese refugee problem. He said that while the relief measures for existing refugees was urgent, it was necessary to take measures to keep Vietnam from expelling refugees.

• All but one of the twenty-two contracts, agreed to by Japanese companies in 1978 and suspended in February 1979, were validated by China. The outstanding contract was still being renegotiated. The Chinese side was not asked for price increases or for penalty payments. By the new terms, payment would be made on a deferred basis, half in Japanese yen and half in US dollars.

July 21 A People's Daily editorial indicated that the Chinese people shared the joys of the Nicaraguan people in their triumphant struggle against the Somoza dictatorship.

• NCNA reported that China was willing to take another 10,000 refugees from Southeast Asia.

July 23 NCNA reported that Vietnamese soldiers fired across the Chinese border, killing civilians and provoking counterfire.

• The Chinese General Civil Aviation Department declared four areas in the sea, east and south of Hainan
Island, as danger zones for air navigation.

July 24 China and France signed, in Beijing, new electronic
project agreements. Three contracts worth FFr. 100
million were for the import of transformers and engineering enterprises.

July 25 The Beijing Chinese Catholic Patriotic Association
elected Michael Fu Tieshan as bishop of Beijing, the
first since the Cultural Revolution. He was consecrated
on December 21.

July 26 NCNA announced that the Chinese Government Dele-
gation, led by Zhao Puchu, would attend the Third
Assembly of the World Conference on Religion and
Peace, scheduled to take place in Princeton, New Jer-
sey from August 29 to September 7.
• Britain and China initialled an air service agreement for regular flights between Beijing, London, and
Hong Kong.
• Premier Hua Guofeng extended China's recognition
to the National Reconstruction Government of Nicaragua.
• China and Pakistan concluded an agreement on
reciprocal registration of trademarks in Beijing.
• The People's Daily commentary called for an end
to "anarchy" in construction in Beijing, calling the
situation "sluggish, disorganized, chaotic and waste-
ful." Lack of planning and coordination had led to
poor quality and waste in the construction sector, the
article said. Factories had been built without adequate
housing, transportation, medical installations, recrea-
tional facilities and other services for the workers.
New housing projects had gone up without the necessary water, electricity, and gas lines to serve them,
so hundreds of thousands of square meters of floor
space were unoccupied.

July 27 The Soviet government formally accepted a Chinese
offer to start talks in mid-September on normalizing
relations.

July 28 NCNA reported that a bronze bell, dating back
nearly 3,000 years, was recently unearthed on a hill

in Jianou county, Fujian province. Archaeological
workers from the Fujian Museum estimated that the
bronze bell belonged to the Western Zhou Dynasty
(around eleventh century-771 B.C.).
• Premier Hua Guofeng met, in Beijing, Edward
Hill, chairman of the Central Committee of the Communist party of Australia (M-L), and Mrs. Joyce Hill.

July 29 NCNA reported that a new air route from Beijing
to Chengdu would be formally commissioned on August 1.

July 30 NCNA reported that the skull of a middle-aged
male and the front of the cranium of a child, both dating back approximately 10,000 years and both quite
well-preserved, were found in Huangyan Cave in Feng-
gai county, Guangdong province.
• The Standing Committee of the NPC appointed
Vice Premier Gu Mu as minister in charge of two commissions, both of which set up the same day, one to
regulate foreign investments, the other to supervise
the PRC's imports and exports.
• China and Vietnam ended their ninth unsuccessful
session of talks in Beijing. The Chinese made clear
their view that no progress would be possible as long
as Vietnamese troops remained in Kampuchea.
• The Chinese Ministry of Foreign Affairs published
documents in support of China's claims to sovereignty
over the Xisha and Nansha islands in the South China
Sea. A week later, the Vietnamese Foreign Ministry
issued a statement claiming sovereignty over the disputed islands, seeking to refute the Chinese claims.

July 31 Ye Jianying met the Parliamentary Delegation from
Bangladesh, led by Speaker Mirza Cholam Hafiz.
• Premier Hua Guofeng sent a message to Charan
Singh, extending warm congratulations on his assump-
tion of the office of prime minister of India.
• The Defense Ministry held a reception at the Great
Hall of the People marking the fifty-second anniversary
of the founding of the PLA.

August 1 The Manila-Guangzhou-Beijing air service, to be
flown by the Philippine Airline, was formally inaugurated.

August 2 Deputy Chairman of the Vietnamese National Assembly Hoang Van Hoan, defected to China while supposedly en route to Eastern Europe for medical treatment. Chairman Hua Guofeng met him on August 9. Hoang Van Hoan gave a press conference in Beijing on August 9 to read his "Message to Vietnamese Compatriots," denouncing the Vietnamese leadership, especially for having invaded and occupied Kampuchea, and mobilized tens of millions of the Vietnamese people for a war against China.

• NCNA reported that the People's Court in China had reexamined 708,000 criminal cases in the eighteen months from January 1978 to June 1979, and found that more than 166,000 cases from the period of the Cultural Revolution involved false accusations or wrong verdicts.

August 3 The Ningxia Hui autonomous region reopened its 158 moslem mosques. These religious centers, which were damaged to varying degrees in the past few years, were being repaired with government funds.

• Beijing newspapers gave front-page prominence to a decision of the Municipal Party Committee, approved by the Central Committee, to exonerate Deng Du, Wu Han and Laio Mosha, who were smeared as the "Three-Family Village anti-Party Group" at the beginning of the Cultural Revolution.

August 4 The People's Daily published an article entitled "Appraise and Treat Urban Collective Ownership Correctly," to stress the importance of urban collectively owned enterprises in China's socialist national economy. It noted that China had to build a large number of big enterprises, equipped with the world's advanced technology, as the backbone for raising the scientific and technological level of the national economy. Yet the more modernized and specialized the big state-owned enterprises became, the larger the coordination and supplementation of the vast numbers of small, collectively owned enterprises became.

• Communication equipment repair shops, set up by the China Ocean Shipping Company in several coastal cities, would serve as representatives of the International Telephone and Telegram Inc. in providing maintenance services according to an agreement signed in Beijing between China Ocean Shipping Company and the ITT Far East and Pacific Inc.

August 5   The Chinese Foreign Ministry, in a note to the
Vietnamese Foreign Ministry, strongly protested against
Hanoi's criminal acts of armed provocation in the border
areas and strongly demanded an end to all violations
of Chinese territory.

August 6   The annual Sino-Soviet trade agreement was
signed in Moscow.   The new agreement was for a total
trade turnover value of 350 million rubles.
   • China and Sudan signed the 1979–80 trade protocol
in Khartoum.

August 7   China and Halsat (Italy) signed a five-year agreement to form joint ventures in China and other developing countries.   Under the terms of the agreement, Halsat would supply the technology while China would provide 400,000 Chinese workers.

August 8   The Chinese authorities were informed that on the
advice of congressional leaders, the Carter administration would delay sending the MFN legislation to Capitol
Hill.

August 9   NCNA reported that China's first automated marine
hydrometeorological buoy was put into operation in the
Yellow Sea at 122.9 degrees east longitude and 32.33
degrees north latitude, off the coast near Shanghai.

August 10   China and Mongolia signed the 1979 protocol on
mutual supply of goods.

August 11   Control of population growth was one of the most
important factors in realizing the Four Modernizations
and remained a major urgent problem awaiting solution,
said Vice Premier Chen Muhua in an article that appeared in the People's Daily.   She said, "In 1949, China
had 540 million people.   Now the population has increased to more than 900 million.   About 360 million
people have been born, or 63% of the total populations.
The natural growth averaged 20 per thousand."   She
then outlined the goals for the population growth control program in two stages, to lower the birth rate from
twelve per thousand to around five per thousand by
1985, and to lower it to zero by the year 2000.
   • Vice Premier Chen Muhua, in the same article,

noted that "now 6% of school-age children are still not enrolled, 12% of the primary school graduates are unable to go on to middle school, and over 50% of the junior middle school graduates are unable to go on to senior middle school. Students who have been enrolled in universities only constitute 5% of senior middle school graduates. This has caused a lot of problems in employment."

August 13   China and Congo signed a protocol in Brazzaville to send Chinese technicians to the naval yard of Congo.
• Prime Minister Ranasingh Premadasa of Sri Lanka, Mrs. Premadasa, and their party visited China August 13-19 at the invitation of the Chinese government. Premier Hua Guofeng met them at the airport, and held talks with them on August 14. Prime Minister Premadasa accepted an interest-free government loan of $160 million.

August 14   The Tenth Plenary Meeting of the Sino-Vietnamese talks was held in Beijing. Han Nianlong categorically refuted the "five points" on opposing hegemonism made by the Vietnamese side at the Seventh Plenary Meeting. He said that the "five points" actually try to cover up hegemonism while purporting to be antihegemonism.

August 15   More than 400 Catholics celebrated "the assumption of the blessed Virgin Mary," one of the four grand Catholic feast days, at Beijing's Nandang cathedral (Cathedral of the Immaculate Conception). Monsignor Michael Fu Tieshan, the new bishop of Beijing, officiated at the mass.

August 16   The Xinhua News Agency and the Yugoslav telegraph agency, Tanjug, signed an agreement for the exchange of news items and cooperation in Belgrade.

August 17   A ceremony was held in Dar Es Salaam to sign the protocol of the Thirteenth Meeting of the Board of Directors of the Chinese-Tanzanian Joint Shipping Company.

August 18   Li Bendong, aged forty-three, was executed by firing squad for the rape and murder of a twenty-six-year-old woman on the evening of November 10, 1978.

- NCNA reported that over 200 Buddhists from different parts of China and overseas had made pilgrimages to Wutai mountain, the well-known Buddhist center in Shanxi province.
- The State Council decided to commend national advanced enterprises and national model workers to mark the thirtieth anniversary of the founding of the PRC. The national advanced enterprises would be honored with commendations and the national advanced workers would be presented with medals and certificates.
- The Xinhua News Agency and the Rumanian news agency, Agerpress, signed an agreement for the exchange of news items and cooperation in Bucharest.

August 19   NCNA reported that China had devised its first electronic monitor for examining the fetus and had begun making this kind of instrument in small quantities.

August 20   Premier Hua Guofeng met the Maltese Parliamentary party, led by Speaker Calcidon Agiua.
- Premier Hua Guofeng sent a message to greet the convening of the UN Conference on Science and Technology for Development in Vienna.

August 21   Hanoi issued a statement to reaffirm the claim to a twelve-mile territorial sea limit and it criticized American attempts to limit this to three. The statement not only confirmed Vietnamese claims to the Paracel and Spratly islands and their adjacent territorial seas, but it also went on to warn that Vietnam "would take appropriate measures to protect these and to defend its interest in other maritime zones and on the continental shelf."
- The Chinese Cycling Association was admitted to the membership of the International Amateur Cycling Federation (FIAC) by a vote of 26–25 with three abstentions in Maastricht, the Netherlands.

August 22   NCNA reported that the seaport of Swatow was made a special zone for international trade and navigation.
- The People's Daily printed, on the front page, a message of congratulations from the Chinese leaders to their Rumanian counterparts to mark the thirtieth anniversary of Rumanian liberation. Premier Hua Guofeng met Rumanian Ambassador to China Florea Dumitrescu.

August 23 Vice Premier Deng Xiaoping met US Senator Henry M. Jackson. Senator Jackson and his party arrived in Beijing on August 7 for his third visit to China. Premier Hua Guofeng met him on August 24. After his visit, Senator Jackson said that he detected a general feeling in the leadership of a state of unhappiness about the delay in sending the MFN legislation to Capitol Hill.

August 24 Japanese Foreign Ministry officials said that the government was ready in principle to advance a direct intergovernmental loan to China. A Chinese request for a loan said to be one trillion yuan ($5 billion) was being studied. The loan would be from the Overseas Economic Cooperation Fund (OECF), which handled low-interest concessional financing to less-developed countries.

• NCNA reported that a portion of a large fossil turtle and a number of dinosaur fossils dating back more than eight million years were unearthed in Inner Mongolia in May and June of this year. The preserved portion of shell of the fossil was about thirty-five centimeters long and forty-five centimeters wide. Unearthed at the same time in mid-June were the teeth of a protoceratops--a primitive, horned dinosaur with a parrotlike beak and the vertebrae of a crocodile.

• Samdech Norodom Sihanouk and Madame Sihanouk arrived in Beijing from North Korea for a week's visit. Vice Premier Deng Xiaoping met him on August 30.

August 25 China's largest opera company opened its new season in Beijing with a stress on traditional classics and historical themes.

• The former party secretary General Zhang Wentian was mourned for at a memorial meeting in Beijing by Chinese party and state leaders. Zhang Wentian died at the age of seventy-six on July 1, 1976 in Wuxi, Jiangsu province, under persecution by Lin Biao and the Gang of Four. Hua Guofeng, Deng Xiaoping, Li Xiannian, Chen Yun and Wang Dongxing, and other party and state leaders attended the memorial meeting. Deng Xiaoping, in the memorial speech, gave an account of the revolutionary activities of Zhang Wentian.

• Premier Hua Guofeng met a visiting parliamentary delegation from Barbados, led by Sir Armott Cato, president of the Senate.

- An earthquake was reported in Wuyan county, Inner Mongolia; it injured more than 100 persons.
- US Vice President Walter F. Mondale began a week-long official visit in China. He made a speech at Beijing University that was televised live throughout China. He said, "Any nation which seeks to weaken or isolate you in world affairs assumes a stance counter to American interests." He held talks with Vice Premier Deng Xiaoping a few times, and met Chairman Hua Guofeng on August 28. Mondale also made this point clear in his talks with Chinese leaders: the US does not have or anticipate a military relationship with China. Before leaving China, Mondale, on August 31, opened the first American consulate in Guangzhou at temporary quarters in the Dong Feng hotel. New accounts on electricity and cultural exchanges were signed. Premier Hua Guofeng accepted an invitation to visit the US the following year.

August 26 King Birendra of Nepal made his fourth visit to China August 26-28 en route to the Non-Aligned Summit Conference in Havana. Premier Hua Guofeng met him on August 27, and Vice Premier Deng Xiaoping met him on August 28. It was announced that in the past year the two countries had completed the joint surveying of their common boundary. The Fourth Session of the China-Nepal Joint Boundary Inspection Committee was held from August 27 to September 3.
- The Second Session of the Fifth People's Congress of the Xinjiang Uighur autonomous region was held in Urumgi from August 26 to September 5. All members of the Second Session of the Fourth Regional Political Consultative Conference, held from August 24 to September 6, attended the People's Congress as non-voting delegates. Ismail Amat was elected chairman of the People's Government of the Xinjiang Uighur autonomous region.

August 29 The eleventh plenary meeting of the Sino-Vietnamese negotiations was held in Beijing.
- Han Nianlong reiterated that so long as the Vietnamese troops did not withdraw from Kampuchea and the Vietnamese authorities did not stop their war of aggression against and military occupation of Kamuchea, China would not cease its support to the Kampuchean people's struggle against Vietnamese aggression.

• Chairman Hua Guofeng said that the policy of mobilizing educated youth to go to the countryside was correct in present circumstances. His remark was made when he received thirty-four representative educated young people. They were attending a meeting in the capital as representatives of educated youth from twenty-one provinces, cities, and autonomous regions.

September 1   Vice Premier Gu Mu visited Japan September 1-12. On September 6, he gave an important press conference in Tokyo in which he explained China's position on joint ventures and on opening of two special districts near Hong Kong and Macao where foreign investors could not only take part in joint undertakings, but also could run enterprises independently. Then he added, "The overwhelming majority of the nearly 1,100 million Chinese and Japanese people who desire to live on the best terms and cooperate closely in the fields of economics, trade, technology, and culture constitutes a mighty force, a tide which no one can dam." A joint venture, with capital investment around 100 million yuan (RMB), between China and Japan's ten major electrical and electronics firms was agreed to in principle.

September 2   Premier Hua Guofeng sent a message to greet the convening of the Sixth Conference of the Heads of State and Government of Non-Aligned Countries held in Havana.

September 3   The southern port of the Huangpu area was opened to foreign investment.
• The Chinese delegation to the Non-Aligned Summit Conference held in Havana, Cuba walked out of the opening session of the meeting when Cuban President Fidel Castro launched a scathing attack on China and the United States.

September 4   The United Nations Development Program (UNDP) opened a permanent field office in Beijing. Vice Premier Deng Xiaoping met the UNDP administrator, Mr. F. Bradford Morse and his party.
• China inaugurated a new flight on a new route, Beijing-Guangzhou-Manila. Under the Sino-Philippines civil aviation agreement, there would be two flights a week.

September 5 NCNA reported that a new concrete highway
bridge was opened to traffic across the upper reaches
of the Huanghe River. The twenty-eight-meter bridge
was located near the county town of Maju, in Gansu
province.

September 6 NCNA reported that a Japanese proposal in
June to engage in joint exploration of the oil resources
near the Senkaku (or Diao Yu) Islands was accepted
by Vice Premier Gu Mu during his visit to Japan.
  • Former British Prime Minister Edward Heath visited
China at the invitation of the Chinese government.
Vice Premier Deng Xiaoping met him on September 17.
  • Collectively owned small shops and some individual-
ly run trades provided needed service to the people,
said a commentary in the People's Daily. As a result,
thousands of collectively owned enterprises, including
restaurants, tea shops, and other service trades, had
sprung up。
  • China and Rumania signed, in Bucharest, an
agreement to cooperate in building a coking plant in
Huo county, Shanxi province.
  • NCNA reported that 600,000 Chinese were taking
university courses by watching television. Twenty-
eight stations in different parts of China were carrying
the classes of the national university which had been
run by the Ministry of Education and the Central
Broadcasting Administration since February 1979.
Courses included those in mathematics, physics, chemistry and English. The university held an end-of-term
examination in August. Students would receive diplo-
mas when they graduated after three years. At the
time, there were 20,000 teachers and instructors involved in the television university.

September 7 The CCP Central Committee and the State
Council were to organize a group of cadres to help
local party organizations and government departments
solve the problems of petitioners who were victims of
the false charges engineered by Lin Biao and the Gang
of Four. There were now approximately 6,000 petitioners in Beijing.

September 8 The third anniversary of the death of Mao
Zedong was marked by the publication of his "Talk to

Music Workers" delivered on August 24, 1956. It rejected both indiscriminate rejections and wholesale absorption of western culture, and advocated learning from the ancients to benefit the living, and learning from foreigners to benefit the Chinese.

• The State Council issued a circular instructing rural government organizations to adopt measures to encourage the peasants to harvest valuable wild plants, which could be used in place of grain, timber and other crops. Plans should be made to make use of these wild plants for making such things as paper, liquor, soap, and paint. The banks were instructed to extend loans to enterprises processing these raw materials. Tax exemptions were also made for those enterprises. The government would subsidize any initial losses.

September 9   The Bank of China announced it had the exclusive right to recover China's unblocked assets in the United States and would then deal with individual claimants.

September 10   Premier Hua Guofeng met the Canadian Parliamentary Delegation, led by Renaude Lapointe, speaker of the Senate, and James Jerome, speaker of the House of Commons.

September 11   China sent documents of its accession to the Convention on the Privileges and Immunities of the United Nations.

• China and Japan agreed to set up a joint venture, the Kyowa Co. Ltd., to run Beijing roast duck restaurants and other undertakings in Japan, including the sale of Beijing art and craft works, and the publication of Beijing recipes.

• The Eleventh Meeting of the Standing Committee of the Fifth NPC was held in Beijing from September 11-13. The meeting delegates discussed and approved "the Law on Environmental Protection of the People's Republic of China," and other resolutions as well as removals and appointments, including Ji Pengfei as vice premier of the State Council and Wei Wenbo as minister of Justice.

• Felix Greene, British writer and filmmaker, held a television interview with Premier Hua Guofeng. The entire script of the interview was released by NCNA on October 17.

September 12 The Queen of Denmark became the first head-of-state of a north European state to visit China when she arrived in Beijing for a ten-day visit. Premier Hua Guofeng met the queen on September 14, and the two nations signed an economic and technological cooperation agreement on the same day.

• A talk by Chairman Hua Guofeng on sports in China was given front-page coverage by the People's Daily. He said that sports not only help develop good health but also are conducive to moral and intellectual development as well."

• More than 3,000 people attended a political discussion at Tiananmen Square on the thought of the late Chairman Mao Zedong.

September 14 Chinese Ambassador to Japan Fu Hao hosted a cocktail party in Tokyo to mark the completion of the new Chinese Embassy building.

• Premier Hua Guofeng sent a message to José Eduardo Dos Santos, interim head of Angola, to express deep condolences on the death of President Agostinho Neto.

• The CCP Central Committee issued twenty-six slogans marking the thirtieth anniversary of the founding of the PRC, including ones to lower the population growth rate to below one percent, "Seek truth from facts," and "Practice is the sole criterion for testing."

September 15 Minister of Education Jiang Nanxiang left Beijing to visit Italy, the Netherlands, and Britain.

• Vice Premier Deng Xiaoping met Mr. Kanichi Kubo, Governor of Nagasaki prefecture in Japan, Mrs. Kubo, and other Japanese friends.

• After nearly five years' construction, a new modern terminal building with two satellite wings was completed in Beijing at the international airport. It was opened to passengers on October 1 when the installation of all interior equipment was completed. The terminal was located in the eastern suburbs some twenty kilometers from Beijing city center. Completed at the same time were a ramp, a hotel, a parking area, a highway, an overpass and a general fuelling station.

- The Fourth National Games, the biggest since 1949, opened in the 80,000-seat Workers Stadium in Beijing. Chairman Hua Guofeng, Vice-Chairmen Deng Xiaoping, Li Xiannian, and Wang Dongxing, and other party and state leaders attended the ceremony together with Queen Margrethe and Prince Henrik of Denmark and their entourage and other foreign guests. The games closed on September 30, after improving eight world and eight Asian records and 102 national records.

September 17 Premier Hua Guofeng met the Cameroon Military Delegation, led by Sadou Daoudou, minister of State for the Armed Forces.
- China and Japan signed a memorandum of science exchange in Tokyo.

September 18 Former US President Richard M. Nixon visited China September 18-22. He met Vice Premier Deng Xiaoping on September 18, Premier Hua Guofeng on September 19, and Ye Jianying, Chairman of the Standing Committee of the Fifth NPC. Nixon said at a banquet, "I consider the opening to China to have been the greatest achievement of my administration as President of the United States."

September 20 Vice Premier Deng Xiaoping met Dixy Lee Ray, governor of Washington State of the United States.
- Chairman Hua Guofeng met all members of the delegation from the Benin People's Revolutionary party.
- The twelfth plenary meeting of the Sino-Vietnamese negotiations was held in Beijing.

September 21 Vice Premier Deng Xiaoping met Akio Morita, chairman of the Board of Directors of the Sony Corporation of Japan, his wife, and his party.
- Hua Guofeng, Ye Jianying and Li Xiannian and other party and state leaders received, at the Great Hall of the People, representatives of advanced youth teams and individuals, and advanced women collectives and individuals from all over the country, and were photographed with them.
- The Sino-Nepalese Rasuwa Bridge was completed over the Dongling-Zangbu River bordering China and Nepal. This was the second bridge ever built by the two countries.

- Chen Chu, at the plenary meeting of the UN General Assembly, stressed that "The Government of Democratic Kampuchea is the sole legal government representing the people of Kampuchea," and that "it is only natural for it to send a delegation to attend the current session of the General Assembly."

September 23 NCNA reported that most adults now were able to read and write and ninety-four percent of the school-age children were enrolled in school. China's 900,000 primary schools now had 146 million students. The 160,000 middle schools had sixty-five million students. China's 598 universities and colleges had 850,000 students.

- The Chinese Government Delegation, led by Vice Foreign Minister Wang Yuping, arrived in Moscow to hold negotiations on problems affecting bilateral relations. This was the first formal attempt at direct intergovernmental negotiations to resolve outstanding issues since Premier Kosygin's visit to Beijing ten years ago. Five plenary meetings were held between September 27 and October 13. The talks lasted until January 19, 1980 without a breakthrough.

September 25 China and Morocco signed a protocol in Rabat to send a Chinese medical team to Morocco.

- Chen Chu spoke in the Fifth Committee of the UN General Assembly on China's rate of assessment. He said that in 1974 China had raised the rate from four percent to 5.5 percent on its own initiative as an indication of its support for the United Nations. This year China had provided statistics which made it possible for the Committee on Contributions to estimate China's rate in accordance with the unified rules of the UN and it was worked out that China's rate of assessment should be 0.95 percent. In order to prevent an immediate increase in the rates of some developed countries, China had accepted an increase of 0.67 percent points over the 0.95 percent rate, making China's rate 1.62 percent.

- Zhao Ziyang and Peng Zhen were elected to the politburo and twelve additional members to the Eleventh CCP Central Committee at the latter's Fourth Plenum held in Beijing from September 25-28. The plenum meeting also approved Ye Jianying's speech to mark the thirtieth anniversary of the founding of the PRC, and endorsed decisions on questions concerning the acceleration of agricultural development.

• Vice Premier Deng Xiaoping met former Prime Minister Pierre Trudeau of Canada. Deng told Trudeau, "the Sino-Soviet talks may go on a very long time without much progress."

September 26 Zhang Haifeng, vice minister of Foreign Affairs, went to the Czechoslovakian Embassy in Beijing, expressing his condolences on the death of General Ludvik Svoboda, former president of Czechoslovakia.

• NCNA reported that China had completed the building of a new oil field at Nanyang in Henan province.

• The Chinese Foreign Ministry issued a statement to reiterate sovereignty over Nansha Islands. It said, "Encroachment upon any part of the Nansha Islands, and exploitative or any other activities undertaken in these areas by any foreign country are illegal and impermissible."

• Ye Jianying, chairman of the Standing Committee of the Fifth NPC, met Their Royal Highnesses Grand Duke Jean and the Grand Duchess of Luxembourg. Chairman Hua Guofeng met them on September 28.

September 27 In general debate at the UN General Assembly, Han Nianlong said that the United Nations must take effective measures to make Vietnam withdraw from Democratic Kampuchea but then the Indo-Chinese question must be solved by the Indo-Chinese people without foreign interference.

• The CPPCC National Committee held a meeting to mark the double thirtieth anniversary of the founding of the PRC and the CPPCC in Beijing. Attending the meeting were a total of 1,400 people, including vice-chairmen, Standing Committee members, and members of the CPPCC National Committee and its staff.

September 28 At a press conference in Beijing, Vice Premier Gu Mu stated, "We are ready to accept loans from all friendly countries and financial organizations provided they do not affect China's sovereign rights and the terms are appropriate." He also stated, "China is ready to accede to the UN Financial Organizations and accept loans from the World Bank and other international financial organizations." He firmly stated, "There is no question about China's ability to repay loans."

• Premier Hua Guofeng gave awards to 222 national model workers and 118 advanced enterprises that had made outstanding contributions to the country's socialist modernization.

• China and Equatorial Guinea signed, in Malabo, two protocols to send a Chinese medical team, and radio technicians to Equatorial Guinea.

September 29   The launching of a three-stage rocket was reported in the Shanghai Liberation Daily. The paper published a photograph of the launching and said the rocket could place in orbit experimental scientific satellites and astronomical satellites.

• The protocol of the 1979 annual meeting of the Sino-Mongolian Border Railway Joint Commission was signed in Huhehot.

• NCNA reported that new highway bridge across the Yellow River in Lanzhou city in northwest China had opened to traffic. The reinforced concrete bridge was 304 meters in length and fifteen meters wide and carried a four-lane road. It also carried a six-meter wide pedestrian walkway.

• At a rally in Beijing marking the thirtieth anniversary of the founding of the PRC, Ye Jianying, chairman of the Standing Committee of the Fifth NPC, delivered a keynote speech. In his nationally televised speech, he made it plain that the Cultural Revolution of 1966-69 had been an outright "calamity." He said, "The Cultural Revolution was launched with the aim of preventing and combating revisionism. But at the time when the Cultural Revolution was launched, no accurate definition was given of revisionism, and an erroneous policy and method of struggle were adopted, deviating from the principle of democratic centralism. Driven by counter-revolutionary motives, Lin Biao, the 'Gang of Four' and other conspirators and careerists exploited these errors, pushed things to the extreme and formulated and pursued an ultra-left line. They engaged in overthrowing everything and launching an all-out civil war, usurping the party leadership and staging a coup to seize power. They attempted to undermine the foundation of our socialist system, subvert the dictator-

ship of the proletariat, destroy the leadership of the
party and adulterate Marxism-Leninism-Mao Zedong
Thought. The havoc which the counter-revolutionary
caused for ten long years spelled calamity for our
people and constituted the most severe reversal to
our socialist cause since the founding of the PRC."
Ye, in his speech, paid Liu Shaoqi, former state chairman, an indirect compliment by mentioning the "great
importance" of a party congress that had been dominated by Liu. There was the sudden reemergence of
Liu in a huge new painting depicting the leaders who
had assembled with Mao Zedong for the proclamation
of the People's Republic of China three decades ago.

September 30   Chairman Hua Guofeng presided over a huge
banquet at the Great Hall of the People in Beijing,
marking the thirtieth anniversary of the founding of
the PRC.
- Premier Hua Guofeng met the visiting Goodwill
Military Delegation from Bangladesh, led by Major General H.M. Ershad.
- Premier Hua Guofeng met the delegation of the
Burundi National Party of Unity and Progress, led by
Emile Mworoha.
- Vice Premier Deng Xiaoping met Takeshi Sakurada,
president of the Japan Federation of Employee's Associations, and Mrs. Sakurada.
- NCNA reported that as preparations for unblocking
all Chinese assets were not yet completed, China and
the US decided to postpone the date for unblocking to
January 31, 1980 (from October 1, 1979).

October 1   The Qin Shi Huang Museum of Soldier and Horse
Tomb Figures was opened to public in Lindong county,
Shaanxi province.
- Mr. Abdullah Rahmin, the deputy director of the
Foreign Affairs Office in the Xinjiang Uighur autonomous
region recounted that during the Chinese punitive attack
on Vietnam, Soviet border units were reinforced and had
been moved into battle positions. Chinese forces were
then arrayed against them.
- Ye Jianying, chairman of the Standing Committee
of the Fifth NPC, sent a message of congratulations to
President Alhaji Shehu Shagari on his assumption of the
president of Nigeria.

- Well over 20,000 people from China's fifty-six nationalities gathered to celebrate the thirtieth anniversary of the founding of the PRC at a colorful carnival in the Great Hall of the People in Beijing. Chairman Hua Guofeng, Vice-Chairmen Deng Xiaoping, Li Xiannian, and other top party and state leaders joined the holiday-makers in enjoying a kaleidoscopic program put on by outstanding artists and sportsmen. Among the presentations were songs and dances, operas and dramas, some of the latest Chinese feature films, ballad singing, instrumental music, puppet shows, acrobatics, gymnastics, table tennis and other sports shows, all going on simultaneously in two auditoriums and a dozen large and small halls.

October 2   Chairman Hua Guofeng, Vice-Chairmen Ye Jianying and Li Xiannian and other party and state leaders received representatives of the various minority nationalities attending the National Day celebrations, along with folk singers and poets attending a forum in Beijing and people working on a minority nationalities exhibition, in the Great Hall of the People.

- Chairman Hua Guofeng, Vice-Chairmen Deng Xiaoping and Li Xiannian, and other party and state leaders met sportsmen who distinguished themselves at the Fourth National Games, along with representatives of sports organizations in the Great Hall of the People.

October 3   Vice Premier Deng Xiaoping met Lord Todd, president of the Royal Society of London, Lady Todd, and their party.

October 4   The China International Trust and Investment Corporation held its first board of directors meeting. Rong Yien was appointed chairman of the forty-four-man board. Ye Jianying, chairman of the Standing Committee of the Fifth NPC, and other party and state leaders received all the directors.

- An agreement on an annual investment of $50 million for three consecutive years of joint ventures in China was signed in Beijing by the China International Trust and Investment Corporation and the Eaton-Sehn Pacific Corporation in San Francisco. Two other US corporations and one Swiss corporation had also entered into agreements for joint ventures.

October 5   A China-US bilateral six-day symposium on poly-
mer chemistry and physics was held at the Science
Hall in the western suburbs of Beijing. The twelve
American polymer chemists and physicists attending the
symposium were headed by Professor Paul J. Flory, a
Nobel Prize winner.

October 6   NCNA reported that an ancient temple, with valuable murals dating back 450 years, was recently discovered in southern Shanxi province. Inscriptions
showed that the authors were all folk artists.

• NCNA reported that China would present the
Japanese people with a second female panda after Lan
Lan, one of the two giant pandas sent to Japan in October 1972, died of nephritis and uremia in September
1979.

October 7   The Eighth Session of the Standing Committee of
the Fifth National Committee of the CPPCC closed in
Beijing. The session called on the CPPCC at all levels
to study and implement the communiqué of the Fourth
Plenary Session of the CCP Eleventh National Congress,
and Comrade Ye Jianying's speech, both documents of
historical importance.

• At his press conference, Premier Hua Guofeng announced that he would soon pay a state visit to four
western European countries--France, West Germany,
Britain, and Italy. He said that he looked forward to
discussing with government leaders of these countries
"international issues of common concern and ways of
further strengthening cooperation, expanding economic
and commercial dealings and broadening scientific, technical and cultural exchanges. He also made the following points: (1) China is opposed to the hegemonist
policies of aggression and expansion, and not to détente; (2) China had just signed contracts with France
for the building of a power station of 600,000 kw and
some equipment for a high-tension transmission line of
500,000 kv; (3) The Gang of Four would not be sentenced to death and they were now alive and would have
to be settled in the due process of law in the not-too-
distant future; (4) We oppose anarchism and the use of
democracy for the purpose of infringing upon the rights
of other people; (5) The Law of Joint Ventures adopted
at the recent NPC showed that China protected the in-

terests of foreign investors. China would continue to
work out supplementary laws and regulations to guarantee the rightful interests of foreign investors. Until
then, the procedure was to sign contracts with foreign
companies and have the contracts cleared by the government to give them legal authority; (6) China
stressed collective leadership. He was not very keen
on publishing his personal life, because this would
create inconveniences for his family, particularly his
children in their work and public activities; (7) A
good way of settling the questions relating to Hong
Kong, Kowloon, and the new territories could be sought
through consultations. Regardless of how the matter
would be settled, China would take notice of the interests of the investors there.

October 8   A "Declaration of Intent" on the development of
agriculture cooperation between China and the Netherlands was signed in The Hague. It pointed out that
opportunities for mutual agricultural cooperation might
exist in the sectors of animal husbandry, horticulture,
manufacturing and processing of animal feed, processing
of agricultural products, land development, land rec-
lamation and water management. The two sides agreed
to establish a joint China-Netherlands agricultural working group and to organize further reciprocal visits of
agricultural delegations.

October 9   Liang Yufan, speaking at the Thirtieth Session
of the Executive Committee of the UN High Commission-
ers for Refugees (UNHCR) in Geneva, urged that effective measures be adopted to stop the creation and
export of the refugees by Vietnam. He said that the
Chinese government had spent a total of $450 million in
assisting the 250,000 refugees driven into Chinese territories by the Vietnamese authorities.

October 10   Vice Premier Deng Xiaoping met the Thai Friendship Delegation, led by Air Marshal Sidhi Savetsila.
    • About 2,000 students of the People's University
paraded through Tiananmen Square in Beijing demanding that army units leave their campus.
    • The Xinhua News Agency and the Iraqi News
Agency signed an agreement on information cooperation.
    • A meeting to mark the sinking of a new high-yield

oil well in the South China Sea was held in Guangzhou
under the auspices of the Ministry of Geology and
Guangdong Provincial Revolutionary Committee. The
new well was located in the basin at the estuary of the
Pearl River on the continental shelf in the South Sea.
The basin, discovered in 1975, covered a total area of
150,000 sq. km.

October 11   NCNA reported that 230-million-year-old fossil
of an ullmannia tree was recently discovered by geologists and paleontologists in Runlian county, Sichuan
province.
    • Eight Democratic parties, and the All-China Feder-
ation of Industrial and Businessmen held their National
Congress in Beijing October 11-12. One thousand five-
hundred deputies attended the meetings to call on the
participants to help make China a powerful modern socialist country and achieve its reunification.
    • Vice Premier Deng Xiaoping met a visiting delegation
from the British Academy, led by Sir Alec Cairneross.

October 12   About 200 university students staged a march in
Beijing to demand that a tobacco company vacate their
campus.
    • The fifth session of the preliminary meeting for the
Sino-Soviet negotiations was held in Moscow. Although
no agreement was reached on the agenda, the two sides
agreed that the preliminary meeting should be concluded
and that formal negotiations should begin next week.
    • Premier Hua Guofeng left Beijing this morning by
special plane for Urumqi, capital of the Xinjiang Uighur
autonomous region, and then proceeded to France for
an official visit (October 15-20), the Federal Republic
of Germany (October 21-28), Britain (October 28 to
November 3), and Italy (November 3-6). This was the
first official visit to Western Europe by the head of the
Chinese government since 1949.

October 13   NCNA reported that Vice Premier Wang Renzhong
visited Yugoslavia, Denmark, the Netherlands and Belgium. He left Brussels for home on October 13.
    • Foreign correspondents reported that about 200
people took part in demonstrations outside Beijing's
Zhongnanhai, demanding to be allowed to return from
the countryside.

October 15   Premier Hua Guofeng arrived in Paris for an official visit from October 15-20.   Welcoming Premier Hua
at Orly Airport, French President Giscard d'Estaing
said that the visit was of "historical significance."   The
two leaders confirmed the trade agreement initialled in
Beijing the previous December.   A number of contracts
under negotiation were to be concluded shortly.   Premier Hua Guofeng had breakfast with Dr. Henry Kissinger at Hôtel De Marigny in Paris on October 17.
The two nations signed the following agreements: (1)
The Development of Economic Relations between China
and France; (2) A joint declaration relating to the opening of consular ports; (3) A program of cultural exchanges between China and France.
   • NCNA reported that Vietnamese armed personnel
were continuing with their provocations along the borders of Yunnan and Guangxi.
   • Vice Premier Deng Xiaoping was interviewed in
Beijing for British television by writer and filmmaker
Felix Greene.   The Vice Premier answered questions on
socialist democracy and the Chinese legal system, population control, environmental protection, development
of the Chinese economy and relations between China
and the Third World.

October 16   NCNA reported that 170,000 kw hydroelectric
power station recent went into operation in a town on
the Wuxi River in Zhejiang province.   The station's
dam was 129 meters high and 440 meters long at the
top.   The water storage capacity of the reservoir was
2,060 million cubic meters.
   • NCNA reported that China's first geological map
of the Qinghai-Tibet plateau was completed this August
. after six months' effort.   The geological map, to a
scale of 1.5 million to one, covered an area of
2,400,000 sq. km, and embraced western Sichuan province, northwestern Yunnan province, and the southern
part of Xianjiang and Gansu, apart from Qinghai and
Tibet.
   • Wei Jingsheng was sentenced to fifteen years' imprisonment at a public trial conducted by the intermediate people's court of Beijing.   He was convicted of supplying a foreigner with Chinese military intelligence
and carrying out counterrevolutionary agitation.   The
court also ruled that after he had served his sentence,

Wei Jingsheng would be deprived of political rights for
three years. Wei Jingsheng, twenty-nine years of age,
was a worker at the Beijing Public Parks Service Company before he was arrested on March 29. He joined
the army in 1969 and was demobilized in 1973.

* Former adviser to the Guomindang Executive Yuan
Deng Peng and his wife met Vice-Chairman Deng Yingchao in Beijing.

October 17   The US Federal District Court ruled that Presi-
dent Carter could not terminate the Mutual Defense
Treaty with the Republic of China (Taiwan) without
Congressional consent. This was overruled by the US
Court of Appeals on December 2, and on December 13,
the Supreme Court upheld, in effect, the position of
President Carter on procedural grounds.

* The first plenary meeting of the Sino-Soviet negotiations was held in Moscow, but no agreement was
reached except to meet again in Beijing in the spring.
It was reported that the Soviet side proposed the issuing of a joint statement on the principles to govern
their state relations. The Chinese side instead suggested a point-by-point discussion of all their differences including those on Indo-China.

* The Beijing intermediate people's court conducted
a public trial of Fu Yuehua, a woman on charges of
libel and violation of public order by organizing mass
disturbances. She was arrested by the Beijing Municipal Public Security Bureau on April 3 on a charge of
violating public order with the approval of the Beijing
municipal people's procuratorate. In an indictment
read at the trial, the public prosecutor accused Fu
Yuehua of bringing a false charge against Geng Yutian,
former acting party secretary of her brigade. In April
1973, Fu Yuehua accused Geng of raping her on the
night of February 14, 1972. The service company conducted an investigation and found the charge groundless and announced the result of the investigation at a
public meeting in her brigade in 1974. Fu Yuehua,
however, continued to make the same charge, the indictment said.

* Chairman Hua Guofeng said in a TV interview (by
Felix Greene on September 11) that the Cultural Revolution was a grave setback for China but he denied the
country was discarding the ideas of former Chairman Mao.

• Vice Premier Deng Xiaoping met the US State Governor Delegation, led by William G. Milliken, governor of Michigan. The delegation included the governors of Hawaii, Montana, Colorado, Minnesota, Iowa, and Vermont.

• A play, Storm Over China, was staged in Beijing. The eleven-scene play, by the Guangzhou PLA Modern Drama Company, covered events from the time of Lin Biao's plane crash in September 1971 to the arrest of the Gang of Four in October 1976.

October 18   Vice Premier Deng Xiaoping met the Asahi Shimbun delegation from Japan, led by director Seiki Watanabe.

• The Chinese Ministry of Agriculture presented three stud hogs from Meishan Jiaxing and Jinhua to the Ministry of Agriculture of France at a ceremony in Shanghai. The gift was part of the effort to promote exchanges of science and technology between the two nations.

• NCNA reported that Erwin Engst and Joan Hinton, two Americans who had been working in China for more than thirty years, were invited to be advisers to the Ministry of Farm Machinery.

October 19   The thirteenth plenary session of the Sino-Vietnamese negotiations was held in Beijing. Han Nianlong said, "If Vietnam does not stop its aggression and expansion in Kampuchea and Laos and its hostile anti-China policy, it will be difficult to re-establish the necessary mutual trust between China and Vietnam and the relations between the two countries cannot be normalized."

• A delegation of Moslems, led by Mohammed Ali Zhang Jie, left Beijing to visit Mecca, the first group of Chinese Moslems to make a pilgrimage since 1949.

• Vice Premier Deng Xiaoping met the Pakistan Airforce Goodwill Delegation, led by Chief of Airforce Marshal Mohammed Shamin.

• China and Thailand signed the 1980 protocol on the importation and exportation of commodities in Bangkok.

• China and Canada exchanged notes to renew the trade agreement (originally signed in October 1973) and signed an economic cooperation protocol in Ottawa.

It was also announced that "effective January 1, 1980, the government of Canada would grant general preferential tariff treatment to China."

October 20 The Chinese Military Delegation, led by Zhang Caiqian, arrived in Islamabad for a ten-day visit to Pakistan.

October 21 Premier Hua Guofeng arrived at Bonn-Cologne from Paris for an official visit October 21-27. Three agreements were signed, covering economic cooperation, cultural and scientific exchanges embracing technology, sports, education and joint exchanges of teachers, scientists and youth, and the setting up of consulates in Hamburg and Shanghai. Also agreed to was a link-up between China and Germany in joint production of goods and materials for the Third World.
  • The Chinese Olympic Committee accepted the proposal made by the International Olympic Committee (IOC) in Puerto Rico on June 29 concerning China's seat in the world body, considering it good and conforming to reality. According to the proposal, the Taiwan sports body would stay in the IOC as a provincial organization of China, under the name of China's Taipei Olympic Committee; and the Taipei Olympic Committee should also change its flag and anthem as a matter of principle.
  • China and Italy signed the 1980-81 cultural, scientific and technical cooperation program.

October 23 President Carter sent the US-China trade agreement to Congress for approval. The agreement contained reciprocal nondiscriminatory treatment--that is, most-favored-nation-treatment--for the imports and exports of both countries.
  • Vice Premier Deng Xiaoping met a noted Japanese public figure Shigeharu Matsumoto.

October 24 NCNA reported that the Capital Cement Plant became the first factory in Beijing to use opinion polls in the appointment of senior administrative personnel. This was a new measure adopted by the plant and was aimed at giving the 3,100 workers more say before appointments were made by the plant leadership. Of the twenty-one chiefs and deputy chiefs in the fifteen of-

fices of the plant, four failed to receive a majority vote
and were removed from office.

• NCNA reported that the State Council raised the
purchasing prices of eighteen main agricultural products
starting last March. The price increases averaged
24.8 percent.

• The Beijing Institute of Political Science and Law
reopened after a suspension of eight years. The Institute enrolled 403 undergraduates and thirty-five
postgraduates this school year.

• Vice President Walter Mondale met Chinese Foreign
Trade Minister Li Qiang and his party at Mondale's
office in the White House.

• Zhu Yunshan was elected Chairman of the Control
Committee of the Revolutionary Committee of the Chi-
nese Guomindang. Shi Liang was elected chairman of
the Central Committee of the China Democratic League.
Hu Ruewen was elected chairman of the Central Committee of the China Democratic National Construction
Association. Zhou Jianren was elected chairman of the
Central Committee of the China Association for Promot-
ing Democracy. Ji Fang was elected chairman of the
Central Committee of the Chinese Peasants and Workers
Democratic party. Huang Dingchen was elected chairman of Jiusan Society. Cao Xiao was elected chairman
of the Council of the General Office of the Taiwan
Democratic Self-Government League. Hu Ziang was
elected chairman of the Executive Committee of the All-
China Federation of Industrialists and Businessmen.

October 25 Vice Premier Deng Xiaoping met Harold Macmillan, chairman of the board of Macmillan Publishing Company and former British prime minister, and his party.
• The second plenary meeting of the Sino-Soviet
negotiations on state relations was held in Moscow.
• NCNA announced that eight Chinese mountain peaks
would be opened to foreign climbers, beginning in 1980.
The eight peaks were: Mount Chomolunga, the world's
highest peak, on China's border with Nepal; Mount
Xisha Bangma in Tibet; Mount Muztag Ata in Xinjiang;
Mount Kongur in Xianjiang; Mount Kongur Tiubie Tagh
in Xinjiang; Mount Bogda in Xinjiang; Mount Gongga
in Sichuan province; and Mount Anyemaqen in Qinghai.

October 26 In a full-page commentator's article on human

rights, the Guangming Daily declared that all those who acted in violation of state law and party discipline and encroached on any citizen's rights would be seriously dealt with, irrespective of their positions.
• The IOC Executive Board unanimously adopted a resolution in Nagoya, Japan, to restore China's seat in the IOC.

October 27   China and Finland signed the 1980 trade agreement in Beijing.
• Premier Hua Guofeng sent a message to Prime Minister Milton Cato, extending congratulations on the independence of St. Vincent and the Grenadines in the eastern part of the Caribbean Sea, and informing him of the Chinese decision to recognize the country.

October 28   NCNA reported that 3,000 participants from all over China were expected at the Fourth National Congress of Writers and Artists, the first such meeting in nineteen years. The gathering was to open on October 30. Positive and negative lessons in China's literary work would be discussed at the fifteen-day meeting. Simultaneous with this Congress would be meetings by the Chinese Associations of Writers, Dramatists, Film Workers, Musicians, Artists, Dancers and Ballad Singers, the Photographic Society and the Society for the Study of Folk Literature and Art.
• The earliest map of the stars to be found in China was discovered in a temple pagoda in Suzhou. The map, dated A.D. 1005 and printed with wood blocks, depicts the twenty-eight "lunar mansions" in ancient China and the zodiacal signs of Babylon on a sanskrit incantation--"Dharani of Great Freedom to be obtained."
• Vice Premier Deng Xiaoping met Air Chief Marshal Harin Hongskula of Thailand. He told the marshal that China would side with the ASEAN countries if Vietnam attacked them; China would side with Thailand if Vietnam attacked it.
• Premier Hua Guofeng arrived in London for an official visit from October 28 to November 2. Hua held talks with Prime Minister Margaret Thatcher at Downing Street on October 29. The two nations signed an air agreement which provided for regular flights between Beijing and London. Hua told Thatcher he would take action to stop the rising flood of illegal Chinese immi-

grants into Hong Kong. Foreign Minister Huang Hua
said investors could rest at ease over Hong Kong's future. Mrs. Thatcher accepted an invitation to visit
China. China finally won the approval of the British
government to purchase a Harrier VTOL aircraft.

October 29   China and West Germany signed an agreement
on technical cooperation in weights and measures in
Bonn.
 • China and Gambia signed a protocol to dispatch
a Chinese medical team to Gambia.
 • Meetings were held to commemorate the ninetieth
birthday of the late Comrade Li Dazhao, one of the
founders of the CCP and a martyr who was murdered
by the Northern Warlord fifty-two years ago.

October 30   In a speech to the Fourth National Congress of
Writers and Artists, Vice Premier Deng Xiaoping called
on China's writers and artists to "make positive contributions to a highly developed socialist civilization" as
part of China's drive for modernization.
 • The Chinese Football Association, in its reply to
the International Football Federation, accepted the
resolution taken by its Executive Committee on the
question of China's representation. The resolution decided to readmit the PRC Association, while retaining
the membership of the Football Association based in
Taiwan on the condition that it would change its name
to "The Chinese Taipei Football Association" and not
use its original symbol.

October 31   Vice Premier Deng Xiaoping met former French
Prime Minister Edgar Faure.
 • Hubei province and the state of Ohio officially became sister states.
 • China and Poland signed a scientific and technical
cooperation protocol in Warsaw.
 • NCNA announced the November 1 price rise, aver-
aging thirty percent, for eight categories of foodstuffs.
This coincided with the issuing of monthly subsidies of
five RMB for urban workers aimed at offsetting the
food price rise. The eight categories involved pork,
beef, eggs, chicken, duck, marine products, milk, and
vegetables. It also announced that forty percent of the
urban work force would receive wage raises this year.

This was the first salary boost since November 1977,
a move which affected about sixty percent of the urban
labor force and which broke a fourteen-year dry spell
during which such wide-scale increases were neglected.

November 1   Yilin (Forest of Translation), a journal devoted
to the translation of foreign literature, began publication by the Jiangsu People's Publishing House.
   • The Berlin Philharmonic Orchestra ended its week
of concerts in China and received prolonged applause
from an audience of 5,000. Herbert Von Karajan conducted a joint performance by his orchestra and the
Chinese Central Philharmonic Orchestra.
   • NCNA reported that the Hairag-Delungha section
of the Qinghai-Tibet railway was opened to passenger
traffic.

November 2   The Chinese city of Nanjing and the US city
of St. Louis became sister cities.
   • The third plenary meeting of the Sino-Soviet negotiations was held in Moscow.
   • The US House of Representative Committee on Foreign Affairs held a hearing on a trade bill concerning
China.
   • Chinese Foreign Trade Minister Li Qiang, after
his ten-day trade mission to seven US cities, held a
press conference in New York. He said that New York
would become the center of China's growing trade efforts with the United States. However, China had not
decided where to situate its first trade mission office.

November 3   The US Defense Secretary Harold Brown said
he would visit China January 6-13 to discuss world
issues with Chinese leaders. However, he excluded
the possibility of arms sales to China.
   • Chairman Hua Guofeng arrived in Rome for an official state visit. The two nations signed two declarations of intent; one for cultural, scientific and technical cooperation, the other in trade and economic
spheres. China and Italy were also to exchange consulates in Milan and Shanghai. In the next year, an
Italian-Chinese committee would meet in Rome to discuss
trade and economic issues.

November 5   Yu Mengjia, at the UN Second Committee meeting, said that China had decided to participate in the Global Environmental Monitoring System (GEMS). China was engaged in constructing shelter belt systems to combat desertification, campaigning to educate the Chinese in better understanding of the environment, and promulgating environmental protection laws.

November 6   Chairman Hua Guofeng had a talk with the director general of the FAO in Rome. Although China had not released official stock figures, the FAO claimed that stocks had steadily increased since 1974 except in 1978, and that a stock of fifty-two million tons would be held by China at the end of 1980.
  • Wei Jingsheng's appeal against his fifteen-year sentence was turned down by Beijing Higher Court.
  • NCNA reported that from October 21-30, Vietnam had made armed provocations on fifty occasions along China's Yunnan and Guangxi border.

November 7   The Chinese Social Science Delegation, led by Hu Qiaomu, visited Rumania November 1-7. The two nations signed a social science cooperation agreement on November 7.
  • Foreign correspondents in Beijing reported that printed wall posters appeared in Beijing urging candidates for local elections to support the policy of allowing Chinese to emigrate abroad freely and to take up jobs overseas.

November 8   The London Times reported that friends of Wei Jingsheng asked British Prime Minister Margaret Thatcher to intercede with Chairman Hua for Wei's freedom.

November 9   Foreign Minister Huang Hua ended a three-day visit to Yugoslavia. During his visit, he held talks with President Tito.
  • The Chinese Academy of Sciences held a policy-making meeting in Beijing from October 25 to November 7. It was attended by 170 people, including some sixty noted Chinese scientists.
  • China and West Germany signed an agreement on broadcasting and television cooperation.
  • "The Long March," the largest jade carving produced in China to date, was recently completed and was

now on display at an arts-and-crafts exhibition in Shanghai.

November 10   Foreign Minister Huang Hua arrived in Bucharest, Rumania for a three-day visit (November 10-12). He held talks with President Nicolae Ceausescu.
   • China and Mali signed, in Banako, a protocol to dispatch a Chinese medical team to Mali.
   • Premier Hua Guofeng returned to Beijing after visiting four West European countries. Vice Premier Deng Xiaoping and other party and state leaders greeted him at the airport. On his way home, Premier Hua Guofeng made a short stopover in Urumqi, Xinjiang Uighur autonomous region.

November 11   China Central Television put out a new language teaching program, "English on Sunday," for viewers who had mastered basic English and wished to improve their standard.
   • China and Jordan signed a cultural cooperation agreement in Amman.
   • At Beijing's Democracy Wall, a group of young people were selling transcripts of the trial of Wei Jingsheng.
   • Vice Foreign Minister He Ying returned home after visiting Somalia, Kenya, Oman, Lebanon, Egypt, the Yemen Arab Republic and Kuwait.
   • The United Nations signed an agreement with the PRC for a grant of $20 million to Beijing to aid the resettlement of more than 250,000 ethnic Chinese who had been expelled from Vietnam.
   • In order to reduce population growth to zero by the year 2000, the Chinese government adopted new regulations aimed at limiting families to one or, at most, two children. It also announced that the current population stood at 960 million, an increase of 400 million in thirty years.

November 12   Greek Prime Minister Constantine Karamanlis paid an official visit to China November 12-16. The People's Daily editorial praised Greece's entry into the EEC, its relations with the Third World and its developing friendship and cooperation among countries in the Balkan and Mediterranean region. On November 15, an agreement was signed for scientific and technical cooperation. Vice Premier Deng Xiaoping held talks with Premier Karamanlis on November 13.

• Chen Chu urged the UN General Assembly to take immediate measures to stop aggression against Democratic Kampuchea, to demand the withdrawal of Vietnamese forces from Kampuchea and to offer all possible assistance to the Kampuchean people.

• The Twelfth Session of the Standing Committee of the Fifth NPC was held in Beijing November 12-29. The members discussed Chairman Hua Guofeng's visit to four Western countries and the effectiveness of laws and decrees and regulations on reeducation through labor. They also appointed Peng Zhen as acting secretary general of the committee, and referred the problem of the Xidan (Democracy) Wall to the Beijing Municipal Revolutionary Committee.

November 13 Liu Qing, editor of the Chinese underground journal, The April 5 Forum, was arrested after he voluntarily went to Beijing's Public Security Bureau to try to help the four arrested at Democracy Wall on November 11. Liu was apparently arrested for his role in publishing a tape-recorded transcript of the trial of Wei Jingsheng.

• Premier Hua Guofeng met Bettino Craxi, general secretary of the Italian Socialist party.

• Jiangsu province established official ties of friendship (sister state) with the State of Victoria of Australia.

November 15 Elections by secret ballot took place in Beijing's East City District, the first step towards a general election. Out of 592 candidates standing, 348 were elected.

November 16 The International Olympic Committee voted, 62-17, to accept a plan under which the PRC would take part in the 1980 Olympic Games. China had not participated in the Olympics since 1949.

• The Fourth National Congress of Writers and Artists closed in Beijing. Chairman Hua Guofeng, Vice-Chairman Li Xiannian, and other party and state leaders met all the participants at the Great Hall of the People. The results of the congress were summarized in a 25,000-character report by Zhou Yang, the newly elected chairman of the federation.

November 17 In Dalian (Liaoning province), the Chinese
Seismological Society's inaugural meeting, held over six
days (November 17-22), reported that casualties in the
great Tangshan earthquake (July 28, 1976) were an
estimated 242,000 people killed and 164,000 seriously
injured.

• China and Bangladesh signed a cultural cooperation
agreement in Beijing. Premier Hua Guofeng met Foreign Minister Muhammad Shamsul Huq.

• A symposium on astro-geodynamics was held in
Wuhan recently to study polar motion, time and latitude
observatories, star catalogue, analysis of time signals
errors in China, and the relationship of these to the
earth's tides.

November 18 NCNA reported that a well-preserved bronze
sword, dating back about 2,300 years, was found on a
tomb of the ancient Chu state in Huaiyang country,
Henan province.

• Premier Hua Guofeng met the delegation from the
Central Committee of the League of Communists of Yugoslavia.

• The CCP Central Committee sent a message of
congratulations to the Rumanian Communist party on
the convocation of its Twelfth National Congress. The
CCP Delegation, led by Ulanfu, attended the Congress.

November 19 Premier Hua Guofeng met the Zaire Popular
Revolutionary Movement Delegation, led by Kithima Rin
Ramazani, political bureau member and executive secre-
tary of the movement.

November 20 Chairman Hua Guofeng met the Delegation of
the Palestine National Council, led by President Khaled
Fahum.

• Vice Premier Deng Xiaoping met Volker Hauff,
minister of Research and Technology of the Federal Republic of Germany.

• The Chinese Ministry of Foreign Affairs issued a
statement to state China's three principles for solving
the Middle East question: (1) the Palestinian people
must realize their national rights, including the right
to return to their homeland, exercise self-determination, and build a Palestinian state; (2) the People of
the Arab countries must recover their lost territories;

and (3) the Middle East question must be solved in an all-round and impartial way.

• NCNA reported that Chinese geologists had discovered animal fossils in the Mashan group strata in Heilongjiang province, estimated to be between fifty-seven and 700 million years old.

• NCNA announced an agreement providing a new kind of joint venture between an industrial company, the Beijing Cotton Textile Company, and a number of rural people's communes and state farms.

• China and Nepal signed a protocol on joint boundary inspection.

• The first consulate general of the PRC in the US was officially inaugurated in Houston, Texas.

• China and Venezuela signed an agreement in Caracas to promote sport exchanges between the two nations (table tennis, gymnastics, archery, softball, and cycling).

November 21 The State Council issued regulations on awards for outstanding scientists who made significant contributions in the area of natural sciences: first class, a medal and 10,000 RMB; second class, a medal and 5,000 RMB; third class, a medal and 2,000 RMB; fourth class, a medal and 1,000 RMB.

• Non-Communist party members won more than a third of the 348 seats in Beijing's East City District Congress in the first multichoice election in the country for twenty-five years.

• Yu Mengjia said in the UN Second Committee meeting that, in China, solar energy was being used and research was being conducted in the use of wind power, geothermal energy, and the possibilities of biomass conversion from small-scale hydroelectric stations.

November 22 The 1976 Tangshan earthquake death toll was announced in Dalian where the Chinese Seismological Society held its inaugural Congress. An estimated 242,000 people were killed and 164,000 were seriously injured.

• The fifth plenary meeting of the Sino-Soviet negotiations on state relations was held in Moscow.

• Chinese writers, artists and professors joined in debate with the nation's leaders over how much creative freedom they should have and whether their work must be limited to serve Communist party interest.

November 23 Premier Hua Guofeng met Belgian Vice Premier
Willy Claes. On the same day, an agreement on the
development of economic, industrial, scientific and technical cooperation was concluded between the PRC and
the Belgium-Luxembourg Economic Union.
  • Chairman Hua Guofeng sent a message congratulating Nicolae Ceausescu on his relection as general secretary of the Rumanian Communist party.

November 24 China held a national scientific and technological conference to discuss how to implement the policy
of readjustment, and how to encourage scientists and
other intellectuals to work for China's socialist modernization.
  • Foreign Minister Huang Hua ended his five-day
visit to Nepal. He signed a Sino-Nepalese boundary
protocol in Katmandu with his Nepalese counterpart,
and expressed satisfaction with the fulfillment of the
first journey survey of the Sino-Nepalese border. He
arrived in Rangoon, Burma on November 24.

November 26 Belgium and China signed an agreement and
two protocols on economic, industrial, scientific and
technical cooperation in Beijing.
  • China and Sri Lanka signed the 1980 protocol governing the exchange of commodities in Beijing.
  • The Chinese Olympic Committee welcomed the International Olympic Committee's decision restoring Chinese rights in the IOC.
  • The Chinese Ministry of Foreign Affairs issued a
statement, expressing concern over the recent developments in Iran-US relations. It said, "We always hold
that the internal affairs of each country should be no
interference by other countries. But at the same time
we hold that the principles guiding international relations and the accepted diplomatic immunities should be
universally respected. We hope that a reasonable and
appropriate solution can be found at an early date
through peaceful consultation in accordance with principles of international law and diplomatic practice."

November 27 The Standing Committee of the Fifth NPC held
a meeting to discuss how to strengthen the socialist
legal system.
  • Premier Hua Guofeng sent a cable to President

Kaunda, expressing support for the Zambian government and people in their struggle against armed incursions by Rhodesian racist forces.
  • NCNA reported that in mid-November, Vietnamese
armed personnel frequently fired or shelled across
China's Yunnan and Guangxi borders and made incursions into China's territory, killing four inhabitants and
wounding many others.
  • At a press conference, the president of the Chinese Olympic Committee, Zhong Shitong, announced
that the committee had decided to send athletes to participate in five events (speed-skating, figure skating,
alpine skiing, cross-country skiing and the winter
biathlon) at the Thirteenth Winter Olympics to be held
at Lake Placid in February. He also announced that
China would participate in the competitions and preliminary contests of fifteen events, including track and
field, swimming, and gymnastics, at the twenty-second
summer Olympics to be held in Moscow the following
July.
  • Chinese Olympic Committee President Zhong Shitong
wrote a letter to the chairman of the Chinese Taipei
Olympic Committee, Shen Chiaming, proposing sports
exchanges between the mainland and Taipei in preparation for the Lake Placid and Moscow Games.

November 28 Syria and China signed a sports agreement on
table tennis, gymnastics, and volleyball.
  • The Second Session of the Sino-Yugoslav Joint
Committee for Industrial Cooperation was held in Belgrade November 22-28.

November 29 On behalf of the Musician's International Mutual Aid Fund of the International Music Council, the
world-renowned violinist Yehudi Menuhin presented
Chinese musicians with a violin when he and his wife
visited the Central Conservatory of Music in Beijing.
  • Premier Hua Guofeng sent a message to the president of the UN Commemoration Conference on the International Day of Solidarity with Palestine People, and
reaffirmed China's support for the struggle of the
Palestine people to regain their national rights.
  • The Twelfth Plenary Session of the Standing Committee of the Fifth NPC appointed Peng Zhen acting
secretary general of the NPC Standing Committee. The

session also passed three resolutions to strengthen law and order.

November 30 The first round of the Sino-Soviet negotiations to improve state relations concluded without positive result in Moscow. According to press reports, Moscow presented a draft statement that called upon each side to pledge, not to attack the other. China, in turn, demanded that the Soviet Union withdraw three divisions from the Mongolian border and end aid to Vietnam. Moscow rejected the Chinese demands. Both sides agreed to convene the next session in Beijing.
  • China held a national conference on mini-computer techniques in Sian, Shaanxi.

December 1 Chen Chu supported the appeal made on behalf of the UN Security Council for the immediate release of the detained American diplomatic personnel in Iran. He also said that although China believed that the internal affairs of each country should be managed by its own people with no outside interference, the principles guiding international relations and the accepted diplomatic immunities should be universally respected.

December 2 The Vietnamese government formally notified the UN Security Council of its charge that China was preparing for another war by accepting 10,000 tribesmen from Laos as refugees.

December 3 China and Sudan signed an agreement in Beijing to extend a Chinese loan to Sudan.
  • Premier Hua Guofeng met General Abdel Magid Khalil, first vice president, minister of Defense and Commander-in-Chief of the Armed Forces of the Sudan.
  • Zhang Guotao, last surviving founder of the CCP, died at age 82 in Canada.

December 4 The Chinese Wushu Troupe ended its visit to Belgium. The troupe had arrived in Belgium on November 22 at the invitation of the Belgium-China Association.

December 5 NCNA reported that 14,000 bronze coins, from 800 to 2,000 years old, were recently unearthed in Jilin province.

• NCNA reported that the People's Construction
Bank of China would give priority in the allocation of
funds and loans to enterprises involved in cooperative
ventures with foreign countries, while ensuring funds
for major construction projects.
• Prime Minister Ohira Masayoshi visited China December 5-9, accompanied by new Foreign Minister Okita
Saburo. He held talks with Premier Hua Guofeng on
December 5 and 6, and with Vice Premier Deng Xiaoping
on December 6. The Japanese pledged $1.5 million in
low-interest loans for six high-priority modernization
projects, namely Shijusuo port construction, Yanzhou-
Shijusuo railway expansion, Qinghuangdao-Beijing railway expansion, Guangzhou-Henyang railway expansion,
Qinghuangdao port expansion, and Wuqiangxi hydroelectric power plant construction. China would become
eligible for the preferential tariff system for developing
countries in the Japanese market beginning April 1980.
Premier Hua Guofeng would make an official visit to
Japan in May. Another Japanese aid project would be
the Japan-China Friendship Hospital to be completed in
the compounds of Beijing Medical College during 1980
at a cost of 15.5 billion yuan. An agreement was signed
on the promotion of cultural, educational, scientific,
art, and sport exchanges, while support "in principle"
was given to a Japanese request that Japanese families
be allowed to visit northwest China to conduct memorial
services for war dead. Agreement was also reached on
December 6 for the joint development of oil and natural
gas deposits in Bohai Bay. On political matters, Premier Hua was said to have rejected Ohira's plea to conduct further military action against Vietnam. Hua was
quoted as saying there was "no possibility" of North
Korea attacking South Korea. Ohira and Hua agreed
to the lessening of tensions on the Korean Peninsula
and to its eventual reunification.

December 6   The Beijing Municipal Revolutionary Committee
issued a notice, to take effect beginning December 8,
banning the posting of large-or-small character posters
in public places other than one site in the outskirts of
the city (Yuetan Park). The notice also announced
that poster authors must register with the committee.

December 8   NCNA reported that the state purchase prices

for farm products had gone up by more than 130 percent in twenty-nine years since 1950, while market prices for farm machinery in the same period had dropped forty-eight percent.

• China and Energy International (an American company) signed an agreement, in the form of letter of understanding, to license China Corp. of Shipbuilding Industry to produce a multifuel engine (developed in the US) for export.

• NCNA reported that a national conference on urban social order and security was held recently in Beijing. It focussed on problems about the social order and discussed the principles, tasks, and measures needed to deal with them.

December 9   China and Iraq signed a sports exchange agreement in Beijing.

• The People's Daily, in an editorial, lashed out at "international reactionaries" who protested against the trial and fifteen-year prison sentence of dissident Wei Jingsheng. The editorial said that the official verdict on Wei was that he was not a dissident but a criminal, and was dealt with accordingly.

• President Hadji Hassan Gouled Aptidon of Djibouti arrived in Beijing for an official visit. He was welcomed at the airport by Premier Hua Guofeng. An agreement on economic and technical cooperation was signed.

December 10   NCNA reported that beginning February 1980, China would take part in the work of the Geneva Committee on Disarmament. China did not take part in meetings of the committee in 1979, but declared that it reserved the right to take part in the committee at an appropriate time.

• A Chinese military friendship delegation left Bangkok for home after an eight-day visit to Thailand.

December 12   China raised oil prices for its crude oil supplies for the October-December shipments to Japan from $21.8 to $24 per barrel.

December 13   The Seventh Municipal Congress of Beijing elected Lin Hujia as mayor of Beijing.

• NCNA reported that some 500 rare Buddhist art

objects from Zhejiang, Jiangsu and Shanghai were now on display in Shanghai, attracting thousands of visitors every day.

• China and Czechoslovakia signed a scientific and technical cooperation protocol in Beijing.

• China opened a consulate general office in San Francisco.

• The People's Daily reported that gang warfare had erupted in Beijing last summer and one fight involved more than 140 men. The article also noted that gang leaders Zheng Guohua and Zhang Huolin were put on trial and given long prison sentences.

December 14   The US Supreme Court voted down (7-2) to hear an appeal for a lower court decision and upheld the Carter administration's abrogation of the US-Taiwan Treaty.

• The Institute de Development Industriel and the Chinese International Trust and Investment Corporation signed an outline agreement in Beijing to help small and medium sized French companies establish themselves in China. The agreement would pave the way for cooperation in joint ventures and compensation trade.

December 16   An agreement for a joint Chinese-Italian film-- Marco Polo--was signed in Beijing.

December 17   NCNA reported that a well-preserved 3,000- year-old dry female corpse found in Xinjiang in September 1978, was on display in Shanghai at an exhibition of ancient Chinese corpses of various dynasties.

December 18   The PRC Ministry of Foreign Affairs, in a note to the Vietnamese Embassy in Beijing, strongly protested a recent incursion by armed Vietnamese personnel in the border areas which killed or wounded a number of Chinese.

• Vice Premier Deng Xiaoping said that China would make another "punitive" strike on Vietnam if its troops crossed into Thailand.

December 19   NCNA reported that China's urban housing construction was expected to exceed forty million square meters in 1979, setting a new annual record.

• Former World Heavyweight Boxing Champion Muhammad Ali arrived in Beijing.

- The US Senate Finance Committee unanimously approved a 1979 trade agreement giving China most-favored-nation trade status.

December 20   China and Egypt signed a scientific cooperation agreement in Cairo.
- The fifteenth session of Sino-Vietnamese talks ended in deadlock. The Chinese side rejected a Vietnamese proposal to sign an agreement "to refrain from armed provocations" beginning January 1, 1980 as "perfunctory and cheating."

December 21   A protocol of the Eighteenth Session of the Sino-Hungarian Commission of Scientific and Technical Cooperation was signed in Budapest.
- A new edition of the late American writer Edgar Snow's Red Star Over China was published.
- Michael Fu Tieshan of the Beijing diocese was consecrated bishop this morning in a two-and-a-half-hour ceremony held at the seventy-five-year-old southern cathedral in Beijing (the site of the Beijing First Catholic Church). The ceremony was not recognized as valid by the Vatican since the prelate was elected by prisoners.
- NCNA announced that construction of China's largest tourist hotel began in Shanghai. The twenty-five story Shanghai Hotel would have a total floor area of more than 43,800 square meters. It would also have 600 rooms, eleven restaurants, a central lobby, and shops.

December 22   The Hong Kong-Beijing chartered flight for tourists was inaugurated.

December 23   NCNA reported that 1,200 newspapers, magazines and journals had been published in China for circulation.
- The People's Daily printed, on the front page, a letter from Yasir Arafat, thanking Premier Hua Guofeng for his message on the UN International Day of Solidarity to the Palestine people, expressing the Chinese people's support for the Palestinian people's just struggle.

December 24   In New York, Chinese and Ecuadorean representatives signed a joint communiqué announcing their decision to establish diplomatic relations at the ambassadorial level.

December 25   A People's Daily article, marking the eighty-sixth anniversary of Chairman Mao Zedong's birth said, "Mao Zedong objected to 'Maoism' and believed that his thought was the result of a collective effort."
  • NCNA reported that editing work on the first comprehensive dictionary of Chinese history began recently in Tianjin under the leadership of the Chinese Academy of Social Sciences with the noted historian Zheng Tianting as editor-in-chief. The dictionary contained 30,000 entries amounting to some ten million words.
  • NCNA reported that tourist hotels were being built in more than twenty cities throughout China; the cities included Kunming, Guilin, Hangzhou and the major cities of Beijing, Shanghai, Chongqing and Harbin. Work on the hotels began in 1978 and most of them were expected to be completed in 1981. All of the hotels could accommodate 500 tourists or more.
  • Fu Yuehua, a thirty-four-year-old activist, was sentenced to two years in prison by the Beijing court for bringing false charges of rape against a superior, and "violating public order" during a protest march last January.
  • NCNA reported that Beijing's Protestant church in the eastern part of the city resounded with the singing and music of Christmas carols at a Christmas eve service attended by more than 200 Chinese and foreign Christians. The newly consecrated Bishop Michael Fu Tieshan presided at Midnight Mass in the city's southern Catholic cathedral.

December 26   An art show of thirty-one avant-garde Chinese artists was held in Beijing.
  • All Beijing papers featured Chairman Mao Zedong's Prefaces to two rural surveys he wrote in 1931, marking the eighty-sixth anniversary of his birth.
  • A survey by the New China News Agency showed that the four most popular consumer products were television sets, wristwatches, bicycles, and sewing machines. From January to November, a total of 210,000 television sets were sold in Beijing, compared with 70,000 in 1978 and 40,000 in 1977, the figure for 1965 was slightly over 1,000. It was estimated that about

thirty-five percent of the families in the city proper now had television sets. In addition, almost every factory, school and government organization had at least one television set, placed in a meeting hall or office.

• The Ministry of Public Security disclosed that China had ten times more juvenile delinquency now than in the early 1960's and traced the problem to the Cultural Revolution.

December 27   NCNA reported that a well-preserved human skeleton from the Stone Age, estimated to have lived in China from 4,000 to 8,000 or 9,000 B.C., was found in Jiangxian county, Shanxi province in late August this year.

December 28   The State Council awarded 340 national model workers and 251 national advanced units in agriculture, finance and trade, scientific research, education and public health for outstanding contributions to socialist construction.

• Premier Hua Guofeng reaffirmed his "first support" for the Khmer Rouge in a message to Khieu Samphan, warmly congratulating him on his assumption of the office of prime minister.

• NCNA reported that China would extend preferential treatment to all foreign companies setting up enterprises or joint ventures in special economic zones in south China's Shenzen and Zhuhai areas in Guangdong province.

• A compensation trade agreement on processing about 60,000 carats of diamond articles a year was signed in Beijing between two Chinese corporations and a firm in West Germany. Under the five-year agreement, the V.K. Narasimhah Company would provide the raw material, subsidiary materials and equipment. Represented by the Beijing Jeweller Branch of Chinese National Arts and Crafts Import and Export Corporation and the Beijing Special Industrial Art Company, the Chinese side would be responsible for building workshops with a floor space of 3,000 square meters and for setting up a technical school to train craftsmen. The Narasimhah Company would get half of the annual processing income as compensation for its investment, which would be paid off in three or four years. This compensation agreement was one of 200 agreements signed this year by China's arts-and-crafts enterprises with other countries and regions.

December 29   NCNA reported that the newly built Harbin Airport, the largest in northeast China, went into operation. The airport, situated in the western suburbs of Harbin, had a runway 3,200 meters long and forty-five meters wide.

• The National Committee of the CPPCC held a meeting in Beijing to assess industry and transport matters. Vice Premier Kang Shien delivered a report including the following points: Along with wage increases forty percent of office and industrial workers, and regional adjustment of wages, the average annual of urban dwellers increased to 700 yuan compared to 662 yuan in 1978. In the rural areas a peasant's average income rose from seventy-four yuan in 1978 to eighty yuan. By the end of this year, 7.5 million urban residents would be provided with jobs.

• Singapore and China signed a trade agreement including the most-favored-nation clause provision.

• China called the Soviet Afghanistan invasion "a threat to Chinese security," and demanded the withdrawal of the Soviet forces.

• Well-known Japanese symphony conductor Seiji Ozawa guided the Chinese Orchestra at the first of a series of three concerts of Beethoven's Ninth (Choral) Symphony in Beijing.

December 30   NCNA reported that popularizing vasectomies and further study of oral contraceptives for men were among a number of recommendations made by Chinese medical scholars at a recent symposium on birth control held in Beijing.

• NCNA reported that Provincial People's Congresses in eight provinces recently elected new leadership and adopted programs for economic development. The eight provinces were: Zhejian, Shandong, Henan, Gansu, Fujian, Heilongjiang, and Sichuan.

• NCNA reported that construction of a 1.6 million kw hydroelectric power station at Longyang gorge in Qinghai province, the biggest such station on the Yellow River, had entered a new stage with the completion of a cofferdam across the river.

December 31 The twenty-five-year-old US-Taiwan Defense
Treaty expired, one year after unilateral notice of
termination from Washington.

● NCNA reported that the twenty-seven-arch water-
discharging gate had been completed as a part of the
first stage of work on the Gezhouba project on the
middle reaches of the Yangzi River in Hubei province.

● Speaking in an interview with Radio Beijing, Ambassador Woodcock said, "I am confident that in late
January or early February, the US Congress will ratify
the trade agreement which will open the door to most-
favored-nation status extended by the United States to
the People's Republic of China."

● According to the China Travel and Tourism Administrative Bureau, more than 800,000 tourists visited
China in 1979, thirty percent more than in 1978.

Appendix A: Bibiographical Sources

This Chronology has been compiled from the following sources:

1. Agence France Presse (AFP) Dispatches from Beijing
2. Asian Record (New Delhi)
3. China Quarterly (London)
4. Beijing Review (Beijing) known as Peking Review before December, 1978
5. Cheng Ming (Contention, Hong Kong)
6. China News Analysis (Hong Kong)
7. Current Background (U.S. Consulate-General, Hong Kong)
8. Daily News Release (Xinhua News Agency, Tokyo)
9. Department of State Bulletin (Washington, D.C.)
10. Far Eastern Economic Review (Hong Kong)
11. Facts on File (Washington, D.C.)
12. Foreign Broadcasting Information Service (FBIS) daily reports--the People's Republic of China, published by National Technical Information, Springfield, Virginia.
13. Guanming Ribao (Beijing)
14. Issues and Studies (Taiwan)
15. Hongqi (Red Flag, Beijing)
16. Jiefangjun Bao (Liberation Army Daily, Beijing)
17. Keesing's Contemporary Archives (London)
18. Kyodo News Agency, dispatches from Beijing and Hong Kong (Tokyo)
19. Le Monde (Paris)
20. New York Times (New York)
21. Renmin Ribao (People's Daily, Beijing)
22. Reuters News Agency, dispatches from Beijing and Hong Kong (Canada)
23. Supplement to the Survey of the China Mainland Maga-

zines (US Consulate-General, Hong Kong)
24. Supplement to the Survey of China Mainland Press (US Consulate-General, Hong Kong)
25. Survey of the China Mainland Magazines (US Consulate-General, Hong Kong)
26. Survey of the China Mainland Press (US Consulate-General, Hong Kong)
27. Survey of the People's Republic of China Magazines (US Consulate-General, Hong Kong)
28. Survey of the People's Republic of China Press (US Consulate-General, Hong Kong)
29. The Times (London)
30. Toronto Globe and Mail (Toronto)
31. US Joint Publication Research Service (JPRS) Translations on the People's Republic of China, known as China Report since mid-1979. The China Report is published in several series: (a) Economic, (b) Agriculture, (c) political.
32. Zhongguo Qingnian (China Youth, Beijing)

Appendix B: Selected Further Readings

Arnold, Eve. In China. New York: Alfred A. Knopf, 1980

Bloodworth, Dennis. The Messiah and The Mandarins: Mao
   Tse-tung and the Ironies of Power. New York: Athene-
   um, 1982

Bonavia, David. The Chinese. New York: Harper & Row,
   1980

Butterfield, Fox. China: Alive in the Bitter Sea. New
   York: Times Books, 1982

Cheng, Peter P. An Annotated Bibliography: The People's
   Repúblic of China. London: CLIO Press, 1984

Coye, Molly J. and Jon Livingston, Editors. China: Yesterday and Today. New York: Bantam, 1979

Diamond, E. Grey. Inside China Today: A Western View.
   New York: Norton, 1983

Garside, Roger. Coming Alive: China After Mao. New
   York: McGraw-Hill, 1981

Goldman, Merle. China's Intellectuals: Advise and Dissent.
   Cambridge, Mass.: Harvard University Press, 1981

Heng, Liang, and Judith Shapiro. Son of the Revolution.
   New York: Alfred A. Knopf, 1983

Hsu, Immanuel C. China Without Mao: The Search for a
   New Order. New York: Oxford University Press, 1983

571

Li, Victor H. Law Without Lawyers: A Comparative View of Law in China and the United States. Boulder, Colo.: Westview Press, 1978

MacDonald, Malcolm. Inside China. New York: Little, Brown, 1981

Mathews, Jay and Linda. One Billion: A China Chronicle. New York: Random House, 1983

Morath, Inge and Arthur Miller. Chinese Encounters. New York: Farrar, Straus & Giroux, 1979

Ronan, Colin A. The Shorter Science & Civilization in China, Vol. I. New York: Cambridge University Press, 1980

Schell, Orville. Watch Out for the Foreign Guests! China Encounters the West. New York: Pantheon, 1981

Saich, Tony. China: Politics and Government. New York: St. Martin's Press, 1981

Short, Philip. The Dragon and The Bear: Inside China and Russia Today. New York: Morrow, 1983

Spence, Jonathan D. The Gate of Heavenly Peace: The Chinese and Their Revolution 1895-1980. New York: Viking, 1981

Spender, Stephen and David Hockney. China Diary. New York: Abrams, 1983

Terrill, Ross. The Future of China: After Mao. New York: Delacorte, 1978

_____. Mao: A Biography. New York: Harper & Row, 1980

_____. The China Difference. New York: Harper & Row, 1980

Wilson, Dick. The People's Emperor: Mao: A Biography of Mao Tse-tung. Garden City, N.Y.: Doubleday, 1980

The dates for Mao Zedong and Zhou Enlai are not listed in the Index due to the frequent appearance of their names throughout the Chronology.

573

Kaunda, Kenneth D.
1970: 10-22
1974: 2-21 (& wife)
1979: 11-27
Kawasaki, Hideji
1971: 9-11
Kawawa, Rashidi Mfaume
1978: 9-28
Kayibanda, Gregoire
1971: 11-9
Kaysone see Phomvihan
Kellezi, Abdyle
1970: 8-13
Kennedy, Edward M.
1973: 2-21
1978: 1-2 (& wife)
Kent, Duke of
1979: 6-5
Kerekon, Mathiu
1976: 7-15
Kergolay, Ronald de
1977: 7-11
Khaddam, Abdel Halim
1972: 5-21
Khalid, Mansour
1973: 10-26
Khalil, Abdel Magid
1979: 12-3
Khalyl, S. E.
1972: 11-24
Khama, Seretae
1976: 7-26
Khan, Audul Rahim
1970: 5-31
Khan, Ghulam Jilani
1979: 2-11
Khan, Yahya p. 1
1970: 3-9; 4-2; 11-10
Khieu Samphan
1974: 4-1
1975: 8-15; 8-21
1976: 4-14; 4-16
1978: 12-6
1979: 12-28
Khrushchev, Nikita
p. 138
1970: 1-1
Kiki, Albert Maori
1975: 1-31
Kim Il Sung
p. 230
1970: 4-5
1971: 8-6
1972: 4-14; 12-22
1973: 6-24
1975: 4-17; 9-21
1976: 7-10

1977: 12-17
1978: 5-5; 9-8
1979: 5-25
Kimura, Takeo
1973: 1-16; 1-17
King, George
1973: 10-21
King, Kenneth
1972: 10-31
Kirchschlaeger, Rudolf
1974: 4-4
Kirti Nidhi Bista
1972: 11-14 (& wife)
1977: 9-18
1978: 9-27
Kissinger, Henry A.
pp. 35-36, 78, 136, 137, 185,
       228-29, 281, 282, 333
1971: 7-9; 7-15; 10-20; 11-29
1972: 2-21; 2-22; 2-27; 6-19;
       6-24; 10-22
1973: 1-15; 6-13; 7-5; 9-25;
       9-29; 10-24; 11-10; 11-14;
       11-24
1974: 5-31; 6-3; 9-6; 11-25
1975: 9-27; 10-19 (& wife)
1976: 9-14
1977: 9-6; 10-5
1979: 4-25; 5-5; 10-15
Klonsky, Michael
1977: 7-20
Ko Tae Un
1973: 7-5
Kohl, H.
1974: 9-3
Kolokassidea, Michael
1973: 9-16 (& wife)
Komoto, Toshio
1978: 9-11
Kono, Ichiro
1979: 3-15
Kosaka, Zentaro
1972: 9-18
Kosh, Gerald E.
p. 184
Kossamak, Sisowath
1975: 4-28
Kosygin, Aleksey
1970: 6-10; 6-13
1978: 3-9
1979: 9-23
Kotsokoane, J. R. L.
1975: 5-19
Kountche, Sebyi (Senyi)
p. 334
1977: 9-18
Kovacevic, Zivorad

1979: 1-20

GHANA
1972: 2-29; 9-8
1974: 6-6
1975: 5-13
1976: 3-3
1977: 12-19
1978: 4-10

GREECE
1972: 6-5
1973: 5-20
1975: 4-19
1978: 9-21
1979: 11-12

GRENADA
1974: 2-8

GUINEA
1970: 2-1; 3-10; 5-20; 10-20
1971: 1-26; 5-17
1972: 1-26; 12-9
1973: 2-16
1974: 2-7; 12-11
1975: 10-18
1977: 3-19; 4-26
1978: 3-17; 10-25

GUINEA-BISSAU
1973: 9-30
1974: 3-20; 9-6
1975: 7-3
1976: 4-15; 5-12
1977: 4-21; 6-10

GUYANA
1971: 8-24; 11-8
1972: 6-27; 10-31
1973: 10-21
1974: 2-15; 10-5; 11-20
1975: 3-12
1976: 5-14
1977: 4-18
1978: 7-21

HEALTH
1970: 1-13
1975: 7-3
1977: 4-5; 7-26
1978: 6-11; 6-12; 6-13; 6-
26; 7-12; 7-22; 11-2
1979: 2-7; 3-1; 6-1; 6-5;
11-11; 12-30

HONDURAS
1977: 1-10

HUNGARY
1970: 7-19
1972: 3-11; 5-10; 11-10
1973: 5-23
1974: 3-23; 10-19
1975: 3-3; 11-5
1976: 3-6; 7-23; 10-23
1977: 4-21; 11-26
1978: 2-27; 11-12
1979: 1-16; 12-21

INDIA
1971: 4-7; 12-16; 12-27; 12-29
1972: 2-28
1973: 12-2
1974: 9-3; 9-11
1975: 4-29; 11-1; 11-3
1976: 6-15; 7-7
1977: 2-13; 3-30; 5-20; 12-4
1978: 2-7; 5-11; 9-27
1979: 2-12; 7-31

INDONESIA
1977: 5-18; 11-11
1979: 2-15

INDUSTRY, CONSTRUCTION, AND
COMMUNICATION
1970: 4-23; 7-1
1971: 1-4; 2-21; 5-16; 8-19;
9-9; 9-27
1972: 10-1; 10-26
1973: 2-18; 4-17; 12-26
1974: 2-28; 4-10; 5-1; 6-24;
9-14; 9-26; 12-18; 12-20;
12-27
1975: 2-4; 2-5; 2-12; 4-1; 4-29;
6-1; 6-30; 7-1; 7-8; 7-18;
7-19; 8-24; 9-8; 9-11;
9-23; 10-5; 11-1; 11-14;
12-1; 12-23
1976: 3-23; 5-13; 5-23; 5-29;
5-31; 6-28; 6-29; 7-30;
7-31; 8-7; 8-24; 8-29;
9-1; 12-14; 12-26
1977: 1-2; 1-3; 1-10; 1-11; 1-
23; 4-11; 4-20; 4-28;
5-1; 5-5; 5-18; 6-5; 7-6;
8-11; 9-20; 11-8; 11-27;
11-28; 12-26; 12-31
1978: 1-1; 1-12; 1-15; 2-18; 4-
2; 4-29; 5-2; 5-5; 5-7;
5-31; 6-1; 6-2; 7-4; 7-
26; 8-13; 10-2; 10-5;
10-6; 10-20; 10-28; 11-9;
11-26; 12-15
1979: 1-17; 1-31; 2-12; 2-15;
2-19; 3-21; 3-23; 4-15;